VIEWPOINT

TEACHER'S EDITION 2

MICHAEL MCCARTHY

JEANNE MCCARTEN

HELEN SANDIFORD

CAMBRIDGE
UNIVERSITY PRESS

CAMBRIDGE
UNIVERSITY PRESS

32 Avenue of the Americas, New York, NY 10013-2473, USA

Cambridge University Press is part of the University of Cambridge.

It furthers the University's mission by disseminating knowledge in the pursuit of education, learning and research at the highest international levels of excellence.

www.cambridge.org
Information on this title: www.cambridge.org/9781107601567

© Cambridge University Press 2014

It is normally necessary for written permission for copying to be obtained in advance from a publisher. The tests and tapescripts at the back of this book are designed to be copied and distributed in class. The normal requirements are waived here and it is not necessary to write to Cambridge University Press for permission for an individual teacher to make copies for use within his or her own classroom. Only those pages that carry the wording '© Cambridge University Press' may be copied.

First published 2014
2nd printing 2014

Printed in the United States of America.

A catalog record for this publication is available from the British Library.

ISBN 978-0-521-13189-6 Student's Book
ISBN 978-1-107-60631-9 Workbook
ISBN 978-1-107-60156-7 Teacher's Edition with Assessment CD/CD-ROM
ISBN 978-1-107-66132-5 Class Audio CDs (4)
ISBN 978-1-107-67577-3 Presentation Plus
ISBN 978-1-107-65967-4 Blended Online Pack (Student's Book + Online Workbook)

Additional resources for this publication at www.cambridge.org/viewpoint
Cambridge University Press has no responsibility for the persistence or accuracy of URLs for external or third-party internet websites referred to in this publication, and does not guarantee that any content on such websites is, or will remain, accurate or appropriate. Information regarding prices, travel timetables, and other factual information given in this work is correct at the time of first printing but Cambridge University Press does not guarantee the accuracy of such information thereafter.

Contents

Introduction

Viewpoint is an innovative new series for adult and young adult learners of English. It is a corpus-informed course, drawing on extensive research into the corpus of North American English in the Cambridge English Corpus – a large database of everyday conversations and texts that show how people actually use English. The database also includes the multimillion-word Cambridge Learner Corpus, which shows us how learners at different levels use English, what problems they have, and what the most common errors are at each level.

Corpus research ensures that learners using *Viewpoint* will encounter the most useful and widely-used words, phrases, and grammar in a range of everyday situations. The research also makes possible the introduction of the important syllabus area of conversation management strategies – for example, how to comment on one's own and others' statements, how to soften opinions, and how to build an argument or avoid topics of conversation. The result is a groundbreaking course of language and skills development that helps learners communicate naturally and effectively.

Easy and enjoyable to teach, *Viewpoint* is full of new and exciting ideas, offering a fresh approach to the teaching and learning of English. Here are some answers to the questions that people have asked us about the *Viewpoint* series.

Viewpoint is a corpus-informed course. What is a corpus exactly?

A corpus is a database of spoken and / or written English. The texts in a corpus can be collected from a variety of sources. For example, texts in a written corpus may come from newspapers, magazines, books, or the Internet, while "texts" in a spoken corpus may come from everyday conversations between friends and family, strangers, coworkers, etc. *Viewpoint* was written using the corpus of North American English in the *Cambridge English Corpus* – a database that currently holds more than a billion words from spoken and written texts.

What kinds of information can you learn from a corpus?

With computer software to analyze a corpus, we can find out the most commonly-used English words and expressions. The use of a corpus is a major innovation that makes it possible to develop an exciting new approach to learning English.

We used the Corpus to answer questions like these:

What are the most frequent words and phrases in English? By analyzing the Corpus, we can identify the most frequent words and expressions in everyday conversation. For example, we can find the top 50, 500, 1,000, or 5,000 words in the spoken Corpus and see how these are different from the most frequent words in the written Corpus. This ensures that students learn the most useful conversational words right from the beginning.

Which English words are most likely to occur together? We can find typical collocations, or words frequently used together, by looking at all the examples of an individual word and seeing what words most often precede or follow it. For example, we can identify the nouns that are most frequently used after the phrasal verb *run out of*. We learn that the top four are *time, money, space,* and *breath.* Another example is adjectives that are modified by *not quite* (*sure, right, true, clear,* and *certain*). This kind of information helps us present phrasal verbs, as well as other words and phrases, in natural and useful collocations.

What are the most common meanings and uses of a particular grammar structure? By using the Corpus, we can search for sophisticated grammatical patterns – for example, the future perfect continuous form – to see exactly when and how they are used and their most common meanings and contexts. We can also find out which adverbs are most commonly used with modal verbs. We can see which structures are more common in speaking than in writing and vice versa. Such information enables us to foreground the patterns and usage that are most frequent and appropriate.

How do people manage conversations effectively? By reading the multitude of conversations in the Corpus, we can see how people interact in real-life situations. For example, we see that people often signal their attitude to what they're saying by using *-ly* adverbs such as *seriously, clearly, luckily*, or *surprisingly*; they soften what they say by using *would* in expressions such as *I would think, I'd say*. We can also see different types of responses people make, for example, *I suppose, I think so, I guess not*. We see how people use rhetorical questions to make a point as well as how people add to or repeat their ideas with expressions like *What I'm saying is, . . .* or *I don't mean . . .* In sum, we learn how people use their grammar and vocabulary resources to create and maintain good relations with their conversational partners. Identifying these conversation strategies has made it possible in *Viewpoint* to teach students useful skills for managing their own conversations in English.

What are the most typical contexts for specific vocabulary and grammar structures? Searching the Corpus helps us find typical situations for using specific grammar structures and vocabulary so that we can present new language in natural contexts. For example, we can see that *be going to* is generally followed by a continuous verb in spoken rather than written English and that the relative pronoun *whom* is over 15 times more frequent in written English than in conversation. Therefore we are able to determine the best contexts, spoken or written, for presentation of structures. The articles, podcasts, conversations, interviews, and listening and reading material that students encounter in the series are constructed in ways that reflect the character and content of the material in the Corpus.

What errors do students make most frequently with grammar or vocabulary? Searching the Learner Corpus helps us find the most frequent and persistent errors that learners typically make. Examples include the uncountable nouns that students have the most problems with or using verbs with two objects correctly. This information from the Learner Corpus enables us to target such problem areas and alert students to them as points to watch out for.

How does this corpus-informed approach help me and my students?

By identifying what language is essential to basic communication and what language allows us to speak and write clearly and precisely, corpus-informed materials can take learners to their goals more quickly and efficiently.

In addition, a study of a spoken corpus teaches us important things about social communication. As a result, activities based on corpus-informed materials can focus on the most important features of listening and speaking skills, making students more effective listeners and communicators. Successful spoken interaction is often called "the fifth skill."

Do I need to know a lot about the Corpus to be able to teach with *Viewpoint*?

Not at all. You don't need any special knowledge of the Corpus to use the course successfully. But you can feel assured that we, as authors, have checked the Corpus carefully to ensure that the language we teach is frequent, natural, and useful, and that the statements we make about language are accurate.

As you teach from *Viewpoint,* you and your students will learn many interesting facts about language coming from our corpus research. Throughout the Student's Books you will see *In conversation* panels, which give useful information about spoken grammar and vocabulary or differences between informal and formal spoken English. There are also *Writing vs. conversation* panels, which point to differences between written and spoken English. On many of the *Vocabulary notebook* pages you will find fun facts about vocabulary, such as the most frequent adjectives that start with *self-*. The *Common errors* panels give useful advice on the common errors to avoid with a particular language item. In the Teacher's Edition we provide additional information about grammar and vocabulary that we feel will be of particular interest to you as a teacher. See pages xviii–xxi in this Teacher's Edition for a list of the 500 words used most frequently in conversation.

What methodology will I be using in *Viewpoint*?

Viewpoint merges the best features of proven and familiar communicative methodologies while, at the same time, offering stimulating activities carefully crafted to focus on the learning process. The *Viewpoint* philosophy maintains that a successful course meets all of the following goals:

1. **It is interaction-based.** An important learning aim in every lesson is to get students talking to each other. This strong emphasis on spoken interaction enables students to use new language immediately in order to communicate with their classmates. In addition, *Viewpoint* devotes a full lesson in every unit to the teaching of conversation strategies so that students can learn the skills needed for effective spoken communication.

2. **It personalizes the learning experience.** *Viewpoint* offers engaging activities that encourage students to talk about their own lives and ideas as they discuss topics relevant to their interests and experiences. Students will enjoy talking about topics such as social networks, life in the future, world issues, getting along with friends and family, nature, and travel. The *About you* icon points out some of these opportunities.

3. **It promotes noticing and inductive learning.** Throughout the series students complete tasks that actively involve them in the learning process. Students are also challenged to notice and figure out (inductive learning) grammar structures or English usage. Solving a problem or figuring something out for oneself is a powerful aid to understanding, and research shows that activities that have students notice and figure things out result in successful learning. *Figure it out* tasks challenge students to think about how target grammar structures are formed and used before they are formally introduced. *Notice* tasks in the *Conversation strategy* lessons encourage students to think about how people manage conversations effectively. *Word sort* tasks and *Vocabulary notebook* pages get students to actively learn new vocabulary.

   Clear learning aims at the start of each unit and *Progress checks* at the end of each Workbook unit enable students to monitor their own learning. Each Teacher's Edition provides a testing program that gives you and your students another valuable tool for assessing progress.

4. **It recognizes the importance of review and recycling.** Language students need constant review, and *Viewpoint* systematically recycles and reviews target language in several sections of the Student's Book – in *Conversation strategy, Reading* and *Listening, Vocabulary notebook,* and *Checkpoint,* as well as in the Workbook. Grammar, vocabulary, and conversation strategies taught in earlier units are recycled in later units. *Recycle* icons throughout the Teacher's Edition point out these and other opportunities for review and recycling.

5. **It offers flexibility to meet the needs of specific classes.** *Viewpoint* can be used with large and small classes. Activities can be done in pairs, groups, or as a whole class, depending on your particular needs. *Viewpoint* can also be adapted to varying course lengths. For shorter courses, the *Vocabulary notebook* pages and many of the *Reading* and *Writing* tasks can be assigned for homework. For longer courses, the Workbook provides additional learning tasks. The Teacher's Edition offers a variety of extra classroom activities to reinforce learning when time allows.

Can I teach the lessons in a unit out of order?

It is highly recommended that Lessons A, B, C, D, and Writing are taught in order. This is because the new structures and vocabulary taught in the earlier lessons are generally recycled and reused in the later lessons. Each lesson in a unit assumes that students have learned the language of the previous lesson(s).

A special thank-you from the authors . . .

We would like to extend a very personal thank-you to all the teachers and students who have provided so many constructive comments during the development of *Viewpoint*. We sincerely hope that you will enjoy using *Viewpoint* and that it will contribute to the success of your English classes. We welcome your feedback and look forward to hearing from you.

With our very best wishes,

Mike McCarthy
Jeanne McCarten
Helen Sandiford

Course components

Each level of *Viewpoint* consists of a Student's Book, a Workbook, a Teacher's Edition with Assessment Audio CD / CD-ROM for the quizzes and tests, and the Class Audio CDs. In addition, teachers can download recordings of grammar charts and readings from the *Viewpoint* website.

Student's Book

There are 12 units in each Student's Book. Each unit consists of:

- four two-page lessons (Lessons A, B, C, and D) that present grammar, vocabulary, and conversation strategies, and include listening, speaking, and reading practice
- a single-page lesson that teaches the language and skills of writing including a special grammar chart about the grammar of writing
- a *Vocabulary notebook* page with practical learning tips to help students catalog new vocabulary, reinforce collocations, and further develop their vocabulary-building skills
- two *Grammar extra* pages at the back of the book that contain additional information and practice exercises on the target grammar of each A and B lesson
- a *Speaking naturally* activity at the back of the book that presents and practices a feature of pronunciation, linked to the language of the unit

Four *Checkpoint* lessons review the language taught in the previous three units.

Unique features of the Student's Book include:

- the *Conversation strategy* lesson, which covers the important syllabus area of conversation management techniques
- the *Vocabulary notebook*, which systematically covers vocabulary-building strategies to ensure effective learning
- *Figure it out* tasks, which involve students in figuring out how target structures are formed and used
- *Word sort* tasks, which encourage students to take an active role in learning new vocabulary
- information panels about differences between conversation and writing

Workbook

The Workbook is a natural extension of the Student's Book, providing reinforcement and consolidation of the material in the Student's Book. There are two pages of activities to practice the grammar from Lessons A and B, a page of vocabulary activities, a page of conversation strategy practice, two pages of reading, and a page of writing practice. In addition, there is an extra page of listening – *Listening extra*. The Workbook provides:

- thorough consolidation and practice of the vocabulary, grammar, and conversation strategies taught in the Student's Book
- extra reading, writing, and listening activities to reinforce these important skills
- a wide variety of activity types, with photos and illustrations to provide context and keep students motivated
- a *Progress check* at the end of the book to help students plan further independent study

Teacher's Edition with Assessment Audio CD / CD-ROM

The interleaved Teacher's Edition contains practical, step-by-step teaching notes for each page of the Student's Book. It also offers:

- *Language notes* that not only provide an overview of the language presented in each unit but also give useful information, drawn from the Corpus, on the frequency of grammatical forms, words, and expressions

- a wide variety of optional interactive classroom tasks geared to both small and large classes
- a photocopiable testing package containing general, writing, and speaking quizzes for every unit, along with answer keys and scripts
- audio scripts for all recorded material from the Student's Book and Workbook
- unit-by-unit language summaries that include the unit vocabulary and expressions
- the Workbook answer key

An Assessment Audio CD / CD-ROM bound into the Teacher's Edition contains:

- general, speaking, and writing tests – one test of each type for Units 1–6, one for Units 7–12, and one for Units 1–12. All tests are available as both PDFs and Word documents.
- PDFs and Word documents of all the general, speaking, and writing quizzes (also available in the printed Teacher's Edition)
- audio recordings, answer keys, and scripts for the *Viewpoint* testing program

Class Audio Program

The Class Audio CDs and downloadable recordings provide students with natural models for speaking and pronunciation as well as the opportunity to listen to a variety of voices and accents. The Class Audio CDs contain all the material for the presentation and listening activities. The grammar charts and the Lesson D reading texts are available as downloadable recordings from www.cambridge.org/viewpoint/audio

Presentation Plus

Viewpoint Presentation Plus allows you to present the contents of *Viewpoint* in a more lively, interactive way by conveniently bringing the following materials together in one place in front of the classroom:

- Student's Book
- Class Audio
- Workbook
- Video Activity Worksheets
- Video Program
- Cambridge Dictionaries Online

Video and Video Resource Book

The *Viewpoint* video, available on DVD, provides video conversations that accompany the Student's Book. The *Video Resource Book* offers video worksheets for each unit. These can be used in class as extension activities.

Online Workbook

The Online Workbook provides the Workbook content as interactive activities. Students complete the activities online and have their answers automatically marked. Teachers can look at scores for the class and for each student.

Online Course

The Online Course uses the same syllabus and learning outcomes as the Student's Book. The material has been carefully adapted and extended to take students through a fully-supported learning program, which can be used to create a wide range of blended learning solutions – from 100 percent classroom learning to 100 percent online learning or anywhere in between.

The Online Course includes newly-created multimedia presentation and personalized, interactive practice. It offers original activities, engaging video clips, and opportunities for students to record their voice, post blogs, write wikis, and leave spoken messages.

For more information about these components, see: www.cambridge.org/viewpoint

Structure of the units in the Student's Book

All units contain the following basic structure. It is important to note that lessons should be taught in A, B, C, D, Writing order. There may be some variety from unit to unit in the exact position of vocabulary, pronunciation, listening, and speaking activities. Below is a typical unit.

Lesson A – Vocabulary, grammar, and speaking

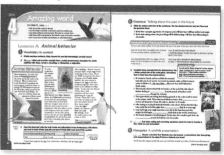

Lesson B – Grammar and listening

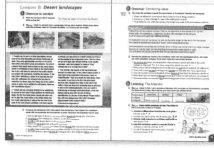

Lesson C – Conversation strategies, listening, speaking, and pronunciation

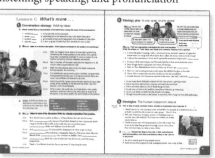

Lesson D – Reading, vocabulary, listening, and speaking

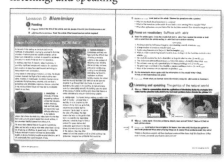

Writing – Writing skills and grammar for writing

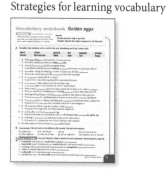

Vocabulary notebook – Strategies for learning vocabulary

After Units 3, 6, 9, and 12

Checkpoint – Review

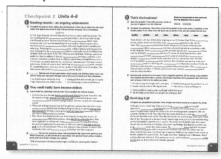

At the back of the Student's Book

Speaking naturally – Pronunciation and intonation

Grammar extra – Information and exercises to extend the grammar in Lessons A and B

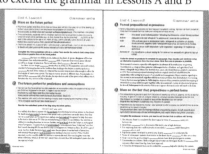

Features of the units in the Student's Book

Lesson A

Lessons A and B present the main grammar points of the unit. Each lesson contains useful vocabulary, and one of the two lessons also teaches the main target vocabulary of the unit. Sometimes these lessons end with a *Viewpoint* group discussion or a *Listening* task. In some lessons, teachers are directed to a *Speaking naturally* pronunciation task at the back of the book.

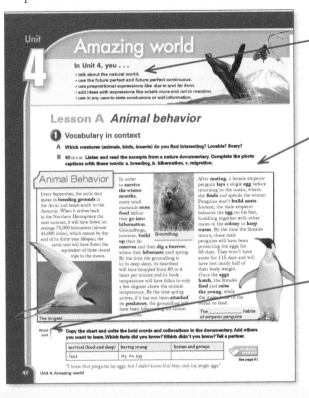

Unit aims
- show the key topics and functional areas, grammar, and strategies that are taught in Lessons A–C

Grammar in context / Vocabulary in context
- presents new grammar in natural contexts such as conversations, interviews, formal discussions, podcasts, articles, questionnaires
- focuses on the most frequent and useful language for everyday communication
- *Vocabulary in context* sections also include target words and / or expressions

Word sort
- helps students organize new vocabulary in meaningful ways to help the learning process
- gives opportunities for students to use the new vocabulary immediately in personalized interactions with classmates

Grammar charts
- provide a clear presentation of new structures with straightforward examples to make the grammar easy to assimilate

Common errors
- provides information from the Learner Corpus about key errors to avoid

Grammar exercises
- give students both controlled and freer practice with the new structure
- offer opportunities to apply the structure in expressing their own thoughts and experiences and to exchange their own personal information

Viewpoint
- includes pair, group, and class discussions and tasks on questions and issues that flow out of the lesson topics and issues raised
- provides an opportunity for students to use the language presented in the unit
- includes expressions that would be useful for the discussion in an *In conversation* information panel (These expressions are recycled from the *Touchstone* series.)
- includes pair, group, and class discussions on questions and issues derived from the reading
- provides an opportunity for students to use the language presented in the unit as well as showing expressions useful for the discussion in an *In conversation* information panel

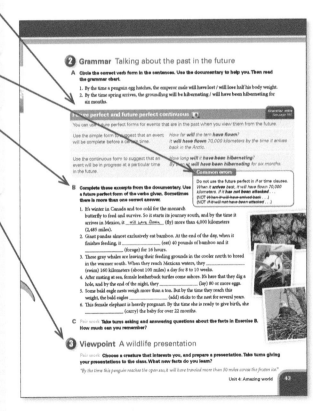

Lesson B

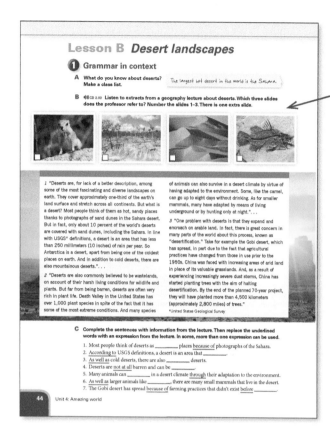

Grammar in context / Vocabulary in context

- presents new grammar in natural contexts such as conversations, interviews, formal discussions, podcasts, articles, questionnaires
- focuses on the most frequent and useful language for everyday communication

Figure it out

- helps students notice the forms and / or uses of the new structure
- challenges students to use their inductive skills before the grammar chart is presented

Listening

- presents expository information on a topic of interest
- includes a task that assesses students' comprehension of the gist of the information
- encourages students to listen again for specific details

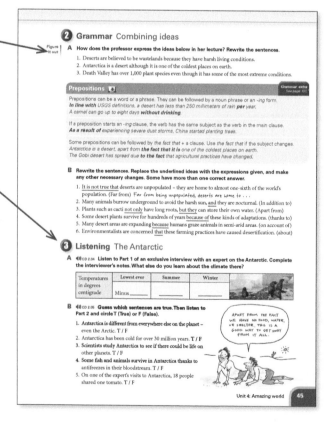

Lesson C

Lesson C teaches conversation management strategies in the *Conversation strategy* and *Strategy plus* sections. It always includes common expressions that are useful in conversation. The final section is a speaking or a listening and speaking activity that practices again and reinforces the conversational language and strategies of the earlier sections. The grammar in this lesson is always recycled and is thus grammar that students already know.

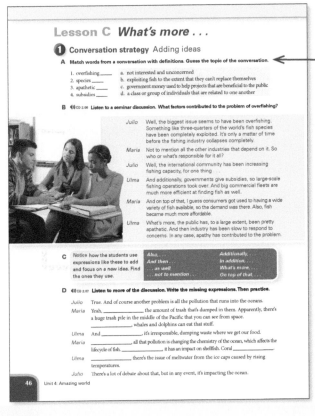

Conversation strategy

- teaches students techniques for managing conversations more effectively in English

- offers an exciting syllabus of strategies drawn from conversations in the Corpus, covering techniques such as checking understanding of what people say, using rhetorical questions to make a point, expressions for drawing conclusions, showing strong agreement, and much more

This section provides a four-step presentation and practice where students:

- First, do schema building, preparation, and / or a vocabulary warmup activity.

- Then, listen and understand the content of the conversation.

- Next, notice the strategy (presentation) and find more examples in the conversation.

- Finally, use the strategy in controlled, then freer, interactive and personalized practice.

Strategy plus

- teaches conversation management expressions chosen for their relevance and frequency such as *No wonder, I think so, I have to say . . . ,* and *You know what?*

- extends and reinforces the material presented in *Conversation strategy*

In conversation

- often includes information panels about the use or frequency of the structure in conversation, sometimes in contrast to its use in writing

Strategies

- provides practice with expressions or skills from *Conversation strategy* and *Strategy plus* within conversations and extracts that are all based on real-life language

- provides an opportunity to use conversation strategies to discuss real-life situations with a partner, group, or whole class

About you

- signals a personalized practice task that allows students to apply their learning

Speaking naturally

- In some units, teachers are directed to a *Speaking naturally* section at the back of the book, where the teaching point from Lesson C is integrated with and uses the expressions taught in the lesson.

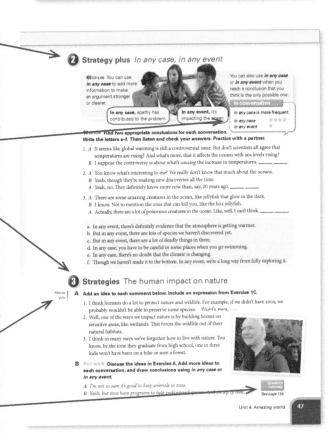

Lesson D

Lesson D focuses on reading skills while also providing additional listening and speaking activities. Most units include a *Reading tip* that helps students become more familiar with conventions of formal writing by providing useful information about techniques writers use to structure texts, create interest, avoid repetition, and so forth.

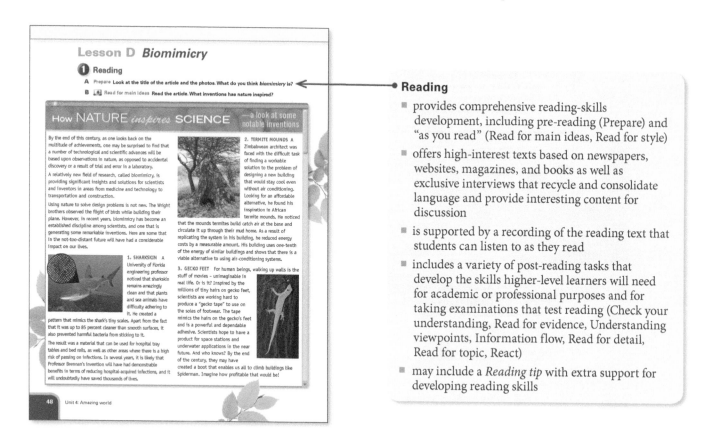

Reading

- provides comprehensive reading-skills development, including pre-reading (Prepare) and "as you read" (Read for main ideas, Read for style)

- offers high-interest texts based on newspapers, websites, magazines, and books as well as exclusive interviews that recycle and consolidate language and provide interesting content for discussion

- is supported by a recording of the reading text that students can listen to as they read

- includes a variety of post-reading tasks that develop the skills higher-level learners will need for academic or professional purposes and for taking examinations that test reading (Check your understanding, Read for evidence, Understanding viewpoints, Information flow, Read for detail, Read for topic, React)

- may include a *Reading tip* with extra support for developing reading skills

Focus on vocabulary

- provides a variety of vocabulary tasks based on the reading text to help students acquire a wider repertoire of vocabulary knowledge for reading and writing, such as using context to guess meaning, word formation, use of synonyms and opposites, collocations and idiomatic expressions, and much more

Listening and speaking

- covers these important complementary skills in the same section

- recycles the key grammar and vocabulary taught in the lesson

- presents conversations and extracts that are all based on real-life language

- mirrors real communication by teaching students to react or respond: Tasks include "listen and choose a good response," "listen and predict," and "listen and decide if you agree"

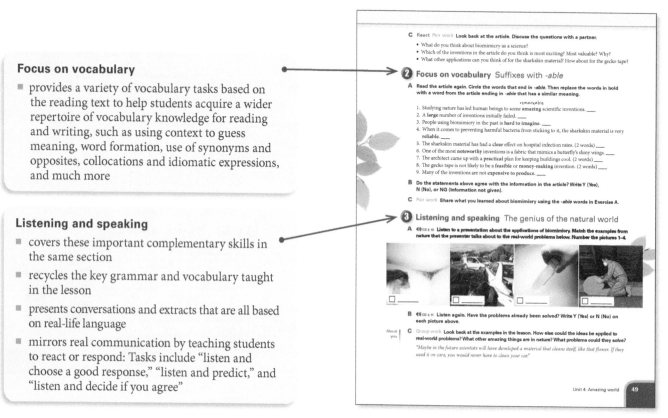

Writing

The one-page *Writing* lesson teaches and develops formal writing skills such as describing charts and graphs, planning an argument, contrasting viewpoints, writing different types of essay (persuasive, descriptive, etc.), and structuring paragraphs and essays. A model text is provided that exemplifies the various teaching points as well as a grammar chart that presents a "grammar for writing" structure. Students are guided through the writing process with tasks requiring brainstorming, organizing, drafting, and checking for errors.

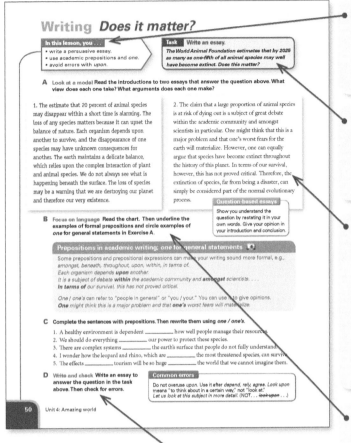

In this lesson, you . . .

- introduces the key writing skill, text-organization point, grammar for writing structure, and error to avoid that will be taught in the lesson as part of completing the writing task

Task

- introduces the writing task that students are about to do, including the type of text students will write (e.g., an article, a paragraph in an essay) and the topic or question to be answered

Look at a model

- illustrates the writing point and grammar structures of the lesson and provides students with a model outcome of the writing task they will undertake at the end of the lesson
- includes real-world writing tasks such as email requests, narratives, reports, short articles, as well as more academically focused paragraphs and essays that students might have to write in examinations
- sometimes includes panels with extra information about text types and structures

Focus on language

- presents a grammar point geared specifically to writing such as verb tenses for narrative writing, expressions (conjunctions and adverbs) for contrasting or adding ideas within and across sentences, and using relative clauses to present key information within a paragraph
- often includes panels with information about the differences in use of language items in written and spoken English

Write and check

- assigns the writing task previewed at the beginning of the lesson, while the accompanying *Common errors* panel alerts students to an error that is often made by learners using the grammar point

Vocabulary notebook

Vocabulary notebook provides a page of enjoyable tasks at the end of every unit to help students organize and write down new vocabulary. It allows students to customize their own vocabulary learning, working in class or at home, and encourages them to learn additional vocabulary in the *Word builder* activities.

Learning tip

- introduces a different useful technique in every unit for writing down and organizing new vocabulary
- covers writing whole expressions or collocations as well as individual words, grouping vocabulary in different ways, using personalization, writing definitions and paraphrasing, and using creative visual techniques like "idea strings" and "word forks" to write down vocabulary

Dictionary tip / Corpus information

- sometimes features a *Dictionary tip* that gives useful advice on how to use dictionaries effectively or an interesting fact about the use of a particular expression using information from the Corpus

Word builder

- includes new vocabulary related to the unit topic for students to look up, study, and learn

Focus on vocabulary

- reinforces new words and expressions first presented in Lesson D

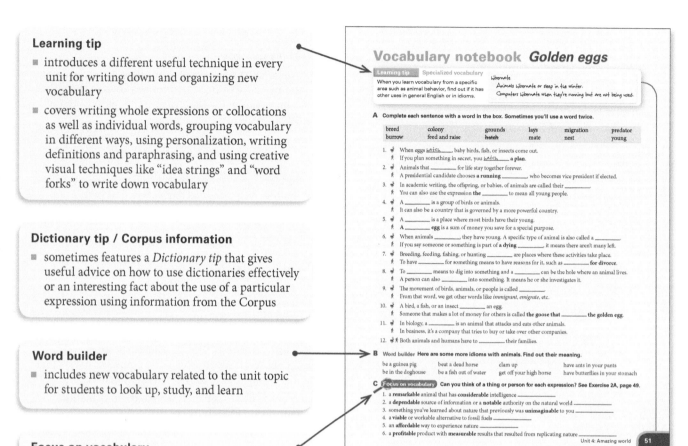

Grammar extra and Speaking naturally

Grammar extra provides information and exercises to extend the grammar from Lessons A and B.
Speaking naturally enables pronunciation and intonation learning and practice.

Unit 4, Lesson A · Grammar extra

① More on the future perfect

- The future perfect describes events that at a future point will be in the past, or in a time leading up to that future point in time. It can emphasize the completion of the events.
  *In two months, it will be winter and many birds **will have migrated** south.* (The migration is complete.)
- Time expressions, especially with *by*, are often used with the future perfect to show the time by which an event will be complete, e.g., *by then, by that time, by the time (that) . . ., by 2030, by the end of the century, by the age of six, within 30 days, within a decade, within the next 20 years.*
  *Within the next 10 years, many species **will have become** extinct.*
- The future perfect has a passive form – *will have been* + past participle – but it is not very common.
  *In the time it takes you to do this lesson, hundreds of sharks **will have been killed**.*

Complete the time expressions with *by* or *within*. Then rewrite the verbs in bold using either the active or passive form of the future perfect.

_____ the time our children reach adulthood, hundreds of species **disappear** off the face of the planet. One study estimated that _____ 2050, 37 percent of terrestrial species **die out** or will be in danger of extinction. That is well over a third _____ the next 30 years.

Sea life is also in danger _____ the time that sea levels rise 50 centimeters (about 20 inches), one-third of nesting beaches in the Caribbean **lose**, leading to the decline in turtle populations. _____ the end of this century, it is believed that seawater temperatures **rise** enough to affect the food supply of some ocean species. This impacts various species in different ways. For example, it is believed that _____ only a few decades, the reproductive cycle of the sperm whale **affect**, which threatens the very survival of the whale itself.

② The future perfect for predictions and assumptions

- You can use the future perfect to state predictions or assumptions about the present or to say what you think has happened in the past. It suggests you are certain.
  *No doubt you **will have read** about the melting ice caps.*
  *Many people **will not have seen** the recent documentary about this.*
- The negative with *won't* with this meaning is mostly used in speaking and informal writing.
  *"A lot of people **won't even have heard** about it."*

Rewrite the underlined parts of the blog using the future perfect.

will not / won't have heard

It is unlikely that there is anyone who <u>has not heard</u> about the threat to certain species on the planet. No doubt you <u>have reacted</u> to the news that species such as polar bears are under threat. But what can we as individuals do? In recent years, perhaps you <u>have noticed</u> the appeals for help that come in the mail or that are on TV. They are certainly having an impact on my children. I'm sure that in addition to sending donations to various charities, you <u>have heard</u> about the "adopt an endangered animal" programs. I suspect what you <u>haven't realized</u> is how expensive these "adoptions" are. Not that I mind donating $50 for my child to adopt an orangutan or a Sumatran rhino. It's all for a good cause. And no doubt donations <u>have saved</u> some obscure species from the brink of extinction, and certainly the programs <u>have motivated</u> many children to become involved. What I hadn't expected was for a cuddly stuffed toy version to arrive in the mail. Now my daughter wants the entire collection, which is all very well – except there are more than 100 endangered species that she can sign up to help!

150 · Grammar extra

Grammar extra

- extends the grammar from Lessons A and B with extra information and activities that can be done in class or for homework
- provides a clear presentation of structures with straightforward examples to make the grammar easy to assimilate
- may include *Common errors* panels with information from the Learner Corpus about key errors to avoid

---

Speaking naturally

- helps students understand and use natural pronunciation and intonation
- is closely integrated with the grammar, vocabulary, or strategies of the main units
- covers the key areas of linking and reduction, stress and intonation, basic grammatical forms, and common problems in listening comprehension
- provides communicative and personalized practice to fully integrate pronunciation into the lesson

---

Speaking naturally

Unit 3, Lesson C · Stress in expressions of contrast

Notice which words are stressed in these expressions introducing a contrasting view.

*It's important to get a college degree, **but even then**, you won't necessarily find a job.*
***Having said that, though**, your chances are better if you finish college.*
*There's a lot of competition for jobs these days. **But then again**, there always has been.*
***Even so**, the competition is probably more intense now than ever.*

A 🔊 Read and listen to the information above. Repeat the example sentences.

B 🔊 Listen. Circle the stressed word in each bold expression. Then listen, check, and repeat.

1. I think you should attend the best college that accepts you. **Having said that, though**, you need to make sure you can afford the housing and tuition costs.
2. I think it's great that people have a shorter workweek than they used to. **But then again**, many people now work two jobs in order to earn enough money to live on.
3. More people are working overtime, **but even then**, many have a hard time paying their bills.
4. I think it's good that people are getting married later, when they're more mature. **But even so**, the divorce rate doesn't seem to be going down.
5. There *is* competition for jobs. **Having said that**, there aren't enough candidates for some jobs.

About you | **C** Pair work Discuss the comments. Which views do you agree with?

Unit 4, Lesson C · Stress in adding expressions

Notice which words are stressed in these expressions that add information.

*Overfishing decreases the fish population, **not to mention** that many fish are killed by pollution.*
***On top of that**, fish consumption continues to increase every year.*
***What's more**, no one seems interested in finding a solution to the problem.*
***In any case**, someday people will have to consume less fish, or there won't be any left to eat.*

A 🔊 Read and listen to the information above. Repeat the example sentences.

B 🔊 Listen to these conversations. Circle the stressed word in each bold expression. Then listen, check, and repeat.

1. *A* No one seems to agree on the causes of global warming. **What's more** they don't agree on any solutions, either.
   B I suppose it's hard to identify the causes, but **in any event**, we need to do something.
   A I agree. I mean, we need to prepare for higher temperatures, **not to mention** extreme weather events like hurricanes. And **on top of that**, there's rising sea levels.
2. *A* The world uses way too much oil, and **what's more**, demand is increasing every year.
   B Yeah. **Not to mention** the fact that the supply of oil is decreasing pretty quickly.
   A And **on top of that**, people aren't trying very hard to develop different energy sources.
   B You're right. **In any case**, we'll need to do something soon. We're running out of oil.

About you | **C** Pair work Practice the conversations. Then discuss the issues. What's your view?

Speaking naturally · 139

This is a list of the top 500 words in spoken North American English. It is based on a sample of four and a half million words of conversation from the *Cambridge English Corpus*. The most frequent word, *I*, is at the top of the list.

1	I	41	with	81	they're
2	and	42	he	82	kind
3	the	43	one	83	here
4	you	44	are	84	from
5	uh	45	this	85	did
6	to	46	there	86	something
7	a	47	I'm	87	too
8	that	48	all	88	more
9	it	49	if	89	very
10	of	50	no	90	want
11	yeah	51	get	91	little
12	know	52	about	92	been
13	in	53	at	93	things
14	like	54	out	94	an
15	they	55	had	95	you're
16	have	56	then	96	said
17	so	57	because	97	there's
18	was	58	go	98	I've
19	but	59	up	99	much
20	is	60	she	100	where
21	it's	61	when	101	two
22	we	62	them	102	thing
23	huh	63	can	103	her
24	just	64	would	104	didn't
25	oh	65	as	105	other
26	do	66	me	106	say
27	don't	67	mean	107	back
28	that's	68	some	108	could
29	well	69	good	109	their
30	for	70	got	110	our
31	what	71	OK	111	guess
32	on	72	people	112	yes
33	think	73	now	113	way
34	right	74	going	114	has
35	not	75	were	115	down
36	um	76	lot	116	we're
37	or	77	your	117	any
38	my	78	time	118	he's
39	be	79	see	119	work
40	really	80	how	120	take

121 even	167 anything	213 twenty
122 those	168 kids	214 after
123 over	169 first	215 ever
124 probably	170 does	216 find
125 him	171 need	217 care
126 who	172 us	218 better
127 put	173 should	219 hard
128 years	174 talking	220 haven't
129 sure	175 last	221 trying
130 can't	176 thought	222 give
131 pretty	177 doesn't	223 I'd
132 gonna	178 different	224 problem
133 stuff	179 money	225 else
134 come	180 long	226 remember
135 these	181 used	227 might
136 by	182 getting	228 again
137 into	183 same	229 pay
138 went	184 four	230 try
139 make	185 every	231 place
140 than	186 new	232 part
141 year	187 everything	233 let
142 three	188 many	234 keep
143 which	189 before	235 children
144 home	190 though	236 anyway
145 will	191 most	237 came
146 nice	192 tell	238 six
147 never	193 being	239 family
148 only	194 bit	240 wasn't
149 his	195 house	241 talk
150 doing	196 also	242 made
151 cause	197 use	243 hundred
152 off	198 through	244 night
153 I'll	199 feel	245 call
154 maybe	200 course	246 saying
155 real	201 what's	247 dollars
156 why	202 old	248 live
157 big	203 done	249 away
158 actually	204 sort	250 either
159 she's	205 great	251 read
160 day	206 bad	252 having
161 five	207 we've	253 far
162 always	208 another	254 watch
163 school	209 car	255 week
164 look	210 true	256 mhm
165 still	211 whole	257 quite
166 around	212 whatever	258 enough

259 next	305 looking	351 stay
260 couple	306 someone	352 mom
261 own	307 coming	353 sounds
262 wouldn't	308 eight	354 change
263 ten	309 love	355 understand
264 interesting	310 everybody	356 such
265 am	311 able	357 gone
266 sometimes	312 we'll	358 system
267 bye	313 life	359 comes
268 seems	314 may	360 thank
269 heard	315 both	361 show
270 goes	316 type	362 thousand
271 called	317 end	363 left
272 point	318 least	364 friends
273 ago	319 told	365 class
274 while	320 saw	366 already
275 fact	321 college	367 eat
276 once	322 ones	368 small
277 seen	323 almost	369 boy
278 wanted	324 since	370 paper
279 isn't	325 days	371 world
280 start	326 couldn't	372 best
281 high	327 gets	373 water
282 somebody	328 guys	374 myself
283 let's	329 god	375 run
284 times	330 country	376 they'll
285 guy	331 wait	377 won't
286 area	332 yet	378 movie
287 fun	333 believe	379 cool
288 they've	334 thinking	380 news
289 you've	335 funny	381 number
290 started	336 state	382 man
291 job	337 until	383 basically
292 says	338 husband	384 nine
293 play	339 idea	385 enjoy
294 usually	340 name	386 bought
295 wow	341 seven	387 whether
296 exactly	342 together	388 especially
297 took	343 each	389 taking
298 few	344 hear	390 sit
299 child	345 help	391 book
300 thirty	346 nothing	392 fifty
301 buy	347 parents	393 months
302 person	348 room	394 women
303 working	349 today	395 month
304 half	350 makes	396 found

397 side	432 hour	467 percent
398 food	433 deal	468 hand
399 looks	434 mine	469 gosh
400 summer	435 reason	470 top
401 hmm	436 credit	471 cut
402 fine	437 dog	472 computer
403 hey	438 group	473 tried
404 student	439 turn	474 gotten
405 agree	440 making	475 mind
406 mother	441 American	476 business
407 problems	442 weeks	477 anybody
408 city	443 certain	478 takes
409 second	444 less	479 aren't
410 definitely	445 must	480 question
411 spend	446 dad	481 rather
412 happened	447 during	482 twelve
413 hours	448 lived	483 phone
414 war	449 forty	484 program
415 matter	450 air	485 without
416 supposed	451 government	486 moved
417 worked	452 eighty	487 gave
418 company	453 wonderful	488 yep
419 friend	454 seem	489 case
420 set	455 wrong	490 looked
421 minutes	456 young	491 certainly
422 morning	457 places	492 talked
423 between	458 girl	493 beautiful
424 music	459 happen	494 card
425 close	460 sorry	495 walk
426 leave	461 living	496 married
427 wife	462 drive	497 anymore
428 knew	463 outside	498 you'll
429 pick	464 bring	499 middle
430 important	465 easy	500 tax
431 ask	466 stop	

Irregular verbs

Base form	Simple past	Past participle
be	was/were	been
beat	beat	beaten
become	became	become
begin	began	begun
bend	bent	bent
bet	bet	bet
bind	bound	bound
bite	bit	bitten
bleed	bled	bled
blow	blew	blown
break	broke	broken
breed	bred	bred
bring	brought	brought
broadcast	broadcast	broadcast
build	built	built
burst	burst	burst
burn	burned/burnt	burned/burnt
buy	bought	bought
cast	cast	cast
catch	caught	caught
choose	chose	chosen
cling	clung	clung
come	came	come
cost	cost	cost
creep	crept	crept
cut	cut	cut
deal	dealt	dealt
dig	dug	dug
do	did	done
draw	drew	drawn
dream	dreamed/dreamt	dreamed/dreamt
drink	drank	drunk
drive	drove	driven
eat	ate	eaten
fall	fell	fallen
feed	fed	fed
feel	felt	felt
fight	fought	fought
find	found	found
fit	fitted/fit	fitted/fit
flee	fled	fled
fling	flung	flung
fly	flew	flown
forbid	forbade	forbidden
forget	forgot	forgotten
forgive	forgave	forgiven
freeze	froze	frozen
get	got	gotten
give	gave	given
go	went	gone
grow	grew	grown
hang (an object)	hung	hung
have	had	had
hear	heard	heard
hide	hid	hidden
hit	hit	hit
hold	held	held
hurt	hurt	hurt
keep	kept	kept
know	knew	known
lay	laid	laid
lead	led	led
leave	left	left
lend	lent	lent
let	let	let
lie (down)	lay	lain
light	lit	lit
lose	lost	lost

Base form	Simple past	Past participle
make	made	made
mean	meant	meant
meet	met	met
mislead	misled	misled
overcome	overcame	overcome
pay	paid	paid
prove	proved	proven/proved
put	put	put
quit	quit	quit
read	read	read
ride	rode	ridden
ring	rang	rung
rise	rose	risen
run	ran	run
say	said	said
see	saw	seen
seek	sought	sought
sell	sold	sold
send	sent	sent
set	set	set
sew	sewed	sewn/sewed
shake	shook	shaken
shine	shone	shone
shoot	shot	shot
show	showed	shown/showed
shrink	shrank	shrunk
shut	shut	shut
sing	sang	sung
sink	sank	sunk
sit	sat	sat
sleep	slept	slept
slide	slid	slid
sling	slung	slung
slink	slunk	slunk
sow	sowed	sown
speak	spoke	spoken
spend	spent	spent
spill	spilled/spilt	spilled/spilt
spin	spun	spun
spread	spread	spread
speed	sped	sped
spring	sprang	sprung
stand	stood	stood
steal	stole	stolen
stick	stuck	stuck
sting	stung	stung
stink	stank	stunk
strike	struck	struck
string	strung	strung
swear	swore	sworn
sweep	swept	swept
swim	swam	swum
swing	swung	swung
take	took	taken
teach	taught	taught
tear	tore	torn
tell	told	told
think	thought	thought
throw	threw	thrown
understand	understood	understood
wake	woke	woken
wear	wore	worn
weep	wept	wept
win	won	won
wind	wound	wound
withhold	withheld	withheld
write	wrote	written

Authors' acknowledgements

The authors would like to thank the entire team of professionals who have contributed their expertise to creating *Viewpoint 2*. We appreciate you all, including those we have not met. Here we would like to thank the people with whom we have had the most personal, day-to-day contact through the project. In particular, Michael Poor, who skillfully and sensitively edited the material and dedicated so much time and professional expertise to help us improve it; Mary Vaughn for her usual sage advice on our syllabus and her excellent contributions to the pronunciation materials; Dawn Elwell for her superb production skills; copy editor Karen Davy for checking through the manuscripts; Sue Aldcorn and Arley Gray for their work on creating the Teacher's Edition; Helen Tiliouine, Therese Naber and Janet Gokay, for creating and editing the testing program; Cristina Zurawski and Graham Skerritt for their comments on some of the early drafts, Mary McKeon, for her series oversight and project management; Melissa Struck for her help on the workbook and project management; Rossita Fernando and Jennifer Pardilla for their roles on the Workbook, Class Audio, and Video Program; Catherine Black for her support on the answer keys and audio scripts and deft handling of the Online Workbook; Tyler Heacock and Kathleen Corley, and their friends and family for the recordings they made, which fed into the materials; Ann Fiddes for corpus support and access to the English Profile wordlists; Dr Cynan Ellis Evans for the interview on page 45, and Kristen Ulmer for the interview which is reported on page 55.

We would also like to express our deep appreciation to Bryan Fletcher and Sarah Cole, who started the *Viewpoint* project with incredible vision and drive; and Janet Aitchison for her continued support.

Finally, we would like to thank each other for getting through another project together! In addition, Helen Sandiford would like to thank her husband, Bryan, and her daughters for their unwavering support.

In addition, a great number of people contributed to the research and development of *Viewpoint*. The authors and publishers would like to extend their particular thanks to the following for their valuable insights and suggestions.

Reviewers and consultants:
Elisa Borges and Samara Camilo Tomé Costa from **Instituto Brasil-Estados Unidos**, Rio de Janeiro, Brazil; Deborah Iddon from **Harmon Hall** Cuajimalpa, México; and Chris Sol Cruz from **Suncross Media LLC**. Special thanks to Sedat Cilingir, Didem Mutçalıoğlu, and Burcu Tezvan from **İstanbul Bilgi Üniversitesi**, İstanbul, Turkey for their invaluable input in reviewing both the Student's Book and Workbook.

The authors and publishers would also like to thank our design and production teams at Cenveo Publisher Services/Nesbitt Graphics, Inc., Page 2, LLC, and New York Audio Productions.

Cambridge University Press staff and advisors:
Mary Louise Baez, Jeff Chen, Seil Choi, Vincent Di Blasi, Julian Eynon, Maiza Fatureto, Keiko Hirano, Chris Hughes, Peter Holly, Tomomi Katsuki, Jeff Krum, Christine Lee, John Letcher, Vicky Lin, Hugo Loyola, Joao Madureira, Alejandro Martinez, Daniela A. Meyer, Devrim Ozdemir, Jinhee Park, Gabriela Perez, Panthipa Rojanasuworapong, Luiz Rose, Howard Siegelman, Satoko Shimoyama, Ian Sutherland, Alicione Soares Tavares, Frank Vargas, Julie Watson, Irene Yang, Jess Zhou, Frank Zhu.

Viewpoint Level 2 *Scope and sequence*

	Functions / Topics	Grammar	Vocabulary	Conversation strategies	Speaking naturally
Unit 1 **A great read** pages 10–19	• Talk about types of literature, reading habits, and favorite authors. • Discuss the pros and cons of reading and writing blogs. • Analyze and interpret a poem.	• Use auxiliary verbs, *to*, *one*, and *ones* to avoid repeating words and phrases.	• Idiomatic expressions for understanding (*I can't make heads or tails of it*) and remembering (*It's on the tip of my tongue*) • Synonyms (*enduring - lasting*)	• Use stressed auxiliary verbs (*do, does*) before main verbs to add emphasis. • Use *if so* to mean "if this is true", and *if not* to mean "if this is not true."	• Stressing auxiliaries for emphasis *page 138*
Unit 2 **Technology** pages 20–29	• Talk about technology and its impact on your life. • Discuss the issue of privacy vs. security. • Evaluate the pros and cons of modern conveniences. • Discuss how you respond to new technologies.	• Add information to nouns with different types of expressions. • Use two-part conjunctions like *either . . . or* to combine ideas.	• Compound adjectives to describe technology (*high-speed, energy-efficient*) • Suffixes (*innovation, radical*)	• Use adverbs like *predictably* and *apparently* to express what you predict, expect, etc. • Emphasize that something is impossible with *can't / couldn't possibly*.	• Stress in noun phrases *page 138*
Unit 3 **Society** pages 30–39	• Talk about different social pressures that you and others face. • Discuss the challenges of starting college and other new experiences. • Discuss how children put pressure on parents. • Evaluate gender differences in language.	• Use participle clauses to link events and add information about time or reason. • Add emphasis with *so . . . that, such . . . that, even,* and *only*.	• Expressions with *take* (*take advantage of, take credit for*) • Synonyms (*often – frequently; show – reveal*)	• Express a contrasting view with expressions like *having said that* and *then again*. • Use *even so* and *even then* to introduce a contrasting idea.	• Stress in expressions of contrast *page 139*
Checkpoint 1 Units 1–3 pages 40–41					
Unit 4 **Amazing world** pages 42–51	• Talk about the natural world. • Present information about a member of the animal kingdom. • Consider the impact that humans have on nature.	• Use future perfect forms to talk about the past in the future. • Use prepositions and prepositional phrases to combine ideas.	• Expressions to describe the behavior of wildlife (*hibernate, predator*) • Suffixes with *-able* (*remarkable, valuable*)	• Use expressions like *What's more* to add and focus on new ideas. • Use *in any case* and *in any event* to strengthen arguments and reach conclusions.	• Stress in adding expressions *page 139*

Listening	Reading	Writing	Vocabulary notebook	Grammar extra
The blogosphere • A presenter shares statistics about blogging. *My interpretation is . . .* • Someone gives an interpretation of a poem.	*A brief history of poetry* • An article about different types of poetry through history	• Write a review of a book you have enjoyed. • Describe, evaluate, and recommend a book. • Coordinate adjectives. • Avoid errors with *yet*.	*Heads or tails* • Think of situations when you can use certain idioms.	• More on auxiliary verbs to avoid repetition • *too, either, so, neither,* and *(to) do so* • More on using *to* to avoid repeating verb phrases • More on *one /ones* to avoid repeating countable nouns *pages 144–145*
Privacy or convenience? • Two friends discuss privacy and fingerprinting. *How do you multitask?* • Three conversations about multitasking	*As technology changes, so do adoption life cycles.* • An article about the willingness of consumers to invest in new technology	• Write a report about Internet use. • Describe graphs, charts, and tables. • Describe and compare statistics. • Avoid errors with *as can be seen*, etc.	*High-tech gadgets* • Use compound adjectives with nouns to say something true about your life.	• Adjectives after nouns • Negative phrases after nouns • More on two-part conjunctions • Two-part conjunctions with phrases and clauses *pages 146–147*
It's an issue . . . • Two people discuss the challenges when kids become more independent. *Language and gender* • A professor introduces a course on language and gender.	*Spring semester courses in Language and Society* • Course outlines of classes about language and society	• Write an evaluation of a course. • Plan and write an evaluative report. • Express results in writing. • Avoid errors with *therefore*.	*Take credit!* • Write sentences that paraphrase the meaning of new expressions.	• Clauses with prepositions and conjunctions + *-ing* • Passive forms of participle and time clauses • More on *so* and *such* • More on *even* and *only* *pages 148–149*

Checkpoint 1 Units 1–3 pages 40–41

Listening	Reading	Writing	Vocabulary notebook	Grammar extra
The Antarctic • An expert answers questions about Antarctica. *The genius of the natural world* • A presenter shares ideas about how biomimicry could solve problems.	*How nature inspires science – a look at some notable inventions* • An article about how nature inspires innovation	• Write a persuasive essay about an environmental concern. • Use academic prepositions and impersonal *one*. • Avoid errors with *upon*.	*Golden eggs* • Notice the use of specialized vocabulary in general English or in idioms.	• More on the future perfect • The future perfect for predictions and assumptions • Formal prepositional expressions • More on *the fact that*; prepositions + perfect forms *pages 150–151*

	Functions / Topics	Grammar	Vocabulary	Conversation strategies	Speaking naturally
Unit 5 **Progress** pages 52–61	• Talk about inventions, progress, and human achievements. • Evaluate the motivation of people who are driven to perform dangerous feats. • Discuss the pros and cons of research. • Discuss inventions and innovations.	• Use adverbs with continuous and perfect forms of the passive. • Use past modals with the passive.	• More formal adjectives (*obsolete, portable*) • Adjectives into nouns (*convenient – convenience; easy – ease*)	• Use expressions like *Let's put it this way* to make a point. • Use expressions like *Maybe (not), Absolutely (not),* and *Not necessarily* in responses.	• Stress in expressions *page 140*
Unit 6 **Business studies** pages 62–71	• Talk about business and retail. • Consider the motivations behind shopping habits. • Evaluate the benefits of online and instore shopping. • Present the advantages of big business and small business.	• Use relative clauses that begin with pronouns or prepositions. • Use *some, any, other, others,* and *another* to refer to people and things.	• Verbs that mean *attract* and *deter* (*entice, discourage*) • Adjectives (*malicious, vulnerable*)	• Use negative and tag questions to persuade others of your point of view. • Use *granted* to concede points.	• Prepositions in relative clauses *page 140*
Checkpoint 2 Units 4–6 pages 72–73					
Unit 7 **Relationships** pages 74–83	• Talk about relationships, marriage, and family life. • Discuss the most important issues to consider before getting married. • Talk about the best ways to meet people. • Evaluate the pros and cons of monitoring family members.	• Use conditional sentences without *if* to hypothesize. • Use *wh-* clauses as subjects and objects.	• Binomial expressions with *and, or, but* (*give and take, sooner or later, slowly but surely*) • Building synonyms (*see – perceive; improve – enhance*)	• Use expressions like *in the end* and *in a word* to summarize or finish your points. • Use *then* and *in that case* to draw a conclusion from something someone said.	• Binomial pairs *page 141*
Unit 8 **History** pages 84–93	• Talk about people and events in history. • Determine what makes a historical event "world-changing." • Talk about the importance of one's family history.	• Use the perfect infinitive to refer to past time. • Use cleft sentences beginning with *It* to focus on certain nouns, phrases, and clauses.	• Adjective antonyms (*lasting – temporary; superficial – profound*) • Metaphors (*sift, bring to life*)	• Use expressions like *Let's not go there* to avoid talking about a topic. • Respond with *That's what I'm saying* to focus on your viewpoint.	• Saying perfect infinitives *page 141*

Listening	Reading	Writing	Vocabulary notebook	Grammar extra
Kristen Ulmer – a world-class extreme skier • A reporter relates her conversation with Kristen Ulmer. *What's the point of research?* • Two people discuss the benefits and drawbacks of research.	*Invention: inspired thinking or accidental discovery?* • An article about how inventions come about	• Write an opinion essay about technological progress. • Compare and contrast arguments. • Use *it* clauses + passive to say what people think. • Avoid errors with *affect* and *effect*.	*Old or ancient?* • Learn synonyms to express basic concepts in formal writing.	• Adverbs in present and past passive verb phrases • Adverbs in perfect verb phrases • Adverbs and past modal verb phrases • Questions with passive past modals *pages 152–153*
Too good to be true? • Four consumer experts talk about special promotions. *The top threats* • A business expert discusses the risks of running a business.	*Data leakage – Are you protected?* • An article about keeping a business's information secure	• Write a report on data security. • Use modals to avoid being too assertive and to make recommendations. • Use expressions to describe cause (*This may be the result of . . .*). • Avoid errors with *can* and *could*.	*It's tempting.* • Write word family charts.	• Pronouns and numbers in relative clauses • Nouns in relative clauses • *other, every other, other than* • More on *another* *pages 154–155*
Checkpoint 2 Units 4–6 pages 72–73				
Bringing up baby? • A student talks about his experience with a "baby simulator." *Keeping tabs on the family* • A family counselor discusses using technology to keep track of family members.	*Technology – is it driving families apart?* • An article about how technology impacts family dynamics	• Write a magazine article about how to enhance friendships. • Express number and amount with expressions like *a number of, a great deal of*. • Avoid errors with *a number of*, etc. • Use expressions like *affect, have an effect on* to describe effects.	*Now or never* • Use expressions in sentences that are personally meaningful.	• More on inversions • More on *what* clauses • *what* clauses with passive verbs and modals in writing *pages 156–157*
Tracing family histories • Two friends talk about their family backgrounds. *Citizen participation projects* • A lecturer describes projects that help uncover the past.	*The Ancient Lives Project* • An article about the collaboration between experts and volunteers in piecing together the past	• Write a narrative essay about your family or someone you know. • Order events in the past. • Avoid errors with *in the end* and *at the end*.	*Deep, low, high* • Look up the synonyms and antonyms of new words.	• More on perfect infinitives • The perfect infinitive after adjectives and nouns • More on cleft sentences with *it + be* • *it + be* + noun phrase in writing *pages 158–159*

	Functions / Topics	Grammar	Vocabulary	Conversation strategies	Speaking naturally
Unit 9 **Engineering wonders** pages 94–103	• Talk about feats, challenges, and developments in engineering. • Evaluate the priorities in research and development. • Discuss the usefulness of robots.	• Use *-ever* words in talking about unknown people or things. • Use negative adverbs (*never, not only*) + inversion to start a sentence for emphasis.	• Vocabulary of engineering projects (*erect, install*) • Verbs (*interact, determine*)	• Use expressions like *given* or *considering* to introduce facts that support your opinions. • Emphasize negative phrases with *at all* and *whatsoever*.	• Intonation of background information *page 142*
	Checkpoint 3 Units 7–9 pages 104–105				
Unit 10 **Current events** pages 106–115	• Talk about the news, who reports it, and how. • Discuss if speed or accuracy is more important in news reporting. • Evaluate how much you trust what you hear or read in the news.	• Use continuous infinitive forms to report events in progress. • Use the subjunctive to describe what should happen, what is important, and to refer to demands and recommendations.	• Noun and verb collocations (*undergo surgery, contain an oil spill*) • Vocabulary to express truth or fiction (*verify, fabricate*)	• Highlight topics by putting them at the start or end of what you say. • Use *this* and *these* to highlight information and *that* and *those* to refer to known information.	• Stress and intonation *page 142*
Unit 11 **Is it real?** pages 116–125	• Talk about whether information is true or not. • Consider how you would handle an emergency. • Talk about white lies and if they're ever acceptable. • Discuss if art forgers are still true artists.	• Use *be to* to refer to fixed or hypothetical future events. • Use passive verb complements.	• Idioms and phrasal verbs with *turn* (*turn over a new leaf, turn around*) • Words in context (*lucrative, laborious*)	• Use expressions like *That doesn't seem right* to express concerns. • Use *to me, to her*, etc. to introduce an opinion.	• Stress in longer idioms *page 143*
Unit 12 **Psychology** pages 126–135	• Talk about being independent, the psychology of attraction, and the brain. • Discuss the differences between online and in-person relationships. • Discuss stereotypes.	• Use objects + *-ing* forms after prepositions and verbs. • Use reflexive pronouns — including to add emphasis — and *each other / one another*.	• Phrasal verbs (*go by, pick up on*) • Expressions with *be, do, go, have, take* (*be close to, have to do with*)	• Use expressions like *I can see it from both sides* and *by the same token*. • Use *to put it* + adverb to indicate your meaning behind an opinion.	• Stress with reflexive pronouns *page 143*
	Checkpoint 4 Units 10–12 pages 136–137				

Listening	Reading	Writing	Vocabulary notebook	Grammar extra
Other amazing feats • Three documentaries describe marvels of engineering. *Is she for real?* • A radio interview about a robot.	*Robots* • An article about the widespread use of robots in society	• Write an essay about whether robots can replace humans. • Express alternatives. • Avoid errors with *would rather / rather than*.	*How do you do it?* • Ask yourself questions using new vocabulary.	• *whatever, whichever,* and *whoever* as subjects and objects • Patterns with *however* and *whatever* • More on inversion • Inversion with modals and in passive sentences *pages 160–161*

Checkpoint 3 Units 7–9   pages 104–105

Listening	Reading	Writing	Vocabulary notebook	Grammar extra
Journalism • A guest on a radio program discusses trends in journalism.	*Establishing the truth: How accurate are news reports?* • An article about issues in news reporting	• Summarize an article. • Use subject-verb agreement. • Avoid subject-verb agreement errors in relative clauses.	*Trust your instincts* • Find multiple verbs that collocate with the same noun.	• Simple vs. continuous infinitives • More on perfect continuous infinitives • More on the subjunctive • The subjunctive and conditional sentences *pages 162–163*
Online lies • Two friends talk about the lies that people tell about themselves online. *Fakes of art!* • A radio program profiles artist John Myatt.	*Authenticating art* • An article about the techniques used to identify art forgeries	• Write an essay about fake designer goods. • Share your views and those of others. • Use academic conjunctions and adverbs. • Avoid errors with *provided that*.	*Use it or lose it.* • Use new vocabulary in imaginary conversations with a friend.	• More on *be to; be due to, be meant to* • *be to* for orders and instructions • More on passive perfect infinitives • *would rather* *pages 164–165*
"Helicopter" parents • A mother and son talk about overprotective parents. *Understanding the brain – outcomes* • Four professionals lecture about the impact of brain research on their fields.	*The developing brain* • An article about how brain development relates to behavior	• Write a report using statistics. • Compare statistics. • Use expressions like *twice as likely, four times more often.* • Avoid errors with *twice.*	*Pick and choose* • Create a thesaurus.	• Common verbs, adjectives, and nouns + object + *-ing* • More on reflexive pronouns • Referring to unknown people *pages 166–167*

Checkpoint 4 Units 10–12   pages 136–137

Introduction: *Viewpoint* Level 2 Scope and sequence   **xxix**

Teaching higher-level learners of English

Viewpoint is intended for higher-level learners of English. At this point, students are considered to have crossed the threshold to becoming independent learners, a qualitative change from the dependent learner at the beginner or elementary level. It is not just a question of learning more language; it is about becoming a different kind of learner. So what happens when students move from intermediate to advanced levels? What substantive changes mark this shift?

Issues for higher-level learners

Higher-level learners have different needs from those at more basic levels. These include the needs to:

- move beyond general language toward more vocational and academic language.
- improve accuracy and confidence in using grammatical structures by understanding their complexities.
- review and correct common grammatical errors.
- learn new structures that are frequent and useful so students feel they are moving forward and covering new ground.
- learn more about appropriateness of use, such as formal and informal grammatical structures, vocabulary, and expressions, and understand which are suitable for writing and which are not.
- be able to operate fluently and confidently in a wider range of speaking situations, not only in informal conversations with friends but also in more formal settings such as the workplace or at seminars or presentations.
- develop skills for how to approach more formal writing and how to structure texts.

Teaching vocabulary

Ideally, students at the threshold of the more advanced levels will already recognize some 4,000 words. Most of the new words encountered in English at this point are fairly uncommon, and students are less likely to encounter them on a regular basis. Phrasal vocabulary is also increasingly important at the advanced level. Here we need to introduce themes and topics that will be relevant to students who typically have vocational, academic, and professional goals. What this means is that a topic such as travel and vacations can be expanded and specialized to include issues such as tourism and its impact on cultures and environments; friendship and socializing in general can make way for more demanding issues such as peer pressures and academic pressures. In *Viewpoint* students are encouraged to take responsibility for their own vocabulary development through a section in each unit called *Vocabulary notebook*. This encourages them to write notes and improve their vocabulary learning strategies as part of the general learning process.

Teaching grammar

The *Viewpoint* presentations and activities expose students to the grammar used in speaking and also, perhaps crucially for these levels, to the grammar of writing. The grammatical syllabus has been organized by careful corpus analysis of the kinds of texts and contexts that more advanced students will need to work with. It has also been influenced by research in how examiners evaluate and assess students' writing.

Teaching speaking

At the advanced levels, students are expected to have a high level of fluency, precision, and spontaneity in speaking. The CEFR, for example, sees the C-level learner as being able to speak "without much obvious searching for expressions," and to be skilled at "differentiating finer shades of meaning even in more complex situations." At this point, we can help students communicate more precisely *and* interactively. As well as helping them maintain the flow of language in their own contribution to the conversation, we have a duty to help students make their speaking turn connect smoothly and coherently with the contributions of other speakers. In short, our task is to help them make the whole conversation flow. *Viewpoint* takes this challenge seriously and, based on real conversation and spoken corpus analysis, offers speaking strategies in every unit that focus on producing a fluent speaking turn, linking and connecting with other speakers to create that sense of flow or confluence that marks successful spoken interaction.

Using groups and pairs to increase opportunities to speak

For students to improve their spoken English, they must have opportunities to practice speaking. *Viewpoint* offers many opportunities for students to work in pairs or groups. Make use of these opportunities by having students work with a partner or putting the class into small groups.

- For group work, groups of three to seven students are best. If a group is too small, there aren't enough participants; if it is too large, students don't have enough opportunities to speak. You can have fixed groups, or change them on a regular basis so that each student has a chance to work with the others. Students can be organized by height, birthday, or a variety of other methods.

- If the task will last more than a few minutes, designate one student to help keep other group members on task. This student can also act as timekeeper and encourage group members to change roles when necessary.

- When putting students into pairs, be sure to introduce variety into the class. Don't have the same students work together all the time. Many activities require students to change roles. Be sure that everyone gets a chance to speak.

- Sometimes speaking activities can be demanding or require some preparation and thought to get the most out of them. Students have to think through not only their ideas, but also the best ways to express them using the new language items. Try to allow some planning time when necessary, especially for in-depth discussions.

Establish and use regular routines to facilitate smooth classroom operations

Higher-level learners respond best when they know what to expect. Set up a series of routines with your students so that they know what is coming next. You can set routines for the beginning of class, the end of class, for small group and pair activities, for homework, and for tests. Be consistent in what you do, when you do it, and how it is done.

- Establish a simple set of teacher signals to indicate specific classroom commands such as *Be quiet, Stop the task you are doing,* and *Time for a task is up.* Some suggestions for signals to use include clapping your hands, ringing a bell or chime, or knocking on the desk.

- Also establish a set of signals for students. For example, students can signal that they have finished a task by raising their hands, placing their textbooks in an upright position on their desks, or putting down their pens or pencils.

Consult with other teachers

Find out what techniques other teachers have used successfully with higher-level learners. Sometimes very simple ideas can have a significant impact on improving the practical aspects of classroom learning. Sharing class management issues and solutions with other teachers is an excellent way of learning from others' experience. Your peers are a wonderful resource.

Unit 1 A great read

Lesson A *Memoirs*

Grammar *Avoiding repetition 1*

(See Student's Book p. 11.)

The unit teaches different aspects of ellipsis (leaving words out) and substitution (using words instead of other words) to avoid repeating the same or similar words when it is clear from the context what is meant. In this lesson, Ss use auxiliary verbs to avoid repetition.

Form

- Avoiding repetition with *be*

  Use the appropriate form (tense, person, number) of *be* when *be* is an auxiliary verb.

  *He's obviously enjoying it – as I **am**. (= **am** enjoying it)*

  You can also use an appropriate form of *be* to avoid repetition when *be* is the main verb.

  *She's clearly confused – as I **am**. (= **am** confused)*

- Avoiding repetition with *do / does (not)* or *did (not)*

  Use *do (not)* or *does (not)* to replace verbs in the simple present. Use *did (not)* to replace verbs in the simple past.

  *I think it's a great idea, but my family **doesn't**. (= **doesn't** think it's a great idea)*

  *She took a risk, which is what I **did**, too. (= **took** a risk)*

- Avoiding repetition with *has / have (not)*

  Use *has / have (not)* to replace verbs in present perfect.

  *I haven't been abroad. My friends **haven't** either. (= **haven't** been abroad)*

Use

- When auxiliaries are used to avoid repetition, the auxiliary can be in the same tense as the first verb, as in the examples above.

- The auxiliary can also be in a different tense when an idea is compared in two different time frames.

  *She obviously changed careers – a lot of people **do** these days. (= **change** careers)*

  *I hope it works out. It **did** for me. (= **worked** out)*

Grammar extra *More on auxiliary verbs to avoid repetition; too, either, so, neither, and (to) do so*

(See Student's Book p. 144.)

Grammar extra looks at ways to use auxiliary verbs with more verb forms and *too, either, so, neither,* and *(to) do so* to avoid repetition.

Lesson B *Favorite books*

Vocabulary in context *Understanding and remembering*

(See Student's Book p. 12.)

The interviews include idiomatic expressions to describe understanding and remembering.

- Students learn idioms such as *It's beyond me* (understanding) and *It's on the tip of my tongue* (remembering) to talk about their thoughts on reading and literature.

Vocabulary notebook *Heads or tails*

(See Student's Book p. 19.)

The Learning tip tells Ss that when they learn a new expression, they should think of and write down a situation where its use would be appropriate. Ss practice with the vocabulary from Lesson B. These expressions are mostly more suitable for speaking and informal writing than formal writing.

- **Focus on vocabulary** reviews and practices the vocabulary introduced in Lesson D (p. 17)

Grammar *Avoiding repetition 2*

(See Student's Book p. 13.)

In Lesson A, students learned to avoid repetition by replacing a repeated idea with an auxiliary verb. This lesson teaches students how to avoid repeating infinitive verb phrases with *to* and to replace countable nouns with *one* or *ones*.

Form

- Avoiding repetition of an infinitive verb phrase

  Use *to* instead of an infinitive verb phrase.

  *I would love to write like her, but I'll never be able **to**. I mean, I'd like **to**, but . . . (write like her is not repeated)*

  *We had to read Shakespeare's plays in college. Well, we were supposed **to**. (read Shakespeare's plays in college is not repeated)*

- Negatives with *try* and *prefer*

  Negatives of most verbs are formed in the usual way with *didn't / did not*.

  *We had to read Shakespeare, but I **didn't want to**.*

  However, with the verbs *try* and *prefer*, the *not* precedes *to*. The same is also true of *decide, tend,* and *choose*.

  *I shouldn't read trashy novels, and I try **not to**, but . . .*

  *I used to read a lot, but these days I prefer **not to**.*

- Avoiding repetition with *one* and *ones*

  The pronoun *one(s)* can replace countable nouns. Use *one* to replace a singular noun and *ones* to replace a plural noun.

  *I don't read a lot of books, but the **ones** I like tend to be non-fiction.*

Use

- *One* and *ones*

  These cannot be used after possessive adjectives (*my*, etc.) or *some*, *any*, or *both* unless there is an adjective.

  *I've read all her books. Her best **one** is . . .*

 Corpus information

Common errors with *one* / *ones*

You can omit *one* / *ones* after *first*, *second*, *next*, and *best* but not after *new*, *big*, *small*, *long*, etc.

  *I hope she writes a new one. (**NOT:** . . . a new.)*

Grammar extra *More on using* to *to avoid repeating verb phrases; More on* one / ones *to avoid repeating countable nouns*

(See Student's Book p. 145.)

Grammar extra looks in more detail at using *to* and *one* / *ones* to avoid repeating ideas.

Lesson C *I do like it.*

Conversation strategy *Emphasizing ideas*

(See Student's Book p. 14.)

- Speakers often add the stressed auxiliary *do* or *does* before a main verb to add emphasis to what they say. This is common when people give opinions they feel strongly about, want to contradict or correct something, want to say that something actually happens, or simply want to highlight something.

- The auxiliary *did* is used for the past. The auxiliary verbs *be* and *have* can also be stressed for the same purpose.

  *I **am** studying hard. (= Don't think otherwise.)*

  *I **have** read it, and I **did** enjoy it.*

 Corpus information

In conversation

The most common phrases with *I **do*** are: *I do think, I do like, I do know, I do want, I do enjoy, I do believe, I do feel, I do agree.*

Strategy plus *If so, if not*

(See Student's Book p. 15.)

- *If so* is used, especially in formal situations, to avoid repetition. It means *if the answer is "yes,"* *if this is true*, or *if this is the case.*

- *If not* functions in a similar way and means *if the answer is "no,"* *if this is not true*, or *if this is not the case*. *If not* can also be used between words or phrases to restate something with more emphasis or precision (e.g., *It's **as** important, if not **more** important; most, if not **all** people; it's **similar**, if not **identical***). This use is recycled in the Writing lesson.

 Corpus information

In conversation

If not is eight times more frequent in spoken English than *if so*. *If so* often introduces a question, especially in journalistic interviews where more than one question is being asked.

Speaking naturally *Stressing auxiliaries for emphasis*

(See Student's Book p. 138.)

Ss practice stressing auxiliary verbs and the verb *be* to emphasize an idea.

Lesson D *Poetry*

Reading tip *Restatement of the theme*

(See Student's Book p. 16.)

The Reading tip explains that at the end of an article, writers often return to the theme raised at the beginning.

Writing *A short yet powerful novel . . .*

(See Student's Book p. 18.)

This lesson teaches Ss to write a review of a book. The grammar for writing presents linking adjectives.

Linking adjectives in writing

- Related or compatible adjectives can be linked with *and* or a comma.

- Adjectives with a contrasting meaning can be linked with *but, yet,* or *though*. *Though* is more common before an adjective phrase. *Albeit* can also be used:

  *Old Man and the Sea is a short **albeit** powerful novel.*

- Use a stronger adjective after *if not* or (*or*) *even.*

  *. . . a dream that will be difficult, **if not** impossible to fulfill.*

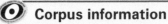 **Corpus information**

Common errors with *yet* and *but*

Yet is a formal word for academic writing. Use *but* in most other cases.

A great read

In Unit 1, you . . .

- talk about literature, reading habits, and favorite authors.
- avoid repeating words by using auxiliary verbs, *to*, and *one(s)*.
- use auxiliary verbs for emphasis.
- use *if so* and *if not* instead of repeating ideas.

Lesson A *Memoirs*

1 Grammar in context

A Read the six-word memoirs below. Can you guess the story behind each memoir?

 Our readers wrote their autobiographies in just six words.

ⓐ **Lindsay** Former accountant now wears chef's apron.	ⓒ **Yoshio** Traveled everywhere. Saw everything. Sadly, broke.	ⓔ **Tim** Every 10 years, I reinvent myself.
ⓑ **Dave** Happily raising three beautiful kids. Exhausted!	ⓓ **Sasha** Studied hard. Good degree. No job.	ⓕ **Stella** The good child – until I wasn't!

B 🔊 CD 1.02 **Listen. Which memoir is each person talking about? Write the letters a–f.**

1. _____ "Like me he seems family oriented. He's obviously enjoying family life – as I am. But he finds it hard. Most people do. I know my sister does. She has three children – all under six!"

2. _____ "Well, she obviously changed careers – a lot of people do these days. But it sounds like she took a risk by choosing a career that's not as lucrative, which is what I did, too. I hope it works out for her. It did for me, but for some people it doesn't."

3. _____ "I'd say this person worked hard in college, which most students do. But it's too bad he or she hasn't gotten any work. I know a lot of graduates who haven't. It's so discouraging."

4. _____ "Sounds like me. I was the perfect kid – made my bed, ate my vegetables, and my brothers never did. At college I went wild, as a lot of kids do. Dyed my hair pink . . ."

5. _____ "This person clearly likes change. Actually, I'm thinking of making a big change in my life. I'm contemplating volunteering. I think it's a great idea, but my family doesn't for some reason."

6. _____ "He must have traveled all over. I'd love to do that. I haven't been abroad once. Most of my friends haven't either. I'm saving up for a trip, and so is one of my friends. So maybe soon."

About you | **C** Pair work **Discuss the questions below. Do you agree?**

Which memoir writer in your view . . .

- seems happiest?
- might be least satisfied?
- has had the best experiences?
- has taken the most risks?

- has had the best education?
- is the most successful?
- seems the most interesting person?
- is most like someone you know?

A great read

Introduce the theme of the unit Tell Ss that in Unit 1 they'll talk about reading materials, that is, the written word. Ask, "When you hear the phrase, 'reading material,' what do you think of?" (e.g., *books, magazines, newspapers, blogs*) Ask, "What makes something a 'great read'?" (e.g., *it's: interesting, informative, short, clever, relevant*) Read the unit aims aloud.

Lesson A *Memoirs*

1 Grammar in context

- **Set the scene** Write on the board:

  memoir   autobiography

  Say, "Both of these are used when someone writes about his or her life. An autobiography is usually the story of a person's entire life. A memoir is often about a particular time or times in a person's life and may contain more reflection. Famous people, e.g., politicians, often write memoirs, setting their lives and actions in a broader historical or political context. A memoir usually involves an accomplishment."

- Tell Ss to raise their hands if they have read a memoir or autobiography. Ask Ss to tell the class who it was about.

A • **Preview and do the task** Ask individual students each to read one of the six-word memoirs aloud. Have Ss call out any vocabulary problems. Have classmates give definitions or explanations of words or expressions they know. Supply definitions for any remaining vocabulary.

- Ask, "Can you guess the story behind each memoir? How about Lindsay?" Have Ss call out ideas (e.g., *She changed her job. She went to cooking school*). Put students in pairs. Say, "Decide on a brief story for each person."

- Have a few pairs call out their ideas for each picture. (Note: If using the Extra Activity below, ask only one pair about one picture.)

Extra activity – groups

Group members read each other's stories aloud. Groups choose their favorite story for each picture.

For each picture, groups present their favorite to the class. The class decides on its favorite story.

B 🔊 CD1, Track 2

- **Preview the task** Read the instructions aloud. Tell Ss to read the things people say. Check for vocabulary problems and help as needed.

- **Play the recording** Ss listen and write the letters a–f.

- **Play the recording again** Ss listen again and check their answers. Check answers with the class.

Answers

1. b	4. f
2. a	5. e
3. d	6. c

About you

C Pair work

- **Preview the task** Read the instructions aloud. Ask a S to read the eight discussion points aloud.

- **Do the task** Have Ss discuss their ideas. Remind Ss to explain the reasons for their choices.

- **Follow up** For each person pictured, have several pairs report their answer and the reason for their answer.

② Grammar

Figure it out

A ⬇ www.cambridge.org/viewpoint/audio

- The grammar charts are available as downloadable recordings from the website above.

- **Preview the task** Ask, "How do the speakers on page 10 avoid repeating the same or similar words? Find these ideas and rewrite the underlined parts of the sentences."

- **Do the task** Have Ss complete the task. Check answers with the class. Read each sentence aloud. Ask a S to read the rewritten version aloud.

Answers

1. Well, she obviously changed careers – a lot of people <u>do</u> these days.
2. I hope it works out for her – it <u>did</u> for me, but for some people it <u>doesn't</u>.
3. She still hasn't gotten any work. I know a lot of graduates who <u>haven't</u>.

- **Focus on the form** Write on the board:

   do   did   does(n't)   have(n't)

   Ask, "What kind of verbs are these?" [auxiliary]

- Ask, "In sentence 1, what does *do* replace?" [change careers] "In sentence 2, what does *did* replace?" [worked out] "Also in sentence 2, what does *doesn't* replace?" [doesn't work out] "In sentence 3, what does *haven't* replace?" [haven't gotten any work]

- **Present the grammar chart** Ask individual Ss each to read a section of the chart aloud. The class listens and reads along. If desired, play the downloadable recording.

- **Understand the grammar** Say, "This chart looks at using auxiliary verbs to avoid repetition." Say, "Notice that sometimes the auxiliary replaces only the verb. Find an example in the chart." [work out] "More often it replaces a similar idea that includes the verb and its object. Look at the examples in the chart."

- Ask, "What auxiliary is used for a verb in simple present?" [do / does] "What auxiliary is used for a verb in simple past?" [did] "What auxiliary is used for a verb in present continuous?" [form of *be*] "How about present perfect?" [has / have]

   (For more information, see Language notes at the beginning of this unit. For more work on auxiliary verbs, go to Grammar extra, p. 144.)

B • **Preview and do the task** Say, "Complete the conversations. Use auxiliary verbs." Have Ss complete the task.

- Say, "To check your answers, practice the completed sentences with a partner." Check answers with the class.

Answers

1. *B* No, I suppose I <u>haven't</u> really. I went to college, as my brother <u>did</u>. . . . I went into dentistry, which is what my dad <u>did</u>, too. . . . I don't like taking risks. My brother <u>does</u>, though. . . .
2. *B* . . . I met the perfect guy. . . , a lot of people <u>don't</u>. And we don't have any financial worries. . . . Many couples <u>do</u> these days.
3. *B* Well, let's see. I had the opportunity to go to China on a school trip, but I didn't go. Some of my friends <u>didn't</u> either. . . . I think they're planning a trip for next year – I hope they <u>are</u>, anyway. . . .
4. *B* Well, I haven't traveled much, though all my friends <u>have</u>. I think it's good to travel, but my parents <u>don't</u>. They worry about me being safe.

About you

C   Pair work

- **Preview and do the task** Read the instructions aloud. Remind Ss to use auxiliary verbs. Have Ss complete the task. Walk around the class, giving help as necessary.

③ Viewpoint

Group work

- **Preview the task** Read the instructions aloud. Have a S read the example memoir.

- **Present *In conversation*** Read the information aloud. Ask a S to read the example answer aloud.

> ### Extra activity – groups
>
> Small groups make lists of *-ly* adverbs that show an attitude. Groups report their list to the class. The group with the most adverbs wins (e.g., *absolutely, clearly, possibly, probably, seriously, undoubtedly*). Write the adverbs called out by Ss on the board.

- **Do the task** Give Ss time to write their memoir. If possible, put Ss in groups with people they don't know well. Have Ss complete the task. Remind Ss to make guesses about the writer and to make comparisons with other people. Walk around class, and give help as needed.

> ### Extra activity – pairs
>
> Ss choose a famous person and write a six-word memoir for that person. Ss take turns reading the memoir to another pair. Pairs guess the person and then comment and make comparisons with other people.

- **Follow-up** Groups report how well they guessed. Have a few groups read memoirs they liked aloud.

2 Grammar Avoiding repetition 1

Figure it out

A How do the speakers in Exercise 1B avoid repeating the same or similar words? Rewrite the underlined parts of the sentences. Then read the grammar chart.

1. Well, she obviously changed careers – a lot of people <u>change careers</u> these days.
2. I hope it works out for her. It <u>worked out</u> for me, but for some people it <u>doesn't work out</u>.
3. She still hasn't gotten any work. I know a lot of graduates who <u>haven't gotten any work</u>.

Auxiliary verbs

Grammar extra
See page 144.

You can avoid repeating words by using auxiliary verbs (e.g., *be, have, do*).

The auxiliary can be in the same tense as the first verb.	*He's obviously enjoying it – as I* **am**. (= am enjoying it) *I think it's a great idea, but my family* **doesn't**. (= doesn't think it's a great idea) *She took a risk, which is what I* **did**, *too*. (= took a risk) *I haven't been abroad. My friends* **haven't** *either*. (= haven't been abroad)
The auxiliary can also be in a different tense	*She obviously changed careers – a lot of people* **do** *these days*. (= change careers) *I hope it works out. It* **did** *for me*. (= worked out)

B Complete the conversations. Use auxiliary verbs. Then practice with a partner.

1. *A* Have you ever taken any risks in life?
   B No, I suppose I haven't really. I went to college, as my brother _____. It was expected, I guess. And I went into dentistry, which is what my dad _____, too. I guess I don't like taking risks. My brother _____, though. He gave up a good career to go into music.

2. *A* So, what's one of the best experiences you've had in life?
   B Well, I guess I've been lucky. I met the perfect guy. And you know, a lot of people _____. And we don't have any financial worries. That's nice. Many couples _____ these days.

3. *A* Have you ever made a decision you regret?
   B Well, let's see. I had the opportunity to go to China on a school trip, but I didn't go. Some of my friends _____, either. But I wish I had. I think they're planning a trip for next year – I hope they _____, anyway. I won't say no next time.

4. *A* Have you traveled much? I mean, where have you been?
   B Well, I haven't traveled much, though all my friends _____. I think it's good to travel, but my parents _____. They worry about me being safe.

About you

C Pair work Ask and answer the questions in Exercise B. Give your own answers.

3 Viewpoint My life

Group work **Write your own six-word "memoir" on a piece of paper. Then mix up the papers and take turns reading each one aloud. What can you guess about the writer? Make comparisons with other people. Can you guess who wrote it?**

Loving life. School. Family. Friends. Basketball.

In conversation . . .

You can use *-ly* adverbs to show your attitude to what you say.

"This person is obviously enjoying life – as I am."

Lesson B *Favorite books*

1 Vocabulary in context

A What are some classic works of literature? Who wrote them? Make a list.

> War and Peace by Leo Tolstoy
> The Tale of Genji by Murasaki Shikibu
> Iracema by José de Alencar

B 🔊 CD 1.03 Listen to people talk about their reading habits. What does each person like to read?

They say young people don't read literature anymore, so we interviewed people to find out.

Who's your favorite author?

"Well, let's see. . . . I love Isabel Allende's novels. Her best one was . . . oh, wait. **It's on the tip of my tongue**, um, . . . *The Stories of Eva Luna*. I would love to write like her, but I'll never be able to. She's so talented, and she tells these amazing, magical stories. I've read every book she's ever written. I hope she writes a new one soon." *– Michael*

What classic literature have you read?

"I enjoy reading Shakespeare. We had to read his plays in college – well, we were supposed to – but they were too difficult, and I **couldn't make heads or tails of** them. It can be hard to **get your head around** the language. But actually, once you **come to grips** with it, you can see how the plots and characters are still relevant today." *– Maiko*

What's your favorite piece of literature?

"Interestingly enough, it's actually a poem. It's one I **learned by heart** when I was a kid. It's about cats, and I can still recite the whole thing. I can't remember who wrote it, though. As kids we used to love reading poems out loud. I still like to, actually." *– Anita*

What did you read most recently?

"**Off the top of my head**, I can't think of anything. Um, let's think. No, nothing **comes to mind**. I don't read a lot of books, but the ones I like tend to be things like biographies, um, nonfiction, where you learn something and **get something out of** it. I don't **see the point** of reading stories that are just made up." *– Carlos*

Is it important to read classic literature?

"Not really. **It's beyond me** why people think you should read the classics. You don't have to. I know I probably shouldn't read trashy novels, and I try not to, but some of my favorite books are just cheap romance novels by unknown authors. They're the ones that **stick in my mind**." *– Sierra*

What are you reading right now?

"Actually, to tell the truth, I don't read much nowadays. I used to. In fact, I was an avid reader; I used to read a lot, but these days I prefer not to. I listen to the radio more, or podcasts, because with, um, sorry . . . I **lost my train of thought**. Um, yeah." *– Jackson*

Word sort

C Complete the idioms in the chart. Use the interviews above to help you. Then ask and answer the questions in Exercise B. Use at least six idioms in your answers.

Understanding	Remembering
I **can't make** _heads or tails of_ it!	It's _____ my tongue.
It's hard to **get your** _____ around it.	We have to **learn it by** _____.
You have to **come to** _____ it.	I don't know off_____ my head.
You want to **get something** _____ it.	Nothing **comes** _____.
It's _____ me.	Sometimes I **lose my** _____.
I don't **see** _____ it.	Her stories _____ in my mind.

"I have lots of favorite authors, but one that comes to mind is Paulo Coelho."

Vocabulary notebook

See page 19.

Lesson B *Favorite books*

1 Vocabulary in context

- **Set the scene** Books closed. Say, "This lesson talks about favorite books. What kinds of books do you enjoy reading?" Elicit genres from the class (e.g., *fiction, nonfiction, mystery, thriller, romance, (auto)biography, poetry, science fiction (sci-fi), technical*).

A • **Preview and do the task** Books open. Ask, "What is a 'classic work' of literature? Have Ss call out ideas. [Classic works of literature are usually older works that are regarded as extremely good and an important part of cultural history.] Read the instructions aloud. Read the examples aloud. Give Ss three or four minutes to complete the task.

- Have Ss call out the names in their list. Write the titles and authors on the board. If a S knows the name of a work, but not its author, ask if any classmates can provide it.

B 🔊 CD1, Track 3

- **Preview and do the task** Read the instructions aloud. Have Ss complete the task. Check the answers with the class.

Answers

1. Michael likes to read Isabel Allende's novels. He likes fiction.
2. Maiko likes reading Shakespeare's plays.
3. Anita likes to read a poem that she learned by heart when she was a child.
4. Carlos likes to read biographies. He likes nonfiction.
5. Sierra likes to read trashy romance novels.
6. Jackson likes to listen to the radio and podcasts rather than read.

Word sort

C • **Preview the task** Say, "Complete the expressions in the sentences in the chart. Use the interviews to help you." Point out that the chart is divided into expressions for understanding and expressions for remembering.

- **Do the task** Have Ss complete the chart. Check answers with the class. Ask individual Ss each to read a completed sentence aloud.

Answers

Understanding:
I can't make heads or tails of it! (Q.2)
It's hard to get your head around it. (Q.2)
You have to come to grips with it. (Q.2)
You want to get something out of it. (Q.4)
It's beyond me. (Q.5)
I don't see the point of it. (Q.4)

Remembering:
It's on the tip of my tongue. (Q.1)
We have to learn it by heart. (Q.3)
I don't know off the top of my head. (Q.4)
Nothing comes to mind. (Q.4)
Sometimes I lose my train of thought. (Q.6)
Her stories stick in my mind. (Q.5)

- Say, "Now work with a partner. Take turns asking and answering the questions in Exercise B. Use at least six expressions in your answer. It's a good idea to check (✓) the expression as you use it."
- Have Ss complete the task. Walk around the class and help as necessary.
- **Follow-up** For each question, have a few Ss report an answer to the class.

Extra activity – groups

Ss look at the lists they made earlier of classical works of literature and the three books mentioned in Exercise 1A.

Write on the board:

Which of these books have you read?

Which book did you like best? Why?

Were there any that you did not like? Why?

Which of these books would you like to read?

Groups discuss the questions and report an interesting part of their discussion to the class. Remind Ss to use at least one expression they have learned to answer each question.

Tell Ss to turn to Vocabulary Notebook on p. 19 of their Student's Books. Have Ss do the tasks in class or assign them for homework. (See the teaching notes on p. T-19.)

2 Grammar

A 🔽 www.cambridge.org/viewpoint/audio

- **Preview and do the task** Ask, "How might the people in the interviews continue this first sentence without repeating words? Use the interviews to help you choose words to delete or change."

- Complete the first sentence as an example with the class. Ask a S to say which words can be changed or deleted. [delete *read a lot of trashy novels*] (If Ss need help, tell them to read the answer to question 1 again.)

- Have Ss complete the task. Check answers with the class: Read a sentence from the exercise aloud. Ask a Ss to read the complete changed sentence aloud.

Answers

these days I'm not able to ~~read a lot of trashy novels~~.
I wasn't supposed to ~~read a lot of trashy novels~~.
I prefer not to ~~read a lot of trashy novels~~ nowadays.
I haven't read one ~~a trashy novel~~ in ages.
the ones ~~trashy novels~~ I like have gotten too trashy.

- **Focus on the form and use** Say, "The new version of each sentence is another example of how to avoid repetition. Look at the sentences on the left in Exercise A. What did you delete from them?" [everything after *to*] "Look at the sentences on the right. How did you change them?" [changed the singular noun phrase – *a trashy novel* – to *one* and the plural – *trashy novels* – to *ones*]

- **Present the grammar chart** Give Ss a few moments to read the chart. If desired, read it aloud or play the recording while Ss read along.

- **Understand the grammar** Say, "This chart demonstrates ways to avoid repeating words when you don't need to because the meaning is clear. Look at the top section of the chart." Ask a S to read the first example sentence aloud. Ask, "Which words from the infinitive verb phrase have been deleted?" [write like her] Have S read the second sentence and say which words have been deleted. [read Shakespeare's plays in college] Say, "Notice that a verb and its object and the phrase 'in college' are deleted."

- Say, "Look at the middle section." Have a S read the information and both examples aloud. Ask, "When you need a negative with the verbs *try* and *prefer*, where is *not* placed?" [between the verb and *to*]

- Have Ss look at the bottom section. Ask a S to read the information and the two examples aloud. Ask, "What part of speech are *one* and *ones* in these examples?" [pronoun] Ask, "What type of noun does *one* replace in the first example?" [a singular countable noun – *book*] Add, "You don't need to use *one / ones* after ordinal numbers like *first* or *second* or after superlative adjectives like *newest* and *biggest*. You do need to use them after basic adjectives like *big* and *small*."

- Ask a S to read aloud the words that cannot be followed by *one* or *ones*. Write several incorrect sentences on the board. Have Ss correct them.

- Write on the board:
    The ones / once I like . . .
  Ask Ss to say which is correct. [ones]
  Say, "Be careful with the spelling of the plural pronoun *ones*."

- **Present *Common errors*** Read the information aloud. (For more information, see Language notes at the beginning of this unit. For more work on avoiding repetition, go to Grammar extra, p. 145.)

B - **Preview and do the task** Read the instructions aloud. Have Ss complete the task. Check answers with the class.

Answers

1. These days I hardly ever pick a book up. Well, I tend not to ~~pick up a book~~. I'd rather read a magazine.
2. There's a lot of literature I haven't read. I've never read *Moby Dick*, but I'd like to ~~read Moby Dick~~ one day.
3. I read plays, especially modern ones. My favorite playwright is Arthur Miller. I've read all his plays. [*no use of* ones *after* his] His best one is *The Crucible*. Though you have to *see* it performed to really get something out of it.
4. In elementary school, we had to learn poems by heart. At least we were supposed to ~~learn poems by heart~~.
5. I read for half an hour in bed every night before I go to sleep. Well, I try to ~~read for half an hour in bed every night~~.
6. I can't see the point of going into bookstores to buy print books. I tend not to ~~go into bookstores to buy print books~~. My books are all downloaded onto a tablet. [*no use of* ones *after* my] It's cheaper.
7. It's beyond me why people don't listen to audio books more. I love autobiographies, and it's a great way to "read," especially long ones. I always get new ones if I'm able to ~~get them~~.
8. I still go to the library to borrow books. The ones I get are usually historical novels. They're the best (ones).
9. I haven't read much classic literature, but I like the work of Jane Austen. Some of her books are also movies, like *Emma* and *Pride and Prejudice*. Both movies are good, but the best (one) is *Emma*. [*no use of* ones *after* both] That sticks in my mind.

C Pair work

- **Preview and do the task** Read the instructions aloud. Have Ss complete the task. Have a few Ss report on the sentences that are also true for them.

Extra activity – pairs

Ss write the first half of five sentences, similar to the sentence to be continued in Exercise 2A. They exchange their sentences with a partner. Ss complete their partner's sentences using the techniques presented in the grammar chart.

② Grammar Avoiding repetition 2

Figure it out

A How might the people in the interviews continue this first sentence without repeating words? Choose words to delete or change. Then read the grammar chart.

I used to read a lot of trashy novels, but . . .

these days I'm not able to read a lot of trashy novels.
I wasn't supposed to read a lot of trashy novels.
I prefer not to read a lot of trashy novels nowadays.

I haven't read a trashy novel in ages.
the trashy novels I like have gotten too trashy.

Infinitive verb phrases; *one, ones* ⬇

Grammar extra
See page 145.

You can avoid repeating infinitive verb phrases by using *to* when it is clear what you mean.
*I would love to write like her, but I'll never be able **to**. I mean, I'd like **to**, but . . .*
*We had to read Shakespeare's plays in college. Well, we were supposed **to**.*

Notice the negatives with *try* and *prefer*.
*I shouldn't read trashy novels, and I try **not to**, but . . .*
*I used to read a lot, but these days I prefer **not to**.*

You can use *one* or *ones* to avoid repeating countable nouns. Don't use them after *my, your, his*, etc., *some, any,* or *both* unless there is an adjective.
*I've read all her books. Her best **one** is . . .*
*Of the books I read, the **ones** I like best are nonfiction.*

> **Common errors**
>
> You can omit *one / ones* after *first, second, next, best*, but not after *new, big, small, long*, etc.
> *I hope she writes a **new one**.* (NOT . . . ~~a new.~~)

B How can you avoid repetition in some of these sentences? Delete words or use *one / ones*. Write *one* or *ones* in parentheses where they are optional.

1. These days I hardly ever pick a book up. Well, I tend not to pick up a book. I'd rather read a magazine.
2. There's a lot of literature I haven't read. I've never read *Moby Dick*, but I'd like to read *Moby Dick* one day.
3. I read plays, especially modern plays. My favorite playwright is Arthur Miller. I've read all his plays. His best play is *The Crucible*. Though you have to *see* it performed to really get something out of it.
4. In elementary school, we had to learn poems by heart. At least we were supposed to learn poems by heart.
5. I read for half an hour in bed every night before I go to sleep. Well, I try to read for half an hour in bed every night.
6. I can't see the point of going into bookstores to buy print books. I tend not to go into bookstores to buy print books. My books are all downloaded onto a tablet. It's cheaper.
7. It's beyond me why people don't listen to audio books more. I love autobiographies, and it's a great way to "read," especially long autobiographies. I always get new audio books if I'm able to get them.
8. I still go to the library to borrow books. The books I get are usually historical novels. They're the best books.
9. I haven't read much classic literature, but I like the work of Jane Austen. Some of her books are also movies, like *Emma* and *Pride and Prejudice*. Both movies are good, but the best movie is *Emma*. That sticks in my mind.

About you

C Pair work Discuss the sentences in Exercise B. Are any of them true for you?

Lesson C *I do like it.*

1 Conversation strategy Emphasizing ideas

A In the last day, how many different things have you read and written? Make two lists.

"I read a friend's blog. I wrote a comment on my friend's social network page."

B ◀))CD 1.04 Listen. What views are mentioned about reading and writing today?

Professor	Not long ago, they were predicting that because of the increase in phone and computer use, people would stop reading and writing. But we haven't. In fact, we're reading and writing more than we did. So, are there implications of this for literature? And if so, what?
Yolanda	Yes, well, it does seem that with social media everybody's writing something these days, like blogs and check-ins and status updates. I know I am.
Elena	Which is a good thing. I mean, I do like the fact that anyone can write a blog. It makes writing, well, . . . more democratic somehow.
Professor	I do think, though, that it gives the impression that anybody can be a writer. But doesn't it take talent to be a good writer? And if not, then does that mean anything goes?
Tariq	Yes, nowadays anyone can publish a novel online, but how do you know if it's any good? How do we evaluate it?
Yolanda	Do you need to, though? I think the real problem is with nonfiction. I mean, how do you determine what information you read on the Internet is accurate and reliable?
Professor	Yes, indeed. That's just as important, if not more important.

C **Notice** how the speakers add a stressed auxiliary verb (*do, does*) before a main verb to add emphasis to what they say. Find more examples in the conversation.

> *It **does** seem that everyone's writing something these days.*

D ◀))CD 1.05 Read the conversations. Add the auxiliary verbs *do* or *does* to add emphasis where possible, and make any other necessary changes. Then listen and check.

> **In conversation . . .**
> The most common phrases with *I do* are:
> *I do think, I do like, I do know, I do want, I do enjoy, I do believe, I do feel, I do agree.*

1. *A* The problem with many of the blogs you read is that they're very poorly written.
   B Yeah. I think it's hard to find ones that are well written. Some have good content, though.

2. *A* You know what I hate? Microblogs. I feel they're a waste of time and not worth reading.
   B Well, I follow some celebrities. I enjoy reading their thoughts on life.

3. *A* I believe that people are much less afraid of writing now. I know I am. It used to be so hard to get your work published, but not anymore. The Internet really makes a difference.
   B But it seems like that's the problem. Anyone can get their work out there.

4. *A* It's interesting how new kinds of writing have come about in recent years. Like those cell phone novels that started in Japan. It makes you wonder why they became so popular.
   B Yeah. It seems unlikely that people would want to read books on a cell phone.

About you **E** **Pair work** Discuss the conversations in Exercise D. Do you agree with the views presented? What other views do you have about each topic?

Lesson C *I do like it.*

1 Conversation strategy

Why emphasize ideas in a conversation?

- In conversation, speakers often use the auxiliaries *do* and *does* to emphasize what they are saying. They may want to give a strong opinion (e.g., *I do like that book!*), contradict or correct something (e.g., *It does take talent to be a writer – don't think just anyone can write.*), emphasize that something actually happens (e.g., *People do write more these days.*), or simply highlight something.

  (For more information, see Language notes at the beginning of this unit.)

- **Set the scene** Books closed. Ask, "How do we decide if something is literature? Or a classic? How old does it have to be? Are you influenced if it's a printed book, an e-book, or just online?" Have Ss give their opinions.

A • **Preview and do the task** Books open. Read the instructions aloud. Ask a S to read the examples aloud. Have Ss complete the task.

- Have Ss report their lists (e.g., *Read: a newspaper, a textbook, a few chapters of a novel; Written: a blog, an email, a homework assignment*).

B ◀)) CD1, Track 4

- **Preview the task** Books closed. Say, "Listen. What views are mentioned about reading and writing today? Write short answers."

- Write on the board: *Professor, Yolanda, Elena, Professor, Tariq, Yolanda, Professor*

  Say, "This is the order of the speakers." Have Ss copy the names.

- **Play the recording** Ss listen and write. Replay the recording if necessary

- **Play the recording again** Books open. Ss listen, read along, and review their answers.

- Check the answers with the class. [The professor says people are reading and writing much more than they used to. He also thinks it gives the impression that anyone can be a writer. He thinks it takes talent to be a good writer.

  Yolanda says that everyone is writing these days, thanks to social media. She thinks it's difficult to determine whether the information you read is accurate and reliable.

  Elena says that it's good that more people are writing these days. She likes the fact that anyone can write a blog. It makes writing more democratic.

  Tariq's view is that it's hard to evaluate what's good and what's not.]

- Have Ss read the conversation again. Check for vocabulary questions.

C • **Present *Notice*** Read the information and the example aloud. Have Ss repeat the example. Tell Ss to find more examples in the conversation. [*Elena:* I mean, I do like the fact that anyone can write a blog. *Professor:* I do think, though, that it gives the impression that . . .]

- **Practice** Tell Ss to practice the conversation twice in groups. Tell Ss to play a different role for the second practice.

- **Present *In conversation*** Ask a S to read the information aloud.

- Have Ss take turns using each phrase to comment on the conversation (e.g., *I do think fewer people are reading works of literature though.*).

D ◀)) CD1, Track 5

- **Preview the task** Say, "Read the conversations. Add the auxiliary verbs *do* or *does* to add emphasis where possible and make any other changes."

- **Play the recording** Say, "Now listen and check your answers."

Answers

1. *B* Yeah. I do think it's hard to find ones that are well written. Some have good content, though.
2. *A* You know what I hate? Microblogs. I do feel they're a waste of time and not worth reading.
   B Well, . . . I do enjoy reading their thoughts on life.
3. *A* I do believe that . . . now. I do know I am. . . . The Internet really does make a difference.
   B But it does seems like that's the problem. . . .
4. *A* It's interesting. . . . It does makes you wonder why they became so popular.
   B Yeah. It does seems unlikely that . . .

About you

E Pair work

- **Preview and do the task** Read the instructions aloud. Have Ss discuss the statements. Walk around the class, giving help as necessary.

- **Follow-up** Have several pairs share the views with the class.

Extra activity – pairs

Pairs choose one of the statements from Exercise 1D and write a conversation. The conversation needs to include four phrases from the *In conversation* box. Pairs present their conversation to another pair. A few pairs present their conversation to the class.

② Strategy plus

Why use *if so* and *if not*?

People use *if so* and *if not* to avoid repetition or to be more concise. *If not* is also used to restate ideas with more emphasis.

(For more information, see Language notes at the beginning of this unit.)

- **Present *Strategy plus*** Books closed. Write on the board:

  If so   If not

- Tell Ss to look at the conversation on p. 14 and find an example of each expression. [*Professor: And if so, what?* *Professor: And if not, then does that mean anything goes?* *Professor: That's just as important, if not more important.*]

- Ask, "What do you think *if so* in the conversation means?" (e.g., *If there are any implications of this for literature; if this is true*) Ask, "What do you think the first *if not* in the conversation means?"(e.g., *if it doesn't take talent to be a good writer; if this isn't true*) Ask, "How is it used in the second?" (e.g., *to repeat and emphasize a point*)

◀))) CD1, Track 6

- **Play the recording** Tell Ss to look at the information box at the top of page 15. Ss listen and read along.

- **Present *In conversation*** Books closed. Ask, "Which is used more often, *if so* or *if not*?" Ss vote with a show of hands. Books open. Have a S read the information aloud.

③ Listening and strategies

A ◀))) CD1, Track 8

- **Preview the task** Say, "Guess the missing words and numbers on the slide." Have several Ss share their guesses with the class.

- Say, "Now listen to a part of a presentation. Write a word or number in each blank."

- **Play the recording** Audio script p. T-268 Ss listen and complete the blanks.

- **Play the recording again** Ss listen and check their answers. Check answers with the class.

Answers

2/3 of blogs are written by men / males.
60% of bloggers are between the ages of 18 and 44.
Bloggers are also more educated.
15% of bloggers spend 10 hours a day blogging.
72% say they don't receive any income / revenue.

B ◀))) CD1, Track 9

- **Preview the task** Read the instructions aloud. Have Ss read the five items before they listen.

- **Play the recording** Audio script p. T-268 Ss listen and take notes.

- **Play the recording again** Ss listen and check their answers. Check answers with the class.

A ◀))) CD1, Track 7

- **Preview the task** Read the instructions aloud. Say, "Before we listen, read each of the professor's responses." Have Ss check for new vocabulary and help as needed.

- **Play the recording** Audio script p. T-268 Say, "Listen to the recording, but don't write. As you listen, scan the responses for ideas that are similar to what you are hearing."

- **Play the recording again** Ss listen and number the responses. Play the recording a third time. Ss listen and check their answers. Check answers with the class.

Answers

a. 4; b. 1; c. 5; d. 3; e. 2

About you

B Pair work

- **Preview the task** Read the instructions aloud. Remind Ss to use *if so* and *if not* in their discussions.

- **Do the task** Ss discuss the questions. Walk around the class, helping as needed and listening for the use of *if so* and *if not*.

Answers

1. sharing their views and opinions
2. more practical
3. the things they believe in
4. want to have influence
5. add advertisements for products that they really believe in

About you

C Pair work

- **Preview and do the task** Read the instructions and the discussion questions aloud. Ask a pair of Ss to read the example aloud. Have pairs complete the task.

- **Follow-up** Have several pairs report on one of the questions they discussed.

Speaking naturally

Tell Ss to turn to Speaking naturally on p. 138. (For more information, see Language notes at the beginning of this unit. See the teaching notes on p. T-138.)

Extra activity – class / groups

Ss take a survey of their classmates. They find who writes blogs and who reads them. They present their findings to a group. Do more classmates read or write blogs?

2 Strategy plus *If so, if not*

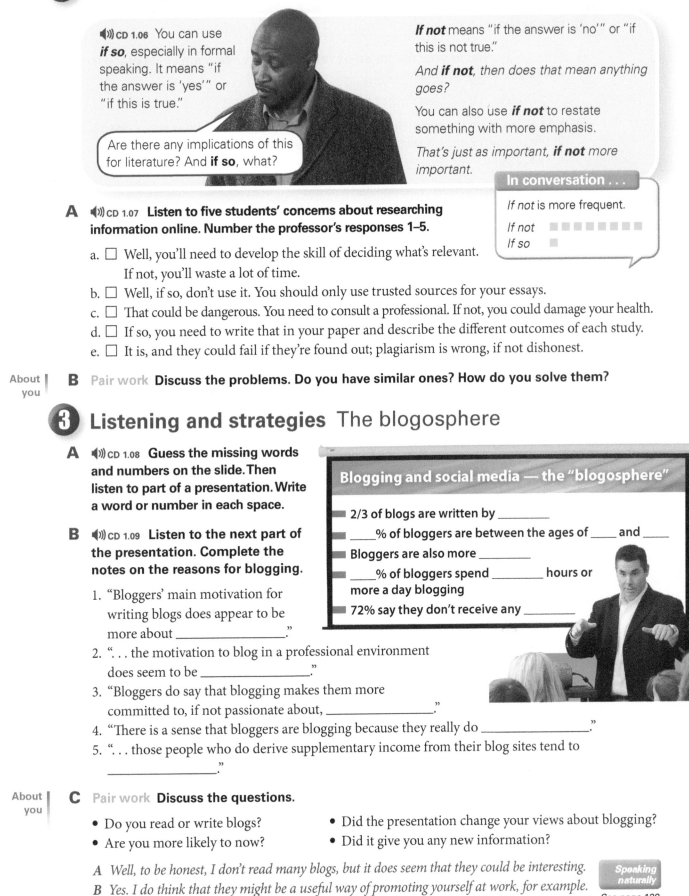

◀)) CD 1.06 You can use *if so*, especially in formal speaking. It means "if the answer is 'yes'" or "if this is true."

Are there any implications of this for literature? And **if so**, what?

If not means "if the answer is 'no'" or "if this is not true."

And **if not**, then does that mean anything goes?

You can also use **if not** to restate something with more emphasis.

*That's just as important, **if not** more important.*

In conversation . . .

If not is more frequent.

If not ■ ■ ■ ■ ■ ■ ■ ■
If so ■

A ◀)) CD 1.07 Listen to five students' concerns about researching information online. Number the professor's responses 1–5.

a. ☐ Well, you'll need to develop the skill of deciding what's relevant. If not, you'll waste a lot of time.

b. ☐ Well, if so, don't use it. You should only use trusted sources for your essays.

c. ☐ That could be dangerous. You need to consult a professional. If not, you could damage your health.

d. ☐ If so, you need to write that in your paper and describe the different outcomes of each study.

e. ☐ It is, and they could fail if they're found out; plagiarism is wrong, if not dishonest.

About you **B Pair work Discuss the problems. Do you have similar ones? How do you solve them?**

3 Listening and strategies The blogosphere

A ◀)) CD 1.08 Guess the missing words and numbers on the slide. Then listen to part of a presentation. Write a word or number in each space.

B ◀)) CD 1.09 Listen to the next part of the presentation. Complete the notes on the reasons for blogging.

> **Blogging and social media — the "blogosphere"**
>
> ■ 2/3 of blogs are written by _____
> ■ ____% of bloggers are between the ages of ____ and ____
> ■ Bloggers are also more _____
> ■ ____% of bloggers spend _____ hours or more a day blogging
> ■ 72% say they don't receive any _____

1. "Bloggers' main motivation for writing blogs does appear to be more about _____."

2. ". . . the motivation to blog in a professional environment does seem to be _____."

3. "Bloggers do say that blogging makes them more committed to, if not passionate about, _____."

4. "There is a sense that bloggers are blogging because they really do _____."

5. ". . . those people who do derive supplementary income from their blog sites tend to _____."

About you **C Pair work Discuss the questions.**

- Do you read or write blogs?
- Are you more likely to now?

- Did the presentation change your views about blogging?
- Did it give you any new information?

A Well, to be honest, I don't read many blogs, but it does seem that they could be interesting.
B Yes. I do think that they might be a useful way of promoting yourself at work, for example.

Speaking naturally

See page 138.

Lesson D *Poetry*

❶ Reading

A **Prepare** **Do you or your friends enjoy reading poetry? Who are some of the famous poets you know of? Make a list.**

"Octavio Paz is a well-known poet here."

B 🔽 **Read for main ideas** **Read the article and the extracts from some poems. What kinds of poetry does it refer to? What are the features of each type?**

A brief history of *poetry*

1 In the Museum of the Ancient Orient in Istanbul, Turkey, there is a small tablet with ancient Sumerian script on it. Few people have been able to read it, but Turkish historian and archaeologist Muazzez İlmiye Çiğ believed that the words on the tablet are those of a lover from 4,000 years ago and that it is the oldest love poem ever found.

2 Of course, love has been one of the enduring themes of poetry for centuries. Additionally, in pre-literate society, poetry was often used as a means of keeping oral history alive, for storytelling, or simply as a way of recording family history or law, for example. Indeed, these societies had no other means of registering important events or cultural information, and reciting poetry was a way to pass what they held dear from generation to generation.

3 Poetry was also valued in religion as a way of remembering teachings and prophecies. Many of the world's sacred scriptures are written in poetic verse. Early agrarian societies used poetry in rituals to encourage a good harvest, while early Chinese poetry evolved from folk songs.

4 One of the earliest known Western poems is Homer's *The Iliad*, written in the eighth century BCE. It is typical of an epic poem and consists of 15,000 lines in a strict rhythmic structure. It tells of the war between the Acheans and Trojans and talks of gods and heroes like Achilles and Patroclus. With themes of war and fate, it is believed that *The Iliad* was learned by heart and repeated as part of passing on cultural values and educational messages.

> **An extract from *The Iliad***
> *Patroclus asks his friend Achilles for permission to join the battle, which Achilles has left.*
>
>
>
> "Give me your armor to put on your shoulders;
> The Trojans might suppose I was you,
> Hold back, and give the Acheans' sons a breather,
> For breathing spells in war are very few.
> Then, with a shout, fresh men might easily
> Turn tired men from the ships toward the city."

5 During the European Renaissance, (late 15th to early 17th century), a poetic form that became popular was the sonnet. This has only 14 lines of verse. William Shakespeare, who was one of the many Renaissance poets, composed 154 of them.

> **An extract from Shakespeare's Sonnet 18**
>
> *Shakespeare is praising the lasting beauty of a woman.*
>
> Shall I compare thee to a summer's day?
> Thou art more lovely and more temperate:
> Rough winds do shake the darling buds of May,
> And summer's lease hath all too short a date:

6 In other cultures, there are different forms of traditional poetry. Japanese *haiku* is structured with 17 syllables in a 5-7-5-syllable pattern. Haiku often describes nature and communicates an abstract idea or a feeling in a moment in time. One eighteenth-century master *haiku* poet – Kobayashi Issa – wrote about his sadness on the death of his third child and then his wife.

> **Haiku**
> **by Kobayashi Issa**
>
> *Ikinokori
> ikinokoritaru
> samusa kana.*

7 While the forms of poetry have changed over time, it has generally retained a style and rhythm that make it different from other forms of writing such as novels, essays, letters, or articles. Nevertheless, one of the continuing debates centers around the issue of "What is poetry?" – a debate that still goes on with the rise of rap culture in the United States. Some see rap as the return of poetry as a performance art – poetry that should be heard rather than read – while critics say that rap should not be considered as poetry at all because it does not use "correct" English. Regardless of the ongoing debate, many rappers do consider themselves as poets. Certainly, the topics of rap songs are those of love, war, life, and death – something that hasn't changed since poetry first established itself as an art form.

> **Reading tip**
>
> In the last sentence or paragraph, writers often return to the theme raised at the start of the piece.

Lesson D *Poetry*

1 Reading

- **Set the scene** Books closed. Say, "This lesson is about poetry." Ask, "What do you know about poetry? Just say anything that comes into your mind." Have Ss call out their answers (e.g., *it's romantic, it tells a story, it rhymes, it paints a picture, it's emotional, it can be the words of a song*).

A Prepare

- **Preview the task** Books open. Ask, "Do any of you enjoy reading poetry?" Ask individual Ss why or why not. Ask, "Is poetry popular among your friends? If so, raise your hand."
- Ask, "Who are some of the famous poets you know of? Make a list." Have a S read the example aloud.
- **Do the task** Have Ss complete their lists. Have Ss call out the names from their lists, and write the names on the board.

B ⬇ www.cambridge.org/viewpoint/audio

- The Lesson D reading texts are available as downloadable recordings from the website above.

Read for main ideas

- **Preview the task** Read the instructions aloud. Say, "Read the article twice. The first time, just read for the main ideas. Don't stop to check vocabulary." If desired, play the downloadable recording. Ss listen and read along.

Extra activity – individuals / class

Ss read the article again and underline any vocabulary they do not know. Ss call out their underlined words and the number of the paragraph that the word is in. Write the words on the board. Call out one of the new words on the board. Ss look for the word and raise their hand when they find it. When all Ss have raised their hands, have one S read the definition aloud. Have other Ss use the word in a sentence to show its meaning.

- **Do the task** Ss read the article again and write their answers. Tell Ss to compare their answers with a partner. Say, "If you have any differences, discuss them with your partner. Use the information in the article."
- Check answers with the class.

Answers

1. epic: lengthy stories in a strict rhythmic structure (para. 4)
2. sonnet: 14 lines of verse with a rhyme at the end (para. 5)
3. haiku: 17 syllables (para. 6)
4. rap: performance art (para. 7)

- **Present *Reading tip*** Have a S read the information aloud. Say, "Scan the first few paragraphs of the article. Which paragraph does the last paragraph refer back to?" [paragraph 2]
- Explain that it can be useful to read the beginnings and endings of articles first, to get a basic idea of what the article is about. It can be a useful study skill to use, for example, when deciding whether an article is on the topic you are researching.

C Read for main ideas

- **Preview the task** Read the instructions aloud. Ask a S to read the seven ideas about poetry aloud. Say, "Read along silently. Raise your hand when you hear a word or phrase you don't know." Explain the vocabulary as needed.
- **Do the task** Have Ss complete the task. Check answers with the class.

Answers

1. Para 3	5. Para 4
2. Para 2	6. Para 1
3. Para 7	7. Para 3
4. Para 6	

2 Focus on vocabulary

- **Present the *tip*** Have a S read the information aloud. Say, "A lot of the vocabulary exercises in the Lesson Ds focus on synonyms because the more words you know, the better reader you will be."

A
- **Preview the task** Read the instructions aloud. Say, "Use the context to help you." Ask a S to read the first sentence and its three choices aloud. Say, "Find the three words and carefully read the sentences they appear in. Which two words have a similar meaning?" Elicit the correct words. [enduring, lasting]
- **Do the task** Have Ss complete the task. Check answers with the class.

Answers

1. enduring / lasting	5. wrote / composed
2. held dear / valued	6. way / means
3. recording / registering	7. ongoing / continuing
4. war / battle	8. verse / poem

B Pair work
- **Preview and do the task** Read the instructions aloud. Have Ss discuss the questions. Walk around the class and help as needed.
- **Follow-up** Have several pairs report on a discussion they had and found interesting.

3 Listening

A ◀)) CD1, Track 10
- **Preview the task** Read the instructions aloud.
- **Play the recording** Ss listen and read along. Ask Ss to say who the poet is talking about. [The poet is talking about someone she loves.]

B ◀)) CD1, Track 11
- **Preview the task** Read the instructions aloud. Make sure the class understands the term *interpretation*. [explanation or opinion]
- **Play the recording** Audio script pp. T-268–T-269 Play the recording twice. The first time, Ss listen only. The second time, they write their answers.
- **Play the recording again** Ss listen and check their answers. Check answers with the class: Have several Ss call out their answers.

Answers

1. She thinks the poem is lovely. She really likes it.
2. She says she can just imagine the silver sky with red-orange colors as the sun rises; and the sky turning a lighter color and seeing a bird fly, and hearing the bells.
3. The poet feels like it's the start of a wonderful new day. She wants to hear the voice of her loved one.
4. It makes her feel calm and encouraged.

About you

C Pair work
- **Preview and do the task** Read the instructions aloud. As Ss discuss their answers, walk around the class and help as needed.
- For each question, ask several pairs for their answer.

Extra activity – groups

Small groups of Ss (four is a good number) write a poem. S1 writes the first line and then passes the paper to S2, who writes the second line. Groups continue in this way until each S has written two lines.

Each group chooses a S to read its poem to the class.

C Read for main ideas **Find the ideas below in the article. Write the paragraph number.**

Which paragraph mentions the following?   **Paragraph**

1. the belief that poetry could improve crop yields   _____
2. how poetry was used to register births and family relationships   _____
3. the controversy surrounding a definition of what poetry actually is   _____
4. how certain poetic forms express ideas that are difficult to define   _____
5. the notion of poets as teachers   _____
6. an example of how romantic poetry has existed for thousands of years   _____
7. the spiritual applications of poetry   _____

2 Focus on vocabulary Synonyms

> **Tip**
>
> Writers use synonyms to avoid repeating the same word. The more synonyms you know, the easier a text is to understand.

A **In each question, circle the two words in bold that are similar in meaning. Use the article to help you. Paragraph numbers are given in parentheses.**

1. What are some of the **abstract (6)** / **enduring (2)** / **lasting (5)** themes of poetry?
2. Why was poetry **retained (7)** / **held dear (2)** / **valued (3)** in early societies?
3. In early societies, poetry was used for **recording (2)** / **consisting of (4)** / **registering (2)** what?
4. What famous poem describes a **war (4)** / **values (4)** / **battle (4)**?
5. Who **wrote (6)** / **evolved (3)** / **composed (5)** sonnets?
6. Which cultures used poetry as a **way (3)** / **fate (4)** / **means (2)** of educating audiences?
7. What is the nature of the **ongoing (7)** / **continuing (7)** / **communicating (6)** debate about rap?
8. Do you have a favorite **verse (3)** / **poem (1)** / **prophecy (3)**?

B Pair work **Discuss the questions in Exercise A. Use the article to help you. Also add your own ideas and views.**

3 Listening My interpretation is . . .

A ◀)) CD 1.10 **Read and listen to the poem. Who is the poet talking about?**

B ◀)) CD 1.11 **Listen to one person's interpretation of the poem. How does the person answer these questions?**

1. What do you think of the poem?   *She thinks . . .*
2. What image does it bring to mind?
3. How do you think the poet feels?
4. How does it make you feel?

About you **C** Pair work **Discuss the questions in Exercise B. Do you agree?**

> **PRIME** by Amy Lowell
>
> Your voice is like bells over roofs at dawn
>
> When a bird flies
>
> And the sky changes to a fresher color.
>
> Speak, speak, Beloved.
>
> Say little things
>
> For my ears to catch
>
> And run with them to my heart.

Writing *A short yet powerful novel . . .*

In this lesson, you . . .
- write a book review.
- link adjectives.
- avoid errors with *yet*.

Task   **Write a review of a book.**

Choose a book that you have enjoyed and write a review of it for the "Book Club" section of a magazine.

A   **Look at a model** Look at the review of a novel. What does the writer think of the novel? Underline adjectives that are linked together.

> A short yet powerful novel, John Steinbeck's *Of Mice and Men* is set in California during the Depression of the 1930s. It tells the story of the friendship of two ranch workers and their hopes and dreams. Lennie, a physically large but gentle man of limited intelligence, and George, his tough yet compassionate and caring friend, share a dream that will be difficult, if not impossible, to fulfill: owning a piece of land.
>
> Throughout the novel, Steinbeck creates an atmosphere that is dark and menacing. It is clear from the start that this is a story that is not going to have a happy ending. Its dramatic, though not entirely unexpected, ending leaves the reader feeling sad but perhaps hopeful that the values of friendship and trust remain stronger than the desperate reality that George and Lennie inhabit.
>
> Brilliantly written, *Of Mice and Men* is compelling, if at times depressing, with themes that are as relevant today as they were then. It is a magnificent work of fiction.

B   **Focus on language** Read the chart. Then choose the best options to complete the sentences below. Sometimes all are correct.

Linking adjectives in writing ⬇

You can link two related or compatible adjectives with *and* or use a comma before a noun.
*George is a **compassionate and caring** friend.* OR *George is a **compassionate, caring** friend.*

Use *but*, *yet*, or *though* to link adjectives with a contrasting meaning. *If* can introduce a negative idea.
*Lennie is a physically **large but gentle** man . . .*   *A **short yet powerful** novel, . . .*
*Its **dramatic, though not unexpected**, ending . . .*   *It is **compelling, if** at times **depressing**.*

You can use *if not* or *(or) even* to add a stronger adjective.
*Their dream will be **difficult, if not / (or) even impossible**, to fulfill.*

Common errors

Use *yet* in academic writing. Use *but* in most other cases.
*I enjoyed the book, **but** it was a little long.* (NOT . . . ~~yet it was . . .~~)

1. It is an engaging **and / , / but** thought-provoking story about two men.
2. The novel has several scenes that are unbearably tense **and / , / if not** disturbing.
3. The lives of the characters are hard, **if not / even / though** desperate.
4. Their dreams are understandable **yet / but / though / if** ultimately unrealistic.
5. The writing is simple **yet / but / ,** deeply symbolic.
6. The ending is moving, **if not / even / but** poignant, with an act that is compassionate, **even / though / if** brutal.

C   **Write and check** Write a short review of a book. Exchange reviews with your classmates.

Writing a book review

Describe the setting, plot, characters, and themes. Evaluate the book. Write a recommendation.

Writing *A short yet powerful novel . . .*

In this lesson

- Ask a S to read the lesson aims (In this lesson, you . . .) aloud. Ask, "Who reads reviews of things like books, movies, plays, or music? Why do people read them? What might they learn from them?" Ask Ss to scan the page to find where each aim is taught. [describe, evaluate, and recommend a book: Activity A; use adjectives: Activities A and B; avoid errors with *yet*: Common errors]

- **Preview the writing** Say, "This lesson looks at writing a review of a book." Point out the writing topic and read it aloud. Explain that Ss will write about a book that they have enjoyed for the Book Club section of a magazine. Say, "As part of writing a book review, you will learn to describe, evaluate, and recommend a book; use adjectives; and avoid common errors with *yet*."

A Look at a model

- **Preview and do the task** Read the first line of the instructions aloud. Have Ss read and then say what the writer thinks of the novel. [it's brilliant, relevant to today, depressing]

- Say, "Read the review again and underline the adjectives that are linked together. Look at the example. What two adjectives are linked?" [short, powerful] "What word links them?" [yet]

- Have Ss complete the task. Check answers with the class: Ask individual Ss each to read one set of linked adjectives.

Answers

short yet powerful
large but gentle
tough yet compassionate and caring
difficult, if not impossible
dark and menacing
dramatic, though not entirely unexpected
sad but perhaps hopeful
compelling, if at times depressing

- Say, "Look at the adjectives you underlined. Circle any that are new to you. Look at the context of the sentence and the adjective your word is linked to. Look at the word or words that link the adjectives. Then guess the meaning. Check your guesses in the dictionary."

B 🔊 www.cambridge.org/viewpoint/audio
Focus on language

- **Present the grammar for writing chart** Read the information in the chart aloud. If desired, play the downloadable recording. Ss listen and read along.

- **Understand the grammar for writing** Have Ss look at the top section of the chart. Say, "These adjectives, *compassionate* and *caring*, are compatible – that means they are similar in strength and meaning. You can join these with *and* or a comma."

- Have Ss look at the middle section. What words link adjectives with a contrasting meaning? [but, yet, though] Say, "You can also use *although* here, but *though* is more common in this position before an adjective phrase."

- Write on the board, underlined as shown: *"Of Mice and Men" is a short albeit powerful novel.* Say, "*Albeit* is a conjunction that can also be used to contrast adjectives."

- Say, "You can link adjectives with *if* when the second adjective is a negative idea. Find the example." [compelling if depressing] "Which word has a positive meaning?" [compelling] "What type of meaning does *depressing* have?" [negative]

- Say, "Look at the bottom section. What expressions can you use to add a second adjective that is stronger than the first one?" [if not; (or) even]

  (For more information, see Language notes at the beginning of the unit.)

- **Preview and do the task** Read the instructions aloud. Ask Ss how they would complete the first sentence. [with *and* or a comma] Have Ss complete the task and compare their answers with a partner. Check answers with the class.

Answers

1. and / ,
2. and / , if not
3. if not / even
4. yet / but / though / if (albeit would fit here, too)
5. yet / but (albeit would fit here, too)
6. if not / even (albeit would fit here, too); though / if

C Write and check

- **Preview the task** Read the instructions aloud.

- Say, "Look at the review again. What does it cover?" [where it takes place, story or plot, the characters, the themes, the writer's opinion] Have a S read the information in the *Writing a book review* box.

- Write *appositive* on the board. Say, "An appositive phrase is a noun phrase that renames or gives more information about another noun. In the review, appositive phrases are used to describe Lennie and George." Ask Ss to find the two appositives. [a physically large but gentle man of limited intelligence (renames Lennie); his tough yet compassionate and caring friend (renames George)]

- **Present *Common errors*** Read the information aloud.

- **Do the task** Have Ss complete the task.

Extra activity – class

Ss leave their book review on their desk for classmates to read. Ss go around the class reading each other's reviews. They make a note of which books they would like to read. Ss share the names of the books that interest them with the class.

Vocabulary notebook *Heads or tails*

If done for homework

Briefly present the Learning tip and the task directions. Make sure Ss understand what they need to do.

If done in class

- **Present *Learning tip*** Read the information aloud. Say, "It is often impossible to guess the meanings of idioms from the individual words in them. You have to remember the idioms as a whole. Thinking of a situation where the idiom is appropriate will help you." Ask a S to read the example aloud.

- Point out that these idioms are mostly more suitable for speaking and informal writing than more formal writing.

A • **Preview and do the task** Read the instructions aloud. Have Ss complete the task. Check answers with the class.

Answers

1. d	4. b
2. a	5. c
3. f	6. e

B • **Preview and do the task** Read the instructions and the first idiom aloud. Ask a few Ss for an example of a situation (e.g., *learning a difficult math concept*). Have Ss complete the task and share their situations with a partner. Have a few Ss report their situation for each expression.

Answers

Answers will vary.

C Word builder

- **Preview and do the task** Read the instructions and the first idiom aloud. Ask if anyone knows the meaning. [help or make you remember something] Ask for an example of a situation (e.g., *You go past a supermarket. It jogs your memory about going shopping for fruit.*) Have Ss complete the task. Say, "Now compare your meanings for each expression with a partner. Tell your partner your situations."

Possible answers

1. Your friend talks about a movie she saw. It jogs your memory about returning a DVD. (= reminds you)
2. Your mother is telling you to wear warm clothes because it's cold outside. You're not listening. It goes in one ear and out the other. (= You don't remember it.)
3. Someone asks you if you remember something. You're not sure you do, but it sounds familiar. It rings a bell. (= sounds familiar)
4. A boyfriend or girlfriend doesn't really want to see you this week. He or she doesn't return your calls. You get the message and understand the person doesn't really want to see you at all. (= understand)
5. Someone tells you something but you don't really understand. You miss the point. (= don't understand the vital piece of information)
6. You have a couple of choices to make. The best choice is really obvious. It's a no-brainer. (= There's nothing to think about.)

D Focus on vocabulary, page 17

- **Preview and do the task** Read the instructions aloud. Say, "First, try to match the words in the box without looking at page 17." Have Ss complete the matching section of the task. Check answers with the class.

Answers

1. value	5. composed
2. lasting	6. means of
3. register	7. continuing
4. battle	8. verse

- Say, "Now write answers to the questions." Have Ss complete the task and read their answers to a partner. For each question, have a few Ss share their answers with the class.

Answers

Answers will vary.

Extra activity – pairs

Pairs write a short conversation using expressions from this page. The conversation should contain at least five expressions. Each pair reads their conversation to another pair. The listening pair counts each expression they hear.

Vocabulary notebook *Heads or tails*

You're trying to follow some instructions to put together a bookshelf.

"I can't make heads or tails of these instructions."

A Match the situations with the expressions. Write the letters a–f.

1. You're taking a class, but you're not sure you're learning anything. _____

2. Someone has just unfriended you on your social networking site – you have no idea why. _____

3. You're trying to remember the name of the author of a book you've just read. _____

4. You have to give a short presentation in class without using any notes. _____

5. You're telling someone a story, but you get distracted. _____

6. You're telling someone about something memorable that happened to you when you were little. _____

a. ***It's beyond me*** *why he did that.*

b. *I have to **learn it by heart**.*

c. *Sorry. I **lost my train of thought**.*

d. *I hope I **get something out of** this.*

e. *That really **sticks in my mind**.*

f. ***It's on the tip of my tongue**.*

B Look at these idioms. Think of a situation when you might use each idiom. Write the situations.

1. _____   "It's hard to get your head around."
2. _____   "I can't come to grips with it."
3. _____   "I really don't see the point of it."
4. _____   "Gosh, I don't know off the top of my head."
5. _____   "Well, nothing really comes to mind."

C Word builder Find the meanings of these idioms. Then write a situation for each one.

1. jog your memory
2. go in one ear and out the other

3. ring a bell
4. get the message

5. miss the point
6. it's a no-brainer

D Focus on vocabulary Write one word from the box that has a similar meaning to the words in bold. Then write answers to the questions. Refer to Exercise 2A on page 17 to help you.

battle	continuing	composed	lasting
means of	register	value	verse

1. What is something that you **hold dear**?
2. What's one of your **enduring** memories from childhood?
3. What information do you have to **record** on a birth certificate?
4. What famous **war** have you learned about in history?
5. When was the last time you **wrote** a poem?
6. What's the best **way of** recording your family history?
7. Do you have any **ongoing** ambitions?
8. Have you ever learned a **poem** by heart?

OF COURSE YOU CAN'T MAKE HEADS OR TAILS OF THE BOOK. YOU'RE HOLDING IT UPSIDE DOWN.

Unit 2 Technology

Lesson A *How private is "private"?*

Grammar *Adding information to nouns*

(See Student's Book p. 21.)

In this lesson, Ss use different types of expressions rather than relative clauses to add information to nouns. It reviews *-ing* forms as "reduced" relative clauses from Viewpoint 1, Unit 9, and active infinitives to describe nouns from Unit 7. They are presented here in the context of a seminar on how to protect your privacy online.

Form

You can add these types of phrases after a noun to add more information. They are similar in meaning to relative clauses.

- Adverb or adverbial phrase

  *You don't know much about the guy **upstairs**.*

- Prepositional phrase

  *You know about the people **on the other side of the world**.*

- Adjective phrase

  *There are lots of people **happy to give away this kind of information**.*

- Active infinitive

  *Privacy is not an easy concept **to define**.*

- Passive infinitive

  A passive infinitive has a future meaning.

  *The subject **to be discussed** is changing attitudes about privacy. (= that will be discussed)*

- Present participle (*-ing* form)

  *There are ads **offering personal recommendations**.*

- Past participle

  A past participle has a passive meaning.

  *What about email applications **programmed to monitor your messages**? (= applications that are programmed)*

Use

Adding information to nouns using expressions other than clauses gives variety to both writing and speaking.

Grammar extra *Adjectives after nouns; Negative phrases after nouns*

(See Student's Book p. 146.)

Grammar extra looks at the adjectives that can follow nouns and adding negative phrases after nouns.

⊙ Corpus information

Writing vs. Conversation

Past participle clauses are more common in writing. In conversation, full relative clauses are up to 12 times more common than past participle clauses.

*You can get applications **that are programmed to monitor your messages**.*

*You can get applications **programmed to monitor your messages**.*

Speaking naturally *Stress in noun phrases*

(See Student's Book p. 138.)

In noun phrases, the primary stress is on a word after the noun or pronoun. The main noun or pronoun gets the secondary stress. In the examples below, the syllable that is in bold and underlined receives the primary stress.

  *infor**ma**tion on**line**

  *infor**ma**tion considered **private***

Lesson B *A smarter home*

Vocabulary in context *Compound adjectives*

(See Student's Book p. 22.)

The article presents compound adjectives in the context of technology in and for the home.

Vocabulary notebook *High-tech gadgets*

(See Student's Book p. 29.)

The Learning tip tells Ss that when they learn a new compound adjective, they should find what other nouns, if any, can also follow it. Ss are encouraged to use the expression to say something true about themselves to help them remember it.

Focus on vocabulary reviews and practices the vocabulary introduced in Lesson D (p. 27).

Grammar *Combining ideas*

(See Student's Book p. 23.)

This lesson teaches ways to combine ideas (two phrases or two clauses) using correlative, or two-part, conjunctions.

Form

either . . . or

  You can use *either . . . or* to list two alternatives.

    *It plays **either** easy-listening music **or** birdsong.*

    *It **either** reads your messages **or** gives you a traffic report.*

both . . . and

You can use *both . . . and* to combine two phrases or clauses in an affirmative context.

> **Both** solar-powered **and** wind-powered energy supplement the regular electricity supply.

- **neither . . . nor**

You can use *neither . . . nor* to combine two phrases or clauses in a negative context.

> Dishwashers and vacuum cleaners are regarded **neither** as remarkable objects **nor** as luxuries.

- **not only . . . but also**

You can use *not only . . . but also* to combine two phrases or clauses in a more emphatic way

> Many homes boast **not only** high-speed Internet connections **but also** high-tech entertainment systems.

Corpus information

Common errors with *both . . . and* vs. *either . . . or*

Use *both . . . and* to emphasize there are two people, things, or events.

Use *either . . . or* (not *both . . . and*) for alternatives when there is a choice.

*Technology has improved **both** our efficiency **and** our quality of life.* (**NOT:** *either . . . or*)

*You **either** love it **or** hate it.*

Grammar extra *More on two-part conjunctions; Two-part conjunctions with phrases and clauses*

(See Student's Book p. 147.) Ss learn and practice more ways to use two-part conjunctions and two-part conjunctions with phrases and time clauses.

Lesson C *Invariably, it's more efficient.*

Conversation strategy *Signaling expectations*

(See Student's Book p. 24.)

Speakers often use adverbs to signal their opinion about something they have to say. These adverbs let the listener know if the speaker is signaling a prediction, an expectation, a presumption, etc.

- Adverbs can express what you:

  predict: *predictably, inevitably, invariably*

  expect: *presumably, supposedly*

  don't expect: *ironically*

  assume to be true: *evidently, apparently, supposedly*

think is possible (in theory): *potentially, theoretically*

think is ideal: *ideally*

Note: All of these adverbs can go at the beginning or end of a sentence (though *invariably* is not common at the end). The most usual position is mid-sentence, i.e., in affirmative sentences between the subject and verb, after *be*, or after a modal or first auxiliary verb.

Strategy plus *can't possibly . . .*

(See Student's Book p. 25.)

People use *can't possibly* or *couldn't possibly* when they want to emphasize that something is impossible. The listener understands that any further suggestions or opinions to the contrary are futile.

Lesson D *Technology adoptions*

Reading tip

(See Student's Book p. 26.)

The Reading tip explains how writers sometimes explain or define a term using *that is, or*, parentheses, or a dash. As well as helping Ss understand a text, this is also useful for Ss to use in their own writing.

Writing *The bar graph illustrates . . .*

(See Student's Book p. 28.)

This lesson teaches Ss to write a report for a business class based on graphs, charts, and tables. The grammar for writing presents ways to refer to, describe, and compare information in charts, diagrams, and graphs. This is a required task in some international examinations.

- Describing

  The graph shows / illustrates . . .

  As can be seen (in the graph), . . .

  . . . as shown (in the table)

  . . . accounted for / represented

- Comparing

  . . . in comparison to (or with) / compared to (or with)

  In comparison / contrast, . . .

Corpus information

Common errors with *as can be seen*, etc.

Do not add *it* to the expressions *as can be seen* and *as is shown*.

As can be seen in the pie chart, most Internet users live in Asia.

(**NOT:** *As it can be seen in . . .*)

Corpus information

Common errors with *that*

Use *that* to introduce a clause, not a noun phrase.

*The graph shows **that** the number of Internet users increased sharply.*

The pie chart shows the number of Internet users by region.

(**NOT:** *The graph shows that the number of Internet users.*)

Technology

In Unit 2, you . . .

- talk about technology and its impact.
- add information to nouns.
- use conjunctions such as *both . . . and . . .* and *neither . . . nor . . .*
- signal expectations with adverbs like *presumably* and *ironically*.
- use *can't / couldn't possibly* to say what is impossible.

Lesson A *How private is "private"?*

1 Grammar in context

A How private do you consider these things to be? What else do you consider as private?

- your cell phone number
- your date of birth
- your marital status
- your mailing address
- favorite websites
- your photographs

B 🔊 CD 1.12 **Listen to a seminar. What invasions of privacy do the students mention?**

> **Professor:** In the college debate next week, the subject to be discussed is changing attitudes toward privacy. Do you think privacy has a different meaning nowadays?

> **Gert:** Yes, definitely. I mean, people put pictures online and share intimate details with hundreds of so-called friends on social networks. You can watch videos of absolutely anything, you know, people brushing their teeth – all kinds of things that were once considered private.

> **Ricard:** Right. And every few minutes, they post updates saying what they're doing. "The cat just bit me," or "Gonna wash my hair." We don't need to know things like that.

> **Lorraine:** True. You can get to know more about people on the other side of the world than about someone next door or the guy upstairs. But I guess it's pretty harmless.

> **Gert:** Maybe, but what about real invasions of privacy? Like online stores bombard you with ads offering personal recommendations because they know what you've searched for. And applications programmed to monitor your email, then on your screen you get those pop-up ads based on what you've just written? They're the ones I find creepy.

> **Lorraine:** Well, you can just ignore ads. What worries me is the information demanded from you if you just want a username for a website – sometimes they want your mailing address, cell phone number, date of birth . . . everything. There must be a lot of people happy to give away all this information, but they have no idea of how it'll be used. They get taken in by websites eager to make money by selling their databases to other companies.

> **Professor:** Privacy is not an easy concept to define. So, let's see if we can come up with a definition of privacy.

C Pair work **Discuss the questions.**

1. What do you think Gert means by "so-called friends"?
2. What is Lorraine referring to when she says "But I guess it's pretty harmless"?
3. Why do you think Gert uses the word *bombard*?
4. Why are some websites a cause for concern, in Lorraine's opinion?
5. Which of the students' views do you agree with?

Technology

Introduce the theme of the unit Tell Ss that this unit looks at technology. Ask, "When I said the word *technology*, what thought first came into your mind? Look at the picture for ideas." Elicit answers (e.g., *smart phones, apps, tablets, computers*). Ask, "Do you ever worry about technology? Why or why not?" Elicit answers (e.g., Yes: *identity theft, hacking, spyware*; No: *Most systems are secure.*). Read the unit aims aloud.

Lesson A *How private is "private"?*

1 Grammar in context

- **Set the scene** Review the worries the Ss mentioned in *Introduce the theme of the unit*. If Ss didn't mention any, ask, "Do you worry about your privacy when you use electronic devices?" Find out how many Ss worry and how many don't.

A • **Preview and do the task** Read the instructions aloud. Ask a S to read the topics aloud.

- Say, "Decide how private these things are and then discuss your answers with a partner. How many do you agree on?"

- Have Ss brainstorm other things that they consider private. Ask Ss to call out their ideas and write them on the board (e.g., *your social security or I.D. number, your passport number, your age, your medical records, your driver's license number*).

- **Follow-up** Call on Ss to say when they have to give out private information (e.g., *when opening a bank account, when applying for a passport*). Ask Ss if they ever refuse to give personal information.

B ◀))) CD1, Track12

- **Preview the task.** Read the instructions aloud.

- **Play the recording** Ss listen and read along. Tell Ss to read the seminar discussion again and identify the invasions of privacy the Ss discuss. Check answers with the class.

Answers

The invasions of privacy the Ss mention include:
- Online stores monitor your purchases and email so they can advertise goods to you.
- Websites ask for personal information when you want a username for the website.
- Websites sell your information to other companies.

- Have Ss call out any vocabulary they don't know. Write it on the board. Have classmates give definitions or explanations of words they know. Supply definitions for any remaining vocabulary.

C Pair work

- **Preview the task** Read the instructions aloud. Ask a S to read the five questions aloud.

- **Do the task** Have Ss discuss the questions. Walk around the class and help as needed.

- Check answers with the class. For each question, have a few pairs report their answers.

Answers

1. Gert is referring to the difference between "friends" on social media networks and real-life friends that you interact with regularly. The expression "so-called" means that someone might be called a friend but is not a true friend in reality.
2. Lorraine means that there isn't a great deal of danger in people putting videos and updates of their everyday lives online.
3. Gert uses *bombard* to suggest that the ads stores send you online are like an attack (of shooting or bombs) and that they are continuous.
4. Some websites ask for a lot of personal information, and people don't know how that information will be used. She mentions that websites might sell the information to make money.
5. Answer will vary.

Extra activity – groups

Write on the board:

People who post personal pictures and information about themselves on social media sites shouldn't have any real expectation of privacy.

Groups discuss the question and report some of their ideas to the class.

Extra activity – pairs

Ask, "What does *privacy* mean?" Have Ss write a definition for *privacy*. Ss share their definitions with the class.

② Grammar

A 📥 www.cambridge.org/viewpoint/audio

- **Preview the task** Say, "This task looks at ways to add information to nouns without using relative clauses." Read the instructions.
- **Do the task** Have Ss complete the task. Check answers.

Answers

1. the guy upstairs
2. websites eager to make money
3. ads offering personal recommendations
4. pop-up ads based on what you've just written

- **Focus on the form** Say, "Compare the way the ideas are expressed in Exercise A with the answers from the seminar. What kind of word was deleted from each one?" [relative pronoun (*who, that*)]
- Ask, "What is the answer to number 1?" [the guy upstairs] "*Upstairs* is an adverb – it tells us where the guy lives. What word comes after *websites* in number 2?" [eager] "*Eager* is an adjective that describes what noun?" [websites] "In number 3, what happened to *offer*?" [changed to *offering*] "What happened to *that are based* in number 4?" [It became just *based*.]
- **Present the grammar chart** Read the information aloud. If desired, play the downloadable recording.
- Say, "Look at the first three examples in the chart. How would you say these as relative clauses?" [guy / someone who lives; people who live / are] "Can you think of other examples like these?" [the guy / people over there, down the street, in the next apartment]
- Say, "In the third example, what kind of word is *happy*?" [adjective] Say, "Adjectives usually go before nouns, but here there is a whole phrase, so it goes after the noun."
- Say, "Look at the fourth and fifth examples. The first infinitive is an active verb. The next infinitive is passive and passive infinitives have a future meaning. This means 'the subject which will be discussed.'"

③ Listening and speaking

A • **Preview and do the task** Ask, "When do people have to give their fingerprints?" Elicit ideas from the class (e.g., *when they commit a crime, to get a visa*). Write the Ss' ideas on the board. Ask, "Are any of these reasonable requests?" Elicit answers.

B 🔊 CD1, Track 14

- **Preview the task** Read the instructions aloud. Say, "Read the five sentences before we listen."
- **Play the recording** Audio script p. T-269 Ss listen and write T or F.
- **Play the recording again** Ss listen and correct the false information. Have Ss compare their answers with a partner. Check answers with the class.

- Say, What types of words come after the nouns *ads* and *applications*?" [present and past participles] Say, "How would you say the first as a relative clause?" [ads that offer . . .] Ask, "Is *offer* an active or passive verb?" [active]. Ask, "How would you say the second sentence as a relative clause?" [applications that are programmed . . .] Ask, "Is *are programmed* an active or passive verb?" [passive] Say, "So a past participle after a noun has a passive meaning."

  (For more information, see Language notes at the beginning of the unit. For more work on ways to add information to nouns, go to Grammar extra, p. 146.)

B 🔊 CD1, Track 13

- **Preview and do the task** Read the first two instructions aloud. Have Ss complete the task and then compare their answers with a partner.
- **Play the recording** Ss listen and check their answers.

Answers

1. . . . matter <u>to discuss</u>. . . . an issue <u>to be taken seriously</u> . . . anyone <u>willing to part with personal information</u> . . . .
2. . . . the items <u>in your basket</u> . . . emails <u>offering you discounts on those same things</u>. . . . emails <u>sent by shopping websites</u> on principle.
3. . . . <u>advertisements targeted at you personally</u>. . . . discount coupons <u>for things you really need</u>.
4. . . . nothing <u>to worry about</u>. . . . The thing <u>to watch</u> is when they want your fingerprints.
5. Friends <u>sharing your personal details with strangers</u> – . . . dangers <u>in social networking</u>. . . . apartment <u>downstairs</u>.

- Read the second part of the instructions aloud. Have Ss discuss the sentences.
- **Follow-up** Have pairs choose one of the items from Exercise 2B and prepare a 30-second presentation about the topic. Tell Ss to include personal anecdotes or similar situations their friends have found themselves in.

Answers

1. F He found out when he got to the front of the line.
2. F The man behind Mark wanted him to go ahead.
3. T
4. T
5. F It was not convenient because they had taken Mark's fingerprints, not hers, so she couldn't open the locker.

About you

C Pair work

- **Preview and do the task** Read the instructions aloud. Have pairs discuss the questions.

Speaking naturally

- Tell Ss to turn to Speaking naturally on p. 138. (For more information, see Language notes at the beginning of this unit. See the teaching notes on p. T-138.)

② Grammar Adding information to nouns

Figure it out

A Write how the students say these things without relative clauses. Then read the chart.

1. the guy who lives upstairs
2. websites that are eager to make money
3. ads that offer personal recommendations
4. pop-up ads that are based on what you've just written

Noun phrases 🔽

Grammar extra
See page 146.

You can add information to nouns with different types of expressions instead of using a relative clause.

An adverb or adverbial phrase	the guy **upstairs** (= who lives upstairs), *someone* **next door**
A prepositional phrase	people **on the other side of the world**
An adjective phrase	people **happy to give away this information**
An active infinitive	an easy concept **to define**
A passive infinitive has a future meaning	the subject **to be discussed**
A present participle (-*ing* form)	ads **offering personal recommendations**
A past participle has a passive meaning	applications **programmed to monitor your messages**

B 🔊 CD 1.13 **Rewrite the comments. Replace the underlined words with the type of phrase given. Do you agree with the comments? Discuss with a partner.**

1. The invasion of privacy is an important matter that we should discuss. (active infinitive) I mean, how to protect our privacy is an issue that should be taken seriously. (passive infinitive) And anyone who is willing to part with personal information is just taking a risk. (adjective phrase)
2. I hate it when online stores monitor the items that you have put in your basket and then bombard you with emails that offer you discounts on those same things. (prepositional phrase, present participle) I delete all emails that are sent by shopping websites on principle. (past participle)
3. It's useful that they send advertisements that they target at you personally. (past participle) Sometimes you get discount coupons that are for things you really need. (prepositional phrase)
4. Giving your phone number in stores to get a refund is nothing that we should worry about. (active infinitive) The thing we should watch is when they want your fingerprints. (active infinitive)
5. Friends who share your personal details with strangers – that's one of the potential dangers that exist in social networking. (present participle, prepositional phrase) For example, I know far too much about the person in the apartment that is downstairs. (adverb)

③ Listening and speaking Privacy or convenience?

A When do people have to give their fingerprints? Is it a reasonable request?

B 🔊 CD 1.14 **Listen to Mark tell Mary about a trip to a theme park. Are the sentences true (T) or false (F)? Correct the false information.**

1. Mark knew beforehand that he would have to give his fingerprint. _____
2. The man behind Mark in the line agreed with Mark's point of view. _____
3. Mary thinks the theme park knows that people will object. _____
4. Mary would rather be inconvenienced than give her personal information. _____
5. Mark's wife thought it was a convenient way of opening the lockers. _____

About you **C** Pair work **What do you think of Mark's story? What would you have done in his position?**

Speaking naturally
See page 138.

Lesson B *A smarter home*

① Vocabulary in context

A What items of technology do most people have in their homes? Make a list.

B 🔊 CD 1.15 Read the article. Are any of the items of technology from your list mentioned?

Who's smarter, YOU or the BUILDING?

In many parts of the world, **labor-saving** appliances such as dishwashers and vacuum cleaners are regarded neither as remarkable objects nor as luxuries. In others, both **solar-powered** and **wind-powered** energy supplement the regular electricity supply, so people can enjoy **energy-efficient** or even **carbon-neutral, air-conditioned** comfort. Many homes boast not only **high-speed** Internet connections but also **high-tech** streaming entertainment systems. It might seem as if there is nothing left to invent nor any domestic task that cannot be automated. Homes are getting smarter, and in the not-too-distant future, the so-called ultra-modern home will be available to all. Here's how your day might look very soon.

7:00 a.m. Your bedside alarm decides when to wake you by checking the schedule downloaded from your computer. It plays either easy-listening music or bird song (or any sound of your choice), getting louder as the lights fade up to just the right level. The blinds open to reveal sparkling **self-cleaning** windows. Meanwhile, in your state-of-the-art kitchen, a **custom-built** robot is preparing your breakfast as you head for the **climate-controlled** shower room. A touch-screen panel in the mirror either reads your messages to you or gives you the traffic and weather reports you'll need for the day.

6:30 p.m. You say, "I'm home" as you get back from work. The hallway lights go on, and the aroma of a **home-cooked** meal wafts out of the kitchen. You enter the kitchen; the lights go on, and off in the hallway. The lifelike robot greets you with a **human-like** "Hello" and serves dinner.

10:30 p.m. The **computer-controlled** system takes over. It not only powers down the lights and the heating, but it also locks down the house and activates the security system. Everything is going well until you make a **last-minute** decision to go out to a late movie. Now . . . what was that top-secret, voice-activated code for overriding the whole smart operating system to unlock the front door?

About you

C Pair work **Discuss the questions.**

1. Which items of technology in the article would you like to have? Why?
2. Which items do you think will become common in the next 10 to 15 years?
3. Are there any items that you think are frivolous or not particularly useful?

Word sort

D **Find compound adjectives in the article to complete the chart. Add seven more from the article. Then use the adjectives to describe technology that you use or know about.**

climate -controlled	custom-	1.	5.
-efficient	home-	2.	6.
-like	high-	3.	7.
-powered	labor-	4.	
air-	last-		
carbon-	self-		

"We have a climate-controlled section in the refrigerator for fresh produce."

Vocabulary notebook

See page 29.

Lesson B *A smarter home*

1 Vocabulary in context

- **Set the scene** Books closed. Say, "The title of this lesson is *A smarter home*. Many of you have 'smart phones.' What can make a home smart?" Elicit ideas from the class and write them on the board (e.g., *a programmable thermostat, a home security service, lights with timers*).

A • **Preview and do the task** Books open. Read the instructions aloud.

- Have Ss call out their ideas, and add them to the board.

B ◀)) CD1, Track 15

- **Preview the task** Tell Ss to read the article without stopping to check vocabulary.

- **Vocabulary help** Write on the board:

    1. boast   a. add something extra
    2. fade up   b. have something to be proud of
    3. supplement   c. get brighter
    4. waft   d. move gently through the air

- Say, "Match each word with the correct meaning. Use the article to help you." Check answers with the class. [1. b; 2. c; 3. a; 4. d] Have Ss call out any other vocabulary problems. Write the words on the board. Have classmates give definitions or explanations of words they know. Supply definitions for any remaining vocabulary.

- **Do the task** Have Ss read the article again and complete the task. Have Ss call out the items that were mentioned earlier.

About you

C Pair work

- **Preview the task** Read the instructions aloud. Ask a S to read the three discussion questions aloud. Ensure that Ss understand the meaning of *frivolous*. [silly or not serious]

- **Do the task** Have Ss complete the task. For each question, have a few pairs share their ideas with the class.

Word sort

D • **Preview the task** Write *climate-controlled* on the board. Say, "A compound adjective is two or more words joined by a hyphen or hyphens. A compound adjective describes a noun."

- Say, "Find compound adjectives in the article to complete the chart. Add seven more from the article." Point out the first example.

- **Do the task** Ss complete the chart. Check answers with the class.

Answers

climate-*controlled*   last-*minute*
energy-*efficient*   self-*cleaning*
human-*like*
solar-*powered*   1. *so-called*
wind-*powered*   2. *ultra-modern*
air-*conditioned*   3. *not-too-distant*
carbon-*neutral*   4. *easy-listening*
custom-*built*   5. *state-of-the-art*
home-*cooked*   6. *top-secret*
high-*tech*   7. *voice-activated*
high-*speed*   8. *touch-screen*
labor-*saving*

- Say, "Now use the adjectives to describe technology that you use or know about. Tell a partner."

- Indicate or rewrite *climate-controlled* on the board. Ask Ss for an example sentence (e.g., *The mall is climate-controlled. It's always comfortable there – no matter what the weather is like.*)

- **Follow-up** Have several pairs tell the class about a technology they know or use.

Extra activity – groups

Write on the board, underlined as shown:

A technology I need

A technology I really want

Groups decide on two technologies they need and two they really want. Groups report to the class. A S records the items on the board. The class decides on the most needed and the most wanted.

Tell Ss to turn to Vocabulary Notebook on p. 29 of their Student's Books. Have Ss do the tasks in class or assign them for homework. (See the teaching notes on p. T-29.)

② Grammar

A 🔊 www.cambridge.org/viewpoint/audio

- **Preview the task** Say, "Use the article to help you rewrite these sentences."
- **Do the task** Have Ss complete the task. Check answers with the class.

Answers

1. Both solar-powered and wind-powered energy supplement the regular electricity supply.
2. Dishwashers are regarded neither as remarkable objects nor luxuries.
3. It not only gradually powers down the lights, but it also activates the security system.

- **Focus on the form and use** Say, "Look at the sentences you wrote. Sentence 1 talks about two things that supplement the electricity supply. What are they?" [solar-powered and wind-powered energy] "How were these ideas combined?" [*both* was added]

- Ask, "In sentence 2, what two things are not true about dishwashers?" [They're not remarkable objects, and they're not luxuries.] "How were these ideas combined?" [with *neither* and *nor*]

- Ask, "In sentence 3, what two things can *it* do?" [power down the lights and activate the security system] "How were these ideas combined?" [with *not only* and *but also*]

- Say, "This activity and grammar chart teach ways to combine ideas."

- **Present the grammar chart** Read the information aloud. If desired, play the downloadable recording. Ss listen and read along.

- **Understand the grammar chart** Say, "Review the chart. Where are two-part conjunctions placed in the sentences?" [The first conjunction precedes the first alternative, and the second conjunction precedes the second alternative.]

- Ask Ss to compare sentence 2 in Exercise 2A with the example sentence in the third section. Say, "Notice that *not* + verb becomes *neither*. Or becomes *nor*."

- **Present *Common errors*** Read the information aloud.
  (For more information, see Language notes at the beginning of the unit. For more work on two-part conjunctions, go to Grammar extra, p. 147.)

B
- **Preview the task** Say, "Rewrite the sentences using the conjunctions given. You may have to change the form or order of words, or leave some words out."

- **Do the task** Ss complete the task. Check answers with the class: Have individual pairs each read a conversation aloud.

Answers

1. **A** . . . that you neither want nor use . . . It not only tells the time, but (it) also gives the temperature outside.
   B . . . I neither open the calendar, nor use the voice-activated calling.
2. **A** . . . my grandmother not only washed . . . by hand, but she also hung it out to dry.
   B . . . they had neither the luxury nor the convenience of all our labor-saving devices.
3. **A** . . . control both the heating system and the lights. . . . turn off either the stove or the coffee . . .
   B . . . you could not only check on your house, but (you could) also water your plants.
4. **A** . . . that can either cook or clean. . . . chores are both boring and a waste of time.
   B . . . It not only saved her time but (it) also did a better job than she did.

- Say, "Now practice the conversations with a partner."

About you

C Pair work

- **Preview the task** Read the instructions aloud.
- **Do the task** Ss complete the task. Walk around the class, giving help as needed. When pairs have completed the activity, have several pairs share their ideas with the class.

Extra activity – groups

Write on the board:

Many functions on high-tech gadgets are frivolous. The companies are just making more money by bringing out newer models every few months.

Groups discuss the idea and then share their conclusions with the class. Conclusions should include all four two-part conjunctions.

❷ Grammar Combining ideas

Figure it out

A **Use the article to help you rewrite these sentences. Then read the grammar chart.**

1. Solar-powered and wind-powered energy supplement the regular electricity supply.
2. Dishwashers are not regarded as remarkable objects or luxuries.
3. It gradually powers down the lights, and it activates the security system.

Grammar extra
See page 147.

either . . . or, both . . . and, neither . . . nor, not only . . . but also

You can use these conjunctions to combine two phrases or clauses in one clause or one sentence.

Use *either . . . or . . .* to list two alternatives.	It plays **either** easy-listening music **or** birdsong. It **either** reads your messages **or** gives you a traffic report.
Use *both . . . and . . .* to combine two phrases or clauses in an affirmative context.	**Both** solar-powered **and** wind-powered energy supplement the regular electricity supply.
Use *neither . . . nor . . .* to combine two phrases or clauses in a negative context.	Dishwashers and vacuum cleaners are regarded **neither** as remarkable objects **nor** as luxuries.
Use *not only . . . but also . . .* to combine two phrases or clauses in a more emphatic way.	Many homes boast **not only** high-speed Internet connections **but also** high-tech entertainment systems.

B **Rewrite the comments using the conjunctions given. You may have to change the form or order of the words, or leave some words out. Then practice with a partner.**

> **Common errors**
>
> Use *both . . . and . . .* to emphasize that there are two people or things.
> Use *either . . . or . . .* when there is a choice of alternatives.
> Technology improves **both** our efficiency **and** our quality of life.
> (NOT . . . ~~improves either . . . or . . .~~)

1. *A* You know what I don't like? High-tech gadgets with all those functions that you don't want or use. (neither . . . nor) Like my alarm clock tells the time and gives the temperature outside. (not only . . . but also)
   B It's like my cell phone. I don't open the calendar, and I don't use the voice-activated calling. (neither . . . nor)

2. *A* You know, chores were much harder for our grandparents' generation. I mean, my grandmother washed everything by hand, and she hung it out to dry. (not only . . . but also)
   B Well, they didn't have the luxury or the convenience of all our labor-saving devices. (neither . . . nor)

3. *A* Imagine running your home from your laptop. You could control the heating system, the lights. (both . . . and) Well, everything, really. Then if you forgot to turn off the stove or the coffee pot, you could just do it when you got to work. (either . . . or)
   B It'd be handy, too, on vacation. I mean, you could check on your house and you could water your plants. (not only . . . but also)

4. *A* I'd love a robot that can cook or clean. (either . . . or) I think chores are boring and a waste of time. (both . . . and)
   B Me too. My friend bought one of those robot vacuum cleaners. It saved her time and did a better job than she did. (not only . . . but also)

About you

C Pair work **What do you think about the views above? Discuss your ideas. Do you agree?**

Lesson C *Invariably, it's more efficient.*

1 Conversation strategy Signaling expectations

A Do you think you're good at multitasking? What two things can you do at the same time?

B 🔊 CD 1.16 Listen. What does the research that Lucia read say about multitasking?

Rashad	All these people with headphones on – working, emailing, messaging . . . I couldn't possibly do that.
Lucia	Me neither.
Rashad	I mean, multitasking is supposedly an essential skill these days, and theoretically, you can pack 12 hours into an 8-hour day, but I'm skeptical. You can't possibly concentrate on more than one thing.
Lucia	Well, I was reading about this recently, and evidently, if you're multitasking, you're either doing things badly or not at all.
Rashad	So there's been research on this, presumably?
Lucia	Yeah. Apparently, they gave people these tasks to do and found that "high multitaskers" weren't just slower; they had poor memories and couldn't switch tasks easily, either. So being able to multitask is really a myth and might even be harmful.
Rashad	Sounds like there's a lot to be said for doing one thing at a time.
Lucia	Well, it's almost invariably more efficient. And ironically, the people who said they were bad at multitasking performed better than those who said they were good at it, and vice versa.
Rashad	Maybe I'd be better at it than I thought, then.

C Notice how Rashad and Lucia use adverbs to signal what they predict, expect, or assume to be true. Find the examples they use in the conversation.

> **Adverbs can express what you . . .**
> predict: *predictably, inevitably, invariably*
> expect: *presumably, supposedly;* don't expect: *ironically*
> assume to be true: *evidently, apparently, supposedly*
> think is possible (in theory): *potentially, theoretically*
> think is ideal: *ideally*

D Rewrite the sentences, replacing the underlined words with the adverb form of the word in bold. Then discuss the information with a partner. Do you agree?

Mothers supposedly spend a lot more time . . .

1. Mothers <u>are **supposed**</u> to spend a lot more time multitasking than fathers, <u>or so people say</u>. The **invariable** <u>belief is</u> that they're making dinner and helping the kids with homework.
2. <u>There is the **potential** that</u> multitasking for a period of time can overload the brain and cause stress. <u>It **appears** that</u> it's harmful to the brain.
3. <u>There is **evidence** that</u> workers distracted by phone calls and email suffer a drop in IQ. <u>The **ideal** thing is</u> you should avoid distractions. <u>The **potential** is</u> it's like losing a night's sleep.
4. Some people think multitasking makes them more productive, <u>which is **ironic**</u>. <u>You have to **presume** that</u> they haven't read the research about its effect on your brain.
5. <u>In **theory**</u>, it's possible for multitasking to be addictive. The **invariable** <u>habit of</u> high multitaskers <u>is to</u> place a high value on new information. They switch from emails to texts to calls because it's exciting to them, <u>which is **inevitable**</u>.

Lesson C *Invariably, it's more efficient.*

1 Conversation strategy

Why signal expectations?

Speakers often use adverbs to signal their attitude to something they have to say. These adverbs let the listener know if the speaker is predicting, anticipating, or presuming, and so on. For example, *"Apparently, multitasking isn't really efficient."* tells the listener that the speaker is reporting something she or he has heard and assumes to be true.

(For more information, see Language notes at the beginning of this unit.)

- **Set the scene** Books closed. Say, "What is *multitasking*?" [doing more than one job at the same time] Ask, "Do you think multitasking is a good skill to have?" Elicit answers and have Ss say why or why not.

A • **Preview and do the task** Books open. Read the instructions aloud.

- Ask, "Who's good at multitasking? Raise your hand if you think you are." Ask several Ss what two things they can do at the same time. Say, "Now that you've heard some examples of multitasking, raise your hand if you think you're good at multitasking."

B 🔊 CD1, Track 16

- **Preview the task** Books closed. Read the instructions aloud. Add, "Write a short answer to the question."
- **Play the recording** Ss listen and write. Replay the recording if necessary. Have Ss compare their answers in pairs.
- **Play the recording again** Books open. Ss listen, read along, and check their answer. Check the answer with the class. [The research says that multitaskers generally do things more slowly. They have poor memories and find it difficult to switch tasks, also. It might even harm the brain. Researchers also say that multitaskers who think they are good at multitasking perform worse than people who think they are bad at it.]

C • **Present *Notice*** Read the information aloud. Read the lists of adverbs aloud. Check that Ss understand the adverbs used in the list.

- Say, "Read the conversation again. Find examples in the conversation." Have a S read them aloud. [*Rashad*: I mean, multitasking is supposedly an essential skill . . . , and theoretically, you can . . . *Lucia*: . . . , and evidently, if you're multitasking . . . *Rashad*: . . . research on this, presumably? *Lucia*: Yeah. Apparently, they gave . . . *Lucia*: Well, it's almost invariably more efficient. And ironically, . . .]
- **Practice** Tell Ss to practice the conversation in pairs, taking turns playing each role.

D • **Preview and do the task** Say, "Rewrite the sentences, replacing the underlined words with the adverb form of the word in bold. Some adverbs can be moved to a different place in the sentence." Have Ss complete the task. Check answers with the class: Have individual Ss each read a sentence aloud.

Note: The key shows the adverbs at the beginning of the sentence and the most common mid-sentence position (before a main verb after *be*, or after a modal or first auxiliary verb). They can also go at the end of the sentence, though *invariably* is not common at the end. The adverbs which replace relative clauses are shown at the end.

Answers

1. Mothers supposedly spend . . . They're invariably making dinner . . . / Invariably, they're making dinner . . .
2. Multitasking for a period of time can potentially overload . . . / Potentially, multitasking for a period of time can overload . . . It's apparently harmful to the brain. / Apparently, it's harmful to the brain.
3. Workers distracted by phone calls and email evidently suffer a drop in IQ. / Evidently, workers distracted by phone calls and email suffer a drop in IQ. You should ideally avoid distractions. / Ideally, you should avoid distractions. It's potentially like losing a night's sleep. / Potentially, it's like losing a night's sleep.
4. Some people think multitasking makes them more productive, ironically. They presumably haven't read the research . . . / Presumably, they haven't read the research . . .
5. It's theoretically possible for multitasking . . . / Theoretically, it's possible for multitasking . . . High multitaskers invariably place a high value . . . / Invariably, high multitaskers place a high value . . . They switch from emails to texts because it's exciting to them, inevitably . . .

- Say, "Now discuss the information with a partner. Do you agree?"
- **Follow-up** For each sentence, have a few Ss give their opinion.

Extra activity – pairs

Pairs write a short conversation similar to Rashad and Lucia's, talking about their attitude toward multitasking. Remind Ss to use at least three adverbs in their conversation. Pairs present their conversation to another pair. Tell Ss to listen carefully and find out if any new ideas are discussed.

② Strategy plus

Why use *can't possibly . . . ?*

In conversation, a speaker may use *can't possibly* or *couldn't possibly* when he or she wants to emphasize that something is impossible. The listener understands that any further suggestions or opinions to the contrary are futile.

(For more information, see Language notes at the beginning of this unit.)

◀))) CD1, Track 17

- **Present *Strategy plus*** Tell Ss to look at Rashad and Lucia's conversation again and find examples of *can't possibly* and *couldn't possibly*. [*Rashad:* I couldn't possibly do that; *Rashad:* You can't possibly concentrate . . .]
- **Play the recording** Ss listen and read along.

A ◀))) CD1, Track 18

- **Preview the task** Read the instructions aloud. Ask a S to read the five summary sentences aloud.
- **Play the recording** Audio script p. T-269 Ss listen and number the sentences. Check answers with the class.

Answers

5 All young people do it.
2 You get less work done.
1 It's dangerous while driving.
3 It affects your concentration.
4 It's actually pretty easy.

B ◀))) CD1, Track 19

- **Preview the task** Read the instructions aloud. Ask Ss to read the five responses aloud. Tell Ss they will hear the people talking about multitasking again. Tell Ss to listen and choose an appropriate response.
- **Play the recording** Audio script p. T-269 Model the activity by pausing after the first comment, and tell Ss to find the best response. Have a S call out the response. [Right. You can't possibly concentrate on driving if you're on the phone.] Tell Ss to write number *1* next to the response. Play the rest of the recording, pausing after each comment. Ss listen and number the responses. Check answers with the class.

Answers

3 Right. You couldn't possibly say that . . .
4 Yeah, it can't possibly be that hard to . . .
1 Right. You can't possibly concentrate on . . .
5 I know. I mean, you can't possibly expect . . .
2 Exactly. But you can't possibly avoid . . .

About you

C ◀))) CD1, Track 20

- **Preview the task** Say, "Listen again. Write your own responses. Include *can't possibly* or *couldn't possibly* in each response you write."
- **Play the recording** Audio script p. T-269 Ss listen and write. Pause the recording after each person speaks to give the Ss time to write. Have Ss compare their answers with a partner.
- **Follow-up** Play the recording again. Pause after each speaker and have several Ss read their responses aloud.

③ Listening and strategies

A ◀))) CD1, Track 21

- **Preview the task** Read the instructions aloud. Tell Ss to write a few words, not complete sentences.
- **Play the recording** Audio script pp. T-269–T-270 Ss listen and write. Play the recording again if necessary.
- Check answers with the class.

Answers

Conversation 1
1. cook
2. remembers orders, cooks, serves customers
3. sometimes burns the food

Conversation 2
1. personal assistant
2. prints out reports, sets up appointments, checks mail
3. writes down the wrong appointment times

Conversation 3
1. high school student
2. watches TV show, updates social network page, does homework
3. gets some of the math problems wrong

B ◀))) CD1, Track 22

- **Preview the task** Read the instructions aloud.
- **Play the recording** Audio script pp. T-269–T-270 Ss listen and write. Check answers with the class.

Answers

1. can't possibly
2. Inevitably
3. Invariably
4. couldn't possibly
5. presumably

About you

C Pair work

- **Preview the task** Read the instructions aloud.
- **Do the task** Ss discuss the comments. Walk around the class, giving help as needed. When pairs have completed the activity, have several pairs share their ideas with the class.

2 Strategy plus *can't possibly . . .*

🔊 **CD 1.17** You can use **can't possibly** or **couldn't possibly** to emphasize that something is impossible.

> You **can't possibly** concentrate on more than one thing.

A 🔊 **CD 1.18** **Listen. Five people talk about multitasking. Number the summaries of their views 1–5.**

☐ All young people do it. ☐ It's dangerous while driving. ☐ It's actually pretty easy.
☐ You get less work done. ☐ It affects your concentration.

B 🔊 **CD 1.19** **Read the responses below. Then listen again and number the responses 1–5.**

_____ Right. You couldn't possibly say that multitasking is a good skill to have, then.
_____ Yeah, it can't possibly be that hard to do two simple everyday tasks at the same time.
_____ Right. You can't possibly concentrate on driving if you're on the phone.
_____ I know. I mean, you can't possibly expect them to do anything different.
_____ Exactly. But you can't possibly avoid phone calls and things, even if you work at home.

About you **C** 🔊 **CD 1.20** **Listen again. Write your own responses. Then compare with a partner.**

3 Listening and strategies How do you multitask?

A 🔊 **CD 1.21** **Listen to three conversations. Write answers for each item below.**

1. Write the job each multitasker has.
2. Write three tasks each multitasker does at the same time.
3. Write the mistake each multitasker admits to.

B 🔊 **CD 1.22** **Listen again to some of the things the speakers say. Complete the comments below with expressions from the box. There are two extra expressions.**

can't possibly   couldn't possibly   inevitably   invariably   ironically   potentially   presumably

1. You _____ expect people to do three or four things at the same time and do each thing properly.
2. _____, I end up making mistakes when I try to do more than one thing at once. It's usually better to take your time.
3. That's what drives me crazy – trying to have a conversation with someone and they're checking messages on their phone. _____, I just make an excuse and leave.
4. I don't know about you, but I _____ just sit and watch a TV show. I have to do other stuff at the same time.
5. I can see you can listen to music and study – it helps you concentrate, _____. I mean, that kind of multitasking seems fine.

> MY WIFE DOESN'T THINK I'M VERY GOOD AT MULTITASKING.

About you **C** **Pair work** **Do you agree with the comments above? Discuss with a partner.**

A *Actually, I agree. You can't possibly expect people to do three or four things at the same time and do each thing properly.*
B *Oh, I totally agree. I mean, invariably you end up making a mistake with something.*

Lesson D *Technology adoptions*

① Reading

A Prepare When new gadgets come onto the market, how many people in the class: a. buy them immediately? b. wait and see what other people say about them? c. never buy them? Take a class vote.

B 📥 Read for main ideas Read the article to see if your class fits the model in the diagram. Complete the labels in the diagram with terms and percentages in the article to help you find out.

As technology changes, so do adoption lifecycles

1 For decades now, conventional marketing wisdom about product adoption cycles has been based on a model first described in the 1950s. The Adoption Process model (also known as the Diffusion of Innovation) illustrates how consumers purchase new products and services (see Rogers, 2003*). It categorizes consumers according to their behavior as early adopters at one end of the cycle and laggards at the other.

2 Until recently, cutting-edge technologies were mainly used by a minority group of "innovators," who accounted for approximately 2 percent of consumers. These were the enthusiasts that tried out every new gadget on the market. They were also the ones who found any bugs or problems in the products, gave honest feedback, and became loyal users. The next group of customers were the more cautious "early adopters," who represented 13.5 percent of consumers. Then came the majority of mainstream consumers, who are described as "early majority" and "late majority" consumers, each group representing 34 percent of the total market. They viewed new technology with more caution. Typically, they waited until a new piece of technology was truly tried and tested and until the price had been considerably reduced. It invariably took several years for this to happen, and at this point, when the majority of consumers had purchased a product, it was said that it had truly penetrated the market and become a mainstream "must-have" item. The remaining 16 percent of consumers are labeled "laggards" – that is, those who are either very late adopters or who never buy high-tech products.

3 However, some researchers are beginning to find that these typical adoption patterns are becoming less relevant in today's marketplace and that mainstream consumers are *all* becoming early adopters. The length of time it takes for a new technology to enter the mainstream market is also shortening. When tablets hit the market in 2010, it was the fastest uptake of any device ever. It was faster than the spread of laptops and faster than the penetration of smart phones. Over 15 million tablets were sold in the first nine months after the initial release – a phenomenal rate by any standards.

4 Furthermore, in the past, advanced technologies often first appeared in the workplace and then migrated into the

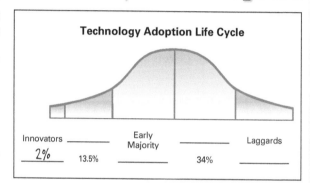

Technology Adoption Life Cycle

Innovators _____ Early Majority _____ Laggards
2%   13.5%   34%

domestic setting as recreational products. That is no longer the case, and it is increasingly the general domestic consumer who is driving what is used in the workplace, as employees show up at work with their new "toys" and expect to be able to use them. Authors of one study point out that the average family is now instrumental in driving recent technology adoptions. Having the latest technology is one way to catalog your children growing up and share it with other family members. Over 85 percent of families with children have cell phones, and they are more likely to have both music and video playback features on their phones.

5 Perhaps part of the reason for the change in how technologies are adopted is that the millennial generation is now a much larger segment of the consumer population. Millennials, that is, children born in the 1980s, grew up with media and digital technologies. Generation Z kids born in the 1990s are even more connected and net-savvy and are often known as "digital-natives." In the near future, they will become the majority of the consumer population, and the only logical assumption is that the technology lifecycle as described in traditional models may well be obsolete and in need of radical revision.

*Rogers, E.M. 2003. *Diffusion of Innovations* (5th Edition). New York: Free Press.

Reading tip

Writers sometimes explain a term using *that is, or,* parentheses ( ), or a dash – . *Millennials, that is, children born in the 1980s , . . .*

Lesson D *Technology adoptions*

1 Reading

- **Set the scene** Books closed. Read the title of the lesson aloud. Ask, "What does it mean to adopt something?" [to accept or start using something new] Ask, "What are some technologies you've adopted in the past?" Have Ss call out their answers (e.g., *a smart phone, a notebook computer, downloading apps*).

A Prepare

- **Preview and do the task** Books open. Read the instructions aloud. Assign a S to count and record the votes. Write the totals on the board and as approximate percentages of the class.
- Call on a few Ss to say why they buy things right away, why they wait to buy, or why they never buy new technologies.

B 🔽 www.cambridge.org/viewpoint/audio
Read for main ideas

- **Preview the task** Read the instructions aloud. Say, "Read the article twice. The first time, just read for the main ideas. The second time, complete the labels in the diagram." If desired, play the downloadable recording.

  Note: The word *laggard* is used here as a marketing term. In general use, *laggard* can be pejorative.

- **Do the task** Ss read and complete the labels. Tell Ss to compare their answers.

Answers

Innovators – 2%
Early adopters – 13.5%
Early majority – 34%
Late majority – 34%
Laggards – 16%

- Ask, "Does our class fit the model?" Write on the board:

  a = Innovators and Early adopters
  b = Early and Late majorities
  c = Laggards

- Have Ss call out the totals from the chart. [*a.* = 15.5%; *b.* = 68%; *c.* = 16%] Add them to the board. Ask, "How does our class compare? Do any of the comparisons surprise you?" Elicit opinions from the class.

- **Present *Reading tip*** Read the information aloud. Ask Ss to scan the article and find the explanation of a *laggard*. [those who are either very late adopters or who never buy high-tech products] Ask, "What did the writer use to show that this was an explanation?" [He or she used a dash and *that is.*] Do the same for *bugs* (para. 2).

- **Vocabulary help** Write on the board:

  1. *domestic*   4. *obsolete*
  2. *innovator*   5. *radical*
  3. *mainstream*   6. *uptake*

  Have Ss scan the article and circle words from the board. As Ss scan, write on the board:

  a. something common, shared by most people
  b. no longer used or needed
  c. extreme
  d. relating to the home
  e. acceptance
  f. one who introduces change and new ideas

  Have Ss use the context to match the words with their definitions. Check answers with the class. [1. d; 2. f; 3. a; 4. b; 5. c; 6. e]

Extra activity – pairs

Pairs write four questions about the information in the article on a separate piece of paper and take note of the answers (without writing the answers on the paper). Pairs exchange papers with another pair and answer the questions. Pairs check each other's answers.

C Check your understanding

- **Preview the task** Read the instructions and sentence 1 aloud. Ask Ss to look at paragraph 1 in the article and find the example answer. [It illustrates how consumers purchase new products and services.]
- **Do the task** Have Ss complete the task. Check answers.

Answers

1. It illustrates how people buy new products and services / the different types of consumers for new products and services.
2. The model categorizes consumers into these types: innovators, early adopters, early majority adopters, late majority adopters, and laggards.
3. The majority of consumers typically purchased a product after it had been tested and after the price had reduced.
4. The "early adopter" group accounts for 13.5% of consumers.

5. Tablets penetrated the market quicker than any other product.
6. Marketers are noticing that there is a fast uptake of products after the initial release.
7. Domestic use is driving technology adoptions more now.
8. Younger people are a larger segment of the consumer population, so this may be the reason for the faster uptake of new technology.

D React / Pair work

- **Preview and do the task** Say, "Ask and answer the questions from Exercise 1C. Then discuss the ideas. Do you recognize the issues and trends described in the article?" Have Ss complete the task.
- **Follow-up** For each question, elicit a few opinions from the class.

2 Focus on vocabulary

A
- Read the information in the Study tip aloud.
- **Preview the task** Read the instructions aloud. Model the first item with the class by reading it aloud. Point out the first given item. Say, "*Innovation* is a noun. *Innovate* is the verb." Point Ss to the word *adopt* in bold. Call on Ss to give the correct form of the word for the second sentence. [adoption] Ask, "Where did you find the words?" [innovation: para. 1; adoption: para. 1]
- **Do the task** Have Ss complete the sentences. Check answers with the class: Have individual Ss each read a completed sentence.

Answers

1. innovation / adoption (both in para. 1)
2. caution (para. 2)
3. penetration / phenomenal (both in para. 3)
4. recreational (para. 4)
5. millennial (para. 5)
6. assumptions (para. 5)
7. radical / revision (para. 5)

B Pair work

- **Preview and do the task** Read the instructions aloud. Tell Ss to use each word in the answers to Exercise 2A in a sentence so that Ss practice using the suffix endings. Walk around the class, listening for the correct usage and helping as needed.

3 Viewpoint

Group work

- **Preview the task** Have Ss read the questions aloud.
- **Present *In conversation*** Read the information aloud. Say, "If you remain silent while you're thinking of how to say something, people might assume you have nothing to say and ask someone else. These expressions are very useful in these discussions." Ask a S to read the example answer for the task aloud.

- **Do the task** Groups discuss the questions. Have several groups share an interesting point from their discussions

Extra activity – pairs

Pairs choose a recent technology and prepare a one-minute presentation about it. Ss should include information about when the technology was launched into the market and information about how it was promoted, etc. Ss have to use at least five new expressions from the lesson in their presentation.

C **Check your understanding** Find words in the article with a similar meaning to the words in bold below. Use those words to answer the questions.

1. What does the product adoption cycle **show**? (para. 1)   It illustrates . . .
2. The model **groups** or **classifies** consumers into five types. What are they? (para. 1)
3. When did the majority of consumers typically **buy** a product? (para. 1)
4. What percentage of consumers does the "early adopter" group **represent**? (para. 2)
5. What product **got into** the market more quickly than any other? (para. 2)
6. What trends are marketers now noticing after the **first launch** of a product? (para. 3)
7. What is driving technology adoptions: the workplace or **home** use? (para. 4)
8. What influence are younger people having as a **section** of the consumer population? (para. 5)

D **React** Pair work Ask and answer the questions in Exercise C. Do you recognize the trends described in the article?

2 Focus on vocabulary Suffixes

A **In this summary of the article, complete the second sentences with a form of the bold words in the first sentences. The words can all be found in the article**

> **Study tip**
>
> Learn suffixes like *-al / -ical* for adjectives and *-tion / -sion* for nouns. In reading, they can help you understand new words. In writing, using different word forms helps you avoid repetition.

1. Technology companies love to **innovate** and hope that consumers will **adopt** their products quickly. However, consumers vary in their approach to innovation_____ and their _____ of new technology.
2. Consumers used to be more **cautious**. Their _____ was due to the high price of gadgets.
3. Tablets immediately **penetrated** the market and became a **phenomenon**. Such a rapid _____ of the market was truly _____.
4. New gadgets used to be for work, not **recreation**. Once they became _____, the market grew.
5. The children who reached adulthood at the **millennium** are now consumers. This _____ generation is less conservative and more net-savvy than older generations.
6. We can no longer **assume** that Bourne's model is still relevant. Our _____ have to change.
7. The market has changed **radically**, and experts are **revising** their theories. Bourne's model therefore needs a _____ _____.

B Pair work **Take turns using the words in Exercise A to discuss your observations about how people buy and use technology.**

3 Viewpoint What type of consumer are you?

Group work **Discuss the questions.**

- How would you describe yourself as a technology consumer? Are you an early adopter? A laggard?
- How about other types of purchases? Do you have the same approach?
- What new technologies have recently been released into the market? Which ones interest you?
- Describe someone you know – anyone who's a different consumer type from you with regard to technology. What do you think of that approach?
- What differences, if any, do you see between the generations and their approach to buying technology?

> **In conversation . . .**
>
> If you need time to think, you can say *Let's see* or *Let me think*.

"Well, let's see, I suppose you could say that I'm in the late majority of consumers. I tend to wait . . ."

Writing *The bar graph illustrates . . .*

Task Write a report about Internet use.

Write a report for a business class or your employer about Internet use. Use graphs, charts, or tables in your report.

A **Look at a model** Look at the graph and complete the paragraph.

The bar graph illustrates the percentage of the population who were Internet users in each geographic region in _____. As can be seen in the graph, North America accounted for the highest percentage of Internet users in comparison with other regions, at _____ %, followed by _____ at 67.8%. In comparison, the region with the lowest percentage was _____, which represents _____ % of Internet users.

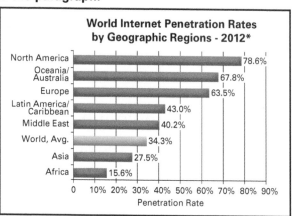

World Internet Penetration Rates by Geographic Regions - 2012*

Region	Penetration Rate
North America	78.6%
Oceania/Australia	67.8%
Europe	63.5%
Latin America/Caribbean	43.0%
Middle East	40.2%
World, Avg.	34.3%
Asia	27.5%
Africa	15.6%

B **Focus on language** Read the chart. Then underline the expressions for describing and comparing in the paragraph in Exercise A.

Describing and comparing information in graphs ⬇

The graph shows / illustrates . . .   *As can be seen* in the graph . . .   *. . . as shown* in the table.
*In 2012, Internet users **accounted for / represented** 32.7 percent of the world population.*
*North America had a high percentage of users **in comparison to / compared** to Africa.*
***In comparison / contrast,** Africa had the lowest percentage of Internet users.*

Common errors

Do not add *it* to the expressions *as can be seen, as is shown.*
***As can be seen** in the pie chart, most Internet users live in Asia.*
(NOT *As it can be seen in the pie chart, . . .*)

C **Write and check** Write a report on Internet use, using the information from the graph in Exercise A and the pie chart below. Then check for errors.

The pie chart shows the percentage of Internet users by world region. As can be seen in the chart, the highest percentage of users are in Asia. They account for 44.8% of the world's users. . . .

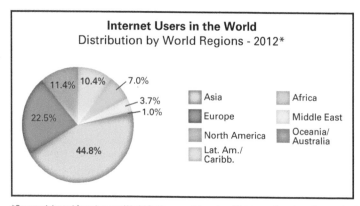

Internet Users in the World
Distribution by World Regions - 2012*

- 11.4%
- 10.4%
- 7.0%
- 3.7%
- 1.0%
- 22.5%
- 44.8%

Asia	Africa
Europe	Middle East
North America	Oceania/Australia
Lat. Am./Caribb.	

*Source: Adapted from Internet World Stats - www.internetworldstats.com/stats.htm. Penetration Rates are based on a world population of 7,012,519,841 and 2,405,510,175 estimated Internet users on June 30, 2012. Copyright © 2012, Miniwatts Marketing Group

Writing *The bar graph illustrates . . .*

In this lesson

- Ask a S to read the lesson aims (*In this lesson, you . . .*) aloud. Say, "Look at Exercise A. What lesson aim is being taught?" [describe graphs, charts, and tables] Ask, "What lesson aim is taught in Exercise B, the grammar for writing chart?" [describe and compare statistics] "What common error is shown?" [Avoid errors with *as can be seen*.]
- **Preview the writing** Say, "In this lesson, you will write a report for a business class or your employer about Internet use." Point out the writing topic in Task and read it aloud. Explain that Ss will end the lesson by writing a report that will practice the three aims presented in this lesson.

A Look at a model

- **Preview and do the task** Read the instructions aloud. Say, "Look at the graph and complete the paragraph." Have Ss complete the task. Check answers with the class.

Answers

The bar graph illustrates the percentage of the population who were Internet users in each geographic region in <u>2012</u>. As can be seen in the graph, North America accounted for the highest percentage of Internet users in comparison with other regions, at <u>78.6%</u>, followed by <u>Oceania / Australia</u> at 67.8%. In comparison, the region with the lowest percentage was <u>Africa</u>, which represents <u>15.6%</u> of Internet users.

B ⬇ www.cambridge.org/viewpoint/audio

Focus on language

- **Present the grammar for writing chart** Read the information in the chart aloud. If desired, play the downloadable recording. Ss listen and read along.
- **Understand the grammar for writing** Say, "When referring to charts, diagrams, and graphs, you will either be describing what happens in them or comparing some aspect of them."
- **Preview and do the task** Read the instructions aloud. Tell Ss to find examples of the expressions from the grammar chart in the paragraph in Exercise 1A and underline them.
- Check answers with the class. Have Ss call out the expressions they underlined.

Answers

<u>The bar graph illustrates</u> the percentage of the population who were Internet users in each geographic region in 2012. <u>As can be seen</u> in the graph, North America <u>accounted for</u> the highest percentage of Internet users in <u>comparison with</u> other regions, at 78.6%, followed by Oceania / Australia at 67.8%. <u>In comparison</u>, the region with the lowest percentage was Africa, which <u>represents</u> 15.6% of Internet users.

C Write and check

- **Preview and do the task** Say, "Look first at the graph in Exercise A. Give me an example of a sentence that describes the graph." (e.g., *As can be seen in the graph, . . .*) Ask the Ss for example sentences comparing some aspect of the pie chart. (e.g., *Oceania / Australia had the lowest percentage of users at 1.1%, followed by the Middle East at 3.4%.*)
- Say, "Now write two sentences about the graph and the pie chart." Have Ss write the sentences. Have several Ss read their sentences aloud. Tell the class to look at the graph and the pie chart as they listen to the sentences and verify the information that is being compared or described.
- **Present *Common errors*** Read the information aloud. Say, "There is another common error to be aware of." Write on the board:

  1. *The graph shows that the number of Internet users increased sharply.*
  2. *The pie chart shows the number of Internet users by region.*
  3. *The graph shows that the number of Internet users.*

- Say, "One of these sentences is incorrect. You can use *that* to introduce a clause but *not* a noun phrase." Ask Ss to call out the incorrect sentence. [3] Ask, "What's the easiest way to correct it?" [Take out *that*.] Strike through *that* in sentence 3 on the board.
- Say, "Now use the graph from Exercise 1A and the pie chart from Exercise 1C, and write a report on Internet use."
- When Ss have finished, have them check their work for errors. Get Ss to switch papers and check each other's work also.

Extra activity – class

Ss read two of their classmates' reports, and check them for errors.

Vocabulary notebook *High-tech gadgets*

If done for homework

Briefly present the Learning tip and the task directions.
Make sure Ss understand what they need to do.

If done in class

- **Present *Learning tip*** Ask what a *collocation* is.
  [A word or phrase that is often used with another word
  in a way that sounds correct to people. For example,
  we say someone has blond hair, but we don't say yellow
  cars are blond.] Read the information aloud. Ask a S to
  read the examples in the box.
- **Present *Dictionary tip*** Read the information aloud.
  Ask a S to read the examples aloud.

A • **Preview and do the task** Say, "Complete each
comment with one adjective in the box." Point out that
the first answer has been done as an example. Have Ss
complete the task. Check answers with the class.

Answers

1. high-speed	4. labor-saving
2. air-conditioned	5. custom-built
3. last-minute	

- Say, "Are any of these sentences true for you? If they are
  not, rewrite them and make them true. With sentence 1,
  for example, you could write, *We have high-speed
  Internet, but we don't have high-speed trains here. Most
  people fly.*" Have Ss complete the task
- **Follow-up** Have Ss compare their sentences in pairs.
  Then have a few Ss share one of their sentences with
  the class.

B • **Preview and do the task** Read the instructions aloud.
Ask for an example from page 22 for *energy-efficient*.
[comfort] Then ask for a noun in Box B. [car] Have Ss
complete the task. Check answers with the class.

Answers

- energy-efficient *comfort* / airline, appliances, car,
  environment, equipment, house, mall, travel
- carbon-neutral *comfort* / airline, appliances, car,
  environment, equipment, house, mall, travel
- climate-controlled (*shower*) room / car, environment,
  house, mall
- home-cooked *meal* / dinner, food
- human-like "*Hello*" or voice / face, sculptures
- solar-powered *energy* / appliances, car, equipment,
  house, mall

C Word builder

- **Preview and do the task** Say, "Complete the
  compound adjective in each pair with the same word."
  Have Ss complete the task. Check answers with the
  class.

Answers

1. powered	4. self
2. efficient	
3. high	

- Say, "Now use each compound noun in a true
  sentence." Have Ss write the sentences and then read
  them aloud to a partner.

D Focus on vocabulary, page 27

- **Preview and do the task** Read the instructions aloud.
  Say, "First try to complete the chart without looking at
  page 27. Then look and check. A gray space in the chart
  means that form of the word isn't required." Have Ss
  complete the task. Check answers with the class.

Answers

Verb	Noun	Adjective
adopt	adoption	—*
—	caution	cautious
assume	assumption	—
innovate	innovation	innovative
—	phenomenon	phenomenal
revise	revision	—

* The adjective *adoptive* is mostly used in the context of
families. *My adoptive parents* = the parents who adopted
me, not my birth parents.

- **Present *Self, self, self!*** Ask a S to read the top
  adjectives with *self* aloud.
- Have Ss write a sentence using each word. Have Ss
  compare their sentences in pairs.

Vocabulary notebook *High-tech gadgets*

not-too-distant future; self-cleaning windows, oven

I hope to graduate in the not-too-distant future.

I'd love a self-cleaning oven and self-cleaning windows.

high-p|	🔍
high-pitched	
high-powered	

A Complete each comment with one adjective from the box. Then make the sentences true for you.

air-conditioned	custom-built	high-speed	labor-saving	last-minute

1. We've had high-speed _____ Internet connections in this country for years. High-speed _____ trains, too.

2. I don't live in _____ comfort. It gets hot in the summer, so I'd love an _____ bedroom.

3. I'm always making _____ decisions. I'm always making _____ changes to plans, too.

4. We don't have too many _____ appliances or gadgets, apart from a washing machine.

5. I'd rather have a _____ kitchen than a _____ robot in the house.

B Find each adjective in Box A in the article on page 22 and write the noun it describes. Then find at least two other nouns in Box B that you can use it with.

A				B	
energy-efficient	_____	_____	_____	airline	face
carbon-neutral	_____	_____	_____	appliances	food
climate-controlled	_____	_____	_____	car	house
home-cooked	_____	_____	_____	dinner	mall
human-like	_____	_____	_____	environment	sculptures
solar-powered	_____	_____	_____	equipment	travel

C Word builder Complete the compound adjectives in each group with the same word.

1. wind-_____; battery-_____; high-_____

2. energy-_____; cost-_____; fuel-_____

3. _____-tech; _____-level; _____-class

4. ___-sufficient; ___-explanatory; ___-conscious

D (Focus on vocabulary) Complete the chart of these words from Exercise 2A on page 27.

Verb	Noun	Adjective
	adoption	
		cautious
	assumption	
innovate		
	phenomenon	
	revision	

Unit 3 Society

Lesson A *Social pressures*

Grammar *Linking events*

(See Student's Book p. 31.)

In this lesson, Ss use participle clauses to link events by adding information about time or reason. They are presented here in the context of people talking about social pressures.

Form

The subject of the participle clause and the main clause is usually the same.

- Present participle clauses

    ***Growing up**, I was always branded a rebel.* = ***When I was growing up**, I was always branded a rebel.*

- Present perfect participle clause

    ***Having built up a successful career**, I'm happy with my life choices.* = ***Because I have built up a successful career**, I'm happy with my life choices.*

Use

Participle clauses can be used to link events and add information about time or reason.

- Present participle clauses – time

    ***Thinking about it**, this is probably going to sound silly.* = ***When I think about it**, this is probably going to sound silly.*

- Present participle clauses – reason

    *I never met anyone, **working as hard as I do.** = I never met anyone because I work hard.*

- Present perfect participle clauses – reason

    *I've never conformed to social norms, **not having had any children.** = I've never conformed to social norms **because I haven't had any children.***

> ### Corpus information
>
> #### In conversation
>
> In conversation, expressions like *generally speaking, thinking about it, bearing in mind, speaking of,* and *talking of* are participle clauses, but they often have a different subject from the main clause.
>
> *Bearing in mind the economy, it's no wonder people feel pressured.*

Grammar extra *Clauses with prepositions and conjunctions + -ing; Passive forms of participle and time clauses*

(See Student's Book p. 148.)

Grammar extra presents and practices more ways to link events and add information about time or reason using clauses with prepositions and conjunctions + *-ing*. Also presented and practiced are passive forms of participle and time clauses.

Lesson B *New experiences*

Vocabulary in context *Take expressions*

(See Student's Book p. 32.)

The article presents expressions with *take* in the context of challenges that Ss face when they start college. Ss learn expressions such as *take care, take charge,* and *take responsibility.*

Vocabulary notebook *Take credit!*

(See Student's Book p. 39.)

The Learning tip tells Ss that when they learn a new expression, they should write it in a sentence that paraphrases its meaning.

Grammar *Adding emphasis*

(See Student's Book p. 33.)

This lesson teaches *so / such . . . that, even,* and *only. So / such . . . that* can be used to emphasize the results or effects of something. *Even* can add emphasis or signal that something is surprising. *Only* means "no one / nothing else."

Form

- *So . . . (that)*

    . . . so + adjective / adverb + (that) . . .

    *You'll be **so** excited **that** you'll only think of the fun ahead.*

    *Time goes **so** fast you won't notice.*

- *Such . . . (that) . . .*

    . . . such + (a / an) + (adjective) + noun + (that)

    *It's **such** an overwhelming experience **that** many students drop out.*

- *Even*

    Even is used before the part of the sentence you want to emphasize. Here it is shown before a main verb (after an auxiliary or modal), before a comparative adjective, and before a noun phrase.

    *You don't **even** realize. (NOT . . . even don't)*

    *It may **even** take a year to adjust to college life.*

    *That will make things **even** worse.*

    ***Even** the best students don't always get A's.*

- **Only**

   Only is used before the part of the sentence you want to emphasize. Here it is shown before a main verb, after a modal, before an adjective, and before a pronoun.

   > You **only** want to take refuge in your room.
   >
   > It will **only** make matters worse.
   >
   > It's **only** natural to feel anxious.
   >
   > **Only** you can take charge of your situation.

Grammar extra More on *so* and *such*; More on *even* and *only*

(See Student's Book p. 149.)

Grammar extra looks at more ways to use *so* and *such* and *even* and *only*.

Lesson C *Having said that . . .*

Conversation strategy *Changing views*

(See Student's Book p. 34.)

The lesson teaches expressions that speakers use to express a contrasting view to one they have just expressed. This is useful in conversations when the speaker changes his or her opinion, realizes he or she said something that was wrong in some way, or simply wants to present another and different point of view on an issue.

Expressions:

> *Having said that, (though) . . .*
>
> *But then,*
>
> *(But) then again,*

Strategy plus *even so, even then*

(See Student's Book p. 35.)

The lesson teaches another way to introduce a contrasting idea.

- *Even so* means "despite what was just said."

   > *. . . some women worked, but **even so**, their options were limited.*

- *Even then* also introduces a contrasting idea. It means "despite the situation that was just described."

   > *You can study and study, but **even then**, you're not guaranteed a job.*

Speaking naturally *Stress in expressions of contrast*

(See Student's Book p. 139.)

In this section, Ss practice stressing words in the expressions they learned in this lesson.

Lesson D *Language and society*

Writing *I recommend it.*

(See Student's Book p. 38.)

This lesson teaches Ss to plan and write an evaluation of a course, including both positive and negative comments. The grammar for writing presents ways to express results. It recycles participle clauses from Lesson A, adding another use (expressing result). It also recycles *so / such . . . that* from Lesson B.

- Expressing results in writing

   You can express result in the following ways:

   Present participle clauses

   so / such . . . that

   Conjunction

   so

   Adverbials

   As a result, Consequently, Therefore

3

Society

In Unit 3, you . . .

- talk about different social pressures.
- use participle clauses to link ideas.
- add emphasis with *only, even, so . . . that,* and *such . . . that.*
- change your view as you speak.
- use *even so* and *even then* to introduce contrasting ideas.

Lesson A *Social pressures*

1 Grammar in context

A What kinds of pressure do people have in their lives? Make a list.

B ◀») CD 1.23 Listen. What pressures does each person talk about? Are any on your list?

WE ASKED PEOPLE,

"What are some of the social pressures you've resisted?"

1. CHELSEA, 30   Toronto, Canada, designer

Growing up, I was always branded a rebel, which is a little unfair. I guess, though, that I've never really conformed to social norms, being single and not having had any children at the ripe old age of 30! I just never met anyone, working as hard as I do. But having built up a successful career, I'm happy with my life choices. People say, "Oh, you'll regret it when you're old and lonely." But looking around, I see plenty of elderly people with families who are still lonely.

2. VICTOR, 36   Cancún, Mexico, ex-PR consultant and restaurant owner

I recently decided to get out of the rat race, having been in it most of my adult life. I'd been thinking about doing something different, but then I got laid off and was offered a generous severance package. So, presented with a golden opportunity to change my life, I bought a small restaurant here. Working in the PR industry, people are under enormous pressure, you know, to look good, have the right clothes, and be "perfect," which is really stressful. Not to mention the work hours. I got out. I'm earning less now, running this place, but I just know I'll be a lot happier going forward.

3. CHIN-SUN, 23   Seoul, South Korea, businesswoman

Thinking about it, this is probably going to sound silly, but I feel tremendous pressure to have an active social life. I don't have that many friends compared to my co-workers, or so it seems. I dread Fridays, when they ask if I'm going out with friends on the weekend. And speaking of friends, with social networking, you're supposed to have hundreds of them, and I don't. I mean, not wanting to be rude or anything, I can't see how you can have that many friends, really.

About you | **C** Pair work **Which of the pressures above are common in your society?**

"I don't think there's a lot of pressure to have kids, but I do think people feel pressure to . . ."

Society

Introduce the theme of the unit Tell Ss that this unit looks at aspects of society. It includes discussions of language, education, and some of the different kinds of pressure that people deal with. Read the unit aims aloud.

Lesson A *Social pressures*

1 Grammar in context

- **Set the scene** Ask, "What is social pressure?" Elicit ideas (e.g., *the feeling you have to do what other people expect you to do*). Ask, "Who can put pressure on other people?" (e.g., *parents, family, teachers, supervisors, co-workers, friends*)

A
- **Preview and do the task** Read the instructions aloud. Have Ss complete the task.
- Have Ss call out their ideas, and write them on the board. Leave the answers on the board for a later activity.

Possible answers

pressure to find work, work long hours, get a high-paying job, get married, stay married, have children, dress nicely, be "perfect," look young, get good grades, get into top colleges, pass exams

B ◀)) CD1, Track 23
- **Preview the task** Read the instructions aloud. Say, "Look at the introduction. What do you think *resist* means?" [to refuse to accept something and try to stop it from happening]
- **Play the recording** Books closed. Tell Ss to listen to the speakers and write brief answers. Have Ss compare their notes with a partner.
- Books open. Tell Ss to read the article to check their answers. (If desired, play the recording again while Ss read along.)
- Check the answers with the class.

Answers

1. Chelsea – talks about the pressure to get married and have children at an earlier age.
2. Victor – talks about the pressure to stay in a career you might not enjoy, the pressure to look good, have the right clothes, be "perfect," and work long hours.
3. Chin-sun – talks about the pressure to have an active social life with lots of friends.

- Have Ss read the article again, and underline any new words. Have Ss call out the words and write them on the board. Call on other Ss to explain the meanings of the new words.

About you

C Pair work
- **Preview and do the task** Read the instructions and the example aloud. Have Ss discuss the question.
- **Follow-up** Have several pairs report to the class.

Extra activity – groups

Write on the board:

Which of these pressures could you resist?

Which, if any, do you not consider a "pressure"?

Group members discuss which of the pressures that are on the board from Exercise 1A they think they could resist.

Extra activity – pairs

Ss look at the list of pressures from Exercise 1A again. This time Ss determine possible results and effects of giving in to each pressure. Have Ss make a list for each pressure. (e.g., *pressure to find work: If people feel pressured to find work, they may end up in a job that they don't want to do. They might miss other opportunities, for example, doing additional training, etc.*)

② Grammar

A 📥 www.cambridge.org/viewpoint/audio

- **Preview the task** Read the instructions aloud.
- **Do the task** Have Ss complete the task. Check answers.

Answers

1. Looking around, . . .
2. . . . being single and not having had any children.

- **Focus on the use** Say, "This is a way to link ideas and add variety to your speaking and writing."

- **Present the grammar chart** Read the information aloud. If desired, play the downloadable recording.

- Ask Ss to look at the examples in the *Present participle* section of the chart. Say, "*Growing up* and *working as hard as I do* are participle clauses." A participle clause starts with the *-ing* form of the verb. Say, "Read the first example. What is the participle clause here?" [growing up] Ask, "Who is 'growing up'?" [the speaker, *I*] Ask, "When was the speaker branded or called a rebel?" [when she was growing up] Say, "So the participle clause here adds more information about the time when she was branded a rebel. Notice that the subject of *growing up* is the same as the main clause – *I*."

- Say, "Read the second example. What is the participle clause here?" [working as hard as I do] Ask, "Who is 'working'?" [the speaker, *I*] Ask, "Why do you think the speaker never met a potential husband?" [She was working too hard.] Say, "So here, the participle clause can express the idea of 'because,' too; it adds a reason."

- Ask Ss to look at the first example in the *Perfect participle* section of the chart. Ask, "Does *Having built up a successful career* add information about time or reason?" [reason] "What is the pattern for the verb?" Write the answer on the board:

    having + past participle

- Say, "Look at the second example. Where does *not* go?" Add *not* to the answer on the board:

    (not) having + past participle

- Say, "Write the four example sentences from the chart, but use *she* as the subject of the main clause. Check for any other changes you need." Have Ss complete the task and compare answers with a partner. Check answers with the class. [Growing up, she was always branded a rebel. She never met anyone, working as hard as she does. Having built up a successful career, she's happy with her life choices. She's never conformed to social norms, not having had any children.]

- **Present *In conversation*** Read the information aloud. Say, "Read the example. What is the participle clause here?" [bearing in mind] Ask, "Is the subject of both clauses the same?" [no] Say, "With these expressions, the subject is different in the two clauses."

- Ask, "When do you think each expression would be useful?" Read out each expression and elicit a possible use. Have Ss write notes about the expressions in their notebooks. [*generally speaking*: to generalize; *thinking about it*: to say more about or remember something, to show you have thought more; *bearing in mind*: to show you need to remember or think about a point or situation; *speaking / talking of*: to add something about a topic you're discussing, to change the topic slightly]

(For more information, see Language notes at the beginning of the unit. For more work on different types of clauses, go to Grammar extra, p. 148.)

B • **Preview the task** Read the instructions aloud. Ask Ss to call out the correct form of *be*. [being]

- **Do the task** Have Ss complete the task and compare their answers with a partner. Check answers with the class: Ask individual Ss each to read what a speaker said.

Answers

1. <u>Being</u> a woman, I feel . . . I mean, <u>not wanting</u> to sound sexist, . . . I think most women do, generally <u>speaking</u>.
2. <u>Growing up</u> in a family where . . . to feel really bad, <u>not being</u> able to afford . . . So now, <u>having experienced</u> that, and you know, <u>bearing</u> in mind that . . .
3. Well, <u>coming</u> from an academic family, . . . when I was 18, <u>having worked</u> hard to get . . . So, <u>having made up</u> my mind to do that, . . . <u>Looking back</u>, it was the best decision I ever made.
4. <u>Staying / Having stayed</u> home and <u>raising / (having) raised</u> a family, I've sometimes felt . . . They probably think that, <u>not having</u> a proper career, . . . I mean, <u>thinking</u> about it, I'd say . . .

C **Pair work**

- **Preview and do the task** Say, "Write your view about each comment in Exercise 2B. Try to include participle clauses in your answers."

- When Ss have finished writing their comments, say, "Now discuss your comments with a partner. What other social pressures are there? Where do these pressures come from?" Ask a S to read the example aloud.

- **Follow-up** For each comment in exercise 2B, have the class discuss their views.

② Grammar Linking events

Figure it out

A How do the people in the article on page 30 express the ideas below? Rewrite the clauses in bold. Then read the grammar chart.

1. **When I look around**, I see plenty of elderly people with families who are still lonely.
2. I've never really conformed to social norms **because I'm single and haven't had any children**.

Participle clauses ⬇

Grammar extra
See page 148.

You can use participle clauses to link events and add information about time or reason.
The subject of the participle clause and the main clause is usually the same.

Present participle   *Growing up, I was always branded a rebel.* (= When I was growing up)
*I never met anyone, **working as hard as I do.*** (= because I work hard)

Perfect participle   *Having built up a successful career, I'm happy with my life choices.*
*I've never conformed to social norms, **not having had any children.***

B Complete the things the people say about pressures in life. Write participle clauses, using the verbs given. Sometimes there is more than one answer.

> **In conversation . . .**
>
> Expressions like *generally speaking, thinking about it, bearing in mind, speaking of,* and *talking of* are participle clauses, but they often have a different subject from the main clause.
>
> *Bearing in mind the economy, it's no wonder people feel pressured.*

1. _____ (be) a woman, I feel a certain pressure to dress well. I mean, _____ (not want) to sound sexist, but unlike my male colleagues, I feel I have to wear something different every day to the office. I think most women do, generally _____ (speak).

2. _____ (grow up) in a family where money was tight, I felt a lot of pressure – especially as a teenager. I used to feel really bad, _____ (not be) able to afford brand-name sneakers or the latest cell phone. So now, _____ (experience) that, and you know, _____ (bear) in mind that kids just want to fit in, I always try to buy my boys the things their friends have.

3. Well, _____ (come) from an academic family, I was to supposed go to a top school. But when I was 18, _____ (work) hard to get the grades I needed, I decided I really wanted to pursue a career as an artist. So, _____ (make up) my mind to do that, I kind of dropped out of formal education altogether. _____ (look back), it was the best decision I ever made.

4. _____ (stay) home and _____ (raise) a family, I've sometimes felt pressure from my friends who work outside the home. They probably think that, _____ (not have) a proper career, I haven't really "done" anything, which is really unfair. I mean, _____ (think) about it, I'd say raising kids is the most important job there is.

> BEING A COLLEGE STUDENT, I FEEL PRESSURE TO RISE TO EXPECTATIONS. JUST NOT THIS EARLY IN THE MORNING.

About you

C Pair work Write your view about each comment in Exercise 2B. Then discuss your comments with a partner. What other social pressures are there? Where do these pressures come from?

"Being a student, I don't really feel any pressure about how to dress. Not having had any fashion sense my entire life, I tend not to worry about these things."

Lesson B *New experiences*

1 Vocabulary in context

A 🔊 CD 1.24 **What challenges might students face before starting college? Make a list. Then read the web page. How many of your ideas are mentioned?**

So you've graduated from high school and you're ready to take the next step in your academic career. You'll probably be so excited that you can only think of the fun ahead. However, going to college can be such an overwhelming experience that some 35 percent of freshmen drop out in the first year and many leave before the end of the first semester. But don't worry! There are **steps** you can **take** to help you face the challenges and make your first semester both successful and enjoyable.

If, in the first few weeks, you feel so anxious that you only want to **take refuge** in your room, don't. That will only make things even worse. It's only natural to feel like this, and you won't be the only one, so talk to someone about it.

> "It takes time to adjust to college life. It may even take most of the first year." —RORY

On the social side, **take advantage of** what college life has to offer. For example, **take part in** extra-curricular activities; take up a new sport or hobby – it's such a great way to meet

people that it's worth the effort. However, don't let your social life **take precedence over** your studies. You are there to get a degree, after all.

> "Remember to take care of yourself by getting enough sleep. The consequences of sleeping only four hours a night are so huge that you don't even realize till it's too late." —CAITLIN

Academically, it's up to you to **take responsibility for** your studies, and you should **take into account** the fact that you may struggle with new academic challenges. **Take the initiative** and talk to a professor about any problems you have.

> "If you don't understand something, ask. **Take charge.**" —ERKAN

In class, learn how to take criticism without taking offense or taking it personally. If you're shy, **take note of** how successful students interact, and use their strategies for participating. If you get a bad grade, **take heart**: it's only one bad grade and is unlikely to throw your studies off course. Even the best students don't always get straight A's.

After the first few weeks, time will go by so fast that your first semester will be over before you know it. Look back and **take stock of** all you've achieved. Then **take credit for** surviving your first semester of college. Good job!

Word sort

B **Find expressions in bold with these meanings, and write them below. Then find other expressions with *take* on the web page. What do they mean? Compare with a partner.**

hide (in) __take refuge (in)__	take priority (over) _____
have courage or confidence _____	reflect and assess _____
participate, be involved (in) _____	notice _____
take control (of) (2 expressions) _____	accept praise for _____
_____	make use of _____
do something positive _____	do something before others do it _____
think about, consider _____	_____

About you

C **Pair work** **Do you agree with the advice given on the web page? What other advice could you give to someone starting college?**

Vocabulary notebook

See page 39.

Lesson B *New experiences*

1 Vocabulary in context

- **Set the scene** Books closed. Say, "The title of Lesson B is *New experiences*. What are some experiences that people have?" Have Ss call out their ideas (e.g., *starting school, getting a job, first girlfriend / boyfriend, getting married, having a baby, traveling*).

Culture note

Many Ss in the United States and Canada leave their hometown to attend college. Most live in dorms, sometimes called *residences*. Some Ss may go and live in a dorm even if the school is in their hometown in order to learn more independence and be able to spend free time with their peer group more easily.

A ◀))) CD1, Track 24

- **Preview the task** Say, "Starting college is a new experience. What challenges might some students face before starting college? Make a list."
- **Play the recording** Books open. Ss listen and read along.
- Ask, "How many of your ideas are mentioned?"

Word sort

B
- **Preview the task** Say, "Find expressions in bold with these meanings and complete the chart. Remember to use the context to help you. Don't use a dictionary yet."
- **Do the task** Point out that the first answer has been given. Say, "Find *take refuge* on the web page." (para. 2) Have a S read the sentence that contains it aloud. Check that Ss understand the activity. Have Ss complete the chart. Check answers with the class.

Answers

hide (in): *take refuge (in)*
have courage or confidence: *take heart*
participate, be involved (in): *take part (in)*
take control (of): *take charge / take responsibility (for)*
do something positive: *take steps*
think about, consider: *take into account*
take priority (over): *take precedence (over)*
reflect and assess: *take stock of*
notice: *take note (of)*
accept praise for: *take credit for*
make use of: *take advantage of*
do something before others do it: *take the initiative*

- Say, "Go through the web page and find other expressions with *take*. Use the context to help you guess what they mean. Then compare with a partner."
- Check answers with the class. Give Ss time to check their dictionaries if necessary.

Answers

take the next step: *go on to the next stage*
take time: *you need time*
take up: *start (e.g., a hobby or sport)*
take criticism: *accept criticism*
take offense: *be offended*
take it personally: *feel criticized / attacked personally*
take care of yourself: *care for, treat well*

Extra activity – pairs

S1 uses a *take* expression from Exercise 1B in a sentence. With book closed, S2 paraphrases the sentence without using a *take* expression (e.g., S1: *Take all of your reading lists and assignments into account when scheduling your time.* S2: *Think about all of your reading lists and assignments when scheduling your time.*) Pairs take turns.

Tell Ss to turn to Vocabulary Notebook on p. 39 of their Student's Books. Have Ss do the tasks in class or assign them for homework. (See the teaching notes on p, T-39.)

About you

C Pair work

- **Preview and do the task** Read the instructions aloud. Ask, "What are some examples of other advice you could give?" Elicit a few examples from the class (e.g., *eating healthful food, don't leave things until the last minute*). Have Ss complete the task.
- **Follow-up** Have Ss say which advice they agree with. Ss call out the other advice they thought of. Write their ideas on the board.

Extra activity – pairs

Pairs choose the five most important pieces of advice from the web page and the ideas on the board. Pairs present their list to another pair. Several pairs present their list to the class.

② Grammar

Figure it out

A ⬇ www.cambridge.org/viewpoint/audio

- **Preview the task** Say, "Add one word to each sentence and cross out the underlined words to keep the same meaning. Use the web page to help you." Do the first sentence with the class: Ask a S to read sentence 1 aloud. Say, "Find a similar sentence on the web page and make the changes to sentence 1." Have a S read the new sentence aloud. [You may get so anxious that you'll take refuge in your room.]

- **Do the task** Have Ss complete the task. Check answers with the class: Ask individual Ss each to read a sentence aloud.

Answers

1. You may get **so** anxious ~~and the result will be~~ that . . .
2. Taking up a new sport is **such** a good way to make friends ~~and the result will be~~ that . . .
3. Adjusting . . . may **even** take a year, ~~which is surprising~~.
4. . . . may **only** think about the fun ahead, ~~and nothing else~~.

- **Focus on the form** Ask, "What did you add to sentence 1?" [so] "What's between *so* and *that*?" [anxious] "What part of speech is *anxious*?" [adjective] Ask, "What did you add to sentence 2?" [such] "What's between *such* and *that*?" [a good way to make friends] "What parts of speech are in *a good way*?" [article + adjective + noun]

- Ask, "What did you add to sentence 3?" [even] What does *even* replace?" [which is surprising] "Where does *even* go in the sentence?" [before *take a year*] Ask, "What did you add to sentence 4?" [only] "What does *only* replace?" [and nothing else] "Where does *only* go in the sentence?" [before *think about the fun ahead*]

- **Present the grammar chart** Read the information aloud. If desired, play the downloadable recording.

- **Understand the grammar chart** Say, "The chart teaches ways to emphasize an idea in a sentence."

- Have Ss look at the top section of the chart. Say, "Notice that *so* emphasizes the adjective or the adverb. If there is a noun after the adjective, use *such a* or *such an*. To introduce the result or effect, you can add the word *that*."

- Have Ss look at the bottom section of the chart. Say, "*Even* and *only* go before the information they emphasize.

If you're emphasizing a verb that has an auxiliary or a modal, put *even* after the auxiliary or modal verb."

(For more information, see Language notes at the beginning of the unit. For more work on *so* and *such*, *even* and *only*, go to Grammar extra, p. 149.)

Extra activity – class

Write on the board:

Going to college is so ____ that ____.
Going to college is such a(n) ____ that ____.
My first week at college was so ____ that ____.
My first week at college was such a(n) ____ that ____.

Ss complete the sentences with their own ideas. Several Ss read a sentence aloud.

About you

B • **Preview and do the task** Read the instructions aloud. Say, "Some blanks don't need a word, so write a dash. Be sure to read each conversation before completing it." Have Ss complete the task and then compare answers with a partner. Check answers with the class.

Answers

1. *A* My friend said he __—__ didn't **even** anticipate how difficult . . . apartment was <u>such</u> hard work <u>that</u> he ended up . . . He <u>only</u> got a place . . . I'd have been <u>so</u> depressed <u>that</u> I . . . It took him <u>so</u> long to settle <u>that</u> he almost . . . But he has <u>such</u> a positive outlook <u>that</u> things always . . .
   B There are probably things you __—__ don't **even** take into account. . . . You're usually <u>so</u> busy when you move that you __—__ don't **even** have time . . .
2. *A* . . . at this job was <u>such</u> a big deal <u>that</u> I couldn't eat. I **even** felt nervous. . . . But you can <u>only</u> do your best to fit in. I worked <u>so</u> hard my first week <u>that</u> it was over . . .
   B Well, I'm pretty outgoing, but **even** I get . . . But it <u>only</u> lasts a few days. . . . Then you'll get <u>so</u> involved <u>that</u> you'll forget you were **even** nervous. In the end, <u>only</u> you can take responsibility . . .

- Say, "Practice the conversations with a partner. Do you agree with the answers? Share your ideas." Have Ss practice and discuss. Have several pairs share their ideas with the class.

③ Viewpoint

Pair work

- **Preview and do the task** Read the instructions aloud. Have a S read the example aloud. Say, "Remember to include some *take* expressions in your advice. Use *so*, *such*, *even*, or *only* to emphasize your points."

- Walk around the class, giving help as needed. When groups have completed the activity, have several pairs present their advice to the class.

② Grammar Adding emphasis

Figure
it out

A **Add one word to each sentence and cross out the underlined words to keep the same meaning. Use the web page to help you. Then read the grammar chart.**

1. You may get anxious, <u>and the result will be</u> that you'll take refuge in your room.
2. Taking up a new sport is a good way to make friends, <u>and the result will be</u> that you won't regret it.
3. Adjusting to college may take a year, <u>which is surprising</u>.
4. Before you go to college, you may think about the fun ahead <u>and nothing else</u>.

---

so . . . that, *such (a / an) . . . (that)*, *even*, and *only* ⬇

Grammar extra
See page 149.

You can use *so . . .* or *such . . . (that)* to emphasize the results or effects of something.
Use *so . . .* + adjective / adverb *(that) . . .* or *such . . . (a / an)* + (adjective) noun *(that) . . .*
You'll be **so excited that** you can only think of the fun ahead. Time goes **so fast** you won't notice.
It's **such an** overwhelming **experience that** many students drop out.

Even can add emphasis or signal that something is surprising. *Only* means "no one else" or "nothing else." Use them before the phrase or part of the sentence you want to emphasize.
You don't **even** realize. (NOT . . . ~~even don't~~ . . .)   You **only** want to take refuge in your room.
It may **even** take a year to adjust to college life.   It will **only** make things worse.
That will make things **even** worse.   It's **only** natural to feel anxious.
Even the best students don't always get A's.   **Only** you can take charge of your situation.

About
you

B **Complete the conversations with *so . . . that, such (a / an) . . . that, only*, or *even*. If none fit, write a dash (–). Then practice with a partner. Do you agree with the answers? Share your ideas.**

1. **What problems do people face when they move to a new city?**
   A My friend said he ___–___ didn't _____ anticipate how difficult it would be until he moved last year. He said finding an apartment was _____ hard work _____ he ended up taking refuge on a friend's couch. He _____ got a place a month ago. I'd have been _____ depressed _____ I would've given up! It took him _____ long to settle _____ he almost moved back. But he has _____ positive outlook _____ things always work out for him.
   B There are probably things you _____ don't _____ take into account – like changing your address on your driver's license. You're usually _____ busy when you move _____ you _____ don't _____ have time to stop and think.

2. **What's it like starting a new job?**
   A You know, my first day at this job was _____ big deal _____ I couldn't eat. I _____ felt nervous the week before I started. But you can _____ do your best to fit in. I worked _____ hard my first week _____ it was over before I knew it.
   B Well, I'm pretty outgoing, but _____ I get nervous in new job situations. But it _____ lasts a few days. I'd say you should take the initiative to get to know people. Then you'll get _____ involved _____ you'll forget you were _____ nervous. In the end, _____ you can take responsibility for how things turn out.

③ Viewpoint Take the initiative

Pair work **Discuss four challenges that people may face in new situations. What advice would you give? Prepare one idea to put on a self-help website.**

"Starting a new job is so stressful for people that they quickly burn out."

Lesson C *Having said that . . .*

1 Conversation strategy Changing views

A What kinds of peer pressure do young people experience? Make a list.

B ◀)) CD 1.25 Listen. What do Carol and Ashley say are the main pressures on young people today?

Carol I do think life was a lot easier when I was your age – for young people, I mean.

Ashley You do? In what way?

Carol Well, there wasn't all this peer pressure to have the latest fashions and cell phones and that sort of thing. But having said that, there were other pressures.

Ashley Like what?

Carol Oh, back in the day, women were expected to stay home and raise a family. I mean, some women worked, but even so, their options were limited.

Ashley Well, I guess that's changed, which is good. But then again, they say women still do more of the household chores.

Carol True.

Ashley I think the worst thing now is like pressure to get good grades. You can study and study, but even then, you're not guaranteed a good job at the end of it.

Carol Yes, there's so much competition for jobs nowadays. But then, I suppose there always was.

C **Notice** how Carol and Ashley change their view and express a contrasting view with expressions like these. Find examples in the conversation.

> *Having said that, (though), . . .*
> *But then, . . .*
> *(But) then again, . . .*

D Link each comment (1–6) with a contrasting view (a–f). Use an expression from Exercise C.

1. There are so many social problems today.
2. You're not cool if you don't have a car.
3. Getting a good job is a real problem.
4. Looks are important, as is keeping up with the latest trends.
5. And you have to have the latest gadgets.
6. There's so much pressure to do well in school.

a. _____, it's hard to live without a cell phone.

b. _____, fashion's always been a big thing for a lot of people.

c. _____, education was the only way for my parents' generation to get ahead, too.

d. _____, you had to have a motorbike to be cool at one time.

e. _Having said that, though_, there have always been issues to fix in society.

f. _____, I don't know anyone who's unemployed.

About you **E** Pair work Take turns starting conversations using the full comments above. Continue each conversation with your own views.

Lesson C *Having said that . . .*

1 Conversation strategy

Why use *Having said that . . .*, etc.?

As they are speaking, people change their opinion about a topic, realize what they just said was wrong in some way, or decide to present a different point of view. They can use the expressions taught in this lesson, such as *Having said that*, to show this.

(For more information, see Language notes at the beginning of this unit.)

- **Set the scene** Books closed.
- Ask, "Who is your peer?" [someone who is the same age and has the same social position in a group]
- Write on the board:

  peer pressure

- Ask, "What do you think peer pressure is?" [pressure to behave the same way as your peers]

A • **Preview and do the task** Read the instructions aloud. Have Ss make their list. Have Ss call out the items from their lists. Write them on the board (e.g., *like the same music, fashion, TV shows*) (Note: If using the Extra Activity that follows Exercise 1E, do not erase the board.)

B 🔊 CD1, Track 25

- **Preview the task** Read the instructions aloud.
- **Play the recording** Write on the board:

  Carol

  Ashley

- Say, "These are the names of the two speakers. Carol speaks first." Ss listen only. Replay the recording. Ss listen and write. Have Ss compare their answers in pairs.
- **Play the recording again** Books open. Ss listen, read along, and check their answers. Check the answer with the class. [Carol believes there is pressure to have the latest fashions and cell phones. She also mentions there's a lot of competition for jobs. Ashley believes there is pressure to get good grades.]
- Ask, "What were peer pressures when Carol was young? [Women were expected to stay home and raise a family.]
- **Follow-up** Ss compare their ideas from the board to the ideas mentioned in the conversation.

C • **Present *Notice*** Read the information and the examples aloud.

- Say, "Read the conversation again. Find the examples." Have a S read them aloud. [*Carol*: But having said that, there were other pressures. *Ashley*: But then again, they say women still do more of the household chores. *Carol*: But then, I suppose there always was.]
- **Practice** Tell Ss to practice the conversation in pairs, taking turns playing each role.

D • **Preview the task** Read the instructions aloud. Ask Ss to read the example answer. Ask, "What ideas do comments 1 and *e* contrast?" [that there are a lot of social problems now and the fact that there were in the past too]

- **Do the task** Have Ss complete the task. Check answers with the class.

Answers

The underlined expressions are example answers. Other expressions from the list in Exercise 1C can also be used.

1. There are so many social problems today.	e. <u>Having said that, though,</u> there have always been issues to fix in society.
2. You're not cool if you don't have a car.	d. <u>Then again,</u> you had to have a motorbike to be cool at one time.
3. Getting a good job is a real problem.	f. <u>Having said that,</u> I don't know anyone who's unemployed.
4. Looks are important, as is keeping up with the latest trends.	b. <u>Thinking about it, though,</u> fashion's always been a big thing for people.
5. And you have to have the latest gadgets.	a. <u>Then again,</u> it's hard to live without a cell phone.
6. There's so much pressure to do well in school.	c. <u>But then, thinking about it,</u> education was the only way for my parents' generation to get ahead, too.

About you

E Pair work

- **Preview and do the task** Read the instructions aloud. Have pairs continue the conversations. Remind Ss to use expressions to change their views. Walk around the class and help as needed.

Extra activity – pairs

Ss choose peer pressures from the board or their own ideas and write a conversation similar to Carol and Ashley's. Pairs join another pair and read their conversation. The listening pair notes how often an expression to change views was used.

② Strategy plus

Why use *even so* and *even then*?

Even so and *even then* can also introduce a contrasting idea. They mean "however" or "despite what was just said."

(For more information, see Language notes at the beginning of this unit.)

◀)) CD1, Track 26

- **Present *Strategy plus*** Read aloud or play the recording of the information and examples. Ss listen and read along.
- Tell Ss to read the conversation on page 34 again and find examples of *even so* and *even then*.

A ◀)) CD1, Track 27

- **Preview the task** Read the instructions aloud. Tell Ss to read the comments. Check for vocabulary questions.
- Have a S read aloud the first comment. Get Ss to guess the topic of the conversation. Repeat with each comment.
- **Play the recording** Audio script p. T-270 Ss listen and number the comments. Have Ss compare their answers.
- **Play the recording again** Ss listen and review their answers. (Answers are checked in Exercise 2B.)

About you

B ◀)) CD1, Track 28

- **Preview and do the task** Say, "Now listen and check your answers. Write notes to remind yourself of the issue."
- **Play the recording** Audio script p. T-270 Check answers with the class.

Answers

3. But even so, they all still want to fit in with their friends.
4. Even then, I'm sure he got lower grades than he could have – deliberately.
2. And even then, they're not guaranteed to get a place in college.
☐. Even so, the major problem is having access to drugs.
1. But even so, we still see some cases of this kind of behavior.

- Read the remaining instructions aloud. Have Ss discuss the issues with a partner.
- **Follow-up** Have Ss share their discussion with the class.

③ Listening and strategies

A ◀)) CD, Track 29

- **Preview the task** Say, "Discuss the sentences. Do you agree?" Have Ss discuss and share answers with the class.
- **Play the recording** Audio script p. T-271 Read the remaining instructions aloud. Ss listen and check (✓) the correct box. Check the answer with the class.

Answers

2. Parents face challenges as their children . . .

B ◀)) CD, Track 30

- **Preview the task** Read the instructions aloud.
- **Play the recording** Audio script p. T-271 Ss listen and write. Play the recording again. Have Ss compare their answers. Check answers with the class.

Answers

1. Even then, you can't be sure they'll be safe.
2. But even so, I think it's too young.
3. Then again, adult drivers do that, too.
4. But then, thinking about it, I guess we caused problems for our parents, too.
5. Having said that, though, my mom probably wouldn't agree!

About you

C Pair work

- **Preview and do the task** Read the instructions aloud. Ask a S to read the example aloud. As Ss discuss their ideas, walk around the class giving help or ideas as needed.
- **Follow-up** Have pairs share their ideas with the class.

Extra activity – pairs

Have Ss choose one of the topics from Exercise 3A. Ss take opposing views and prepare to debate the topic to the class. When Ss have had chance to prepare, have pairs present their debates. Ss in the class vote on the view they agree with.

Speaking naturally

- Tell Ss to turn to Speaking naturally on p. 139. (For more information, see Language notes at the beginning of this unit. See the teaching notes on p. T-139.)

② Strategy plus *even so, even then*

🔊 CD 1.26 You can use **even so** to introduce a contrasting idea. It means, "despite what was just said."

A similar expression is **even then**, which means "despite the situation that was just described."

> . . . *some* women worked, but **even so**, their options were limited.

> You can study and study, but **even then**, you're not guaranteed a job.

A 🔊 CD 1.27 **Read the comments below. Then listen to people talking about various issues. Predict which comment each person makes next. Number the comments 1–4. There is one extra.**

_____ But even so, they all still want to fit in with their friends.

_____ Even then, I'm sure he got lower grades than he could have – deliberately.

_____ And even then, they're not guaranteed to get a place in college.

_____ Even so, the major problem is that too many kids skip school.

_____ But even so, we still see some cases of this kind of behavior.

About you

B 🔊 CD 1.28 Pair work **Listen and check your answers. Then discuss the issues with a partner. Do you see these types of problems and peer pressures in your society?**

③ Listening and strategies It's an issue . . .

A 🔊 CD 1.29 **Discuss the sentences below. Do you agree? Then listen to a conversation. Which sentence best summarizes the main topic of the discussion? Check (✓) the box.**

☐ 1. Parents are just not aware of the issues young people face.
☐ 2. Parents face challenges as their children grow up and become more independent.
☐ 3. Parents and children never used to have conflicts about how children should behave.

B 🔊 CD 1.30 **Listen again. Complete the contrasting views the speakers give next.**

1. Troy: You shouldn't let kids drive till they're 21.
   Even then, you can't be sure they'll be safe.

2. Troy: Yeah. They're legally old enough at 16 or 17.
   _____

3. Lucy: You even hear of kids texting at the wheel.
   _____

4. Troy: A lot of my friends have stories about their kids growing up too fast. _____

5. Lucy: I think I was an easy kid to raise.
   _____

About you

C Pair work **Discuss the opinions in Exercise B. Do you agree? How else do kids pressure parents? What would you do to resist pressure if you were a parent?**

"Actually, I agree that young people should wait before learning to drive. Though having said that, I guess some kids need to drive at 16, like if they've started working. Even so, it might be better . . ."

Speaking naturally
See page 139

Lesson D *Language and society*

1 Reading

A **Prepare** When you study a language, what kinds of things do you learn? Make a list.

B ⬇ **Read for main ideas** Read the course outlines. Write the title of each course in the space provided. There are two extra titles.

Language and Social Roles   Accent and Dialect   Right or wrong? Can technology help?
Language and Education   Language Change   What is bilingualism?

Spring semester courses in LANGUAGE and SOCIETY

| HOME | PEOPLE | RESEARCH | STUDY | COURSES | RESOURCES |

Participants should gain an understanding of how language reflects social structure and social change.

Course 101: _____

1 Language is constantly in development, and this course looks at one aspect of this: neologisms, i.e., new words. New words enter the language, sometimes pushing old words out of use. New words are very seldom completely new and are typically made up of existing words or segments of them. Scientific terms such as *nanotechnology* and *psychotherapy* combine classical Latin and Greek roots in new ways. Computer and Internet terminology reuses familiar everyday words, giving them novel meanings (*mouse, friend, memory stick, paste*), and new words are formed from the initial letters of existing words (*RAM, USB*). Sometimes names such as trade names form new words (*to Google*), or words change word class (*a big ask, a must-have*). On other occasions, English simply borrows from other languages (*pizza, sushi*). Such developments reveal a great deal about changes in society.

Course 102: _____

2 The purpose of this course is to examine styles of speaking and their social and professional consequences. Everyone speaks with an accent. When we say someone "has no accent," we usually mean the person is using the one associated with people of high social status or education. The term *non-standard accent* refers to geographical / regional varieties of speech, none of which is either inherently superior or inferior to any other. Even so, research shows that people do evaluate regional accents as being more, or less, friendly and pleasant, even judging whether people are suitable for certain types of jobs on the basis of their accent. Additionally, geographical regions and social groups frequently possess their own distinct grammar and vocabulary. However, accents and dialects are increasingly coming under pressure from mass media and centralization, threatening their very existence.

Course 103: _____

3 Correct grammar is usually seen as the grammar employed by educated people of higher social status, such as great writers, or those in power. In this course, we use a corpus (a large computer database of recorded  conversations and written texts) and dedicated software to investigate thousands of examples of people from every social and educational background speaking and writing. We find there is consensus in that people generally follow the same rules of grammar. Nevertheless, we can also observe numerous cases where everyone seems to "break the rules" without comment. When everyone ignores a grammatical convention, is the rule still valid – or should we rethink it?

Course 104: _____

4 Many languages utilize different forms, titles, and names to address people who are friends and intimates, as compared to strangers, superiors, or people with whom a more formal relationship is appropriate. In this course, we examine how English creates, reflects, and maintains social relations. We ask: What is politeness? What is the status of titles and forms of address such as *Professor, Sir, Ma'am*? How do changes in English mirror shifts in social perceptions and relationships? For instance, using gender-marked vocabulary such as *fireman, waitress, chairman* is now regarded as outdated and even offensive by many, and neutral alternatives such as *firefighter, server,* and *chair(person)* are considered more acceptable. What kinds of social structures, therefore, does contemporary English reflect?

Lesson D *Language and society*

1 Reading

- **Set the scene** Books closed. Write the title of the lesson on the board. Say, "When you think about language and society, what do you think of?" Elicit answers (e.g., *correct grammar, slang, formal language, peer group language*).

A Prepare

- **Preview and do the task** Ask, "When you learn a language, what kinds of things do you learn?" Have Ss call out their ideas (e.g., *grammar, vocabulary, pronunciation, culture*).

B 🔽 www.cambridge.org/viewpoint/audio

Read for main ideas

- **Preview the task** Books open. Read the instructions aloud. Have a S read the course titles aloud. Help with any vocabulary questions. If desired, play the downloadable recording. Ss listen and read along.

- **Do the task** Ss read and write the names of the course titles. Tell Ss to compare their answers with a partner. Check the answers with the class.

Answers

Course 101: Language Change
Course 102: Accent and Dialect
Course 103: Right or wrong? Can technology help?
Course 104: Language and Social Roles

- Have Ss skim through the course outlines again and underline any new words. Have Ss call out the new words and write them on the board. Call on Ss to give the meanings of any words they know. Alternatively, have Ss check meanings in their dictionaries.

- **Follow up** Have Ss tell a partner which of the four courses they would prefer to study and say why. Call on a few Ss to share their answers with the class.

Extra activity – pairs

Ss take turns asking five questions about the course outlines. S1 asks a question. S2 answers without looking at his or her book. Ss then change roles. (e.g., *A: What's a neologism? B: It's a new word.*)

C Read for detail

- **Preview and do the task** Ask, "Which course covers these questions? Write the course number." Have Ss read the six questions.

- Do the first question as an example with the class. Ask, "Which course covers question 1?" Have Ss complete the task. Check answers with the class.

Answers

1. 102	4. 102
2. 103	5. 101
3. 104	6. 103

- Say, "Now discuss the questions with a partner."
- **Follow-up** Have a short class discussion about the questions.

2 Focus on vocabulary

- **Preview the task** Say, "Synonyms are important to learn because exams use synonyms to test comprehension."

- Say, "Find synonyms in the course outlines to replace the words in bold. The numbers in parentheses refer to the course number where the synonyms can be found." Point out that the first answer has been done for them.

- **Do the task** Have Ss complete the task and compare answers with a partner. Check answers with the class.

Answers

1. frequently
2. seldom
3. accent, reveal
4. regarded / considered (no as), inherently, superior to
5. inferior
6. evaluate, consensus
7. conventions
8. distinct

- Say, "Now discuss the questions with a partner about your language. Give examples, if possible."
- Start the discussion by asking question 1. Elicit answers from the class. Walk around the class and give help as needed.
- **Follow-up** For each question, have a few Ss share their answers and examples with the class.

3 Listening and speaking

A ◀)) CD1, Track 31

- **Preview the task** Ask, "What's a course in language and gender about?" [language of men and women]

- Say, "Now read the outline and predict the missing words." Give Ss time to write. Have Ss share ideas with the class.

- **Play the recording** Audio script pp. T-271–T-272 Ss listen and write. Play the recording again so Ss can check their answers.

- Check answers with the class. Write the correct words on the board so Ss can check their spelling.

Answers

A controversial and <u>sensitive</u> area, . . . facts or <u>evidence</u>. . . . Do men <u>talk</u> more than women? . . . or less <u>confident</u>? . . . we find <u>little or no</u> difference . . . people of a <u>high social status</u> . . . between the sexes is <u>cross-cultural (communication)</u>. . . . one type of talk is <u>inherently superior to</u> another?

B ◀)) CD1, Track 32

- **Preview the task** Read the instructions aloud. Say, "Read the six questions to answer carefully. 'Write notes' means brief notes. Don't try to write full sentences."

- **Play the recording** Audio script pp. T-271–T-272 Ss listen and write.
- **Play the recording again** Ss complete and check their notes. Check the answers with the class.

Answers

1. Other books are not reliable because they are not based on research.
2. Are women better listeners?
3. Because traditionally in society men have been dominant, higher status
4. policeman, actresses, male nurse
5. Because men and women have been raised differently and come from different cultures
6. The differences between different people in the same situation

C Pair work

- **Preview and do the task** Read the instructions aloud. Have Ss discuss the questions. Walk around the class and give help as needed.

- **Follow-up** Find out (with a show of hands) which lecture most Ss think sounds most interesting. Have a few Ss give the reason for their choice. Have Ss share their opinions on the other questions.

C Read for detail Which course covers these questions? Write the course number. Then discuss the questions with a partner.

1. Does television affect the way people adapt or change the language they use? _____
2. How can examples of actual language be studied? _____
3. Is it possible to avoid sexist language? _____
4. Does the way you speak affect your career prospects? _____
5. What words from foreign languages have been introduced? _____
6. Do native speakers make mistakes? Is this acceptable? _____

2 Focus on vocabulary Synonyms

Find synonyms in the course outlines to replace the words in bold. Then discuss the questions with a partner about your language. Give examples, if possible.

frequently

1. Are new words **often** invented in your language? What are some examples? (101)
2. Which words are **rarely** used anymore? (102)
3. What do you think your **way of speaking** can **show** about you? (102 / 101)
4. Are some accents **seen** as **essentially** good, even **better than** others? (104 / 102 / 102)
5. Are some accents seen as **less good**? (102)
6. Which accents, if any, do people **assess** as being more "friendly"? (102)
   Is there general **agreement** on that? (103)
7. Are there **rules** for addressing people of different social status, gender, or age? (103)
8. Do people of higher social status use language that is **different**? (102)

3 Listening and speaking Language and gender

A ◀⬤) CD 1.31 **Read the outline below. Can you predict the missing words? Then listen and complete each sentence with one, two, or three words.**

Course 105 Language and Gender

A controversial and _____ area, this course analyzes language and gender on the basis of facts or _____. Questions include: Do men _____ more than women? Are women less assertive or less _____? Researching such questions, we find _____ difference between the sexes, so should we instead consider who is dominant? Put simply, people of a _____ talk more. We also look at "sexist" language and whether communication between the sexes is _____. Finally, we ask: Do comparisons imply that one type of talk is _____ another?

B ◀⬤) CD 1.32 **Listen again and answer the questions. Write notes.**

1. Why does the professor advise the students to read only the books on the reading list?
2. In Lecture 1, what question will be considered in addition to the ones in the outline?
3. Lecture 2 will cover studies that found that men talk more. Why is that?
4. In Lecture 3, what is one of the examples given of possibly "sexist" language?
5. Lecture 4 is about Tannen's work. Why does she say men and women's language is different?
6. In Lecture 5, what does the professor say should be studied instead of male–female differences?

C Pair work **Discuss which lecture you think sounds most interesting. What views do you have on men and women's language? Are there issues of sexist language in your language?**

"Actually the Language and Gender course sounds really interesting. Not having studied it before, I think I'd learn a lot about how men and women communicate."

Writing *I recommend it.*

In this lesson, you . . .
- plan and write an evaluative report.
- express results in writing.
- avoid errors with *therefore*.

Task **Write a report on a course.**

Write an evaluation of an international summer course you attended, taking into account other students' positive and negative views. Make a recommendation for future students.

A Look at a model Look at some students' comments on a course. Check (✓) the comments that are included in the report. Would you put the other points in paragraph 2 or 3? Write the number.

STUDENTS' COMMENTS

☐ Good food, accommodations
☐ We enjoyed the group work
☐ Some lectures were too long
☐ One professor talked too fast
☐ Too much reading
☐ Campus too far from city
☐ Good social program and good to meet other students
☐ Difficult assignments

The purpose of this report is to evaluate the residential Business Management Program, which I attended in July. As requested, I will report on both the positive and negative aspects.

On the positive side, the course was extremely well designed, giving all students an opportunity to take part. Group work was an integral part of the program. As a result, the classes were lively and varied. In terms of the social program, everyone enjoyed meeting people from other countries, making many new friends in the process.

On the negative side, some students complained that there was too much reading, leaving little time for evening activities. A further complaint was that one professor spoke so quickly that some students could not understand her.

In conclusion, the course was both useful and enjoyable. Having said that, there are some aspects which should be changed, such as the amount of reading. Even so, it was an excellent course, and I would therefore recommend it to other students.

B Focus on language Read the chart. Then underline the examples of results in Exercise A.

Expressing results in writing 📥

You can express a result in writing with present participle clauses, *so / such . . . that . . .*, or *so*.
*There was too much reading, **leaving little time for evening activities**.*
*She spoke **so** quickly **that** students could not understand her.* OR *She spoke quickly, **so** students . . .*

You can also use *as a result, consequently,* or *therefore.*
*Group work was part of the course. **As a result, / Consequently,** the classes were lively.*
*It was an excellent course, and I would **therefore** recommend it.*

Writing vs. Conversation

■ Conversation
■ Academic writing

as a result
therefore
consequently

C Rewrite the sentences, using the structures given.

1. The teacher spoke too fast. This made it difficult for students to follow. (participle)
2. The campus was too far from the city. We were only able to go there once. (*so . . . that* or *so*)
3. Some lectures were too long. This left no time for questions. (participle)
4. There was a good mix of nationalities. English was widely used. (*Consequently* or *As a result*)
5. The accommodations were excellent. We recommend staying on campus. (*therefore*)

D Write and check Write an evaluation of a course that you have taken. Use Exercises A and C to help you. Then check for errors.

Common errors

Do not use *therefore* by itself to join two clauses.
*It was excellent. **Therefore**, I would recommend it.* OR
*It was excellent, **and therefore,** I would recommend it.*
(NOT ~~It was excellent therefore I would recommend it.~~)

Writing *I recommend it.*

In this lesson

- Ask a S to read the lesson aims (*In this lesson, you . . .*) aloud. Say, "Can you use a present participle clause to express a result?" [yes]

- Ask, "When might you have to write a report?" (e.g., *for school, for business*) Ask, "What type of report might you have to write for business?" (e.g., *a report on sales, market research*) "What kind of report might you write for school?" (e.g., *a report on a survey, on your research*) Tell Ss that some international exams ask you to write a report on information they give you.

- **Preview the writing** Ask, "What does it mean to evaluate something?" [to judge something and decide if it is good or bad] Point out the writing topic in Task and read it aloud.

A Look at a model

- **Preview and do the task** Have Ss look at *Students' comments* on the left. Ask, "What did the Ss like or not like about the program?" [Liked: good food, accommodation, the group work, the social program; Didn't like: the lectures were too long, one professor talked too fast, the amount of reading, the campus too far from city, the difficult assignments] Ask, "Do you think this course should be recommended?" Have Ss vote with a show of hands.

- Have Ss read the report and students' comments on the left.

- Read the instructions aloud. Have Ss complete the task. Check answers with the class.

Answers

2 Good food, accommodations
☑ We enjoyed the group work
3 Some lectures were too long
☑ One professor talked too fast
☑ Too much reading
3 Campus too far from city
☑ Good social program and good to meet other students
3 Difficult assignments

- Ask, "How did you decide which paragraphs to put the comments in?" [Positive comments are in paragraph 2 because it's about the positive side of the course. Negative comments are in paragraph 3 because it's about the negative.]

- Ask, "How is the report structured? What are Paragraphs 1 and 4?" [introduction and conclusion]

B 📥 www.cambridge.org/viewpoint/audio
Focus on language

- **Present the grammar for the writing chart** Read the information in the chart aloud. If desired, play the downloadable recording. Ss listen and read along.

- **Understand the grammar for writing** Say, "In Lesson A, we looked at participle clauses to link events in terms of time and reason. In this example, too much reading is linked to evening activities. The idea that the participle clause expresses here is a result. The result of the reading was that there was little time for evening activities."

- Say, "In Lesson B, we looked at *so* and *such that* to add emphasis to the results or effects of something." Ask, "What is the result of the professor speaking quickly?" [The students could not understand her.]

- Say, "The expressions *as a result*, *consequently*, and *therefore* can also be used." Ask, "What do you need if they start a sentence?" [a comma]

- **Present *Writing vs. Conversation*** Have Ss look at the chart. Say "*Therefore* is used much more often than *consequently* or *as a result*, especially in academic writing. Notice also that the three expressions are used far less in conversation than in academic writing."

- **Do the task** Say, "Now underline the examples of results in Exercise A." Have Ss complete the task. Check answers with the class.

Answers

giving all students an opportunity to take part: As a result, the classes were lively and varied; making many new friends in the process; leaving little time for evening activities; so quickly that some students could not understand her; would therefore recommend it to other students

C
- **Preview and do the task** Read the instructions aloud. Have Ss complete the task. Check answers with the class.

Answers

1. The teacher spoke too fast, <u>making</u> it difficult for students to follow.
2. The campus was <u>so</u> far from the city <u>that</u> we were only able to go there once. OR The campus was too far from the city, <u>so</u> we were only able to go there once.
3. Some lectures were too long, <u>leaving</u> no time for questions.
4. There was a good mix of nationalities. <u>Consequently</u> / <u>As a result</u>, English was widely used.
5. The accommodations were excellent. <u>Therefore, we</u> / <u>We therefore</u> recommend staying on campus.

D Write and check

- **Preview the task** Read the instructions aloud.

- **Present *Common errors*** Read the information aloud. Add, "In addition to this error with *therefore*, Ss often forget the final *e*, so check your spelling."

- **Do the task** Have Ss complete the task.

Vocabulary notebook *Take credit!*

If done for homework

Briefly present the Learning tip and the task directions. Make sure Ss understand what they need to do.

If done in class

- **Present *Learning tip*** Read the information aloud. Add, "It's a good idea to underline or highlight the paraphrase. You'll be able to focus on it quickly." Ask a S to read the examples in the box.

A • **Preview and do the task** Read the instructions aloud. Have Ss complete the task. Check answers with the class. Ask individual Ss each to read a sentence aloud.

Answers

1. take part in
2. take advantage of
3. take into account
4. take responsibility for
5. take credit for

B • **Preview and do the task** Read the instructions aloud. Elicit ideas for a sentence for *take heart*. (e.g., *If you find a class hard, take heart. Others in the class probably do, too.*)

Answers

Answers will vary.

- **Follow-up** Have Ss form small groups and read their sentences to each other.

C Word builder

- **Preview and do the task** Read the instructions aloud. Elicit ideas for a paraphrase for *take action* (e.g., *do something positive, for example, about a problem*). Remind Ss to use a good dictionary or online dictionary.

- Have Ss complete the task. Check the answers with the class: Have a few Ss call out their paraphrase for each expression. Ask individual Ss each to read his or her sentence for each expression.

Example answers

1. It's important to <u>take action</u> and do something when things are not going well in your life.
2. I <u>take exception to</u> and really don't agree with people who are rude to others.
3. I like to <u>take into consideration</u> and think about everyone's ideas before I make a decision.
4. My friend's wedding <u>took place</u> in Hawaii. It was held in a resort.
5. I just took some allergy medicine, and it <u>took effect</u> really quickly. It made a difference right away.
6. I have to call the professor and make sure I got into the class. I don't want <u>to take it for granted</u>.
7. She wasn't happy with my decision. She <u>took issue with</u> the fact that I'd never visited the campus.

- **Present *What we take!*** Have Ss cover the box. Say, "Look at all the *take* expressions on this page. Write three that you think are used more often than others." Ss write their guesses. Have Ss uncover the box. Ask a S to read the information aloud. How many did Ss guess correctly?

D Focus on vocabulary, page 36

- **Preview and do the task** Read the instructions aloud. Say, "First write any words that you know or remember. Then look at page 36." Have Ss find the words. Check answers with the class.

Answers

1. seldom, frequently
2. consensus
3. regard / consider (no *as*)
4. reveals
5. convention
6. evaluate, accent
7. distinct
8. inherently
9. superior to, inferior to

- Say, "Now write sentences using the words and giving examples." Have Ss complete the task. Ss form groups and take turns reading their sentences aloud."

Vocabulary notebook *Take credit!*

take the initiative
 I need to take the initiative on a project at work, and
 start it without waiting for my co-workers.

A Complete the sentences with the correct expressions from the box. Use the underlined paraphrases to
help you.

take advantage of	take credit for	take into account	take part in	take responsibility for

1. It's good to _____ events that your friends organize and join in what they are doing.
2. I should _____ being single and make the most of the fact that I have few responsibilities.
3. When you see some teens behaving badly, you should _____ how easily they can be
   influenced and consider the peer pressure they are under.
4. If I do something wrong, I have to _____ it and take the blame for it.
5. You should _____ the good things you do in your community because it's important to know
   how to accept praise and be recognized.

B Use each expression in a sentence and paraphrase its meaning.

1. take heart _____
2. take precedence _____
3. take refuge in _____
4. take steps _____
5. take stock of _____
6. take note of _____

C Word builder Find the meanings of these expressions. Write each one in a sentence, and write a
paraphrase of its meaning.

take action	take place	take for granted
take exception to	take effect	take issue (with)
take into consideration		

What we take!

The top collocations of *take* include:
*take care, advantage, place, seriously, step(s),
precedence, for granted, account, action.*

D Focus on vocabulary Look at the course outlines on page 36. Find words for the paraphrases in
bold. Then write sentences using the words and giving examples. Refer to Exercise 2 on page 37
to help you.

Give an example of . . .
1. something you **don't often** do and something you **often** do.
2. an issue on which there is **agreement** in your group of friends.
3. something you **think of** as very important in life.
4. something you do that **shows or makes evident** your personality.
5. a **way that something is usually done** in society that you don't agree with.
6. how people **judge** you by your **way of speaking** or how you dress.
7. an area in your country that has very **different** pronunciation.
8. something that you feel is **essentially** dangerous.
9. a thing you own that is **better than** a friend's and something that is **not as good**.

Checkpoint 1 *Units 1–3*

1 Peer pressure

A Circle the correct auxiliary verb. Then complete the sentences with an appropriate adverb from the box. Sometimes there is more than one answer.

evidently	inevitably	ironically	presumably
ideally	invariably	potentially	supposedly

1. *A* My friend says she feels a lot of pressure from her parents, as I **am / do**, really. You know, to take all these extra classes, play an instrument, do a sport. I mean, do you?
   B Oh, yeah. _____, our parents never did all this stuff._____, they just want us to have more opportunities than they **did / are**. Well, I know my mom **is / does**.

2. *A* There's _____ all this bullying in schools. But you know, I've never experienced it. And I know my friends **haven't / have**, either. Have you?
   B Well, _____, a lot of it happens online. So _____, you don't see a lot of it. And our school has a strict policy on bullying, which a lot of schools **does / do**, I suppose.

3. *A* I don't really feel any strong peer pressure, though my best friend **does / is**. Do you?
   B Well, there's _____ some. My friends are all pretty confident, but I **do / am**, too.
   A That's good. I mean, _____, you want supportive friends. Well, I **have / do**. Some people are always worrying about what others think – as my friend **is / are**. And _____, that's bad for you.

About you

B Pair work **Ask and answer the questions in Exercise A. Use *even so* and *even then*.**

"Actually, my parents don't pressure me at all. But even so, I still want to do well so I don't disappoint them. So yeah, I try to get good grades and everything."

2 Using technology

A Complete the comments using *to, not to, one,* or *ones*. Complete the underlined idioms.

1. There's software on my computer that I don't know how to use. And I'll probably never be able _____. I mean, I'd like _____, but . . . it's _____ me.
2. You know, my phone has all these useless functions. Like the most useless _____ for most people is the stock market report. I don't <u>see _____ it</u>.
3. I can't use the remote to record anything. Well, I could, but I prefer _____. I can't make <u>heads _____ it</u>. And I always mess up the satellite channels when I try _____.
4. We want to get one of those things that cleans your floors. Well, we were going _____. Oh, what are they called? <u>It's on the tip _____</u> – those, um, robot things.
5. We never had calculators in my day. Not like the _____ they have now. You had to <u>learn all your math tables by _____</u>. You just had to <u>come _____ with it all</u>.
6. A gadget I can't live without? I don't know <u>off the top _____</u>. <u>Nothing comes _____</u>. I'd like to get a scooter, but I'll never be able _____. The _____ I want is so expensive.

About you

B Pair work **Discuss the comments above. Are any true for you? Express a contrasting view with expressions like *Having said that, But then,* and *(But) then again*.**

"I have no idea how to use spreadsheets, but I'd like to. Having said that, I'm not sure I need to."

Checkpoint 1 Units 1–3

- Before you begin the Checkpoint, write the following on the board:

	Grammar	Vocabulary	Conversation strategies
Unit 1			
Unit 2			
Unit 3			

- Say, "How well do you think you know these areas in Units 1–3? Write down each subject area. Then write the percentage that you think you know." Tell Ss that they will look at the figures again after completing the Checkpoint tasks to see if they would still choose the same percentages.

1 Peer pressure

↩ This task recycles avoiding repetition with auxiliary verbs, the conversation strategies of using adverbs for signaling expectations, and *even so* and *even then* to contrast ideas.

A (1A Grammar; 2C Conversation strategy)

- **Preview and do the task** Read the instructions and the adverbs in the box aloud. Have Ss complete the task and then compare answers in pairs. Check answers.

Answers

1. A My friend says . . . from her parents, as I <u>do</u>, really. . . .
   B Oh, yeah. <u>Ironically / Evidently / Presumably</u>, our parents . . . <u>Presumably / Evidently</u>, they just want . . . they <u>did</u>. Well, I know my mom <u>does</u>.
2. A There's <u>supposedly / presumably</u> all this bullying . . . my friends <u>haven't</u>, either. . . .
   B Well, <u>evidently / supposedly</u>, a lot of it happens online. So <u>invariably / inevitably</u>, you don't . . . , which a lot of schools <u>do</u>, I suppose.

3. A . . . though my best friend <u>does</u>. Do you?
   B Well, there's <u>inevitably / invariably</u> some. . . . confident, but I <u>am</u>, too.
   A . . . I mean, <u>ideally / presumably</u>, you want . . . Well, I <u>do</u>. . . . others think – as my friend <u>is</u>. And <u>potentially</u>, that's bad for you.

About you

B (3C Strategy plus) **Pair work**

- **Preview and do the task** Read the instructions aloud. Ask a S to read the first question in Exercise 1A aloud. Ask another S to read the example answer aloud.

- **Follow-up** For each question, have a few pairs present their question and answer to the class.

2 Using technology

↩ This task recycles avoiding repetition with *to*, *not to*, *one(s)*, idioms for understanding and remembering, and the strategy of using expressions such as *Having said that* to express contrasting views.

A (1B Grammar; 1B Vocabulary)

- **Preview the task** Read the instructions aloud. Tell Ss to complete comment 1 and then compare their answer with a partner. Check the answer with the class.

- **Do the task** Have Ss complete the task. Check answers with the class.

Answers

1. . . . I'll probably never be able <u>to</u>. I mean, I'd like <u>to</u>, but . . . <u>it's beyond me.</u>
2. . . . Like the most useless <u>one</u> for most people . . . I don't <u>see the point of it.</u>
3. . . . Well, I prefer <u>not to</u>. I <u>can't make heads or tails of it.</u> . . . when I try <u>to</u>.
4. . . . Well, we were going <u>to</u>. Oh, what are they called? It's on the <u>tip of my tongue</u> – . . .

5. . . . Not like the <u>ones</u> they have now. You had to <u>learn</u> all your math tables <u>by heart</u>. You just had to <u>come to grips with</u> it all.
6. . . . I don't know <u>off the top of my head</u>. <u>Nothing comes to mind.</u> . . . I'll never be able <u>to</u>. The <u>one</u> I want is so expensive.

About you

B (3C Conversation strategy) **Pair work**

- **Preview and do the task** Read the instructions aloud.

- Have Ss complete the task. Give help as needed.

- **Follow-up** Ask several Ss to tell the class about one of their contrasting views.

Extra activity – pairs

Ss write the names of three gadgets on a piece of paper and exchange it with a partner. Ss choose one of the gadgets and talk about it using the comments in Exercise 2A as a model. Encourage Ss to express a contrasting view in their comment.

3 Bookworms

🔄 This task recycles conjunctions, participle clauses, expressions with *take*, and auxiliary *do* for emphasis.

A (3B Vocabulary; 3A Grammar; 2B Grammar)

- **Preview and do the task** Say, "Read both interviews to get the main idea of each one. Then complete the *take* expressions." Have Ss complete the take expressions and compare answers with a partner.
- Say, "Now, in interview 1, write participle clauses using the verbs given." Ask a S to give the first one as an example.
- Say, "In interview 2, write *both . . . and, either . . . or, neither . . . nor,* or *not only . . . but also.*"
- Have Ss complete the task. Check answers.

Answers

1. Growing up, I was always a bookworm. Reading always took precedence over everything else. If I take stock of all my successes in life, it's probably due to reading. My mom has to take credit for teaching us to read. Not having [had] a career, she stayed home and took responsibility for our education. She used to take note / charge of how much we read every day. And living near a library, we always took advantage of it. By the age of 10, I had a wide vocabulary, having read / reading as much as I did. I often won the local spelling bees when

I took part in them. Also, having read / reading all the classics, I was good at general knowledge quizzes, too. These days, working as much as I do, I still like to take refuge in a book. It's a great way to escape from life!

2. I haven't read either a book or a magazine in months. Well, unless you take into account the books I read to my kids. They want me both / not only to read every night, and / but also to tell them stories about when I was a kid. So I read and tell stories every single night. Sometimes I have neither the time nor the energy after a day's work. But even if you are busy, you can take steps to help your kids read. Like now they have electronic readers for kids, which are great. They're both fun and educational. Kids can both read and listen at the same time. If they don't know how to say a word, they can either ask me or point to it and hear it. It's a great way to get kids to take the initiative and read.

About you

B (1C Conversation strategy) Pair work

- **Preview and do the task** Read the instructions aloud. Ask a S to read the example. Have Ss discuss the ideas in Exercise A.
- **Follow-up** Ask the class to share their ideas about interview 1. Then have them share their ideas about interview 2.

4 Solar power

🔄 This task recycles *only*, post-noun modifiers, compound adjectives, using *so / such a / an . . . that, even,* and *can't possibly* to say something is impossible, and using *if so* or *if not* to mean *if this is* or *is not true.*

A (2B Vocabulary; 2C Strategy plus)

- **Preview and do the task** Ask, "How many different compound adjectives do you remember?" (e.g., *self-cleaning, high-speed*). Have Ss make their lists and write them on the board.
- Say, "Now use the words to discuss different technologies with a partner. Use *can't possibly* or *couldn't possibly.*" Ask a S to read the example aloud. Have Ss discuss the technologies. Walk around the class, listening and helping as needed.
- **Follow-up** Call out words from the board. Have a few Ss report their discussion to the class.

B (1C Strategy plus; 3B Grammar)

- **Preview and do the task** Read the instructions aloud. Have Ss complete the task. Check answers.

Answers

Worried . . . ? If so, why not install solar panels . . . ? They are now so affordable that everyone . . . And what's just as important, if not more important, is that it's such a clean source of power that . . . With some

systems, you can even get paid . . . The panels only take . . . fall so rapidly that you'll be pleased that you've made such a great investment.

C (2A Grammar)

- **Preview and do the task** Read the instructions aloud. Do the first example with the class. Ask, "Where in sentence 1 will you add *happy to pay*?" Elicit the correct answer. [I know there are a lot of people happy to pay for solar energy.]
- Have Ss complete the task and then compare their answers with a partner. Check the answers.

Answers

1. I know there are a lot of people happy to pay for solar energy.
2. Solar power is not a cheap technology to install, or so I heard.
3. The people next door have it, and they said it cost a fortune.
4. Solar panels on the roof change the look of your home.
5. It's definitely something to be considered because it saves money.
6. People hoping to get their money back quickly will be disappointed.
7. I also heard that some homes built before a certain date can't have it.

3 Bookworms

A Complete the *take* expressions in both interviews. Then in 1, write participle clauses using the verbs given. In 2, write *both . . . and, either . . . or, neither . . . nor,* or *not only . . . but also.*

1. _____ (grow up), I was always a bookworm. Reading always **took** _____ **over** everything else. If I **take** _____ **of** all my successes in life, it's probably due to reading. My mom has to **take** _____ **for** teaching us to read. _____ (not have) a career, she stayed home and **took** _____ **for** our education. She used to **take** _____ **of** how much we read every day. And _____ (live) near a library, we always **took** _____ **of** it. By the age of 10, I had a wide vocabulary, _____ (read) as much as I did. I often won the local spelling bees when I **took** _____ **in** them. Also, _____ (read) all the classics, I was good at general-knowledge quizzes, too. These days, _____ (work) as much as I do, I still like to **take** _____ **in** a book. It's a great way to escape from life!

2. I haven't read _____ a book _____ a magazine in months. Well, unless you **take into** _____ the books I read to my kids. They want me _____ to read every night _____ to tell them stories about when I was a kid. So I read and tell stories every single night. Sometimes I have _____ the time _____ the energy after a day's work. But even if you are busy, you can **take** _____ to help your kids read. Like now they have electronic readers for kids, which are great. They're _____ fun _____ educational. Kids can _____ read _____ listen at the same time. If they don't know how to say a word, they can _____ ask me _____ point to it and hear it. It's a great way to get kids to **take the** _____ and read.

About you **B** Pair work **Discuss the ideas above. Use expressions like *I do think* to add emphasis.**

"I do think it's good for parents to read to their kids."

4 Solar power

A How many compound adjectives do you remember? Make a list. Then use them to discuss different technologies with a partner. Use *can't possibly* and *couldn't possibly.*

"I bet a lot of people couldn't possibly live without their labor-saving devices."

B Circle the correct options to complete the information from a website selling solar-power panels.

Worried about heating costs? **If so, / If not**, why not install solar panels in your home to reduce your energy bills? They are now **such / so** affordable that everyone can benefit from them. And what's just as important, **if not / if so** more important, is that it's **such / so** a clean source of power that you'll be helping to reduce pollution, too. With some systems, you can **even / so** get paid for the energy you produce. The panels **such / only** take a day to install. Your heating bills will fall **so / such** rapidly that you'll be pleased that you've made **so / such** a great investment.

C Rewrite the comments using the phrases in parentheses.

1. I know there are a lot of people for solar energy. (happy to pay)
2. Solar power is not a cheap technology, or so I heard. (to install)
3. The people have it, and they said it cost a fortune. (next door)
4. Solar panels change the look of your home. (on the roof)
5. It's definitely something because it saves money. (to be considered)
6. People will be disappointed. (hoping to get their money back quickly)
7. I also heard that some homes can't have it. (built before a certain date)

Unit 4 Amazing world

Lesson A *Animal behavior*

Vocabulary in context *Animal behavior*

(See Student's Book p. 42.)

Language to talk about animal behavior, for example, *mating* and *hibernation*, is presented in the context of excerpts from a nature documentary.

Vocabulary notebook *Golden eggs*

(See Student's Book p. 51.)

The Learning tip tells Ss that when they learn vocabulary from a specific subject area, they should check for other uses of the word in general English. For example, both animals and computers hibernate.

Grammar *Talking about the past in the future*

(See Student's Book p. 43.)

In this lesson, Ss use future perfect and future perfect continuous to talk about the past as it is seen from the future.

Form

* Future perfect

  will / won't + have + past participle

  *How far **will** the tern **have flown**?*

  *It **will have flown** 70,000 kilometers by the time it arrives back in the Arctic.*

* Future perfect continuous

  will / won't + have + been + -ing form

  *How long **will** it **have been hibernating**?*

  *By then, it **will have been hibernating** for six months.*

Use

* Future perfect

  The future perfect is used for events that are in the past when you "view" them from the future. It is often used to talk about things that you expect to be finished or achieved by a certain future time.

* Future perfect continuous

  The future perfect continuous is used to suggest that an event will be in progress when it is "viewed" at a particular time in the future.

Grammar extra *More on the future perfect; The future perfect for predictions and assumptions*

(See Student's Book p. 150.)

Grammar extra presents more ways to use the future perfect, including with time expressions and the passive form. Also presented and practiced is the use of the future perfect for predictions and assumptions.

> ### Corpus information
>
> **Common errors with *if* and time clauses**
>
> Ss may incorrectly use the future perfect in *if* or time clauses. They should use the present or present perfect.
>
> *When it **arrives** back, it will have flown 70,000 kilometers.* (**NOT:** ~~When it will have arrived back~~ . . .)
>
> *If it **has not been attacked**, . . .* (**NOT:** ~~If it will not have been attacked~~, . . .)

Lesson B *Desert landscapes*

Grammar *Combining ideas*

(See Student's Book p. 45.)

This lesson teaches ways to combine ideas using prepositions and prepositional phrases.

Form

* Preposition + noun / *-ing* form

  A preposition or prepositional phrase is followed by a noun, pronoun, or an *-ing* form of a verb.

  ***In line with** USGS definitions, a desert has less than 250 millimeters of rain **per** year.*

  *A camel can go up to eight days **without** drinking.*

* Preposition + *-ing* clause

  A preposition or prepositional expression can start an *-ing* clause.

  ***As a result of** experiencing severe dust storms, China started planting trees.*

* *The fact that* + clause

  Some prepositions and prepositional phrases can be followed by *the fact that* + a clause.

  *Antarctica is a desert, apart from **the fact that** it is one of the coldest places on earth.*

Use

* Preposition + *-ing* clause

  If a preposition starts an *-ing* clause, the subject of the verb in the *-ing* clause should be the same as in the main clause.

  ***As a result of** experiencing severe dust storms, China started planting trees.*

  China is the subject of both *experiencing* and *started*.

- *The fact that* + clause

  If the subjects of the main clause and the *-ing* clause are different, you can often use *the fact that* to link the ideas.

  *The Gobi desert has spread owing to **the fact that** agricultural practices have changed.*

  Prepositional phrases that often precede *the fact that* include: *apart from, because of, besides, despite, due to, in spite of, in light of, in view of, owing to,* and *thanks to.*

Grammar extra *Formal prepositional expressions; More on* the fact that; *prepositions + perfect forms*

(See Student's Book p. 151.)

Grammar extra presents more ways to combine ideas with formal prepositions, *the fact that,* and prepositions + perfect forms.

Lesson C *What's more . . .*

Conversation strategy *Adding ideas*

(See Student's Book p. 46.)

Speakers use expressions such as *what's more* and *on top of that* to add ideas as they speak and think of other things they wish to say. These expressions can also have the effect of focusing on an idea. They are useful when speakers are building an argument, describing a situation, or adding to other people's ideas. The expressions *In addition* and *Additionally* are more frequent and therefore more useful in formal and academic settings, such as seminars and tutorials.

Expressions taught are:

> *Also, . . .*
> *And then . . .*
> *. . . as well,*
> *. . . not to mention . . .*
> *Additionally, . . .*
> *In addition, . . .*
> *What's more . . .*
> *On top of that . . .*

Strategy plus *In any case, in any event*

(See Student's Book p. 47.)

In conversation, *in any case* can be used to add more ideas and to make an argument stronger or clearer. *In any case* and *in any event* can both introduce a conclusion that the speaker considers to be the only one possible given what has just been said.

 Corpus information

In conversation

The expression *in any case* is more frequent in writing and formal speaking than informal conversation. *In any event* is more frequent than *in any case* in formal spoken English and less frequent than *in any case* in academic written English.

Speaking naturally *Stress in adding expressions*

(See Student's Book p. 139.)

In this section, Ss practice stress in the expressions they learned in this lesson.

Lesson D *Biomimicry*

Writing *Does it matter?*

(See Student's Book p. 50.)

This lesson teaches Ss to write a persuasive essay that argues a particular case. The grammar for writing presents prepositions that are particularly frequent in academic writing and can therefore make writing sound more formal. It also teaches the use of the generic pronoun *one* to mean "people in general" or "you" and its possessive form, *one's.*

- Prepositions
  amongst
  beneath
  throughout
  upon
  within
  in terms of

Corpus information

Common errors with *upon*

Ss often overuse *upon,* so they should be encouraged to use it only in academic writing and especially after the verbs *depend, rely,* and *agree.*

Another error is to use *look upon* instead of *look at. Look upon* means "to think about in a certain way." For example: *You can look upon climate change as either inevitable or as a disaster.* In other cases, *look at* should be used.

Let us look at this subject in more detail. (**NOT:** *look upon*)

Amazing world

In Unit 4, you . . .
- talk about the natural world.
- use the future perfect and future perfect continuous.
- use prepositional expressions like *due to* and *far from*.
- add ideas with expressions like *what's more* and *not to mention*.
- use *in any case* to state conclusions or add information.

Lesson A *Animal behavior*

1 Vocabulary in context

A Which creatures (animals, birds, insects) do you find interesting? Lovable? Scary?

B 🔊 CD 2.02 Listen and read the excerpts from a nature documentary. Complete the photo captions with these words: a. breeding, b. hibernation, c. migration.

Animal Behavior

Every September, the arctic tern leaves its **breeding grounds** in the Arctic and heads south to the Antarctic. When it arrives back in the Northern Hemisphere the next summer, it will have flown on average 70,000 kilometers (almost 44,000 miles), which means by the end of its thirty-year lifespan, the arctic tern will have flown the equivalent of three round trips to the moon.

The longest _____

In order to **survive the winter months**, many small mammals **store food** before they **go into hibernation**. Groundhogs, however, **build up** their fat reserves and then **dig a burrow**, where they **hibernate** until spring. By the time the groundhog is in its deep sleep, its heartbeat will have dropped from 80 to 4 beats per minute and its body temperature will have fallen to only a few degrees above the outside temperature. By the time spring arrives, if it has not been **attacked** by **predators**, the groundhog will have been hibernating for almost six months.

Groundhog
_____

After **mating**, a female emperor penguin **lays** a single **egg** before returning to the ocean, where she **feeds** and spends the winter. Penguins don't **build nests**. Instead, the male emperor balances the **egg** on his feet, huddling together with other males in the **colony** to **keep warm**. By the time the females return, these male penguins will have been protecting the eggs for 65 days. They won't have eaten for 115 days and will have lost nearly half of their body weight. Once the **eggs hatch**, the females **feed** and **raise the young**, while the males head to the ocean to feed.

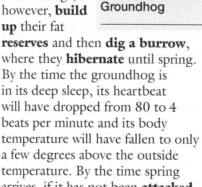
The _____ habits of emperor penguins

Word sort

C Copy the chart and write the bold words and collocations in the documentary. Add others you want to learn. Which facts did you know? Which didn't you know? Tell a partner.

survival (food and sleep)	having young	homes and groups
feed	lay an egg	

Vocabulary notebook

See page 51.

"I knew that penguins lay eggs, but I didn't know that they only lay single eggs."

Amazing world

Introduce the theme of the unit Say, "In Unit 2, we looked at the theme of technology that makes our world amazing. This unit is about another aspect of our amazing world." Say, "Look at the pictures on page 42. What do you see?" [a whale, a butterfly, a bird/tern, a groundhog, a penguin] "What aspect of the world will this unit cover?" (e.g., *the world of nature*) Have a S read the unit aims aloud.

Lesson A *Animal behavior*

1 Vocabulary in context

- **Set the scene** Books closed. Ask, "When you think about animal behavior, what comes to mind?" Elicit answers from the class (e.g., *pets that are loyal, mother cats training their kittens, animals hunting other animals*)

A • **Preview and do the task** Write as column headings on the board:

> *Interesting*
>
> *Loveable*
>
> *Scary*

Ask, "Which creatures – that is, animals, birds, or insects – do you find most interesting? loveable? scary?"

- Have Ss call out their ideas. If using the Extra Activity below, write them on the board under the appropriate column heading.

Extra activity – groups

Ss look at which type of creature dominates each list. Groups decide what makes a creature interesting, lovable, or scary. Groups report their ideas to the class.

B ◀)) CD2 Track 2

- **Preview and do the task** Books open. Read the instructions aloud. Ensure that Ss know the meanings of *breeding, hibernation,* and *migration.*
- **Play the recording** Ss listen, read along, and write their answers. Check the answers with the class.

Answers

The longest <u>migration</u> (c)
Groundhog <u>hibernation</u> (b)
The <u>breeding</u> habits of emperor penguins (a)

Word sort

C • **Preview the task** Say, "Copy the chart and write the bold words and collocations in the documentary. Add others you want to learn."

- **Do the task** Have Ss complete the task. Walk around the class and help as needed.
- Check answers with the class. For each column in the chart, have Ss call out the answers.

Answers

Survival (food and sleep)
feed
hibernate
migration
keep warm
store food
build up (fat) reserves
be attacked by predators
survive the winter months
go into hibernation

having young
lay an egg
breeding grounds
breeding habits
eggs hatch
mate
raise young

homes and groups
a colony
build a nest
dig a burrow

- Review the words in the chart. For each word, have Ss call out the meaning. Tell Ss to look at the words in context. Have Ss call out any words they want to learn. Write them on the board. Ask other Ss to call out any definitions they know. Help with remaining vocabulary.
- Ask, "Which facts did you know? Which didn't you know?" Ask a S to read the example aloud. Say, "Now tell your partner."
- **Follow-up** Have pairs report one thing they knew and one thing they didn't know to the class.

> Tell Ss to turn to Vocabulary Notebook on p. 51 of their Student's Books. Have Ss do the tasks in class or assign them for homework. (See the teaching notes on p. T-51.)
>
> *Vocabulary notebook*

② Grammar

A   🔊   www.cambridge.org/viewpoint/audio

- **Preview the task**   Say, "Circle the correct verb forms to complete the sentences. Use the documentary to help you. Find similar sentences."
- **Do the task**   Have Ss complete the task. Check answers with the class.

Answers

1. will have lost
2. will have been hibernating

- **Focus on the use**   Say, "The verb form in example 1 is the future perfect. The future perfect describes the past from the point of view of the future. It is used to talk about things you expect to be finished by a certain time in the future. In example 2, the future perfect continuous is used to talk about events that will be in progress at a certain time in the future."
- **Focus on the form**   Review the future perfect. Write on the board, underlined as shown:

  The emperor male <u>will have lost</u> half his body fat.

  Ask, "Why is the auxiliary *will* used?" [to indicate future] Point out *have lost*. Ask, "What verb form is it like?" [present perfect] Ask, "What is the pattern for the future perfect form of the verb?" Write on the board:

  will / won't + have + past participle

- Write on the board, underlined as shown:

  The groundhog <u>will have been hibernating</u> for six months.

  Point out the underlined section. Ask, "What is the pattern for the future perfect form of the verb?" Write on the board:

  will / won't + have + been + -ing form

- **Present the grammar chart**   Read the information aloud. If desired, play the downloadable recording. Ss listen and read along.
- Say, "Look at the example questions and answers in both sections of the chart. What preposition do the answers have in common?" [by] Say, "*By* and a reference to a future point in time is often used with future perfect forms."

- **Present *Common errors***   Read the information aloud. (For more information, see Language notes at the beginning of the unit. For more work on future perfect forms, go to Grammar extra, p. 150.)

B
- **Preview the task**   Read the instructions aloud. Ask a S to read excerpt 1 aloud. Point out the example answer. Ask, "Why is future perfect correct here?" [When the butterfly arrives in Mexico, its journey will be complete.]
- **Do the task**   Have Ss complete the task and then compare their answers with a partner. Check answers with the class.

Answers

1. will have flown
2. will have eaten; will have foraged / will have been foraging
3. will have been swimming / will have swum
4. will have laid
5. will have been adding
6. will have carried / will have been carrying

C   Pair work

- **Preview and do the task**   Read the instructions aloud. Say, "Decide who is Student A and who is Student B. B Students close your books. A Students ask questions about three of the excerpts. Then reverse roles. B Students ask questions about the remaining three excerpts." Have Ss complete the task.

Extra activity – individuals / class

Write on the board:

What will you have done by 2020?

What will you have been doing for (amount of time) in 2020?

Ss write two predictions for each question. They walk around the class and tell each other. Several S tell one of their predictions to the class.

---

③ Viewpoint

Pair work

- **Preview the task**   Say, "Choose a creature that interests you and prepare a presentation. You can choose one from the documentary on p. 42 or use your own idea." Say, "Imagine everyone is watching a film of the creature you are talking about. Use the future perfect or future perfect continuous in your presentation to describe the things it will have done or will have been doing by a future time." Ask a S to read the example aloud.

- **Do the task**   Ss prepare their presentation. If the classroom has Internet access, have Ss show pictures of their chosen creature.
- Have pairs give their presentations to the class. After each presentation, ask, "What new facts did you learn?"

2 Grammar Talking about the past in the future

A Circle the correct verb form in the sentences. Use the documentary to help you. Then read the grammar chart.

1. By the time a penguin egg hatches, the emperor male **will have lost / will lose** half his body weight.
2. By the time spring arrives, the groundhog **will be hibernating / will have been hibernating** for six months.

Future perfect and future perfect continuous 📥

Grammar extra
See page 150.

You can use future perfect forms for events that are in the past when you view them from the future.

Use the simple form to suggest that an event will be complete before a certain time.	How far **will** the tern **have flown**? It **will have flown** 70,000 kilometers by the time it arrives back in the Arctic.
Use the continuous form to suggest that an event will be in progress at a particular time in the future.	How long **will** it **have been hibernating**? By then, it **will have been hibernating** for six months.

Common errors

Do not use the future perfect in *if* or time clauses.
When it **arrives** back, it will have flown 70,000 kilometers. If it **has not been attacked** . . .
(NOT ~~When it will have arrived back . . .~~)
(NOT ~~If it will not have been attacked . . .~~)

B Complete these excerpts from the documentary. Use a future perfect form of the verbs given. Sometimes there is more than one correct answer.

1. It's winter in Canada and too cold for the monarch butterfly to feed and survive. So it starts its journey south, and by the time it arrives in Mexico, it ___will have flown___ (fly) more than 4,000 kilometers (2,485 miles).
2. Giant pandas almost exclusively eat bamboo. At the end of the day, when it finishes feeding, it _____ (eat) 40 pounds of bamboo and it _____ (forage) for 16 hours.
3. These gray whales are leaving their feeding grounds in the cooler north to breed in the warmer south. When they reach Mexican waters, they _____ (swim) 160 kilometers (about 100 miles) a day for 8 to 10 weeks.
4. After mating at sea, female leatherback turtles come ashore. It's here that they dig a hole, and by the end of the night, they _____ (lay) 80 or more eggs.
5. Some bald eagle nests weigh more than a ton. But by the time they reach this weight, the bald eagles _____ (add) sticks to the nest for several years.
6. This female elephant is heavily pregnant. By the time she is ready to give birth, she _____ (carry) the baby for over 22 months.

C Pair work Take turns asking and answering questions about the facts in Exercise B. How much can you remember?

3 Viewpoint A wildlife presentation

Pair work **Choose a creature that interests you, and prepare a presentation. Take turns giving your presentations to the class. What new facts do you learn?**

"By the time this penguin reaches the open sea, it will have traveled more than 50 miles across the frozen ice."

Lesson B *Desert landscapes*

1 Grammar in context

A What do you know about deserts? Make a class list.

> The largest hot desert in the world is the Sahara.

B ◀))CD 2.03 **Listen to extracts from a geography lecture about deserts. Which three slides does the professor refer to? Number the slides 1–3. There is one extra slide.**

1 "Deserts are, for lack of a better description, among some of the most fascinating and diverse landscapes on earth. They cover approximately one-third of the earth's land surface and stretch across all continents. But what is a desert? Most people think of them as hot, sandy places thanks to photographs of sand dunes in the Sahara desert. But in fact, only about 10 percent of the world's deserts are covered with sand dunes, including the Sahara. In line with USGS* definitions, a desert is an area that has less than 250 millimeters (10 inches) of rain per year. So Antarctica is a desert, apart from being one of the coldest places on earth. And in addition to cold deserts, there are also mountainous deserts."...

2 "Deserts are also commonly believed to be wastelands, on account of their harsh living conditions for wildlife and plants. But far from being barren, deserts are often very rich in plant life. Death Valley in the United States has over 1,000 plant species in spite of the fact that it has some of the most extreme conditions. And many species of animals can also survive in a desert climate by virtue of having adapted to the environment. Some, like the camel, can go up to eight days without drinking. As for smaller mammals, many have adapted by means of living underground or by hunting only at night."...

3 "One problem with deserts is that they expand and encroach on arable land. In fact, there is great concern in many parts of the world about this process, known as "desertification." Take for example the Gobi desert, which has spread, in part due to the fact that agricultural practices have changed from those in use prior to the 1950s. China was faced with increasing areas of arid land in place of its valuable grasslands. And, as a result of experiencing increasingly severe dust storms, China has started planting trees with the aim of halting desertification. By the end of the planned 70-year project, they will have planted more than 4,500 kilometers (approximately 2,800 miles) of trees."

*United States Geological Survey

C **Complete the sentences with information from the lecture. Then replace the underlined words with an expression from the lecture. In some, more than one expression can be used.**

1. Most people think of deserts as _____ places <u>because of</u> photographs of the Sahara.
2. <u>According to</u> USGS definitions, a desert is an area that _____.
3. <u>As well as</u> cold deserts, there are also _____ deserts.
4. Deserts are <u>not at all</u> barren and can be _____.
5. Many animals can _____ in a desert climate <u>through</u> their adaptation to the environment.
6. <u>As well as</u> larger animals like _____, there are many small mammals that live in the desert.
7. The Gobi desert has spread <u>because of</u> farming practices that didn't exist <u>before</u> _____.

Lesson B *Desert landscapes*

1 Grammar in context

- **Set the scene** Books closed. Write *Desert landscapes* on the board. Say, "This is the topic of this lesson. What is a landscape?" Elicit the answer (e.g., *the appearance of an area / what an area looks like*). Ask, "What image does the phrase *desert landscape* bring to mind?" Elicit answers (e.g., *sand, an oasis, a camel*).

A • **Preview and do the task** Books open. Read the instructions and the example aloud. Have Ss complete the task. Have several Ss call out an item from their list.

Possible answers

- Deserts can be hot or cold, like Antarctica.
- Deserts have very low rainfall.
- Some well-known deserts around the world are the Gobi, the Atacama, Kalahari, the Great Sandy Desert.
- Some deserts have a wide variety of animal and plant life.

B ◀)) CD2, Track 3

- **Preview the task** Read the instructions aloud. Write on the board:

  arable   encroach

  diverse   wasteland

  Have classmates give definitions or explanations of words they know. Supply definitions for any remaining vocabulary. [*arable*: suitable for growing crops; *diverse*: varied, different; *encroach*: take over gradually without being noticed; *wasteland*: land that cannot be used]

- Have Ss look at the four slides. Call on Ss to describe what they see. [a gopher, desert erosion (desertification), sand dunes, a fossil]

- **Play the recording** Ss listen along and number the slides. Check the answers with the class.

Answers

Slides, l-r: 2, 3,1, □

- Check for remaining vocabulary problems.

C • **Preview and do the task** Read the instructions aloud. Say, "Several of the expressions highlighted in the lecture are similar in meaning. Add these to your notes." Write on the board:

  thanks to: as result of, on account of, because of, and owing to

  as well as: in addition to

- Have Ss complete the task and compare their answers in pairs.

Answers

1. Most people think of deserts as hot, sandy places thanks to / as a result of / on account of / due to photographs of the Sahara.
2. In line with USGS definitions, a desert is an area that has less than 250 millimeters (10 inches) of rain per year.
3. In addition to cold deserts, there are also mountainous deserts.
4. Deserts are far from (being) barren and can be very rich in plant life.
5. Many animals can survive in a desert climate by means of / by virtue of their adaptation to the environment.
6. Apart from / In addition to larger animals like camels, there are many small mammals that live in the desert.
7. The Gobi desert has spread due to / on account of / as a result of farming practices that didn't exist prior to the 1950s.

Extra activity – pairs

Ss take turns "testing" each other on desert facts from the lecture. S1 asks six questions. S2 answers without looking at his or her book. Ss then change roles and see who can answer the most questions correctly.

Extra activity – pairs

Pairs choose a desert and find out three facts about it. Pairs make a 20-second presentation about the desert to present to another pair or to the class.

② Grammar

Figure it out

A ⬇ www.cambridge.org/viewpoint/audio

- **Preview the task** Say, "This task looks at more ways to combine ideas. How does the professor express the ideas below in her lecture? Rewrite the sentences."
- **Do the task** Have Ss complete the task. Check answers.

Answers

1. Deserts are believed to be wastelands, <u>on account of</u> their harsh living conditions.
2. Antarctica is a desert <u>apart from being</u> one of the coldest places on earth.
3. Death Valley has over 1,000 plant species <u>in spite of the fact that</u> it has some of the most extreme conditions.

- **Focus on the form** Ask, "What does *on account of* replace in sentence 1?" [because they have] Ask, "What follows *on account of*: a clause or a noun phrase?" [noun phrase]
- Ask, "What does *apart from* replace in sentence 2?" [although it is] Ask, "Why did *is* change to *being*?" [You need an *-ing* form of a verb after a preposition.]
- Ask, "What replaces *even though* in sentence 3?" [in spite of the fact that] Ask, "Can you use *in spite of*?" [no] "Why not?" [*in spite of* is a preposition and needs a noun after it; it can't be followed by a clause]
- **Present the grammar chart** Read the information aloud. If desired, play the downloadable recording.
- Say, "The top section of the chart gives examples of prepositions followed by a noun or an *-ing* form. The second section shows a preposition that starts an *-ing* clause. Ask, "What is the subject of *experiencing*?" [China] "And the main clause?" [China] Say, "Notice that the subject of the *-ing* clause and the main clause are the same."

- Say, "Use *the fact that* after a preposition when the subject of the main clause and the subject of the *-ing* clause are different."

  (For more information, see Language notes at the beginning of the unit. For more work on prepositions, go to Grammar extra, p. 151.)

B - **Preview the task** Read the instructions aloud. Tell Ss to look at sentence 1 and its example answer.
- **Do the task** Have Ss complete the task and then compare their answers with a partner. Check answers with the class. Remind Ss that some sentences have more than one correct answer. A S with a different answer should read it aloud.

Answers

1. <u>Far from being unpopulated</u>, deserts are home . . .
2. <u>In addition to burrowing underground</u> . . . , <u>many animals</u> are nocturnal.
   <u>In addition to the fact that they</u> burrow underground . . . , <u>many animals</u> are nocturnal.
3. <u>Apart from having long roots</u>, plants such as cacti can store their own water.
   <u>Apart from the fact that they</u> have long roots, plants such as cacti can store their own water.
4. Some desert plants survive . . . <u>thanks to these kinds of adaptations</u>. / <u>thanks to the fact that they have made</u> these kinds of adaptations.
5. Many desert areas are expanding <u>on account of the fact that</u> humans graze animals in semi-arid areas.
6. Environmentalists are concerned <u>about</u> these farming practices <u>having</u> caused desertification.
   Environmentalists are concerned <u>about the fact</u> that farming practices <u>like these</u> have caused desertification.

③ Listening

A 🔊 CD2, Track 4

- **Preview the task** Read the instructions aloud. Say, "Guess the temperatures before we listen." Write several Ss' guesses on the board.
- **Play the recording** Audio script p. T-272 Ss listen and take notes.
- **Play the recording again** Ss listen and check their answers. Check answers with the class.

Answers

Lowest ever	Summer	Winter
Minus 89.6	Minus 20	Minus 60

It's very much the driest part of the planet.
It's all ice and snow, so it's a very cold desert.
It's also incredibly windy in very large parts of the continent.

B 🔊 CD2, Track 5

- **Preview the task** Read the instructions aloud. Say, "Read the five sentences before we listen and guess whether each one is true or false. Write your guesses in your books."
- **Play the recording** Audio script p. T-272 Ss listen and circle T or F.
- **Play the recording again** Ss listen and check their guesses. Check answers with the class.

Answers

All answers are true.

② Grammar Combining ideas

Figure
it out

A How does the professor express the ideas below in her lecture? Rewrite the sentences.

1. Deserts are believed to be wastelands because they have harsh living conditions.
2. Antarctica is a desert although it is one of the coldest places on earth.
3. Death Valley has over 1,000 plant species even though it has some of the most extreme conditions.

Prepositions

Grammar extra
See page 151.

Prepositions can be a word or a phrase. They can be followed by a noun phrase or an *-ing* form.
In line with USGS definitions, a desert has less than 250 millimeters of rain **per** year.
A camel can go up to eight days **without drinking**.

If a preposition starts an *-ing* clause, the verb has the same subject as the verb in the main clause.
As a result of experiencing severe dust storms, China started planting trees.

Some prepositions can be followed by *the fact that* + a clause. Use *the fact that* if the subject changes.
Antarctica is a desert, apart from **the fact that it is** one of the coldest places on earth.
The Gobi desert has spread due **to the fact** that agricultural practices have changed.

B Rewrite the sentences. Replace the underlined ideas with the expressions given, and make any other necessary changes. Some have more than one correct answer.

1. It is not true that deserts are unpopulated – they are home to almost one-sixth of the world's population. (Far from) Far from being unpopulated, deserts are home to . . .
2. Many animals burrow underground to avoid the harsh sun, and they are nocturnal. (In addition to)
3. Plants such as cacti not only have long roots, but they can store their own water. (Apart from)
4. Some desert plants survive for hundreds of years because of these kinds of adaptations. (thanks to)
5. Many desert areas are expanding because humans graze animals in semi-arid areas. (on account of)
6. Environmentalists are concerned that these farming practices have caused desertification. (about)

③ Listening The Antarctic

A ◀))CD 2.04 Listen to Part 1 of an exclusive interview with an expert on the Antarctic. Complete the interviewer's notes. What else do you learn about the climate there?

Temperatures in degrees centigrade	Lowest ever	Summer	Winter	
	Minus _____	_____	_____	

B ◀))CD 2.05 Guess which sentences are true. Then listen to Part 2 and circle T (True) or F (False).

1. Antarctica is different from everywhere else on the planet – even the Arctic. **T / F**
2. Antarctica has been cold for over 30 million years. **T / F**
3. Scientists study Antarctica to see if there could be life on other planets. **T / F**
4. Some fish and animals survive in Antarctica thanks to antifreezes in their bloodstream. **T / F**
5. On one of the expert's visits to Antarctica, 18 people shared one tomato. **T / F**

APART FROM THE FACT WE HAVE NO FOOD, WATER, OR SHELTER, THIS IS A GOOD WAY TO GET AWAY FROM IT ALL.

Lesson C *What's more . . .*

1 Conversation strategy Adding ideas

A Match words from a conversation with definitions. Guess the topic of the conversation.

1. overfishing _____
2. species _____
3. apathetic _____
4. subsidies _____

a. not interested and unconcerned
b. exploiting fish to the extent that they can't replace themselves
c. government money used to help projects that are beneficial to the public
d. a class or group of individuals that are related to one another

B ◀))CD 2.06 **Listen to a seminar discussion. What factors contributed to the problem of overfishing?**

Julio Well, the biggest issue seems to have been overfishing. Something like three-quarters of the world's fish species have been completely exploited. It's only a matter of time before the fishing industry collapses completely.

Maria Not to mention all the other industries that depend on it. So who or what's responsible for it all?

Julio Well, the international community has been increasing fishing capacity, for one thing . . .

Ulma And additionally, governments give subsidies, so large-scale fishing operations took over. And big commercial fleets are much more efficient at finding fish as well.

Maria And on top of that, I guess consumers got used to having a wide variety of fish available, so the demand was there. Also, fish became much more affordable.

Ulma What's more, the public has, to a large extent, been pretty apathetic. And then industry has been slow to respond to concerns. In any case, apathy has contributed to the problem.

C Notice how the students use expressions like these to add and focus on a new idea. Find the ones they use.

Also, . . .	Additionally, . . .
And then . . .	In addition, . . .
. . . as well	What's more, . . .
. . . not to mention . . .	On top of that, . . .

D ◀))CD 2.07 **Listen to more of the discussion. Write the missing expressions. Then practice.**

Julio True. And of course another problem is all the pollution that runs into the oceans.

Maria Yeah, _____ the amount of trash that's dumped in them. Apparently, there's a huge trash pile in the middle of the Pacific that you can see from space. _____, whales and dolphins can eat that stuff.

Ulma And _____, it's irresponsible, dumping waste where we get our food.

Maria _____, all that pollution is changing the chemistry of the ocean, which affects the lifecycle of fish. _____, it has an impact on shellfish. Coral _____.

Ulma _____ there's the issue of meltwater from the ice caps caused by rising temperatures.

Julio There's a lot of debate about that, but in any event, it's impacting the ocean.

Lesson C *What's more . . .*

1 Conversation strategy

Why use expressions to add ideas?

In any kind of speaking, people add ideas to what they just said. This is especially true of formal or academic discussions, when people build arguments or make a case for their point of view. The lesson teaches common expressions that speakers use to add and focus on ideas, both while making a case and to add to a previous speaker's contribution.

(For more information, see Language notes at the beginning of this unit.)

- **Set the scene** Ask, "What happens in a typical college seminar?" Elicit answers (e.g., *A small group of Ss discuss a topic from the class or a reading assignment.*)

A • **Preview and do the task** Tell Ss to cover the conversation. Read the instructions and the four words aloud. Have a S read the definitions aloud.
- Have Ss complete the task and compare their answers with a partner. Check the answers with the class.

Answers

1. b   2. d   3. a   4. c

- Say, "What do you think the topic of the conversation is?" Elicit ideas (e.g., *problems with commercial fishing; too many fish are being caught; the government has to help the fishing industry*).

B 🔊 CD2, Track 6
- **Preview the task** Books closed. Read the instructions aloud. Say, "Just listen for the first time."
- **Play the recording** Ss listen. Say, "Listen again and take short notes." Replay the recording. Ss listen and write. Have Ss compare their notes and add to each other's answers.
- **Play the recording again** Books open. Ss listen, read along, and check their notes. Check the answer with the class: Have Ss call out the factors they made notes of. Write them on the board. [efforts to increase fishing capacity by the international community / creation of subsidies for large-scale fishing operations / big commercial fleets are more efficient at finding fish / increased demand by consumers / fish became affordable / public apathy]

C • **Present *Notice*** Read the information and the examples aloud.
- Say, "Read the conversation again. Find examples in the conversation." Have Ss complete the task. Have a S read them aloud. [*Maria*: Not to mention all the other industries that depend on it. *Ulma*: And additionally, governments . . . And big commercial fleets are much

more efficient at finding fish as well. *Maria*: And on top of that, I guess consumers . . . Also, fish became much more affordable. *Ulma*: What's more, the public has, . . . And then industry has been slow . . .]

- **Practice** Tell Ss to practice the conversation in threes, taking turns playing each role.

D 🔊 CD2, Track 7
- **Preview the task** Say, "Listen to more of the discussion. Write the missing expressions."
- **Play the recording** Ss listen and write. Replay the recording so Ss can check their answers. Check answers with the class: Have three Ss read the discussion aloud.

Answers

Julio True. And of course . . .
Maria Yeah, not to mention the amount of trash that's dumped in them. Apparently, . . . from space. Also, whales . . .
Ulma And on top of that, it's irresponsible, . . .
Maria What's more, . . . the lifecycle of fish. In addition, it has . . . shellfish. Coral, as well.
Ulma And then there's the issue of meltwater . . .
Julio There's a lot . . .

- Have Ss practice in threes.

Extra activity – groups

In groups of three, Ss use one of the suggestions below and write a conversation similar to Julio, Maria, and Ulma's. Write on the board:

Confronting climate change

Protecting endangered species

Your own idea

Have several groups present their conversation to the class.

② Strategy plus

Why use *in any case* and *in any event*?

In conversation, a speaker may use *in any case* to add more information to make an argument stronger or clearer. *In any case* and *in any event* can introduce a conclusion that the speaker considers to be the only one possible.

(For more information, see Language notes at the beginning of this unit.)

◀)) CD2, Track 8

- **Present *Strategy plus*** Tell Ss to look at both parts of the conversation on page 46 again and find examples of *in any case* and *in any event*. [*Ulma*: In any case, apathy has contributed to the problem.]
- **Play the recording** Ss listen and read along.
- **Present *In conversation*** Books closed. Ask, "Which of these two expressions is used more often in conversation?" Have Ss vote. Books open. Ask a S to read the information aloud.

③ Strategies

About you

A • **Preview and do the task** Read the instructions aloud. Ask Ss to read comment 1 and its example expression. Tell Ss they can choose a different expression to begin the idea they add. Tell Ss to write a few words, not a complete sentence.

Possible answers

1. What's more, zoos and places like that often rescue injured animals and rehabilitate them and return them to the wild.
2. In addition, it often puts animals, like bears, at risk because they encounter humans more often and we end up tranquilizing them and removing them from the area.
3. Not to mention that they know little about nature or even learn about it in school.

A ◀)) CD2, Track 9

- **Preview the task** Say, "Read the conversations. Find two appropriate conclusions for each conversation. Write the letters a to f." Ask a S to read the six conclusions aloud. Have Ss complete the task.
- **Play the recording** Ss listen and check their answers.

Answers

1. a, e
2. b, f
3. c, d

- Have Ss practice the conversations. Ss take turns playing each role.

B **Pair work**

- **Preview and do the task** Read the instructions aloud. Have a pair of Ss read the example aloud.

Extra activity – groups

Write on the board:

  It's more important to preserve farmlands than wetlands.

Groups discuss the issue and present the major arguments for and against to the class.

Speaking naturally

- Tell Ss to turn to Speaking naturally on p. 139. (For more information, see Language notes at the beginning of this unit. See the teaching notes on p. T-139.)

2 Strategy plus *In any case, in any event*

🔊 CD 2.08 You can use *in any case* to add more information to make an argument stronger or clearer.

In any case, apathy has contributed to the problem.

In any event, it's impacting the ocean.

You can also use *in any case* or *in any event* when you reach a conclusion that you think is the only possible one.

In conversation . . .

In any case is more frequent.

In any case	■ ■ ■ ■
In any event	■

🔊 CD 2.09 **Find two appropriate conclusions for each conversation. Write the letters a–f. Then listen and check your answers. Practice with a partner.**

1. *A* It seems like global warming is still a controversial issue. But don't scientists all agree that temperatures are rising? And what's more, that it affects the oceans with sea levels rising?
   B I suppose the controversy is about what's *causing* the increase in temperatures. _____ _____

2. *A* You know what's interesting to me? We really don't know that much about the oceans.
   B Yeah, though they're making new discoveries all the time.
   A Yeah, no. They definitely know more now than, say, 20 years ago. _____ _____

3. *A* There are some amazing creatures in the ocean, like jellyfish that glow in the dark.
   B I know. Not to mention the ones that can kill you, like the box jellyfish.
   A Actually, there are a lot of poisonous creatures in the ocean. Like, well, I can't think. _____ _____

   a. In any event, there's definitely evidence that the atmosphere is getting warmer.
   b. But in any event, there are lots of species we haven't discovered yet.
   c. But in any event, there are a lot of deadly things in there.
   d. In any case, you have to be careful in some places when you go swimming.
   e. In any case, there's no doubt that the climate is changing.
   f. Though we haven't made it to the bottom. In any event, we're a long way from fully exploring it.

3 Strategies *The human impact on nature*

About you

A Add an idea to each comment below. Include an expression from Exercise 1C.

1. I think humans do a lot to protect nature and wildlife. For example, if we didn't have zoos, we probably wouldn't be able to preserve some species.   *What's more, . . .*

2. Well, one of the ways we impact nature is by building homes on sensitive areas, like wetlands. That forces the wildlife out of their natural habitats.

3. I think in many ways we've forgotten how to live with nature. You know, by the time they graduate from high school, one in three kids won't have been on a hike or seen a forest.

B Pair work Discuss the ideas in Exercise A. Add more ideas to each conversation, and draw conclusions using *in any case* or *in any event*.

A I'm not so sure it's good to keep animals in zoos.
B Yeah, but zoos have programs to help endangered species. And on top of that, . . .

Speaking naturally

See page 139.

Lesson D *Biomimicry*

① Reading

A **Prepare** **Look at the title of the article and the photos. What do you think *biomimicry* is?**

B ⬇ **Read for main ideas** **Read the article. What inventions has nature inspired?**

How NATURE *inspires* SCIENCE —a look at some notable inventions

By the end of this century, as one looks back on the multitude of achievements, one may be surprised to find that a number of technological and scientific advances will be based upon observations in nature, as opposed to accidental discovery or a result of trial and error in a laboratory.

A relatively new field of research, called biomimicry, is providing significant insights and solutions for scientists and inventors in areas from medicine and technology to transportation and construction.

Using nature to solve design problems is not new. The Wright brothers observed the flight of birds while building their plane. However, in recent years, biomimicry has become an established discipline among scientists, and one that is generating some remarkable inventions. Here are some that in the not-too-distant future will have had a considerable impact on our lives.

1. SHARKSKIN A University of Florida engineering professor noticed that sharkskin remains amazingly clean and that plants and sea animals have difficulty adhering to it. He created a pattern that mimics the shark's tiny scales. Apart from the fact that it was up to 85 percent cleaner than smooth surfaces, it also prevented harmful bacteria from sticking to it.

The result was a material that can be used for hospital tray tables and bed rails, as well as other areas where there is a high risk of passing on infections. In several years, it is likely that Professor Brennan's invention will have had demonstrable benefits in terms of reducing hospital-acquired infections, and it will undoubtedly have saved thousands of lives.

2. TERMITE MOUNDS A Zimbabwean architect was faced with the difficult task of finding a workable solution to the problem of designing a new building that would stay cool even without air conditioning. Looking for an affordable alternative, he found his inspiration in African termite mounds. He noticed that the mounds termites build catch air at the base and circulate it up through their mud home. As a result of replicating the system in his building, he reduced energy costs by a measurable amount. His building uses one-tenth of the energy of similar buildings and shows that there is a viable alternative to using air-conditioning systems.

3. GECKO FEET For human beings, walking up walls is the stuff of movies – unimaginable in real life. Or is it? Inspired by the millions of tiny hairs on gecko feet, scientists are working hard to produce a "gecko tape" to use on the soles of footwear. The tape mimics the hairs on the gecko's feet and is a powerful and dependable adhesive. Scientists hope to have a product for space stations and underwater applications in the near future. And who knows? By the end of the century, they may have created a boot that enables us all to climb buildings like Spiderman. Imagine how profitable that would be!

Lesson D *Biomimicry*

1 Reading

- **Set the scene** Books closed. Write *mimic* on the board. Say, "This word is both a noun and a verb. Does anyone know what *to mimic* means?" Have Ss call out their ideas. [to copy or imitate]

A Prepare

- **Preview and do the task** Books open. Read the instructions aloud. Elicit ideas from the class. If Ss need a little help guessing, write *biology* on the board and remind them that it is the study of living things.
- Give the definition to the class. [Biomimicry is a science that studies things in nature and mimics and applies the ideas to solve human problems.]

B www.cambridge.org/viewpoint/audio
Read for main ideas

- **Preview the task** Read the instructions aloud. Say, "Read the article twice. The first time, just read for the main ideas. Don't stop to check vocabulary. The second time, write down the inventions that nature has inspired." If desired, play the downloadable recording. Ss listen and read along.
- **Do the task** Ss read and make their list. Tell Ss to compare their answers with a partner. Say, "If your partner's list is missing an invention, point it out in the article." Check the answers with the class.

Answers

planes
a bacteria-resistant material
a cooling system for buildings that is an alternative to air
    conditioning
an adhesive tape

- **Vocabulary help** Write on the board:

1. *multitude*	5. *adhering*
2. *trial and error*	6. *replicating*
3. *discipline (n)*	7. *application*
4. *generating*	

  Have Ss scan the article and circle the words from the board. As Ss scan, write on the board:

  a. *producing*
  b. *trying different things and learning from mistakes*
  c. *copying or repeating*
  d. *large number of people or things*
  e. *a particular use*
  f. *sticking to*
  g. *an area of study at college or university*

  Have Ss use the context to match the words with their definitions. Check answers with the class. [1. d; 2. b; 3. g; 4. a; 5. f; 6. c; 7. e]

Extra activity – class

Ss write a new sentence for each of the vocabulary items learned in *Vocabulary help*. For each item, a few Ss read their sentence aloud.

C React / Pair work

- **Preview the task** Read the instructions aloud. Have Ss discuss the questions. Walk around the class and help as necessary.
- **Follow-up** For each question, ask several pairs to share their ideas with the class.

2 Focus on vocabulary

A
- **Preview and do the task** Say, "Read the article again. Circle the words that end in -*able*." Ss read and circle.
- Ask, "What kind of words are these?" [adjectives] Say, "Now replace the words in these sentences in bold with a word from the article ending in -*able* that has a similar meaning." Point out the example given for sentence 1. Add, "Sometimes two -*able* words may be correct in one sentence."
- Have Ss complete the task and compare their answers with a partner. Check answers with the class. Ask individual Ss each to read a sentence aloud.

Answers

1. remarkable
2. considerable
3. unimaginable
4. dependable
5. demonstrable / measurable
6. notable
7. viable / workable
8. viable or profitable
9. affordable

B
- **Preview and do the task** Read the instructions aloud. Have Ss complete the task. Check answers with the class.

Answers

1. Y
2. NG
3. N
4. Y
5. Y
6. NG
7. Y
8. N
9. NG

C Pair work

- **Preview the task** Read the instructions aloud. Add, "This is also a good opportunity to use the expressions to add information that you learned on page 46."
- **Do the task** Have Ss take turns talking about things they have learned about biomimicry. Ask several Ss, "What is the most remarkable thing you've learned?"

3 Listening and speaking

A ◀») CD2, Track 10
- **Preview the task** Read the instructions aloud. Say, "Work with a partner. Talk about what you see in each picture." (Useful vocabulary: *black mold, multi-car pileup, a test tube, fiberglass insulation*)
- **Play the recording** Audio script pp. T-272–T-273 Ss listen and number the pictures. Check the answers with the class.

Answers

3, 1, 2, 4

B ◀») CD2, Track 11
- **Preview the task** Read the instructions aloud.
- **Play the recording** Audio script pp. T-272–T-273 Ss listen and write *yes* or *no*. Check the answers with the class.

Answers

(*from left to right*)
Picture 1: yes
Picture 2: no
Picture 3: yes
Picture 4: yes

About you

C Group work

- **Preview and do the task** Read the instructions aloud. Ask a S to read the example aloud.
- **Follow-up** Read each question aloud again, one at a time. Have groups share their answers and ideas with the class.

Extra activity – groups / class

Groups rank the four ideas presented in the listening from most useful to least useful. Groups present their final list to the class. The class does a final ranking.

C **React** Pair work **Look back at the article. Discuss the questions with a partner.**

- What do you think about biomimicry as a science?
- Which of the inventions in the article do you think is most exciting? Most valuable? Why?
- What other applications can you think of for the sharkskin material? How about for the gecko tape?

② Focus on vocabulary Suffixes with -able

A **Read the article again. Circle the words that end in -able. Then replace the words in bold with a word from the article ending in -able that has a similar meaning.**

remarkable

1. Studying nature has led human beings to some **amazing** scientific inventions. ____
2. A **large** number of inventions initially failed. ____
3. People using biomimicry in the past is **hard to imagine**. ____
4. When it comes to preventing harmful bacteria from sticking to it, the sharkskin material is very **reliable**. ____
5. The sharkskin material has had a **clear** effect on hospital infection rates. (2 words) ____
6. One of the most **noteworthy** inventions is a fabric that mimics a butterfly's shiny wings. ____
7. The architect came up with a **practical** plan for keeping buildings cool. (2 words) ____
8. The gecko tape is not likely to be a **feasible** or **money-making** invention. (2 words) ____
9. Many of the inventions are not **expensive to produce**. ____

B **Do the statements above agree with the information in the article? Write Y (Yes), N (No), or NG (Information not given).**

C Pair work **Share what you learned about biomimicry using the -able words in Exercise A.**

③ Listening and speaking The genius of the natural world

A 🔊CD 2.10 **Listen to a presentation about the applications of biomimicry. Match the examples from nature that the presenter talks about to the real-world problems below. Number the pictures 1–4.**

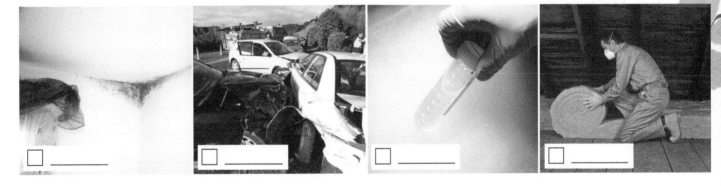

☐ _____   ☐ _____   ☐ _____   ☐ _____

B 🔊CD 2.11 **Listen again. Have the problems already been solved? Write Y (Yes) or N (No) on each picture above.**

About you

C Group work **Look back at the examples in the lesson. How else could the ideas be applied to real-world problems? What other amazing things are in nature? What problems could they solve?**

"Maybe in the future scientists will have developed a material that cleans itself, like that flower. If they used it on cars, you would never have to clean your car."

Writing *Does it matter?*

In this lesson, you . . .
- write a persuasive essay.
- use academic prepositions and *one*.
- avoid errors with *upon*.

Task | **Write an essay.**

The World Animal Foundation estimates that by 2025 as many as one-fifth of all animal species may well have become extinct. Does this matter?

A **Look at a model** Read the introductions to two essays that answer the question above. What view does each one take? What arguments does each one make?

1. The estimate that 20 percent of animal species may disappear within a short time is alarming. The loss of any species matters because it can upset the balance of nature. Each organism depends upon another to survive, and the disappearance of one species may have unknown consequences for another. The earth maintains a delicate balance, which relies upon the complex interaction of plant and animal species. We do not always see what is happening beneath the surface. The loss of species may be a warning that we are destroying our planet and therefore our very existence.

2. The claim that a large proportion of animal species is at risk of dying out is a subject of great debate within the academic community and amongst scientists in particular. One might think that this is a major problem and that one's worst fears for the earth will materialize. However, one can equally argue that species have become extinct throughout the history of this planet. In terms of our survival, however, this has not proved critical. Therefore, the extinction of species, far from being a disaster, can simply be considered part of the normal evolutionary process.

Question-based essays

Show you understand the question by restating it in your own words. Give your opinion in your introduction and conclusion.

B **Focus on language** Read the chart. Then underline the examples of formal prepositions and circle examples of *one* for general statements in Exercise A.

Prepositions in academic writing; *one* for general statements ⬇

Some prepositions and prepositional expressions can make your writing sound more formal, e.g., *amongst, beneath, throughout, upon, within, in terms of.*
Each organism depends **upon** another.
It is a subject of debate **within** the academic community and **amongst** scientists. . . .
In terms of our survival, this has not proved critical.

One / one's can refer to "people in general" or "you / your." You can use it to give opinions.
One might think this is a major problem and that **one's** worst fears will materialize.

C Complete the sentences with prepositions. Then rewrite them using *one / one's.*

1. A healthy environment is dependent _____ how well people manage their resources.
2. We should do everything _____ our power to protect these species.
3. There are complex systems _____ the earth's surface that people do not fully understand.
4. I wonder how the leopard and rhino, which are _____ the most threatened species, can survive.
5. The effects _____ tourism will be so huge _____ the world that we cannot imagine them.

D **Write and check** Write an essay to answer the question in the task above. Then check for errors.

Common errors

Do not overuse *upon*. Use it after *depend, rely, agree. Look upon* means "to think about in a certain way," not "look at."
Let us look at this subject in more detail. (NOT. . . ~~look upon~~ . . .)

Writing *Does it matter?*

In this lesson

- Ask a S to read the lesson aims (*In this lesson, you . . .*) aloud. Ask, "What is a persuasive essay?" [It persuades the reader to believe something.] Ask, "How do you persuade people?" Elicit ideas (e.g., *use good arguments, use facts*).
- **Preview the writing** Point out the writing topic in Task and read it aloud. Explain that Ss will end the lesson by writing an essay that will practice the three aims presented in this lesson.

A Look at a model

- **Preview and do the task** Read the instructions aloud. Tell Ss to review the essay question before they begin. Say, "Write brief notes on each introduction."
- Have Ss complete the task and discuss their answers with a partner. Check answers with the class.

Possible answers

The first essay introduction takes the view that the extinction of species is disastrous to our own survival because it disrupts the balance of life on earth. The second essay introduction takes the view that the extinction of species is not cause for alarm because many species of plants and animals become extinct with no detrimental effect on humans.

- **Present *Question-based essays*** Read the information aloud.
- Ask, "How does introduction 1 restate the question and give an opinion?" [The writer repeats the question but uses *20 percent* instead of *one-fifth*. The writer states that this is alarming.]
- Ask, "What does the writer of introduction 2 do?" [The writer makes several substitutions: *dying out* instead of *extinct*; *large proportion* instead of *one-fifth*. The writer shows an opinion by using the verb *claim* – which suggests that no proof exists.]
- Say, "When an essay topic asks a question, you need to do four things: (1) explain what you understand by the question; (2) state your opinion in a thesis statement in your introduction; (3) give reasons and examples in the following paragraphs; and (4) restate your view in your final concluding paragraph." Write the four points on the board.

B ⬇ www.cambridge.org/viewpoint/audio
Focus on language

- **Present the grammar for writing chart** Read the information in the chart aloud. If desired, play the downloadable recording. Ss listen and read along.
- **Understand the grammar for writing** Tell Ss to look at the top section of the chart. Say, "An academic essay should use more formal language, and these prepositions are more common in academic writing." Ask a S to read the first example aloud. Ask, "What's the usual preposition here?" [on]

- Say, "In writing you can use *one* instead of *you* to write about people in general. It is considered very formal."
- **Do the task** Read the instructions aloud. Have Ss complete the task. Check answers with the class.

Answers

1. The estimate that . . . may disappear <u>within</u> a short time is alarming. . . . Each organism depends <u>upon</u> another to survive, . . . The earth maintains a delicate balance, which relies <u>upon</u> the complex . . . We do not always see what is happening <u>beneath</u> the surface. . . .
2. The claim that . . . great debate <u>within</u> the academic community and <u>amongst</u> scientists in particular. ⓐOne might think . . . that ⓐone's worst fears . . . However, ⓐone can equally argue . . . extinct <u>throughout</u> the history of this planet. <u>In terms of</u> our survival, . . .

C
- **Preview and do the task** Read the instructions aloud. Have Ss complete the task. Check answers.

Answers

1. A healthy environment is dependent <u>upon</u> how well people manage their resources.
   A healthy environment is dependent upon how well <u>one</u> manages <u>one's</u> resources.
2. We should do everything <u>within</u> our power to protect these species.
   <u>One</u> should do everything within <u>one's</u> power to protect these species.
3. There are complex systems <u>beneath</u> the earth's surface that people do not fully understand.
   There are complex systems <u>beneath</u> the earth's surface that <u>one</u> does not fully understand.
4. I wonder how the leopard and rhino, which are <u>amongst</u> the most threatened species, can survive.
   <u>One must</u> wonder how the leopard and rhino, which are amongst the most threatened species, can survive.
5. The effects <u>upon</u> tourism will be so huge <u>throughout</u> the world that we cannot imagine them.
   The effects upon tourism will be so huge throughout the world that <u>one</u> cannot imagine them.

D Write and check

- **Preview the task** Read the instructions aloud.
- **Present *Common errors*** Read the information aloud. Say, "Look at introduction 1 in Exercise 1A. Find two examples of *upon*." [Each organism depends upon another . . . ; The earth maintains a delicate balance which relies upon . . .]
- **Do the task** Have Ss complete the task.

Extra activity – class

Ss leave their essays on their desk for classmates to read. Ss go around the class reading each other's work. Ss decide if any of the essays could persuade them to change their opinion.

Vocabulary notebook *Golden eggs*

If done for homework

Briefly present the Learning tip and the task directions. Make sure Ss understand what they need to do.

If done in class

- **Present** *Learning tip* Read the information aloud. Say, "Learning vocabulary from a specific subject area can help you with your reading ability generally." Add, "It's a good idea to write sentences that illustrate the different uses clearly." Ask a S to read the example in the box.

A • **Preview and do the task** Read the instructions and the words in the box aloud. Ask a S to read the completed example sentences aloud. Have Ss complete the task. Check answers with the class. Ask individual Ss each to read a pair of sentences aloud.

Answers

1. hatch	7. grounds
2. mate	8. burrow
3. young	9. migration
4. colony	10. lays
5. nest	11. predator
6. breed	12. feed and raise

B Word builder

- **Preview the task** Read the instructions aloud. Have a S read the idioms aloud. Say, "Raise your hand if you've heard or seen any of these idioms before." Ask any S who raises his or her hand to explain the idiom.

- **Do the task** Have Ss complete the task. Check answers with the class.

Answers

be a guinea pig: be the subject of an experiment
be in the doghouse: be in trouble
beat a dead horse: waste your time on something
be a fish out of water: not fit in, be out of place
clam up: not say anything, perhaps because you feel uncomfortable
get off your high horse: stop being superior
have ants in your pants: be anxious or excited to do something
have butterflies in your stomach: be nervous

Extra activity – class / pairs

Ss write one sentence for each idiom. Ss read their sentences to a partner. For each idiom, a few Ss read their sentence to the class.

C Focus on vocabulary, page 49

- **Preview and do the task** Read the instructions aloud. Say, "There are no single correct answers here. Look at page 49 if you need help with the vocabulary." Have Ss find the words. Check answers with the class: Have a few Ss read their answers aloud.

Example answers

1. dolphin / octopus / horse
2. *National Geographic*
3. fish and creatures at the bottom of the ocean
4. solar power / wind power
5. visit national parks
6. shark skin can be replicated and used for sanitary surfaces

Extra activity – pairs

Ss tell their partner why they chose each thing or person in Exercise C.

Vocabulary notebook *Golden eggs*

hibernate
Animals hibernate or sleep in the winter.
Computers hibernate when they're running but are not being used.

A   Complete each sentence with a word in the box. Sometimes you'll use a word twice.

breed	colony	grounds	lays	migration	predator
burrow	feed and raise	~~hatch~~	mate	nest	young

1. 🦌 When eggs _hatch____, baby birds, fish, or insects come out.
   🏃 If you plan something in secret, you _hatch____ **a plan**.

2. 🦌 Animals that _____ for life stay together forever.
   🏃 A presidential candidate chooses **a running** _____, who becomes vice president if elected.

3. 🦌 In academic writing, the offspring, or babies, of animals are called their _____.
   🏃 You can also use the expression **the** _____ to mean all young people.

4. 🦌 A _____ is a group of birds or animals.
   🏃 It can also be a country that is governed by a more powerful country.

5. 🦌 A _____ is a place where most birds have their young.
   🏃 **A** _____ **egg** is a sum of money you save for a special purpose.

6. 🦌 When animals _____, they have young. A specific type of animal is also called a _____.
   🏃 If you say someone or something is part of **a dying** _____, it means there aren't many left.

7. 🦌 Breeding, feeding, fishing, or hunting _____ are places where these activities take place.
   🏃 To have _____ for something means to have reasons for it, such as _____ **for divorce**.

8. 🦌 To _____ means to dig into something and a _____ can be the hole where an animal lives.
   🏃 A person can also _____ into something. It means he or she investigates it.

9. 🦌 The movement of birds, animals, or people is called _____.
   🏃 From that word, we get other words like *immigrant*, *emigrate*, etc.

10. 🦌 A bird, a fish, or an insect _____ an egg.
    🏃 Someone that makes a lot of money for others is called **the goose that** _____ **the golden egg**.

11. 🦌 In biology, a _____ is an animal that attacks and eats other animals.
    🏃 In business, it's a company that tries to buy or take over other companies.

12. 🦌🏃 Both animals and humans have to _____ their families.

B   Word builder Here are some more idioms with animals. Find out their meaning.

be a guinea pig	beat a dead horse	clam up	have ants in your pants
be in the doghouse	be a fish out of water	get off your high horse	have butterflies in your stomach

C   (Focus on vocabulary) Can you think of a thing or person for each expression? See Exercise 2A, page 49.

1. a **remarkable** animal that has **considerable** intelligence _____
2. a **dependable** source of information or a **notable** authority on the natural world _____
3. something you've learned about nature that previously was **unimaginable** to you _____
4. a **viable** or workable alternative to fossil fuels _____
5. an **affordable** way to experience nature _____
6. a **profitable** product with **measurable** results that resulted from replicating nature _____

Unit 5 Progress

Lesson A Out with the old

Vocabulary in context *Formal adjectives*

(See Student's Book p. 52.)

More formal adjectives are taught to express key concepts, for example, *small* vs. *compact*, in the context of a blog.

Vocabulary notebook *Old or ancient?*

(See Student's Book p. 61.)

The Learning tip helps Ss learn more ways to express basic concepts like *big* and *small* to use in formal writing.

The Dictionary tip tells Ss that when they use the thesaurus in their word-processing software to find a synonym, they should check its meaning and use in a dictionary.

Grammar *Information focus 1*

(See Student's Book p. 53.)

In this lesson, Ss learn the position of adverbs *within* continuous and perfect passive verb phrases. Many adverbs can also go before the verb phrase or after it, but this is not addressed here. The most common position for adverbs is generally after the first auxiliary verb. This is a very complex area and variations are often possible. However, the positions of adverbs presented in the chart are the most frequent.

Form

- Adverb after the first auxiliary

  Time / frequency adverbs (e.g., *already, continually, finally, just, long, still*), attitude adverbs (e.g., *fortunately, sadly),*

and the adverbs *also, probably, apparently, reportedly* usually follow the first auxiliary.

> GPS **has** already **been incorporated** into aircraft.
>
> It **had** originally **been developed** for military purposes.

- Adverb before the participle

  Adverbs that say "how" or "how much" or that describe the participle (e.g., *badly, intensively, seriously, largely, greatly, widely*) often go before the participle.

  > It **has been** widely **used**.

- Adverb in either position

  Some adverbs (*increasingly, previously, largely, originally, initially, continually, generally*) can go either after the first auxiliary or before the participle.

  > GPS **is** increasingly **being used** . . . OR GPS **is being** increasingly **used** . . .
  >
  > It **has** previously **been used** . . . OR It **has been** previously **used** . . .

Grammar extra *Adverbs in present and past passive verb phrases; Adverbs in perfect verb phrases*

(See Student's Book p. 152.)

Grammar extra presents the positions of adverbs in present and past passive verb phrases and in perfect verb phrases.

Lesson B What drives us?

Grammar *Information focus 2*

(See Student's Book p. 55.)

This lesson reviews past modal active sentences and teaches the passive form of past modal sentences. The affirmative sentences are shown with adverbs after the modal verb. It also shows the different complementation patterns of the causative verb *make* in active and passive sentences.

Form

- Active sentence with a past modal

  Affirmative

  Subject + modal + (adverb) + *have* + past participle

  > A *motorist* **could** easily **have killed him.**

  Negative

  Subject + modal + *not* + *have* + past participle

  > They **shouldn't have permitted** him to do it.

  With *ought to*

  > They **ought (not) to have allowed** it.

- Passive sentence with a past modal

  Affirmative

  Subject + modal + (adverb) + *have been* + past participle (+ *by* phrase)

  > He **could** easily **have been killed (by** a *motorist*).

  Negative

  Subject + modal + *not* + (*to*) *have been* + past participle (+ *by* phrase)

  > He **shouldn't have been permitted** to do it.
  >
  > It **ought not to have been allowed.**

- Patterns with *make*

  In active sentences, the base form of the verb is used after *make*:

  Subject + *make* + object + verb

  > They **made** him <u>sleep</u> in police cells.

  In passive sentences, the infinitive form is used:

  Subject + *be made* + *to* + verb

  > He **was made** <u>to sleep</u> in police cells.

Lesson C *Just think . . .*

Conversation strategy *Making a point*

(See Student's Book p. 56.)

The lesson teaches different expressions to introduce a point. *(Just) think (about it)* invites the listener to consider an idea; *One way to look at it, (Let's) put it this way, (I) look at it this way* can introduce one perspective on an idea. Speakers can repeat, reformulate, or clarify ideas by using expressions such as *To put it another way* or *Let me put it another way.*

Strategy plus *Absolutely (not), not necessarily*

(See Student's Book p. 57.)

In a conversation during which different points are being argued, speakers can agree or disagree to varying degrees. People use *absolutely* or *definitely* to make a *yes* response stronger. *Absolutely not* or *definitely not* can make a *no* response stronger. If a speaker doesn't want to commit strongly in a response, he or she can use *probably (not)* or *maybe (not)*. They can also be used together: *Yeah, well . . .*

maybe. Maybe not. The response *not necessarily* means "that is not completely or always true."

Expressions

Absolutely (not)	*Maybe (not)*
Definitely (not)	*Not necessarily*
Probably (not)	

Speaking naturally *Stress in expressions*

(See Student's Book p. 140.)

In this section, Ss practice saying expressions that introduce different perspectives on an issue. The primary stress (underlined below) is on the determiners, and the secondary stress is on the verbs.

> <u>**One**</u> way to <u>**look**</u> at it is that space exploration is a good investment.

Lesson D *Smart ideas*

Reading tip *Starting with a quote*

(See Student's Book p. 58.)

The Reading tip explains that writers sometimes use a quotation from a famous person or a saying to start and set the theme of an article. This introduces the topic, creates interest, and lends credence to the writing.

Writing *It is often said . . .*

(See Student's Book p. 60.)

This lesson teaches Ss to write an opinion essay that compares and contrasts arguments. The grammar for writing presents a typical use of the passive in academic writing, i.e., in *it* clauses. These are often used to introduce what people say or think as common beliefs (*It is often said that; It is generally believed that*) or to report research (*It has been suggested that*). Clauses such as *It has been shown that* are also useful to refer back to an argument or result that has been presented in the same academic paper.

- *It* clauses

  > *It is . . . often said . . . , generally accepted / believed . . . ,*
  > *widely recognized . . . , well known . . . ,*
  > *widely assumed / known . . . ,*
  > *generally agreed / accepted . . . ,*
  > *well established . . . , commonly accepted . . .*
  > **It is often said** *that technological progress is important.*

  > *It has also been reported / shown / suggested that . . .*

  A regular passive can also be used to make the noun the main theme of a sentence.

  Compare:

  > *It is often said that technological progress is important.*
  > *Technological progress <u>is often said</u> to be important.*

- Expressions for contrast

  These expressions are used to introduce contrasting ideas or opinions.

  > *While / whereas*
  > *Although*
  > *However, . . .*
  > *In contrast, . . .*
  > *Nevertheless, . . .*

> **⊙ Corpus information**
>
> **Common error with *affect* and *effect***
>
> Ss often confuse *affect* and *effect. Affect* is a verb; *effect* is a noun.
>
> *Progress **affects** everyone.* (**NOT:** ~~Progress effects . . .~~)
>
> *Progress has several positive **effects**.* (**NOT:** . . . ~~several positive affects.~~)

Grammar extra *Adverbs and past modal verb phrases; Questions with passive past modals*

(See Student's Book p. 153.)

Grammar extra looks at the placement of adverbs in past modal phrases. It also presents questions with passive past modals.

Progress

In Unit 5, you . . .

- talk about inventions, progress, and human achievements.
- use adverbs with continuous and perfect passives.
- use modal verbs with passive forms.
- make a point with expressions like *I look at it this way.*
- use expressions like *absolutely not* to make responses stronger.

Lesson A *Out with the old*

1 Vocabulary in context

A What are some common gadgets people use these days? Why are they useful? Make a list.

B ◀)) CD 2.12 Read the article from a hiker's blog. Which items in the photos are mentioned?

The most **rudimentary** instrument that has been widely used for centuries to find direction is the magnetic compass. It was probably invented by the Chinese and was based on the metal lodestone, which had long been admired for its ability to point toward north. **Countless** lives have undoubtedly been saved over the centuries on land and at sea thanks to the compass, which functions equally well in daylight, darkness, or thick fog. Even in our electronic age, magnetic compasses are still being made, and their basic design has not changed for centuries. They are **compact**, **functional**, and **portable**.

Toward the end of the twentieth century, alternatives to the compass were being intensively developed, and **significant** advances were made – thanks to satellite technology. GPS* is

now an **integral** part of our daily lives, making moving maps, communicating with smartphones, and offering handheld location devices. It had originally been developed for military purposes, but it soon became part of everyday technology, and **innovative** ways to use GPS – from tracking migrating birds to helping golfers judge their shots – are continually being found through ongoing research. The system has already been incorporated into aircraft and ship design as **standard**, and many other technologies also derive considerable benefit from it.

But what about the **humble** compass? Is it **obsolete** now? Has it been completely forgotten? We'd like to hear your views.

*Global Positioning System

C Find more formal adjectives in the blog with similar meanings to the words in the chart.

Vocabulary notebook

See page 61.

easy-to-carry	portable	creative		useful	
important		out-of-date		usual	
modest		basic		"a lot of"	
necessary		small			

About you **D** Pair work **Take turns using the adjectives you found to talk about everyday objects you own.**

"My cell phone is becoming a bit obsolete. It's one of those older flip-phones, but it's functional."

Progress

Introduce the theme of the unit Say, "When you see or hear the word *progress*, what do you think of?" Elicit answers (e.g., *technology, personal success, moving forward*). Say, "In this unit, we'll talk about different types of progress and achievement." Have a S read the unit aims aloud.

Lesson A *Out with the old*

1 Vocabulary in context

- **Set the scene** Books closed. Write on the board:

  "Out with the old, in with the new."

  Ask Ss what the expression means (e.g., *get rid of old things when they can be replaced with newer models*). Ask Ss if they have a similar expression in their language. Say, "When you hear about a newer model of something, do you usually get it? Can you think of any examples where you preferred an old model to a newer one?" Have short class discussion.

A • **Preview and do the task** Books open. Read the instructions aloud. Have a S read the example aloud.

- Have Ss make their lists. Tell Ss to compare their answers with a partner and give each other more ideas. Have Ss call out their lists of gadgets and uses.

Possible answers

GPS devices – useful for finding your way around in big cities
Cell phones – useful for sending text messages
Food processors – useful for slicing foods
Noise reducing headphones – useful for sleeping on planes
Digital Video Recorders (DVRs) – useful for pausing programs or replaying parts you want to watch again

B ◀)) CD2, Track 12

- **Preview the task** Read the instructions aloud. Elicit or give the names of the four objects and make sure Ss understand what they are. [from left to right: *a compass*: used to tell directions; *a pedometer*: used to count steps and distances; *(a) GPS (device / system)* used for finding places; *a telescope*: used for looking at distant objects, usually in the sky.]

- **Play the recording** Ss listen, read along, and check (✓) the things that are mentioned. Check the answers with the class.

Answers

the magnetic compass
the GPS device

Word sort

C • **Preview the task** Say, "This activity focuses on more formal alternatives to common adjectives. These are useful to help you read and write more effectively." Read the instructions aloud.

- Point out the first example. Say, "Look at the words in bold to find the correct formal adjective." Say, "The last item in the chart is in quotes because *a lot of* isn't an adjective."

- **Do the task** Have Ss complete the task and compare their answers with a partner. Say, "If you and your partner have a different answer, reread the sentences that have the word you each chose. Decide which one of you is correct."

- Check answers with the class.

Answers

easy to carry: portable
important: significant
modest: humble
necessary: integral
creative: innovative
out of date: obsolete
basic: rudimentary
small: compact
useful: functional
usual: standard
"a lot of": countless

About you

D **Pair work**

- **Preview and do the task** Read the instructions and the example aloud. Say, "Every time you use a word from the chart, put a check (✓) beside it so you'll know you've used all of them."

- **Follow-up** Have several Ss tell the class about an object they own.

Tell Ss to turn to Vocabulary Notebook on p. 61 of their Student's Books. Have Ss do the tasks in class or assign them for homework. (See the teaching notes on p. T-61.)

Extra activity – groups

Groups write each new, formal adjective from the chart on separate slips of paper. Ss close their books and place the slips facedown on the table. Group members take turns picking up a slip and using the word in a sentence. The meaning of the adjective should be obvious from the sentence.

Figure it out

A ⬇ www.cambridge.org/viewpoint/audio

- **Preview the task** Briefly review the passive. Ask, "When do you use the passive?" [when you don't know who did an action or if it's not important; when you want to make the receiver of an action the main focus of the sentence] If necessary, briefly review the main forms the passive.

- Say, "Write these sentences in the passive. Find similar sentences in the blog to help you, and underline them. Notice each verb phrase has an adverb." Have Ss identify the four adverbs. [continually, still, completely, originally] Say, "Look for these adverbs and notice how they are used with passive verbs."

- **Do the task** Have Ss complete the task. Check answers.

Answers

1. New applications for GPS are continually being found.
2. The compass was still being used by all serious hikers until very recently.
3. Has the compass been completely replaced by GPS?
4. The compass had originally been developed by the Chinese.

- **Focus on the form** Say, "Look at the sentences you wrote. In sentences 1 and 2, where is the adverb?" [after the first auxiliary] Ask, "Where is the adverb in sentence 3?" [before the participle] "Where is it in sentence 4?" [after the first auxiliary]

- **Focus on the use** Say, "This lesson teaches the most common positions of adverbs *inside* a verb phrase."

- **Present the grammar chart** Read the information aloud. If desired, play the downloadable recording.

- Say, "Look at the top section of the chart. Which of the adverbs listed here show attitude?" [fortunately, sadly] Have Ss look at the first line of the examples. Ask, "What verbs forms are these?" [present and past continuous passive] "How many verbs are there in the verb phrases in bold?" [3] "Which are the adverbs?" [still, continually] "Where are they?" [after *are, were* – the first auxiliary verb]

- Have Ss look at the middle section of the chart. Say, "Adverbs that tell you how something is done, or how much or to what degree, usually go before the participle." Ask, "Which are the participles in the examples?" [developed, used] "Which adverbs in this section describe how something is done?" [badly, intensively, seriously] "Which tell you how much?" [largely, greatly, widely, completely]

- Have Ss look at the bottom section of the chart. Say, "Some adverbs can go either after the first auxiliary or before the participle." Ask a S to read out which ones.

  (For more information, see Language notes at the beginning of the unit. For more work on adverbs and verb phrases, go to Grammar extra, p. 152.)

B • **Preview the task** Read the instructions aloud. Do the first underlined section with the class. Ask a S to change it to passive. [Well, the material had been developed by NASA.] Ask, "Where should the adverb be placed?" [after *had* or before *developed*]

- **Do the task** Have Ss complete the task and compare their answers with a partner. Check answers.

Answers

1. . . . Well, the material had originally been developed by NASA / the material had been originally developed by NASA to improve . . . And now, of course, memory foam is generally being incorporated / is being generally incorporated into . . . foam beds, which are increasingly being used / are being increasingly used in hospitals. Countless lives have apparently been saved because . . . And the lives of these patients have fortunately been greatly improved.

2. . . . Many of them had initially been devised by inventors / Many of them had been initially devised by inventors for other purposes. While these products were still being developed, no one . . . They had apparently been produced in the 1970s to . . . Now they are increasingly being installed / are being increasingly installed as standard . . .

3. The abacus is a tool that has long been used for . . . even today, abacuses are currently being used in many parts of the world. People think that they had originally been invented by the Chinese / had been originally invented by the Chinese. . . . But counting boards had already been constructed in Roman times, and (they) had reportedly been widely used across Europe. Although the abacus has been largely overtaken by calculators / the abacus has largely been overtaken by calculators, it's interesting that it has not been made completely obsolete [by calculators / them].

About you

C Pair work

- **Preview and do the task** Say, "Read the information again. Then take turns retelling the information. Use adverbs within a passive verb phrase when possible."

- Ask, "What other examples of progress can you think of? Give as much information as you can."

- **Follow-up** Ask a few Ss to share their ideas.

Extra activity – individuals

Write *time*, *attitude*, *how*, and *how much* as column headings on the board for Ss to copy into their notebooks. Call out random adverbs from the chart. With books closed, Ss write them under the correct heading. Ss call out the adverbs for each column.

2 Grammar Information focus 1

Figure it out

A **Write these sentences in the passive. Find similar sentences in the blog to help you, and underline them. Then read the grammar chart.**

1. They are continually finding new applications for GPS.
2. All serious hikers were still using the compass until very recently.
3. Has GPS completely replaced the compass?
4. The Chinese had originally developed the compass.

Adverbs within continuous and perfect passive verbs

Grammar extra
See page 152.

The most common position for adverbs is after the first auxiliary verb (*am / is / are / was / were; has / have / had*). Time and attitude adverbs, e.g., *already, always, continually, currently, finally, just, long, since, still; fortunately, sadly,* etc., and the adverbs *also, probably, apparently, reportedly* are usually in this position.
Compasses **are still being made**. They **were continually being improved** in the last century.
GPS **has already been incorporated** into aircraft. It **had originally been developed** for military use.

Adverbs that say "how" and "how much" or that describe the participle often go before the participle, e.g., *badly, intensively, seriously, largely, greatly, widely, completely.*
Alternatives to the compass **were being intensively developed**. It **has been widely used**.

Some adverbs can go in both positions, e.g., *increasingly, previously, largely, originally, initially, continually, generally.*
GPS **is increasingly being used** . . . OR GPS **is being increasingly used** . . .
It **has previously been used** . . . OR It **has been previously used** . . .

B **Look at these examples of progress. Rewrite the underlined parts of the sentences in the passive. Add the adverbs given — sometimes there are two — and use *by* if necessary.**

1. Do you know how memory foam was developed? Well, <u>NASA had developed the material</u> (originally) to improve the safety of aircraft cushions. And now, of course, <u>they are incorporating memory foam</u> (generally) into a whole range of everyday products, like memory-foam beds, which <u>they are using</u> (increasingly) in hospitals. <u>They have saved countless lives</u> (apparently) because foam beds reduce pressure sores when patients are bedridden for long periods of time. And <u>they have improved the lives of these patients</u> (fortunately, greatly).

2. It's interesting when you think about a lot of the things we use in everyday life. Inventors <u>had devised many of them</u> (initially) for other purposes. While <u>they were developing these products</u> (still), no one really thought about spin-offs. Take, for example, smoke detectors. <u>They had produced them</u> (apparently) in the 1970s to help detect toxic gases in the space station. Now <u>they are installing them</u> (increasingly) as standard in newly built homes all over the world.

3. The abacus is a tool that <u>we have used</u> (long) for counting and in fact even today, <u>they are using abacuses</u> (currently) in many parts of the world. People think that <u>the Chinese had invented them</u> (originally). And I guess the ones that we are familiar with today were. But <u>they had constructed similar counting boards</u> (already) in Roman times, and <u>they had used them</u> (reportedly, widely) across Europe. Although <u>calculators have overtaken the abacus</u> (largely), it's interesting that <u>they have not made it obsolete</u> (completely).

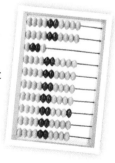

About you

C Pair work **Read the information again. Then take turns retelling the information. What other examples of progress can you think of?**

Lesson B *What drives us?*

1 Grammar in context

A One kind of progress is when people push the limits of what the human body can do. Why do you think people take on challenges like running marathons or walking across deserts?

"I guess people like to test their limits." "Well, people also do these things to raise funds for charity."

B 🔊 CD 2.13 **Listen. What dangers did Beaumont face on his expedition?**

AN AMAZING ACHIEVEMENT

In 2008, a 25-year-old Scottish man, Mark Beaumont, set a new record by cycling around the world in 195 days. Although it was an incredible feat, things did not always go smoothly. Pedaling across difficult terrain was often extremely painful. On top of that, his wallet and camera were stolen, and at one point he could easily have been killed in the United States when a motorist drove through a red light. In fact, the whole trip might well have been cut short at several points, owing to sickness, flooded roads, and mechanical problems. Sometimes, when traveling through particularly dangerous regions, he was made to sleep in grim police cells for his own protection.

Beaumont was lucky. He put his life in danger and survived. Others who pursued incredible feats, like climbing Mt. Everest, have died in their attempts. Indeed, the majority of people who have died on Everest were young people with families and partners, so what drove them? They must have known the dangers, so why did they consciously choose to put themselves in harm's way? Some would argue that

adventurers like these should not have been permitted to attempt such dangerous expeditions. After all, there are easier – and safer – ways to challenge yourself, raise money for charity, or break world records. Did Mark Beaumont feel that he might not have been given another opportunity to make his mark on the world and pursue his ambition if he hadn't taken this chance?

C Pair work **Answer the questions.**

About you

1. What drives people like Mark Beaumont?
2. What do you think of people who attempt feats like this? Are they adventurous, or reckless and irresponsible?
3. What does *make your mark on the world* mean? How do other people make their marks on the world?
4. If you had an opportunity to follow a dream, what would you do?
5. Would you ever follow a dream that put you in harm's way?

Lesson B *What drives us?*

1 Grammar in context

- **Set the scene** Books closed. Ask, "Can you think of things people do that require great effort both mentally and physically?" Elicit ideas from the class (e.g., *being an Olympic athlete, sailing across an ocean alone*) Say, "This lesson talks about people who do these kinds of things."

A • **Preview and do the task** Books open. Read the instructions and the example aloud. Get ideas from the class.

B 🔊 CD2, Track 13

- **Preview the task** Books closed. Say, "You are going to hear about Mark Beaumont. He rode his bicycle around the world in 195 days. What dangers do you think he faced?" Have Ss call out ideas (e.g., *thieves, wild animals, bad weather, dangerous drivers*).

- Say, "Listen. What dangers did he face on his expedition? Take brief notes."

- **Play the recording** Ss listen and make notes. Have Ss compare their notes with a partner.

- **Play the recording again** Books open. Ss listen, read along, and check their answers. Check answers with the class.

Answers

He faced the following dangers: injury, people stealing from him, sickness, floods, mechanical problems, accidents.

- Have Ss call out any vocabulary they don't know. Write it on the board. Have classmates give definitions or explanations of words they know. Supply definitions for any remaining vocabulary.

C Pair work

- **Preview and do the task** Read the instructions aloud. Ask a S to read question 1 aloud. Say, "Now that you've read the article, what does *drives* mean in this context?" [gives someone determination to do something difficult]

- Have Ss discuss the questions. Walk around the class and help as needed.

Answers

1. A desire to do something challenging; break world records, push themselves to their limits; raise money for charity.
2. Answers will vary.
3. *Make your mark on the world* means do something important that other people will notice or have an effect in some way.
4. Answers will vary.
5. Answers will vary.

- **Follow-up** For each question, ask a few pairs to report their ideas to the class.

Extra activity – pairs

Partners think of someone they've heard of who achieved something amazing. Using what they know, they prepare a short presentation about that person and what he or she accomplished.

Extra activity – pairs

Ss prepare for a debate on whether people should risk their lives in pursuit of dangerous achievements like cycling or sailing around the world solo. Ss think of for and against arguments. Have Ss debate their arguments for the class.

2 Grammar

A ⬇ www.cambridge.org/viewpoint/audio

- **Preview the task** Say, "Read the sentences. What is the verb form used?" [past modals, active] Say, "Rewrite the sentences in the passive, starting with the words given. Use similar sentences in the article to help you."
- **Do the task** Have Ss complete the task and then compare their answers with a partner. Check answers.

Answers

1. Beaumont might well have been injured.
2. The trip could easily have been cut short.
3. He shouldn't have been allowed to do it.

- **Focus on the form** Write on the board:

   1. Something might have injured Beaumont.

   2. Beaumont might have been injured.

   Ask, "In sentence 1, what form is the underlined verb phrase?" [past modal] "Is it active or passive?" [active] Ask, "How about sentence 2?" [passive past modal]

   Ask, "Where does *well* go in both sentences?" [after the modal] Add *well* to both sentences on the board.
- Go through the other sentences in a similar way.
- **Present the grammar chart** Read the information aloud. If desired, play the downloadable recording.
- Ask, "What is the pattern for most active past modal sentences?" Write the pattern on the board.

   subject + modal (+ not) + have + past participle

   Ask, "What's the pattern with *ought to*?"

   subject + ought (+ not)+ to have + past participle
- Ask, "What are the patterns for passive past modal sentences? Write the patterns on the board.

   subject + modal (+ not) + have been + past participle

subject + ought (+ not) + to have been + past participle

Ask "Where does the adverb go?" [after the modal]

- Point out the last section of the chart. Ask, "What is the pattern for *make* in the active sentence?"

   subject + make + person + verb
- Ask, "How about when *make* is in a passive sentence?"

   subject + be + made + to + verb

(For more information, see Language notes at the beginning of the unit. For more work on adverbs and past modal phrases, go to Grammar extra, p. 153.)

B • **Preview the task** Read the instructions aloud. Tell Ss to look at sentence 1 and its example answer. Ask, "What change was made to the verb phrase?" [*Could bury* became *could have been buried*.] "Where was the adverb added?" [after the modal]

- **Do the task** Have Ss complete the task and then compare their answers with a partner. Check answers with the class.

Answers

1. a. She could easily have been buried alive . . . .
   b. Her attempt might well have been postponed . . . .
   c. She shouldn't have been encouraged to do it.
2. a. He could easily have been blown off by the wind.
   b. He should also have been made to wear a . . . .
   c. He should never have been allowed to do it.
3. a. He shouldn't have been arrested, and he shouldn't have been thrown in jail, either.
   b. Someone could well have been killed if he'd fallen.
   c. He might have been sponsored for advertising . . . . His stunt shouldn't have been given so much press.

C Pair work

- **Preview and do the task** Read the instructions aloud. Have Ss discuss the feats and add their ideas.
- **Follow-up** Have pairs share their ideas.

3 Listening

A 🔊 CD2, Track 14

- **Preview the task** Ask, "What is extreme skiing?" (e.g., *skiing down slopes that are longer and steeper, usually in areas that are mountainous*). Read the instructions and the six topics aloud.
- **Play the recording** Audio script pp. T-273–T-274 Ss listen and number the topics. Play it again and check answers.

Answers

2 childhood 1 college 5 giving up extreme skiing □ marriage 3 travel 4 film career

B 🔊 CD2, Track 15

- **Preview the task** Read the instructions aloud. Say, "First read the sentences and options."

- **Play the recording** Audio script pp. T-273–T-274 Ss listen and circle *a*, *b*, or *c*. Play again, then check answers.

Answers

1. b; 2. c; 3. a; 4. b; 5. b; 6. c

About you

C Pair work

- **Preview and do the task** Read the instructions aloud. Have pairs discuss the question. Have pairs share their ideas with the class.

2 Grammar Information focus 2

Figure it out

A Rewrite the sentences in the passive, starting with the words given. Use similar sentences in the article to help you. Then read the grammar chart.

1. Something might well have injured Beaumont. Beaumont . . .
2. Something could easily have cut the trip short. The trip . . .
3. They shouldn't have allowed him to do it. He . . .

Grammar extra
See page 153.

Past modals and the passive; the verb *make* in the passive ⬇

Active sentences	**Passive sentences**
A motorist **could** easily **have killed** him.	He **could** easily **have been killed** (**by** a motorist).
Sickness **might** well **have cut short** the trip.	The trip might well **have been cut short** (**by** sickness).
They **shouldn't have permitted** him to do it.	He **shouldn't have been permitted** to do it.
They **ought (not) to have allowed** it.	It **ought (not) to have been allowed**.

The verb *make* has a different pattern in the active and passive when it is followed by a verb.
Active: *They made him* **sleep** *in police cells.*   **Passive:** *He was made* **to sleep** *in police cells.*

B Look at more feats and things people might have said *beforehand*. Rewrite the sentences as what people might have thought *afterward*. Add the adverbs, where given.

1. **Kristen Ulmer, an extreme skier, skied down the face of Grand Teton, U.S., in 1997.**
   a. An avalanche could bury her alive. *She* _could easily have been buried alive by an avalanche_. (easily)
   b. They might postpone her attempt due to bad weather. *Her attempt* _____. (well)
   c. They shouldn't encourage her to do it. *She* _____.
2. **Philippe Petit walked a tightrope between the twin towers in New York City in 1974.**
   a. The wind could blow him off. *He* _____. (easily)
   b. They should make him wear a safety harness. *He* _____. (also)
   c. They should never allow him to do it. *He* _____.
3. **Alain Robert got arrested in 2010 after climbing the Lumiere skyscraper in Sydney.**
   a. They shouldn't arrest him, and they shouldn't throw him in jail, either. *He* _____.
   b. He could kill someone if he falls. *Someone* _____. (well)
   c. A company might sponsor him for advertising. They shouldn't give his stunt so much press.
   He _____. *His stunt* _____.

C Pair work Discuss the feats in this lesson. What else might have happened to the people?

3 Listening *Kristen Ulmer on extreme skiing*

A ◀ CD 2.14 Listen to a reporter talk about her recent meeting with Kristen Ulmer. Number the topics in the order the speaker mentions them (1–5). There is one topic the interviewer doesn't mention.

☐ childhood   ☐ college   ☐ giving up extreme skiing   ☐ marriage   ☐ travel   ☐ film career

B ◀ CD 2.15 Listen again. Circle a, b, or c to complete the sentences.

1. Kristen started doing dangerous skiing   a) as a child.   b) in college.   c) for movies.
2. As a child, she   a) was made to ski.   b) was an expert skier.   c) enjoyed skiing.
3. Her rule in Asia was   a) never discuss skiing.   b) tell everyone about skiing.   c) look good.
4. In Asia, she might have   a) gotten sick.   b) lost her life.   c) killed someone by accident.
5. While she was filming, she was   a) not well known.   b) almost killed.   c) badly paid.
6. Now she wants to   a) transform her performance.   b) keep filming.   c) coach other athletes.

About you

C Pair work **Would you ever do the kinds of things Kristen has done?**

Lesson C *Just think . . .*

1 Conversation strategy Making a point

A How has humanity progressed in the last 100 years? Share ideas with the class.

B ◀))CD 2.16 Listen. What does Alba think about space exploration? How about Jack?

Alba I see another rocket's just been launched. All this money that's being wasted on going into space. Just think what could have been done with those billions of dollars!

Jack Yes, . . . but one way to look at it is that all kinds of things have been discovered through space exploration.

Alba Like what?

Jack Well, satellite technology, more accurate weather forecasting – they've both come from space programs. And you can't say that we don't need those things.

Alba Absolutely not. But I look at it this way: there are other things we could spend the money on. Don't you think it would have been better spent on things like schools?

Jack Not necessarily. But anyway, things like the space program encourage kids to go into science and engineering. It makes it exciting. I mean, life would be very limited if we never looked beyond our immediate environment.

Alba Well, let me put it another way: maybe we *should* explore space but not till we've made our own world a better place.

Jack Maybe. Maybe not.

C **Notice** how Alba and Jack use expressions like these to make their points. Find the expressions they use in the conversation.

(Let's) put it this way: . . .   *One way to look at it is (that) . . .*
To put it another way: . . .
Let me put it another way: . . .   *Just think.*
(I) look at it this way: . . .   *(Just) think about it.*

D ◀))CD 2.17 Listen to the rest of Alba and Jack's conversation. Write the expressions you hear.

Alba Well, _____ what could have been done to research alternative fuels, for example, if we'd had all those billions of dollars. _____: there are better things to spend money on.

Jack Yeah, possibly. But _____: Plenty of countries don't have space programs, but they don't necessarily spend their money on better things.

Alba I'm not sure that's entirely true. I mean, some countries are way ahead in terms of using alternative energies. I mean, _____: that in itself does more for the planet.

Jack Well, _____ not only have better technologies been developed, but also new medicines are being discovered. _____ – all that research that's done in space.

About you | **E** Pair work **Practice the whole conversation. Whose opinions do you agree with?**

Lesson C *Just think . . .*

1 Conversation strategy

Why use expressions to make a point?

Speakers often use particular expressions to introduce a point or argument they wish to make. For example, they can invite the listener to consider an idea (*just think*), introduce one perspective or aspect of an idea (*One way to look at it*), or repeat, reformulate, or clarify ideas (*To put it another way*).

(For more information, see Language notes at the beginning of this unit.)

- **Set the scene** Books closed. Ask, "What do you think daily life was like when your great-grandparents were your age?" Have Ss share their ideas.

A
- **Preview and do the task** Books open. Read the instructions aloud. Have Ss call out their ideas. (e.g., *Advances in medical technology have saved many lives. Improvements in transportation – air, rail, car – have made travel easier and faster.*)

B ◀))) CD2, Track 16
- **Preview the task** Tell Ss to cover the conversation and look at the picture. Ask, "What are these people looking at?" [a rocket launch] Ask, "Do you think space exploration is good or useful?" Elicit answers from the class.
- Read the instructions aloud. Tell Ss to keep the conversation covered and to make brief notes to answer the questions.
- **Play the recording** Ss listen only. Replay the recording. Ss listen and write. Have Ss compare their notes in pairs.
- **Play the recording again** Ss uncover the conversation, listen, read along, and check their answers. Check the answer with the class. [*Alba*: it's a waste of money; there are better things to spend money on (schools); we should make our own world better first. *Jack*: many things have been discovered (satellite technology, weather forecasting); encourages kids to go into science and engineering]

C
- **Present *Notice*** Read the information and the examples aloud.
- Say, "Read the conversation again. Find the examples." Have a S read them aloud. [*Alba*: **Just think** what could have been done . . . *Jack*: Yes, . . . but **one way to look at it is that** all kinds . . . *Alba*: But **I look at it this way:** there are other . . . Well, **let me put it another way:** maybe we should explore . . .]
- **Practice** Tell Ss to practice the conversation in pairs, taking turns playing each role.

D ◀))) CD2, Track 17
- **Preview the task** Read the instructions aloud. Ask Ss to read through the rest of the conversation and to review the expressions in Notice.
- **Play the recording** Ss listen and write. Have Ss compare their answers with a partner. Play the recording again and have Ss check their answers. Check answers with the class.

Answers

Alba   Well, <u>think</u> what could have been done . . . <u>Let's put it this way</u>: there are better things . . .
Jack   . . . But <u>look at it this way</u>: plenty of . . .
Alba   . . . I mean, <u>think about it</u>: that in itself . . .
Jack   Well, <u>one way to look at it is that</u> not only have . . . <u>Just think</u> – all that research . . .

About you

E Pair work
- **Preview and do the task** Read the instructions aloud. Have Ss practice both parts of the conversation in Exercises 1B and 1D and then discuss the opinions.
- **Follow-up** Using a show of hands, find out how many Ss agree with Alba and how many agree with Jack. Ask several Ss to give reasons for their choice.

Extra activity – pairs

Have pairs write a conversation where two people discuss space tourism and whether trips to the International Space Station would be a worthwhile experience.

Pairs present their conversation to another pair. The listening pair notes which expressions from Exercise 1C were used.

② Strategy plus

Why use *absolutely (not)* and *not necessarily?*

In a conversation during which different points are being argued, speakers can agree or disagree to varying degrees. Using *absolutely (not)* or *definitely (not)* strengthens a yes (or no) response, while *probably (not)* or *maybe (not)* can be used if a speaker wants to remain more noncommittal. A response of *not necessarily* expresses the idea that something is not completely or always true.

(For more information, see Language notes at the beginning of this unit.)

◀))) CD2, Track 18

- **Present *Strategy plus*** Read aloud or play the recording of the information and examples. Ss listen and read along.
- Tell Ss to read Alba and Jack's conversation on page 56 again and find examples of these responses. [*Alba:* Absolutely not. But I look at it . . . *Jack:* Not necessarily. But anyway, things like . . . *Jack:* Maybe. Maybe not.]

About you

- **Preview and do the task** Say, "Read statements 1 to 5. Then read responses *a* to *e*, and match each statement with the correct response." Have Ss complete the task and compare their answers with a partner. Check answers with the class.

Answers

1. b;   2. e;   3. c;   4. d;   5. a

- Have Ss practice with the class. Say, "Now practice again, but this time give your own responses to the comments. Try and carry on the conversations as long as you can."
- **Follow-up** Ask Ss to tell the class any interesting ideas they added to the comments and responses.

③ Listening and strategies

About you

A ◀))) CD2, Track 19

- **Preview the task** Read the instructions and the topics aloud. Ask, "What does *applications of research* mean here? [how the results of the research are used in practical ways]
- **Play the recording** Audio script p. T-274 Ss listen and check (✓) the topics. Replay the recording if necessary. Check answers with the class.

Answers

education, agriculture, medicine

B ◀))) CD2, Track 20

- **Preview the task** Read the instructions aloud. Say, "Look at the chart. Think about the information you need as you listen." Ask, "In this chart, what does *application* mean?" [a use for]
- Have Ss predict the missing words in the chart. Have Ss call out possible ideas.
- **Play the recording** Audio script p. T-274 Ss listen and write. Play the recording again to give Ss more time to write and complete their answers. Have Ss compare their answers with a partner. Check answers with the class.

Answers

Research questions: How far can crickets walk in a day? How much crop damage in a day do they do?

Possible application of research: To ensure food security

Research question: How do snails learn and remember?

Possible applications of research: To improve people's ability to learn

To help people after a brain injury or disease

About you

C Pair work

- **Preview and do the task** Read the instructions aloud. Ask a S to read the questions aloud. As Ss discuss their ideas, walk around the class giving help or ideas as needed.
- **Follow-up** Have several pairs share some of their ideas with the class. (Note: If using the Extra Activity, write the ideas on the board or ask a S to write them on the board.)

Extra activity – groups

Using the ideas on the board from Exercise 3C or their own ideas, groups attempt to reach a final answer to each question in Exercise 3C. Groups present their answers to the class, including reasons and examples.

Speaking naturally

- Tell Ss to turn to Speaking naturally on p. 140. (For more information, see Language notes at the beginning of this unit. See the teaching notes on p. T-140.)

2 Strategy plus *Absolutely (not), not necessarily*

◀))CD 2.18 You can use **Absolutely (not)** or **Definitely (not)** to make a *yes* (or *no*) response stronger.

Use **Probably (not)** and **Maybe (not)** if you do not want to commit strongly to a response.

If you want to say something is not completely or always true, you can say **Not necessarily**.

> You can't say we don't need those things.

> Absolutely not.

About you

Match the statements with the responses. Write the letters a–e. Then practice with a partner. Practice again, giving your own responses.

1. Space exploration is certainly not a waste of money or a waste of time, as some people say. _____
2. Do you think we'll ever discover life on other planets? _____
3. Don't you think we should send humans to Mars, no matter how much it costs? _____
4. Another thing about space programs is they promote international cooperation, which is good. _____
5. Life wouldn't be as exciting if we didn't explore space. _____

a. Probably not. Though there are still plenty of things to explore on earth.
b. Absolutely not. For every dollar spent on space, $8 of economic benefit has reportedly been generated.
c. Definitely. I mean, they've successfully landed a spacecraft there, so why not a human.
d. Not necessarily. I mean, if you want to keep your technology a secret, then it's not good.
e. Maybe. Maybe not. But imagine if we did find other life forms. There'd be a lot of issues to consider.

3 Listening and strategies *What's the point of research?*

A ◀))CD 2.19 **Listen to a conversation. What applications of research do they mention? Check (✓) the topics. There are two extra topics.**

☐ education   ☐ social studies   ☐ agriculture   ☐ climate   ☐ medicine

B ◀))CD 2.20 **Listen again. What specific research do the speakers mention? Complete the chart.**

Research questions:	**Research question:**
How far can crickets _____ ?	How do snails _____ ?
How much _____ do they do?	**Possible applications of research:**
Possible application of research:	To improve _____
To ensure _____	To help people after _____

About you

C Pair work Discuss these questions. Give examples or reasons to support your ideas.

- What research has contributed most to society in the last 10 years?
- Which areas deserve more research? What outcomes would you like to see?
- What subjects do you feel should not be researched? Why?
- Who should pay for research?

Speaking naturally
See page 140.

> DO YOU THINK I COULD BE THE FIRST PERSON TO DISCOVER AN ALIEN LIFE FORM?

> ABSOLUTELY. WHY DON'T YOU START BY LOOKING IN YOUR ROOM?

Lesson D *Smart ideas*

① Reading

A Prepare **Scan the article. What is the focus of the article? Check (✓) one topic.**

☐ How to become an inventor
☐ How to market a new invention

☐ How different inventions come about
☐ Why some inventions fail

B 🔽 **Read for main ideas** **Read the article. Where do these sentences fit in the article? Write the correct letters in the spaces.**

a. There is seemingly no end to the number of inventions we can look forward to in the future.
b. Necessity is the mother of invention – or so the saying goes.
c. The smartphone app is another good example.
d. It is generally believed that inventions are the result of focused effort by inventors seeking specific solutions to specific problems.
e. Clearly, many inventions have come about from a mix of astute observation and inspired thinking.
f. In reality, most people probably will never invent something as world-changing as the steam engine.

INVENTION: INSPIRED THINKING OR ACCIDENTAL DISCOVERY?

❶ "To invent, you need a good imagination and a pile of junk," or so Thomas Edison, one of the world's most famous inventors, is quoted as saying. Yet how do successful inventions come about? How have inventions been achieved in the past? What makes something a brilliant invention?

❷ _____ Brilliance, however, is not enough, and obviously, hard work and persistence need to follow. James Dyson noticed his vacuum cleaner would frequently clog up and stop picking up dirt. On a visit to a local factory, he observed how dust was removed from the air by large industrial cyclones, and it inspired him to try the same principles on a smaller scale in a vacuum cleaner. He developed over 5,000 prototype designs before finally succeeding with his invention: the first cyclonic bagless vacuum cleaner.

❸ _____ Surprisingly, many innovations that have enhanced the efficiency, comfort, and convenience of everyday life have often been discovered by accident. The steam engine, superglue, artificial sweeteners, and synthetic dyes, to name but a few, all came about when their inventors' minds were being applied to quite different problems. If Dr. Percy Spencer had not noticed that a candy bar had melted in his pocket as he was testing microwave radiation for use in radar, the microwave oven may never have been invented.

❹ _____ No invention is more true of this proverb than the ice-cream cone. When an ice-cream seller ran out of plates on which to serve his ice cream, he used a rolled-up waffle instead. The ice-cream cone had inadvertently been created, and with great success.

❺ _____ Few will have the skills to engineer something like a vacuum cleaner or microwave oven. Even so, when you consider some of the everyday things that have been developed, it's clear that inventions do not have to be complex or life-changing to be hugely successful and incredibly marketable. Tags that label your electrical cords, silly bands for kids, or suitcases with wheels are all examples of inventions that gained huge popularity and left people wondering, "Why didn't I think of that?"

❻ _____ By 2011, there were already more than half a million of them, many of which were incredibly simple and straightforward, and many of which had actually been invented by ordinary people and even children. One, nine-year-old Ding Wen from Singapore, invented a drawing app that allows users to draw with their fingers across a touch screen and then shake the device to clear the screen. Another was 14-year-old Robert Nay, an eighth grader from Utah, whose Bubble Ball physics game had reportedly been downloaded more than two million times within two weeks of its launch. What these apps had in common was originality, simplicity, ease of use, and wide demographic appeal.

❼ Nevertheless, no matter how inventions come about, whether by sheer brilliance or by a stroke of luck, one thing is clear. _____ What's more, our willingness to adopt them, whether for their effectiveness or simply for our own amusement, means that there will be always be a ready market.

Reading tip

Writers sometimes use a quotation from a famous person or a saying to start and set the theme of an article.

Lesson D *Smart ideas*

1 Reading

- **Set the scene** Books closed. Ask Ss to work in pairs and say, "Think of five inventions that changed the world." Have pairs report their choices to the class.

A Prepare

- **Preview and do the task** Books open. Read the instructions and four topics aloud. Check that Ss know the meaning of *market* [promote and sell] and *come about* [happen]. Say, "You have 30 seconds to scan and choose your answer." After 30 seconds, check the answer with the class. [How different inventions come about]

B ⬇ www.cambridge.org/viewpoint/audio

Read for main ideas

- **Preview the task** Read the instructions aloud. Ask individual Ss to read sentences *a* to *f* aloud and check for vocabulary problems. Write on the board:

    seemingly

    seeking

    astute

    Ask Ss to provide definitions.

- **Do the task** Ss read the article and complete the task. If desired, play the downloadable recording. Ss listen and read along. Tell Ss to compare their answer with a partner. Check the answer with the class.

Answers

2. e; 3. d; 4. b; 5. f; 6. c; 7. a

- Have Ss give reasons why the answers are correct and which words give them the clues.

2. The paragraph says *Brilliance, however, is not enough,* which follows *astute observation and inspired thinking* in the missing sentence.

3. The belief that inventions are always the result of a focused effort in the missing sentence is contrasted with the surprising idea that sometimes they happen by accident in the paragraph.

4. The paragraph refers to *this proverb,* which is the same as *a saying* in the missing sentence.

5. The missing sentence refers to *world-changing* inventions and the paragraph lists two (*vacuum cleaner* and *microwave oven*).

6. The missing sentence introduces the theme of apps, which are discussed in the paragraph.

7. Both the missing sentence and the paragraph refer to the future.

- **Present *Reading tip*** Read the information aloud. Ask, "Why is this a good strategy?" Elicit answers (e.g., *it captures the reader's interest, it introduces the topic, it makes the writer sound well-informed*).

② Focus on vocabulary

- Say, "This lesson teaches some suffixes that turn adjectives into nouns." Read the information in the box aloud. Say, "Pay attention to the nouns that end in -ance, -ence, and -ency. The vowel in these is unstressed, so it's easy to misspell them."

A • **Preview the task** Say, "Complete the sentences below with the noun form of the adjectives given. Use the article to help you."

- **Do the task** Have Ss complete the task and compare their answers with a partner. Check answers with the class.

Answers

1. willingness, popularity
2. convenience, originality, amusement
3. brilliance, simplicity, comfort
4. efficiency, ease, effectiveness

- Say, "Now match the pictures with the sentences. Write the letters a to d." Have Ss complete the task. Check answers with the class.

Answers

1. b; 2. c; 3. a; 4. d

B **Pair work**

- **Preview and do the task** Read the instructions aloud. Walk around the class and give help as needed.
- **Follow-up** For each question, have a few Ss share their answers with the class.

③ Viewpoint

Pair work

- **Preview the task** Ask a S to read the instructions and the descriptions for discussions aloud.
- **Present *In conversation*** Ask a S to read the information aloud. Add, "Listen to the example. The speaker wants to sound less assertive (forceful) or direct." Have a S read the example aloud.
- **Do the task** Have Ss complete the task. As Ss discuss, walk around the class and help as needed.
- **Follow-up** For each item, have pairs share their ideas with the class. (If using the Extra Activity, write the answers on the board or have a S write them.)

Extra activity – groups / class

Write on the board:

What invention has changed the world most? Why?

Which is the most useful or convenient app?

What simple invention do you most wish you had thought of?

What invention would you most like to see?

Small groups discuss the questions using the ideas on the board or new ideas of their own. Groups try to agree on one answer for each question.

Groups present their choices to the class.

The class finds out if more than one group had the same final answer for any of the questions.

2 Focus on vocabulary Adjectives into nouns

A Complete the sentences below with the noun form of the words given. Use the article to help you. Then match the pictures with the sentences. Write the letters a–d.

a. a bladeless fan

b. a doodling app

c. mop slippers

d. sticky notes

☐ 1. With the _____ (willing) of millions to download these, their _____ (popular) is clear. What apps have you downloaded? How useful are they?

☐ 2. The _____ (convenient) of this invention is evident, and it certainly wins a prize for _____ (original). It also provides plenty of _____ (amuse). But would you really buy something like this?

☐ 3. The sheer _____ (brilliant) of this invention is clear, and the _____ (simple) of its design is appealing. It also improves the _____ (comfortable) of our everyday lives. What other inventions have made life better?

☐ 4. This simple invention certainly improved the _____ (efficient) of many people's working lives. It's _____ of use (easy) and _____ (effective) are part of its winning formula. What other inventions have contributed to a better workplace?

B Pair work **Discuss the questions above. Think of as many ideas as you can.**

3 Viewpoint The best ideas . . .

Pair work **Think of ideas for each description below and see if you agree on any of them. Discuss why you made your choices and how the inventions have impacted people's lives.**

Think of . . .

- an invention that improves efficiency in travel.
- an invention that has changed the world.
- an app that is really convenient to have.
- a device that you couldn't live without.
- a simple invention that you wish you had thought of.
- an invention that you'd like to see.
- an app that you would like to develop.

"I guess high-speed rail has really improved the efficiency in travel. The convenience of jumping on a train rather than going to the airport is one reason high-speed trains are so widely used."

In conversation . . .

You can use *I guess, I think,* or *I suppose* to sound less direct or assertive.

Writing *It is often said . . .*

In this lesson, you . . .
- compare and contrast arguments.
- use *it* clauses + passive.
- avoid errors with *affect* and *effect*.

Task **Write an opinion essay.**

Some people argue that technological progress is always positive. Others dispute this. What is your view and why?

A **Look at a model** Look at the introduction to an essay responding to the question above. Underline the thesis statement. Circle the topics that the student will discuss in the essay.

It is often said that technological progress is important and can only have positive or beneficial effects on our lives. Progress, it is argued, especially in the fields of medicine, communications, and infrastructure, has improved the quality of life for human beings. In contrast, others disagree, saying that progress mostly has a negative impact, in particular on the environment. While progress can have both positive and negative effects, I would argue that the positive effects of progress outweigh the negative.

To compare opinions, include:

Introduction – outline the issues and give your view

Opinion 1 with reasons and examples

Opinion 2 with reasons and examples

Conclusion – summarize the arguments and restate your view

B **Focus on language** Read the chart. Then rewrite the underlined parts of the sentences below using *it* clauses and the adverbs given.

it clauses with the passive in academic writing

You can use *it* clauses with the passive to introduce what people say or think. Adverbs like *often, generally, well, widely* emphasize what is commonly said.
It is often said that technological progress is important.
It is generally accepted . . . / *widely recognized* . . . / *well known* . . .
It has also been reported / shown / suggested that . . .

Useful expressions

while / whereas
although
However, . . .
In contrast, . . .
Nevertheless, . . .
On the one / other hand, . . .

1. People accept that progress is inevitable, but we should examine this carefully. (generally)
2. People recognize that progress in industry can cause pollution. (widely) On the other hand, people understand that some industries are making efforts to become "greener." (also)
3. Scientists have shown that life expectancy is increasing as a result of medical advances, although some people suggest that this is only the case in wealthier societies. (also)
4. People know that progress in communications leads to a better-functioning society. (well) Nevertheless, they recognize that privacy and security issues are a growing problem. (widely)
5. People have suggested that technological progress often comes out of military programs. However, people believe that developments like the Internet benefit everyone. (generally)
6. People have reported that so-called industrial progress adversely affects the poor. In contrast, people say that the wealthy become wealthier. (often)

C **Write and check** Now write your own opinion essay for the question. Then check for errors. Read a classmate's essay. Do you share the same views?

Common errors

Do not confuse *affect* and *effect*. *Affect* is a verb; *effect* is a noun.
*Progress **affects** everyone.* (NOT ~~Progress effects everyone.~~)
*Progress has several positive **effects**.* (NOT . . . ~~several positive affects.~~)

Writing *It is often said . . .*

In this lesson

- Ask a S to read the lesson aims (*In this lesson, you . . .*) aloud. Say, "The first lesson aim is compare and contrast arguments. When you write an opinion essay, you can compare two opinions that are in contrast with each other." Ask, "What's presented in the grammar for writing chart?" [*it* clauses with the passive in academic writing]
- **Preview the writing** Say, "In this lesson, you will write an opinion essay that discusses contrasting opinions." Point out the writing topic in Task and read it aloud. Ask Ss to share their view and to brainstorm reasons. Write Ss' answers on the board, divided into arguments "for" and "against."
- Explain that Ss will end the lesson by writing an essay that will practice the three aims presented in this lesson.

A Look at a model

- **Preview the task** Read the instructions aloud. Tell Ss it is a good idea to read through the entire paragraph before answering. Check that Ss understand *infrastructure*. [basic systems (e.g., transportation, communication) that a country / organization uses to work effectively]
- **Do the task** Have Ss complete the task. Check answers with the class. Ask, "What is the writer's view?" You could also see if any of the arguments Ss brainstormed above are in it.
- Ask, "What is the writer's view of technological progress?" [The positive effects outweigh the negative.] Ask Ss to look at the board and call out any of the ideas there that are also in the model.

Answers

It is often said that technological progress is important and can only have positive or beneficial effects on our lives. Progress, it is argued, especially in the fields of (medicine), (communications), *and* (infrastructure) *has improved the quality of life for human beings. In contrast, others disagree, saying that progress mostly has a negative impact, in particular on the* (environment). *While progress can have both positive and negative effects, I would argue that the positive effects of progress outweigh the negative.*

- Have a S read the information in the box. Choose a topic from the model and have Ss think of reasons and examples the writer can give for both options. Say, "You can contrast ideas in each paragraph or you can write a set of paragraphs with one argument followed by a paragraph giving the other argument."

B 📥 www.cambridge.org/viewpoint/audio
Focus on language

- **Present the grammar for writing chart** Read the information in the chart aloud. If desired, play the downloadable recording. Ss listen and read along.

- **Understand the grammar for writing** Say, "When you want to write what people generally say or think – a common belief or generality – you can use an *it* clause with a passive verb."
- Say, "Here is a list of other *it* clauses often used with the passive in academic writing." Write on the board and have Ss copy into their books:

  It is. . .
  widely assumed / known
  generally agreed / accepted
  well established
  commonly accepted

- Say, "You can also use a regular passive to make the noun the main theme of a sentence." Write on the board, underlined as shown:

  Technological progress is often said to be important.

- **Present *Useful expressions*** Ask, "In the introduction above, what did the writer use to begin the contrasting opinion?" [In contrast] Say, "These expressions are also useful to show contrast. Using a variety in the same essay will give your work more style." Ask a S to read them aloud.
- **Preview and do the task** Read the instructions aloud. Have Ss complete the task. Check answers with the class.

Answers

1. It is generally accepted that . . .
2. It is widely recognized that . . . On the other hand, it is also understood that . . .
3. It has been shown (by scientists) that . . . although it is also suggested that . . .
4. It is well known that . . . Nevertheless, it is widely recognized that . . .
5. It has been suggested that . . . However, it is generally believed that . . .
6. It has been reported that so-called . . . In contrast, it is often said that . . .

C Write and check

- **Preview the task** Say, "Write an essay to answer the question in the task above. Then check for errors."
- **Present *Common errors*** Read the information aloud. Write some incomplete sentences with forms of *effect* and *affect* on the board and have Ss complete them.
- **Do the task** Say, "Look at the model again. The box on the right contains the guidelines you'll need for this essay." Have Ss write their essay and check for errors.
- Have Ss read a classmate's essay. Several Ss say if they share the classmate's view.

Extra activity – class

Ss leave their essays on their desk for classmates to read. Ss read two other essays. They look for the number of *it* clauses each essay contains.

Vocabulary notebook *Old or ancient?*

If done for homework

Briefly present the Learning tip and the task directions. Make sure Ss understand what they need to do.

If done in class

- **Present *Learning tip*** Read the information aloud. Add, "Learning synonyms will also help you with reading, especially more formal types of texts." Say, "It's always a good idea to write sentences using the synonyms you find." Ask a S to read the examples in the box.

- **Present *Dictionary tip*** Read the information aloud. Say, "A thesaurus may present synonyms that are only similar in meaning, but which don't fit all contexts, so it's important to check a dictionary and write an example sentence. For example, look at the examples for *bad*. *Inferior* suggests a comparison, but *poor* doesn't."

A • **Preview and do the task** Read the instructions aloud. Point out that the first answer has been done as an example. Have Ss complete the task. Check answers with the class.

Answers

1. portable
2. functional
3. compact
4. integral
5. countless
6. obsolete

B • **Preview and do the task** Read the instructions aloud. Ask for an example from page 52 for "modest, ordinary." [humble] Say, "Don't look at the exercise on page 52 until you've tried to write the remaining synonyms." Have Ss complete the task. Check answers with the class.

Answers

1. humble
2. innovative
3. rudimentary
4. significant
5. standard

- Have Ss read their sentences to a partner.

C Word builder

- **Preview the task** Read the instructions and the six words aloud. Have Ss complete the task. Check the answers with the class.

Answers

archaic: obsolete (Ex. A, #6)
elementary: rudimentary (Ex. B, #3)
everyday: standard (Ex. B, #5)
groundbreaking: innovative (Ex. B, #2)
major: significant (Ex. B, #4)
practical: functional (Ex. A, #2)

D Focus on vocabulary, page 59

- **Preview and do the task** Read the instructions aloud. Say, "First try to complete the chart without looking at page 59. Then look and check." Have Ss complete the task. Check answers with the class.

Answers

Adjective	Noun
willing	willingness
popular	popularity
convenient	convenience
original	originality
amusing	amusement
brilliant	brilliance
simple	simplicity
comfortable	comfort
efficient	efficiency
easy	ease of use
effective	effectiveness

Vocabulary notebook *Old or ancient?*

Learning tip   Building synonyms

It's useful to learn more than one way to express basic concepts like *big, small, many, important, good, bad*, etc., especially for formal writing.

bad= inferior, poor
   With recent advances in GPS, older versions now seem inferior.
   You can be fired for poor performance at work.

Dictionary tip

Your word-processing software probably has a thesaurus to help you find synonyms, but check them in a dictionary before you use them.

A   **Choose a synonym from the box for these words. Then complete the example sentences.**

| compact | countless | functional | integral | obsolete | ✓ portable |

1. easy to carry = portable   We have a portable _____ grill that we barbecue on.
2. useful = _____   Kitchen appliances should be both _____ and attractive.
3. small = _____   With gas prices so high, people are now buying _____ cars.
4. essential = _____   Having ideas is an _____ part of making progress.
5. many, a lot of = _____   There have been _____ inventions that didn't work.
6. out of date = _____   The typewriter has more or less become _____.

B   **Write synonyms for these adjectives. Then write a sentence that uses the synonym you came up with.**

1. modest, ordinary = _____   _____
2. creative, new = _____   _____
3. simple, basic = _____   _____
4. important, big = _____   _____
5. usual, not special = _____   _____

C   **Word builder These words are all synonyms of one or more words in Exercises A and B. Find their meanings. Then write them next to their synonyms above.**

| archaic | elementary | everyday | groundbreaking | major | practical |

D   **Focus on vocabulary** **Look back at the article on page 58. Look for the words there and in Exercise 2A on page 59 to help you complete the chart below.**

Adjective	Noun
willing	willingness
popular	
	convenience
original	
amusing	
	brilliance
simple	
	comfort
efficient	
easy	
	effectiveness

Unit 6 Business studies

Lesson A *A case study*

Grammar *Adding and modifying information*

(See Student's Book p. 63.)

In this lesson, Ss learn to use more complex relative clauses beginning with pronouns or prepositions. They are presented here in the context of a case study of *Groupon*, an online coupon company.

Form

Relative clauses can begin with pronoun + *of* + *which* / *whom* or preposition + *which* / *whom*.

Which is used for things, and *whom* is used for people.

- Pronouns + *of* in relative clauses

  Examples of pronouns + *of* are: *all of, some of, most of, many of, a few of.*

  > In three years, the company had more than 85 million merchants, **all of whom** "opt in" to the site.

  > The Internet provided a new opportunity to coupon businesses, **many of which** have been successful.

- Prepositions

  Examples of prepositions are: *to, from, for, with, between, among.*

  > Mason had an idea: attract subscribers **to whom** you email special deals.

  > Shoppers clip coupons from newspapers, **with which** they can save money.

Use

Relative clauses beginning with these pronouns modify the noun in the main clause by saying what proportion of the noun the information applies to (e.g., *all, a few, some,* etc.).

Prepositions can also go at the end of a relative clause, but in formal writing, they are generally used to start the relative clause. Compare:

> Shoppers clip coupons **that / which** they can save money **with**.

> Shoppers clip coupons **with which** they can save money.

The second one is more formal.

⊙ Corpus information

Writing vs. Conversation

Relative clauses with pronoun + *of whom / of which* are approximately 10 times more common in academic writing than in conversation.

Grammar extra *Pronouns and numbers in relative clauses; Nouns in relative clauses*

(See Student's Book p. 154.)

Grammar extra presents more relative clauses beginning with pronouns, numbers, and nouns.

Speaking naturally *Prepositions in relative clauses*

(See Student's Book p. 140.)

In this section, Ss practice reducing the preposition *of* in relative clauses with pronoun + *of whom / of which*. The pronoun receiving the primary stress is underlined in the example below.

> Online coupons bring in new customers, **some** *of whom* become regular customers later on.

Lesson B *Bringing in the customers*

Vocabulary in context *Attracting and deterring*

(See Student's Book p. 64.)

The article presents verbs with the meanings of attracting or deterring (customers) in the context of a podcast on changes in retail patterns. Ss learn verbs such as *tempt, draw in, discourage,* and *alienate.*

Vocabulary notebook *It's tempting.*

(See Student's Book p. 71.)

The Learning tip tells Ss that when they learn a new verb, they should find other words in the same word family. They are also warned that some words are mostly used as verbs and may not have other forms. Ss get more practice with the vocabulary from Lesson B.

- **Focus on vocabulary** reviews and practices vocabulary introduced in Lesson D (p. 69).

Grammar *Referring to people and things*

(See Student's Book p. 65.)

This lesson teaches Ss more uses of common pronouns and determiners: *some, any, other, others,* and *another.*

Use

- *Some*

  The "strong" form of *some* [/sʌm/] before a noun or as a pronoun can mean "certain" or "some but not all." It suggests a contrast with other people or things.

  > Cheaper prices will tempt **some** people. (= but not everyone; other people won't be tempted).

  It can also be used with singular nouns to mean "an unknown person or thing" and is often slightly derogatory (*Some store assistant came up to me*). In conversation, it can also be used to praise, or say something was special in some way.

  > That was **some** shopping trip! (= e.g., good, long, or expensive)

- *Any*

  The stressed form of *any* (/ˈen·i/) before a noun means "any person or thing – it doesn't matter which."

  > ***Any** store that makes people feel at home will probably generate more business. (= every or any, it doesn't matter which store)*

- *Other / Others*

  Other can be used before a plural or uncountable noun. It can be used after the definite article (*the*), possessives (*your*, *his*, etc.), quantifiers (*some*, *a few*, etc.), and demonstratives (*this*, *those*, etc.), to refer to additional, extra, or different people or things.

  > *[Lower prices aren't enough.] Stores need to find **other** ways to attract customers.*

  Others is a pronoun. It cannot be used before a noun.

  > *. . . but **others** know they can probably get what they want cheaper online. (= other people)*

- *Another*

  Another is used before a singular countable noun or as a pronoun to refer to "a different or additional one."

Another store might offer self-service ordering. Yet another might create a "third place."

Corpus information

Common errors with *another* and *others*

Ss often use *another* incorrectly before a plural noun.

*Retail stores need to find **other ways** to attract customers.* (**NOT:** ~~another ways~~)

Ss often use *others* before a noun.

Other stores have more high-tech facilities. (**NOT:** ~~others stores~~)

Grammar extra Other, every other, other than; *More on* another

(See Student's Book p. 155.)

Grammar extra presents more ways to refer to people and things using *other*, *every other*, *other than*, and *another*.

Lesson C *Don't you think . . . ?*

Conversation strategy *Persuading*

(See Student's Book p. 66.)

The lesson teaches using negative questions (*Don't you think . . . ?*) and tag questions (*. . . can't it?*), which strongly suggest to the listener that he or she should agree. These are both useful strategies for persuading people of a point of view – as here – or course of action.

Strategy plus *Granted*

(See Student's Book p. 67.)

Granted can be used when a speaker wants to concede that another speaker has made a good point, including when the point is not strong enough to change an opinion. *Granted* often comes at or near the beginning of a sentence or clause, but it can also come at the end as well as mid-sentence.

Lesson D *Organizational threats*

Writing *It can occur in any company.*

(See Student's Book p. 70.)

This lesson teaches Ss to plan and write a report on data security, identifying causes of a problem and proposing possible solutions to it. The grammar for writing presents ways to use modal verbs to avoid being too assertive in describing situations or problems and ways to make recommendations. It also gives phrases for introducing sentences describing cause. The topic recycles vocabulary from Lesson D.

Using modal verbs

- Avoid being too assertive.

  Modal verbs can be used as hedges (softening expressions) to avoid sounding too direct or assertive. Compare:

  > *These factors **cause** data leakage.* (simple, bold assertion of a fact that there is no doubt about)

  > *These factors **can** cause data leakage.* (suggests they are known to have caused this; that it is a strong probability)

  > *These factors **might / may / could** cause data leakage.* (It is possible, but far from 100 percent certain.)

- Make recommendations

  Polite recommendations can be made with modal verbs, including *would* and *could*.

  > *It **would** be advisable not to allow employees to take work home.* (*It would be advisable* is less direct than *It is advisable*.)

  > *We **could** also enforce the rules on using private computers.* (*Could* proposes a recommendation as a possibility. Note: Using *should* here would be a more assertive statement of what needs to be done.)

Corpus information

Common errors with *could*

Ss sometimes use *could* for things that in fact do happen.

Employees can access their personal email. = They do this, we know.

(**NOT:** ~~Employees could access . . .~~)

However, *could* is correct here, meaning "It would be possible."

Employees could access their email if we allowed it.

Business studies

In Unit 6, you . . .

- talk about business, retail, and threats to companies.
- use relative clauses that begin with pronouns and prepositions.
- use determiners and pronouns like *some, any, other(s), another*.
- persuade people of your views using negative and tag questions.
- *say granted* when someone makes a good point.

Lesson A *A case study*

1 Grammar in context

A   **How do people get discounts when they shop? Make a list.**

B   ◀)) CD 2.21   **Read the case study for an online coupon company. How does the business work?**

A CASE STUDY – Online coupons

For decades savvy shoppers have been clipping coupons from newspapers and magazines, with which they can save money on everything from groceries to spa treatments. The emergence of the Internet provided a new opportunity to coupon businesses, many of which have been very successful. Then came *Groupon*.

BACKGROUND

Like many start-up companies, *Groupon* was founded by a forward-thinking entrepreneur, in this case, Andrew Mason. As with many such entrepreneurs, some of whom have become overnight multimillionaires, Mason had a deceptively simple idea: attract subscribers to whom you email special deals. These daily promotions give subscribers steep discounts, some of which may exceed 50 percent, on a range of goods and services. The success of any deal depends on the extent to which people sign up. If the number of people who sign up falls short of the target, the deal doesn't go through.

GOALS AND GROWTH

Some of the main goals for the company were to grow their subscriber base in key cities around the world; sell daily deals, which was revolutionary in the coupon business; and create awareness of the brand in national and international markets.

In just three years, it had more than 85 million global customers, all of whom "opt in" to the site. The company also had more than 55,000 merchants from whom deals were sought.

A SUCCESS STORY

Over 90 percent of participating companies, most of which are small businesses, said the *Groupon* promotion attracted new customers, and 87 percent reported increased awareness of their product or service in the community. *Groupon* may not be suitable for every enterprise, but for plenty of small business owners, many of whom struggle to grow, it can be a lifesaver, especially in an uncertain economy. One such small business, a bakery in New York, offered half-price cupcakes. More than 9,000 coupons were purchased, new customers came in, and business spread by word of mouth, all of which has to be good for the bottom line!

C   Pair work   **Discuss these questions about the article.**

1. What does the writer mean by "savvy" shoppers?
2. Why does the writer refer to the idea behind *Groupon* as "deceptively simple"?
3. Why was *Groupon* "revolutionary" in the coupon business? What did it do?
4. What kinds of successes do small businesses report after using *Groupon*?
5. Why is *Groupon* a "life saver" for some businesses? Why is it good for the "bottom line"?

Business studies

Introduce the theme of the unit Tell Ss that this unit looks at aspects of business. It includes the story of how one business became successful, it discusses approaches to selling, and it talks about how online technology threatens business today. Read the unit aims aloud.

Lesson A *A case study*

① Grammar in context

- **Set the scene** Books closed. Say, "A case study is a report of how something develops in a period of time. This lesson contains a case study of a well-known business. A case study is a report that gives us an example of how a simple idea was successful."

A • **Preview and do the task** Read the instructions aloud. Have Ss make a list.

- Have Ss call out their ideas, and write them on the board (e.g., *sales, promotions, coupons, bargaining, rebates*).

Culture note

In the U.S., at most stores it's not typical to bargain. Occasionally, for large-ticket items such as houses or cars, buyers will try to bargain down the prices. Consumers also often ask for discounts or use coupons to obtain better prices at retail stores. In some stores, rebate programs allow customers to apply for a rebate on products (such as electronic items or contact lenses). Customers have to complete information and provide evidence of their purchase, and approximately six weeks later, customers receive a rebate check in the mail.

B ◀)) CD2, Track 21

- **Preview and do the task** Ask, "What is a coupon?" [a small piece of printed paper that gives you a discount or other deal on an item or service; found in stores, magazines, newspapers]

- Read the instructions aloud. Say, "First, read and make brief notes to answer the question. Don't stop to check the meaning of new vocabulary." If desired, play the downloadable recording. Ss listen and read along.

- Have Ss complete the task and compare their answer with a partner. Check the answer with the class.

- As Ss complete the task, write the vocabulary check activity below on the board.

Answer

Groupon works by attracting large numbers of subscribers with special deals on a variety of products and services from businesses that participate. The website lets customers know about daily deals that they can take advantage of. If enough subscribers sign up for a deal, then the deal goes through. If not, then the subscribers don't get the deal.

- Say, "Find these words in the case study. Use the context to match the words to the meanings." Write on the board:

1. *savvy*	a. *to choose to join*
2. *emergence*	b. *appearance*
3. *an entrepreneur*	c. *a business*
4. *steep*	d. *knowledgeable / smart*
5. *to opt in*	e. *looked for*
6. *sought*	f. *large*
7. *an enterprise*	g. *someone who takes risks to start a business*
8. *bottom line*	h. *profit or loss*

- Have Ss complete the task and then compare their answers with a partner. Check the answers with the class. [1. d; 2. b; 3. g; 4. f; 5. a; 6. e; 7. c; 8. h]

C Pair work

- **Preview and do the task** Read the instructions aloud. Have Ss discuss the questions. Walk around the class and help as needed.

- Check answers with the class.

Answers

1. By "savvy," the writer means shoppers who are smart in the way they shop, always looking for good bargains.
2. By "deceptively simple," the writer means that *Groupon* takes the traditional idea behind coupons and adapts it for the electronic age. It looks simple, but it's a complicated and clever idea.
3. It was revolutionary because it offered subscribers daily deals, many of which are very attractive. Also, it only works if large numbers of people sign up for it.
4. Small businesses report having new customers, an increased awareness of what they do and what they offer, and more business.
5. It can help boost a company's revenue, and profits can be invested back into the company to help it expand and grow. It's good for the bottom line because more money makes a company more profitable.

Extra activity – groups

Ss say why they would or would not use *Groupon*. Ss who would use it say what kinds of deals they would look for. Ss who would not use it give their reasons

2 Grammar

A ⬇ www.cambridge.org/viewpoint/audio

- **Preview the task** Read the instructions.
- **Do the task** Have Ss complete the task and compare with a partner. Check answers with the class.

Answers

1. The emergence of the Internet provided a new opportunity to coupon businesses, <u>many of which</u> have been very successful.
2. The company also had more than 55,000 merchants <u>from whom</u> deals were sought.

- **Focus on the form** Have Ss look at sentence 1. Ask, "What did *Many of these coupon businesses* change to?" [many of which]
- Have Ss look at sentence 2. Ask, "What did *from these merchants* change to?" [from whom] Ask, "Does *whom* refer to things or people?" [people]
- **Present the grammar chart** Read the information.
- Ask Ss look at the first three example sentences in the chart. Say, "The relative pronoun in each of these sentences has been modified with a pronoun + *of* to give an idea of number or amount. *All of* expresses the idea that every one of the 85 million customers opted in. *Many of* and *most of* makes it clearer that the sentence is true for a majority. *Some of* is true for a minority, or a smaller percentage."
- Write *of whom* on the board. Ask, "Why is *whom* used in the example?" [because it is an object]

- Have Ss look at the last two example sentences. Say, "You can also put the prepositions at the end of the sentence. However, in formal writing, it is considered more correct not to.
- **Present *Conversation vs. Writing*** Read the information aloud.

  (For more information, see Language notes at the beginning of the unit. For more work on pronouns, numbers, and nouns in relative clauses, go to Grammar extra, p. 154.)

B • **Preview and do the task** Read the instructions aloud. Have Ss complete the sentences and compare their answers with a partner. Check answers.

Answers

1. . . . capital with <u>which</u> he was hoping . . .
2. . . . ideas, some <u>of which</u> had potential, but . . .
3. . . . several banks, all <u>of which</u> turned down . . .
4. The friends to <u>whom</u> he turned . . .
5. . . . advisers, most <u>of whom</u> advised him . . .
6. . . . business for <u>which</u> he needed . . . There were several places in his area, most <u>of which</u> charged . . .
7. . . . special offer, to <u>which</u> over 100 people. . . .
8. . . . 40 customers, many <u>of whom</u> became . . .

C Pair work

- **Preview and do the task** Books closed. Read the instructions aloud. Have Ss complete the task. Books open. Ss check to find which details they forgot.

3 Listening and speaking

A 🔊 CD2, Track 22

- **Preview the task** Read the instructions aloud. Ask, "What is a *promotion*?" [an activity or special offer that is supposed to increase sales] Have Ss look at the list of goods and services and the list of promotions. Check that Ss understand the vocabulary.
- **Play the recording** Audio script pp. T-274–T-275 Ss listen and match. Have Ss compare answers with a partner.
- **Play the recording again** Ss listen and check their answers. Check answers with the class.

Answers

1. b; 2. a; 3. c; 4. e

B 🔊 CD2, Track 23

- **Preview the task** Read the instructions aloud. Remind Ss not to write full sentences.
- **Play the recording** Audio script pp. T-274–T-275 Ss listen and write. Replay if necessary. Check answers.

Answers

1. Most people forget to send the rebate receipts in, so they don't benefit from the discount. Or they send the receipts in too late.
2. People spend a lot on appetizers and desserts, so they don't really end up saving money.
3. People buy clothes because they are on sale, but then don't like them and never wear them.
4. People end up giving a tip because they feel guilty about getting something for free.

About you

C Pair work

- **Preview and do the task** Have Ss discuss the questions.

Speaking naturally

- Tell Ss to turn to Speaking naturally on p. 140. (For more information, see Language notes at the beginning of this unit. See the teaching notes on p. T-140.)

② Grammar Adding and modifying information

Figure it out

A **How does the writer of the case study express the ideas below? Rewrite each pair of sentences as one sentence. Then read the grammar chart.**

1. The emergence of the Internet provided a new opportunity to coupon businesses. Many of these coupon businesses have been very successful.
2. The company also had more than 55,000 merchants. Deals were sought from these merchants.

Pronouns and prepositions in relative clauses

Grammar extra
See page 154.

You can add pronouns + *of*, e.g., *all of, some of, most of, many of*, etc., or prepositions to relative clauses. Use *whom* for people and *which* for things.

*In three years, the company had more than 85 million customers, **all of whom** "opt in" to the site.*
*The Internet provided a new opportunity to coupon businesses, **many of which** have been successful.*
*Over 90 percent of companies, **most of which** are small businesses, said the promotion attracted customers.*
*Mason had an idea: Attract subscribers **to whom** you email special deals.*
*Shoppers clip coupons from newspapers, **with which** they can save money.*

Conversation vs. Writing

Relative clauses with pronoun + *of whom / of which* are approximately 10 times more common in academic writing than in conversation.

B **Complete the relative clauses from another case study.**

1. An entrepreneur needed capital with which_____ he was hoping to start his own business.
2. He'd had several ideas, some _____ had potential, but they needed a lot of capital up front.
3. He applied for loans to several banks, all _____ turned down his applications.
4. The friends to _____ he turned for financial help were unable to lend him any money.
5. He talked to several advisors, most _____ advised him not to borrow without a business plan.
6. He finally decided to start a business for _____ he needed very little money – auto detailing. There were several places in his area, most _____ charged very high prices.
7. He sent out flyers for an introductory special offer, to _____ over 100 people replied.
8. Within three weeks, he had serviced cars for 40 customers, many _____ became regular clients.

C Pair work **Take turns retelling details from Exercise B. How much can you remember?**

③ Listening and speaking Too good to be true?

A ◀))CD 2.22 **Listen to four consumer experts talk about special promotions. Draw lines to match the goods with the promotions they talk about. There is one extra promotion.**

Goods or services
1. electronics
2. restaurants
3. clothes
4. neck massage

Promotions
a. "buy one, get one free"
b. a mail-in rebate promotion
c. "buy one, get one for 50% off"
d. kids eat free
e. try it for free

B ◀))CD 2.23 **Listen again. What problems does each expert mention? Take notes.**

About you

C Pair work **Which of the promotions in Exercise A do you think work best? Why? Which promotions have you used? What did you buy?**

Speaking naturally
See page 140.

Lesson B *Bringing in the customers*

1 Vocabulary in context

A How many ways do you shop? What's your favorite way to shop? Take a class vote.

online from a major retailer   online from smaller companies   online at auction sites
in store from a superstore   in store from locally owned stores   other ways?

B ◀))) CD 2.24 **Listen to the podcast. What changes in retail does the speaker predict?**

PODCAST   LISTEN   READ   WATCH   Share

STATIONS

ABOUT

SUPPORT

LOG IN

SIGN UP

How do you **lure** people into a retail store? Lower prices will **tempt** some people, and some will be **attracted** by special offers, but others know they can probably get what they want cheaper online. In most developed economies, online shopping has grown steadily by about 20 percent a year, while in-store shopping has more or less remained stagnant. To compete, retail stores need to find other ways to **persuade** customers to leave their computers, and **convince** them that there's a better shopping experience in store.

But **coaxing** people to come in and buy is not so easy. Some retailers have found that an effective way of **wooing** customers is to create a store that combines conventional décor and layout with high-tech facilities. Such an environment may look very traditional but also offers facilities like self-service checkouts. Another store might have terminals with self-service ordering for home delivery. Yet another might **entice** customers by creating a social space – a so-called "third place" between work and home – where people can enjoy coffee or read in a relaxed setting without feeling **pressured into** buying things they don't need. Any store that makes people feel at ease will probably generate more business. No store wants to **scare** people **off** or **discourage** them from buying products by creating a cold, unfriendly atmosphere. Some evidence points to the fact that in-store music relaxes customers. Other evidence suggests it can actually irritate people. Equally, no store wants to be so overwhelming that it **puts** people **off** or even **alienates** them. There's a fine balance between **deterring** customers and **drawing** them **in**.

The atmosphere needs to **appeal** to *you*, be like your *home* – not some other unfamiliar place. And since most people don't live in homes the size of aircraft hangars, a store with a small footprint will be less likely to **intimidate.** The superstores of the late twentieth century may well have had their day. Such places were good for browsing a vast range of goods, but we can now browse the whole shopping world online. So in retail, small may prove to be beautiful after all.

Word sort

C **Make a chart of verbs in the podcast for attracting people and deterring them. Then use at least six new verbs to tell a partner what attracts you to stores and what deters you.**

Attract	Deter
lure	

Vocabulary notebook

See page 71.

Lesson B *Bringing in the customers*

1 Vocabulary in context

- **Set the scene** Books closed. Say, "The title of Lesson B is *Bringing in the customers*. In Lesson A we talked about various kinds of promotions that businesses use to attract customers. Can you think of other ways that stores do this?" Have Ss call out their ideas (e.g., *hire people who know the merchandise, have attractive displays*).

A • **Preview the task** Books open. Read the instructions aloud. Ask a S to read the different ways of shopping aloud. Check that Ss understand each way to shop.

- Assign a S to record numbers on the board. Using a show of hands, Ss say which way they shop. Ask, "What's your favorite way to shop?" Again, using a show of hands, Ss vote for their favorite way.

- Call on Ss to tell the class their favorite way to shop. Ask Ss to say why. Have other Ss call out advantages of each way of shopping, and possible disadvantages.

B ◀)) CD2, Track 24

- **Preview the task** Read the instructions aloud. Say, "Write brief notes to answer the question."

- **Play the recording** Books closed. Ss listen and write. Replay the recording. Ss add to their notes and compare their answers with a classmate.

- **Play the recording again** Books open. Ss listen, read along, and check their notes. Check the answer with the class. [The speaker predicts that the superstores of the late twentieth century will be replaced by smaller stores.]

Word sort

C • **Preview the task** Say, "Make a chart of verbs in the podcast for attracting people and deterring them." Make sure that Ss understand the verb *deter*. [to make someone less likely to do something] Say, "Use the context to help you."

- **Do the task** Do an example with the class. Say, "Find *lure* in the first paragraph. Which column does it belong in?" [attract] "Why?" [The sentence is about bringing people *into* a store.] Have Ss complete the chart and compare their answers with a partner. Check answers with the class.

Answers

Attract

lure	woo
tempt	entice
be attracted by	be pressured into
persuade	draw in
convince	appeal
coax	

Deter

scare off	alienate
discourage	deter
put off	intimidate

Extra activity – groups

Group members review the verbs in the chart. Ss ask each other for any help they need with definitions. Ss provide definitions they know. Ss check their dictionaries for remaining vocabulary.

Extra activity – pairs

Have Ss take turns making sentences about stores they know using each of the words in the chart.

Tell Ss to turn to Vocabulary Notebook on p. 71 of their Student's Books. Have Ss do the tasks in class or assign them for homework. (See the teaching notes on p. T-71.)

2 Grammar

A ⬇ www.cambridge.org/viewpoint/audio

- **Preview the task** Say, "Find words in the podcast to replace the ideas in bold. There may be more than one correct answer." Do the first sentence with the class: Ask a S to read sentence 1 aloud. Say, "Find a similar sentence in the podcast and make the changes to sentence 1. Have a S read the new sentence aloud. [Cheaper prices will attract **some** people, and **some / others** will find special offers appealing.]

- **Do the task** Have Ss complete the task and compare their answers with a partner. Check answers with the class. Ask individual Ss each to read a sentence aloud.

Answers

1. Cheaper prices will attract <u>some</u> people, and <u>some / others</u> will find special offers appealing.
2. <u>Any</u> store that creates a good atmosphere will do well.
3. Lowering prices is one way to attract customers, but stores need to find <u>other / some other</u> ways, too.
4. One store might have nice music. <u>Another</u> might have a restaurant.

- **Focus on the use** Ask, "What words did you find in the podcast to replace the ideas in bold?" [*some, any, other, others, some other*, and *another*]

- **Present the grammar chart** Read the information aloud. If desired, play the downloadable recording.

- **Understand the grammar chart** Say, "The chart teaches some new meanings of common determiners and pronouns."

- Say, "Look at the top section of the chart. The 'strong' or stressed form of *some* before a noun or as a pronoun can mean 'certain' or 'some but not all.' It suggests a contrast with other people or things." Have Ss read the first example aloud and make sure they say some as /sʌm/, not /səm/.

- Say, "The 'strong' or stressed form of *any* is typically used before a singular countable or an uncountable noun and means 'any person or thing.'"

- Have Ss read the second example aloud, stressing *any*.

- Ask Ss to look at the middle section of the chart. Say, "*Other* can be used before a plural or uncountable noun. It can be used after the definite article (*the*), possessives (*your, his*, etc.), quantifiers (*some, a few,* etc.) and demonstratives (*this, those*, etc.) to refer to additional, extra, or different people or things. *Others* is a pronoun. It cannot be used before a noun." Ask, "How can you write the last example without *others*?" [other people]

- Have Ss look at the bottom section of the chart. Say, "*Another* can be used before a singular count noun. In this case, it means 'one more' or 'a different one.' *Another* can be used alone as a pronoun to replace a singular count noun." Have a S read the examples.

- **Present *Common errors*** Read the information aloud. (For more information, see Language notes at the beginning of the unit. For more work on determiners and pronouns, go to Grammar extra, p. 155.)

B
- **Preview the task** Say, "Complete the sentences with *some, any, other, others, some other,* or *another*. There may be more than one answer." Point out "24/7" in sentence 1 and "limited selection" in sentence 4. Ask Ss if they know what they mean. [*24/7*: 24 hours a day, 7 days a week (never closed); *limited selection*: small number of choices] Tell Ss that "24/7" is said "twenty-four seven."

- **Do the task** Have Ss complete the task and then compare answers with a partner. Check answers with the class.

Answers

1. <u>Some</u> retailers are staying open 24/7 to . . .
2. <u>Some</u> retail experts say . . . there are <u>some</u> customers . . . <u>Others / Some</u> want to . . . <u>Any</u> store that . . .
3. One way stores . . . <u>Another</u> way is . . . <u>Some</u> stores . . . cookies that <u>any</u> customer . . . <u>Other / Some</u> stores offer . . .
4. . . . there needs to be <u>some</u> choice. <u>Another</u> suggestion is . . . Once a retailer has <u>any</u> customer . . . don't go to <u>another / some other</u> store.

- Say, "Now discuss in pairs. Would the ideas entice you to shop in store?" Have Ss discuss. Ask several pairs to share their ideas with the class.

3 Viewpoint

Pair work

- **Preview the task** Read the instructions aloud. Have a S read the four questions aloud. Say, "Remember to include *some, any, other, others, some other,* or *another* in your discussions."

- **Present *In conversation*** Read the information aloud. Say, "Remember to use rising intonation." Have Ss discuss the questions. Walk around the class, giving help as needed. When groups have completed the activity, have several pairs share their ideas with the class.

Extra activity – groups

Each group decides on a type of retail business they want to operate in a local mall. Ss decide how they will entice and keep customers.

2 Grammar Referring to people and things

Figure it out

A Find words in the podcast to replace the ideas in bold. There may be more than one correct answer. Then read the grammar chart.

1. Cheaper prices will attract **certain** people, and **certain people** will find special offers appealing.
2. **Every (and it doesn't matter which)** store that creates a good atmosphere will do well.
3. Lowering prices is one way to attract customers, but stores need to find **additional** ways, too.
4. One store might have nice music. **A different store** might have a restaurant.

Grammar extra
See page 155.

some, any, other, others, another

Some and *any* have "strong" forms. You can use the strong form of *some* to talk about "certain but not all" people or things. The strong form of *any* means "it doesn't matter which."
Lower prices will tempt **some people**, and **some** will be attracted by special offers.
Any store that makes people feel at ease will probably generate more business.

Use *other* before a plural or uncountable noun, after *the, your, this, some,* etc.
Stores need to find **other** ways to attract customers.
Other evidence suggests music can actually irritate people.
It needs to be like your home, not **some other** unfamiliar place.

Common errors

Don't use *another* with a plural noun.
*Retail stores need to find **other ways** to attract customers.* (NOT ~~another ways~~)

Others is a pronoun. Don't use it before a noun.
. . . but **others** know they can probably get what they want cheaper online. (OR **other people**)

Use *another* before a singular count noun or as a pronoun to replace a singular count noun.
Another store might offer self-service ordering. Yet **another** might create a "third place."

B Complete the sentences with *some, any, other, others, some other,* and *another.* There may be more than one answer. Then discuss the ideas in pairs. Would they entice you to shop in store?

1. _____ retailers are staying open 24/7 to draw customers in to compete with online stores.
2. _____ retail experts say stores need to attract customers by becoming "idea centers." For example, there are _____ customers who want to see kitchen appliances in a kitchen layout. _____ want to touch products before buying. _____ store that doesn't create an experience may not last.
3. One way stores can compete is to give excellent customer service. _____ way is for stores to provide services you *can't* get online. _____ stores entice people with home-baked cookies that _____ customer can take. _____ stores offer special deals only to in-store customers.
4. There are so many choices for consumers online. Stores could offer a limited selection, but there needs to be _____ choice. _____ suggestion is for retailers to offer shopping advice. Once a retailer has _____ customer in the store, it needs to keep them so they don't go to _____ store.

3 Viewpoint *Online or in store?*

Pair work Discuss the questions.

- What are the advantages of shopping online? Are there any disadvantages?
- In what other ways can regular stores compete with online stores?
- What kinds of services do you think shoppers will demand in the future?
- What other changes do you think there will be in the retail business?

In conversation . . .

You can ask *You know what I mean?* to check that others agree with or understand you.

Lesson C *Don't you think . . . ?*

1 Conversation strategy Persuading

A Do people you know ever boycott, or refuse to patronize a company on principle? Is corporate social responsibility, the idea that companies should be charitable, popular?

B 🔊 CD 2.25 **Listen. What is "buycotting"? Do Erkan and Dion agree that it works?**

Erkan	Have you heard that expression "to buycott"?
Dion	Not sure. What is it?
Erkan	It's when you buy a company's products because you support its corporate policies. Like if they support a cause you believe in or if they do business ethically. It's like the opposite of *boycott*.
Dion	Oh, right. Does it work? I mean, consumers don't have that much influence, do they?
Erkan	But don't you think companies *should* listen to their customers?
Dion	Well, to some extent, maybe.
Erkan	I think people want businesses to give something back to the community and to have ethical practices. It makes sense for any corporation to do that, doesn't it?
Dion	Well, granted the notion of corporate social responsibility is very popular. It's fine in theory. In practice it's more complex than that, isn't it? And in any event, don't companies only do what's good for their bottom line?

C **Notice** how Erkan and Dion use negative questions and tag questions to persuade each other that their opinions are right. Find examples in the conversation.

> *Don't you think companies* should *listen to their customers?*
> *It makes sense for any corporation, doesn't it?*

D **Read more excerpts from the conversation. Rewrite each first question as a negative question, and add a tag question to each response. Then practice with a partner.**

1. *Erkan* But do you believe corporate social responsibility is a good thing?
   Dion Yes. But it's not what drives a company, _____ ?

2. *Dion* And is a company's responsibility to its shareholders, rather than doing good?
   Erkan Well, it's not just a case of either-or. Any business can do both, _____ ?

3. *Erkan* Do workers feel better when their company stands for something they believe in?
   Dion Perhaps. But many companies are just struggling to survive, _____?

4. *Dion* Are companies having a hard time as it is, without moral pressure from interest groups?
   Erkan Well, it depends. They should still do business ethically, _____?

About you **E** **Pair work** **Do you agree with any of the opinions in the conversation and Exercise D? Discuss the ideas. Use negative and tag questions to persuade your partner.**

A *Don't you believe corporate social responsibility is a good thing? I mean, I do.*
B *Actually, I do, too. More companies should do business ethically, shouldn't they?*

Lesson C *Don't you think . . . ?*

❶ Conversation strategy

Persuading

In conversation, people often use a negative question (e.g., *Doesn't it make sense for a corporation to help?*) when they want or expect another person to agree. In the same way, tag questions (e.g., *It makes sense for a corporation to help, doesn't it?*) strongly suggest that the other person should agree. Negative questions and tag questions can both be used to try to persuade others.

(For more information, see Language notes at the beginning of this unit.)

- **Set the scene** Books closed. Ask, "Do you think big companies have a responsibility to help society, or is there only responsibility to their employees and their investors?" Elicit opinions from the class.

A • **Preview and do the task** Write *boycott* on the board. Ask, "Do people ever boycott companies, that is, not buy their goods and services on principle?" Elicit answers from the class. If any Ss answer *yes*, have them give an example.

- Ask, "What does it mean for a company to give back to the community?" [to use some of their profits to help or benefit the community] Ask, "Is corporate social responsibility – the idea that companies are ethical or give back to their communities – popular?" Elicit answers from the class. If any Ss answer *yes*, have them give an example of a socially responsible corporation.

B 🔊 **CD2, Track 25**

- **Preview the task** Write *complex* and *ethical practices* on the board. Tell Ss they will hear these words in the conversation. Check that Ss know the meanings. [*complex*: complicated; *ethical practices*: doing things in a morally correct way]

- Write *buycott* on the board. Read the instructions aloud. Say, "Write brief answers."

- **Play the recording** Write on the board:

  Erkan

  Dion

  Say, "These are the names of the two speakers. Erkan speaks first." Ss listen only. Replay the recording. Ss listen and write. Have Ss compare their answers in pairs.

- **Play the recording again** Books open. Ss listen, read along, and check their answers. Check the answer with the class. [*Buycotting*: buying a company's product because you support its corporate policies. Erkan thinks it makes sense for corporations to give back to the community and to have ethical practices. Dion thinks it's a good theory, but it's more complex in practice, and companies only do what's good for their bottom line.]

C • **Present *Notice*** Read the information and the examples aloud.

- Say, "Read the conversation again. Find the examples." Have a S read them aloud. [*Dion*: I mean, consumers don't have that much influence, do they? *Erkan*: But don't you think companies *should* listen to their customers? . . . It makes sense for any corporation, doesn't it? *Dion*: In practice it's more complex than that, isn't it? And in any event, don't companies only do what's good for their bottom line?]

- **Practice** Tell Ss to practice the conversation in pairs, taking turns playing each role.

D • **Preview the task** Briefly review the forms of negative and tag questions, if necessary. Say, "Read more excerpts from Dion and Erkan's conversation. Rewrite each first question as a negative question, and add a tag question to each response."

- **Do the task** Have Ss complete the task. Check answers with the class

Answers

1. *Erkan* But don't you believe . . . ?
   Dion Yes. But . . . , is it?
2. *Dion* And isn't a company's . . . ?
   Erkan . . . do both, can't it?
3. *Erkan* Don't workers . . . ?
   Dion Perhaps . . . to survive, aren't they?
4. *Dion* Aren't companies . . . ?
   Erkan . . . ethically, shouldn't they?

- Have Ss practice the excerpts with a partner.

About you

E **Pair work**

- **Preview and do the task** Read the instructions aloud. Ask a pair of Ss to read the example aloud. Walk around the class and help as needed.

- **Follow-up** Have several pairs share their opinions with the class.

Extra activity – pairs

Ss discuss the following argument: Every company should be required to give 10 percent of its profits to a charitable organization or give back to the community in some way. Do you agree? How about for individuals? Have Ss discuss and then prepare a short, 30-second conversation illustrating their ideas. Ss present their conversations to another pair or to the class.

2 Strategy plus

Why use *granted*?

When debating a topic with someone, a speaker can use *granted* to acknowledge that another person has made a good point. It sometimes suggests that no matter how good the point is, it's not enough to change the speaker's opinion.

(For more information, see Language notes at the beginning of this unit.)

🔊 CD2, Track 26

- **Present Strategy plus** Read aloud or play the recording of the information and example. Ss listen and read along.

- Tell Ss to read Erkan and Dion's conversation on page 66 again and find the example. Ask, "What good point is Dion recognizing?" [the notion that social responsibility is very popular]

- **Present In conversation** Read the information aloud. Say, "You'll see examples in the responses in Exercise 2A."

A 🔊 CD2, Track 27

- **Preview the task** Say, "Match the statements with the responses. Write the letters *a* to *e*. When you

finish, we'll listen and check." Tell Ss to read the five statements and the five responses. Check for any vocabulary questions. Have classmates help with any definitions or examples they know. Provide other definitions as needed.

- **Do the task** Have Ss complete the task and compare their answers with a partner.

- **Play the recording** Ss listen check their answers.

Answers

1. d; 2. c; 3. e; 4. b; 5. a

About you

B Pair work

- **Preview and do the task** Read the instructions aloud. Check that Ss understand the meaning of *controversial*. Have Ss discuss the questions.

- **Follow-up** Have several pairs say which statements they found controversial and why.

3 Strategies

About you

A • **Preview the task** Read the instructions aloud. Have Ss read the conversations. Check for vocabulary problems.

- **Do the task** Have Ss complete the task. Walk around the class and help as needed.

- Check answers with the class. Remind Ss that there will be different answers. Have several Ss read their B responses.

Possible answers

There are many different answers as each A statement can be a negative or tag question (see #1 as an example). The negative questions could also begin Don't you think / believe that . . . ?

1. A Isn't it better to support small, local businesses? / It's better to support small, local businesses, isn't it? / Shouldn't we all support our neighborhood stores? / We should all support our neighborhood stores, shouldn't we?
   B Well, yeah, granted it's nice to buy things at small stores and everything. But sometimes they don't have as much choice as bigger stores.
2. A Don't big companies typically employ a lot of people? That's a good thing, isn't it?
   B Yeah, I guess. I mean, granted they do provide a lot of jobs, but they don't always pay very well.
3. A The trouble with those big-box stores, you know, the huge superstores, is that they've driven out small business owners, haven't they?
   B Well, granted that can happen. But competition is a good thing. It keeps prices down.

4. A Don't small clothing stores tend to give you better personal service? I mean, they have more time for you, don't they?
   B Well, it's true, granted. But some of the big companies give really good customer service, too.
5. A Isn't the biggest advantage of small stores, like small shoe stores, that you can find things that are different? You can also usually find better-quality things, can't you?
   B Well, granted the quality of the products is usually good at small stores. But you pay for it. I can't always afford to shop at small exclusive stores.

B Pair work

- **Preview and do the task** Read the instructions aloud. Ask a pair of Ss to read the example. Remind Ss to use negative and tag questions and *granted*.

- **Follow-up** Have a few pairs present their debate to the class. (Note: If using the Extra activity below, have several pairs present. Tell the class to take brief notes on the debates.)

Extra activity – class / groups

After listening to the debating pairs, groups use their notes to decide whether big or small businesses have the advantage using reasons from the debates.

Finally, the class votes to decide which one has the advantage.

❷ Strategy plus *Granted*

🔊 CD 2.26 You can use *granted* when someone makes a point that is good, but it doesn't change your opinion.

> Well, **granted** the notion is very popular . . .

In conversation . . .

Granted often comes near the beginning of what people say, but it can also come in other places.

A 🔊 CD 2.27 **Match the statements with the responses. Write the letters a–e. Then listen and check.**

1. Don't you think companies often forget that it's their employees that make them successful? _____
2. Manufacturers need to make sure that they're environmentally friendly, don't you think? _____
3. Doesn't the research show that people prefer to buy from socially responsible businesses? _____
4. Don't you believe companies should give a percentage of their profits to charity? _____
5. It's interesting to see the gender and racial balance of people on a company's website. _____

    a. They can tell you a lot, granted, but it doesn't mean that they reflect who the company actually employs.
    b. Well, granted it's nice to give something back to the community. But you can't make it law, can you?
    c. Well, they should, granted. But there's the cost, isn't there? The cost of going green can be prohibitive.
    d. People should come first. Granted. But it's often the staff that gets laid off when times are tough.
    e. Um, they might *say* that, granted, but when it comes down to it, they probably buy what's cheap.

About you   **B**   Pair work   **Discuss the statements above. Do you think any are particularly controversial?**

❸ Strategies Big business vs. small business

About you   **A**   **Rewrite the conversations below. Write A's comments using a negative question or a tag question. Add *granted* to B's responses and then complete the idea.**

1. *A* It's better to support small, local businesses. We should all support our neighborhood stores.
   B Well, yeah, it's nice to buy things at small stores and everything. But . . .
2. *A* Big companies typically employ a lot of people. That's a good thing.
   B Yeah, I guess. I mean, they *do* provide a lot of jobs, but . . .
3. *A* The trouble with those big-box stores, you know, the huge superstores, is that they've driven out small-business owners.
   B Well, that can happen. But . . .
4. *A* Small clothing stores tend to give you better personal service. I mean, they have more time for you.
   B Well, it's true. But . . .
5. *A* The biggest advantage of small stores, like small shoe stores, is you can find things that are different. You can also usually find better-quality things.
   B Well, the quality of the products is usually good at small stores. But . . .

THE PROBLEM WITH MY SMALL BUSINESS IS IT KEEPS GETTING BIGGER AND BIGGER.

Lemonade 10¢

B   Pair work   **What are the advantages of big businesses versus small businesses? Prepare a debate to present to the class.**

A Don't you think that generally it's better to support small, local businesses?
B Not necessarily. I mean, granted, small business is good for a community, but . . .

Lesson D *Organizational threats*

① Reading

A **Prepare** How might a company "leak" or lose electronic data (information)? Make a list.

B **Read for main ideas** Read the article. How many of your ideas are mentioned? What types of data leakage can you find? What are the reasons for it?

Data leakage – are you protected?

1 Like any company, your business is no doubt one in which technology is widely used. Online banking, sales, networked collaboration, and communication are central to your operation, and your IT professionals carefully safeguard your electronic data. But how secure is that data? You might well have software that protects you from the external threats of hacking and industrial espionage, but are you overlooking another threat that's closer to home?

2 You probably encourage your staff to take work home. With laptops, portable storage devices, and smartphones, it's easy for employees to finish off that report at night or reply to email on the train to work. Thanks to technology, you have a productive workforce that works for you during off hours. However, this means your confidential company data is out "in the open," outside of your premises. It's less secure and is vulnerable to misuse and theft. And you don't need reminding that the loss or leaking of sensitive financial data, strategic plans, and intellectual property could not only cost your company its competitive edge but could ruin it completely.

THE ENEMY WITHIN?

3 Research* commissioned by Cisco® and carried out by InsightExpress in 10 countries estimated that within a two-year period, over 250 million confidential records were either lost or stolen. The research also revealed the extent to which employee behavior, both innocent and malicious, can put company data at risk. While insiders were responsible for 21 percent of electronic crimes – as opposed to 58 percent for outsiders – the companies surveyed estimated that 33 percent of insider crimes were costly or damaging.

REASONS FOR DATA LEAKAGE

4 Yet, even without crime, there are many more mundane reasons for data leakage. The report paints a worrisome picture of employee behaviors, among which is using company computers to access personal email. Even though many employers do not allow this, almost 80 percent of employees do it, over 60 percent of whom do it at least once a day. Unauthorized applications for email, online banking, or shopping can put your computers at risk from theft or viruses from malicious sites.

5 Other common behaviors are when employees knowingly bypass or change security settings to access sites for personal use and also when they fail to use passwords or log off correctly. According to the report, one-third of employees leave their computers on without logging off when they leave their desks, including overnight, and a fifth leave logon information in insecure places, often next to their computers.

6 Remote working also causes problems if employees transfer or copy data from company computers to home computers, to which others may have access and many of which may not have the same level of security. Computers and storage devices can be lost or stolen when used in public, and the practice of discussing sensitive company information in public, where others can overhear, is widespread. Incredibly, 25 percent of employees admit to sharing such information with friends, family, and strangers.

WHAT'S TO BE DONE?

7 The practices described above may not even be considered problematic by employees, many of whom would see their actions as entirely legitimate. Training and insistence upon the observance of security protocol is one way to handle it.

Continued on the next page …

* http://www.cisco.com/en/US/solutions/collateral/ns170/ns896/ ns895/white_paper_c11-499060.html

Lesson D *Organizational threats*

❶ Reading

- **Set the scene** Books closed. Write the title of the lesson on the board. Say, "What do you think this lesson title refers to?" Elicit ideas (e.g., *poor sales, corporate spying / espionage, hackers*).

A Prepare

- **Preview and do the task** Read the instructions aloud. Ask, "In the business and corporate world, what is a 'leak'?" [when confidential company information is made public or somehow stolen by the competition] Have Ss write their lists. Ask Ss to call out their ideas and write them on the board (e.g., *hackers, poor Internet security, viruses, employee theft, employees losing laptops*).

B 🔽 www.cambridge.org/viewpoint/audio
Read for main ideas

- **Preview the task** Books open. Say, "Read through the article once. Don't stop to check your dictionary. Instead, circle or underline any new words."

- After Ss have read the article once, ask them to call out any vocabulary they don't know. Write it on the board. Have classmates give definitions or explanations of words they know. Supply definitions for any remaining vocabulary.

- Say, "Read the article again. How many of your ideas from Exercise A were mentioned? What types of data leakage did you find? What were the reasons for it?" If desired, play the downloadable recording. Ss listen and read along.

- **Do the task** Have Ss complete the task and compare their answers with a partner. Ask Ss to say how many of their ideas were mentioned. Ask, "What types of data leakage did you find?" [theft, viruses, loss of computer / storage device] "What are the reasons for it?" [using company computers for personal uses, bypassing / changing security settings, failing to use passwords, logging off incorrectly or not at all, leaving logon information in insecure locations, transferring data to home computers, discussing sensitive information in public]

Extra activity – groups

Write on the board:

> Which problem had you never considered dangerous before?
>
> Which problem do you think is probably most common in large companies?
>
> Which problem do you think is easiest to solve? most difficult?

Groups discuss the questions and report to the class.

C Understanding inference

- **Preview the task** Read the instructions aloud. Have Ss read each question aloud.
- **Do the task** Have Ss complete the task. Tell Ss to compare their answers in pairs. Then check answers with the class.

Answers

1. It's written for business owners to alert them to the issue of data security and how important information may be leaking from their companies.
2. " . . . another threat that's closer to home" means a threat in the company, not an external threat.
3. Sixty percent of employees log onto their personal email every day from a work computer.

2 Focus on vocabulary

A
- **Preview and do the task** Say, "This exercise focuses on adjectives. Learning more ways to express ideas will improve both your reading and writing skills."
- Read the instructions aloud. Have Ss complete the task and compare answers. Check answers.

Answers

1. g; 2. f; 3. a; 4. b; 5. c; 6. e; 7. d

About you

B Pair work
- **Preview and do the task** Read the instructions aloud. Have Ss rephrase the questions and compare their questions with a partner.

3 Listening and speaking

A ◀)) CD2, Track 28
- **Preview the task** Say, "Look at these threats to organizations." Check for vocabulary questions.
- Say, "Guess the top five threats companies fear." Have Ss call out their guesses.
- Read the instructions aloud.
- **Play the recording** Audio script p. T-275 Ss listen and number the threats 1 to 5. Replay the recording. Ss listen and review. Check answers with the class.

Answers

1 unplanned IT and telecom outages
2 loss or theft of confidential information
3 malicious software and other cyber attacks
4 adverse weather
5 interruption to utility supplies

- Have Ss call out how many of their guesses they got right. Ask Ss if any of the answers surprised them.

B ◀)) CD2, Track 29
- **Preview the task** Read the instructions. Have Ss think of ways the threats may impact a business.

4. The writer points out that insider crime may be less common than external crime, but is still damaging.
5. The writer finds it hard to believe that so many employees share information outside the company.
6. They don't see it as a problem.

- Ask, "What other solutions do you think the writer might suggest in paragraph 7?" Have Ss call out their ideas.

About you

D React
- **Preview and do the task** Read the instructions aloud. Have a class discussion to answer the questions.

Answers

What are <u>legitimate</u> uses of an employer's computer? What's not <u>legitimate</u>?
How <u>widespread</u> do you think hacking is these days?
Are you personally <u>vulnerable</u> to attack by <u>malicious</u> software?
How do you keep your private information <u>secure</u>, especially online?
Do you ever feel that really <u>confidential</u> information about you is <u>insecure</u> online?

- Say, "Now discuss the questions with a partner."

- **Play the recording** Audio script p. T-275 Ss listen and make notes. Have Ss compare their notes.
- **Play the recording again** Ss check their notes.

Answers

1. Unplanned IT and telecom outages impact business because companies are so dependent on their computer systems that they can't do business without them.
2. The loss or theft of confidential information impacts business because, for example, a company's plans for a new product can be stolen, or crucial original information can be lost forever.
3. Malicious software or cyber attacks impact business because companies can lose hundreds of working hours trying to get the systems fixed.
4. Adverse weather can cause damage to data or physical products like the goods stored in warehouses.
5. Interruption to utility supplies – gas, water, electricity – can close down businesses because they rely on these utilities to operate; no power, no business.

C Pair work
- **Preview and do the task** Read the instructions aloud. Have Ss discuss the questions.
- **Follow-up** Have pairs share their ideas with the class.

C Understanding inference **Answer the questions about the article. Then compare with a partner.**

1. Who is the article written for? What is it trying to do? Why does the title ask that question?
2. What does the writer mean by ". . . another threat that's closer to home"?
3. What do 60 percent of employees do every day?
4. What point is the writer trying to make by quoting the percentages of insider crime?
5. What does the writer think about employees sharing information outside the company?
6. Why might employees think their use of a company computer is "legitimate"?

About you **D** React **What did you read in the article that surprised you about data leakage? Will the information make you change any of your behaviors in the future?**

② Focus on vocabulary Adjectives

A **Find the words below in the article. Can you figure out their meanings? Then match them to the words in the second column with a similar meaning. Write the letters a–g.**

1. secure (para. 1) and insecure (para. 5) _____
2. confidential and sensitive (para. 2) _____
3. vulnerable (para. 2) _____
4. malicious (para. 3) _____
5. mundane (para. 4) _____
6. widespread (para. 6) _____
7. legitimate (para. 7) _____

a. open to attack
b. harmful
c. everyday, unexciting
d. acceptable
e. common, affecting many people or places
f. private and not to be discussed openly
g. safe and unsafe

About you **B** Pair work **Use the adjectives above to rephrase the questions. Then discuss with a partner.**

• What are acceptable uses of an employer's computer? What's not acceptable?
• How common do you think hacking is these days?
• Are you personally open to attack by harmful software?
• How do you keep your private information safe, especially online?
• Do you ever feel that really private information about you is unsafe online?

③ Listening and speaking The top threats

A ◀)) CD 2.28 **Look at these threats to organizations. Guess the top five threats companies fear. Then listen to an interview and check your guesses. Number the threats 1–5.**

☐ unplanned IT and telecom outages
☐ industrial disputes
☐ malicious software and other cyber attacks
☐ interruption to utility supplies

☐ adverse weather
☐ loss of personnel talent
☐ loss or theft of confidential information
☐ new laws or regulations

B ◀)) CD 2.29 **Listen again. In what specific way can each threat impact a business? Write notes on a separate piece of paper.**

C Pair work **How could the other threats described in Exercise A disrupt business? What other threats might organizations face?**

Writing *It can occur in any company.*

- write about causes of and solutions to a problem.
- use modals to avoid being too assertive.
- avoid errors with *can* and *could*.

Task Write a report on data security.
Write a report for your boss, describing the possible causes of data leakage. Propose some potential solutions in your workplace.

A **Look at a model** Brainstorm some ideas about the causes of and solutions to data leakage for a report. Then look at the extracts from a report below. Does it include any of your ideas?

Leakage of sensitive data is a serious problem, which can occur in any company for a number of reasons. One reason may be the fact that employees take work outside of the office on portable devices. Some of these devices might be shared with other people or may not be as secure as company computers. Second, employees can access their personal email and other websites from work computers and they may fail to observe security procedures when doing so. This could allow malicious software to attack company servers. Another cause of data leakage is thought to be . . .

All of the above factors can cause data leakage, which could potentially damage the company's profits and image. To prevent data leakage, a number of security measures should be employed, many of which are simple to implement.
1. As a company, we need to control what data leaves the building. It would be advisable not to allow employees to take work home.
2. We could also enforce the rules on using private computers.
. . .

B **Focus on language** Read the chart and underline the modal verbs in Exercise A.

Using modal verbs in writing

You can use modals to avoid being too assertive in describing situations.
*These factors **can** cause data leakage.* (= they can and do)
*Some devices **might / may / could** be shared with others.* (it is possible)

You can also use modals to make polite recommendations.
*It **would** be advisable not to allow employees to take work home.*
*We **could** also enforce the rules on using private computers.*

Describing cause

One reason for this might be . . .
A possible cause could be . . .
This may be a result of . . .
It can be caused by . . .

C Rewrite the underlined parts of each sentence below using the modal verbs given.

1. Security is improved if procedures are in place. Data leakage is a result of poor security. (can, may)
2. A possible cause of data leakage is that employees don't realize that they should not discuss work with friends and family. One reason for this is a lack of training. (could, may, might)
3. Data leakage is also caused by employees' use of instant-messaging programs. (might)
4. Certain Internet sites are infected by viruses, so it is advisable to limit access to them. (may, would)
5. Employees' laptops infect company computers, which causes data loss. (might, may)
6. One possible solution is to check employees' devices on a regular basis for malware. (could)

D **Write and check** Write the report on data leakage in the task above. Then check for errors.

Common errors

Do not use *could* for things which in fact do happen.
Employees can access their personal email. = They do this, we know.
(NOT *Employees could access* . . ., except in sentences like this:
Employees could access their email if we allowed it. = It would be possible.)

Writing *It can occur in any company.*

In this lesson

- Ask a S to read the lesson aims (*In this lesson, you . . .*) aloud. Say, "When you write about problems and their causes and solutions, what is the first step?" [Identify the problem and its causes.] Ask, "What do you do next?" [Present solutions to the problem.]

- **Preview the writing** Books closed. Say, "In this lesson, you will plan and write a report on data security." Point out the writing topic in Task and read it aloud. Explain that Ss will end the lesson by writing a report that will practice the three aims presented in this lesson.

A Look at a model

- **Preview and do the task** Say, "Brainstorm some ideas about the causes of and solutions to data leakage for a report. Make a list." Have Ss complete the task. Have Ss call out their ideas and write them on the board. Do not erase.

- Books open. Say, "Now look at the extracts from a report below. Does it include any of your ideas?" Have Ss complete the reading. Call on a few Ss to say if their ideas were mentioned. Check for vocabulary questions in the extracts.

B ⬇ www.cambridge.org/viewpoint/audio
Focus on language

- **Present the grammar for writing chart** Read the information in the chart aloud. If desired, play the downloadable recording. Ss listen and read along.

- **Understand the grammar for writing** Ask, "What does it mean *to be assertive*?" [to be direct and to say what you think in a strong and confident way] Say, "Speaking or writing assertively informs people that you feel confident that your information is correct and true. Being too assertive can make you appear to be bossy, pushy, or aggressive. When writing reports that describe situations, you can use modal verbs that allow you to sound less assertive and more reasonable."

- Write on the board, underlined as shown:

  1. These factors *cause* data leakage.
  2. These factors *can cause* data leakage.
  3. These factors *might / may / could cause* data leakage.

  Say, "Compare the three sentences. Sentence 1 has no modal verb. It is a simple statement of a fact that there is no doubt about. Sentence 2 includes the modal verb *can*. Now the sentence suggests that the factors are known to have caused this, and the probability is strong. In sentence 3, the modal verbs suggest that it is possible, but it is far from 100 percent certain."

- Say, "You can also use modal verbs to make recommendations." Write on the board:

  1. It *would be advisable* not to allow employees to take work home.

  2. We *could* also enforce the rules on using private computers.

  Say, "In sentence 1, *It would be advisable* is less direct than *It is advisable*. In sentence 2, using *could* suggests that the recommendation is a possibility."

- **Present *Describing cause*** Say, "Here are some ways of describing causes. The expressions contain modal verbs so that the writer is not too assertive."

- **Preview and do the task** Read the instructions aloud. Have Ss complete the task. Check answers with the class.

Answers

Leakage . . . which <u>can</u> occur . . . One reason <u>may</u> be the fact . . . Some . . . <u>might</u> be shared . . . or <u>may</u> not . . . Second, employees <u>can</u> access . . . they <u>may</u> fail . . . This <u>could</u> allow . . .
All . . . <u>can</u> cause . . . which <u>could</u> potentially . . . To prevent data leakage, a number of security measures <u>should</u> be . . .
1. . . . It <u>would</u> be advisable . . .
2. We <u>could</u> also enforce . . .

C
- **Preview and do the task** Read the instructions aloud. Have Ss complete the task. Check answers with the class.

Answers

1. Security <u>can be</u> improved . . . Data leakage <u>may be</u> a result . . .
2. . . . leakage <u>could be</u> that employees <u>may not realize</u> that . . . One reason for this <u>might be</u> . . .
3. Data leakage <u>might</u> also <u>be</u> caused . . .
4. . . . sites <u>may be</u> infected . . . , so it <u>would be</u> advisable . . .
5. . . . laptops <u>might infect</u> company computers, which <u>may cause</u> . . .
6. One possible solution <u>could be</u> to check . . .

D Write and check

- **Preview the task** Read the instructions aloud.
- **Present *Common errors*** Read the information aloud.
- **Do the task** Have Ss complete the task.

Extra activity – class

Ss leave their reports on their desk for classmates to read. Ss go around the class reading each other's work. Ss note two problem causes and their solutions to report to the class.

Vocabulary notebook *It's tempting.*

If done for homework

Briefly present the Learning tip and the task directions. Make sure Ss understand what they need to do.

If done in class

- **Present *Learning tip*** Read the information aloud. Say, "A chart like this is extremely useful because of the different suffixes English uses in its word families." Tell Ss to look at the example with the word family for *tempt*. Ask a S to read the three forms aloud. Say, "Notice the column for *Mostly as verb*. It contains the word *coax*. Some words either only have a verb form or are mostly used as verbs."

A • **Preview and do the task** Read the instructions aloud. Say, "The gray area in the chart should be left blank." Have Ss complete the task and compare their charts with a partner. Check answers with the class.

Answers

Verb	Noun	Adjective
convince	conviction (= a belief)	convincing
deter	deterrent / deterrence	—
discourage	discouragement	discouraging / discouraged
persuade	persuasion	persuasive
pressure	pressure	pressured

Mostly used as verbs:
put off
scare off
woo

B • **Preview and do the task** Read the instructions aloud. Say "Use you dictionary if you need help." Have Ss complete the task and compare their charts with a partner. Check answers with the class.

Answers

Verb	Noun	Adjective
alienate	alienation	alienated
appeal	appeal	appealing
attract	attraction	attractive
entice	enticement	enticing
intimidate	intimidation	intimidating / intimidated

Mostly used as verbs:
coax
draw in
lure

C **Word builder**

- **Preview and do the task** Read the instructions aloud. Remind Ss to use a good dictionary or online dictionary.
- Have Ss complete the task. Check the answers with the class.

Answers

attract: induce, prompt, urge
deter: dissuade, unnerve

D **Focus on vocabulary, page 69**

- **Preview and do the task** Read the instructions aloud. Do the first one with the class. Ask, "What nouns do you know with the same meaning as *secure* and *insecure*?" [*security* and *insecurity*] Have Ss complete the chart and compare with a partner. Check answers with the class.

Answers

Adjectives	Nouns	Adverbs
1. secure / insecure	security	securely / insecurely
2. confidential	confidentiality	confidentially
3. sensitive	sensitivity	sensitively / insensitively
4. vulnerable	vulnerability	vulnerably (rare)
5. malicious	malice	maliciously
6. mundane	mundaneness / mundanity (rare)	mundane
7. widespread	—	—
8. legitimate	legitimacy	legitimately / illegitimately

Vocabulary notebook *It's tempting.*

Learning tip   Word families

When you learn a new verb, use a dictionary to help you find other words in the same family. Write them in a chart. *Note*: Some words are only or mostly used as verbs and don't have other forms.

Verb	Noun	Adjective		Mostly as verb
tempt	temptation	tempting		coax

A   Complete the charts with verbs from the podcast on page 64. Then add nouns and adjectives from the same word family to the chart on the left.

Verb	Noun	Adjective(s)	Mostly used as verbs
	conviction (= a belief)		put off
deter			scare off
		discouraging / discouraged	woo
persuade			
	pressure		

B   Make a chart with these verbs.

alienate   appeal   attract   coax   draw in   entice   intimidate   lure

C   Word builder Find the meaning of these verbs. Are they verbs that mean "attract" or verbs that mean "deter"?

dissuade   induce   prompt   unnerve   urge

D   (Focus on vocabulary) Which of the adjectives below have other forms in the same family with the same meaning? What are they? Write them in the chart. Use Exercise 2A on page 69 to help you.

	Adjectives	Nouns	Adverbs
1.	secure / insecure		
2.	confidential		
3.	sensitive		
4.	vulnerable		
5.	malicious		
6.	mundane		
7.	widespread		
8.	legitimate		

Checkpoint 2 *Units 4–6*

1 Breaking records – an ongoing achievement

A Complete the passive verbs, adding the adverbs given. There may be more than one word order. Then replace the words in bold with synonyms, changing *a* to *an* if necessary.

significant

In 1954, Roger Bannister achieved a **big** milestone: he ran a mile in under four minutes. This was something that had _____ (see, previously) as almost impossible, though **a lot of** people had tried. The four-minute barrier has _____ (break, since) numerous times and is now the **normal** time for most medium-distance runners. In fact, records in track are _____ (achieve, still) today, largely thanks to **creative, new** technology. Technology has _____ (use, widely) to enhance performance in the sport. Running shoes are _____ (improve, continually) and are far different from the **basic** rubber-soled shoes of the 1950s, which are now **out of date**. Clothing is much more **useful**, too. Even the **ordinary** T-shirt has _____ (redesign, completely) so that it removes sweat from an athlete's body. In addition, **easy-to-carry** and **small** devices, such as GPS watches, can monitor heart rate, etc., and are now a **necessary** part of tracking a runner's performance. Further advances in sports technology are _____ (make, currently). It's a **continuing** process, and it may only be a matter of time before we see the headline, "The three-minute-mile barrier has _____ (shatter, finally)."

B Pair work Discuss each of the topics below about sports and athletics today. Use *In any case* to make your argument stronger and *In any event* to reach your final conclusion.

- use of performance-enhancing drugs
- high salaries that some athletes receive
- training children from an early age to compete
- use of technology to improve performance

2 They could easily have become extinct.

A Unscramble the underlined verb phrases. Then complete the relative clauses.

1. In the last few years, the tiger <u>been have could wiped off easily</u> the planet by poachers. But the extinction of tigers <u>prevented may been have well</u> by innovative programs, some _____ focus on preserving tiger habitats. How else can we protect endangered species?

2. When some endangered species were first brought into captivity, there were critics, many _____ believed that breeding endangered animals in captivity <u>have not been should permitted</u>. Although some programs <u>failed well might have</u>, many didn't. What is your view on keeping animals in captivity?

3. News reports have detailed specific cases of wild animals attacking their trainers, all _____ suffered severe injuries, which <u>killed have could easily</u> them. Other reports highlight how wild animals, many_____ are losing their habitats, encroach into neighborhoods and are shot. In other cases, animals <u>have been to perform made</u> in jobs and entertainment. What is your response to this treatment of animals? How can people protest, and to_____ should they send their complaints?

B Pair work Discuss the questions above. Use expressions like *Apart from anything else, What's more,* etc., to add and focus on new ideas. Use *granted* if your partner makes a good point that doesn't change your opinion.

"Well, it's important to educate people about tigers in addition to preserving their habitats."

Checkpoint 2 Units 4–6

Tell Ss to look through Viewpoint Checkpoint 2. Ask, "Which tasks look easy to you? Which ones look hard?" Tell Ss to choose a task that they think will be hard for them, go back to the unit where the language is taught, and review it before beginning the Checkpoint. (See Unit and lesson reference in parentheses.)

1 Breaking records – an ongoing achievement

↻ This task recycles adverbs with continuous and perfect forms in the passive. It also recycles formal adjectives for describing new gadgets and technology. During the pair work discussion, Ss review using *In any case* to strengthen an argument and *In any event* to reach a conclusion to an argument.

A (5A Grammar; 5A Vocabulary)

- **Preview and do the task** Read the instructions aloud. Say, "Complete the verbs and add the adverbs first. Then go back and replace the words in bold." Point out that the first adjective has been replaced as an example. Have Ss complete the task and then compare answers in pairs. Check answers with the class.

Answers

Note: These adverbs can also go after the verb phrase.
In 1954, Roger Bannister achieved a significant milestone: . . . This was something that had previously been seen / had been previously seen as almost impossible though countless people had tried. The four-minute barrier has since been broken . . . now

the standard time . . . In fact, records in track are still being achieved today, largely thanks to innovative technology. Technology has been widely used* to enhance . . . Running shoes are continually being improved / are being continually improved and are far different from the rudimentary rubber-soled shoes of the 1950s, which are now obsolete. Clothing is much more functional, too. Even the humble T-shirt has been completely redesigned so that it . . . In addition, portable and compact devices, such as . . . are now an integral part of . . . Further advances in sport technology are currently being made. It's an ongoing process, . . . "The three-minute-mile barrier has finally been shattered."
* *has widely been used is possible, but far less frequent*

B (4C Strategy plus) Pair work

- **Preview the task** Read the instructions aloud. Ask a S to read the four topics aloud. Check that Ss understand what a *performance-enhancing* drug is.
- **Do the task** Ss work in pairs to discuss the topics.
- **Follow-up** For each topic, have a few pairs present their ideas to the class.

2 They could easily have become extinct.

↻ This task recycles passive past modal verb phrases as well as relative clauses beginning with pronouns and prepositions. It also recycles the conversation strategy of using expressions to add and focus on a new idea and *granted* to say that someone's point was good but not opinion changing.

A (5B Grammar; 6A Grammar)

- **Preview the task** Read the instructions aloud. Ask Ss to read section 1. Ask Ss to unscramble the verb phrase in the first sentence. [could easily have been wiped off] Ask Ss to fill in the first blank to complete the relative clause. [of which]
- **Do the task** Have Ss complete the task. Check answers with the class.

Answers

1. . . . the tiger could easily have been wiped off / could have easily been wiped off the planet by poachers. But . . . may well have been prevented by innovative programs, some of which focus on . . .

2. . . . there were critics, many of whom believed that . . . captivity should not have been permitted. Although some programs might well have failed, many didn't. . . .
3. . . . all of whom suffered severe injuries, which could easily have killed / could have easily killed them. Other . . . many of which are losing . . . In other cases, animals have been made to perform in jobs . . . How can people protest, and to whom should . . . ?

B (4C Conversation strategy; 6C Strategy plus) Pair work

- **Preview and do the task** Read the instructions aloud. Have a S read the example aloud. Have Ss complete the task. Walk around the class and help as needed. Listen for the use of the conversation strategies.
- **Follow-up** For each question, have several pairs share their opinion with the class.

Extra activity – individuals / pairs

Individual Ss write four more sentences: two about sports issues and two about animal rights issues. Ss discuss their ideas in pairs. Encourage Ss to use expressions to add and focus on new ideas as they did in Exercise 2B.

3 That's the business!

This task recycles future perfect and future perfect continuous, *some, any, other, others,* and *another* as determiners and pronouns, verbs meaning attract or deter, negative questions and tag questions to persuade, expressions such as *Just think* to make a point.

A (6B Vocabulary)

- **Preview and do the task** Read the instructions aloud. Point out the example words. Remind Ss that some of the verbs are phrasal verbs. Have Ss complete the task. Have Ss read their words to a partner and add to or correct each other's lists.
- Check answers and write the words on the board.

Answers

Woo	*Deterred*
lure	intimidated
tempt	scared off
attract	put off
persuade	alienated
convince	discouraged
coax	
entice	
pressure	
draw in	
appeal to	

B (4A Grammar; 6B Grammar)

Culture note

In the United States, "Black Friday" falls on the last Friday of November. It is the biggest shopping day of the year and the beginning of December holiday shopping.

- **Preview and do the task** Read the instructions aloud. Have Ss complete the task and compare their answers with a partner. Check answers.

Answers

. . . By the time Black Friday <u>arrives</u>, retailers . . . Most stores <u>will have been preparing</u> for the sales for weeks.

4 Surviving it all

This task recycles prepositions, prepositional phrases, and vocabulary for animal behavior.

(4B Grammar; 4A Vocabulary)

- **Preview and do the task** Read the instructions aloud. Tell Ss to read the entire paragraph before they begin. Have Ss complete the task and compare answers with a partner. Check answers with the class.

They <u>will have stocked / will have been stocking</u> their shelves . . . When the doors <u>open,</u> <u>any</u> store that is not ready . . . Stores <u>will have been advertising / will have advertised</u> their deals for days. <u>Some</u> reduce prices . . . <u>Others</u> take up to . . . By the time the doors open, <u>some</u> customers <u>will have been waiting / will have waited</u> in line for several hours. <u>Other</u> shoppers <u>will have been camping out / will have camped out</u> for more than . . . <u>Some</u> stores advertise deals, . . . <u>Another</u> tactic is to sell old goods. <u>Another</u> is to sell products made just for the sale. By the time stores close, they <u>will have served</u> millions of customers. They <u>will have taken in</u> millions . . . customers <u>will have spent</u> more than they intended to.

C (6C, 5C Conversation strategy; 5C Strategy plus)

- **Preview and do the task** Say, "Rewrite each comment in two ways: (1) as a negative question and (2) by adding a tag question." Have Ss rewrite the comments. Check answers with the class.

Answers

1. <u>Don't you think it's crazy / Isn't it crazy</u> to . . . ?
   It's crazy . . . , <u>isn't it?</u>
2. <u>Doesn't it make sense / Don't you think it makes sense</u> for stores . . . ?
   It makes sense . . . , <u>doesn't it?</u>
3. <u>Don't people / Don't you think people</u> buy . . . ?
   People buy . . . , <u>don't they?</u>
4. <u>Aren't sales / Don't you think sales</u> are just . . . ?
   Sales are just . . . , <u>aren't they?</u>

- Read the remaining instructions aloud. Ask a pair of Ss to read the example aloud. Have Ss discuss their answers.
- **Follow-up** Have a class discussion.

Extra activity – pairs

Using verbs to attract and deter from Exercise 3A, pairs prepare a short presentation on a topic connected to "Black Friday" or an equivalent big sale day they know about. Pairs present to the class.

Answers

Bald eagles . . . which may not be <u>in line with</u> most people's expectations. <u>Apart from being</u> the national symbol . . . Northern eagles . . . breeding <u>ground</u> year after year and <u>mate</u> for life. They often build their <u>nests</u> near water <u>on account of</u> the . . . They <u>lay</u> . . . eggs, which <u>hatch</u> . . . The eagles . . . <u>keep</u> the eggs . . . attacked by <u>predators</u> . . . The parents initially <u>raise</u> the young . . . parents stop <u>feeding</u> them and they may go <u>up to</u> several . . . <u>Far from being</u> neglectful, . . . Once out of their nests, . . . fat <u>reserves</u> and . . . can survive . . . Bald eagles don't <u>store</u> food or <u>hibernate</u>, . . . Their presence . . . unwelcome <u>owing to the fact that</u> they . . . <u>colonies.</u>

3 That's the business!

> Stores use smart tactics to **woo** customers. Don't be **deterred**! But be careful.

A Read the headline. Then write as many words as you can to replace *woo* and *deterred*.

attract   intimidate

B Complete the sentences. Use a form of the future perfect of the verbs given, if possible, or the simple present if not. More than one form may be correct. Then add the words from the box.

| another | another | any | other | others | some | some | some |

"Black Friday" is the start of the holiday shopping season. By the time Black Friday _____ (arrive), retailers need to be ready. Most stores _____ (prepare) for the sales for weeks. They _____ (stock) their shelves with goods at low prices. When the doors _____ (open), _____ store that is not ready may end up not making a profit for the whole year. Stores _____ (advertise) their deals for days. _____ reduce prices by 50 percent. _____ take up to 75 percent off. By the time the doors open, _____ customers _____ (wait) in line for several hours. _____ shoppers _____ (camp out) for more than 24 hours to get the best deals. However, not all are genuine. _____ stores advertise deals, but there's only one item at this price. _____ tactic is to sell old goods. _____ is to sell products made just for the sale. By the time stores close, they _____ (serve) millions of customers. They _____ (take in) millions of dollars in revenue, and no doubt some customers _____ (spend) more than they intended to.

C Rewrite each comment in two ways: (1) as a negative question; (2) by adding a tag question. Then discuss the ideas with a partner. Use strong responses and expressions like *Just think* and *Let's put it this way* to make your point.

1. It's crazy to camp out all night until a store opens.
2. It makes sense for stores to offer big discounts.
3. People buy things just because they're on sale.
4. Sales are just a clever marketing tool.

A *Don't you think it's crazy to camp out all night until a store opens?*
B *Oh, absolutely not! Just think: you can get some really great deals.*

4 Surviving it all

Complete the prepositional phrases. Then choose the correct words to complete the article.

Bald eagles are not actually bald, which may not be in _____ with most people's expectations. _____ from being the national symbol of the United States, it is a protected species. Northern eagles migrate but return to the same breeding **ground / young** year after year and **mate / hibernate** for life. They often build their **nests / burrows** near water on _____ of the fact that they feed mostly on fish. They **dig / lay** between one and three eggs, which **mate / hatch** after 35 days. The eagles sit on the nest to **keep / store** the eggs warm and also to prevent them being attacked by **predators / reserves** such as squirrels. The parents initially **hatch / raise** the young in the nest, but once the chicks have feathers, the parents stop **feeding / breeding** them and they may go up _____ several days without eating. Far _____ being neglectful, the parents are simply encouraging the chicks to leave the nest and learn to fly. Once out of their nests, the chicks are fed by the parents to build up their fat **reserves / habits** and are taught to hunt so they can **survive / migrate** the winter months. Bald eagles don't **store / build up** food or **hibernate / breed**, and they often hunt other birds. Their presence in an area can be unwelcome _____ to the fact that they can destroy other birds' **colonies / grounds**.

Unit **7** Relationships

Lesson A *Parenting*

Grammar *Hypothesizing*

(See Student's Book p. 75.)

In this lesson, Ss learn to make conditional sentences without *if*. They are presented here in the context of a podcast on parenting classes.

Form

Conditional sentences without *if* can be made using imperative . . . *and*; inversions with *were, had, should*; and *otherwise*.

- Imperative . . . *and*

  The "condition" clause begins with an imperative. It is followed by a result clause beginning with *and*.

  Ask *any new parent this question,* ***and*** *you'll get the answer, "Absolutely!"* (= *If you ask . . . , you'll . . .*)

- Inversions

  Here, inversion means reversing the normal statement word order of subject + verb to verb + subject.

  Were + subject (+ infinitive)

  Were I *in charge of education, I would make this class mandatory.* (= *If I were in charge of . . .*)

  Were she to have *another baby, she would be better prepared.* (= *If she had / were to have . . .*)

Had + subject + past participle

Had I known *it would be this hard, I would have waited.* (= *If I had known, . . .*)

Should + subject + verb

Should you think *your experience will be any different, think again.* (= *If you thought / should think . . .*)

- Otherwise

  Otherwise is an adverb. It has the meaning, "if not."

  Let's make them mandatory. ***Otherwise****, parents will be unprepared.* (= *If we don't, . . .*)

Use

These structures can introduce a hypothetical idea without using *if*.

> ### ⊙ Corpus information
> #### Writing vs. Conversation
> Inversions are much more common in writing and formal speaking than in conversation.

Grammar extra *More on inversions*

(See Student's Book p. 156.)

Grammar extra reviews, extends, and practices using inversions for hypothesizing.

Lesson B *Questions to ask*

Vocabulary in context *Binomials*

(See Student's Book p. 76.)

The article presents binomials – words in the same part of speech paired together and joined by *and, or,* or *but*. Examples are *stop and think, sooner or later,* and *slowly but surely*. These are presented in the context of an article that discusses issues couples should talk about before marriage.

Vocabulary notebook *Now or never*

(See Student's Book p. 83.)

The Learning tip tells Ss that when they learn a new expression, they should use it in a personalized sentence that will help them remember it. Ss get more practice with the vocabulary from Lesson B.

- **Focus on vocabulary** reviews and practices vocabulary introduced in Lesson D (p. 81).

Grammar *Information focus*

(See Student's Book p. 77.)

This lesson teaches *wh-* clauses as the subject or object of a verb. Here, a *wh-* clause means a clause that starts with a question word (*What, Where,* etc., as well as *How*).

Form

The word order for *wh-* clauses used this way is *wh-* word + statement word order.

- *Wh-* clauses as subjects in questions

  When the sentence is a question, the verb from the main clause and the *wh-* clause are inverted.

  Is ***how you spend money*** *a problem right now?*

- *Wh-* clauses as subjects in statements

  What many couples fail to do *is (to) discuss the important issues.*

  How you resolve differences *can be critical.*

- *Wh-* clauses as objects in statements and questions

  Tell each other now ***whether / if you intend to work long hours.***

  Agree now on ***what your financial goals are.***

  Can you agree ***how often your partner's family can visit*** *without arguing?*

Use

Using a *wh-* clause as the subject gives extra emphasis to it.

Corpus information

In conversation

In conversation, *whether or not* is also used when there is a choice of two options. The parentheses show the possible places *or not* can go. It should not be used twice in this sentence.

Discuss **whether (or not)** *you would both move to another city* **(or not)**.

Grammar extra *More on* **what** *clauses;* **what** *clauses with passive verbs and modals in writing*

(See Student's Book p. 157.)

Grammar extra presents and practices more uses and forms of *what* clauses as the subject or object in sentences.

Speaking naturally *Binomial pairs*

(See Student's Book p. 141.)

In this section, Ss practice saying binomial pairs.

The primary stress is on the second word of the pair and the secondary stress on the first. *And* and *but* are reduced in these binomial expressions.

Lesson C *In the end*

Conversation strategy *Finishing a point*

(See Student's Book p. 78.)

Speakers sometimes conclude a point or argument they are making with a summary or restatement of what they have said. The expressions taught are *at the end of the day, in the end, when all's said and done, in a word,* and *in a nutshell. In a nutshell* and *in a word* allow a speaker to summarize, present, or restate the main points of an argument. An expression such as *in the end* signals a concluding point and can tell the listener that speaker's turn is coming to an end.

Strategy plus *. . ., then*

(See Student's Book p. 79.)

In conversation, speakers often end a response with *then* when they draw a conclusion from what someone has just said. It can be used to state a conclusion at the end of a statement (e.g., *A: I'm going out tonight. B: I'll call you tomorrow,* **then**.) or in a question to check information or understanding (e.g., *B: So, you're not coming over to my house,* **then***?*). People also use *in that case,* which also means "because of what was just said."

 Corpus information

In conversation

In conversation, the most common expressions are *in the end* and *at the end of the day*. In writing, you can use *in a word* and *in a nutshell* or the more formal *in the final analysis*.

 Corpus information

In conversation

In conversation, *in that case* usually comes near the beginning of what people say.

Lesson D *Smart families*

Reading tip *Explaining terms*

(See Student's Book p. 80.)

The Reading tip explains that writers sometimes give their own views in a question. For example, *Is it any different from four people reading their own books?* This allows the writer to give an opinion in a less assertive or less explicit way.

Writing *It just takes a little thought.*

(See Student's Book p. 82.)

This lesson teaches Ss to plan and write a magazine article on the topic of friendship. This is a "how-to" article, which requires suggesting ideas and describing effects. The grammar for writing presents ways to express number and amount in academic writing. It also gives phrases for expressing effect.

Expressing number and amount

- With plural countable nouns

    a (large / huge / small) number of; a (wide) variety of; a (wide) range of; several / many / various; a few (= some; a "positive idea"); *few* (= not many; a "negative idea")

When the noun phrase that contains the above expressions is the subject of a verb, the verb should be plural.

> *There are* **a number of** */* **several** *factors that* **lead** *to improved relationships.*

- With uncountable nouns

    a great deal of; a(n) (large / small) amount of; a little (= some; a "positive idea"); *little* (= not much; a "negative idea")

    They don't take **a great deal of** *time / effort. It takes* **little** *time /* **a little** *thought.*

 Corpus information

Common errors with *a number of*

Even advanced Ss sometimes use a singular instead of a plural verb after a noun phrase that begins with *a number of, several,* etc., + plural noun. The error is also common with *There is* instead of *There are* to introduce a noun phrase with *a number of* or *several*.

There **are** *a number of factors that* **lead** *to . . .*

(**NOT**: *There* ~~is~~ *a number of factors that* ~~leads~~ *to . . .*)

Relationships

In Unit 7, you . . .

- talk about relationships, marriage, and family life.
- express the idea of *if* in different ways.
- use *wh-* clauses as subjects and objects to focus information.
- finish a point with expressions like *in the end*.
- say *then* and *in that case* in responses to draw a conclusion.

Lesson A *Parenting*

1 Grammar in context

A **What's the best age to become a parent? Tell the class your views.**

B 🔊 CD 3.02 **Listen to the podcast. What's the speaker's main proposal about parenting?**

STATIONS • ABOUT • SUPPORT • LOG IN • SIGN UP

PODCAST LISTEN LIVE 🎧   👍 | 👎 | 🖨 | ⬚ | SHARE

Our Family Season continues with Rachel Birken's take on the topic of parenting.

A friend of mine struggling with sleepless nights after the birth of her daughter recently said to me, quote, "Had I known having a baby would be this hard, I might have waited a few more years. Why aren't parenting classes mandatory, especially in high school?" Which got me thinking: Why *aren't* they?

Ask any new parent this question: "Would you have benefited from parenting classes?" and you'll probably get the answer, "Absolutely!" Most parents experience problems with sleepless nights, anxiety about their baby's health, and as their children grow, issues with behavior and setting boundaries. Should you think your experience will be any different, think again. Parenting is a skill to be learned.

Some school districts have recognized this and introduced programs where students take care of a computerized baby doll that behaves like a real baby. It cries in the night and needs to be changed and comforted. It helps young people understand what is involved in starting a family.

One college senior I know who did this told me it was a cool experience and that had he not taken that class, he wouldn't have realized what hard work a baby is.

Were I in charge of education, I would make all students from the age of 12 do this for a whole weekend every year.

Should you need further evidence that parenting classes are a good idea, school and city districts all over the country are expanding programs that offer workshops in parenting skills – not to students – but to *parents* of their students. Clearly, there is a need out there.

So let's make parenting classes mandatory. Otherwise, we run the risk of creating a generation of parents who are unprepared to tackle the most important job of their lives.

C Pair work **Discuss the questions.**

- What reasons does the speaker give or imply for her proposal? What are they?
- What gave her the idea in the first place?
- How does the baby doll program work? What is its goal?
- Why do you think parenting classes are offered by city and school districts?

Relationships

Introduce the theme of the unit Tell Ss the title of the unit. Say, "We all have business, professional, and personal relationships. The lessons in this unit deal with various types of personal relationships." Read the unit aims aloud.

Lesson A *Parenting*

1 Grammar in context

- **Set the scene** Books closed. Say, "The noun *parenting* has only been around since the late 1950s. What do you think a good definition for *parenting* might be?" Elicit ideas from the class (e.g., *raising a baby or child; teaching a baby or child the things he or she needs to know*). Ask, "Do you think there's a big difference between the parenting of today and when your grandparents were young?" Have a short class discussion.

A • **Preview and do the task** Ask, "What's the best age to become a parent?" Have Ss call out their opinion. Write the ages on the board. Have a few Ss say why they chose a particular age.

B 🔊 CD3, Track 2

- **Preview the task** Write on the board:

  mandatory

  anxiety

  to tackle (a job)

  Say, "If you know the meaning of any of these, tell the class." Write the correct Ss' definitions on the board. [*mandatory*: something that must be done; *anxiety*: the feeling of being very worried; *to tackle (a job)*: try to deal with (a job)]

- Read the instructions aloud. Add, "In this case, a *proposal* is a suggestion."

- **Play the recording** Books closed. Tell Ss to listen to the podcast and write brief answers. Have Ss compare their notes with a partner.

- Books open. Tell Ss to read the article and find the answer. (If desired, play the recording again while Ss read along.)

- Have Ss complete the task. Check the answer with the class. [Parenting classes should be mandatory before people become parents.]

Culture Note

These "baby doll" programs vary. Some are weekend only, and some are for a week. They run in high schools with students aged 14 to 17. When the "baby" cries, the caregiver – like a real parent – must figure out why. The "baby" will continue to cry until the caregiver finds the correct solution.

C Pair work

- **Preview and do the task** Read the instructions aloud. Ask a S to read the questions aloud. Check that Ss understand them.

- Have Ss discuss the questions. Walk around the class and help as needed. Have several pairs report to the class.

Answers

- *What reasons does the speaker give or imply for her proposal? What are they?*
  - Having a baby is hard work; it would be good if would-be parents knew this beforehand. (implied in example)
  - Parents often encounter problems with sleeplessness, anxiety, and children's behavior (stated), and so people without kids need to know that they, too, will encounter these problems eventually. (implied)
  - Some school districts have programs where students take care of a computerized baby, and one student said he wouldn't have realized what hard work having a baby was if he hadn't taken the class. (stated)
  - School districts perceive a need to educate parents after they have had children. (stated)
- *What gave her the idea in the first place?*
  - A friend who said that having a baby was hard and she might have waited if she'd known how hard it was.
- *How does the baby doll program work? What is its goal?*
  - Students take care of a computerized doll that acts like a real baby and needs to be taken care of. It helps young people understand what is involved in starting a family.
- *Why do you think parenting classes are offered by city and school districts?*
  - *Answers will vary. Possible answers include:* It helps people understand better the challenges involved in caring for a baby and raising children.

- **Follow-up** Say, "At the beginning of this lesson, you decided on the best age to be a parent. Has anything you read or talked about changed your mind? If you have changed your mind, raise your hand." Ask Ss who raise their hand if they have raised or lowered the age and ask why.

Extra activity – groups

Write on the board:

Is the baby doll program a good idea?

How realistic do you think it is?

Should parenting classes be mandatory?

Groups discuss the baby doll program. Groups report their ideas to the class.

2 Grammar

A 🔲 www.cambridge.org/viewpoint/audio

- Ask, "What is *hypothesizing*?" [proposing an idea that is possible but not yet proven] Say, "We are going to look at ways of introducing a hypothetical idea."
- **Preview the task** Say, "Rewrite these phrases without *if*. Use the podcast to help you."
- Do the first one with the class.
- **Do the task** Have Ss complete the task and compare answers with a partner. Check answers with the class

Answers

1. Ask any new parent this question, and . . .
2. Had I known having a baby would be this hard, . . .
3. Should you need further evidence . . .
4. Otherwise, we run the risk . . .

- **Focus on the use** Ask, "What do we often call sentences that begin with *If*?" [conditional]
- **Present the grammar chart** Read the information aloud. If desired, play the downloadable recording.
- Say, "The chart presents ways to express hypothetical ideas, without using *if*.
- Have Ss look at the example in the first section of the chart. Ask, "What does the first clause begin with?" [an imperative, *ask*] Ask, "How about the second clause?" [and] Ask, "Which clause introduces the hypothetical idea?" [the first]
- Have Ss look at the next section. Say, " *Inversion* means changing the order of two things. What inversion is in the first two examples?" [the subject and the verb] Ask, "How can you say these sentences with *if*?" [If I were in charge of . . . ; If she had another baby, . . .]

- Ask Ss to look at the example sentence with *Had I*. Ask, "What inversion takes place in this example?" [the subject and the auxiliary verb, *had*] "What follows the subject?" [past participle] Point out the example with *should*. Say, "*Should* in a hypothetical sentence means 'if it happens' or 'if by chance.' *Should* and the subject are inverted."
- Tell Ss to look at the last section. Ask, "What does *otherwise* mean?" [if they're not mandatory]
- **Present *Writing vs. Conversation*** Say, "Cover the page. Do you think inversions are more frequent in writing or conversation?" Read the information aloud.

  (For more information, see Language notes at the beginning of the unit. For more work on conditional sentences without *if*, go to Grammar extra, p. 156.)

B • **Preview and do the task** Read the instructions aloud. Have Ss complete the task. Check answers with the class.

Answers

1. Had I had the chance to . . .
2. Were I to become a school principal, . . .
3. Make parenting classes mandatory and students . . .
4. Were I to become a parent in the next year, . . .
5. Ask most kids . . . and they'll say, "It's easy."
6. Teaching kids . . . is a good idea. Otherwise, how do . . .
7. I'd want . . . like personal finance, should that be possible.
8. Had I known more about life . . .

C Pair work

- **Preview and do the task** Read the instructions and the example sentence aloud. As pairs discuss the sentences, walk around the class, listen, and give help as needed.
- **Follow-up** Ask Ss to share their view with the class.

3 Listening and speaking

A 🔊 CD3, Track 3

- **Preview the task** Read the instructions aloud. Make sure the class understands what a *baby simulator* is. [a doll designed to function like a real baby]
- **Play the recording** Audio script pp. T-275–T-276 Ss listen. Replay the recording. Ss listen and write. Have Ss compare their notes to make more complete answers.
- **Play the recording again** Ss listen and check their answers. Check the answers with the class. [Brandon took care of a baby simulator as part of a required health class. He thought it was a positive experience, although it was a lot of work.]

B 🔊 CD3, Track 4

- **Preview the task** Read the instructions aloud. Have Ss read the six sentences before they listen.
- **Play the recording** Audio script pp. T-275–T-276 Ss listen and complete the task. Have Ss compare their answers

with a partner. Replay the recording. Ss listen and check their answers. Check answers with the class.

Answers

1. T
2. F – He thought it was going to be easy.
3. F – Having to wake up during the middle of the night at least three or four times was the worst part.
4. T
5. T
6. F – He thinks it's a great program for his age group.

C Pair work

- **Preview and do the task** Read the instructions aloud. Elicit ideas for types of classes (e.g., *budgeting, investing*). Have Ss complete the task.
- **Follow-up** Have several pairs report their four choices to the class.

2 Grammar Hypothesizing

Figure it out

A **Rewrite these phrases without *If*. Use the podcast to help you. Then read the grammar chart.**

1. If you ask any new parent this question, . . .
2. If I had known having a baby would be this hard, . . .
3. If you need further evidence that parenting classes are needed, . . .
4. If we don't do this, we run the risk . . .

Conditional sentences without *if* 🖥

Grammar extra
See page 156.

You can use these structures to introduce a hypothetical idea without using the word *if*.

Imperative . . . *and* . . .	**Ask** any new parent the question, **and** you'll get the answer, "Absolutely!"
Inversions *Were* + subject (+ infinitive) *Had* + subject + past participle *Should* + subject + verb	**Were I** in charge of education, I would make this class mandatory. **Were she** to have another baby, she would be better prepared. **Had I known** it would be this hard, I would have waited. **Should you think** your experience will be any different, think again.
Otherwise	Let's make them mandatory. **Otherwise,** parents will be unprepared.

Writing vs. Conversation

Inversions are much more common in writing and formal speaking than in conversation.

B **Change the *if* clauses, using the words or structure given.**

Had I had

1. ~~If I had~~ the chance to take care of a doll in school, I would have said, "No way." (*Had*)
2. If I were to become a school principal, I would make parenting classes mandatory. (*Were*)
3. If you make parenting classes mandatory, students will hate them. (imperative)
4. If I were to become a parent in the next year, I'd be very happy. (*Were*)
5. If you ask most kids what it's like to have children, they'll say, "It's easy." (imperative)
6. Teaching kids about relationships is a good idea. If we don't, how do they learn? (*Otherwise*)
7. I'd want my kids to take other "life" classes like personal finance, if that were possible. (*should*)
8. If I had known more about life when I left school, things would have been easier. (*Had*)

About you

C **Pair work** **Do you agree with the sentences above? Change them to express your own views.**

"Had I had the chance to take care of a doll in high school, I would have done it."

3 Listening and speaking Bringing up baby?

A ◀))CD 3.03 **Listen. What was Brandon's class? Was it a positive experience?**

B ◀))CD 3.04 **Listen again. Are the sentences true or false? Write T or F. Then correct the false sentences.**

1. It was a mandatory class. _____
2. He knew before he did it how hard it would be. _____
3. He found changing diapers the worst part. _____
4. It taught him how much time a baby needs. _____
5. His friends said how annoying it was to do. _____
6. He's not sure if it's a good idea for his age group. _____

About you

C **Pair work** **Agree on four classes you would make mandatory to help students prepare for life.**

Lesson B *Questions to ask*

① Vocabulary in context

A ◀)) CD 3.05 **What issues do you think couples should discuss and agree on before they get married? Make a list. Then read the article. Which of your ideas are mentioned?**

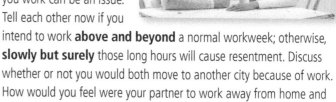

Getting married? *Don't just wait and see what happens.*

So you've met the man or woman of your dreams and decided to become **husband and wife**. You're probably **sick and tired** of reading the divorce statistics, but they're not encouraging. In many Western countries, around 40 percent of marriages end in divorce. Why divorce rates are so high is not clear. But what many couples fail to do is to discuss the important issues before the wedding. So, **stop and think** now – you'll save yourself **time and energy** and maybe avoid a lot of **pain and suffering**.

MONEY

Is how you spend money a problem right now? When you're married, it will likely become a problem **sooner or later**. Agree now on how much you will spend – for example, on rent, vacations, entertainment, etc. – and what your financial goals are. Do you know if you'll keep separate bank accounts?

WORK

How many hours a week you work can be an issue. Tell each other now if you intend to work **above and beyond** a normal workweek; otherwise, **slowly but surely** those long hours will cause resentment. Discuss whether or not you would both move to another city because of work. How would you feel were your partner to work away from home and commute **back and forth** on weekends?

CONFLICTS

Every relationship has its **ups and downs**, but **in this day and age**, marriage is all about **give-and-take**. How you resolve differences can be critical and may predict the **success or failure** of a marriage. Can you agree without arguing how often your in-laws can visit?

You can't always **pick and choose** where you **live and work**, but can you compromise should you have different views? [MORE...]

About you

B **Complete the expressions with words from the article. Then discuss the comments with a partner. Do you agree with the views given?**

1. I know that divorce causes a lot of pain _____, but it takes a lot of time _____ to discuss these questions, too. I think you should just get married if you want to and then wait _____ what happens.

2. I don't think people stop _____ before getting married. There are a lot more things to agree on above _____ the ideas in the article.

3. Sooner _____ everyone argues. You can't avoid it as husband _____.

4. All couples have their ups _____. You can't agree on everything, so pick _____ what you argue about.

5. I agree marriage is about give _____, but I like to get my own way, and slowly _____ I usually do.

6. In this day _____, we don't need advice about marriage. I'm sick _____ of reading articles like this.

7. It's not a problem to live _____ in two places. It'd be fun to travel back _____.

Word sort

C **Make a chart of the expressions in bold in the article. Add more ideas.**

and	but	or
wait and see		

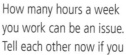
Vocabulary notebook

See page 83.

Lesson B *Questions to ask*

1 Vocabulary in context

- **Set the scene** Books closed. Write *whirlwind romance* on the board. Say, "A whirlwind romance is a short but intense relationship. Sometimes, the couple involved in a whirlwind relationship gets married after knowing each for only a few months. Do you think marriage after dating for such a short time is a good idea? Why or why not?" Have a short class discussion.

A 🔊 CD3, Track 5

- **Preview the task** Say, "What issues do you think couples should discuss and agree on before they get married? Make a list." Have Ss write their list. Ask several Ss to share their ideas with the class. Write them on the board.
- **Play the recording** Books open. Ss listen and read along. Check for vocabulary questions.
- Ask, "How many of your ideas are mentioned?"
- Call on Ss to give their opinion of the article and if they agree with the ideas in it.

About you

B • **Preview and do the task** Say, "The vocabulary in this lesson is expressions with *and*, *but*, and *or*. Complete the expressions with words from the article." Have Ss complete the task and compare answers with a partner. Check answers with the class.

Answers

1. I know . . . lot of pain <u>and suffering</u>, . . . a lot of time <u>and energy</u> . . . I think . . . then wait <u>and see</u> what happens.
2. . . . stop <u>and think</u> before . . . There are . . . agree on above <u>and beyond</u> the ideas in the article.
3. Sooner <u>or later</u> everyone . . . You . . . as husband <u>and wife</u>.
4. . . . ups <u>and downs</u>. . . . , so pick <u>and choose</u> . . .
5. . . . about give <u>and take</u>, . . . and slowly <u>but surely</u> I usually do.
6. In this day <u>and age</u>, . . . I'm sick <u>and tired</u> of . . .
7. . . . problem to live <u>and work</u> in . . . It'd be fun to travel back <u>and forth</u>.

- Say, "Now discuss the comments with a partner. Do you agree with the views given?"

Word sort

C • **Preview and do the task** Read the instructions aloud. Say, "An example of two words joined by *and* has been done for you." Have Ss make a chart like the one in the book, and then complete the task. (Note: If using the Extra Activity to the right, write the words on the board while Ss complete their charts.) Check answers with the class.

Answers

and	but
wait and see	slowly but surely
husband and wife	
sick and tired	
stop and think	
time and energy	or
pain and suffering	sooner or later
above and beyond	success or failure
back and forth	
ups and downs	
in this day and age	
give-and-take	
pick and choose	
live and work	

Extra activity – pairs

Choose five expressions and then write the first part of the expression on the board, with the second part of the expression mixed up in a second column:

Column 1
research and (development)
health and (safety)
life and (death)
supply and (demand)
day and (night)
heart and (soul)
buy and (sell)
again and (again)
here and (there)
nothing but (praise)
gently but (firmly)
slow but (steady)
small but (significant)
simple but (effective)
success or (failure)
make or (break)
give or (take)
here or (there)
now or (never)
over and (above)

Pairs match the first part of the expression in Column 1 with the second half of the expression. Pairs compare their answers with another pair. Then answers are checked as a class. Ss then make sentences using each of the five expressions.

Tell Ss to turn to Vocabulary Notebook on p. 83 of their Student's Books. Have Ss do the tasks in class or assign them for homework. (See the teaching notes on p. T-83.)

❷ Grammar

A 🔊 www.cambridge.org/viewpoint/audio

- **Preview and do the task** Read the instructions aloud. Have Ss complete the task. Check answers with the class. Ask individual Ss each to read a sentence aloud.

Answers

1. Is how you spend money a problem right now? (para. 2)
2. Why divorce rates are so high is not clear. (para. 1)
3. Do you know if you'll keep separate bank accounts? (para. 2)
4. You can't always pick and choose where you live and work. (concluding sentence)

- **Focus on the form and use** Write on the board:

  Why divorce rates are so high is not clear.

  Circle *is*. Ask, "What's the subject of *is* in this sentence?" [why divorce rates are so high] Underline the *wh-* clause on the board. Say, "A *wh-* clause can be the subject of a sentence. A *wh-* clause means a clause that starts with a question word, including *how*."

- Say, "Using a *wh-* clause as the subject can be very effective when you want to give extra emphasis to an idea."

- Write on the board:

  You can't always pick and choose where you live.

  Circle *pick and choose*. Ask, "What's the object of *pick and choose* in this sentence?" [where you live] Underline the *wh-* clause on the board. Say, "A *wh-* clause can be the object of a sentence."

- **Present the grammar chart** Read the information aloud. If desired, play the downloadable recording.

- **Understand the grammar chart** Say, "The chart shows ways to focus on information or emphasize an idea in a sentence."

- Have Ss look at the chart. Ask, "What's the word order in the *wh-* clauses?" [*wh-* word + statement order]

- Ask Ss to look at the *Subjects* section of the chart. Ask, "How do you make a question with a *wh-* clause as

subject?" [Invert the verb from the main clause with the *wh-* clause.]

- Have Ss look at the *Objects* section of the chart. Ask, "How do you make a question with a *wh-*clause as object?" [Invert the subject and verb from the main clause.]

- **Present *In conversation*** Read the information aloud. Say, "*Or not* can also go at the end of the sentence."

(For more information, see Language notes at the beginning of the unit. For more work on *wh-* clauses as subjects and objects, go to Grammar extra, p. 157.)

B • **Preview and do the task** Read the instructions aloud. Ask a S to read sentence 1 and its example answer aloud. Ask, "What changed in the first sentence?" [*this* was deleted] Ask, "What happened in the second sentence?" [The question order was changed to statement order.] Have Ss complete the task and then compare answers with a partner. Check answers with the class.

Answers

1. Should you tell your husband or wife which of his or her friends you don't like?
2. Why couples divorce is usually obvious, don't you think?
3. How many hours a week you work can easily become a problem, can't it?
4. It's important to discuss if / whether you both want children.
5. You should also decide how many children you both want to have.
6. You need to find out if / whether your partner has different religious or political views.
7. Who does the chores will become an issue sooner or later.
8. Is it important to decide how often you will go out separately with your own friends.

C **Pair work**

- **Preview and do the task** Read the instructions aloud. Have Ss complete the task. Walk around the class, giving help as needed. When groups have completed the activity, have several pairs tell the class about the views they did not share.

❸ Viewpoint

- **Preview the task** Read the instructions and issues aloud. Check that Ss understand what each issue is.

- **Present *In conversation*** Read the information aloud. Tell pairs to read the example conversation aloud. Say, "Now read it again without using the softening expressions. Notice that the exchange sounds more direct, assertive – even abrupt – when the expressions are not used."

- **Do the task** Have Ss complete the task. Walk around the class and give help as needed.

- **Follow-up** For each issue, have a few pairs share their ideas with the class. Ask Ss to call out the ideas they

added. (Note: If using the Extra Activity below, write the ideas on the board.)

Extra activity – groups

Groups consider the ideas on the board and in the Student's Book. They choose the five most important issues to discuss before marriage. Groups present their choices to the class and give reasons.

Speaking naturally

- Tell Ss to turn to Speaking naturally on p. 141. (For more information, see Language notes at the beginning of this unit. See the teaching notes on p. T-141.)

2 **Grammar** Information focus

Figure it out

A **Underline the sentences in the article with these meanings.**

1. How do you spend money? Is it a problem right now?
2. Why are divorce rates high? It's not clear.
3. Will you keep separate bank accounts? Do you know?
4. Where do you live and work? You can't always pick and choose.

Wh– clauses as subjects and objects

Grammar extra
See page 157.

A wh– clause can be the subject or object of a verb. Using a wh– clause as the subject gives extra emphasis to it. Notice the statement word order in the wh– clause.

Subjects
Is **how you spend money** a problem right now?
What many couples fail to do is (to) discuss the important issues.
How you resolve differences can be critical.

Objects
Can you agree **how often your partner's family can visit** without arguing?
Tell each other now **whether / if you intend to work long hours**.
Agree now on **what your financial goals are**.

> **In conversation . . .**
> You can also say whether or not when there is a choice of two options.
> Discuss **whether or not** you would both move to another city.

B **Rewrite the two sentences as one sentence. Keep the clauses in the same order.**

1. Should you tell your husband or wife this? Which of his or her friends don't you like?
   Should you tell your husband or wife which of his or her friends you don't like?
2. Why do couples divorce? It's usually obvious, don't you think?
3. How many hours a week do you work? It can easily become a problem, can't it?
4. It's important to discuss this. Do you both want children?
5. You should also decide this. How many children do you both want to have?
6. You need to find this out. Does your partner have different religious or political views?
7. Who does the chores? This will become an issue sooner or later.
8. Is it important to decide this? How often will you go out separately with your own friends?

About you

C Pair work **Discuss the questions and statements above. Do you have the same views?**

3 **Viewpoint** A manifesto for marriage

Pair work **Discuss the 10 most important issues you need to agree on before you get married. Use these ideas and add your own.**

chores	money	visiting in-laws
leisure time	raising children	work

A How you spend money is the first thing to discuss, I would say.
B Yes. It seems to me you should agree on what you spend money on.

> **In conversation . . .**
> You can soften opinions with I would say, I would think, I would imagine, and It seems to me.

Speaking naturally
See page 141

OF COURSE I'LL MARRY YOU! HERE'S A LIST OF CHANGES I'LL NEED YOU TO MAKE FIRST.

Lesson C *In the end*

① Conversation strategy Finishing a point

A 🔊 CD 3.06 **What are the advantages and disadvantages of Internet dating sites? Make a list. Then listen. What do Tara and Carmen think about them?**

Tara	Did I tell you I'm going out on a date tonight?
Carmen	No. Who with?
Tara	This guy I met on an Internet dating site.
Carmen	Is that . . . all right?
Tara	Oh, yeah. Talk to anybody these days, and you'll probably find they're using dating sites.
Carmen	So you think it's OK, then?
Tara	I do. Really and truly. It's just like being at a party. You see somebody you like, you arrange to meet and –
Carmen	But you don't *really* know who they are. I mean, when all's said and done, surely it's better to get to know them a little first.
Tara	Well, you do. You email or call. It's so convenient. And in the end, you don't waste time on people you're not interested in.
Carmen	I guess.
Tara	You know, all the time I spend working, I'll never meet anybody otherwise.
Carmen	Well, in that case, do you have time to date? I mean, at the end of the day, if you're always working, you probably don't have time for a boyfriend.

B **Notice** how Carmen and Tara summarize and finish their points with expressions like these. Find examples in the conversation.

at the end of the day	**in a word**
in the end	**in a nutshell**
when all's said and done	

In conversation . . .

The most common expressions are *in the end* and *at the end of the day*. In writing, you can use *in a word* and *in a nutshell* or the more formal *in the final analysis*.

About you

C 🔊 CD 3.07 **Listen. Complete Tara's comments with the expressions you hear. Then discuss the views with a partner. Do you agree with her?**

1. People don't go out to meet people – it takes time. _____, we're all too busy.
2. I read an academic article about Internet dating that said, "Online daters are just like face-to-face daters. _____, there is no difference between them."
3. You can email and call or video chat before you first meet. So really, _____, you're already friends.
4. You don't need to go out and spend money on movies or restaurants. _____, it's a lot cheaper.
5. And because you do it from home, you don't get into difficult situations. _____, it's safer, too.
6. There are lots of people that you can get to know online. _____, you don't have to choose just one.

Lesson C *In the end*

1 Conversation strategy

Why use expressions to finish a point?

Speakers often structure what they say in some way. They sometimes conclude a point or argument they are making with a summary or restatement of what they have said. *In a nutshell*, for example, allows them to summarize, present, or restate the main points of the argument. An expression such as *in the end* signals a concluding point and can tell the listener that the speaker's turn is coming to an end.

(For more information, see Language notes at the beginning of this unit.)

- **Set the scene** Books closed. Ask, "How do people find dates these days?" Elicit ideas from the class. Mention Internet dating sites if Ss did not. Ask, "What do you know about them? How do they work? Do you know people who use them?" Have S call out their ideas.

A ◀)) CD3, Track 6

- **Preview and do the task** Read the instructions aloud. Write *advantages* and *disadvantages* on the board as column headings. Have Ss call out their opinions. Write them on the board under the appropriate heading.

- Tell Ss to make brief notes to answer the questions. Say, "These are the speakers." Write on the board:

    Tara

    Carmen

    Say, "Tara speaks first."

- **Play the recording** Ss listen only. Replay the recording. Ss listen and take notes. Have Ss compare their notes in pairs.

- **Play the recording again** Books open. Ss listen, read along, and check their answer. Check the answer with the class. [*Tara:* She thinks they're good. They're convenient and you don't waste time on people you're not interested in. *Carmen:* She's suspicious because you don't really know who the people are.]

B • **Present *Notice*** Read the information and the examples aloud.

- Say, "Read the conversation again. Find the examples." Have a S read them aloud. [*Carmen:* I mean, **when all's**

said and done, surely it's better to get to know them a little first. *Tara:* And **in the end**, you don't waste time on people you're not interested in. *Carmen:* I mean, **at the end of the day**, if you're always working, . . .]

- **Practice** Tell Ss to practice the conversation in pairs, taking turns playing each role.

About you

C ◀)) CD3, Track 7

- **Preview the task** Say, "Listen. Complete Tara's comments with the expressions you hear."

- **Play the recording** Ss listen and write. Have Ss compare their answers with a partner. Play the recording again and have Ss check their answers. Check answers with the class.

Answers

1. . . . In a nutshell, we're all too busy.
2. . . . In the final analysis, there is no difference between them.
3. . . . So really, when all's said and done, you're already friends.
4. . . . In the end, it's a lot cheaper.
5. . . . In a word, it's safer, too.
6. . . . At the end of the day, you don't have to choose just one.

- Say, "Now discuss the views with a partner. Do you agree with Tara?" As Ss discuss their views, walk around the class, listening for the expressions and giving help as needed.

- **Follow-up** Have several Ss share their opinions with the class.

Extra activity – pairs

Ss write a conversation similar to Tara and Carmen's on the topic of Internet dating using ideas from Exercise C or their own ideas. Pairs present their conversation to another pair. The listening pair notes when expressions to summarize and finish the point were used.

Why use . . ., *then*?

In conversation, speakers often end a response with *then* when they draw a conclusion from what someone has just said. They use it to state a conclusion at the end of a statement or at the end of a question to check. People also use *in that case*, which means "because of what you just said."

(For more information, see Language notes at the beginning of this unit.)

🔊 CD3, Track 8

- **Present *Strategy plus*** Read aloud or play the recording of the information and example. Ss listen and read along.
- **Present *In conversation*** Read the information aloud.
- Tell Ss to read Tara and Carmen's conversation on page 78 again and find these expressions. [*Carmen:* So you think it's OK, **then**?; Well, **in that case**, do you have time to date?]

③ Strategies

A
- **Preview and do the task** Say, "Circle the best options to complete the rest of Carmen and Tara's conversation. Sometimes both are correct." Tell Ss to read through the conversation before they begin.
- Have Ss complete the task. Check answers with the class.

Answers

Carmen So, if there are hundreds of people on the site, how do you choose one, ⟨then⟩?

Tara Well, you fill out a long questionnaire about yourself and the site gives you a short list. ⟨At the end of the day⟩, they do all the hard work and match potential dates.

Carmen So ⟨in that case / in a word⟩, the computer chooses someone?

Tara No. Well, kind of. I mean, it gives you a selection to choose from based on your questionnaire. I mean, ⟨when all's said and done⟩, it's pretty efficient.

Carmen That's one way of putting it. But I suppose it's just like regular dating. I guess ⟨in the end⟩, it's really no different from meeting a stranger at a party.

A
- **Preview and do the task** Say, "Read comments 1 to 6. Then read responses a to f." Check for vocabulary questions. Say, "Match each comment with the correct response." Have Ss complete the task and compare their answers with a partner. Check answers with the class.

Answers

1. b; 2. e; 3. a; 4. f; 5. c; 6. d

- Say, "Now practice the comments and responses with a partner."

About you

B Pair work
- **Preview and do the task** Read the instructions aloud. Have Ss complete the task.
- **Follow-up** For each comment, ask a few Ss to give their response.

About you

B Pair work
- **Preview and do the task** Read the instructions and the ideas aloud. Ask, "What advantages or disadvantages does each one have? Could the different ways be better for some people than others?" Have Ss complete the task.
- **Follow-up** Have pairs share interesting points with the class.

Extra activity – pairs

Write on the board:

1. *Couples should date for at least two years before getting married.*
2. *Long engagements are a good idea.*
3. *Couples shouldn't spend much on wedding ceremonies.*

Ss choose one topic and discuss their views. Tell Ss to use the expressions they have learned from the lesson.

2 Strategy plus ..., then

◀)) CD 3.08 You can end a response with **then** to draw a conclusion from what someone just said.

So you think it's OK, **then**?

You can also say **In that case**, which means "because of what was just said."

In conversation ...

In that case usually comes near the beginning of what people say.

A Match the comments with the responses. Write the letters a–f. Then practice in pairs.

1. Some research shows that 94 percent of online daters go out more than once. _____
2. Apparently, only 5 percent of people who use online dating actually establish a relationship. _____
3. Online daters prefer instant messaging to email because it's more like a real conversation. _____
4. They tend not to use their webcams, though. _____
5. What a lot of people do is to email or chat for weeks before they actually meet. _____
6. Look at the people using Internet dating sites, and you'll find mostly middle-aged people. _____

a. That's interesting. Email isn't considered a good way to get to know somebody, then.
b. Well, in that case, you've got a good chance of getting at least a couple of dates.
c. OK, so in that case, what do they have to talk about when they get together?
d. So it's not just young people, then?
e. Well, in that case, it doesn't have a very high success rate, then, does it?
f. So in that case, you don't need to look your best when you're dating online.

About you | **B** Pair work **Take turns reading the comments. Use your own responses with *then* or *in that case*.**

3 Strategies

A Circle the best options to complete the rest of Carmen and Tara's conversation. Sometimes both are correct. Then practice in pairs.

Carmen: So if there are hundreds of people on the site, how do you choose one, **then / in a word**?

Tara: Well, you fill out a long questionnaire about yourself and the site gives you a short list. **In that case / At the end of the day,** they do all the hard work and match potential dates.

Carmen: So **in that case / in a word,** the computer chooses someone?

Tara: No. Well, kind of. I mean, it gives you a selection to choose from based on your questionnaire. I mean, **in that case / when all's said and done,** it's pretty efficient.

Carmen: That's one way of putting it. But I suppose it's just like regular dating. I guess **in the end / in that case,** it's really no different from meeting a stranger at a party.

About you | **B** Pair work **What are the best ways to meet people? Discuss the ideas below and add your own.**

online dating   through friends   at work / school   through parents   at clubs

Lesson D *Smart families*

1 Reading

A Prepare **Look at the title of the article and the photo. Brainstorm ideas, words, and expressions that you expect the writer to include. What arguments do you expect to read?**

B Read for main ideas **Read the article. How many of your ideas were included?**

TECHNOLOGY –
is it driving families apart?

1 Look inside any family home in the evening, and you might see a typical enough scene: Mom and Dad, each on their own laptop or tablet, streaming movies, catching up on work, or maybe answering email on their smartphones. Meanwhile, one child is chatting online with one school friend while texting another. The other is playing a video game with a friend on the other side of the city at the same time as playing chess against an uncle in another state. Each member of the family is totally absorbed in his or her own piece of technology. How you interpret such a scene might depend on your attitude toward technology. Do you see a close family that is enjoying "quality time" together? Or do you perceive this family unit as "together" only in a physical sense, as a dysfunctional family whose members are isolated from one another, inhabiting parallel virtual worlds?

2 For some, the effect of technology on human relationships is worrisome. It appears to be the case that many people would much rather spend time with their gadgets than with one another. Technology, they claim, becomes a substitute for face-to-face human relationships, which is a cause for concern.

3 According to some experts, technology is changing how people interact with each another, and for the worse. Some teachers say it is difficult to get students' attention and they have to compete with texting and surfing the Web to such an extent that many schools now require students to leave mobile devices in their lockers. In the same way, young people try to get their parents' attention but have to contend with smartphones, tablets, and other technology.

4 However, a report from the Pew Internet and American Life Project offers a more hopeful and encouraging view, suggesting that far from replacing human contact, new technology can actually enhance family relationships.

Just over half of the 2,253 people surveyed agreed that technology had enabled them to increase their contact with distant family members and 47 percent said it had improved the interactions with the people they live with.

5 Thanks to more sophisticated, lighter, and more portable tablet, smartphone, and computer technology, family members who might otherwise have sat in separate rooms can now be in the same one while still occupying a different mental space. Look back at our typical family scene above. Is it any different from four people reading their own books? Does the fact that each person is immersed in a screen rather than a paper page make their activity any less sociable?

6 Moreover, even the closest of families and couples need time away from each other at some point to pursue their own interests. Technology allows people to be both present and absent simultaneously.

7 Where technology will lead us remains to be seen. How it affects the quality of our family relationships is up to all of us.

> **Reading tip**
> Writers sometimes give their own views in a question. *Is it any different from four people reading their own books?*

Lesson D *Smart families*

1 Reading

- **Set the scene** Books closed. Ask Ss, "What is *quality time*?" [time spent in a meaningful way with a person or people you feel close to] "What is your idea of good quality family time? What would you be doing?" Elicit ideas from the class (e.g., *cooking or eating together, watching a movie, playing a game, going on a trip*).

A Prepare

- **Preview and do the task** Books open. Read the instructions aloud. Make sure Ss understand the meaning of *drive families apart*. [cause families to be less close] Have Ss complete the task. If preferred, have Ss work with a partner.

- Ask, "What ideas, words, and expressions do you expect?" Have Ss call out their ideas. Write them on the board (e.g., *Internet, notebook, chat room, download, fun, share, alone, separate*, and so on).

- Ask, "What arguments do you expect to read?" Elicit ideas and write them on the board (e.g., *technology separates families, everyone is doing something on their own, there's no more sharing, there's more sharing, family members can teach / show each other new ideas / computer skills*).

- Ask Ss if they have read articles on the topic of technology and families before. Ask Ss to tell the class what information they learned from the articles they have read previously.

Extra activity – class

Ss close their books (or cover the article) and vote on whether they think the answer to the title question will be *yes* or *no*. Ss give opinions for their choices, using the ideas on the board.

B www.cambridge.org/viewpoint/audio
Read for main ideas

- **Preview the task** Read the instructions aloud. If desired, play the downloadable recording. Ss listen and read along.

- **Do the task** Ss read the article. Ask, "How many of your ideas were included? How many ideas from the board were included?"

- **Present *Reading tip*** Read the information aloud. Ask, "Why is this a good strategy for writers?" Elicit answers. (e.g., *It engages the reader by asking a question the reader can answer. It also allows the writer to give an opinion in a less assertive way, or to give an opinion without being explicit.*)

C Read for inference

- **Preview and do the task** Read the instructions aloud. Have Ss complete the task and compare their answers with a partner.
- Say, "Compare your answers and reasons with a partner. If an answer is different, show your partner where you found your reason."
- Check answers with the class.

Answers

Is technology driving families apart? *No. In some ways, it's bringing them closer together.*
Is reading books better for family relationships? *No. It's no better and no worse.*
Should families spend as much of their free time together as possible? *No. They need time to pursue their own interests.*

2 Focus on vocabulary

A • **Preview and do the task** Read the instructions aloud. Have Ss complete the task and compare their answers with a partner. Check answers with the class.

Answers

1. . . . how did you <u>interpret</u> the family scene?
   Did you <u>perceive</u> a <u>dysfunctional family</u>?
2. . . . technology is <u>a substitute for</u> . . . ?
   Is this <u>worrisome / a cause for concern</u>?
3. When have you had to <u>contend</u> with . . . ?
4. Can technology <u>enhance</u> family . . . ?
5. Is it rude to be <u>immersed</u> in a screen . . . ?
6. How often . . . technology <u>simultaneously</u>?
7. . . . families to <u>pursue</u> . . . ? Why? Why not?

3 Listening and speaking

A ◀)) CD3, Track 9

- **Preview the task** Read the title aloud. Ask if anyone knows what *keep tabs on* means. [watch someone to know where they are and what they're doing] Say, "Look at some ways of monitoring people." Ask, "Which family members might use them and why?" Elicit ideas.
- **Play the recording** Audio script p. T-276 Say, "Check (✓) the devices the expert describes."
- **Play the recording again** Ss listen and check their answers. Check answers with the class.

Answers

☑ a screen-time control device
☑ a GPS tracking device for the car
☑ a device that detects body movement

B ◀)) CD3, Track 10

- **Preview the task** Read the instructions aloud.
- **Play the recording** Audio script p. T-276 Ss listen and complete the chart. Replay the recording if necessary. Have Ss compare answers. Check answers with the class.

Do we know where technology will lead us? *No. It remains to be seen.*
Is it the responsibility of families to decide what impact technology has on their relationships? *Yes. It's up to all of us in our own families.*

D Read for detail

- **Preview the task** Read the instructions aloud. Check that Ss understand all the questions. Have Ss complete the task and compare answers with a partner.
- Check answers with the class.

Answers

1. NG   2. T (para. 2)   3. F (para. 6)   4. NG
5. T (para. 5)   6. NG

About you

B Pair work

- **Preview and do the task** Read the instructions aloud. Walk around the class and help as needed.
- **Follow-up** For each question, have a few Ss share their answers with the class.

Answers

Checked: a screen-time control device; *Who might use it?* parents of young children; *What does it do?* limits amount of time they can spend on electronic devices
Checked: a GPS tracking device for the car; *Who might use it?* parents of teen drivers; *What does it do?* tracks the car, tells if they are speeding or texting while driving
Checked: a device that detects body movement; *Who might use it?* children of elderly parents; *What does it do?* texts or calls you if someone isn't moving for a long period of time, e.g., after a fall

About you

C Pair work

- **Preview and do the task** Read the instructions aloud. Have Ss discuss the questions.
- **Follow-up** Have Ss give their views to the class.

C Read for inference Do you think the writer would answer "yes" or "no" to these questions? Give reasons for your answers.

- Is technology driving families apart?
- Is reading books better for family relationships?
- Should families spend as much of their free time together as possible?
- Do we know where technology will lead us?
- Is it the responsibility of families to decide what impact technology has on their relationships?

D Read for detail Are the sentences true (T), false (F), or is the information not given (NG)? Find evidence in the article for your answers. Then compare with a partner.

1. The writer believes the family in the example is dysfunctional. _____
2. Some people believe that we prefer the company of our computers to being with other people. _____
3. Teachers who can't get their students' attention resort to using technology. _____
4. The Pew study says that technology makes family relationships more distant. _____
5. Technology allows people to do their own thing in the same part of the house. _____
6. Reading is better for family life than using computers. _____

2 Focus on vocabulary Building synonyms

A Replace the words in bold with expressions from the article. You may have to change the form.

1. When you read the first paragraph, how did you **understand** the family scene? (para. 1)
   Did you **see** a **family that doesn't get along**? (2 expressions, para. 1)
2. Do you think technology is **replacing** face-to-face relationships? (para. 2)
   Is this **something that you worry about**? (2 expressions, para. 2)
3. When have you had to **compete** with technology to get someone's attention? (para. 3)
4. Can technology **improve** family relationships, in your opinion? (para. 4)
5. Is it rude to be **absorbed** in a screen when you are with other people? (para. 5)
6. How often do you use more than one piece of technology **at the same time**? (para. 6)
7. Do you think it's important for families to **do** different activities? Why? Why not? (para. 6)

About you **B** Pair work Ask and answer the questions above. Use all the new expressions in your answers.

3 Listening and speaking Keeping tabs on the family

A CD 3.09 Look at the ways of monitoring people. Which family members might use them and why? Then listen to a radio show and check (✓) the devices the expert describes.

	Who might use it?	What does it do?
☐ parental controls on a computer		
☐ a screen-time control device		
☐ a GPS tracking device for the car		
☐ a camera in the living room		
☐ a device that detects body movement		

B CD 3.10 Listen again and answer the questions in the chart. Write one example for each item.

About you **C** Pair work Do you agree with the expert's views? What do you think about each monitoring device in the chart? Would you ever use one? How would you feel if someone monitored you?

Writing *It just takes a little thought.*

In this lesson, you . . .
- write a magazine article.
- use expressions like *a number of* and *a little*.
- avoid errors with *a number of*, etc.

Task Write a magazine article.

A college magazine has asked you to write an article called *Enhancing friendships – a how-to guide*.

A **Look at a model** Look at the extract from an article. Which topics does it cover? Write them in the article. Brainstorm other ideas that the article could include.

being considerate   communication   remembering birthdays, etc.   spending time together

Relationships with friends are very important to our well-being. However, many of us often take the people closest to us for granted, which can result in losing friends. There are a number of factors that lead to improved relationships, including _____, _____, and support. With just a little thought, you can enhance any friendship. . . .

There are a variety of ways to keep in touch with people. Social networks, texts, and phone calls enable us to find out what is happening in our friends' lives and update them about events in our own. They don't take a great deal of effort but do contribute to a feeling of closeness.

Not seeing friends can have a negative impact on your relationship. Therefore, it's important to spend a certain amount of time with them.

B **Focus on language** Read the chart. Underline examples of the expressions in the article above.

Expressing number and amount in writing

With plural countable nouns, you can use: *a (large / huge / small) number of, a (wide) variety of, a (wide) range of, several, many, various; a few* (= some), *few* (= not many).
There are **a number of / several** factors that lead to improved relationships.

With uncountable nouns, you can use: *a great deal of, a(n) (large / small) amount of; a little* (= some), *little* (= not much).
They don't take **a great deal of** time / effort. It takes **little** time / **a little** thought.

Expressing effect
contribute to, create, lead to, result in, affect, have an effect / impact on, as a result, . . .

Common errors
Use a plural verb with *a number of, several,* etc. + plural noun.
There **are** a number of factors that **lead to** . . .   (NOT There ~~is~~ . . . that ~~leads to~~ . . .)

C Circle the best expressions to complete the article. Sometimes there are two.

Spending quality time together doesn't need to cost **a huge amount of / a number of / various** money. It just takes **little / a little / a small amount of** imagination. **Few / A few / A variety of** friendships can survive without regular contact, and there are **various / a great deal of / a variety of** ways you can spend meaningful time together. Here are just **a little / a few / few** ideas: Take a walk. Go to a museum. Exercise.

Sending a message to say "Hi" doesn't take **a great deal of / several / little** time, either, but it can create **a number of / an enormous amount of** goodwill. Don't just send messages on birthdays or other special occasions. A birthday card may have **little / several / a few** effect if you are not in regular contact. You can find **a range of / various / few** websites that have fun greeting cards to send at any time of year.

D **Write and check** Look at the Task at the top of the page. Write your article. Then check for errors.

Writing *It just takes a little thought.*

In this lesson

- Ask a S to read the lesson aims (*In this lesson, you . . .*) aloud. Say, "The magazine article you'll write will be a 'how-to' guide. What do you expect to find in a how-to article?" Elicit ideas (e.g., *steps, instructions, methods*). Say, "Scan the page. Tell a partner one new thing you'll learn." Ask several Ss to say what they told their partner.

- **Preview the writing** Say, "In this lesson, you will write a magazine article." Point out the writing topic in Task and read it aloud. Explain that Ss will end the lesson by writing a magazine article that will practice the three aims presented in this lesson.

A Look at a model

- **Preview and do the task** Say, "Look at the extract from the article. Read the first paragraph. What does it mean to *take someone for granted*?" Elicit ideas from the class. [assume that someone will continue to be a friend without thinking about it or considering their needs]

- Say, "Read the entire extract. What topics from the box does it cover?" Have a S read the four topics given aloud. Tell Ss to write the topics in the article. Check answers with the class. [communication, spending time together]

- Say, "Notice that the first paragraph introduces the themes of the article. The second and third paragraphs pick up these themes and expand them. This technique is also very useful in academic writing."

- Have the class brainstorm other ideas that the article could include (e.g., *being supportive, introducing old friends to new friends, respecting confidences*). Write the Ss' ideas on the board. (Do not erase.)

B 📥 www.cambridge.org/viewpoint/audio

Focus on language

- **Present the grammar for writing chart** Read the information in the chart aloud. If desired, play the downloadable recording. Ss listen and read along.

- **Understand the grammar for writing** Say, "The chart shows you more appropriate ways to express the ideas of *a lot of* and *not a lot of* before nouns in formal writing."

  Write on the board

  > *It is possible to improve friendships in _____ ways.*
  >
  > *It takes _____ thought.*

  Ask, "What kind of noun is *ways*?" [plural, countable] "What expressions can I write here to mean *a lot of*?" [a (large) number of, a (wide) variety of, a (wide) range of, several, many, various] "How can I express the idea of *some* or *not a lot of*?" [a (small) number of, a few]

  Then ask, "What kind of noun is *thought*?" [uncountable] "What expressions can I write here to mean *a lot of*?" [a great deal of, a(n) (large) amount of]

- Say, "It is also important to remember the differences in meaning between *few* and *a few* and *little* and *a little*.

A few and *a little* mean 'some' – they express quantity as a positive idea. *Few* and *little* express the idea of 'not a lot' as a negative – *not many / much*."

- **Preview and do the task** Read the instructions aloud. Have Ss complete the task. Check answers with the class.

Answers

. . . However, <u>many</u> of us . . . There are <u>a number of</u> factors that lead to . . . With just <u>a little</u> thought, . . . There are <u>a variety of</u> ways to . . . They don't take <u>a great deal of</u> effort but . . .

. . . Therefore, it's important to spend <u>a certain amount of</u> time with them.

- **Present *Common errors*** Write on the board:

  > *There is / are a number of ways to improve friendships.*
  >
  > *A number of factors leads / lead to better friendships.*
  >
  > *There is / are several reasons for this.*

- Ask a Ss to circle the correct verbs [are, lead, are] and say why [the noun is plural].

- Read the information aloud. Say, "This error is common even among advanced students. Remember to check your verb if you use *a number of* or *several* + plural noun."

- **Present *Expressing effect*** Ask a S to read the expressions aloud. Remind Ss of the difference between *affect* (verb) and *effect* (noun).

C
- **Preview and do the task** Read the instructions aloud. Have Ss complete the task. Check answers with the class.

Answers

Spending quality time . . . cost <u>a huge amount of</u> money. It just takes <u>a little</u> / <u>a small amount of</u> imagination. <u>Few</u> friendships . . . , and there are <u>various</u> / <u>a variety of</u> ways you can . . . Here are just <u>a few</u> ideas: . . .

Sending a message . . . take <u>a great deal of</u> time, either, but it can create <u>an enormous amount of</u> goodwill. . . . A birthday card may have <u>little</u> effect if . . . You can find <u>a range of</u> / <u>various</u> websites . . .

D Write and check

- **Preview and do the task** Read the instructions aloud. Say, "You can use the ideas on the board from Exercise A." Have Ss complete the task.

Extra activity – class

Ss leave their magazine articles on their desk for classmates to read. Ss go around the class reading each other's work. Ss decide on three how-to pieces of advice that they will make a point of remembering.

Vocabulary notebook *Now or never*

If done for homework

Briefly present the Learning tip and the task directions. Make sure Ss understand what they need to do.

If done in class

- **Present *Learning tip*** Read the information aloud. Ask a S to read the example in the box. Ask the class for more examples of sentences containing the expression *pain and suffering*.

A • **Preview and do the task** Read the instructions and the expressions in the box aloud. Ask Ss which expression completes sentence 1. [wait and see] Have Ss complete the task. Check answers with the class. Ask individual Ss each to read a sentence aloud.

Answers

1. wait and see
2. sick and tired
3. above and beyond
4. success or failure
5. back and forth
6. live and work

B • **Preview and do the task** Read the instructions aloud. Have Ss complete the task. Ss read their sentences aloud to a partner. Have a few Ss read their sentences aloud to the class.

Possible answers

1. I don't have the time and energy to go to the gym in the evenings.
2. Sometimes I say things I don't mean. I should stop and think first.
3. Everyone has ups and downs in life.
4. I've always believed that relationships are give-and-take.
5. Sooner or later, someone is going to knock me off my bike. Drivers are crazy!
6. I'm getting rid of the clutter in our house slowly but surely.

C Word builder

- **Preview the task** Read the instructions aloud. Have a S read the expressions aloud.
- **Do the task** Have Ss complete the task. Check answers with the class.

Possible answers

1. My sister is far and away the best basketball player on her team.
2. I want to thank my teachers, my classmates, and, last but not least, my parents.
3. I like to go to the movies now and then.
4. I should change my career. It's now or never really – before I get too old!
5. I need to get out and about more. I spend too much time at home.
6. That movie was over and above the best I've seen in five years.
7. There are a lot of people walking to and from in my neighborhood today.

D Focus on vocabulary, page 81

- **Preview and do the task** Read the instructions aloud. When Ss have completed the questions using the words in the box, check answers with the class. Have a few Ss read the questions aloud.
- Then have Ss write true answers to the questions. Ss compare their answers in pairs. Call on a few Ss to share answers with the class.

Answers

1. Why do you think some families are dysfunctional? What can enhance their relationships?
2. Is a long email from a friend a good substitute for having a conversation with that person?
3. Do you perceive any differences in the way that older and younger people use technology?
4. Do you find it worrisome that people spend so much time on their computers?
5. Do you ever have to contend with television to get the attention of your family?
6. Do you ever get so immersed in your work that you forget to have dinner?
7. What two things can you do simultaneously?
8. Are there any interests you'd like to pursue when you're older?

Extra activity – pairs

Ss ask and answer the questions in Exercise D.

Vocabulary notebook *Now or never*

pain and suffering
    Divorce can cause a lot of pain and suffering, and I feel lucky that my parents never got divorced.

A   Use the expressions in the box to complete the sentences.

| above and beyond | live and work | success or failure | back and forth | sick and tired | wait and see |

1. I'm not sure how I did on my last exam. I'll just have to _____.
2. People are always throwing trash around in my neighborhood. I'm _____ of it.
3. My dad is so great. If I ever ask a favor, he always goes _____ what I ask for.
4. What determines the _____ of a relationship is your ability to communicate.
5. When I'm working on a project with classmates, we send each other files _____ all day.
6. I'm lucky that I get to _____ in the same city.

B   Write personalized sentences for these expressions.

1. time and energy _____
2. stop and think _____
3. ups and downs _____
4. give-and-take _____
5. sooner or later _____
6. slowly but surely _____

C   Word builder Find the meanings of these expressions. Then use each one in a personalized sentence.

| far and away | now and then | out and about | to and from |
| last but not least | now or never | over and above | |

I think communication is far and away the most important thing in any relationship.

D   (Focus on vocabulary) Complete the questions with the words in the box. Then write true answers. Refer to Exercise 2A on page 81 to help you.

| contend dysfunctional enhance immersed perceive pursue simultaneously substitute worrisome |

1. Why do you think some families are _____ ? What can _____ their relationships?
2. Is a long email from a friend a good _____ for having a conversation with that person?
3. Do you _____ any differences in the way that older and younger people use technology?
4. Do you find it _____ that people spend so much time on their computers?
5. Do you ever have to _____ with television to get the attention of your family?
6. Do you ever get so _____ in your work that you forget to have dinner?
7. What two things can you do _____ ?
8. Are there any interests you'd like to _____ when you're older?

Unit 8 History

Lesson A *People in history*

Grammar *Referring to past time*

(See Student's Book p. 85.)

In this lesson, Ss use perfect infinitives to refer to the past. They are presented here in the context of people talking about historical figures they wish they could have met.

Form

The pattern for perfect infinitives is *to* + *have* + past participle.

Perfect infinitives follow verbs like *seem*, *appear*, and *happen*; verbs like *acknowledge*, *believe*, *consider*, and *know* when they are passive; and verbs like *would like / love / hate* for events that did not happen.

- After verbs like *seem*, *appear*, *happen*

  He seems to have had a lot of respect for older people.

- After verbs such as *acknowledge*, *consider*, etc., in the passive

  She is considered to have formed some extremely effective political alliances.

- After *would like / love / hate*, etc., for events that did not happen

  I'd love to have met Leonardo da Vinci.

  Reiko would like to have spoken face-to-face with Confucius.

Use

The perfect infinitive can be used for events in a period of time that leads up to the time expressed by the main verb.

In this lesson, it is used after present tense verbs. *Bolivar is acknowledged to have helped achieve independence.* (*It is still acknowledged that he helped . . .*). It is also commonly used to describe hypothetical events after *would like*, etc.

> ### Corpus information
> **In conversation**
>
> In conversation, people generally say, for example, *I would have liked to do it*, not *I would like to have done it*. Some also say *I would have liked to have done it*.

Grammar extra *More on perfect infinitives; The perfect infinitive after adjectives and nouns*

(See Student's Book p. 158.)

Grammar extra presents perfect infinitives after verbs in the present and past, negative forms, and after adjectives and nouns.

Speaking naturally *Saying perfect infinitives*

(See Student's Book p. 141.)

In this section, Ss practice saying perfect infinitives (*to* + *have* + past participle). In this pattern, *to* is not reduced, but *have* is reduced.

Lesson B *Events that changed the world*

Vocabulary in context *Antonyms*

(See Student's Book p. 86.)

The podcast presents adjectives (and their antonyms or opposites) to describe degrees of impact, change, and effect caused by world-changing events. Ss learn antonyms such as *lasting / temporary* and *imperceptible / apparent*.

Vocabulary notebook *Deep, low, high*

(See Student's Book p. 93.)

The Learning tip tells Ss that when they learn a new word, they should also look up its synonyms and antonyms. It warns that some words, such as *deep*, have more than one meaning and that different meanings may have different synonyms and antonyms.

Grammar *Giving ideas extra focus*

(See Student's Book p. 87.)

This lesson teaches *it*-cleft sentences. A cleft sentence is a sentence in which a single clause has been split into two clauses to emphasize an idea.

Form

- *It*-cleft + noun

  It + *be* + noun + *who / that* + clause

  It was scientists who / that started alerting us to the fact that the world climate was changing. (= *Scientists started alerting us to the fact that the world climate was changing.* Here, *scientists* has extra focus or emphasis.)

- *It*-cleft + phrase

  It + *be* + phrase + *that* + clause

  Generally, it is not the small things that we worry about. (= *Generally, we don't worry about the small things.*)

- *It* + *be* + clause + *that* + clause

  It is only when we are personally affected that we describe events as "world-changing." (= *We describe events as "world-changing" only when we are personally affected.*)

Negative statements are also possible.

  It's not the big things that we worry about.

Use

Cleft sentences allow writers and speakers to give extra emphasis to the idea within the *it* clause.

Grammar extra *More on cleft sentences with it + be; It + be + noun phrase in writing*

(See Student's Book p. 159.)

Grammar extra looks at more ways to give ideas extra focus using cleft sentences with *it* + *be* + noun phrase in writing.

Lesson C *Don't get me started.*

Conversation strategy *Avoiding a topic*

(See Student's Book p. 88.)

The lesson teaches expressions that speakers can use to avoid topics that they don't want to talk about. *Don't get me started (on . . .)* and *Let's not go there* suggest the topic is one that the speaker finds annoying or has a number of very strong opinions about. They also suggest it may take a long time to talk about it. *(But) that's a whole other story* suggests that the point just made is only one aspect of a much larger discussion, which, again, may take too much time to discuss. *I'd rather not talk about it / that* is a clear signal that the speaker is seriously uncomfortable with discussing the topic for some reason.

Expressions:

> *Don't get me started (on . . .).*
>
> *(But) that's another / a whole other story.*
>
> *Let's not go there.*
>
> *Let's not get into / talk about politics / that.*
>
> *I'd rather not talk about it / that.*

Corpus information

In conversation

In conversation, people say *Don't get me started* about a topic they find annoying and often before they do in fact say more about it. *I'd rather not talk about it* is a more serious way to show you want to avoid a topic.

Strategy plus *That's what I'm saying.*

(See Student's Book p. 89.)

In conversation, people use *That's what I'm saying* in responses to introduce and focus on or reinforce their opinion. You can use it when you agree or disagree with someone.

A Everybody should study history — it's important.

B Yeah we need to learn from it.

A That's what I'm saying. It teaches us lessons. (agree)

A History's important, but we never learn from it.

B But can't we learn from mistakes people have made?

A That's what I'm saying. We don't learn. (disagree)

Corpus information

In conversation

In conversation, people also say *That's what I mean / meant.*

Lesson D *Unearthing the past*

Reading tip *Cataphoric reference*

(See Student's Book p. 90.)

The Reading tip explains that writers sometimes use a pronoun in a way that means the reader has to read on to find out what it refers to. For example, the writer may begin a sentence with a pronoun subject and the name or noun to which it refers may be in a later clause or sentence.

Writing *In the end, . . .*

(See Student's Book p. 92.)

This lesson teaches Ss to plan and write a historical narrative. The grammar for writing brings together and recycles structures to vary the way the order of past events is presented. It recycles time clauses from Unit 3, Grammar extra; participle clauses from Unit 3, Lesson A; and adverb placement from Unit 5, Lesson A.

* Ordering events in writing

  Ss can use these structures:

  Time clauses

  > *After / Once / As soon as the war ended, they married.*
  > *On arriving at the station, she met my father.*
  > The subject of both clauses must be the same here and in participle clauses, below.

  Participle clauses

  > *Arriving at the station, she met my father.*

  Adverbs

  > *She had previously lived in the city.*

  Adverbial phrases

  > *In the end, / After a while, they married.*

Corpus information

Writing vs. Conversation

Time clauses with a preposition + *-ing* are not common in conversation. They are much more a feature of writing.

Conversation

Writing

Corpus information

Common errors with *at the end*, *in the end*, and *finally*

Students often confuse *at the end*, *in the end*, and *finally*. Use *at the end of* + a noun.

> *At the end of the war*, they got married.

In the end refers to the conclusion of all the events.

> *In the end*, they retired.

Use *finally* at the end of a series of other events.

> *She finally found happiness.*

In Unit 8, you . . .
- talk about events in history and famous historical figures.
- use the perfect infinitive after verbs like *seem* and *would like*.
- use *it*-cleft sentences to focus on information.
- avoid topics of conversation with expressions like *Let's not go there*.
- say *That's what I'm saying* to focus on your viewpoint.

Lesson A *People in history*

1 Grammar in context

A Who are the most famous figures in your country's history? Why are they famous?

"Atatürk is probably one of the most famous, being the founder of the Republic of Turkey."

B 🔊 CD 3.11 Listen to four people talk about historical figures they wish they could have met. What reasons do they give?

WHICH HISTORICAL FIGURE WOULD YOU LIKE TO HAVE MET AND WHY?

For me it would definitely be Leonardo da Vinci. I'd love to have met him; he was such a creative genius and not just an artist. He seems to have foreseen a number of inventions that only came about hundreds of years later, like flying machines and types of weapons. I'd like to tell him he really did see the future.

Naomi, Chicago

I'd choose Cleopatra – the last pharaoh of ancient Egypt. She is thought to have been very beautiful and is generally considered to have formed some extremely effective political alliances. Not many women were that influential in ancient times. I'd like to have seen how she did it.

Lucinda, Nairobi

I'm Latin American, so I would nominate Simón Bolívar as the person I would like to have known. He's supposed to have been a very charismatic, courageous leader and is acknowledged to have helped achieve independence for several countries in Latin America in the nineteenth century.

Patricio, Caracas

I studied philosophy, so I would like to have spoken face-to-face with the Chinese philosopher Confucius. I'd like to have discussed with him his political philosophy and his ideas about family values. He seems to have had a lot of respect for older people, and even though he lived more than a thousand years ago, his beliefs are still relevant.

Li-yun, Shanghai

About you

C Pair work Discuss the questions about the people above. Give reasons for your views.

Which figure do you think . . .

1. attracted admiration and gained the most respect?
2. was the most intelligent and the most talented?
3. had ideas that could be applied nowadays?
4. was particularly clever at political relations?
5. accomplished the most?
6. would make the best role model?

History

Introduce the theme of the unit Tell Ss that this unit looks at aspects of history. Ask, "What are the factors that go into history?" Elicit ideas (e.g., *events, wars, people, leaders, politics, social history*). Say, "History is interesting. Look at the lessons and decide which one looks most interesting to you." Have Ss look through the unit and then call out the lesson they decided on. Read the unit aims aloud.

Lesson A *People in history*

1 Grammar in context

- **Set the scene** Books closed. Say, "This lesson is about people in history. What kinds of things earn people a place in history?" Have Ss call out their ideas (e.g., *inventing something important, discovering something important, bringing about some important social change, their political impact on a country*).

A • **Preview and do the task** Books open. Ask a S to read the example aloud. Read the instructions aloud. Have Ss complete the task.

- Have Ss call out their ideas, and write the names on the board. (Note: If using the Extra Activity at the end of this lesson, do not erase.)

B 🔊 CD3, Track 11

- **Preview the task** Books closed. Read the instructions aloud. Write on the board:

Leonardo da Vinci	*Simón Bolívar*
Cleopatra	*Confucius*

  Say, "The people talk about these four historical figures. What do you know about them?" Have a short class discussion.

Culture note

Leonardo da Vinci: (1452–1519) Italian painter, sculptor, inventor, and scientist, among other talents. One of his famous works is the *Mona Lisa*.

Cleopatra: (69 BCE–30 BCE) Ruler / Queen / Pharaoh of Egypt from 48 BCE. Romantic involvements with the Roman leaders Julius Caesar and Marc Anthony helped her keep the throne.

Simón Bolívar: (1783–1830) Venezuelan military and political leader instrumental in achieving independence from Spain for many South American countries.

Confucius: (551BCE–479 BCE) Chinese philosopher and teacher. He taught self-discipline and a moral approach to living. He is credited with "The Golden Rule" – *Do unto others as you would have done unto yourself.*

- **Play the recording** Tell Ss to listen to the speakers and write brief answers. Have Ss compare their notes with a partner.
- Books open. Tell Ss to read the article for the main ideas. (If desired, play the recording again while Ss read along.) Say, "Don't stop to check the meaning of new vocabulary. Then read the article again and check your answers to the question."

- Have Ss complete the task. Check answers with the class.

Answers

Naomi says Leonardo da Vinci was a creative genius who foresaw a number of inventions.
Lucinda says that Cleopatra was an influential woman who formed effective political alliances.
Patricio says that Simón Bolívar was charismatic and courageous and helped several countries in Latin America gain independence.
Li-yun says that Confucius had respect for older people and a philosophy in favor of family values.

- Check for vocabulary questions.

About you

C Pair work

- **Preview and do the task** Read the instructions aloud. Ask a S to read the six questions aloud. Have Ss discuss the questions.
- **Follow-up** For each question, ask several pairs which figure they chose and why.

Extra activity – pairs

Ss discuss questions from Exercise 1C, but using historical figures from their own country. Ss choose a name on the board from Exercise 1A or choose another figure.

Several Ss tell the class about the person they discussed with their partner.

2 Grammar

A ▸ www.cambridge.org/viewpoint/audio

- **Preview the task** Say, "This activity is about another way to refer to past time. Complete the answers to the questions with the correct verb form. Use the interviews to help you."
- **Do the task** Have Ss complete the task and compare answers with a partner. Check answers with the class.

Answers

1. He seems to have been a very charismatic, courageous leader.
2. Yes, she is acknowledged to have formed some extremely effective political alliances.
3. She'd like to have met Leonardo da Vinci.

- **Focus on the form** Say, "Look at the verbs given to begin the three answer sentences. Which ones are active?" [1 and 3] "Which one is passive?" [2] "Which one is hypothetical?" [3] Say, "Look at the correct verb forms in the completed sentences. What is the pattern for all of them?" [*to* + *have* + past participle] Write the pattern on the board.
- **Focus on the use** Say, "This verb form is the perfect infinitive. It is used for an action or state that happened before the time of the main verb."
- **Present the grammar chart** Read the information aloud. If desired, play the downloadable recording.
- **Present *In conversation*** Ask a S to read the information aloud. Say, "*I would have liked to do it* is an alternative to *I would like to have done it*. The second example, *I would have liked to have done it* is heard often but is not generally considered correct. It's best to avoid it in writing. Be sure to use the form given in the chart."

(For more information, see Language notes at the beginning of the unit. For more help on perfect infinitives, go to Grammar extra, p. 158.)

3 Viewpoint

Group work

- **Preview and do the task** Read the instructions aloud and the example aloud. Have Ss complete the task. Remind Ss to use a perfect infinitive when possible. Walk around the class and give help as needed.
- **Follow-up** Have groups report the three people they chose and say why. (Note: If using the Extra Activity to the right, write the names of the people each group chose on the board.)

Extra activity – class

The class agrees on five people they would like to have met. Ss repeat their reasons to support their choices.

B • **Preview the task** Read the instructions aloud. Ask Ss to read through the four answers. Check for any vocabulary questions. Complete the first answer as a class: Have a S give the answer for the first blank. [I would love to have met]

- **Do the task** Have Ss complete the sentences and compare their answers with a partner. Check answers with the class.

Answers

1. I <u>would love to have met</u> Mozart. He <u>seems to have been</u> a brilliant musician, and he's <u>said to have started</u> composing music . . . He's <u>thought to have died</u> from some kind of fever.
2. I'd <u>like to have traveled</u> with Neil Armstrong, . . . The moon landing <u>is acknowledged to have been</u> a major event . . . My father <u>happens to have met</u> one of the astronauts.
3. I'd <u>like to have interviewed</u> the captain . . . The disappearance of everyone on board <u>is considered to have been</u> one of the . . . The entire crew <u>seems to have disappeared</u> . . .
4. I'd <u>love to have spent</u> a day with Catherine . . . and <u>is acknowledged to have helped</u> Russia . . . She <u>seems to have been</u> very intelligent.

About you

C Pair work

- **Preview and do the task** Read the instructions aloud. Tell Ss to discuss more things they know about each person. (e.g., *Mozart's father taught his son to play piano. He seems to have been a talented musician, too.*) Tell Ss to think of one question they would like to have asked each person.
- **Follow-up** For each famous person in Exercise 2B, have the class discuss their comments.

Speaking naturally

- Tell Ss to turn to Speaking naturally on p. 141. (For more information, see Language notes at the beginning of this unit. See the teaching notes on p. T-141.)

② Grammar Referring to past time

Figure it out

A Use the interviews to help you complete the answers. Then read the grammar chart.

1. What type of leader was Simón Bolívar? He seems _____.
2. Was Cleopatra good at politics? Yes, she is acknowledged _____.
3. Who does Naomi wish she could have met? She'd like _____.

The perfect infinitive 🔽

Grammar extra
See page 158.

Use the perfect infinitive for events in a period of time that lead up to the present or to a point in the past.
You can use the perfect infinitive after verbs like *seem, appear,* and *happen.*
He seems **to have had** *a lot of respect for older people.*

You can use the perfect infinitive after verbs such as *acknowledge, believe, consider, know, say,* and *think*
when they are in the passive, and after *be supposed to.*
She is considered **to have formed** *some extremely effective political alliances.*

You can use the perfect infinitive after *would like / love / hate,* etc., for events that did not happen.
I'd love **to have met** *Leonardo da Vinci.*
Li-yun would like **to have spoken** *face-to-face with Confucius.*

> **In conversation . . .**
> People generally say, e.g., *I would have liked to do it,* not *I would like to have done it.* Some also say, *I would have liked to have done it.*

B Complete the sentences using the verbs given and a perfect infinitive. Some verbs are passive.

What famous person or people would you like to have met?

1. _____ (would love / meet) Mozart. He _____ (seem / be) a brilliant musician, and he _____ (say / start) composing music at the age of five, which is amazing. He _____ (think / die) from some kind of fever.
2. I _____ ('d like / travel) with Neil Armstrong, one of the astronauts that landed on the moon. The moon landing _____ (acknowledge / be) a major event in our history. My father _____ (happen / meet) one of the astronauts.
3. I _____ ('d like / interview) the captain of the *Mary Celeste.* The disappearance of everyone on board _____ (consider / be) one of the strangest mysteries of all time. The entire crew _____ (seem / disappear) from the ship for no reason at all.
4. I _____ ('d love / spend) a day with Catherine the Great of Russia. She became empress after the death of her husband, Peter III, and _____ (acknowledge / help) Russia become a great power. She _____ (seem / be) very intelligent.

About you

C Pair work Do you agree with the comments above? What would you have asked each person?

③ Viewpoint *I'd like to have met . . .*

Group work Discuss the questions. Agree on three people that you would all like to have met.

- What famous person from history would you like to have met?
- What contribution is he or she said to have made to history?
- What kind of person is he or she believed to have been?
- What interesting things is he or she supposed to have done?
- What one question would you like to have asked that person?
- How would you like to have spent the day with him or her?

Speaking naturally
See page 141.

"I'd love to have met John Lennon. He's generally acknowledged to have been a great songwriter."

Lesson B *Events that changed the world*

1 Vocabulary in context

A What twentieth-century events do you think most changed the world? Make a list.

"I think the invention of the Internet changed the world most. We just can't live without it now."

B 🔊 CD 3.12 Listen to the podcast. What two broad kinds of historical change are mentioned?

HOME   SUBSCRIBE   EPISODE GUIDE   MEET THE CAST   CONTACT

▶ PODCAST

Many events are said to have been "world-changing," and it's not only headline writers who use this phrase. But what does it mean? In most cases, planet Earth as a whole remains the same, even after a **major** event such as a natural disaster. That said, a catastrophic asteroid impact millions of years ago is believed to have destroyed almost all life – an event that can genuinely be said to have been **universal** and world-changing. However, as a rule, even significant events have mostly **local** effects and only a **superficial** or **temporary** impact on the vast majority of people outside the affected region. Perhaps it is only when we are personally affected that we describe such events as "world-changing."

Occasionally, events do have a **profound** impact, such as the revolution in travel and communications in the twentieth century. For example, it was the invention of the airplane that made it possible to cross continents in a matter of hours, and it was when Internet use became widespread that the world turned into a global village. These innovations brought about **massive** changes, and many would now consider it impossible to live without them.

Equally, change can also be **gradual** or **imperceptible**. It was more than 30 years ago that scientists started alerting us to the fact that the world climate was changing, but the change was neither immediately **apparent** nor **sudden**. Events that may seem **minor** or **insignificant** – for example, **slight** or **minute** changes in average global temperatures over a number of years – can make it difficult to predict **lasting** or **long-term** effects. Generally, it is not the small things that we worry about. We react to **visible** or **rapid** change, and it is the events with **immediate** effects that get the headlines.

C Pair work **Answer the questions about the podcast.**

1. Why does the speaker mention an asteroid strike?
2. What do the airplane and the Internet have in common, from the writer's viewpoint?
3. Why is climate change a different kind of event from the invention of the Internet?

Word sort **D** **Find adjectives in the podcast that are the opposite of the adjectives below. Can you think of an example of each type of change, effect, or impact?**

lasting effects	temporary	**massive** changes	or
significant events		**gradual** change	or
local effects		**imperceptible** change	or
superficial impact			
major event		**long-term** effects	

"The oil spills in the Gulf of Mexico had lasting effects on the tourist industries."

Vocabulary notebook

See page 93.

Lesson B *Events that changed the world*

① Vocabulary in context

- **Set the scene** Books closed. Say, "The title of Lesson B is *Events that changed the world*. What kinds of events can be world-changing?" (*e.g., a war / revolution, technological discoveries, inventions*)

A • **Preview and do the task** Books open. Read the instructions and the example aloud. Ask Ss to make their list.

- **Follow-up** Have the class call out the events they chose.

B ◀)) CD3, Track 12

- **Preview the task** Books closed. Write on the board:

  1. catastrophic

  2. asteroid

  3. global village

- Ask if any Ss can give a definition or explanation. Provide definitions if necessary. [1. Causing a lot of suffering and / or destruction; 2. Large rocky objects from less than one kilometer to over 900 kilometers wide, which circle the sun; 3. All of the countries of the world when thought of as being closely connected by modern communication and trade.]

- Read the instructions aloud. Ask, "What does *broad kind of change* mean?" [general kind of change] Say, "Just listen the first time for the answer. Write brief notes the second time."

- **Play the recording** Ss listen only. Replay the recording. Ss listen and write. Have Ss compare their answer with a partner.

- **Play the recording again** Books open. Ss listen, read along, and check their answer. Check the answer with the class. [Profound changes and gradual, or imperceptible, changes.]

C Pair work

- **Preview and do the task** Read the instructions aloud. Have Ss work together to answer the questions. Check answers with the class.

Answers

1. It is an example of a universal and world-changing event, as it is believed to have destroyed almost all life.
2. Both have contributed to making the world into a global village.
3. Its results are more gradual or imperceptible.

Word sort

D • **Preview the and do task** Say, "The podcast teaches adjectives that are useful for reading and more formal writing or discussions. Find adjectives in the podcast that are the opposite of the adjectives below, and complete the chart. Remember to use the context to help you."

Have Ss complete the chart and compare their answers with a partner. Check answers with the class.

Answers

lasting effects ≠ temporary

significant events ≠ insignificant

local effects ≠ universal

superficial impact ≠ profound

major event ≠ minor

massive changes ≠ slight or minute

gradual change ≠ rapid or sudden / immediate

imperceptible change ≠ visible or apparent

long-term effects ≠ immediate

- Ask, "Can you think of an example of each type of change, effect, or impact?" Ask Ss to write their examples. Explain that this will help them remember the vocabulary. Ask Ss to call out their examples.

Extra activity – groups

Groups decide on a current event that they think will have a lasting effect on the world today. Groups prepare a short presentation explaining the event and their reasons for choosing it.

Groups make presentations to the class.

Tell Ss to turn to Vocabulary Notebook on p. 93 of their Student's Books. Have Ss do the tasks in class or assign them for homework. (See the teaching notes on p. T-93.) *Vocabulary notebook*

② Grammar

A 🔽 www.cambridge.org/viewpoint/audio

- **Preview the task** Ask, "How are these ideas expressed in the podcast? Write sentences." Do the first sentence with the class: Ask a S to read sentence 1 aloud. Say, "Find a similar sentence in the podcast and make the changes to sentence 1." Have a S read the new sentence aloud. [It was the invention of the airplane that made it possible to cross continents.]

- **Do the task** Have Ss complete the task. Check answers with the class: Ask individual Ss each to read a sentence aloud.

Answers

1. It was the invention of the airplane that made it possible to cross continents.
2. It's not only headline writers who use this phrase.
3. It was when Internet use became widespread that the world turned into a global village.

- **Focus on the form** Say, "Look at the three new sentences. What do they all begin with?" [*It* and a form of *be*] Ask, "What follows *be* in sentence 1?" [a noun phrase – *invention of the airplane*] "What follows *be* in sentence 2?" [a phrase – *not only the headline writers*] Ask, "What about sentence 3? What follows *be*?" [a time clause with *when* – *when Internet use became widespread*]

- Ask, "What is the final structure in sentences 1 and 2?" [a relative clause] "And sentence 3?" [a *that* clause]

- **Focus on the use** Say, "Read each pair of sentences again. What do you think is the effect of using *It + be*?" [The ideas following *It + be* have extra focus.]

- **Present the grammar chart** Read the information aloud. If desired, play the downloadable recording.

- **Understand the grammar chart** Say, "The chart teaches ways to give ideas extra focus in cleft sentences. A cleft sentence is a sentence in which a single clause has been split into two clauses to emphasize an idea."

- Ask Ss to look at the *Noun* section of the chart. Say, "See how *Scientists started* is split into two clauses: *It was scientists* and *who / that started*."

- Have Ss look at the *Phrase* section of the chart. Say, "Look at the example sentences. What does *not* make negative in the original sentence?" [worry] Ask, "What happened to the negative in the cleft sentence?" [It makes *be* negative.]

- Tell Ss to look at the examples in the section on clauses. Ask, "How do you give a clause extra focus?" [Use *It + be* + the clause you want to focus on. Add *that* + the rest of the sentence.]

(For more information, see Language notes at the beginning of the unit. For more work on cleft sentences, go to Grammar extra, p. 159.)

B - **Preview and do the task** Read the instructions aloud. Do the first item with the class. Ask, "What's underlined?" [a noun – *a British scientist*] Have Ss rewrite the sentence. Ask a S to read the cleft sentence aloud. [The Internet is a global phenomenon, but **it was a British scientist**, working in a physics lab in Geneva, Switzerland, **who / that** invented it.]

- Have Ss complete the task and compare their answers with a partner. Check answers with the class.

Answers

A.

(1) The Internet is a global phenomenon, but it was a British scientist, working in a physics lab in Geneva, Switzerland, who / that invented it.
(2) It is perhaps the Internet that has changed the way . . .
(3) It was only after his bosses rejected his proposal that he took it to the masses.
(4) It was at 2:56:20 p.m. on August 6, 1991, that he posted . . .
(5) It was because he persisted with his idea that he succeeded . . .
(6) It was this universal revolution that brought . . .

B.

(1) It was on April 25, 1953, that two scientists, . . . published an article, which answered . . .
(2) It was this discovery that enabled us . . .
(3) It is thanks to their work that significant . . .
(4) However, it wasn't until 1987 that DNA . . .

- Say, "Now practice telling the information to a partner."

Extra activity – pairs

Have Ss write cleft sentences for these three items to share with the class.

Noun: television

Phrase: communicating on social networks

Clause: when air travel became affordable

Extra activity – pairs

Ss write a noun, a phrase, and a clause on a piece of paper. Pairs exchange papers and write a cleft sentence for each structure. Pairs read their sentences to each other.

About you

C Pair work

- **Preview and do the task** Read the instructions aloud. Have a S read the example aloud. Say, "Remember to include cleft sentences where possible when you are justifying your choices."

- Walk around the class, giving help as needed. After pairs have compared ideas with another pair, have several Ss present their choices to the class.

② Grammar Giving ideas extra focus

Figure it out **A** How are these ideas expressed in the podcast? Write sentences. Then read the grammar chart.

1. The invention of the airplane made it possible to cross continents.
2. Headline writers aren't the only ones who use this phrase.
3. The world turned into a global village when Internet use became widespread.

Cleft sentences ⬇

Grammar extra
See page 159.

You can give extra focus to a single noun, phrase, or clause by putting it at the beginning of the sentence, after *it + be*. After nouns, use a relative pronoun – usually *who* or *that*. After other items, use a *that* clause.

Noun *Scientists started alerting us to the fact that the world climate was changing.*
→ **It was scientists who / that** *started alerting us to the fact that the world climate was changing.*

Phrase *Generally, we don't worry about the small things.*
→ *Generally,* **it is not the small things that** *we worry about.*

Clause *We describe events as "world-changing"* **only when we are personally affected.**
→ **It is only when we are personally affected that** *we describe events as "world-changing."*

B Rewrite the numbered sentences as cleft sentences with *it + be* to give extra focus to the underlined words. Then practice telling the information to a partner.

Writing vs. Conversation

It-cleft sentences are about eight times more common in writing.

A. (1) The Internet is a global phenomenon, but a British scientist working in a physics lab in Geneva, Switzerland, invented it. (2) Perhaps the Internet has changed the way people communicate today more than anything else. Tim Berners-Lee devised a new way for scientists to share data by linking documents over the Internet. (3) He took it to the masses only after his bosses rejected his proposal. (4) He posted his idea to an online bulletin board as the "WWW project" at 2:56:20 p.m. on August 6, 1991. (5) He succeeded in creating the World Wide Web because he persisted with his idea. (6) This universal revolution brought us search engines and websites.

B. (1) Two scientists, Francis Crick and James Watson, published an article on April 25, 1953, which answered an age-old question. They had discovered the nature of DNA. (2) This discovery enabled us to understand how parents pass on characteristics, like eye and hair color, to their children. (3) Significant advances in medicine have been possible thanks to their work. In addition, the discovery allowed for the development of criminal forensics. (4) However, DNA wasn't used to convict someone in a criminal case until 1987 in Florida, USA.

About you **C** Pair work Think of six people or events that have had the most profound effect on our lives. Make a list. Then compare ideas with another pair. Justify your choices.

"We chose the discovery of penicillin because it was penicillin that changed medicine and led to the discovery of other antibiotics."

Lesson C *Don't get me started.*

1 Conversation strategy Avoiding a topic

A Are you interested in history? Why? Why not? Share your ideas with the class.

B ◀))CD 3.13 Listen. What does Tom think about history? How about Celia?

Tom	You know, I never did like history in school. It just wasn't a subject I enjoyed, remembering all those dates. I didn't see the point.
Celia	Well, I guess it's not just about learning dates. It's about trying to understand why people did things or what society was like through the ages.
Tom	But I mean, so often the facts get distorted, like what happened in the last war. But don't get me started on that.
Celia	Well, yeah. But that doesn't mean we shouldn't try to find out the truth and then learn from it so we don't repeat the same mistakes.
Tom	But that's what I'm saying. We don't learn, do we? I mean, look at what's happening around the world today. We seem to have learned absolutely nothing. It's like history repeating itself. But that's another story.
Celia	Yeah, but even if we still have disputes, maybe we'll deal with them in a different way. I mean, engage in dialog . . . negotiate.
Tom	But most of the time, talks just break down and don't go anywhere. But anyway, let's not get into politics.

C **Notice** how Tom uses expressions like these to avoid talking about certain topics. Find examples in the conversation.

> *Don't get me started (on . . .).*
> *(But) that's another / a whole other story.*
> *Let's not go there.*
> *Let's not get into / talk about politics / that.*
> *I'd rather not talk about it / that.*

In conversation . . .

People say *Don't get me started* about a topic they find annoying, and often before they say more about it. *I'd rather not talk about it* is a more serious way to show you want to avoid a topic.

D ◀))CD 3.14 Listen to more of the conversation. Complete the expressions that you hear. Then practice the whole conversation with a partner.

Celia I know. There've been some terrible events in recent history, as you know.

Tom I know, _____. We probably won't agree on anything, so _____.

Celia OK, but it's amazing how little people know of their own country's history _____.

Tom Yeah, but there'll always be different versions of events, like the latest peace talks. _____.

Celia Yeah. They seem to have collapsed. _____. You know, I wonder how future generations will see us.

Tom Greedy and aggressive, I'd say. You know what I think. _____.

Lesson C *Don't get me started.*

① *Conversation strategy*

Why use expressions to avoid a topic?

In conversation, people may want to avoid talking about certain topics, either because they find them annoying, too complex to deal with in the time available, or too sensitive. The lesson includes expressions to signal all of these. *Don't get me started (on . . .)* and *Let's not go there* suggest a topic is a lengthy one, which the speaker finds annoying or has a number of very strong opinions about. *(But) that's a whole other story* suggests that the point just made is only one facet of a much larger discussion. *I'd rather not talk about it* says that the speaker is serious about not wanting to discuss a topic.

(For more information, see Language notes at the beginning of this unit.)

- **Set the scene** Books closed. Ask, "During a conversation, what topics do you think people may want to avoid talking about?" Elicit ideas (e.g., *politics, religion, very personal information, salaries*). Ask, "Why do you think people avoid certain topics?" (e.g., *They might cause strong arguments / bad feelings / offense. The topic is too big. The topic is too personal.*)

A • **Preview and do the task** Read the instructions aloud. Have a class discussion.

B 🔊 CD3, Track 13

- **Preview the task** Write on the board:

    to see the point

    distorted

    dispute (n)

    to negotiate

- Tell Ss they will hear these words in the conversation. Check that Ss know the meanings. [*to see the point*: understand the importance of / reason for something; *distorted*: changed so that it's not true or realistic; *dispute*: a disagreement; *negotiate*: try to make or change an agreement through discussion]

- Read the instructions aloud. Say, "Write brief answers."

- **Play the recording** Tell Ss to listen only the first time. Replay the recording. Ss listen and write. Have Ss compare their answers in pairs.

- **Play the recording again** Books open. Ss listen, read along, and check their answers. Check the answers with the class. [Tom didn't like history in school. He didn't see the point of learning all the dates. He thinks facts often get distorted. Celia thinks history is about understanding why people did things and what society was like through the ages. She thinks it's useful so that we don't repeat the same mistakes.]

C • **Present *Notice*** Read the information and the examples aloud.

    Say, "Read the conversation again. Find the examples." Have a S read them aloud. [*Tom*: . . . like what

happened in the last war. But don't get me started on that.; It's like history repeating itself. But that's another story.; But anyway, let's not get into politics.]

- **Present *In conversation*** Ask a S to read the information aloud.

- **Practice** Tell Ss to practice the conversation in pairs, taking turns playing each role.

D 🔊 CD3, Track 14

- **Preview the task** Say, "Listen to more of the conversation. Complete the expressions that you hear."

- **Play the recording** Ss listen and write. Play the recording again. Ss listen and check their answers. If necessary, play the recording a third time, pausing between speakers to give Ss time to write. Check answers with the class.

Answers

Celia I know. . . .

Tom   I know, <u>but let's not go there</u>. We probably won't agree on anything, so <u>I'd rather not talk about it</u>.

Celia OK, but it's amazing . . . country's history. <u>But that's another story</u>.

Tom   Yeah, but . . . latest peace talks. <u>But don't get me started on that</u>.

Celia Yeah. They seem to have collapsed. <u>But let's not get into that</u>. You know, I wonder how . . .

Tom   Greedy and aggressive, I'd say. You know what I think. <u>Don't get me started</u>.

- Say, "Now practice the whole conversation with a partner."

Extra activity – pairs

Pairs write a conversation similar to Tom and Celia's using a topic of their choice (e.g., *politics* or a current controversial event). Pairs present their conversation to another pair. The listening pair notes the expressions for avoiding a topic that the other pair uses.

2 Strategy plus

Why use *That's what I'm saying?*

In conversation, people use *That's what I'm saying* in responses to introduce and focus on or reinforce their viewpoint. Speakers often follow *That's what I'm saying* with a brief summarizing statement. Speakers use it both when they want to agree and when they want to disagree with someone.

(For more information, see Language notes at the beginning of this unit.)

🔊 CD3, Track 15

- **Present Strategy plus** Read aloud or play the recording of the information and example. Ss listen and read along.
- Tell Ss to read Tom and Celia's conversation on page 88 again and find the example. Ask, "What viewpoint is Tom focusing on?" [History in school was pointless because we don't learn from our mistakes.]
- **Present In conversation** Read the information aloud. Say, "You'll see examples in the responses in the next exercise."

🔊 CD3, Track 16

- **Preview the task** Say, "Complete each conversation with two responses from the box. Write *a* to *f*. When

you finish, we'll listen and check." Tell Ss to read the three conversations and the six responses before they begin. Check for any vocabulary questions. Have classmates help with any definitions or examples they know. Provide other definitions as needed.

- **Do the task** Have Ss complete the task and compare their answers with a partner.
- **Play the recording** Ss listen check their answers.

Answers

1. a, d;   2. b, e;   3. c, f

- Say, "Practice the three conversations with a partner twice to use the two responses. Then practice again. Student B, give your own answers to the questions. Student A, give an appropriate response. Be sure to include *That's what I'm saying* or *That's what I mean / meant*."
- Walk around the class and give help as needed.

Extra activity – pairs

Pairs choose one (or more) of the questions and continue the conversation as long as they can.

3 Listening and strategies

A 🔊 CD3, Track 17

- **Preview the task** Read the instructions aloud. Have Ss read the choices for the five sentences. Check for vocabulary problems.
- **Play the recording** Audio script p. T-277 Tell Ss to listen only the first time they listen.
- **Play the recording again** Ss listen and circle *a* or *b*. Tell Ss to compare their answers with a partner. Check answers with the class.

Answers

1. a;   2. a;   3. a;   4. a;   5. b

B 🔊 CD3, Track 18

- **Preview the task** Read the instructions aloud. Tell Ss to read the three questions.
- **Play the recording** Audio script p. T-277 Tell Ss to listen only the first time they listen.
- **Play the recording again** Ss listen and write. Replay the recording if necessary. Have Ss compare their answers with a partner. Check answers with the class.

Answers

1. He mentions that he is adopted.
2. He's talking about knowing your family history and where you came from. He thinks it's important.
3. How being adopted affected him and had a profound impact on him

About you

C Pair work

- **Preview and do the task** Read the instructions aloud. Have Ss complete the task.
- **Follow-up** Have a brief class discussion on each question.

2 Strategy plus *That's what I'm saying.*

CD 3.15 You can use **That's what I'm saying** in responses to focus on your viewpoint.

> But **that's what I'm saying**. We don't learn, do we?

In conversation . . .

People also say *That's what I mean / meant.*

CD 3.16 **Complete each conversation with two responses from the box. Write a–f. Then listen and practice. Practice again, this time giving your own answers to the questions.**

a. That's what I meant. There's something in it for everyone.
b. Yeah. That's what I'm saying. You need to know the context.
c. That's what I'm saying. And literacy is an important part of that. And now, of course, there's the Internet.
d. That's what I'm saying. It's such a broad area that it includes anything and everything.
e. Exactly. That's what I mean. You need to know how it's developed to interpret it.
f. Right. That's what I'm saying. Beliefs, opinions, philosophy – they all shape our actions.

1. *A* History is an interesting area because you can study the history of anything, can't you?
   B I suppose it involves everything from everyday life to great political events and wars and so on.
   A ☐☐

2. *A* Do you think you need to know the history of art to appreciate it?
   B Well, all art builds on the past, either by developing or rejecting it.
   A ☐☐

3. *A* I guess I'm interested in the history of ideas, like how ideas spread. Isn't that what's important?
   B Yeah. I guess new ideas help us develop and keep history moving.
   A ☐☐

3 Listening and strategies *Tracing family histories*

A CD 3.17 **Listen to two friends talk about family histories. Complete the sentences. Circle a or b.**

1. Jennifer's great-grandmother was   a) reluctant to emigrate.   b) 80 when she emigrated.
2. Jennifer's great-grandfather   a) was a baker by profession.   b) enjoyed baking as a hobby.
3. She found out her family history   a) from the Internet.   b) from papers in the attic.
4. Patrick would like to have known   a) who his biological mother was.   b) what his original last name was.
5. He says states should help   a) parents raise adopted children.   b) children find their birth family.

B CD 3.18 **Listen again. Answer the questions.**

1. What fact does Patrick mention when he says, "But that's another story"?
2. When Patrick says, "That's what I mean," what is he talking about?
3. Patrick says, "Let's not get into that." What doesn't he want to talk about?

About you

C Pair work **Discuss the questions.**

1. Is it important for people to know about their family history? Why? Why not?
2. Have you or any of your friends tried to trace your family history? Was it successful?
3. What do you know of your family history? Are there any interesting stories?
4. Do you think adopted children should be able to contact their biological family? Why? Why not?

Lesson D · *Unearthing the past*

1 Reading

A **Prepare** **You are going to read an article about ancient texts. Match the terms on the left with their definitions on the right. Then compare answers with a partner.**

1. archaeology _____
2. papyrus _____
3. anthropology _____
4. manuscript _____
5. paleography _____

a. the study and interpretation of ancient writing
b. a document written by hand rather than printed
c. a kind of paper made from a plant that was common in Ancient Egypt
d. the study of human societies based on material evidence left behind
e. the study of human societies and cultures and how they develop

B **Read for main ideas** **Read the article. What is the Ancient Lives Project? How does it work?**

THE ANCIENT LIVES PROJECT

1 They may not have had computers, databases, social networking sites, or spreadsheets, but the ancient Egyptians are known to have kept careful written records, not only of important people and events but also of the minute details of everyday life. In 1896–1897, hundreds of thousands of fragments of papyrus with writing on them were found on the edge of a ruined Egyptian city, in a place which is believed to have been the city's landfill. The fragments, which filled 700 boxes, were taken back to Oxford, England. The manuscripts, written in ancient Greek, now belong to the Egypt Exploration Society – an organization that was established over 125 years ago to carry out archaeological fieldwork and research in Egypt.

2 As a rule, it is archaeologists, anthropologists, and paleographers who sift the evidence of our distant past, feed our hunger for knowledge about our ancestors, bring to life dead languages, and paint a detailed picture of ancient life for us. However, in this case, there were simply not enough experts to read all those tantalizing fragments of ancient Greek, so they mostly remained undisturbed in their boxes. Those pieces that the experts did decipher revealed a fascinating picture of ancient Egyptian life: Literary, religious, and philosophical texts sat alongside bits of gossip, receipts, marriage certificates, personal letters, love potions, wills, sports reports, and other everyday texts.

3 It is not uncommon for archaeologists to involve non-specialists in their work. The two men who discovered the papyrus fragments hired local labor in Egypt. Every year, volunteers take part in archaeological digs, spending hours on their hands and knees, delicately scraping in the sand and soil of lost cities or the remains of our ancestors' homes. It is this slow, painstaking work that helps archaeologists piece together the jigsaw puzzle of the past. It can also be fun: Working with a team at an archaeological site is how many young people choose to spend their vacations.

4 In 2011, a groundbreaking project was rolled out that allowed volunteers all over the world to help reveal the past while sitting at home in front of a computer screen. The Ancient Lives Project grew from a simple idea – log in at its website, look at a papyrus fragment on your screen, check each symbol you see against an on-screen keyboard of ancient Greek letters, click when you think you have a match, and after a few minutes' work, upload the results to the project's paleographers. It is this imaginative use of the collective labor of thousands of volunteers and "armchair archaeologists" that now enables the experts to read and share with us the hundreds of thousands of manuscripts so that we can look into a window on the past. And who knows? We may even see our own reflection.

> **Reading tip**
> Writers sometimes use a pronoun in a way that means you have to read on to find out what it means, as with the first word of the article *(They . . .).*

Lesson D *Unearthing the past*

1 Reading

- **Set the scene** Books closed. Write *Unearthing the past* on the board and read it aloud. Say, "The verb *unearth* has two uses. One of them means 'to find something in the ground by digging.' The other means 'to find something that has been secret or hidden.' Given that this unit is named 'History,' what can you guess about the article?" Have Ss call out their ideas.

A Prepare

- **Preview and do the task** Books open. Read the instructions aloud. Read the five terms aloud. (word stress: archaeOLogy; paPYrus; anthroPOLogy; MANuscript; paleOGraphy)
- Have Ss complete the task and compare their answers with a partner. Check answers with the class.

Answers

1. d; 2. c; 3. e; 4. b; 5. a

B [⤓] www.cambridge.org/viewpoint/audio

Read for main ideas

- **Preview the task** Read the instructions aloud. Say, "Read the article twice. The first time, just read for the main ideas. Don't stop to check new vocabulary – just circle it. The second time, write your answers." If desired, play the downloadable recording. Ss listen and read along.

- **Do the task** Ss read the article and write their answers. Tell Ss to compare their answers with a partner. Say, "If your partner's answer is different, point out your information in the article." Check the answers with the class. [The Ancient Lives Project is an effort to have amateurs and volunteers contribute to archaeology by interpreting pieces of ancient text. Volunteers look at a piece of manuscript, look for a match in a set of symbols, and record the results online.]

- **Present *Reading tip*** Have a S read the information aloud. Say, "Look at paragraph 1. Who is *they*?" [the ancient Egyptians]

Extra activity – groups

Group members take turns saying a vocabulary item they circled and the paragraph it's found in. A group member defines the item, if known. Otherwise, group members work together and use the context to guess the meaning. The group checks their guess with a dictionary.

C Check your understanding

- **Preview the task** Read the instructions aloud. Tell Ss to read the sentences before they begin. Check that Ss understand each sentence.

- **Do the task** Have Ss complete the task and compare their answers with a partner. Say, "If your answers are different, show your partner where you found your answer." Check answers with the class.

Answers

1. F – They had been dumped in what was believed to have been a landfill. (para. 1)
2. T – (para. 2)

② Focus on vocabulary

A
- **Preview and do the task** Read the instructions. Read sentence 1 aloud. Point out that *sift* is the metaphor that replaces *look carefully through.*

- Say, "Now replace the words in bold in these sentences with a metaphor from the article."

- Have Ss complete the task and compare their answers with a partner. Check answers with the class. Ask individual Ss each to read a sentence aloud.

Answers

1. sift; 2. bring to life dead languages; 3. feed our hunger
4. paint a detailed picture of; 5. sat; 6. piece together the jigsaw puzzle; 7. was rolled out; 8. look into a window on

③ Listening

A 🔊 CD3, Track 19

- **Preview the task** Explain, "Citizen participation projects are projects like the Ancient Lives Project, where a large number of people – citizens – volunteer time to do something that is extremely labor-intensive. What do you think are some ways that people can get involved in projects like these?" Elicit ideas from the class.

- Say, "Read the sentences in Exercise B first. Looking at these questions before you listen will give you a sense, or idea, about what you'll hear in the talk. After you read the questions, come back to Exercise A. Work with a partner and talk about what you see in each picture."

- Say, "Now, having read the questions and looked at the photos, can you predict any of the words or expressions you might hear?" Have Ss call out their ideas (e.g., *navy, records, climate, whale song, whale pods, cosmos, universe, astronomer, telescope, grunt, parenting, instinct, craters, moonscape, astronaut, satellite*). Write them on the board.

- Read the instructions aloud.

- **Play the recording** Audio script p. T-277 Ss listen and check (✓) the pictures. Check the answers with the class.

Answers

Ships' records; Whales communicating;
The surface of the moon

---

3. F – There were many everyday documents such as letters, sports reports, etc. (para. 2)
4. T – (para. 3)
5. F – It is volunteer work. (para. 4)
6. F – Anyone can log in and check the symbols against an on-screen keyboard of ancient Greek letters. (para. 4)

D React / Pair work

- **Preview and do the task.** Read the sentence aloud. Have Ss discuss the question. Walk around the class and help as necessary.

- **Follow-up** Ask several pairs to share their ideas with the class.

B Pair work

- **Preview and do the task** Read the instructions aloud. Have Ss discuss the question. Walk around the class and give help as needed.

Extra activity – groups

Ss form groups not including their partner from Exercise B. They decide on the four most important reasons to "unearth the past." Groups present their choices to the class.

B 🔊 CD3, Track 20

- **Preview the task** Read the instructions aloud. Say, "You may not hear the exact words that you see on the page in this activity, so listen for and understand the whole context. This is helpful because this type of activity is included in some international examinations."

- **Play the recording** Audio script p. T-277 Ss listen and write. Ask Ss to compare their answers with a partner. Play the audio again. Ss listen and check their work. Check the answers with the class.

Answers

1. a major contribution
2. ordinary everyday people
3. less than six
4. old weather records
5. future weather patterns
6. very important historically

C Pair work

- **Preview and do the task** Read the instructions aloud. Say, "Give reasons for your answers."

- **Follow-up** Have several Ss report to the class.

C Check your understanding Are the statements true (T) or false (F) based on the article?

1. The papyrus fragments had been carefully stored away by the Egyptians. _____
2. For a long time, nobody read most of the manuscripts that were found. _____
3. The manuscript fragments were largely official documents. _____
4. Archaeologists often get non-professionals to help with physical work. _____
5. You can earn money by taking part in the Ancient Lives Project. _____
6. You need to be able to understand ancient Greek to participate. _____

D React Pair work **What would the documents you throw away or delete each week reveal to future generations about life today? Discuss.**

2 Focus on vocabulary Metaphors

A Find metaphors in the article to replace the words in bold.

1. Archaeologists **work carefully through** the evidence of our distant past. (para. 2) sift
2. Paleographers **translate languages that no one speaks anymore.** (para. 2)
3. Archaeologists **satisfy our desire** for knowledge about our ancestors. (para. 2)
4. They **describe in detail** ancient life. (para. 2)
5. Religious and philosophical texts **were found** alongside bits of gossip, receipts, etc. (para. 2)
6. Volunteers help archaeologists to **build a detailed picture** of the past. (para. 3)
7. In 2011, a project **began** that allowed volunteers to help decipher the manuscripts. (para. 4)
8. The translations of the manuscripts will allow people to **observe** the past. (para. 4)

B Pair work **How important is it to "unearth the past"? Discuss, using the metaphors above.**

3 Listening Citizen participation projects

A ◀))CD 3.19 **Listen to a talk about citizen participation projects. Check (✓) the ones described.**

☐ Ships' records   ☐ Whales communicating   ☐ Visible stars   ☐ The language of apes   ☐ The surface of the moon

B ◀))CD 3.20 **Listen again. Complete each sentence with three words.**

1. The work of volunteers has made _____ to the Ancient Lives Project.
2. The volunteers who sit at their computers doing this kind of work are _____.
3. A project that would have taken 28 years can be done in _____ months with the help of citizen volunteers.
4. In the Old Weather Project, people are looking at _____ from World War I.
5. The data from the Old Weather Project will be used to predict _____.
6. Discovering stories from these ships is also _____.

C Pair work **Which projects seem most interesting? Would you like to take part in one?**

Writing *In the end, . . .*

In this lesson, you . . .
- write a narrative essay.
- order events in the past.
- avoid errors with *in the end* and *at the end*.

Task | **Write a historical narrative.**

You have been asked to write a history of your family, a family member, or someone in the community for a website. Write a short essay.

A **Look at a model** **Look at the extracts from a narrative essay. Order the events 1–4.**

☐ Annie left her hometown.   ☐ Annie got married.   ☐ The war started.   ☐ Annie's parents died.

My mother, Annie Mason, left the city where she lived shortly after the war started and went to work on a farm in the country. Prior to leaving home, she had lost both her parents in the war. Shocked and saddened by this tragedy, she decided to leave the city. As the train took her away from her old life, she felt sad and lonely. . . .

On arriving at the country station, she met a young man who offered to carry her bags. This was the man who eventually became my father. It was love at first sight. Finally, she had a chance of happiness.

They moved back to the city once the war had ended. As soon as they found jobs, they married and subsequently had four children, all of whom were successful. In the end, they retired to a small house near the railroad station where they'd first met. . . .

B **Focus on language** **Read the chart. Then underline examples of ordering events in Exercise A.**

Ordering events in writing

You can use these structures to vary the way you present the order of events.

Time clauses	***After / Once / As soon as*** *the war ended, they married.* ***On arriving at the station,*** *she met my father.*
Participle clauses	***Arriving at the station,*** *she met my father.* ***Saddened by this tragedy,*** *she decided to leave the city.*
Adverbs and adverbial phrases	*She had **previously** lived in the city.* *They **subsequently / eventually** had four children.* ***In the end, / After a while,*** *they married.*

Writing vs. Conversation

Prepositions + *-ing* are more common in writing.

- Conversation
- Writing

C **Rewrite these sentences, using the word(s) given and making any other changes.**

1. My father met my mother, and then he applied for a job in California. (after)
2. He had lived in the U.S., but he moved back to Mexico when his contract came to an end. (previously)
3. He arrived back in his hometown and met the woman who became my mother. (as soon as / eventually)
4. After they were married, they moved to San Diego. (once)
5. My mother found out that she was pregnant before their fifth wedding anniversary. (prior to)
6. They had three more children and were happy living in the U.S. (after a while)
7. They moved back to Mexico and left their "American life" behind them. (in the end / participle clause)
8. When he walked into his new home, my father vowed he would never leave again. (on)

D **Write and check** **Now write a short essay as described in the Task above. Then check for errors.**

Common errors

Use *at the end of* + a noun. ***At the end of the war,*** *they got married.*

In the end refers to the conclusion of all the events. ***In the end,*** *they retired.*

Use *finally* at the end of a series of other events. *She **finally** found happiness.*

Writing *In the end, . . .*

In this lesson

- Ask a S to read the lesson aims (*In this lesson, you . . .*) aloud. Ask, "What does a narrative do?" [tell a story]
- **Preview the writing** Say, "In this lesson, you write a historical narrative." Read the topic in Task aloud.

A Look at a model

- **Preview and do the task** Read the instructions aloud. Tell Ss to read the four events in Annie's life first.
- Have Ss complete the task. Check the answers.

Answers

3 Annie left her hometown.
4 Annie got married.
1 The war started.
2 Annie's parents died.

B 🔽 www.cambridge.org/viewpoint/audio

Focus on language

- **Present the grammar for writing chart** Read the information in the chart aloud or play the recording.
- **Understand the grammar for writing** Point out the time clauses. Ask, "What other words can begin a time clause?" [before, while, since, when, as, until] Write them on the board. Ask, "Does a time clause always come first?" [no]
- Ask Ss to look at the example that begins with *On arriving*. Ask, "What type of word is *on*?" [preposition]. Ask, "What is the subject of the two clauses?" [she] "Is the subject the same in each clause?" [yes]
- Have Ss look at the example for participle clauses. Ask, "Does the subject have to be the same in each clause?" [yes] "Is the subject given in the participle clause?" [no; in the main clause] Explain, "Using this structure says that the events happened very close together in time."
- Point out the example sentences with adverbs. Ask, "What other adverbs related to time can you find in the model?" [shortly, finally] Elicit others from the class (e.g., *ultimately, already, recently*).
- Ask Ss to look at the example with adverbial phrases. Elicit more examples (e.g., *for several years, after a few dates, before the summer*).
- **Present *Writing vs. Conversation*** Books closed. Read the information aloud. Ask, "How much more frequent do you think these preposition + *-ing* clauses are in writing than in conversation? Have a few Ss guess. Books open. Point out the bar graph and say, "These are 16 times more common. These types of time clauses, as well as participle clauses, will make your writing sound more formal or academic."
- **Do the task** Read the instructions aloud. Have Ss complete the task and compare their answers with a partner. Check answers with the class.

Answers

My mother, . . . she lived <u>shortly after the war started</u> and went to work . . . <u>Prior to leaving home</u>, she had lost . . . <u>Shocked and saddened by this tragedy</u>, she decided . . . <u>As the train took her away from her old life</u>, she felt sad and lonely. . . .

<u>On arriving at the country station</u>, she met . . . This was the man who <u>eventually</u> became my father. . . . <u>Finally</u>, she had a chance of happiness.

They moved back to the city <u>once the war had ended</u>. <u>As soon as they found jobs</u>, they married and <u>subsequently</u> had four children, . . . <u>In the end</u>, they retired to a small house . . .

C

- **Preview and do the task** Read the instructions aloud. Have Ss complete the task. Check answers with the class.

Answers

1. <u>After</u> my father met my mother, he applied . . . / <u>After meeting</u> my mother, my father applied . . .
2. He had <u>previously</u> lived in the U.S, but he . . . / He had lived in the U.S <u>previously</u>, but he . . .
3. <u>As soon as</u> he arrived . . . he met the woman who <u>eventually</u> became my mother.
4. <u>Once</u> they were married, they moved . . .
5. My mother found out . . . <u>prior to</u> their . . .
6. <u>After a while</u>, they had three more . . .
7. <u>In the end, leaving their "American life" behind them</u>, they moved back to Mexico. <u>In the end</u>, they moved back to Mexico, <u>leaving their "American life" behind them</u>.
8. <u>On walking</u> into his new home, my father . . .

D Write and check

- **Preview the task** Read the instructions aloud.
- **Present *Common errors*** Books closed. Write *at the end, in the end,* and *finally* on the board. Then write:

  _____ *of the war, they got married.*
  She _____ *found happiness.*
  _____ , *they retired.*

- Say, "Complete each sentence with one of the expressions." Tell Ss to open their books and look at the *Common errors* to check their answers. Say, "*At the end of* is used before a noun. Be sure to use *of*. *In the end* introduces the conclusion to events, perhaps after some problems or complications. *Finally* emphasizes that what follows is the end of a series of events. It can also be used to start the last sentence on the board."
- **Do the task** Have Ss complete the task.
- **Follow-up** After Ss have read some classmates' essays, have them tell the class about one of them.

Extra activity – class

Ss leave their essays on their desk for classmates to read. Ss go around the class reading each other's work. This time, they find out how often each structure in the Grammar for Writing chart was used.

Vocabulary notebook *Deep, low, high*

If done for homework

Briefly present the Learning tip and the task directions. Make sure Ss understand what they need to do.

If done in class

- **Present *Learning tip*** Read the information aloud. Add, "It's a good idea to write synonyms and antonyms for different meanings." Ask a S to read the examples in the box.

A • **Preview and do the task** Read the instructions aloud. Have Ss complete the task and compare their answers with a partner. Check answers with the class.

Answers

1. **significant** meaningless insignificant (considerable) unimportant
2. **local** universal global foreign (nearby)
3. **superficial** detailed (meaningless) profound thorough
4. **imperceptible** (unseen) conspicuous striking apparent
5. **lasting** (permanent) temporary brief fleeting

B • **Preview the task** Read the instructions aloud. Say, "There are different possible answers."

- **Do the task** Have Ss complete the task. Tell Ss to compare their answer with a partner: Each partner reads his / her synonym and antonym. If a partner doesn't agree with the word that was chosen, the other partner consults a dictionary.
- Check answers with the class: Ask a few Ss and write their answers on the board.

Possible answers

	Synonym	Antonym
1. major	huge	minor
2. gradual	slow	fast
3. long-term	lengthy	short-term
4. massive	huge	tiny

C Word builder

- **Preview the task** Read the instructions and the five words aloud.
- **Do the task** Have Ss complete the task. Check answers with the class.

Answers

abrupt ≠ gradual
deep ≠ superficial
miniature ≠ massive
obvious ≠ imperceptible
transient ≠ lasting

Extra activity – class / pairs

Ss write one sentence for each word in Exercise C. Ss read their sentences to a partner. For each word, a few Ss read their sentence to the class.

D Focus on vocabulary, page 91

- **Preview and do the task** Read the instructions aloud. Remind Ss to use a dictionary if they need help. Have Ss complete the task. Check answers with the class.

Answers

1. b; 2. d; 3. a; 4. e; 5. h; 6. g; 7. f; 8. c

E **Preview the task** Read the instructions aloud. Work through the first example with the class. Ask, "What does *wind something down* mean?" [end something gradually] Say, "The opposite idea is *roll out*."

- **Do the task** Have Ss complete the task and compare their answers with a partner. Check answers with the class.

Answers

1. roll out
2. feed a hunger
3. bring to life
4. look into a window on the past
5. sift (through) / paint a detailed picture

Vocabulary notebook *Deep, low, high*

When you learn a new word, look up its synonyms (words with similar meanings) and antonyms (words with opposite meanings). Be careful: Different meanings of a word can have different synonyms and antonyms.

> a deep conversation = meaningful, profound
> ≠ trivial, light-hearted
> a deep voice = a low voice
> ≠ a high-pitched voice

A   **Underline three antonyms to the words in bold below. Circle the synonym.**

1. **significant**	meaningless	insignificant	considerable	unimportant
2. **local**	universal	global	foreign	nearby
3. **superficial**	detailed	meaningless	profound	thorough
4. **imperceptible**	unseen	conspicuous	striking	apparent
5. **lasting**	permanent	temporary	brief	fleeting

B   **Write a synonym and an antonym for each of these words.**

	Synonym	Antonym
1. major	_____	_____
2. gradual	_____	_____
3. long-term	_____	_____
4. massive	_____	_____

C   **Word builder These words are all antonyms of words in Exercises A and B. Find their meanings and add them to the examples above.**

abrupt	deep	miniature	obvious	transient

D   (Focus on vocabulary)   **Match the metaphors from the article on page 91 with their meanings.**

Metaphor

1. bring something to life _____
2. sift (through), e.g., evidence, facts _____
3. feed a hunger for knowledge _____
4. paint a detailed picture _____
5. sit alongside _____
6. piece together a jigsaw puzzle of something _____
7. roll out (a project) _____
8. look into a window on _____

Meaning

a. satisfy the desire to learn
b. make something interesting or current
c. observe
d. work carefully through
e. explain or describe in detail
f. begin or put into practice
g. figure out a mystery or problem
h. be (together) with

E   **Now look at these metaphors. Write the metaphor from Exercise D that means the opposite of each.**

1. wind something down roll out _____
2. starve someone of something _____
3. kill an idea _____
4. look into a crystal ball _____
5. brush over something _____

THEY SAY PEOPLE WHO DON'T LEARN FROM HISTORY ARE DOOMED TO REPEAT IT.

THEN WE BETTER STUDY. I DON'T WANT TO REPEAT THIS CLASS.

Unit 9 Engineering wonders

Lesson A *Engineers change the world.*

Grammar *Talking about unknown people and things*

(See Student's Book p. 95.)

In this lesson, Ss learn to use *-ever* words, such as *whatever*, *whoever*, and *however*, which are presented here in the context of a college web page describing the types of work that engineers do.

Form and use

You can add *-ever* to *wh-* words to give them a meaning of "any at all" or "it doesn't matter which, where, etc."

- *Whatever* and *whichever* (determiners or pronouns)

    *Engineers work on **whatever** task needs to be done.*

    *Engineers work on **whatever** needs to be done.*

    ***Whatever** goes wrong, one can turn to an engineer.*

    ***Whichever** (field) you choose, you will make an impact.*

- *Whoever* (pronoun)

    ***Whoever** you are, you have the potential to impact society.*

- *Whenever*, *wherever*, and *however* (adverbs)

    ***Whenever** there is a problem, an engineer will fix it.*

***Wherever** you look, you'll see the work of an engineer.*

***However** you look at it, a career in engineering is exciting.*

Corpus information

In conversation

In conversation, *whatever* is the most frequent. It is often used in the vague expressions *or / and whatever*.

*We're not all cut out to be engineers **or whatever**.*

Grammar extra *whatever, whichever, and* whoever *as subjects and objects; Patterns with* however *and* whatever

(See Student's Book p. 160.)

Grammar extra presents using *whatever*, *whichever*, and *whoever* as the subject or object of a verb, as well as patterns with *however*, and *whatever the* + noun.

Lesson B *Incredible feats*

Vocabulary in context *Construction*

(See Student's Book p. 96.)

The article presents vocabulary related to construction, including materials (*concrete*), building (*construct*), moving (*maneuver*), and schedules (*fall behind*).

Vocabulary notebook *How do you do it?*

(See Student's Book p. 103.)

The Learning tip tells Ss to put new vocabulary into a question to ask themselves in order to provide a meaningful context for learning it.

- **Focus on vocabulary** reviews and practices vocabulary introduced in Lesson D (p. 101).

Grammar *Emphasizing ideas*

(See Student's Book p. 97.)

This lesson teaches Ss how to emphasize ideas by starting a sentence with a negative adverb.

Use

Starting a sentence with a negative adverb (*never*, *not only*, etc.) emphasizes the idea that follows it and gives it more focus.

Form

If you use a negative adverb to start a clause or sentence for emphasis, the verb comes before the subject. With simple present and simple past, auxiliary verbs *do*, *does*, *did* are used. With *be*, no auxiliary verb is needed.

- Sentences or clauses with *be*

    Invert *be* and its subject.

    Negative adverb + *be* + subject

    ***Not only was it** the tallest road bridge, but it was also the most challenging to design.*

- Sentences or clauses in simple present

    Use *do / does* before the subject.

    Negative adverb + *does / do* + subject + verb

    ***Not only does it ease** traffic congestion, but it has become a landmark.*

- Sentences or clauses in simple past

    Use *did* before the subject.

    Negative adverb + *did* + subject + verb

    ***Not once did the engineers fail** to find a solution.*

- Sentences with perfect verbs

    Negative adverb + *have* + subject + past participle

    ***Never** before **had engineers attempted** to build a bridge like this.*

- *Little*, *rarely*, and *only* + prepositional phrase

    Use the same inversions as above after the adverbs *little*, *rarely*, and *only* + prepositional phrase.

    ***Only** by elevating the highway **were the architects** able to achieve the stunning visual impact.*

Grammar extra *More on inversion; Inversions with modals and in passive sentences*

(See Student's Book p. 161.)

This Grammar extra reviews, extends, and practices using negative adverbs and inversions.

Lesson C *It makes no sense whatsoever.*

Conversation strategy *Supporting ideas*

(See Student's Book p. 98.)

The lesson teaches these expressions to introduce facts to support a thought or opinion:

> *considering (that / the fact that)*
>
> *given (that / the fact that)*
>
> *in view of (the fact that)*
>
> *in light of (the fact that)*
>
>> *That's kind of surprising, given the weather.*
>>
>> *That's kind of surprising, given (the fact) that the weather was so bad.*

Strategy plus *at all, whatsoever*

(See Student's Book p. 99.)

At all and *whatsoever* are used to make a negative phrase more emphatic.

> *Some places got* **no rain at all***.*
>
> *I mean,* **none whatsoever***.*

Corpus information

In conversation

In conversation, *whatsoever* is typically used after *none, nothing,* or these nouns with *no, not any,* etc.: *problem(s), reason, sense, evidence, doubt(s), impact, effect.*

Speaking naturally *Intonation of background information*

(See Student's Book p. 142.)

Ss practice fall-rise intonation to give information that is background or that a listener is expected to know, using the expressions: *considering . . . ; given (that / the fact that) . . . ; in view of (the fact that) . . . ; in light of (the fact that) . . .*

Lesson D *Robotics*

Writing *A good alternative*

(See Student's Book p. 102.)

This lesson teaches Ss to plan and write a classification essay.

The lesson presents expressions to write about alternatives such as *rather than, as opposed to,* and *be an alternative to* and ways to state preference, such as *would rather . . . than.* It also gives expressions for classifying.

- Classifying

> *There are a number of . . .*
>
> *One is . . . Another is . . . Yet another . . .*
>
> *They can be classified into the following types: . . .*
>
> *They can be divided into four groups / categories. The first is . . .*

- Stating alternatives

> *in place of / instead of* + noun or *-ing* form
>
> *rather than* + noun, verb, *-ing* form, adjective, or prepositional phrase
>
> *as opposed to* + noun or *-ing* form
>
> *be an alternative to / a substitute for*

Corpus information

As opposed to

As opposed to usually follows a noun (more than 65 percent of cases), followed by an adjective, adverb, and verb.

- Expressing preference

> *. . . would rather* + verb *. . . than* + verb or noun *. . .*
>
> *. . . be no substitute for . . .*

Corpus information

In writing

Rather than joins nouns, verbs, prepositional phrases, adjectives, or adverbs. Notice the verb forms after *rather than.*

Rather than **use** / **using** *humans for these tasks, we should use robots.*

Corpus information

Common errors with *would rather / rather*

Ss sometimes incorrectly use *prefer* after *would rather.* They also use *rather* before *than* in basic comparisons.

I **would rather be** *cared for by a robot.*
(**NOT:** *I* ~~would rather prefer to be~~ *. . .*)

Robots are more suited to heavy work **than** *humans.*
(**NOT:** *. . .* ~~work rather than~~ *. . .*)

Unit 9

Engineering wonders

In Unit 9, you . . .

- talk about engineering feats, challenges, and developments.
- use *whoever, whatever,* etc., to talk about unknown people or things.
- start sentences with negative adverbs for extra emphasis.
- give facts using expressions like *considering* and *given (that)*.
- use *at all* and *whatsoever* to emphasize negative ideas.

Lesson A *Engineers change the world.*

1 Grammar in context

A ◀))CD 3.21 **Do you know what engineers do? Make a list. Then read the college web page and see how many of your ideas are mentioned.**

Change the world – be an engineer!

Wherever you look, you'll see the work of a talented engineer who has designed, tested, and improved the objects around you. Whatever goes wrong or whenever there is a problem to be solved, however complex, one can rely on engineers to apply their knowledge of math and science – along with some creativity – to come up with a solution. So, what do engineers do? Here's just a sample of their work.

CHEMICAL ENGINEERS Whenever you wash your jeans, remember it was a chemical engineer that developed the fade-resistant dye. Pick up any game console – that scratchproof plastic was made by these engineers. Chemical engineers also help produce medicines and cosmetics, and find solutions to damage caused by harmful chemicals.

CIVIL ENGINEERS These engineers are at the heart of urban planning and transportation design. Wherever you go and whatever you do today, you'll encounter their work. The system of pipes that brings water to your shower, the roads you drive on, the bridges you cross, the buildings you occupy – these are all examples of civil engineering work.

MATERIALS SCIENCE ENGINEERS
Engineers in this field work with materials such as ceramics, plastics, and metals. Their work is central to engineering as a whole. Materials science engineers process, design, and test whatever materials are used in all other branches of engineering.

BIOMEDICAL ENGINEERS
Bringing together the fields of engineering and medicine, biomedical engineers work on whatever needs to be done to improve health care. They design anything from artificial body parts and lifesaving equipment to drug and gene therapies.

However you look at it, a career in engineering is exciting and rewarding. Whoever you are and whichever field of engineering you choose, you have the potential to design and develop products that will have an enormous impact on society.

B Pair work **Discuss the questions.**

1. What skills do engineers need, according to the web page?
2. What types of activities do the different fields have in common?
3. Which field of engineering sounds most interesting? Which is most valuable to society?
4. Does the web page succeed in getting people to consider engineering as a career, in your view?

Engineering wonders

Introduce the theme of the unit Tell Ss that this unit looks at aspects of engineering. Tell Ss to look at the three photos. Ask, "What field does each picture represent?" Elicit ideas (e.g., *Picture 1: technology, electronics; Picture 2: biology, microbiology, medicine; Picture 3: energy, hydroelectric power, large-scale construction*). Say, "Engineers are involved in all of these fields." Read the unit aims aloud.

Lesson A *Engineers change the world.*

1 Grammar in context

- **Set the scene** Books closed. Say, "As we just talked about, engineers are involved in many fields. This lesson contains a web page that discusses some of the things that engineers do."

A ◀)) CD3, Track 21

- **Preview the task** Read the instructions aloud. Have Ss make a list.
- Have Ss call out their ideas and write them on the board (e.g., *construction, building, mechanical / machines, medical research*).
- Say, "Now listen to the information from a college web page. How many of your ideas are mentioned? How many of the class's ideas?"
- **Play the recording** Ss listen for their ideas.
- Books open. Tell Ss to read the case study. (If desired, play the recording again while Ss read along.) Say, "Don't stop to check the meaning of new vocabulary."
- Ask, "Which fields did you not guess? Were any surprising to you?" Have a short class discussion.
- Check for vocabulary questions. Have Ss supply definitions or examples when possible.

B Pair work

- **Preview and do the task** Read the instructions aloud. Tell Ss to read the four questions. Check that they understand the questions.
- Have Ss discuss the questions. Walk around the class and help as needed.
- Check answers with the class: For each question, have a few pairs share their ideas with the class.

Possible answers

1. They need a knowledge of math and science, creativity, and problem-solving skills.
2. They all find solutions to problems and design, and they develop and test products.
3. Civil engineering sounds interesting to me. Figuring out how to build a skyscraper sounds like a real challenge. Biomedical engineering sounds like a valuable field. There's a great need to improve medical machinery, etc., so doctors can detect diseases earlier and treat them more successfully.
4. I think so. I didn't know much about engineering before reading it, so in that sense it gets your interest.

Extra activity – class / pairs

Ss call out the names of items they use every day. Write them on the board. For each item, pairs decide which type of engineer was involved.

Extra activity – pairs

Ss think of other examples for each kind of engineering on the web page. Ss then share their ideas with the class. Ss listen and check if they agree that the product is made by that type of engineer.

Figure it out

A 📥 www.cambridge.org/viewpoint/audio

- **Preview the task** Ask, "How does the web page express these ideas? Write the phrases."
- **Do the task** Have Ss complete the task and compare their answers with a partner. Check answers with the class.

Answers

1. <u>Whatever</u> goes wrong . . .
2. <u>Whenever</u> there is a problem to be solved . . .
3. <u>However</u> you look at it . . .

- **Focus on the form and use** Say, "Look at the first word in each of the three phrases. What do these words have in common?" [They're all *Wh-* words. They all end in *-ever*.] Say, "You can use the words to talk about unknown people and things. They have the meaning 'any at all' or 'It doesn't matter *what, when,* or *how*.'"
- **Present the grammar chart** Read the information aloud. If desired, play the downloadable recording.
- Have Ss look at the section on *whatever* and *whichever*. Say, "These words can be determiners or pronouns." Remind Ss that determiners are words that go before nouns and help identify them. They can be words like *the, my,* and *this*. Pronouns are words that are used instead of nouns, for example, *that, him, they,* and *something*. Write on the board, underlined as shown:

  1. *These engineers work on <u>whatever</u> task needs to be done.*
  2. *These engineers work on <u>whatever</u> needs to be done.*

  Say, "In which sentence on the board is *whatever* a pronoun?" [sentence 2]
- Have Ss look at the section on *whoever*. Say, "*Whoever* can only be used as a pronoun." Point out that *whoever* cannot be used as a determiner. Say, "A common error is to write *whoever* as two words, *who* and *ever*. Make sure of your spelling."
- Have Ss look at the bottom section. Say, "These words with *-ever* are adverbs. They refer to when, where, or how you do something."
- **Present *In conversation*** Read the information aloud. Have a S read the example. Ask, "What other expressions like *or whatever* do you know?" (e.g., *and things like that, and that kind of thing*)

(For more information, see Language notes at the beginning of the unit. For more work on *-ever* words, go to Grammar extra, p. 160.)

B 🔊 CD3, Track 22

- **Preview the task** Say, "Complete the sentences with *-ever* words." Tell Ss to read the all of the conversations before they begin. Check for vocabulary questions and help as needed.

- **Play the recording** Ss listen and check their answers. Ask individual pairs each to read a conversation aloud.

Answers

1. *A* Do you really understand what engineers do?
   B Well, . . . I mean, <u>whenever</u> someone . . .
   C I do – well, kind of. My friend's . . . told me that <u>whenever</u> I use . . . TV or <u>whatever</u>, that's . . .
2. *A* Do you have what it takes to be an engineer?
   B Sure. <u>Whenever</u> there's a problem . . .
   C Me? . . . <u>Whichever / Whatever</u> way I look at it, . . .
3. *A* Do you think engineering . . . career?
   B Oh, definitely. <u>Whoever</u> says it's . . . I mean, <u>whichever / whatever</u> field of engineering . . .
   C It depends. . . space stations or <u>whatever</u> sounds fun.
4. *A* Do you . . . and <u>whatever</u> actually get built?
   B Yes. <u>Whenever</u> I see a new bridge . . . or <u>whatever</u> being built, I think <u>whoever</u> designed . . .
   C Yeah. <u>Whatever</u> you think . . . admire <u>whoever</u> built them.

About you

C Group work

- **Preview and do the task** Read the instructions aloud. Have groups discuss the questions. Have several groups report their answers.

Extra activity – class / pairs

The class brainstorms more professions that require particular skills and training. Partners take turns choosing one of the professions and asking questions similar to those in Exercise 2B. Ss give their own answers.

Extra activity – pairs

Ss choose one field of engineering and prepare a 30-second presentation to give to their classmates. Ss talk about what the engineers do and possibilities for the future of the field.

2 Grammar Talking about unknown people and things

Figure it out

A How does the web page express these ideas? Write the phrases. Then read the grammar chart.

1. It doesn't matter what goes wrong. . . .
2. At any time at all when there is a problem to be solved . . .
3. It doesn't matter how you look at it. . . .

---

whatever, whichever, whoever, whenever, wherever, however 📥

Grammar extra
See page 160.

The *-ever* words have the meaning "any at all" or "it doesn't matter what, who, where, etc."

Whatever, whichever can be determiners or pronouns.	**Whatever** goes wrong, one can turn to an engineer. *These engineers work on* **whatever** *(task) needs to be done.* **Whichever** *(field) you choose, you will make an impact.*
Whoever is a pronoun.	**Whoever** *you are, you have the potential to impact society.*
Whenever, wherever, however are adverbs.	**Whenever** *there is a problem, an engineer will fix it.* **Wherever** *you look, you'll see the work of an engineer.* **However** *you look at it, a career in engineering is exciting.*

In conversation . . .

Whatever is the most frequent. It is often used in the vague expressions *or / and whatever.*
We're not all cut out to be engineers **or whatever.**

B 🔊 CD 3.22 **Complete the sentences with *-ever* words. Then listen and check.**

1. *A* Do you really understand what engineers do?
   B Well, I didn't until now. I mean, _____ someone said they were studying engineering, I never really understood what they were doing.
   C I do – well, kind of. My friend's an electrical engineer, and he told me that _____ I use like a cell phone or satellite TV or _____, that's the kind of thing he's worked on.

2. *A* Do you have what it takes to be an engineer?
   B Sure. _____ there's a problem at home, I can usually fix it.
   C Me? Absolutely not. _____ way I look at it, I'm not cut out to be an engineer.

3. *A* Do you think engineering could be an exciting career?
   B Oh, definitely. _____ says it's boring doesn't know what they're talking about. I mean, _____ field of engineering you look at, there's something interesting.
   C It depends. I mean, designing things for space stations or _____ sounds fun.

4. *A* Do you ever think about how roads and bridges and _____ actually get built?
   B Yes. _____ I see a new bridge or skyscraper or _____ being built, I think _____ designed all that must be a genius. It's amazing how it's all planned and managed.
   C Yeah. _____ you think of high-rise buildings, you have to admire _____ built them.

About you

C Group work **Take turns answering the questions. Who knows the most about engineering? Who would be most suited to a career in engineering?**

Lesson B *Incredible feats*

1 **Vocabulary in context**

A CD 3.23 **Read the article. Why was constructing the bridge so challenging?**

The Millau Viaduct in southern France has been called "the freeway in the sky." On stormy days, it looks as though it is floating above the clouds. No wonder. When constructed, it was the world's tallest road bridge at 343 meters (1,125 feet) at its highest point above the River Tarn. Never before had engineers attempted to build a bridge of this size and scale. At the outset, little did they realize how much the project would push the boundaries of engineering to its limits. Nor did they know how many problems they would face. However, not once did the engineers fail to find a solution.

The viaduct is a four-lane highway across one of the deepest valleys in France. Not only does it ease the congestion of the north–south routed traffic between Paris and Spain, but it has become one of the country's most celebrated projects – a landmark in itself.

Engineers faced three challenges in building the viaduct. They had to:

- **construct** the tallest **concrete** bridge piers (supporting towers) in the world;
- **assemble** and **maneuver** a 36,000-tonne (40,000-ton), 2.5-kilometer (1.5-mile) freeway, rolling it out to **position** it onto the top of the towers;
- **erect** seven massive **steel** pylons, each weighing 700 tonnes (770 tons), and **install** 11 pairs of steel cables.

In addition, not only did this dangerous work have to be done way above the ground at a height taller than the Eiffel Tower, but it had to be completed in four years! Nowhere else on Earth had engineers accomplished a project of this magnitude **in** such **a short time frame**. By comparison, one of the longest bridges in the world – the Akashi-Kaikyo in Japan – took 10 years to complete. However, under no circumstances could the project **fall behind schedule**. Any **delays** would have cost the construction company $30,000 a day in penalties. Not only did they **complete** it **on time**, but the viaduct opened a month **ahead of schedule**.

The biggest challenge of all, apart from **engineering** the bridge to be strong enough to withstand the elements, was to make it blend into the beautiful landscape. Only by **elevating** the highway so far above ground and slimming down the towers and road deck were the architects able to achieve such a delicate and stunning visual impact.   [more]

B **Complete the chart with vocabulary in the article. Add other items you want to learn. Then tell a partner about engineering feats you know of.**

Word sort

materials	build	move	schedules	other
	construct			

"Well, one that comes to mind is the airport they constructed in Hong Kong. They built an island to put it on."

Vocabulary notebook
See page 103.

Lesson B *Incredible feats*

1 Vocabulary in context

- **Set the scene** Books closed. Say, "The title of Lesson B is *Incredible feats*. We are going to look at some of the amazing structures that engineers have given us."
- Have Ss brainstorm some amazing structures and feats of engineering and call them out to the class.

A ◀)) CD3, Track 23

- **Preview the task** Books open. Say, "Look at the pictures. What do you expect to read about?" [building a bridge] Write *viaduct* on the board and ask Ss what it means. [a high road or railroad bridge across a valley] Say, "Read the article. Why was building the bridge – the Millau Viaduct – so challenging? First read for the main ideas and then write brief notes."
- **Do the task** Have Ss read the article and write notes, then compare their answers with a partner. Check the answer with the class. [Constructing the bridge was challenging because of the overall size and height of the viaduct (it was the tallest ever built); because of the amount of time they had to build it (four years); and because it had to blend in to the landscape and look good.]

Word sort

B
- **Preview the task** Read the instructions and the column headings in the chart aloud. Point out the example, *construct*, in the "build" category. Say, "Write the items you want to learn in the column for *other*."
- **Do the task** Have Ss complete the chart. Check answers with the class.

Answers

materials	*move*
concrete	maneuver
steel	position
	elevate
build	
construct	*schedules*
assemble	in a short time frame
erect	fall behind schedule
install	delays
engineer	complete on time
	ahead of schedule

- Ask Ss to call out the items they added to the *other* column. Write them on the board. Have classmates give definitions or explanations of words they know. Supply definitions for any remaining vocabulary.
- Say, "Now think of other engineering feats you've heard of and tell a partner about them." Walk around class and offer any help as needed.
- **Follow up** Call on pairs to tell the class about the feats they discussed.

Tell Ss to turn to Vocabulary Notebook on p. 103 of their Student's Books. Have Ss do the tasks in class or assign them for homework. (See the teaching notes on p. T-103.)

Extra activity – class / pairs

Ss choose (at least) one item from each category in the chart and write a sentence about a building, bridge, or other structure they are familiar with.

Pairs read each other's sentences and, if possible, guess the structure they are reading about.

2 Grammar

A ⬇ www.cambridge.org/viewpoint/audio

- **Preview the task** Say, "Underline the sentences in the article that express the same ideas as the sentences below."
- **Do the task** Have Ss complete the task. Check answers.

Answers

1. <u>Not only did</u> they complete it on time, but the viaduct . . .
2. <u>Never before had</u> engineers attempted to build . . .
3. <u>Little did they</u> realize how much the project would . . .

- **Focus on the form** Say, "Look at the sentences in the article. What is the pattern?" [negative adverb + verb + subject] Point out the addition of *did* for the simple past in #1 and #3.
- **Focus on the use** Say, "You can add emphasis by starting sentences like this."
- **Present the grammar chart** Read the information aloud. If desired, play the downloadable recording.
- **Understand the grammar chart** Say, "Negative adverbs are words like *never, not only,* and *not once.* When you use them to start a sentence, you put the verb before the subject. With the simple present, you add *do* or *does* before the subject." Ask a S to read the simple present example. Ask, "With a sentence or a clause in the simple past, what do you add before the subject?"[did]

Have a S read the simple past example aloud. Say, "The final sentence in this group is in the past perfect. What comes before the subject?" [the auxiliary, *had*]

Have Ss look at the last section of the chart. Say, "Use the same inversion rules when you begin a sentence with one of these words." Have a S read the example aloud.

Present *Writing vs. Conversation* Books open. Ask a S to read the information aloud.

(For more information, see Language notes at the beginning of the unit. For more work on inversion, go to Grammar extra, p. 161.)

B 🔊 CD3, Track 24

- **Preview the task** Say "Rewrite the sentences starting with the words given. Make any other necessary changes." Have Ss complete the task.
- **Play the recording** Say, "Now check your answers."

Answers

1. <u>Not only did they have</u> to erect seven towers . . .
2. <u>Only by building</u> a concrete factory on-site <u>were they able to supply</u> the concrete.
3. <u>Rarely have engineers</u> constructed freeways . . .
4. <u>Never before had engineers built</u> such a . . .
5. <u>Nor had anyone</u> positioned a road . . .
6. <u>Little did they realize</u> how difficult . . .
7. <u>Never do you hear</u> of projects . . .

- Say, "Close your book. How much information can you remember? Tell a partner."

3 Listening

A 🔊 CD3, Track 25

- **Preview the task** Ask Ss to look at the photos and say what they know about each project. Ask, "Why do you think these are considered as engineering feats?" Elicit ideas. Read the instructions aloud. Tell Ss to look at the photos as they listen.
- **Play the recording** Audio script p. T-278 Ss listen and number the pictures. Check the answers.

Answers

3 the Queen Mary 2
1 Churaumi Aquarium, Japan
2 Channel Tunnel, Britain / France

B 🔊 CD3, Track 26

- **Preview the task** Have Ss read the four questions first. Say, "Write brief notes."
- **Play the recording** Audio script p. T-278 Ss listen and write. Replay the recording, if necessary. Check answers.

Answers

1. *Churaumi Aquarium, Japan*
   1. Building the gigantic window for the aquarium.
   2. To build a tank that held 7 ½ million liters of water, that was earthquake-proof, and that would hold three of the largest species of whale shark.
   3. It had the largest window of its kind in the world.
   4. Two to 3 million people.
2. *Channel Tunnel, England / France*
   1. Digging a tunnel 50 meters below the seabed.
   2. To build two railway lines for high-speed trains and a third emergency tunnel.
   3. It was the longest undersea tunnel in the world.
   4. Approximately 15 million people travel through it.
3. *the Queen Mary 2*
   1. Making the ship profitable.
   2. To make her bigger than any other liner; to make her fit under a New York bridge and through the Panama Canal.
   3. It would be the largest and most luxurious liner in the world.
   4. Ninety-one thousand seven hundred (91,700) people cross the Atlantic aboard the *Queen Mary 2* every year.

C Pair work

- **Preview and do the task** Read the instructions aloud. Have Ss prepare and give their presentation to the class.

② Grammar Emphasizing ideas

Figure it out

A Underline the sentences in the article that express the same ideas as the sentences below. Then read the grammar chart.

1. They not only completed it on time, but the viaduct opened a month ahead of schedule.
2. Engineers had never before attempted to build a bridge of this size and scale.
3. They didn't realize how much the project would push the boundaries of engineering.

Negative adverbs and word order

Grammar extra
See page 161.

If you use a negative adverb (e.g., *never, not*) to start a sentence for emphasis, put the verb before the **subject**. Use *do* or *does* for simple present and *did* for simple past verbs.
Not only **does it ease** traffic congestion, but it has become a landmark.
Not once **did the engineers fail** to find a solution.
Never before **had engineers attempted** to build a bridge like this.

Use the same inversion after *little, rarely,* and *only* + prepositional phrase.
Only by elevating the highway **were the architects able** to achieve the stunning visual impact.

Writing vs. Conversation

The inverted forms are about three times more common in formal writing than in conversation.

B ◀)) CD 3.24 **Rewrite the sentences starting with the words given. Make any other necessary changes. Listen and check. Then close your book. How much information can you remember?**

1. They not only had to erect seven towers taller than the Eiffel Tower, but they also had to make sure the towers were at exactly the right point. *Not only . . .*
2. They supplied the concrete by building a concrete factory on-site. *Only . . .*
3. Engineers have rarely constructed freeways out of steel. *Rarely . . .*
4. Engineers had never before built such a tall bridge. *Never before . . .*
5. No one had positioned a road onto towers in this way. *Nor . . .*
6. They didn't realize how difficult it would be. *Little . . .*
7. You never hear of projects like this going according to schedule. *Never . . .*

③ Listening Other amazing feats

A ◀)) CD 3.25 **Listen to three extracts from a documentary. What project is being described? Number the pictures 1–3. There is one extra.**

☐ the Queen Mary 2   ☐ Palm Islands, Dubai   ☐ Churaumi Aquarium, Japan   ☐ Channel Tunnel, Britain / France

B ◀)) CD 3.26 **Listen again. Answer the questions about each project.**

1. What was the main challenge of the project?
2. What specific aims were engineers trying to accomplish?
3. What world record did it break at the time?
4. How many people use the facility annually?

C Pair work **Choose an engineering feat from the lesson or another you know about. Prepare a presentation to give to the class.**

Lesson C *It makes no sense whatsoever.*

1 Conversation strategy Supporting ideas

A What are the biggest challenges engineers will face in the next century? Make a list.

Not only will there be more people, but there'll be more cars. So building roads will be a challenge.

B ◀))CD 3.27 **Listen. What challenges do Sonia and Scott talk about?**

Sonia I was just listening to a report on the radio about engineering challenges for the next century.

Scott Yeah? Let me guess. Is one of them building a colony on Mars? I mean, it makes no sense whatsoever, but . . .

Sonia No, and in view of the fact that it takes about seven months to get there, that's a long way off.

Scott Right. OK. Well, let's see, um, considering the price of gas, maybe finding cheaper sources of fuel?

Sonia Yeah, there were a couple about energy – like making solar energy economical. But there's one that's kind of surprising, given the weather.

Scott Uh-huh. Yeah?

Sonia Providing access to clean water.

Scott Oh, right. That's pretty basic considering we're in the twenty-first century. But I guess it makes sense in light of the fact that some places got no rain at all last year. I mean, none whatsoever.

Sonia Yeah, they were saying one in six people don't have access to clean water for whatever reason.

C **Notice** how Sonia and Scott use facts to support their opinions and thoughts, using expressions like these. Find the examples in the conversation.

> considering
> given (that / the fact that)
> in view of / in light of (the fact that)

D ◀))CD 3.28 **Listen. Complete the sentences with the expressions you hear.**

1. _____ the world's population is growing, I predict there'll be a crisis over water one day.
2. For some regions, access to water should be relatively easy, _____ the technology to extract water from underground already exists.
3. Having clean water is a really pressing problem, especially _____ something like 80 percent of illnesses in developing countries are linked to poor water conditions.
4. _____ over 90 percent of the world's water is in the ocean, we should find a way to use more sea water for drinking water.
5. _____ everyone needs water, you'd think more people would be concerned about it.
6. _____ how precious clean water is, we should pay more for it and people should be fined if they waste it.

About you

E **Pair work** **Discuss the statements in Exercise D. What are your views?**

A I think there will definitely be a crisis over water supplies in the future.

B Especially considering it's such a basic need. Some people say it will even lead to conflicts.

Lesson C *It makes no sense whatsoever.*

1 Conversation strategy

Introducing supporting ideas

In conversation, people often use facts to support their opinions and to add information. You can introduce facts with expressions such as *given the fact that* and *in view of*.

(For more information, see Language notes at the beginning of this unit.)

- **Set the scene** Books closed. Say, "In the conversation, Scott and Sonia are talking about engineering challenges. What are some factors that could lead to challenges, for example, bigger populations?" Elicit opinions from the class (e.g., *people who want to build something bigger and better than anyone else; new drug-resistant germs / illnesses; going into outer space; need for new food sources*).

A • **Preview and do the task** Read the instructions and the example sentences aloud. Have Ss make a list.

   • Check answers with the class. Have Ss call out their ideas. Write them on the board.

B ◀)) CD3, Track 27

   • **Preview the task** Say, "Listen. What challenges do Sonia and Scott talk about? Just listen to the conversation first. Then we'll listen again. Write brief answers."

   • **Play the recording** Ss listen only. Replay the recording. Ss listen and write. Have Ss compare their answers in pairs.

   • **Play the recording again** Books open. Ss listen, read along, and check their answers. Check the answer with the class. [Sonia and Scott talk about the challenges of building a colony on Mars, finding cheaper sources of fuel, and having access to clean water.]

C • **Present *Notice*** Read the information and the examples aloud. Write on the board and explain:

   1. considering / given / in view of / in light of + noun phrase

   Say, "The expressions in pattern 1 on the board can be used before a noun phrase. When they do, don't use *that*. For example, *Given the price of gas, we should look for cheaper sources of fuel.*"

   2. given / considering (+ that) + clause

   Say, "The expressions in pattern 2 can be used before a clause. When they are, you can use *that*, but it's optional. Sometimes people leave out *that* in conversation, but it's often best to use it to make your meaning clear. For example, *Considering that gas is expensive, we should look for cheaper sources of fuel.*"

   3. considering / given / in view of / in light of (+ the fact that) + clause

   Say, "The expressions in pattern 3 can be used before a noun phrase, for example, *In view of / In light of the price of gas, we should look for cheaper sources of fuel.* If you want to use a clause after them, use *the fact that*

as in, *In view of the fact that gas is expensive, we should look for cheaper sources of fuel.*"

   • Say, "Read the conversation again. Find the examples." Have a S read them aloud. [*Sonia:* No, and in view of the fact that it takes about seven months to get there, that's a long way off. *Scott:* Well, let's see, um, considering the price of gas, maybe find cheaper sources of fuel? *Sonia:* But there's one that's kind of surprising, given the weather. *Scott:* That's pretty basic considering we're in the twenty-first century. But I guess it makes sense in light of the fact that some places got no rain at all last year.]

   • **Practice** Tell Ss to practice the conversation in pairs, taking turns playing each role.

D ◀)) CD3, Track 28

   • **Preview the task** Read the instructions aloud. Say, "Read the six sentences before we begin." Check for vocabulary questions.

   • **Play the recording** Ss listen and write. Play the recording again. Ss check their answers. Check answers with the class

Answers

1. In light of the fact that the world's . . .
2. For some regions, . . . given that the technology . . .
3. Having clean . . . especially in view of the fact that something like 80 . . .
4. Considering that over 90 percent . . .
5. Given that everyone needs water, . . .
6. Considering how precious clean water is, . . .

About you

E Pair work

   • **Preview and do the task** Read the instructions aloud. Ask a pair of Ss to read the example aloud. Walk around the class and help as needed.

   • **Follow-up** Have several pairs share their opinions with the class.

Extra activity – pairs

Pairs choose one of the challenges they brainstormed in Exercise 1A and write a conversation supporting the opinions they give using expressions to introduce their facts. Pairs present their conversation to another pair. The listening pair notes the expressions used.

② Strategy plus

Why use *at all* and *whatsoever*?

In conversation, a speaker can use *at all* or *whatsoever* to emphasize a negative phrase. *Whatsoever* is used mostly after *no . . .* , *not any . . .* , or *none*.

(For more information, see Language notes at the beginning of this unit.)

🔊 **CD3, Track 29**

- **Present *Strategy plus*** Read aloud or play the recording of the information and example. Ss listen and read along.

- Write on the board, underlined as shown:

    I have none at all.

    I have none whatsoever.

    Say, "*At all* and *whatsoever* follow *none* directly because *none* is a pronoun. So, for example, you can say "*I have none at all* or *I have none whatsoever.*"

- Write on the board, underlined as shown:

    There is no problem at all.

    There aren't any mistakes whatsoever.

- Say, "But, in expressions with *no* and *not any, at all* and *whatsoever* must follow nouns." Ask a S to read the examples from the board.

- Tell Ss to read the conversation on page 98 again and find the examples. [*Scott*: I mean, it makes no sense

whatsoever, but . . . ; . . . some places got no rain at all last year. I mean, none whatsoever.] Say, "Notice how Scott uses *at all* to emphasize the fact that some places had no rain. He then makes an already emphatic statement even more emphatic by saying, "*I mean, none whatsoever.*"

- **Present *In conversation*** Read the information aloud. Say, "You'll see more examples in the responses in the next exercise."

About you

- **Preview the task** Tell Ss to read the three comments. Check for vocabulary problems. For each comment, ask Ss if they agree or disagree and to give reasons.

- **Do the task** Tell Ss to read the six responses. Say, "Find two responses for each comment. Write the letters *a* to *f*." Have Ss complete the task and compare their answers with a partner. Check answers with the class.

Answers

1. d, f;   2. a, c;   3. b, e

- Say, "Practice the comments and responses with a partner. Continue the conversations." Walk around the class and give help as needed.

③ Strategies

A • **Preview and do the task** Say, "Circle the correct options to complete the conversations. Circle both options if they are both correct." Have Ss complete the task. Check answers with the class.

Answers

1. **A** I wonder . . .
   B Well, mapping . . . I mean, given / considering that we know so little . . .
   A Oh, there's no doubt whatsoever. . . . I mean, they have no cure whatsoever / at all for . . .
2. **A** What's the most immediate . . . ?
   B Well, they need to . . . Considering / In light of the fact that so many . . .
   A True. And there's no reason at all not to . . .
3. **A** Do you think developing . . . ?
   B I . . . any impact whatsoever on our daily lives. . . . might be good, given that we've . . .

- Say, "Now practice with a partner. Then practice again using different expressions."

About you

B Pair work

- **Preview and do the task** Read the instructions aloud. Remind Ss to use the expressions taught in this lesson.

- **Follow-up** For each conversation, have a few pairs share their answers with the class. (Note: If using the Extra Activity below, have several pairs share ideas. Tell the class to take brief notes on the ideas they hear.)

Extra activity – groups

After listening to the ideas presented in Exercise 3B, groups use their notes to decide on a final answer to each question in Exercise 3B.

Speaking naturally

- Tell Ss to turn to Speaking naturally on p. 142. (For more information, see Language notes at the beginning of this unit. See the teaching notes on p. T-142.)

2 Strategy plus *at all, whatsoever*

◀)) **CD 3.29** You can use *at all* or *whatsoever* to emphasize a negative phrase.

Whatsoever is more emphatic. It is mostly used after *no . . .,* *not any . . .,* or *none*.

Some places got **no** rain **at all**. I mean, **none whatsoever**.

In conversation . . .

Whatsoever is typically used after *none, nothing,* or these nouns: *(no / any) problem(s), reason, sense, evidence, doubt(s), impact, effect*.

About you

Find two responses for each comment. Write the letters a–f. Then practice in pairs. Continue the conversations.

1. Engineering is so important, yet it's not a subject you can take in high school. _____ _____
2. It seems that either money or politics gets in the way of finding solutions to most problems. _____ _____
3. It takes years before engineering breakthroughs affect most people's lives. _____ _____

a. Right. But there's no doubt whatsoever that we can solve these issues.
b. Yes, a lot of them have no impact on us whatsoever.
c. Right. It makes no sense whatsoever. I mean, we should just get on with it and sort these things out.
d. I know. There are no classes in it at all. There was nothing whatsoever like that when I was a kid.
e. Well, I don't see much evidence at all for that. It depends what advances you mean.
f. Yeah, and there shouldn't be any problem at all including it in the curriculum.

3 Strategies *More priorities*

A **Circle the correct options to complete the conversations. Circle both options if they are both correct. Then practice with a partner. Practice again, using different expressions.**

1. *A* I wonder what some of the other engineering challenges are. Do you have any ideas?
   B Well, mapping the brain would be a huge breakthrough. I mean, **given / considering** that we know so little about diseases like Alzheimer's.
   A Oh, there's no doubt **whatsoever / in view of the fact that**. If they could treat brain disorders, that would be huge. I mean, they have no cure **whatsoever / at all** for migraines, even.

2. *A* What's the most *immediate* challenge, do you think?
   B Well, they need to update a lot of the infrastructure in many cities. **Considering / In light of** the fact that so many of the subways and sewers are so old, that should be a priority.
   A True. And there's no reason **considering / at all** not to do that now. They know how to.

3. *A* Do you think developing space technology and exploring Mars is a priority?
   B I don't know. I don't think it has any impact **whatsoever / given** on our daily lives. Though I guess studying asteroids might be good, **in view of / given** that we've been hit by asteroids in the past.

About you

B Pair work **Ask and answer the questions in Exercise A. Give your own answers.**

Speaking naturally

See page 142.

Lesson D *Robotics*

1 Reading

A **Prepare** **What do you know about robots? How are robots used? Make a list. Then scan the article to see if your ideas are mentioned.**

Robots are used in the medical field for things like keyhole surgery.

B 📥 **Read for main ideas** **Read the article. Then check (✓) the best title for the article.**

1. ☐ Robots cause unimaginable problems
2. ☐ The future is here and it's robotic
3. ☐ Home is where your robot is

1 Robots are probably not high on the list of priorities for the average consumer. The nearest they might come to a robot is a robotic vacuum cleaner, which maneuvers its way around the home picking up dust. For most people, not only is the thought of interacting with a humanoid robot in their kitchen highly unlikely, but it also seems a little absurd. Some even consider it positively creepy, which may in part be because people are unsure how to relate to a robot. Such reluctance might also be explained by the ethical dilemmas posed by using robots instead of real people for certain tasks. Is it acceptable, for example, to have robots babysitting our children or looking after our elderly?

2 Robots have of course played a critical part in society for decades. In the 1960s, robots transformed the automotive industry by performing hazardous and repetitive tasks and working more efficiently and more accurately than humans. They could also work longer hours, which undoubtedly had an enormous impact on the profitability of the industry. Since then, industrial robots have been deployed in various manufacturing and electronics industries. Many of the products we purchase have been assembled or handled in some way by robots. Little do consumers realize how much their lives are actually already influenced by robotics.

3 If you consider the robotics industry today, there doesn't seem to be a field that is *not* influenced by robotics in significant ways. Indeed, robotics now plays a role in everything from agriculture and forestry to mining and construction – even to warfare.

Medical robotics

4 For years now, surgeons have been using robots in performing different types of operations. Not only is robotic surgery less invasive, but recovery for the patient is much quicker. More recent groundbreaking developments may have a profound impact on identifying and treating

serious diseases. For example, ETH Zürich researchers have developed micro-robots that are the size of bacteria. While more research needs to be conducted, possible applications include carrying medicine to specific areas of the body and treating heart disease.

Search and rescue

5 Whatever challenges responders face when they arrive at a large-scale disaster site – for example, after an earthquake – one of the greatest is determining where victims may still be trapped. Germany's Fraunhofer Institute has been developing a robotic "spider" that can easily move through the debris of collapsed buildings and send rescuers live images or even sense hazards such as leaking gas. The advantages of using robots as opposed to humans in these situations are obvious.

Ocean exploration

6 U.S. Navy-backed research has produced a robotic "jellyfish" that can power itself using hydrogen from seawater. Possible applications include monitoring oceans for signs of pollution or for security purposes, and for exploration of otherwise inaccessible ocean waters.

7 However you look at it, robots will increasingly be part of our lives in the future. The field of robotics is rapidly expanding, and scientists are forging ahead with developing robots that can see, speak, think, and even make decisions based on the environment around them. The applications of robotics seem unlimited, and certainly the general public might perceive the advantages of using robots in specialized areas. The question remains: How accepting will we be of having robots rather than humans, as caregivers for our families?

Lesson D *Robotics*

1 Reading

- **Set the scene** Books closed. Read the lesson title aloud and write it on the board. Ask, "What is *robotics*?" [the science of making and using robots] Ask, "What is a robot?" [a machine controlled by a computer, which can move and do different tasks] Say, "This reading is about robots and the science of robotics."

A Prepare

- **Preview and do the task** Ask, "What do you know about robots? How are robots used? Make a list of your ideas." Have Ss make their lists. Ask Ss to call out their ideas (e.g., *Robots are used for finding victims in natural disasters, such as earthquakes; for carrying equipment such as cameras, etc. in outer space; for investigating suspicious packages that may be bombs; for manufacturing or making products; for cleaning homes*).

- Books open. Say, "Now scan the article to see if any of your ideas are mentioned. Use the photos in the article to help you."

- Have Ss say which, if any, of their ideas are in the article.

B ⬇ www.cambridge.org/viewpoint/audio
Read for main ideas

- **Preview the task** Read the instructions aloud. Say, "Read the article for the main idea. Don't stop to check vocabulary. Then check (✓) the best title." If desired, play the downloadable recording. Ss listen and read along.

- **Do the task** Ss read and make their choice. Check the answer with the class. [The future is here, and it's robotic.]

- Check for any vocabulary questions.

Extra activity – groups

Groups discuss the final paragraph of the article. Write on the board:

How do you feel about the role of robots in the future?

Can you think of any disadvantages of robots as caregivers?

How about advantages?

Groups share some of their ideas with the class.

C Understanding inference

- **Preview the task** Read the instructions aloud. Tell Ss to read the statements before they begin. Walk around the class and help as necessary.
- **Do the task** Have Ss complete the task and compare their answers with a partner. Say, "If you and your partner have a different answer, go back to the article and read that section again." Check answers with the class.

Answers

1. N (para. 1)
2. Y (para. 2)
3. NG
4. NG
5. Y (para. 6)
6. N (para. 7)

② Focus on vocabulary

A
- **Preview and do the task** Read the instructions aloud. Do the first word with the class. Say, "Read paragraph 1. What verb has a similar meaning to *communicate*?" [interact]
- Have Ss complete the task and compare their answers with a partner. Check answers with the class. Ask individual Ss each to read a sentence aloud.

Answers

1. . . . can we really <u>interact</u> or <u>relate to</u> them?
2. If you were to <u>conduct</u> a survey of friends, . . . ?
3. Can you <u>identify</u> the ways in which . . . ?
4. . . . robots are <u>deployed</u>? What jobs do they <u>perform</u>?
5. . . . robots will <u>transform</u> the workplace . . . ?
6. How would you <u>determine</u> if robots . . . ?
7. Will we need to <u>monitor</u> robots to . . . ?

About you

B Pair work

- **Preview and do the task** Read the instructions aloud. Have Ss complete the task.
- **Follow-up** Call on Ss to share their ideas with the class.

③ Listening

A
- **Preview and do the task** Ask Ss to look at the picture of the robot. Ask, "Does this robot have any resemblance to your idea of a 'human' robot?" Have Ss give their opinion. Read the instructions aloud. Say, "On a separate piece of paper, write a few words for your guesses." Have Ss complete the task.

B ◄)) CD3, Track 30

- **Preview the task** Read the instructions aloud.
- **Play the recording** Audio script pp. T-278–T-279

  Ss listen and check (✓) the questions. Replay the recording. Ss listen and check their answers. Check the answers with the class.

Answers

2. ☑ What can "she" do?
4. ☑ How do people react to her?
5. ☑ What applications does she have?
7. ☑ Do people want robots as friends?

C ◄)) CD3, Track 31

- **Preview the task** Read the instructions aloud.
- **Play the recording** Audio script pp. T-278–T-279

  Ss listen and write. Have Ss compare their answers with a partner.
- **Play the recording again** Ss listen and check their work. Check answers with the class.

Answers

2. She can sing, smile, frown, and interact with people.
4. People are curious, interested, and fascinated. She was a big hit in Hong Kong.
5. She could be a substitute teacher or a caregiver.
7. It depends. It may be cultural. In Japan, people are more accepting of robots.

④ Viewpoint

Group work

- **Preview the task** Read the instructions aloud. Ask a S to read the example aloud.
- **Present *In conversation*** Read the information aloud. Ask, "In the example, what idea was introduced with *The thing is*?" [the possibility of having the flowers cut down] Say, "You can refer to and introduce an idea about the past with *The thing was*. You can also add positive or negative adjectives such as *the great thing is* or *the terrible thing was . . . The only thing* almost always introduces a problem or a negative idea."

- **Do the task** Have Ss discuss their ideas. Walk around the class and help as needed.
- **Follow-up** Have each group present their ideas to the class. (If using the Extra Activity below, suggest the class take notes on the groups' presentations.)

Extra activity – groups / class

The class forms new groups. Ss discuss the ideas they heard, including advantages and disadvantages. They decide on the most important five applications.

Groups present their final list to the class. The class does a final ranking.

C Understanding inference **Do the statements below agree with the information in the article? Write Y (Yes), N (No), or NG (Information not given).**

1. The average consumer really wants to get a robot for their home. _____
2. It's generally more efficient to use robots in industry. _____
3. Patients who have robotic surgery live longer. _____
4. The robotic spider decides where it should go to find victims of earthquakes. _____
5. The robotic jellyfish can go to places where humans can't normally go. _____
6. Robots will always play a limited part in our lives in the future. _____

2 Focus on vocabulary Verbs

A **Find verbs with similar meanings to the verbs in bold. Rewrite the questions, using the correct forms of the verbs and making any other changes needed.**

1. Given that robots have no emotions, can we really **communicate** or **connect with** them? (para. 1)
2. If you were to **do** a survey of friends, do you think they would want a robot in their home? (para. 4)
3. Can you **recognize** the ways in which humanoid robots are lacking? (para. 4)
4. What industries do you know of where robots are **used**? What jobs do they **do**? (para. 2)
5. How do you think robots will **change** the workplace in the future? (para. 2)
6. How would you **decide** if robots could make good caregivers or teachers? (para. 5)
7. Will we need to **watch** robots to make sure that they don't become more powerful than humans? (para. 6)

About you **B** Pair work **Discuss the questions above. Think of as many ideas as you can.**

3 Listening *Is she for real?*

A **Read the questions about a humanoid robot. Can you guess the answers?**

1. ☐ How did they build "her"?
2. ☐ What can "she" do?
3. ☐ How much did she cost to build?
4. ☐ How do people react to her?
5. ☐ What applications does she have?
6. ☐ What are the ethical issues of "human" robots?
7. ☐ Do people want robots as friends?

B ◀)) CD 3.30 **Listen to a radio interview. Which questions does the guest answer? Check (✓) the boxes.**

C ◀)) CD 3.31 **Listen again. Write one detail to answer the questions you checked in Exercise B.**

Geminoid F

4 Viewpoint Applications for the future

Group work **Imagine there are no technological barriers whatsoever. How could robots be useful? Discuss your ideas about specific applications. What are your top 10 ideas?**

"You could have a robot that mows lawns – kind of like a robot vacuum cleaner. The thing is you'd have to make sure it didn't cut down all your flowers."

In conversation . . .

You can use *The thing is . . .* to introduce ideas or problems.

Writing *A good alternative*

In this lesson, you . . .
- write a classification essay.
- express alternatives.
- avoid errors with *would rather / rather than*.

Task **Write an essay.**
Can robots replace human beings in all activities? Give reasons and examples in your response.

A Look at a model **Look at these extracts from an essay. Think of a topic to add to each paragraph.**

. . . There are a number of fields in which robots can and should be used as opposed to human beings. These can be classified into the following types: dangerous activities; tasks requiring extreme precision; tedious, repetitive work; and activities that require huge computing power. One area is in heavy industry, where robots are already used instead of human beings. Not only can they do dangerous or unpleasant jobs, they are also more efficient. Another example of where robots are a good alternative to humans is in space exploration. . . . Yet another is . . .

. . . On the other hand, there are some fields where a robot, however smart, would be no substitute for a human being. One example of this is caring for people in hospitals. Although robots can now perform surgery, human caregivers rather than robots are best at satisfying the psychological needs of patients. In fact, most patients would rather be cared for by a human caregiver than a robot. An additional area is . . .

Classifying

There are a number of . . .
One is . . . Another . . . Yet another . . .

They can be classified into the following types: . . .

They can be divided into four groups / categories. The first is . . .

B Focus on language **Read the chart. Then underline the expressions for stating alternatives and preference in the paragraphs in Exercise A.**

Stating alternatives and preference in writing 🔽

You can use these expressions to write about alternatives.
Robots are used in industry **in place of / instead of / rather than** humans.
Human caregivers **as opposed to** robots are best at caring for patients.
Robots are a good **alternative to / substitute for** humans in space.

Would rather, be preferable to, and *be no substitute for* express preference.
Most people **would rather** have a human caregiver **than** a robot.
Robots **are no substitute for** humans in some areas.

In writing . . .

Rather than joins nouns, verbs, prepositional phrases, adjectives, or adverbs. Notice the verb forms after *rather than*.

*Rather than **use / using** humans for these tasks, we should use robots.*

C **Complete the sentences with expressions from the chart. How many correct answers are there?**

1. In jobs where conditions are dangerous, robots are the obvious _____ human workers.
2. The construction industry could easily use robotic devices _____ human beings.
3. There are many industrial jobs where robots would be a better _____ humans.
4. Manufacturers _____ use robotic technology because it _____ employing people.
5. _____ using human mechanics, some companies now use robots that repair themselves.
6. In teaching, however, _____ use robots as teachers, we should always employ humans.
7. Robots are _____ people when it comes to jobs such as hotel receptionists.

D Write and check **Now write your essay as described in the Task above. Then check for errors.**

Common errors

Do not use *prefer* after *would rather*.
I would rather be cared for by a robot. (NOT *I ~~would rather prefer to be~~* . . .)

Avoid using *rather* before *than* in basic comparisons.
*Robots are more suited to heavy work **than** humans.* (NOT . . . *~~work rather than~~* . . .)

Writing *A good alternative*

In this lesson

- Ask a S to read the lesson aims (*In this lesson, you . . .*) aloud. Ask, "What do you do when you classify things?" [sort them by type or category] Say, "A classification essay sorts ideas into different categories."

- **Preview the writing** Say, "In this lesson, you will plan and write a classification essay." Point out the writing topic in Task and read it aloud. Explain that Ss will end the lesson by writing a report that will practice the three aims presented in this lesson.

A Look at a model

- **Preview and do the task** Books closed. Say, "This extract is from an essay that talks about jobs that robots could or should do as opposed to jobs that are better suited to humans. Which jobs are better for robots?" Have Ss call out their ideas. Write them on the board. Ask, "How about jobs for humans?" Write Ss' ideas on the board.

- Books open. Read the instructions aloud. Say, "Try to think of topics that aren't on the board." Have Ss read the extracts. Check for vocabulary questions. Have Ss complete the task. Ask, "What topics on the board were mentioned in the extract?" Have Ss call them out.

- Ask, "What new topic did you think of for fields that are more suited to robots?" Have Ss call out their ideas. Add them to the board. [Possible answers for paragraph 1: Yet another is in the military or in areas of combat (e.g., bomb detection and defusing). / in the medical field in surgery, for example / in rescue operations (e.g., after earthquakes, etc.) / in manufacturing (e.g., in car assembly)]

- Ask, "What new topic did you think of for fields that are more suited to humans?" Have Ss call out their ideas. Add them to the board. [Possible answers for paragraph 2: An additional area is where there is high unemployment and people need jobs no matter how tedious or repetitive. / in service industries – for example, at hotel reception areas where guests like to speak to real people / in customer support, where people like interaction with real human beings]

- **Present *Classifying*** Say, "These expressions are used in classification essays." Read the information aloud. Say, "Look at the extracts again. Which ones are used?" [paragraph 1: There are a number of fields . . . ; These can be classified into . . . ; One area is in . . . ; Another example of where robots . . . ; Yet another is . . . paragraph 2: One example of this is caring . . . ; An additional area is . . .]

B ⬇ www.cambridge.org/viewpoint/audio

Focus on language

- **Present the grammar for writing chart** Read the information in the chart aloud (or play the recording, if using). Ss listen and read along.

- **Understand the grammar for writing** Say, "*in place of, instead of, rather than,* and *as opposed to* are prepositional expressions. They are usually followed by a noun phrase, pronoun, or *-ing* form."

- Say, "Notice the last example shows the verb phrase *be an alternative to / substitute for.* When you use one of these expressions to write about alternatives, pay attention to the preposition you need."

- Say, "When you write or talk about the alternative that you prefer, you can use *would rather, be preferable to,* or *be no substitute for.* The expression *would rather* usually has a human subject. Use *than* to introduce the second alternative."

- **Present *In writing*** Say "*Rather than* joins nouns, verbs, prepositional phrases, adjectives, or adverbs. Look at paragraph 2 in the model. What does *rather than* join?" [two nouns – (human) caregivers and robots] Say, "Notice the verb forms after *rather than.*" Have a S read the example aloud. Ask, "What forms are used?" [base form and *-ing* form]

- **Do the task** Say, "Now underline the expressions for stating alternatives and preferences in the paragraphs in Exercise A." Have Ss complete the task. Check answers with the class.

Answers

Para 1 There are . . . should be used <u>as opposed</u> to human beings. . . . One area is . . . where robots are already used <u>instead of</u> human beings. . . . Another example of where robots <u>are a good alternative to</u> humans . . .

Para 2 On the other hand, . . . would <u>be no substitute</u> for a human being. . . . Although . . . human caregivers <u>rather than</u> robots are best at . . . In fact, most patients <u>would rather</u> be . . . caregiver <u>than</u> a robot. . . .

C

- **Preview and do the task** Read the instructions aloud. Have Ss complete the task. Check answers with the class.

Answers

1. alternative to / substitute for
2. in place of / instead of / rather than / as opposed to
3. alternative to / substitute for
4. would rather . . . is preferable to
5. In place of / Instead of / Rather than
6. rather than
7. no substitute for

D Write and check

- **Preview the task** Read the instructions aloud.

- **Present *Common errors*** Read the information aloud.

- **Do the task** Have Ss complete the task.

Extra activity – class

Ss leave their essays on their desk for classmates to read. Ss go around the class reading each other's work. Ss note the most mentioned activities for robots.

Vocabulary notebook *How do you do it?*

If done for homework

Briefly present the Learning tip and the task directions. Make sure Ss understand what they need to do.

If done in class

- **Present *Learning tip*** Read the information aloud. Add, "Think of a question and answer that are true or have meaning for you." Ask a S to read the example in the box.

A • **Preview and do the task** Read the instructions aloud. Have Ss complete the task. Check answers with the class. Ask a few Ss to read their sentences aloud.

Possible answers

1. There's not much <u>concrete</u> in the homes in our neighborhood. They're mostly built of wood.
2. Not really. It's hard to <u>maneuver</u> my car into my garage at home.
3. Not only do I <u>complete</u> my homework in <u>on time</u>, I usually do it a few days beforehand.
4. There aren't any <u>elevated</u> highways near my home.
5. Yes. I had to <u>assemble</u> an office chair once, and the instructions made no sense at all.

B • **Preview and do the task** Read the instructions aloud. Elicit ideas for a question for *construct*. (e.g., *What kinds of buildings have been* **constructed** *in your neighborhood?*)

Answers

Answers will vary.

- **Follow-up** Have Ss read their questions and answers to a partner.

Extra activity – pairs

Ss answer each other's questions from Exercise B.

C **Word builder**

- **Preview the task** Say, "Find the meaning of these words from the article on p. 96." Do the first word with the class. Tell them to find *to blend into* in the last paragraph of the article. Say, "Use the context to find the meaning." Elicit an answer from the class. [to merge into so it doesn't stand out] Say, "Use the context to find the meanings. If necessary, look at a dictionary or online dictionary."

- **Do the task** Have Ss complete the task. Check the answers with the class

Answers

to blend into: to merge into so it doesn't stand out
to float: to lie above something else; hang in the air
a landmark: an important feature such as a tower or bridge
a landscape: an area of land, usually in the countryside; valleys and hills, for example
a lane: a section on a freeway for one line of traffic
a penalty: a fee you pay as a punishment for breaking a rule or regulation
a pylon: a tower, for example, one that holds electricity cables
a viaduct: an elevated road high above a valley

Say, "Now write questions and answers for the words." Have Ss complete the task. Have a few Ss read their questions and answers to the class. Alternatively, put Ss in pairs to answer each other's questions.

D **Focus on vocabulary, page 101**

- **Preview and do the task** Read the instructions aloud. Say, "First write any words that you know or remember. Then look at page 101." Have Ss find the words. Check answers with the class.

Answers

1. What's the best way to <u>determine</u> which courses you should take in college?
2. What single thing would <u>transform</u> your life?
3. How do you <u>relate to</u> people generally? Are you good at <u>interacting</u> with others?
4. What jobs in your home would you let a robot <u>perform</u>?
5. Are you able to <u>identify</u> your own strengths and weaknesses?
6. Have you ever had to <u>conduct</u> a survey for a school project?
7. Which industries are robots best <u>deployed</u> in?
8. How does your boss or professor <u>monitor</u> your performance?

- Say, "Now write answers to the questions." Have Ss complete the task.

- **Follow-up** Assign individual Ss to ask the questions in Exercise D. The S asking the question elicits a few answers from the class.

Vocabulary notebook *How do you do it?*

Learning tip   Ask a question

When you learn new vocabulary, put it into a question to ask yourself. Thinking of the question and answer can help you remember it.

Q What's made of steel in the kitchen?
A The silverware / knives and forks.

A **Answer the questions. Use the words in bold in your answers.**

1. Is there any **concrete** in the building where you live? _____
2. Are you good at **maneuvering** a car into a small space? _____
3. Are you usually able to **complete** your assignments **on time**? _____
4. Is there an **elevated** highway near your home? _____
5. Have you ever tried to **assemble** flat packed furniture? _____

B **Write questions and answers for these words.**

1. construct _____
2. erect _____
3. engineer _____
4. install _____
5. position _____
6. fall behind schedule _____
7. delay _____
8. in a short time frame _____
9. ahead of schedule _____

C **Word builder Find the meanings of these words from the article on page 96. Write questions and answers for them.**

| to blend into | to float | a landmark | a landscape | a lane | a penalty | a pylon | a viaduct |

A How can new buildings blend into the natural environment?
B Well, using materials in the same colors as those naturally found in an area can help.

D **Focus on vocabulary Read the questions below. Replace the verbs in bold with words from the box. Then write your own answers to the questions. Refer to Exercise 2A on page 101 to help you.**

| conduct | deployed | determine | identify | interacting | monitor | perform | relate to | transform |

1. What's the best way to **decide** which courses you should take in college?
2. What single thing would **change** your life **completely**?
3. How do you **get along with** people generally? Are you good at **communicating** with others?
4. What jobs in your home would you let a robot **do**?
5. Are you able to **recognize** your own strengths and weaknesses?
6. Have you ever had to **do** a survey for a school project?
7. Which industries are robots best **used** in?
8. How does your boss or professor **watch and check on** your performance?

Checkpoint 3 *Units 7–9*

① Is life easier now?

A Rewrite the underlined parts of the sentences, starting with the words in bold. Then complete the missing parts of the expressions.

In this _____ age, many young people may think that life is hard. They **not only** find it difficult to get work, but that it takes time _____ even to get an interview. Young people have **never before** found it so difficult to buy their first home. But maybe we need to _____ think for a moment, because it's **only** by looking back in history that we are able to gain a different perspective.

In the 1930s, people were accustomed to the _____ downs of the stock market, but when it crashed on October 29, 1929, it initiated the Great Depression. The U.S. had **never before** experienced such a catastrophic economic loss, which was coupled with a drought and failure of crops. The Depression **not only** affected the economy, but it also had a huge social impact. People had **rarely** had so little money. It was a time of great pain _____.

Unemployment rates rose above and _____ anything seen previously. Many young men **not only** had to wait to find work before marrying, but many, sick _____ of not being able to find work, migrated in the thousands to other states. Divorce rates had **rarely** been as low as in the 1930s. However, _____ wives often ran away from their marriages. Homelessness became a huge problem. Some people were able to find a roof over their heads **only** by moving in with their relatives.

History shows us that _____ later things can change, and for the 1930s generation, they did – slowly _____. We'll have to _____ see what the next decades will bring us. But one thing is for sure: we move back _____ between good times and hard times.

B Pair work **Do you think life is difficult for young people? In what ways is life today easier than a hundred years ago? Summarize your points with expressions like *At the end of the day*.**

". . . When all is said and done, life is a lot easier today than a hundred years ago."

② Learning lessons from history

Cross out one word to correct the underlined phrases. Rewrite sentences beginning with a bold phrase as a cleft. Rewrite the *italic* sentences without using *if*.

View: How do we approach problems in the world needs to change. We should analyze precisely what are the problems are. Then we should consider whether have there have been similar problems in history. What we do we fail to do is learn lessons from history.

Comment 1: **Sir Winston Churchill said,** "Those who fail to learn from history are doomed to repeat it." **When we are faced** with a world crisis, we look back and consider how did it happened. **Only several decades ago,** our country suffered a crisis that threatened our security. Yet most people have no idea why do things like that happen. **When people's lives are directly affected,** they pay attention to what's going on in the world.

Comment 2: If we had learned anything from the twentieth century, this century might be more peaceful. We should look back before any crisis looms. If we don't, we are doomed. And if you should think our problems are new, think again. If you ask any historian, they'll tell you the same problems occur throughout history. If I were in a position of influence, I'd make history a required subject every year of school.

Checkpoint 3 *Units 7–9*

Before you begin the Checkpoint, say, "As you do the tasks, circle the items you aren't sure about. When we check the answers, circle any incorrect answers that surprise you. This will help you see things you need to study more."

1 Is life easier now?

↻ Exercise A recycles negative adverbs and word order. It also recycles words in the same part of speech joined by *and*, *or*, or *but* (binomials). During the pair work discussion in Exercise B, Ss review using expressions to summarize and finish points, such as *at the end of the day* and *when all is said and done*.

A (9B Grammar; 7B Vocabulary)

- **Preview and do the task** Read the instructions aloud. Say, "Rewrite the underlined parts of the sentences, starting with the words in bold." Do the first item with the class. Write *Not only* . . . on the board. Ask, "How do you finish rewriting the underlined part of the sentence?" [Not only do they find it]

- Say, "Then go back and complete the missing parts of the expressions. Look at the first blank. How do you complete the expression?" [day and] Have Ss complete the task and then compare answers in pairs. Check answers with the class.

Answers

In this <u>day and age</u>, many . . . <u>Not only do they find it</u> difficult . . . it takes time <u>and energy</u> even to get an interview. <u>Never before have young people found it</u> so difficult . . . we need to <u>stop and</u> think . . . because <u>only by looking back in history are we able</u> to gain a different perspective.

In the 1930s, . . . the <u>ups and downs</u> of the stock market, . . . <u>Never before had the U.S. experienced</u> such a . . . <u>Not only did the Depression affect</u> the economy, . . . <u>Rarely had people had</u> so little money. It was a time of great pain <u>and suffering</u>.

Unemployment rates rose above and <u>beyond</u> . . . <u>Not only did many young men have</u> to wait . . . but many, sick <u>and tired</u> of not . . . <u>Rarely had divorce rates been</u> as low as in the 1930s. However, <u>husbands and wives</u> often . . . <u>Only by</u> . . . relatives <u>were some people able to find</u> . . .

History shows us that <u>sooner or</u> later things . . . , they did – slowly <u>but surely</u>. We'll have to <u>wait and see</u> what . . . But one thing is for sure: we move <u>back and</u> forth between good times and hard times.

B (7C Conversation strategy)

Pair work

- **Preview the task** Read the instructions aloud. Ask a S to read the example aloud.

- **Do the task** Ss work in pairs to discuss the questions.

- **Follow-up** Have several pairs present their summarized points to the class.

2 Learning lessons from history

↻ This task recycles the following grammar points: conditional sentences without *if* (imperative . . . *and*; inversions; *otherwise*), *wh-* clauses as subjects and objects; cleft sentences.

(7A Grammar; 7B Grammar; 8B Grammar)

- **Preview the task** Read the instructions aloud. Tell Ss to read the view and the two comments before they begin. Say, "Follow the instructions in the order they are written."

- **Do the task** Have Ss complete the task and compare their answers with a partner. Check answers with the class.

Answers

View: <u>How ~~do~~ we approach</u> problems . . . We should analyze precisely <u>what ~~are~~ the problems are</u>. Then we should consider <u>whether ~~have~~ there have been</u> similar problems in history. What <u>we do ~~we~~ fail</u> to do is learn lessons from history.

Comment 1: <u>It was Sir Winston Churchill who said</u>, "Those . . . repeat it." <u>It is when we are faced</u> with . . . consider how <u>~~did~~ it happened</u>. <u>It was only several decades ago that our country</u> . . . Yet most people have no idea <u>why ~~do~~ things like that happen</u>. <u>It is when people's lives are directly affected that they</u> . . .

Comment 2: <u>Had we</u> learned anything from the twentieth century, . . . We should look back before any crisis looms. <u>Otherwise</u>, we are doomed. And <u>should you</u> think our problems are new, think again. <u>Ask</u> any historian, <u>and</u> they'll tell you the same problems occur throughout history. <u>Were I</u> in a position of influence, . . .

Extra activity – pairs

Each pair chooses three historical events that they would encourage people to study and say why.

3 Improve your relationships

⟳ Exercise A recycles the -ever words: *whatever, whichever* (pronoun / determiner), *whoever* (pronoun), and *whenever, wherever,* and *however* (adverbs). It also recycles synonyms that describe degrees of impact, change, and effect. The conversation strategy of using expressions such as *considering* and *in light of (the fact that)* to introduce facts that support a thought or opinion is practiced in Exercise 3B.

A (9A Grammar; 8B Vocabulary)

- **Preview the task** Read the instructions aloud. Ask Ss to read the entire article before they begin. Say, "Write in all the -*ever* words first. Then replace the words in bold."

- **Do the task** Have Ss complete the task. Tell Ss to compare their answers with a partner. Check answers with the class. Have individual Ss each read a tip aloud.

Answers

. . . Wherever you look, . . .
1. Whatever you do, . . . how insignificant / minor / minute it may seem. If it's a minor / an insignificant / a minute issue, . . . Whoever is at fault, . . . You'll notice an immediate / a rapid / a sudden . . .

2. Whenever you have . . . about something superficial, but . . . So focus on whatever *that* problem might be, and whenever you . . . don't just fire off a rapid / an immediate / sudden answer. . . You might see a sudden / a rapid / an immediate change . . . and a visible difference in the outcome. Bad moods are universal. If . . . it's probably temporary. Remember that while there's a slight chance . . . So whenever it's apparent that . . .

3. Whatever the problem, however you solve it, use it as a life lesson. Solving even minute / minor / insignificant problems can create profound and . . .

B (9C Conversation Strategy)

Pair work

- **Preview and do the task** Read the instructions aloud. Ask, "What other expressions do you remember?" Have Ss call out the expressions. Ask a pair of Ss to read the example aloud. Have Ss complete the task.

- **Follow-up** Have several pairs share their ideas with the class.

4 Construction projects

⟳ Exercise A recycles vocabulary for talking about construction. Exercise B recycles perfect infinitives and the conversation strategies for drawing a conclusion from what someone said, avoiding topics, responses to focus on your viewpoint, and emphasizing a negative phrase.

A (9B Vocabulary)

- **Preview and do the task** Read the instructions aloud. Point out the cue word in parentheses and the example answer. Tell Ss to read the entire paragraph before they begin. Have Ss complete the task and compare answers with a partner. Check answers with the class.

Answers

Many . . . made of steel and concrete. Sometimes they are constructed or assembled in one place . . . to be maneuvered into position or erected. After that, all the services need to be installed. . . . complete projects in a short time frame, their schedules often fall behind schedule. This can be because of a delay in getting . . . , roads that are elevated above cities are particularly complex. However, . . . is not completed on time.

B (8A Grammar; 8C Conversation Strategy; 7C, 8C Strategy plus)

- **Preview the task** Say, "Use the verbs given with perfect infinitives." Check that Ss understand the structure: Ask, "What will you write in the first blank?" [seems to have changed]

- **Do the task** Have Ss change the verbs indicated. Say, "Now add the expressions in the box. There may be more than one correct answer." Have Ss add the expressions and then compare their answers with a partner. Check answers with the class.

Answers

. . . , the city seems to have changed completely. The old stores appear to have gone – I mean, there are none left whatsoever. The old neighborhoods are supposed to have been really beautiful, so in that case / then, why did they . . . But don't get me started / let's not go there. I would love to have met the planners . . . the city, then?" They . . . cars, which are said to have been more environmentally . . . But don't get me started / let's not go there. We've just lost so much. That's what I'm saying.

- Ask, "Do you have similar views about your city?" Have short class discussion.

Extra activity – groups

Write on the board:

The trend in many cities is to demolish the older parts of town to build high-rise condos and shopping malls. What could some of the positive and negative consequences of this be?

Groups discuss the question and report their ideas to the class.

3 Improve your relationships

A Complete the article with *whatever, whenever, whoever, whichever, however,* and *wherever*. Then replace the words in bold with one word with a similar meaning.

Problems with a relationship? _____ you look, you'll find advice. But have you tried these tips?

1. _____ you do, don't ignore a problem – no matter how **unimportant** it may seem. If it's a **small** issue, talk it through right away. _____ is at fault, ask what *you* can do to help solve the problem. You'll notice an **instant** change in attitude from your partner.

2. _____ you have an argument, figure out what it is *really* about. Many times they seem to be about something "**on the surface**," but often there's a deeper problem. So focus on _____ *that* problem might be, and _____ you are having an argument about the same old topic, don't just fire off a **quick** answer. Try a different response. You might see a **quick** change in the direction of the argument and a **clear** difference in the outcome. Bad moods are **common**. If your partner is in a bad mood, just remember it's probably **for a short time**. Remember that while there's a **small** chance it's about you, most likely it's not. So _____ it's **obvious** that he or she needs some space, give it to them.

3. _____ the problem, _____ you solve it, use it as a life lesson. Solving even **tiny** problems can create **deep** and lasting changes in your relationships in the future.

B Pair work **Discuss the advice in Exercise A. What other advice do you have? Use expressions like *considering* and *in light of (the fact that)* to support your opinions.**

A *However you look at it, you can't really ignore any problem in a relationship.*
B *Right. I mean, given the fact that you live with someone day after day, it's important to solve problems.*

4 Construction projects

A Complete the paragraph with words and expressions. Use the cues given to help you.

Many modern buildings are made of ~~steel~~ and _____ (materials). Sometimes they are _____ (built) or _____ (put together) in one place and then brought to the construction site to be _____ (moved) into position or _____ (put up). After that, all the services need to be _____ (put in). Construction scheduling is a huge challenge. Even though companies agree to complete projects _____ (quickly), their schedules often _____ (are late). This can be because of a _____ (lateness) in getting materials or because the project is complex. For example, roads that are _____ (lifted up) above cities are particularly complex. However, companies often have to pay penalties if the project is not _____ (finish punctually).

B Use the verbs given with perfect infinitives. Then add the expressions in the box. There may be more than one correct answer. Do you have similar views about your city?

don't get me started	in that case	let's not go there	then	what I'm saying	whatsoever

Everything's different now. If you look at old photos, the city _____ (seem / change) completely. The old stores _____ (appear / go – I mean, there are none left _____. The old neighborhoods _____ (be supposed to / be) really beautiful, so _____, why did they demolish all the old wooden houses? It's terrible. But _____. I _____ (would love / meet) the planners and asked, "Why did you destroy the character of the city, _____?" They also took out all the trolley cars, which _____ (be said to / be) more environmentally friendly than cars. We need to think about the environment. But _____. We've just lost so much. That's _____.

Unit **10** Current events

Lesson A *Breaking news*

Vocabulary in context *News collocations*
(See Student's Book p. 106.)

This lesson teaches collocations commonly used in news stories. It presents verb + noun combinations (*contain the oil spill*) and noun + verb combinations (*a bomb goes off*) in the context of the home page of an online news site.

Vocabulary notebook *Trust your instincts.*
(See Student's Book p. 115.)

The Learning tip tells Ss that when they learn a new verb + noun expression, they should find other verbs that collocate with the noun. For example, people *perform / undergo / have* routine surgery. When looking up the word *surgery*, Ss should read all of the examples included with the entry.

Grammar *Reporting events in progress*
(See Student's Book p. 107.)

In this lesson, Ss use continuous infinitive forms with and without *to* to report events in progress in the present, past, or future.

Form

- Continuous infinitive with *to* after present and past verbs
  (*not*) + *to be* + *-ing* form

  *Efforts to contain the spill appear **to be working**.*
  *The senator seems **not to be announcing** her campaign just yet. (OR doesn't seem **to be announcing** . . .)*
  *Police were said **to be searching** for a red pickup truck.*
- Perfect continuous infinitive with *to*
  to have been + *-ing* form
  *Markets are said **to have been gaining** confidence.*

- Continuous infinitive without *to* after modals
  modal + (*not*) + *be* + *-ing* form

  *A young politician **may be preparing** to run for office.*
  *The president **will be undergoing** routine surgery.*
- Past modal continuous form
  modal + (*not*) *have been* + *-ing* form
  *Investors **might have been worrying** unnecessarily.*

Use
Continuous infinitives describe events as ongoing, temporary, or possibly incomplete.

> ### ⊙ Corpus information
> **Writing vs. Conversation**
>
> In writing, continuous infinitive forms with *to* often come after the verbs *seem, appear, be supposed to,* and *have to.* They are less common in academic writing. In conversation, they are also often used after *be going to, need, want,* and *(have) got to.*

Grammar extra *Simple vs. continuous infinitives; More on perfect continuous infinitives*
(See Student's Book p. 162.)

Grammar extra presents more ways to report events using single and continuous infinitives and perfect continuous infinitives.

Lesson B *"Old" news*

Grammar *Describing what should happen*
(See Student's Book p. 109.)

This lesson teaches ways to use the subjunctive to say what is important or what should happen.

Form
The subjunctive uses the base form for all persons – including third person singular – after certain verbs, nouns, and adjectives.

- Verbs

  Examples of verbs are *demand, insist, require, request, ask, suggest,* and *recommend.*

  *The judge demands that the jury **reach** its verdict.*
  *They insist that everything **be edited**.*
- Nouns

  Examples of nouns are *demand, requirement, insistence, suggestion,* and *recommendation.*

  *The requirement that a journalist **check** the facts can mean time is lost.*
- Adjectives

  Examples of adjectives are *important, crucial, necessary, advisable,* and *essential.*

  *It is important the story **be** instantly available.*
- Negatives

  Not is used before the verb in the subjunctive.

  *It is essential that its reputation **not be damaged**.*

Use

Use the subjunctive after certain verbs, nouns, and adjectives to refer to demands, suggestions, and recommendations. The subjunctive is used to say what is important or to say what should happen in an ideal world.

Grammar extra *More on the subjunctive; The subjunctive and conditional sentences*

(See Student's Book p. 163.)

Grammar extra presents more uses of the subjunctive to refer to the past, with passive verbs, and in conditional sentences.

 Corpus information

Writing vs. Conversation

The subjunctive is rare in conversation. People say:

*The judge asked the jury **to reach** its verdict.*

*It's important that the story **should be** accurate.*
OR ***is** accurate.*

Lesson C *Those news tickers*

Conversation strategy *Highlighting topics*

(See Student's Book p. 110.)

In conversation, speakers sometimes introduce and then highlight what they're saying by using a noun to identify the topic and then referring to it with the appropriate pronoun. ***My girlfriend, she** watches news channels all the time.* It is also possible to use a pronoun at the beginning of the sentence and put the topic at the end.

*It drives me crazy, **hearing the same thing all the time.***

 Corpus information

In conversation

When speakers put a topic at the end, it's usually after an evaluative comment, such as *It drives me crazy.*

Note: These structures are for use in conversation only. They should not be used in writing.

Strategy plus *this, that, these, those*

(See Student's Book p. 111)

In conversation, people often use *this* and *these* to introduce and highlight important information, for example: *This guy at work, he has all these new apps.* This makes the topic sound more "immediate" and, therefore, more important. People use *that* and *those* to refer to something specific. It can be something that they have already mentioned or something they expect the listener to know about. (*Did you hear that report?*) People also use *that* and *those* to sound negative about a topic. (*Those news tickers, they're another thing I hate.*) It may help to compare *this / these* and *that / those* to articles. *This* and *these* have a similar meaning to *a* and *some*, whereas *that* and *those* have a similar meaning to *the*.

Speaking naturally *Stress and intonation*

(See Student's Book p. 142.)

Ss look at how longer sentences can be broken up into parts. Each part has a primary stress, where the intonation changes, and often a secondary stress, as well.

Ss also practice fall–rise intonation for background information and falling intonation for new information.

Lesson D *Reporting the news*

Reading tip *Starting with an example*

(See Student's Book p. 112.)

The Reading tip explains that writers sometimes start an article with a short story to illustrate what they are going to write about. This provides an example of the facts or ideas that will follow in the article.

Writing *In short, . . .*

(See Student's Book p. 114.)

This lesson teaches Ss to write a summary of an article they have read. The main teaching points about summary writing include telling Ss to use main points only, not to add new ideas, and not to include a personal opinion. Because the Ss will be summarizing the article they read in Lesson D, that vocabulary is also recycled. The grammar for writing reviews subject-verb agreement in writing and focuses on persistent errors that even advanced Ss make.

- Singular verbs
  Singular verbs are used after:
  uncountable nouns (*news, information*)
  most singular nouns that refer to a group (*the public*)
  a main noun in a phrase that is singular (***The number** of websites . . . **has** grown.*)

- Plural verbs
  Plural verbs are used:
  - when the subject is two nouns – even two uncountable nouns — joined by *and* (*reporting and campaigning*).
  - when the main noun in a phrase is plural. (*A number of websites have appeared.*) Remember that the phrase *A number of* means "a lot of" and introduces a plural noun.
  - after an irregular plural noun (*people*).

- Expressions
  After expressions like *the majority of* and *half of*, the verb agrees with the second noun.
  *The majority of the **population wants** . . .*
  *The majority of **people want** . . .*

 Corpus information

Common errors with relative clauses

Ss often make errors with subject-verb agreement when the subject and its verb are in different clauses.

*The number of websites that **check** news **has** grown.*

- *websites* is the subject of *check*, so the verb is plural.
- *the number* is the subject of *has grown*, so the verb is singular.

Current events

In Unit 10, you . . .

- talk about news and how it is reported.
- use continuous infinitives to report ongoing events.
- use the subjunctive to write what should happen.
- use *this* and *these* or *that* and *those* in conversation.

Lesson A *Breaking news*

1 Vocabulary in context

A **Look at the four headlines. What do you think they are about?**

a. *Region still struggling to recover*

c. *Bomb squad too late*

b. *Conflict over the economy*

d. *New contender to enter race?*

B ◀)) CD 4.02 **Read the home page of an online news site. Write the headlines in Exercise A in the news articles. Are there any similar events in the news at the moment?**

| HOME | U.S. | WORLD | POLITICS | JUSTICE | ENTERTAINMENT | LIVING | TRAVEL | OPINION | MONEY | SPORTS > |

1. _____

Efforts to **contain the oil spill** on the south coast appear to be working. But the oil giant responsible for the disaster could be facing more difficulties. Local businesses were rumored yesterday to be **considering legal action**, claiming for loss of income and livelihood. "People are going to be suing people over this," said one fisherman. A spokesperson for the oil company said they are committed to **compensating victims** affected by the spill. [Full story]

2. _____

A blast in the downtown area has caused extensive damage. Investigators are not sure what **caused the explosion** but have not **ruled out the possibility** that it was a terrorist attack. Three people were reported to have been acting suspiciously in the financial district, and police were said to be searching for a red pickup truck that was seen in the area. A **bomb went off** in the same area two years ago. [Full story]

3. _____

Three years after becoming the first female senator from her state, a young politician may be preparing to run for office in the upcoming presidential election. While the senator seems not to be **announcing** her **campaign** just yet, an appearance on a Sunday morning talk show has **fueled speculation**. [Full story]

RELATED The president's press secretary announced that the president will be **undergoing routine surgery** later this week and might not be able to greet a trade delegation of Chinese officials. [Full story]

4. _____

Investors might have been worrying unnecessarily after the **stock market plunged** to an all-time low last month. **Stocks** are now **making** a modest **recovery** as **markets** are said to have been gaining in confidence over the last two weeks. However, there are still concerns over the state of the economy and the huge deficits. Protesters are said to be planning more demonstrations in the capital. The marches seem to have been going peacefully so far. However, police say that they will be **mobilizing riot squads** if **tensions escalate**. [Full story]

Word sort

C **Make a chart like this of the collocations in bold in the article. Then take turns telling the news stories in Exercise B to a partner.**

verb + noun	noun + verb
contain the oil spill	a bomb goes off

Vocabulary notebook

See page 115.

Current events

Introduce the theme of the unit Ask, "What are current events?" [Events that are in the news right now] Say, "In this unit, we're going to talk about different aspects of news reporting and the things that influence it."

Lesson A *Breaking news*

① Vocabulary in context

- **Set the scene** Books closed. Write the lesson title on the board:

  Breaking news

  Ask Ss if they know what this means. Elicit guesses. ["Breaking news" is news that is becoming known to the public for the first time.]

A • **Preview and do the task** Books open. Read the instructions aloud. Have a S read the four headlines aloud. Say, "Write a short paraphrase for each headline." Remind Ss that headlines only use key words to get their meaning across, so they don't usually include articles *a / an* or *the* or auxiliary verbs, and they often omit main verbs.

- Have Ss complete the task. Ask several Ss to call their paraphrase for each one. [(a) An area is trying hard to return to the way it was after a difficulty. (b) There is serious disagreement over the economy, perhaps about politicians. (c) A bomb exploded before the specialists arrived to defuse it. (d) A new person may try to win an election for political office.]

B 🔊 CD4, Track 2
- **Preview the task** Say, "Read the home page of an online news site."
- **Play the recording** Ss listen and read along. Say, "Now write the headlines in Exercise A in the news articles." Check answers with the class.

Answers

1. (a) Region still struggling to recover
2. (c) Bomb squad too late
3. (d) New contender to enter race?
4. (b) Conflict over the economy

Word sort

C • **Preview the task** Say, "Make a chart like this of the collocations in bold in the article. Write them as word lists." Point out that the base form of the verb is used in the verb + noun column and the present tense is used in the noun + verb column. Say, "When you've finished, compare your chart with a partner."

- **Do the task** Have Ss complete the task. Check answers with the class.

Answers

verb + noun	*noun + verb*
contain the oil spill	a bomb goes off
consider legal action	the stock market plunges
compensate victims	stocks make a recovery
cause the explosion	tensions escalate
rule out the possibility	
announce his / her campaign	
fuel speculation	
undergo routine surgery	
make a recovery	
mobilize riot squads	

- Say, "Cover the news articles and take turns telling the news stories in Exercise B to a partner."

Extra activity – pairs

Pairs make a list of new vocabulary from the news website in Exercise B. They exchange lists with another pair and provide definitions or examples using their own knowledge or a dictionary.

Pairs explain the vocabulary to each other.

Extra activity – individuals / pairs

Write on the board (without the answers in parentheses) these incomplete expressions. Have Ss complete the lists. In pairs, Ss say which expressions they could use to report the week's news. Ss share ideas with the class.

face _____ (difficulties)
extensive _____ (damage)
a _____ (terrorist) attack
act _____ (suspiciously)
_____ (run) for office
plunge to _____ (an all time low)
make a _____ (modest) recovery
gain _____ (in confidence)
(huge) _____ deficits

Tell Ss to turn to Vocabulary Notebook on p. 115 of their Student's Books. Have Ss do the tasks in class or assign them for homework. (See the teaching notes on p. T-115.)

② Grammar

Figure it out

A 🔊 www.cambridge.org/viewpoint/audio

- **Preview the task** Ask, "How are the ideas below expressed in the article? Underline the sentences in the article, and compare them with the sentences below."

- **Do the task** Have Ss complete the task. Check answers with the class.

Answers

1. Protestors are said to be planning more demonstrations in the capital.
2. Local businesses were rumored yesterday to be considering legal action.
3. The marches seem to have been going peacefully.
4. Investors might have been worrying unnecessarily.

- **Focus on the form** Say, "Compare the two versions of sentences 1 and 2. What do you notice about the forms of the verbs?" [In the article, the first verbs – *are said* and *were rumored* – are passive; the second verbs – *to be planning* and *to be considering* are continuous forms.] Say, "These are continuous infinitive forms." Say, "In sentence 3, the article makes *marches* the subject; the verb after *seem* is *to have been going*. This is a continuous perfect infinitive." Say, "The idea of *It's possible* in sentence 4 is expressed in the article with the modal verb *might*, which is followed by the continuous form *have been worrying*."

- **Focus on the use** Say, "Read the sentences from the article again. Are the events ongoing?" [yes] "Are they complete?" [no] Say, "You can use continuous infinitive forms to describe events in progress and events which are not yet complete."

- **Present the grammar chart** Read the information aloud. If desired, play the downloadable recording. Ss listen and read along.

- Say, "Look at the top section of the chart. The example sentences describe events that are ongoing, temporary, or possibly incomplete. Read the example sentences. Are continuous infinitive forms used after active or passive verbs, or both?" [both] Ask, "In negative statements, where does *not* go?" [before *to*] Say, "You can also make the main verb negative: *She doesn't seem to be announcing . . .*"

- Write on the board, underlined as shown:
  Markets are said to be gaining confidence.
  Markets are said to have been gaining confidence.
  Ask, "What is the difference in meaning?" [*Are said to be gaining* means that they are gaining confidence now. *Are said to have been gaining* shows that they were gaining confidence before now, too.]

- Have Ss look at the bottom of the chart. Say, "Modals can be followed by *be + -ing*." Ask a S to read the example aloud. Say, "To talk about the past, or the past up to now, use *have been + -ing*." Ask a S to read the example aloud.

(For more information, see Language notes at the beginning of the unit. For more work on simple vs. continuous infinitive forms, go to Grammar extra, p. 162.)

B • **Preview the task** Read the instructions aloud. Do the first item with the class. Ask a S for the correct form of continuous infinitive. [be preparing] Ask, "Why isn't *to* used?" [It follows a modal.]

- **Do the task** Have Ss complete the task and then compare their answers with a partner. Check answers with class.

Answers

1. The president . . . may <u>be preparing</u> to step down. . . . his health appears <u>to have been deteriorating</u>, and the company is now rumored <u>to be searching / to have been searching</u> for a successor. . . . "We're going to <u>be making</u> an announcement soon."
2. After a month of protests, which seem <u>to have been having / to be having</u> little effect, . . . The workers might <u>have been trying</u> to get . . . appeared <u>not to be listening / not to have been listening</u> to their demands.
3. An actor from a popular sitcom might <u>not be appearing</u> on the show again. TV executives are believed <u>to be considering</u> legal action . . . When told the show may <u>be canceling</u> his contract, the actor said, "You've got to <u>be joking</u>."
4. A senator who . . . she should <u>have been attending</u> . . . An opposition spokesperson said that she was supposed to <u>be representing / have been representing</u> voters . . .

③ Viewpoint

Pair work

- **Preview and do the task** Read the instructions aloud. Ask a S to read the example aloud. Say, "Brainstorm a few news stories with your partner. Choose one that you feel comfortable talking about and that you know enough facts about."

- Have Ss complete the task. Walk around the class and help as necessary.

- Have pairs present their news report to the class. Alternatively, put Ss in groups to present their report. (If using the Extra Activity below, tell Ss to make notes of questions they would like to ask the presenters.)

2 Grammar Reporting events in progress

Figure it out

A How are the ideas below expressed in the article? Underline the sentences in the article, and compare them with the sentences below. Then read the grammar chart.

1. They say protesters are planning more demonstrations in the capital.
2. There were rumors yesterday that local businesses are considering legal action.
3. It seems the marches have been going peacefully.
4. It's possible investors have been worrying unnecessarily.

Continuous infinitive forms ⬇

Grammar extra
See page 162.

Continuous infinitives describe events as ongoing, temporary, or possibly incomplete.
*Efforts to contain the oil spill appear **to be working**.*
*The senator seems **not to be announcing** her campaign just yet.*
*Police were said **to be searching** for a red pickup truck.*
*Markets are said **to have been gaining** confidence.*

Modals can be followed by *be + -ing* or *have been + -ing*.
*The president **will be undergoing** routine surgery.*
*Investors **might have been worrying** unnecessarily.*

Writing vs. Conversation

In writing, continuous infinitive forms with *to* often come after the verbs *seem, appear, be supposed to, have to*. They are less common in academic writing. In conversation, they are also often used after *be going to, need, want, (have) got to*.

B Complete the news reports using continuous infinitives of the verbs given with or without *to*. Sometimes there is more than one correct answer.

1. The president of an international microchip corporation may _____ (prepare) to step down. Over the last year, his health appears _____ (deteriorate), and the company is now rumored _____ (search) for a successor. A company spokesperson said, "We are going to _____ (make) an announcement soon."
2. After a month of protests, which seem _____ (have) little effect, steel workers agreed yesterday to go back to work. The workers might _____ (try) to get a bigger pay increase, but the company refused to negotiate and appeared _____ (not listen) to their demands.
3. An actor from a popular sitcom might _____ (not appear) on the show again. TV executives are believed _____ (consider) legal action after the actor failed to show up for filming on several occasions. When told the show may _____ (cancel) his contract, the actor said, "You've got to _____ (joke)!"
4. A senator who was filmed last week at a nightclub when she should _____ (attend) government meetings would make no comment today. An opposition spokesperson said that she was supposed to _____ (represent) voters in her state that evening.

> HMM. IT SAYS HERE THAT NEW COFFEE YOU'RE DRINKING MAY BE KEEPING YOU UP AT NIGHT.

3 Viewpoint

Pair work Choose a story that's in the news at the moment. Prepare a news report to present to the class. Give as much detail as you can.

"Fans of the biggest sitcom on television may have been protesting unnecessarily. The show's producers announced that they are going to be bring the show back for at least one more season."

Lesson B *"Old" news*

① Grammar in context

A Where do you get your news from? Conventional, mainstream sources or via social networking? Do a class survey.

"I tend to read the headlines on my phone every morning."

B ◀))CD 4.03 **Read the editorial column. What is "old" news? How does the writer regard it?**

Why it is essential that "old" news survive

In the United States, in the trial of a celebrity on a murder charge, a judge demands that the jury reach its verdict. On the other side of the world, a devastating earthquake strikes. In Europe, the winning goal is scored in a crucial soccer game. All three events are instantly broadcast around the world – not via conventional news media, but through text messages, microblogs, social network postings, emails, and blogs that are passed on, person to person, within seconds. The major news organizations receive the same news from their reporters, but because of their insistence that everything be written and edited to broadcast standards, by the time it is broadcast or posted on the Web, it has become "old" news, if only by a few minutes.

In a world where readers and viewers get news via their smartphones and social media, it is important that the story be instantly available. Meanwhile, the requirement that a journalist check the facts more conscientiously can mean precious time is lost. In the case of major breaking news, the mainstream news organizations may insist that a controversial story be investigated, even if this means a delay in broadcasting some of the details. In dangerous situations, it may be advisable that a foreign correspondent not go to the scene immediately. It is essential that the reputation of the organization not be damaged and that the safety of the reporter be guaranteed.

In light of this situation, there is a danger that the major news organizations are perceived as a source of old news, which only a few might turn to for the fuller details of events they already know about. However, it is essential that there be a place for news that, while slower, is ultimately more measured, in-depth, and trustworthy. Ultimately, this comes down to money and whether the public is prepared to pay for such meticulously researched content. It is crucial that this issue be taken seriously by all consumers of news before we lose something precious.

C Pair work **Discuss the questions.**

1. Why are conventional news sources sometimes slower?
2. What qualities does "old" news have?
3. Do you recognize the picture the editorial paints of news? Do you think it's accurate?
4. What do you think is the real purpose of the editorial? What does it want you, the reader, to do?
5. What do you think about the recommendation?

Lesson B *"Old" news*

1 Grammar in context

- **Set the scene** Books closed. Write *"Old" news* on the board. Say, "This is the topic of this lesson. Why do you think *old* has quotation marks around it?" Elicit ideas. (e.g., *"Old" is being used in an unusual way. "Old" has more than one meaning.*) Ask, "What is 'old' news?" Elicit answers (e.g., *news that isn't "breaking"; news that everyone already knows; something that isn't interesting anymore; something that's finished*).

A • **Preview and do the task** Books open. Read the instructions aloud. Explain that "conventional, mainstream sources" are the traditional sources used by most people. Ask, "What do you consider to be conventional, mainstream sources?" Have Ss call out their ideas (e.g., *major national broadcasters and news corporations*). Ask Ss to name the social networking sites they use. Assign a S to write all the sources on the board.

- Assign a S to conduct the survey. He or she calls out each source listed on the board. Ss who use that source raise their hand and get counted. The totals are listed on the board.

Extra activity – groups

Groups discuss the results of the survey. Write on the board:

Which sources are more likely to report "old" news?

Which ones are more likely to report "breaking" news?

Which do you prefer? Why?

Ss illustrate their preference with references to recent events in the news, if possible.

B 🔊 CD4, Track 3

- **Preview the task** Write on the board:

  verdict

  broadcast standards

  foreign correspondent

  in-depth

  meticulously

  Have Ss give definitions or explanations of words they know. Supply definitions for any remaining vocabulary. [*verdict*: final decision in a court of law (guilty or not guilty); *broadcast standards*: level of quality required for a radio or TV news program; *foreign correspondent*: reporter / journalist working abroad; *in-depth*: very detailed; *meticulously*: extremely careful with details]

- Read the instructions aloud. Tell Ss to write brief answers to the questions.

- Ss read and write. Have Ss compare their ideas with a partner. Check the answers with the class. ["Old" news is news from major news organizations that has been written to broadcast standards. It is referred to as "old" because it generally appears after news that is spread by social media. The writer regards this news as something precious that should not be lost because it has higher standards of reporting.]

- Check for remaining vocabulary problems.

C Pair work

- **Preview and do the task** Read the instructions aloud. Tell Ss to read the discussion questions before they begin. Have Ss discuss the questions.

- For each question, have a few pairs share their answer with the class.

Answers / Possible answers

1. Conventional news sources are sometimes slower because news organizations insist that everything be written and edited to broadcast standards, so by the time stories are broadcast, they are old news.
2. In "old" news, journalists check facts conscientiously, stories are investigated, reporters' safety is more important than getting the story in dangerous situations, and the reputation of news organizations is not damaged.
3. *Answers will vary. Possible answer*: It seems accurate in that conventional news does often lag behind other electronic media, such as email, blogs, and social networks.
4. *Answers will vary. Possible answer*: The real purpose of an editorial is for someone to express his or her opinion. The writer would like to convince readers that his or her opinion is valid.
5. *Answers will vary. Possible answer*: It is good to bring attention to the importance of conventional news media because ultimately it is more accurate and reliable than media that brings information very quickly.

Figure it out

A [↓] www.cambridge.org/viewpoint/audio

- **Preview the task** Say, "Write the form of the verb given that the editorial writer uses to express these ideas."

- **Do the task** Have Ss complete the task. Check answers with the class: Have individual Ss each read an answer aloud.

Answers

1. The judge demands that the jury <u>reach</u> its verdict.
2. The requirement that a journalist <u>check</u> the facts can mean time is lost.
3. It is important that the story <u>be</u> instantly available.

- **Focus on the form** Ask, "What form of the verb did you use for each answer?" [base form] "Is that surprising?" [yes, because the subjects are all third person singular] Say, "This form is called the subjunctive form."

- **Present the grammar chart** Read the information aloud. If desired, play the downloadable recording. Ss listen and read along.

- Say, "The subjunctive is used, often in *that* clauses, after certain verbs, nouns, or adjectives in the main clause to stress something is important or urgent. A verb in the subjunctive doesn't show past, present, or future. It doesn't change for singular or plural subjects."

- Ask Ss to look at the *Verbs* section of the chart. Ask a S to read the two examples. Ask, "Which of the two bold verbs is active?" [reach] Ask, "How do you make the subjunctive in passive voice?" [*be* + past participle]

- Say, "The ideas of demands and suggestions can also be expressed with nouns and adjectives." Have Ss read the two examples. Call on Ss to replace the noun and adjective in the examples with others from the list and read out the examples again.

- Have Ss look at the bottom section of the chart. Ask, "What do you do when you need a subjunctive verb to be negative?" [use *not* before the verb in base form]

- **Present *Writing vs. Conversation*** Ask a S to read the information aloud.

- Tell Ss that the subjunctive is also tested in some international language tests. For example, the test might ask Ss to rewrite sentences using the subjunctive.

  (For more information, see Language notes at the beginning of the unit. For more work on subjunctive, go to Grammar extra, p. 163.)

B - **Preview the task** Read the instructions aloud. Tell Ss to look at comment 1. Ask, "What verb is underlined?" [are]. Say, "Read the first sentence in the editorial extract. How will you complete the first blank?" [with *be*] Say, "Read each comment and its extract before you complete the extract."

- **Do the task** Have Ss complete the task and then compare their answers with a partner. Check answers with the class.

Answers

1. Parents are demanding that their children <u>be</u> well-informed about world events. Many feel it is important that children from sixth grade on <u>be exposed</u> to reputable news sources. Their insistence that the school curriculum <u>teach</u> students current events is right. It is our recommendation that every school <u>make</u> this a priority.
2. Students feel it is essential that the news media's attitude toward young people <u>change</u>. Their recommendation that the news <u>include</u> more items that are relevant to their concerns seems justified. Student leaders have suggested that our local TV station <u>have</u> more coverage of student politics as one example. We would recommend that their suggestions <u>not be ignored</u>.
3. It is crucial to the well-being of society that newspapers <u>not die</u>, but they do need to change. The suggestion that the traditional business model <u>be changed</u> should be taken seriously. It is time to insist that the consumer <u>pay</u> more for access to high-quality news reports.

About you

C - **Preview and do the task** Read the instructions aloud. Say, "Brainstorm a few topics and a few supporting details for each topic. Choose one and write. Your editorial should be about 50 words. Be sure to use the subjunctive. Try to use it in a *that* clause and after a verb, a noun, and an adjective."

- **Follow-up** Have a few Ss read the editorial aloud. Find out if the class agrees or disagrees with points made.

Extra activity – groups

Ss form small groups and take turns reading their editorials aloud. Group members debate the issues brought up in the editorials. Groups share the issues they debated with the class.

2 Grammar Describing what should happen

Figure it out

A Write the form of the verb given that the editorial writer uses to express these ideas. Then read the grammar chart.

1. The judge demands that the jury _____ its verdict. (reach)
2. The requirement that a journalist _____ the facts can mean time is lost. (check)
3. It is important that the story _____ instantly available. (be)

Grammar extra
See page 163.

The subjunctive

The subjunctive uses the base form of the verb. Use it for all persons – including third person singular – after certain verbs, nouns, and adjectives. You can use it to refer to demands, suggestions, and recommendations; to say what is important; or to say what should happen in an ideal world

Verbs: *demand, insist, require, request, ask, suggest, recommend*	*The judge demands that the jury* **reach** *its verdict.* *They insist that everything* **be edited**.
Nouns: *demand, requirement, insistence, suggestion, recommendation*	*The requirement that a journalist* **check** *the facts can mean time is lost.*
Adjectives: *important, crucial, necessary, advisable, essential*	*It is important that the story* **be** *instantly available.*
The negative form is *not* + verb.	*It is essential that its reputation* **not be damaged**.

Writing vs. Conversation

The subjunctive is rare in conversation. People say:
The judge asked the jury **to reach** *its verdict.*
It's important that the story **should be / is** *accurate.*

B Read the comments below. Then complete the editorial extracts that reflect these views. Use the subjunctive form of the underlined verbs in the comments.

1. Parents say: "Our kids aren't aware of world events." "They're not exposed to 'proper news' early enough." "We want schools to teach current events." "They should make it a priority."

Parents are demanding that their children _____ well-informed about world events. Many feel it is important that children from sixth grade on _____ to reputable news sources. Their insistence that the school curriculum _____ students current events is right. It is our recommendation that every school _____ this a priority.

2. Students say: "Local news needs to change." "They should include more news about us." "The local TV station should have reports on our activities." "Don't ignore us."

Students feel it is essential that the news media's attitude toward young people _____. Their recommendation that the news _____ more items that are relevant to their concerns seems justified. Student leaders have suggested that our local TV station _____ more coverage of student politics as one example. We would recommend that their suggestions _____.

3. Media experts say: "Newspapers shouldn't die." "They should change their business model." "The consumer should pay more for access to online news."

It is crucial to the well-being of society that newspapers _____, but they do need to change. The suggestion that the traditional business model _____ should be taken seriously. It is time to insist that the consumer _____ more for access to high-quality news reports.

About you

C Write an editorial about an issue that you feel strongly about. Share it with the class.

Lesson C *Those news tickers*

1 Conversation strategy Highlighting topics

A How often do you listen to or watch the news? Are you a "news junkie"?

B ◀))) CD 4.04 Listen. How do Jill and Kyung get their news?

Jill Have you noticed how some people seem almost addicted to news? Like, this guy at work, he has all these news apps on his phone, but he never knows what's going on, really.

Kyung Yeah. My girlfriend, she watches news channels all the time. But I don't think she really listens, you know what I mean? It's just background noise.

Jill I know. Those TV channels, they just repeat the same news over and over. It drives me crazy, hearing the same thing all the time.

Kyung Me too. And those news tickers, they're another thing I hate. It's so distracting, trying to listen with those things going across the screen at the same time.

Jill Yeah. Public radio, that's what I like. They have some really interesting in-depth reports, too.

Kyung Speaking of which, did you hear that report about that huge investment company? It seems to be going under.

C **Notice** how Jill and Kyung highlight the topics they talk about. Sometimes they put the topic at the start of a sentence and then use a pronoun. Sometimes they put the topic at the end. Find more examples in the conversation.

> **My girlfriend, she** watches news channels all the time.
> **It** drives me crazy, **hearing the same thing all the time.**

In conversation . . .

When speakers put a topic at the end, it's usually after an evaluative comment such as *It drives me crazy*.
Note: These structures are for use in conversation only. Do not use them in writing.

D ◀))) CD 4.05 **Guess the missing topics in these sentences. Then listen and write the topics.**

1. _____, that's another thing people listen to but can never remember afterwards.
2. _____ these days, it always seems to be reporting what's going to happen. It's annoying.
3. _____, that's beyond me. I don't understand anything about the markets and trade.
4. _____, it's more informative than TV news. The reports are just more in-depth.
5. _____, they're all I read these days. I never have time to read the full articles or news stories.
6. It's fantastic, having _____ on your phone. You can keep up with the news wherever you are.
7. It takes up so much airtime, _____. Especially if you're not interested in football or whatever.
8. They're so dirty and difficult to handle, _____. I don't miss them at all.

About you **E** Pair work **Discuss the statements in Exercise D. Do you agree?**

Lesson C *Those news tickers*

① Conversation strategy

Highlighting a topic in conversation

In conversation, speakers sometimes introduce and highlight what they're saying by using a noun to identify the topic and then referring to it with the appropriate pronoun. For example, *My girlfriend, she watches news channels all the time.* It is also possible to use a pronoun at the beginning of the sentence and put the topic in a noun phrase at the end, especially in evaluative comments: *It's so distracting, trying to listen with those things going across the screen at the same time.*

(For more information, see Language notes at the beginning of this unit.)

- **Set the scene** Books closed. Write *news ticker* on the board. Read the title of the lesson aloud. Say, "A news ticker is also known as a 'crawl' or a 'slider.' Where do you see news tickers?" [on TV, news websites, smart phone screen, or a broadcast on any platform] "What are they used for?" Ss call out their ideas (e.g., *breaking news, news headlines, weather warnings, sports scores*).

A • **Preview and do the task** Write *junkie* on the board. Ask, "What's a junkie?" [an addict – someone who can't get enough of something] Ask several Ss, "How often do you listen to or watch the news?" Ask, "Are you a 'news junkie'?" Using a show of hands, find out how many Ss consider themselves to be "news junkies."

Extra activity – groups

Groups decide on a definition / description of "news junkie." Ideas: How often / How many hours a day does a news junkie listen to / read / watch news? How many news sources does the person use? How much of his / her conversation is based on news stories?

Groups share their description with the class.

B 🔊 CD4, Track 4

- **Preview the task** Read the instructions aloud. Tell Ss to make brief notes to answer the questions.
- **Play the recording** Ss listen only. Replay the recording. Ss listen and take notes. Have Ss compare their notes in pairs.
- **Play the recording again** Books open. Ss listen, read along, and check their answers. Check the answer with the class. [Jill and Kyung get their news from public radio.]

C • **Present *Notice*** Read the information and the examples aloud.

- Say, "Read the conversation again. Find the examples." Have a S read them aloud. [*Jill*: Like, this guy at work, he has all these apps on his phone, . . . Those TV channels, they just repeat the same news over and over. It drives me crazy, hearing the same thing all the time. Public radio, that's what I like. *Kyung*: My girlfriend, she watches news channels all the time. . . . And those news tickers, they're another thing I hate. It's so distracting, trying to listen with those things going across the screen at the same time.]

- **Practice** Tell Ss to practice the conversation in pairs, taking turns playing each role.

D 🔊 CD4, Track 5

- **Preview the task** Say, "Guess the missing topics in these sentences." For each sentence, ask a few Ss for their guess.
- **Play the recording** Say, "Now listen and write the topics." Ss listen and write. Have Ss compare their answers with a partner. Play the recording again and have Ss check their answers. Check answers with the class.

Answers

1. The weather forecast
2. The news
3. Economic news
4. Radio news
5. The headlines
6. news apps
7. sports news
8. newspapers

About you

E Pair work

- **Preview and do the task** Read the instructions aloud. Have Ss discuss the questions.
- **Follow-up** For each sentence, have a few Ss say whether they agree or not, giving reasons.

② Strategy plus

Using *this, that, these, those*

In conversation, people often use *this* and *these* to introduce and highlight important information, for example, *This guy at work, he has all these new apps.* It makes the topic sound more "immediate" and, therefore, more important. People use *that* and *those* to refer to something specific. It can be something that they have already mentioned or something they expect the listener to know about. (*Did you hear that report?*) People also use *that* and *those* to sound negative about a topic. (*Those news tickers, they're another thing I hate.*) It may help to compare *this / these* and *that / those* to articles. *This* and *these* have a similar meaning to *a* and *some*, while *that* and *those* have a similar meaning to *the*.

(For more information, see Language notes at the beginning of this unit.)

🔊 CD4, Track 6

- **Present *Strategy plus*** Read aloud or play the recording of the information and examples. Ss listen and read along.

- Tell Ss to read Jill and Kyung's conversation on page 110 again and find these expressions. [*Jill:* Like, **this** guy at work, he has all **these** news apps . . . **Those** TV channels, they just repeat the same news . . . *Kyung:*

And **those** news tickers, they're another thing I hate. It's so distracting, trying to listen with **those** things . . . Speaking of which, . . . **that** huge investment company?]

A 🔊 CD4, Track 7

- **Preview the task** Say, "Complete these comments with *this, that, these,* or *those*. Look at the information in parentheses at the end of each sentence. It tells you how these words are being used." Have Ss complete the task and compare their answers with a partner.

- **Play the recording** Ss listen and check their answers. Check answers with the class.

Answers

1. There's <u>this</u> show . . . It has <u>these</u> really . . .
2. There were all <u>these</u> . . .
3. You know <u>that</u> talk show host . . .
4. I hate <u>those</u> magazines that make up . . .

About you

B Pair work

- **Preview and do the task** Read the instructions aloud. Have Ss complete the task.

③ Strategies and listening

A • **Preview the task** Read the instructions aloud. Tell Ss to read the six issues. Have a S read the example answer aloud.

- **Do the task** Have Ss complete the task and compare their ideas with a partner. Check answers with the class: For each issue, elicit Ss' ideas. (e.g., *1. With sliders and news apps for smart phones, news can be reported instantaneously. 2. Costs can include paper, computers, websites, and salaries as well as the cost of sending foreign correspondents overseas or reporters to the scene of an event. 3. People use their smart phones to photograph or video events and post them to the Web or send them to news services or social networks. 4. Twenty-four-hour news TV and radio stations are more interested in breaking news, so they don't report in-depth. 5. Some people find photos of violent acts or death upsetting. 6. Reporters' bias might have an effect.*)

B 🔊 CD4, Track 8

- **Preview the task** Read the instructions aloud. Say, "Just listen the first time."

- **Play the recording** Audio script p. T-279 Ss listen. Replay the recording. Ss listen and check (✓) the topics. Check answers with the class.

Answers

☑ 1. ☑ 3. ☑ 5. ☑ 6.

C 🔊 CD4, Track 9

- **Preview the task** Say, "Listen again. Circle the correct option to complete each sentence. Before we listen, read the four questions and their choices." Check for vocabulary questions.

- **Play the recording** Audio script p. T-279 Ss listen and circle. Have Ss compare their answers with a partner. Replay the recording if necessary. Check answers with the class.

Answers

1. b; 2. a; 3. d; 4. c

- Say, "Discuss the expert's views with a partner. Do you agree?" Have Ss discuss. Walk around the class and help as needed.

- **Follow-up** Have several Ss say which view(s) they disagree with and give reasons.

Extra activity – pairs

Pairs write a conversation similar to Jill and Kyung's on the topic of newspaper news vs. rolling news reports. Pairs present their conversation to another pair. The listening pairs notes the strategies used.

Speaking naturally

- Tell Ss to turn to Speaking naturally on p. 142. (For more information, see Language notes at the beginning of this unit. See the teaching notes on p. T-142.)

2 Strategy plus *this, that, these, those*

◀)) CD 4.06 You can use *this* and *these* to introduce and highlight important information.

You can use *that* and *those* to refer to something specific, which you have mentioned or expect your listener to know about.

You can use *that* and *those* to sound negative about a topic.

This guy at work, he has all **these** news apps.

Did you hear **that** report?

Those news tickers, they're another thing I hate.

A ◀)) CD 4.07 **Complete these comments with *this, that, these,* or *those*. Use the cues in parentheses. Then listen and check.**

1. There's _____ show on the radio called *Radio Lab*. It has _____ really interesting, creative reports on things like time, or ants, or numbers. It's so cool. Do you listen to the radio much? (*highlight*)

2. There were all _____ students in my high school who had no idea what was going on in the world. (*highlight*) To them, international news was boring. Do you follow international news?

3. You know _____ talk show host on late night TV? I don't like her interview style. (*sound negative*) I don't think talk show hosts should be aggressive. What do you think?

4. I hate _____ magazines that make up news like celebrity gossip or stuff that you *know* isn't true. (*be specific*) Don't you?

About you **B** Pair work **Ask and answer the questions at the end of each comment above.**

3 Strategies and listening *Journalism*

A **Look at some of the issues in journalism. What do you think they refer to?**

"The first issue is probably about the fact that news is often reported instantaneously."

1. ☐ The speed at which news is reported
2. ☐ The cost of publishing news stories
3. ☐ The increase in the number of news sources
4. ☐ 24-hour rolling news reports are superficial.
5. ☐ The use of graphic photos
6. ☐ The influence of reporters on events

B ◀)) CD 4.08 **Listen to a radio show. Which trends do the speakers refer to? Check (✓) the topics in Exercise A.**

C ◀)) CD 4.09 **Listen again. Circle the correct option to complete each sentence. Then discuss the expert's views with a partner. Do you agree?**

1. The radio presenter suggests that journalists' work is often _____.
   a. mundane   b. risky   c. boring   d. fun

2. The expert says that journalists often publish their reports _____.
   a. as events take place   b. through agencies   c. 24 hours later   d. before something happens

3. The expert suggests that the reason news organizations use some pictures is _____.
   a. they want to shock   b. it's ethically right   c. to show the truth   d. to compete

4. The expert believes that journalists can _____.
   a. change situations   b. have a huge impact   c. have limited influence   d. give no personal views

Speaking naturally
See page 142.

Lesson D *Reporting the news*

1 Reading

A Prepare **Are some sources of news more trustworthy than others? In what ways?**

"I think the news on public radio is pretty reliable because . . ."

B Read for main ideas **Read the article. What kinds of information does the writer question in terms of its accuracy? Why is information sometimes not accurate?**

Establishing the truth: How accurate are news reports?

1 Following one of the worst natural disasters in recent U.S. history – Hurricane Katrina – journalists and newscasters swarmed the area to report on the extraordinarily terrible events. There were stories of chaos: widespread looting, gunshots, murders, and other violent crimes. While there was indeed disorder, it turned out that much of the initial reporting was either exaggerated, misleading, or plain wrong. The murder victims didn't materialize, and it became apparent there was no widespread increase in violent crime, either.

2 This episode raises some important questions. How does such "news" get reported? Can we believe what we hear on breaking news, or is news reporting so overstated that we are being at best misinformed and at worst deceived? How do we ultimately know whether any of the so-called facts in a news report are true or misrepresented? And perhaps more importantly, how can we verify what we read or hear in news reports?

3 In the case of Hurricane Katrina, a complex mix of circumstances may have created a degree of misinformation. Immediately after the storm, power outages and breakdowns in communications systems caused news "blackouts," making reliable information extremely difficult, if not almost impossible, to establish. News was spread by word of mouth, and it seems that facts became distorted as they were passed along. However, some of the blame may also lie with how news organizations operate. On the air 24/7, they are under pressure to fill airtime and win viewer ratings by being the one with the "hottest" or latest story. It is easy to see how, under such pressure, events are reported without the facts being painstakingly checked.

4 Such distortions are not limited to headline news events. During an election year, one takes for granted that candidates try to boost their ratings in the opinion polls in an effort to swing the race. The public is used to hearing claims from candidates, such as how their policies have led to an increase in manufacturing jobs or how the opposition has created massive national debt. What the public is never quite certain of is what is truth, half-truth, or untruth. Not surprising, then, that an entire industry exists to answer these very questions. Enter the fact-checkers, who check the claims that are made and the accuracy of the statistics that are presented.

5 Indeed, websites have sprung up whose business is purely and simply to check information in the public sphere – whether it be in a news report, a magazine article, or an urban myth. Other consumer sites aim to reduce the level of deception in politics, and some claim to be able to show the extent to which you can believe certain speechmakers. Cable networks also realize that the public is increasingly concerned about being able to trust what they hear, and use slogans to impress on their viewers the fact that they present honest news that is balanced and without bias. While many have jumped on the bandwagon of truth, one enterprising website has done the complete opposite. Rather than publish verifiable facts, it prides itself on featuring satirical news stories which are completely fabricated. Unfortunately, not all media outlets have realized this, and on occasion they have cited reports from the website as though they were true. Sorting fact from fiction just became even more of a challenge.

> **Reading tip**
> Writers sometimes start an article with a short story to illustrate what they are going to write about.

Lesson D *Reporting the news*

1 Reading

- **Set the scene** Books closed. Say "Some people worry that news sources are more concerned with being first with news than with being accurate with news. What do you think?" Have a short class discussion.

A Prepare

- **Preview and do the task** Books open. Read the instructions aloud. Ask a S to read the example aloud. Write each news source the Ss mention on the board. Ask, "Which ones do you consider trustworthy? Which ones do you consider less or not trustworthy?" Elicit opinions and the reasons for them.

B 🔽 www.cambridge.org/viewpoint/audio

Read for main ideas

- **Preview the task** Read the instructions aloud. If desired, play the downloadable recording. Ss listen and read along.

- **Do the task** Ss read the article and answer the questions. Have Ss compare their answers with a partner.

- Ask, "What kinds of information does the writer question in terms of its accuracy?" [The writer questions information passed by word of mouth – which isn't always accurate because, in a rush to get the news in print or on air, the facts are not always confirmed – and the claims made by politicians during election cycles – which are often made in an effort to boost their polling numbers and swing political races in their favor.] Ask, "Why is information sometimes not accurate?" [News spread by word of mouth may become distorted. Events are reported without being fact-checked.]

- Write on the board:

    chaos (1)

    looting (1)

    power outage (3)

    distort (3)

    urban myth (5)

    fabricate (5)

- Say, "The number in parentheses indicates the paragraph where this vocabulary is found. Use the context to try to guess the general meaning of each word or expression. Compare your ideas with a partner." Have Ss complete the task.

- Check the answers with the class. [*chaos:* total confusion / no order whatsoever; *looting:* stealing from houses / shops during a time of unrest; *power outage:* the supply of electricity suddenly stops; *distort:* change information so it is no longer true or realistic; *urban myth:* a story that many people believe, but which may not be true; *fabricate:* make up]

- **Present *Reading tip*** Read the information aloud. Ask, "How does the story about Hurricane Katrina illustrate the article?" Elicit answers. (e.g., *It talks about how the media reported serious crimes being committed. Ultimately, it turned out that there was no such widespread crime. The article gives reasons things like this happen with news stories.*)

Extra activity – pairs

Pairs discuss news sources again. They decide if their level of trust for different news sources has changed. Ss say which information in the article or in discussions influenced them.

C Understanding idioms

- **Preview and do the task** Read the instructions aloud. Have Ss complete the task and compare answers with a partner. Check answers with the class.

Answers

1. There were periods when there was no news because of the breakdown in communications systems.
2. News was passed along from person to person – each retelling the news stories.
3. They were trying to have the race go in their favor.
4. Websites have quickly appeared.
5. Many have joined in the trend of pursuing the truth.

D Read for inference

- **Preview and do the task** Read the instructions aloud. Ask Ss to read all of the statements before they begin. Check that Ss understand the statements. Have Ss complete the task and compare answers with a partner.
- Check answers with the class.

② Focus on vocabulary

A
- **Preview the task** Say, "Find ways in the article to express the ideas below." Do the first one with the class. Say, "Look in paragraph 2 and find another way to express *make sure something is true*." [verify]
- **Present Tip** Read the information aloud. Ask, "What words do you know with the prefix *mis-*?" Elicit some examples (e.g., *misspell, mislead, misapply, misbehave, mismanage*).
- **Do the task** Have Ss complete the task and compare their answers with a partner. Check answers with the class.

Answers

Talking about truth . . .	*. . . and lies*
make sure something is true = verify	giving a wrong impression = misleading
to find out (facts) = establish	exaggerated = overstated
truth or correctness = accuracy	lied to = deceived
believe in = trust	presented in a false way = misrepresented
	wrong information = misinformation
	changed to be untrue = distorted
	an untrue story = a myth
	made up = fabricated

B
- **Preview and do the task** Read the instructions aloud. Have Ss complete the task. Walk around the class and give help as needed. Check answers with the class.

Answers

- ☑ 2. There are several reasons why the facts are sometimes misrepresented.
- ☑ 3. It is difficult to tell truth from fiction in modern news reporting.
- ☑ 5. The general public needs consumer websites to know if politicians are telling the truth.

Answers

Noun	Adjective	Verb
1. verification	—	verify
2. establishment	—	establish
3. accuracy	accurate	—
4. trust	trustworthy / trusting / trusted	trust
5. —	misleading	mislead
6. —	overstated	overstate
7. deception	deceptive / deceiving	deceive
8. misrepresentation	—	misrepresent
9. misinformation	—	misinform
10. distortion	distorted	distort
11. myth	mythical	mythologize
12. fabrication	fabricated	fabricate

Extra activity – pairs

Each pair writes two nouns, two adjectives, and two verbs on a separate piece of paper. Pairs exchange papers with another pair and write a sentence for each word. Pairs read their sentences aloud to another pair, which identifies the word from the chart for each sentence.

About you

C Pair work

- **Preview and do the task** Read the instructions aloud. Have Ss discuss the questions. Walk around the class and help as needed.
- **Follow-up** For each question, have a few pairs report to the class. Alternatively, put two pairs together to share their opinions.

C Understanding idioms **What does the writer mean by saying . . .**

1. breakdowns in communications systems caused news "blackouts"? (para. 3)
2. news was passed by "word of mouth"? (para. 3)
3. in an effort to "swing the race"? (para. 4)
4. websites have "sprung up"? (para. 5)
5. many have "jumped on the bandwagon" of truth? (para. 5)

D Read for inference **Check (✓) the statements that the writer would agree with.**

1. ☐ Hurricane Katrina caused an increase in crime.
2. ☐ There are several reasons why the facts are sometimes misrepresented.
3. ☐ It is difficult to tell truth from fiction in modern news reporting.
4. ☐ It is only major events that are not reported truthfully.
5. ☐ The general public needs consumer websites to know if politicians are telling the truth.
6. ☐ These websites really make politicians more truthful.
7. ☐ It is much easier these days to determine if information is accurate.
8. ☐ The news on one satirical news website is more truthful than from other media outlets.

② Focus on vocabulary Truth or fiction?

> **Tip**
>
> Prefixes sometimes help you understand meanings: *mis-* often means "badly."

A Find alternative ways in the article to express the ideas below. Compare with a partner.

Talking about truth . . .
make sure something is true (para. 2)
find out (facts) (para. 3)
truth or correctness (para. 4)
believe in (para. 5)

. . . and lies
giving a wrong impression (para. 1)
exaggerated (para. 2)
lied to (para. 2)
presented in a false way (para. 2)
wrong information (para. 3)
changed to be untrue (para. 3)
an untrue story (para. 5)
made up (para. 5)

B Make a chart like the one below of the words you found in Exercise A. Add other forms. Write (–) if you cannot make the word into a noun, an adjective, or a verb.

Noun	Adjective	Verb
verification		

C Pair work **Discuss the questions. Try to use at least six of the new words.**

About you

- Does the situation the article describes apply to news organizations you follow?
- Do you always trust everything you hear or read?
- Have you ever found something in the news to be exaggerated or misleading?
- Do you think news stories about celebrities are fabricated? What else is?
- Which news channels do people trust most?
- Do you enjoy satirical news websites or TV shows? If so, which ones?

Writing *In short, . . .*

In this lesson, you . . .
- summarize an article.
- choose singular or plural verbs.
- avoid errors with verbs in relative clauses.

Task Write a summary.

Write a summary of the article on page 112 in no more than 150 words.

A **Look at a model** Read the summary below of the article on page 112 and the notes. Cross out two sentences in the summary that are <u>not</u> suitable. Then circle the correct verbs.

Writing a summary

Use your own words.
Include main points only.
Do not add new ideas.
Do not add an opinion.

It is crucial that news reporting be accurate. The dramatic news reports after Hurricane Katrina, some of which **was / were** later shown to be inaccurate, **is / are** an example of the difficulties of news reporting. The reasons for inaccurate news coverage **varies / vary**. In complex situations, news **is / are** easily misreported, owing to a variety of factors.

Social networks seem to be taking over news reporting. People often **pass / passes** on inaccuracies in word-of-mouth reporting, while in places of conflict, there can be failures in power and communications. News organizations **bear / bears** some responsibility for inaccurate reporting because they do not always verify facts. Political reporting and campaigning **is / are** also in danger of misleading the public and **has / have** led to the need for professional fact-checkers. The number of websites which **checks / check** facts in the news **has / have** grown as a result of increasing public concern.

B **Focus on language** Read the chart. Then complete the sentences below with simple present verbs.

Subject-verb agreement in writing

Use singular verbs after uncountable nouns and most singular nouns that refer to a group.
*News **is** easily misreported. **Information needs** to be checked. **The public is** concerned.*

Use a singular verb if the main noun in a phrase is singular, but not in expressions that mean "a lot of."
*The **number** of websites . . . **has** grown.* BUT *A **number of** websites **have** appeared.*

Use a plural verb after noun *and* noun, when the main noun is plural, and after an irregular plural noun.
*Political **reporting and campaigning are** in danger of misleading the public.*
*The **reasons** for inaccurate news coverage **are** varied. **People pass** on inaccuracies.*

1. People _____ to be able to trust the organizations that _____ news. (need / broadcast)
2. The main reason for inaccuracies _____ that news reports and broadcasts _____ live. (be)
3. The number of reporters who _____ accurate accounts of stories _____ every year. (give / grow)
4. Accurate news and information _____ hard to find. The pressure on reporters _____ huge. (be)
5. A number of journalists _____ always _____ news accurately. (not report)
6. The population generally _____ to know the truth, even if the truth _____ not easy to hear. (want / be)
7. The use of social networks _____ news reporting. (affect)

C **Write and check** Write a summary of the article on page 112. Then check for errors.

Common errors

Be careful with the verbs in relative clauses.
*The number of websites which **check** news **has** grown. (NOT . . . ~~checks . . . . have~~)*

Writing *In short, . . .*

In this lesson

- Ask a S to read the lesson aims (*In this lesson, you . . .*) aloud. Ask, "What do you do when you summarize?" [report the main points or ideas] Say, "Scan the page. How many points are there to remember when you summarize?" [four] Say, "Scan the page again. What grammar point is reviewed in the lesson?" [subject-verb agreement in writing]
- **Preview the writing** Say, "In this lesson, you will write a summary." Point out the writing topic in Task and read it aloud. Explain that Ss will end the lesson by writing a summary that will practice the three aims presented in this lesson.

A Look at a model

- **Present *Writing a summary*** Books closed. Ask, "What guidelines do you think are involved when you write a summary?" Elicit ideas from the class. Books open.
- **Preview the task** Say, "Read the summary below of the article on page 112 and cross out two sentences in the summary that are not suitable. Refer to the points in Writing a Summary to help you decide."
- **Do the task** Have Ss complete the task and compare their answers with a partner. Check answers with the class. Ask Ss for a reason for their choices.

Answers

It is crucial that news reporting be accurate. (opinion)
Social networks seem to be taking over news reporting. (new idea)

- Say, "Read through the summary again. Circle the correct verbs." Have Ss complete the task and compare their answers with a partner. Check answers with the class.

Answers

~~It is crucial that news reporting be accurate.~~ The dramatic news reports after Hurricane Katrina, some of which <u>were</u> later shown to be inaccurate, <u>are</u> an example of the difficulties of news reporting. The reasons for inaccurate news coverage <u>vary</u>. In complex situations, news <u>is</u> easily misreported, owing to a variety of factors. ~~Social networks seem to be taking over news reporting.~~ People often <u>pass</u> on inaccuracies in word-of-mouth reporting, while in places of conflict, there can be failures in power and communications. News organizations <u>bear</u> some responsibility for inaccurate reporting because they do not always verify facts. Political reporting and campaigning <u>are</u> also in danger of misleading the public and <u>have</u> led to the need for professional fact-checkers. The number of websites which <u>check</u> facts in the news <u>has</u> grown as a result of increasing public concern.

B ⬇ www.cambridge.org/viewpoint/audio

Focus on language

- **Present the grammar for writing chart** Read the information in the chart aloud. If desired, play the downloadable recording. Ss listen and read along.

- **Understand the grammar for writing** Say, "The chart reviews subject-verb agreement with a focus on some areas where even advanced Ss make mistakes."
- Ask Ss to look at the section on uncountable nouns. Ask, "Why is there a singular verb after *news*?" [It's uncountable.] "How about after *information*?" [also uncountable] Say, "Most singular nouns that refer to a group use a singular verb, especially in writing, for example *public*, *government*, *military*, *company*, *family*, and *class*. Sometimes plural verbs are used when the group is thought of as a number of individuals, but singular verbs are used when the group is thought of as one body. For example, *police* more often takes a plural verb."
- Have Ss look at the second point. Say, "*Number* in *The number of* is the main subject here – it refers to the total, which is singular. *A number of* is like a determiner, such as *a lot of* or *several*, and the noun after it is plural. Therefore, the verb is plural."
- Tell Ss to look at the next point. Say, "Remember that when the subject is part of a phrase, check to see if the main noun is singular or plural."
- Say, "Now write the correct simple present form of the verbs in the sentences below. Use the verbs in parentheses." Have Ss complete the task. Check answers with the class.

Answers

1. need; broadcast
2. is; are
3. give; grows
4. are; is
5. do not; report
6. wants; is
7. affects

C Write and check

- **Preview and do the task** Read the instructions aloud.
- **Present *Common errors*** Books closed. Write on the board:

   The number of websites that check news has grown.

- Ask, "What's the subject of *check*?" [websites] Ask, "What's the subject of *has grown*?" [the number]
- Books open. Read the information aloud. Say, "This error is common even among advanced students. Remember to check the subject and its verb."
- Have Ss complete the task.

Extra activity – class

Ss leave their summaries on their desk for classmates to read. Ss go around the class reading each other's work. Ss check for subject-verb agreement in the summaries.

Vocabulary notebook *Trust your instincts.*

If done for homework

Briefly present the Learning tip and the task directions. Make sure Ss understand what they need to do.

If done in class

- **Present *Learning tip*** Read the information aloud. Ask a S to read the example in the box. Say, "For example, people can *perform*, *undergo*, and *have* routine surgery."
- **Present *Dictionary tip*** Say, "Read all the examples in a dictionary entry for a word. They often give clues to collocations. For example, if you look up the word *surgery*, you might find different verbs in the example."

A • **Preview and do the task** Read the instructions aloud. Ask Ss which two verbs go with *oil spill*. [*a* and *c*] Have Ss complete the task. Check answers with the class.

Answers

1. a, c	5. a, c
2. b, c	6. a, b
3. a, c	7. a, c
4. b, c	8. b, c

Extra activity – class / pairs

Ss write the nouns from Exercise A on a separate piece of paper and then close their Student's Books. Ss write the verbs they remember beside each noun. Ss exchange papers with another S. Ss check each other's papers and give one point for each correct verb.

B • **Preview and do the task** Read the instructions aloud. Have Ss complete the task. Ss read their sentences aloud to a partner. Check answers with the class.

Answers

1. Bombs can explode or go off.
2. The stock market can plummet or plunge.
3. Protest marches can go or start peacefully.
4. Riot squads can be called in or mobilized.
5. Tensions can arise or escalate.

C Focus on vocabulary, page 113

- **Preview and do the task** Read the instructions aloud. Do the first item with the class. Ask, "What word is similar to *confirm* and *prove*?" [verify] Have Ss find the words. Check answers with the class.

Answers

1. verify
2. establish
3. trust
4. overstate
5. deceive
6. misrepresent
7. distorted, misleading
8. myth
9. fabricate

Vocabulary notebook *Trust your instincts.*

When you learn a new verb + noun expression, find other verbs that collocate with the noun.

perform / undergo / have / routine surgery

Dictionary tip

Read all the examples in a dictionary entry for a word. They often give clues to collocations.

surgery /ˈsɜr·dʒə·ri/ *n* [C/U]

the treatment of injuries or diseases by cutting open the body and removing or repairing the damaged part, or an operation of this type:

[U] *He had undergone open-heart surgery two years ago.*

[U] *I'm recovering from back surgery, so it's going to be awhile before I can ride a horse again.*

[C] *She has undergone several surgeries and will require more.*

A **Which two verbs go with each noun in bold below? Circle a, b, or c.**

1. a. contain	b. hold	c. prevent	**an oil spill**
2. a. rule	b. contemplate	c. consider	**legal action**
3. a. compensate	b. create	c. protect	**victims**
4. a. mobilize	b. trigger	c. cause	**an explosion**
5. a. explore	b. edit	c. rule out	**the possibility**
6. a. run	b. announce	c. determine	**a campaign**
7. a. fuel	b. make	c. cause	**speculation**
8. a. do	b. make	c. see	**a recovery**

B **Find two verbs in the box that can be used to complete each sentence below.**

arise	called in	escalate	explode	go	go off	mobilized	plummet	plunge	start

1. Bombs can _____ or _____.
2. The stock market can _____ or _____.
3. Protest marches can _____ or _____ peacefully.
4. Riot squads can be _____ or _____.
5. Tensions can _____ or _____.

C **Focus on vocabulary** **Complete the vocabulary notes with words from Lesson D on page 113. Look for words with similar meanings to the words in bold.**

1. **confirm** or **prove** or _____ the accuracy of a story, someone's identity
2. **find out** or _____ the facts, the truth, someone's identity
3. **believe (in)** or _____ your instincts, your judgment
4. **exaggerate** or _____ the impact or benefits of something
5. **lie to** or _____ the public, consumers, voters
6. **not tell the truth about** or _____ information, facts, someone's position or view
7. paint an **unclear** or _____ picture or give a **false** or _____ impression
8. create or perpetuate an **untrue story** or an urban _____
9. **make up** or _____ evidence, stories, an account, a report

Unit **11** Is it real?

Lesson A *Imagined threats?*

Grammar *Talking about the future*

(See Student's Book p. 117.)

In this lesson, Ss learn expressions with *be to* for talking about future events.

Form

- Fixed events in the immediate future

  Subject + *be to* + verb

  *A TV documentary **is to air** later this week.*

- Conditionals and hypothetical future events

  If + subject + *be to* + verb

  *If we **are to survive** a catastrophe, we'd better shape up.*

  *If society **were to collapse**, these people are well prepared.*

- Be about / bound / set to

  Subject + *be about / bound / set to* + verb

  *Civilization **is not about to collapse**.*

  *There's **bound to be** debris falling on us.*

- Future seen from the past

  Subject + *be* (past) + *to* + verb

  *They said the world **was to end** in 2012.*

  *It **was bound to happen**, they said.*

Use

You can use *be to* to refer to events in the immediate future, especially those that are fixed or decided. It is rarely used in conversation and is much more a feature of writing. You can also use the future with *be to* in conditional sentences and for hypothetical events in the future. Related expressions include *be about to*, which is used to describe events that will happen very soon, and *be bound to* or *be set to*, which express the idea of certainty. These structures can also be used to talk about the future as it was seen in the past.

Grammar extra *More on* be to; be due to, meant to; be to *for orders and instructions*

(See Student's Book p. 164.)

Grammar extra presents more ways to use *be to* and related expressions, including for instructions.

Lesson B *Hard to believe*

Vocabulary in context *Expressions with* turn

(See Student's Book p. 118.)

Ss learn idioms and phrasal verbs with *turn*. Examples are *turn down*, *turn to*, and *turn over a new leaf*. These are presented in the context of an article about the life of Frank Abagnale, a one-time master forger who turned his back on crime.

Vocabulary notebook *Use it or lose it*

(See Student's Book p. 125.)

The Learning tip tells Ss that when they learn new words and expressions, they should put them into a conversation that they can imagine having with a friend. Ss get more practice with the vocabulary from Lesson B.

- **Focus on vocabulary** reviews and practices vocabulary introduced in Lesson D (p. 123).

Grammar *Information focus*

(See Student's Book p. 119.)

This lesson reviews and extends Ss' knowledge of passive verb complements — verbs in a passive form that are used after other verbs. Passive verb complements can be base forms of verbs, infinitives, perfect infinitives, and *-ing* forms.

Form

- Base form

  The base form is *be* + past participle.

  Use base forms after *had better, would rather,* and modal verbs.

  *He'd rather **be remembered** for his work with the FBI.*

- Passive infinitive

  The passive infinitive form is *to be* + past participle. The perfect passive infinitive form is *to have been* + past participle.

  Use infinitives after *appear, claim, deserve, expect, love,* etc.; *seem, want, 'd like*.

  *Abagnale deserves **to be admired**.*

  *A 12-year prison term appears **to have been considered** harsh even then.*

- Passive *-ing*

  The passive *-ing* form is *being* + past participle

  Use *-ing* forms after *avoid, be worth, enjoy, love,* etc.; *mind, recall, remember, regret.*

  *He avoided **being apprehended** for several years.*

Use

Passive verbs are generally used when the doer of an action is not known or not important or to focus on the receiver of an action.

Notice the difference in meaning between active and passive verb complements.

*He'd **rather remember** his work for the FBI.* (active)

(= He prefers to remember it himself.)

*He'd **rather be remembered** for his work with the FBI.* (passive)

(= He prefers other people (who are unknown) to remember him for his work with the FBI.)

The movie makers *appear **to have exaggerated** events.*
(focus on movie makers)

*The events appear **to have been exaggerated**.*
(focus on the events)

Grammar extra *More on passive perfect infinitives; would rather*

(See Student's Book p. 165.)

Grammar extra looks at passive perfect infinitive verb complements and *would rather* + passive.

Speaking naturally *Stress in longer idioms*

(See Student's Book p. 143.)

Ss have learned that phrasal verbs are usually stressed on the particle. In this section, Ss practice stress in idioms that are phrasal verbs with a noun object. In these, the object has the primary stress. The primary stress is underlined in the examples below.

> *I **turned** a**round** and looked in the mirror.*
>
> *I realized that I needed to **turn** my **life** around.*
>
> BUT *I **turned** it a**round**.*

Lesson C *That's my concern.*

Conversation strategy *Expressing concerns*

(See Student's Book p. 120.)

In conversation, there are times when a speaker may not like or approve of either something that is said or an action that is described. The speaker can use expressions that express concern or disapproval but that are not too strong or harsh. Expressions like *That doesn't sit right with me* or *I'm not comfortable with that* indicate concern. An expression like *That's not good* is more direct but still not overly harsh.

Strategy plus *To me, . . .*

(See Student's Book p. 121.)

You can use *to me* to mean "that's how it seems to me / that's my view." It often indicates a different feeling or reaction. You can also use *to* + other pronouns or nouns to report another person's feeling or attitude, as in, *To her / my friend, it was no big deal.*

Lesson D *Artistic fakes*

Reading tip *Problems and solutions*

(See Student's Book p. 122.)

The Reading tip explains that writers often use the first paragraph of a text to set out a problem to which the rest of the text will offer a series of possible solutions. Understanding this problem-solution pattern can help Ss read faster and more efficiently.

Writing *So what if it's fake?*

(See Student's Book p. 124.)

This lesson teaches Ss to plan and write an opinion essay on the topic of producing or selling fake designer goods. This essay requires Ss to report the views of other people and state their own view. The grammar for writing presents more formal equivalents of basic conjunctions and adverbs that are useful in academic writing. It also gives phrases for giving personal views. The topic recycles vocabulary from Lesson D.

- Conjunctions and adverbs in academic writing

  "If": *as long as, assuming (that); provided / providing (that)*

  "But + despite this": *Yet*

  "Because": *considering (that), in view of / light of [the fact (that)], given (that)*

  "Despite": *regardless of, irrespective of, no matter (who / what / how, etc.)*

- Expressions to give your view

  I believe (that) . . .

  I consider (something) to be . . .

  I regard (something) as . . .

  I would argue (that) . . .

  Clearly, . . .

 Corpus information

Common errors with *yet* and *however*

Even advanced Ss sometimes confuse *yet* and *however*.

Yet is a formal word and has the meaning of "despite this."

*I once bought a bag from a street vendor. **However**, I didn't know it was a fake item.*

(**NOT**: ~~Yet~~, I didn't know . . .)

11 Is it real?

In Unit 11, you . . .

- talk about whether information is true or not.
- use *be to* expressions to talk about the future.
- use passive verb complements.
- express concerns with expressions like *That's my concern.*
- give your opinion using *To me.*

Lesson A *Imagined threats?*

1 Grammar in context

A What kinds of threats to society are there? What could disrupt life as we know it? Make a list.

B ◀)) CD 4.10 **Read the blog. What threats does it mention? Are any of the threats on your list?**

WHAT ARE WE TO BELIEVE?

Recently I saw a trailer for a TV documentary that is to air later this week. It's about families known as "preppers." These are people who are so convinced that life as we know it is to end or that civilization is about to collapse that they are preparing for the day it happens. So they're stockpiling food, water, and survival equipment, which no one is to touch until the day when some unknown disaster occurs – like the failure of the national grid, a natural disaster, even an asteroid strike – which they say is bound to happen eventually. I have to admit: If society were to collapse tomorrow, or if food and energy supplies were to be threatened, they are certainly better prepared than my family. We have barely three cans of baked beans and a pack of birthday candles between us. If we are to survive a catastrophe, we'd better shape up.

If the doomsayers are correct, the world as we know it is to end sooner than we think – which kind of got me thinking about what threats to our lives are real and which are imagined.

For example, remember Y2K? At the turn of this century, there was a great panic that computer systems around the world were about to crash because of the way computers recognized dates. The Year 2000, or Y2K, as it became commonly known, was set to be the biggest systems failure the world had ever experienced. It never happened.

Another perceived threat is an asteroid strike. Is one imminent? If so, shouldn't we all be panicking? Didn't the last one wipe out the dinosaurs? Well, according to experts at NASA*, earth is not about to be hit by an asteroid. They do say that there's bound to be debris from space falling on us at some point, although given the fact that around 70 percent of the earth's surface is water, there's little chance it's going to fall on me as I head for the supermarket.

There's always some disaster that's about to happen. And it truly is hard to know what's real and what's not. So what's the average family like us to do? Maybe the next time I go to the supermarket, I'll buy a few more cans of baked beans and some large white regular candles. Just in case.

END OF WORLD AHEAD

*National Aeronautics and Space Administration

C Pair work **Discuss the questions.**

1. What kind of blog is this? Instructive? Lighthearted? Informative?
2. What kinds of things are "preppers" stockpiling? What other things might they need?
3. Why does the writer suggest we ought to be panicking? Do situations like that cause you to panic?
4. Have you prepared in any way for problems that may arise in the future? How?

Is it real?

Introduce the theme of the unit Tell Ss the title of the unit. Say, "Sometimes it's difficult to know what's real and what's not. We all know about the existence of online scammers. They try to convince us that a phishing request for personal information is real. They may try to sell investment opportunities that aren't real. But trying to convince people that a thing is real doesn't just happen online. What other examples can you think of? Look at the pictures for ideas." Elicit answers from the class. Ask a S to read the unit aims aloud.

Lesson A *Imagined threats?*

1 Grammar in context

- **Set the scene** Books closed. Say, "An ancient calendar from the Mayan people said that the world was going to end in December 2012. Do you know anyone who took that threat seriously? How did the people you know react?" Have a short discussion with the class.

A
- **Preview and do the task** Books open. Read the instructions aloud. Make sure Ss understand the meaning of *disrupt*. [stop something from continuing as it should] Tell Ss to write their lists.

- Ask a few Ss to say what kind of threats there are. Ask what could disrupt life as we know it (e.g., *breakdown in communications, cyber warfare, asteroid strike, nuclear explosion, natural disasters like earthquakes, floods*). Write their ideas on the board.

B 🔊 CD4, Track 10
- **Preview the task** Books closed. Write on the board:

  (TV / movie) trailer

  stockpile

  doomsayer

  imminent

  Say, "If you know the meanings of any of these, tell the class." Write the correct Ss' definitions on the board. [*trailer*: short parts of a TV program or movie that are shown to advertise it; *stockpile*: collect a large number of things that may be used in the future; *doomsayer*: someone who predicts serious problems or disasters; *imminent*: happening very soon] Help with any definitions Ss don't know.

- Say, "Listen to the blog. What threats does it mention? Are any of the threats on your list?" [The blog mentions threats such as power failures (the national grid), natural disasters, and an asteroid strike.]

- **Do the task** Read the instructions aloud. Tell Ss to check (✓) any ideas on their list that they read about. Have Ss compare their notes with a partner.

- Ask, "Which of the threats are on your list? Which are on the board?" Have Ss call out answers.

- Check for any remaining vocabulary questions. Elicit definitions from the class. Provide definitions where necessary.

C Pair work
- **Preview and do the task** Read the instructions aloud. Ask a S to read the questions aloud. Check that Ss understand *lighthearted*. [amusing and not serious]

- Have Ss discuss the questions. Walk around the class and help as needed. Have several pairs report to the class.

Answers

1. This blog is mostly lighthearted and informative in parts.
2. They are stockpiling food, water, and survival equipment. They might need sleeping bags, flashlights, batteries, tools, clothes, matches, books, etc.
3. The writer suggests we ought to panic especially about an asteroid strike because it is believed that is what wiped out the dinosaurs, and another one could be imminent.
4. *Answers will vary.*

Extra activity – pairs
Pairs can stockpile as much as they want of six items. Pairs decide which six they want. Pairs decide and tell the class which items they want.

② Grammar

A 🔽 www.cambridge.org/viewpoint/audio

- **Preview the task** Say, "How does the blog express the underlined ideas? Rewrite the sentences."
- **Do the task** Have Ss complete the task and compare answers with a partner. Check answers with the class.

Answers

1. Life as we know it is to end.
2. Civilization is about to collapse.
3. There's bound to be debris from space.

- **Focus on the use** Ask, "Are these sentences about the past, present, or future?" [future]
- **Focus on the form** Ask, "What structures are used in the sentences in the exercise to refer to the future?" [*will* and *going to*] Ask, "In sentence 1, what is *will end* replaced with?" [is to end] Ask, "What was *is going to collapse very soon* replaced with in sentence 2?" [is about to collapse] "In sentence 3, what did *It's certain there will be* change to?" [There's bound to be]
- **Present the grammar chart** Read the information aloud. If desired, play the downloadable recording.
- Say, "The chart presents ways to talk about the future using *be to*."
- Have Ss look at the first section. Ask, "What pattern do you see?" [Subject + *be to* + verb] Write it on the board. Say, "The event in the example sentence is fixed or decided. How do you know?" [It's about a TV schedule.]
- Have Ss look at the second section. Ask, "What pattern do you see?" [*If* + subject + *be to* + verb] Write it on the board. Have Ss suggest different main clauses.
- Ask Ss to look at the third section. Ask, "What pattern do you see?" [Subject + *be about / bound / set to* + verb] Have Ss say true things that are about to happen or they think are bound to happen soon.
- Ask Ss to look at the bottom of the chart. Ask, "What pattern do you see?" [Subject + *be* (past) + *to* + verb] Ask, "When did 'they' say these things?" [before the end of 2012] Have Ss say other things that were to happen.

Say, "The future with *be to* is rare in conversation. It's more common in writing; *be bound to* and *be about to* are used in conversation."

(For more information, see Language notes at the beginning of the unit. For more work on *be to*, *be due to*, *be meant to*, go to Grammar extra, p. 164.)

B
- **Preview and do the task** Write on the board:

  flu pandemic

  infiltrate

- Check that Ss understand the meanings. [*flu pandemic:* when the flu affects a lot of people in a country, region, or throughout the world; *infiltrate:* secretly join a group or organization so you can learn more about them] Check for any other vocabulary questions.
- Say, "Complete the sentences from a survey using the words given. Be sure to think about tense and if the verb is singular or plural." Complete the first blank with the class. Ask, "What form of *be* do you need?" [is] "How do you complete the blank?" [is bound to] Have Ss complete the task and compare answers with a partner. Check answers with the class.

Answers

1. If scientists are right . . . pandemic is bound to occur sooner or later . . . virus that was set to affect . . . If another pandemic were to / was to occur . . . ?
2. A super volcano . . . is set to explode . . . It's not . . . if past patterns are to be repeated. If you were about to travel . . . ?
3. Doomsayers predict that cyber-warfare is bound to happen soon. They're not . . . systems are set to fail . . . Some experts say that if cyber-terrorists were to attack, we would not be prepared.

Extra activity – pairs / groups

Ss imagine that one of these events is about to happen. Write on the board:

Internet services are to be suspended for a week from midnight.

All public transportation is to be canceled tomorrow.

There is to be a general strike next weekend.

Ss write a TV report.

③ Viewpoint

- **Preview the task** Read the instructions aloud. Ask a S to read the five discussion points. Check for vocabulary questions and provide definitions as needed.
- **Present *In conversation*** Read the information aloud. Ask a S to read the example aloud. Ask Ss to

brainstorm some adverbs that might be useful here (e.g., *strangely (enough), realistically, fortunately, unfortunately, obviously*).

- **Do the task** Have groups discuss the questions. Walk around the class and give help as needed.

2 Grammar Talking about the future

Figure it out

A Find the underlined ideas in the blog and rewrite the sentences. Then read the chart.

1. Life as we know it will end.
2. Civilization is going to collapse very soon.
3. It's certain there will be debris from space.

Expressions with *be to* ⬇

Grammar extra
See page 164.

You can use *be to* to refer to the immediate future, especially events that are fixed or decided.
*A TV documentary **is to air** later this week.*

You can also use *be to* in conditional sentences and for hypothetical events in the future.
*If we **are to survive** a catastrophe, we'd better shape up.*
*If society **were to collapse**, these people are well prepared.*

Be about to means something will happen very soon; *be bound to* or *be set to* suggest certainty.
*Civilization **is not about to collapse**. There's **bound to be** debris falling on us.*

These expressions can also be used to talk about the future as it was seen in the past.
*They said the world **was to end** in 2012. It **was bound to happen**, they said.*

B Complete the sentences from a survey using the words given. Then ask and answer the questions. Do situations like these concern you?

1. If scientists are right, a global flu pandemic _____ (bound) occur sooner or later. Some years ago, a flu virus that _____ (set) affect millions of people turned out to be less disastrous than predicted. If another pandemic _____ (be) occur, would you panic?
1. A super volcano in North America _____ (set) explode sometime in the future. It's not known when, but an eruption is 40,000 years overdue if past patterns _____ (be) be repeated. If you _____ (about) travel to that area soon, would you cancel your trip?
1. Doomsayers predict that cyber-warfare _____ (bound) happen soon. They're not the only ones who think that computer systems _____ (set) fail as a result of infiltration. Security experts say that if cyber-terrorists _____ (be) attack, we would not be prepared.

3 Viewpoint *Are you prepared?*

Group work **Discuss the questions below.**

In conversation . . .
You can introduce what you say with an adverb (e.g., *clearly, fortunately*) to show your attitude.

- Have you ever had to evacuate a building for any reason? Do you know what you're supposed to do in a fire drill?
- If communications systems were to shut down around the country, what would you do? How would it affect you?
- Do you know what people are to do if utility supplies shut off for any reason? What problems would the loss of utilities be bound to cause?
- If you were to hear of an impending crisis (such as a hurricane), how would you prepare?
- What supplies should people have ready in these situations?

"Interestingly enough, we had to evacuate our office building one time. Luckily, it was OK in the end."

Lesson B *Hard to believe*

1 Vocabulary in context

A 🔊 CD 4.11 **Read the article. What is Frank Abagnale known for — now and in the past?**

Why Frank W. Abagnale deserves to be admired

Frank Abagnale is a well-respected businessman, but **turn back the clock** several decades and you will find a notorious past – a past that he probably never expected to be **turned into** a Hollywood movie. But it's his work over the last four decades with the FBI* and other agencies – after he **turned his back on** a life of crime – that he'd rather be remembered for.

As one of the world's most respected authorities on security and fraud prevention, Abagnale is the person to **turn to** when you need to understand the crimes of check forgery and embezzlement. That's because he was an expert at these activities. In his youth, Abagnale was an extraordinary con artist, successfully conning people into thinking he was an airline pilot, a pediatrician, and a college professor – without ever being qualified in any of these fields. He lived a jet-setting lifestyle, but it **turned out** that he had funded all his activities by forging checks across the globe. He successfully avoided being apprehended for several years but was finally caught at the age

of 21 by French authorities. He served prison time in three different countries. It was a **turning point** in his life.

Abagnale recalls being devastated by his parents' divorce, shortly after which he started his life of deception. His crimes, committed between the ages of 16 and 21, earned him a 12-year U.S. prison term, which seems to have been considered harsh even back then. He ended up being released early after agreeing to assist U.S. federal law enforcement agencies. It was an offer Abagnale was smart enough not to **turn down**, and it allowed him to **turn over a new leaf** in his life.

Even if you can't **turn a blind eye** to his past, Abagnale deserves to be admired for the way he **turned** his life **around**. On his website, he states that he regrets being drawn into illegal and unethical activities. He comments, too, on the movie *Catch Me If You Can*, which is loosely based on his life. Abagnale wants it to be known that it's not a true biography. Indeed, many of the events appear to have been exaggerated, which can only be expected. After all, it is a movie.

_____

*the Federal Bureau of Investigation – a U.S. government agency

Word sort

B **Find idioms and phrasal verbs with *turn* in the article that have the meanings below.**

1. stop being involved in _____
2. become _____
3. stop a bad habit _____
4. ignore _____
5. a moment of change _____
6. refuse _____
7. go back in time _____
8. become apparent _____
9. make something better _____
10. go to, approach _____

C Pair work **Discuss the questions. How many *turn* expressions can you use?**

1. Why does Frank Abagnale have a "notorious" past? Why is he now a respected authority on security?
2. When did he begin his life of deception? How did he turn his life around?
3. What do you think about the way Abagnale turned over a new leaf?
4. Have you seen *Catch Me If You Can*? If not, would you like to?

Vocabulary notebook

See page 125.

Lesson B *Hard to believe*

1 Vocabulary in context

- **Set the scene** Books closed. Write *con artist* on the board. Ask, "Do you know what a con artist is?" Find out if any Ss know. If yes, have them tell the class. If no, say, "*Con* is short for *confidence*. Con artists gain your confidence and then trick you into giving them money. Once they have your money, you never hear from them again."

A 🔊 CD4, Track 11

- **Preview the task** Books open. Say, "What is Frank Abagnale known for – now and in the past? Write brief notes of the answers you read."
- **Do the task** Ss read and write. Have Ss compare their notes with a partner.
- **Play the recording** Books open. Ss listen, read along, and check their answers. Check for vocabulary questions.
- Check the answer with the class. [Abagnale is known for his work with the FBI in helping to prevent fraud and check forgery. He is an authority on security. In the past, he was a con artist.] Check for vocabulary questions.

Word sort

B • **Preview and do the task** Read the instructions aloud. Have Ss complete the task and compare answers with a partner. Check answers with the class.

Answers

1. turn your back on
2. turn into
3. turn over a new leaf
4. turn a blind eye to
5. a turning point
6. turn down
7. turn back the clock
8. turn out
9. turn around
10. turn to

Extra activity – pairs

Ss write five *turn* expressions on a separate piece of paper and then exchange papers with a partner. Ss write a sentence for each expression and read the sentences to their partner. The partner decides if the expression has been used correctly.

C Pair work

- **Preview and do the task** Read the instructions aloud. Say, "Read the questions before you begin." Deal with any vocabulary questions.
- Have Ss complete the task. Check answers with the class.

Possible answers

1. If you turn back the clock, you see that Frank Abagnale has a notorious past because as a youth he was a con artist and a check forger. He turned his back on a life of crime and turned his life around after his time in prison, which was a turning point in his life. He is now a respected authority on security because government agencies turn to him to help identify check forgeries and embezzlement.
2. He began his life of deception shortly after his parents' divorce. He turned his life around by agreeing to assist U.S. federal law enforcement agencies in identifying crimes similar to the ones he committed.
3. *Answers will vary.*
4. *Answers will vary.*

> Tell Ss to turn to Vocabulary Notebook on p. 125 of their Student's Books. Have Ss do the tasks in class or assign them for homework. (See the teaching notes on p. T-125.)

Extra activity – groups

Write on the board:

> *What other methods do you know to trick people into giving away money?*
>
> *Are there any people who are more vulnerable than others?*

Groups discuss the questions and report their ideas to the class.

Figure it out

A 🔽 www.cambridge.org/viewpoint/audio

- **Preview the task** Ask, "Which of the two options in each sentence is the idea that is expressed in the article?" Have Ss choose the correct option and compare their choice with a partner. Check answers with the class.

Answers

1 be remembered for
2. to be turned
3. to have been exaggerated
4. being drawn

- **Focus on the form and use** Ask, "What's the difference in meaning between the two options in sentence 1?" [The first option means Abagnale wants to remember; the second means he wants other people to remember him.] Ask, "How about sentence 2?" [The first option means other people turned his past into a movie; the second suggests he made the movie.] Ask, "How about sentence 4?" [The first option means Abagnale drew others into illegal activities; the second means other people drew him in.] Ask, "Are sentences 1, 2, and 4 in the active or passive?" [passive] Ask, "What are some reasons for using passive instead of active?" [The doer of an action is not known or is not important. You want to focus on the receiver of the action.]

- **Present the grammar chart** Read the information aloud. If desired, play the downloadable recording.

- **Understand the grammar chart** Say, "A verb complement is a verb that comes after another verb. For example, in *I like watching* or *to watch movies*, the verb *watching* or *to watch* is a complement. These are active. Complements can also be passive, and this is what this chart presents. Passive verbs focus on information about the receiver of the action rather than the doer of the action. The chart shows how this is expressed in verb complements."

- Have Ss look at the chart. Ask, "What is the pattern for passive verb complements in base form?" [*be* + past participle] Ask, "What is the pattern for passive infinitive verb complements?" [*to be* + past participle] Say, "Tell me the pattern for perfect passive infinitive verb complements." [*to have been* + past participle] Say, "Finally, what pattern do you use with a passive *-ing* form?" [*being* + past participle]

- Have Ss look at the bottom section of the chart. Say, "Use this section as reference when you're deciding which passive verb complement to use."

(For more information, see Language notes at the beginning of the unit. For more work on passive verb complements and information about *would rather*, go to Grammar extra, p. 165.)

B - **Preview and do the task** Read the instructions aloud. Ask, "What form of the passive will you use in the first blank?" [base form / *be played*] Ask why. [It follows *would rather*.] Have Ss complete the task and then compare answers with a partner. Check answers with the class.

Answers

1. I'd rather <u>be played</u> by Chris Rock . . . I want <u>to be remembered</u> for . . . I wouldn't mind <u>being played</u> by Eddie Murphy, either.
2. . . . like <u>to be known</u> for . . . I'd rather <u>be remembered</u> for . . .
3. . . . That deserves <u>to be included</u> in . . .
4. . . . I never expected <u>to be fired</u>. I hate <u>being told / to be told</u> . . . but it wasn't worth <u>being fired</u> for.
5. . . never <u>be told</u> is . . . Fortunately it seems <u>to have been forgotten / to be forgotten</u>. I'm sure she'd rather not <u>be reminded</u> of it in the movie.
6. I've always avoided <u>being made</u> to . . . That's one thing I'd like <u>to be said</u> about me.
7. I'd like <u>to be given</u> the . . . I might <u>be nominated</u> for "best director." I'd enjoy <u>being presented</u> with an award!

About you

C - **Preview and do the task** Read the instructions aloud. Ask a S to read the example sentence aloud. Have Ss complete the task. Walk around the class and help as needed.

- Say, "Share your ideas with a partner." Have pairs read their sentences to each other.

Extra activity – pairs

Pairs choose a well-known figure from any field and write a brief article about his / her life. Pairs read their article to another pair.

Speaking naturally

- Tell Ss to turn to Speaking naturally on p. 143. (For more information, see Language notes at the beginning of this unit. See the teaching notes on p. T-143.)

2 Grammar Information focus

Figure it out

A Which of the two options in each sentence is the idea that is expressed in the article? What's the difference in meaning between the two options? Then read the grammar chart.

1. It's his work for the FBI that Abagnale would rather **remember / be remembered for**.
2. He has a notorious past, which he never expected **to be turned / to turn** into a movie.
3. Many of the events appear **to be exaggerated / to have been exaggerated**.
4. He regrets **drawing others / being drawn** into illegal activities.

Passive verb complements ⬇

Grammar extra See page 165.

Base forms, infinitives, and *-ing* forms can have passive forms after some verbs and expressions.

Base form	*He'd rather **be remembered** for his work with the FBI.* (= i.e., that others remember him.)
	*He'd rather **remember** his work with the FBI.* (= He prefers to remember it himself.)
Infinitives	*Abagnale deserves **to be admired**.* (= Other people should admire him.)
	*A 12-year prison term appears **to have been considered** harsh even then.*
-ing form	*He avoided **being apprehended** for several years.*

Use base forms after *had better, would rather*, and modal verbs.
Use infinitives after *appear, claim, deserve, expect, love, etc., seem, want, 'd like*.
Use *-ing* forms after *avoid, be worth, enjoy, love, etc., mind, recall, remember, regret*.

B Complete what these people say about a movie of their lives. Use passive verb complements of the verbs given. Sometimes there is more than one correct answer.

If they made a movie of my life, . . .

1. I'd rather _____ (play) by Chris Rock than anyone else. I want _____ (remember) for my humor, and he's a funny guy. I wouldn't mind _____ (play) by Eddie Murphy, either.
2. One thing I'd really like _____ (know) for is being kind to people. I'd rather _____ (remember) for that than for the hours I spend at work.
3. I took my math exams three times to improve my grade. That deserves _____ (include) in a movie about me!
4. Don't show my first job – I never expected _____ (fire). I hate _____ (tell) what to do and I argued with my boss. I was right, but it wasn't worth _____ (fire) for.
5. One story about me that should never _____ (tell) is the time I stole money from my mother's purse. Fortunately, it seems _____ (forget). I'm sure she'd rather not _____ (remind) of it in the movie.
6. I've always avoided _____ (make) to do things that I don't want to do. That's one thing I'd like _____ (say) about me.
7. I'd like _____ (give) the chance to direct the movie. I might _____ (nominate) for "best director." I'd enjoy _____ (present) with an award!

About you

C Imagine a movie being made of your life. Make the sentences above true for you. Then share your ideas with a partner.

"I think one thing I'd really like to be known for is being a good friend."

Speaking naturally See page 143.

Lesson C *That's my concern.*

1 Conversation strategy Expressing concerns

A A "white lie" is often told to be tactful or polite. In what kinds of situations might someone tell a "white lie"? Would you ever call someone on telling a white lie? (= point it out)

"For example, if an older person asked me to guess their age, I might say they're younger."

B ◀))CD 4.12 Listen. What does Tania think about telling lies? How about Tom?

Tania	You know, it's interesting. A friend of mine was telling her 12-year-old son about how it's not good to tell lies, and then he caught her telling a lie.
Tom	He did not.
Tania	Oh, yeah. They were going into an amusement park, and she told them he was 11 to get the reduced rate. And her son called her on it.
Tom	Well, yeah. I mean, that doesn't seem right.
Tania	Yeah. And she's like, "It's just a white lie." I guess, to her, it was no big deal. But you know, I'm not comfortable with that. To me, it was a lie.
Tom	Yeah, very much so, but . . . did you tell her that?
Tania	No. I just laughed it off.
Tom	See, that doesn't sit quite right with me.
Tania	But what are you supposed to do? Say, "That's wrong"?
Tom	Yeah, but I mean, if you don't say anything, that's kind of a lie, too. That would be my concern, anyhow.

C Notice how Tania and Tom use expressions like these to express their concerns. Find the examples they use in the conversation.

That's not good.	*I'm not too happy about (that).*
That's my concern.	*I'm not comfortable with (that).*
That doesn't seem right.	*That doesn't sit right with me.*

D ◀))CD 4.13 Listen. Complete the conversations with the expressions you hear.

1. *A* You know what I don't like? When people realize they've done something wrong, and then they don't tell the whole story – you know, to try and hide it. _____.
   B Yeah. _____. That's kind of like lying, too, when you don't tell the whole story.

2. *A* What do you do if you find out your friend's boyfriend is cheating on her? Do you tell her?
   B No. _____. I mean, it's not your business. It's better not to get involved.
   A Yeah, but _____ – not saying something.

3. *A* So if someone asks you, "Does this look good?" and it looks awful, what would you say? I mean, you can't say it looks terrible. You'd hurt their feelings. _____.
   B Yeah, but you can still say it looks awful but in a tactful way. Like, "Your other one looks way better."

About you | **E** Pair work Discuss the conversations above. What are your views?

Right Way ← Wrong Way →

Lesson C *That's my concern.*

① Conversation strategy

Expressing concerns in conversation

In conversation, there are times when a speaker may not like or approve of either something that is said or an action that is described. The speaker can use expressions that express concern or disapproval but that are not too strong or harsh. Expressions such as, *That doesn't sit right with me* or *I'm not comfortable with that* indicate concern. An expression such as *That's not good* is more direct but still not overly harsh.

(For more information, see Language notes at the beginning of this unit.)

- **Set the scene** Books closed. Say, "Imagine you're having a conversation, and someone asks or says something that you disapprove of. Do you say anything? What do you say?" Have a short class discussion.

A • **Preview and do the task** Books open. Read the instructions aloud. Ask a S to read the example aloud. Tell Ss to close their books again. Elicit situations where Ss tell "white lies." Ask Ss if they would ever call someone on a "white lie." Ask, "In what kind of situation would you point out the white lie?" Get examples from the class.

B 🔊 CD4, Track 12

- **Preview the task** Read the instructions aloud. Tell Ss to make brief notes to answer the questions.

- **Play the recording** Ss listen only. Replay the recording. Ss listen and take notes. Have Ss compare their notes in pairs.

- **Play the recording again** Books open. Ss listen, read along, and check their answers. Check the answers with the class. [Neither Tania nor Tom are comfortable about telling lies, even white lies.]

C • **Present *Notice*** Read the information and the examples aloud.

- Say, "Read the conversation again. Find the examples." Have a S read them aloud. [*Tom:* I mean, **that doesn't seem right**. *Tania:* But you know, **I'm not comfortable with that**. *Tom:* See, **that doesn't sit quite right with me**. . . . **That would be my concern**, anyhow.]

- **Practice** Tell Ss to practice the conversation in pairs, taking turns playing each role.

D 🔊 CD4, Track 13

- **Preview the task** Read the instructions aloud. Have Ss read the three conversations before they listen.

- **Play the recording** Ss listen and write. Have Ss compare their answers with a partner. Play the recording again and have Ss check their answers. Check answers with the class.

Answers

1. *A* You know what I don't like? . . . I'm not comfortable with that.
   B Yeah. That's not good. . . .
2. *A* What do you do if . . . Do you tell her?
   B No. That doesn't seem right. . . .
   A Yeah, but that doesn't sit right with me – not saying something.
3. *A* . . . You'd hurt their feelings. That would be my concern.
   B Yeah, but you can still . . .

About you

E **Pair work**

- **Preview and do the task** Say, "Now discuss the conversations with a partner. What are your views?" As Ss discuss, walk around the class, listening for the expressions and giving help as needed.

- **Follow-up** Have several Ss share their opinions with the class.

Extra activity – pairs

Pairs choose one of the situations exemplified by the conversations in Exercise D and write a conversation similar to Tania and Tom's. Pairs present their conversation to another pair.

② Strategy plus

Using *To me*, . . .

You can use *to me* to mean "That's how it seems to me" or "that's my view." You can also use *to* + other pronouns or nouns to report another person's feeling or attitude, as in *To her / my friend, it was no big deal.*

(For more information, see Language notes at the beginning of this unit.)

🔊 CD4, Track 14

- **Present *Strategy plus*** Read aloud or play the recording of the information and examples. Ss listen and read along.
- Tell Ss to read Tania and Tom's conversation on page 120 again and find these expressions. [*Tania:* I guess, **to her**, it was no big deal. . . . **To me**, it was a lie.]

A 🔊 CD4, Track 15

- **Preview the task** Read the instructions aloud. Tell Ss to read the five responses before they listen. Check for vocabulary questions.
- **Play the recording** Audio script p. T-279 Ss listen and number the responses. Have Ss compare their answers

with a partner. Play the recording again if necessary. Check answers with the class.

Answers

2 Right. And you don't want to risk . . .
5 Maybe to them, it's a way of trying . . .
1 Yeah. To him, that's not a lie. . . .
4 Very much so. In any case, . . .
3 I agree. Saying something's nice is . . .

About you

B 🔊 CD4, Track 16
Pair work

- **Preview the task** Read the instructions aloud.
- **Play the recording** Audio script p. T-279 Pause the recording after each response long enough to give the Ss time to discuss it.
- **Follow-up** For each response, ask a few Ss whether or not they agreed and the reason for their decision.

③ Listening and strategies

A 🔊 CD4, Track 17

- **Preview and do the task** Say, "Read the start of the conversation. Can you guess the missing words?" Tell Ss to read through the conversation before they begin.
- Have Ss complete the task. Have Ss read the conversation with their guesses to a partner. Ask a few Ss to share their conversation with the class.
- Say, "Now listen and write the missing information."
- **Play the recording** Audio script pp. T-279–T-280 Ss listen and write the missing words. Replay the recording, if needed. Ss compare their answers with a partner. Check answers with the class.

Answers

A Do you think most people post . . . that are untrue?
B Not sure. I know I have. I've listed a fake birthday, and I actually use a nickname. And to me, that's OK. I'm just protecting my identity. . . .
A So have you changed other information, like, you know, your qualifications or . . . ?

B 🔊 CD4, Track 18

- **Preview the task** Read the instructions aloud. Ask a S to read the five questions aloud. Say, "First, listen only. Then listen again and write brief answers."
- **Play the recording** Audio script pp. T-279–T-280 Ss listen only. Replay the recording. Ss listen and write. Have Ss compare their answers in pairs.
- **Play the recording again** Ss listen and check their answers. Check answers with the class.

Answers

1. It's easier to lie online than in person because face-to-face, people can usually tell if you're lying, and it's harder to tell that in a text or an email.
2. People say, "I'm fine" when you ask how they are.
3. People lie about their height and what they earn and how attractive they are.
4. Men are more likely to tell white lies.
5. People don't look at you when they're speaking or they touch their nose a lot.

About you

C Pair work

- **Preview and do the task** Read the instructions aloud. Have a pair of Ss read the example conversation aloud. Have Ss complete the task.
- **Follow-up** Have pairs share interesting points with the class.

Extra activity – pairs

Write on the board:

Have you ever caught someone telling you a "white lie"? How did it make you feel? What did you do?

Have you ever been caught telling someone a "white lie"? How did you feel when you got caught? What did the person do?

Ask Ss to share their experiences in these situations with their partners.

2 Strategy plus *To me, . . .*

🔊 **CD 4.14** You can use **to me** to mean "that's how it seems to me," "that's my view."

To me, it was a lie.

You can also use **to** + other pronouns or nouns.

To her, / To my friend, it was no big deal.

A 🔊 **CD 4.15** **Listen to five people talk about white lies. Number the responses 1–5.**

☐ Right. And you don't want to risk your friendship over something so minor. To me, it's not worth it.
☐ Maybe to them, it's a way of trying to make friends, like saying, "Look, I'm worth knowing."
☐ Yeah. To him, that's not a lie. He's just telling a story, and he's getting a bit carried away.
☐ Very much so. In any case, is that really a lie? To me, it's just a case of believing in yourself.
☐ I agree. Saying something's nice is a relatively minor thing to me. Like, it doesn't hurt anyone

About you

B 🔊 **CD 4.16** *Pair work* **Listen again and discuss each response. Do you agree with the speakers?**

3 Listening and strategies Online lies

A 🔊 **CD 4.17** **Read the start of a conversation. Can you guess the missing words? Then listen and write the missing information.**

A Do you think most people post things on social network sites that are untrue?
B Not sure. I know I have. I've listed a _____, and I actually use a _____. And to me, that's OK. I'm just protecting _____. I mean, some people change things like their marital status. But that doesn't sit right with me – saying you're single when you're actually married.
A So have you ever changed other information, like, you know, your _____ or . . . ?

B 🔊 **CD 4.18** **Listen to the rest of the conversation. How do the speakers answer the questions below?**

1. Why is it easier to lie online than in person?
2. What's the biggest lie people tell face-to-face?
3. What kinds of white lies do people tell on online dating sites?
4. Are men or women more likely to tell white lies?
5. How can you tell if someone is lying in person? What do they do?

About you

C *Pair work* **Discuss the questions in Exercises A and B. What are your views? Give examples of people you know or stories you've heard.**

A I know people who have posted stuff on their profiles that's not true. But it seems silly to me.
B Well, the problem is everyone has access to that information and . . .

Lesson D *Artistic fakes*

1 Reading

A Prepare **Look at the title of the article and the photographs. Brainstorm 10 words that you might read in the article. Make a list.**

painting
forgery

B ⬇ Read for main ideas **Read the article. What techniques are used to authenticate art?**

Authenticating ART

1 When a work of art sells at auction for millions of dollars, the buyer needs to be certain of its authenticity. Establishing this is not always straightforward, and therefore it is not uncommon for forged works of art to change hands for large sums of money, earning the forger or corrupt dealer huge profits. Forgery can be a lucrative business. Museums, galleries, and private collectors all over the world have repeatedly been taken in by art forgeries despite their best efforts to authenticate the artwork, as this almost unbelievable story illustrates.

2 Several decades ago, a New York art dealer bought three watercolors, which he believed to have been painted by the famous Russian artist Marc Chagall. The fact that they were fakes may never have come to light had the dealer not met with the artist that very same day, entirely by chance. Chagall reportedly declared the paintings to be fake immediately on seeing them. The man who sold the art, and who also happened to be the forger, served several years in prison as a result of his dishonesty.

3 However, most dealers are not this fortunate, and in most cases experts are unable to rely on the word of the actual artist to determine whether a piece of artwork is authentic. In the past, it was art experts and academics who were the main sources for authentication, rather than scientific proof. Other methods of authenticating art include tracing its ownership, a laborious and often unreliable process, especially if the work is several centuries old.

4 While these methods of verifying a work of art remain important, experts also rely on a variety of other techniques, such as analyzing the handwriting of the artist's signature. More technological approaches include carbon dating the pigments in the paint or the age of a canvas. In one case of a painting whose origin was uncertain but thought to be that of Leonardo da Vinci, a high-resolution multi-spectral camera was used to identify a faint fingerprint on the canvas. The fingerprint was then matched to another on a known work of da Vinci's. Carbon dating of the canvas also matched with material of the same period – around 1500. With such techniques, the painting's authenticity seemed to have been confirmed, although there are still those who fiercely contest it.

5 More recently, experts have turned to digital-imaging techniques to examine works of art in fine detail, such as the brushstroke patterns in a painting. In one study, analysts scanned 23 genuine van Gogh works into a computer and studied the number of brushstrokes they had, their length and how steadily they had been made. Statistical models were then developed to create a unique "signature" of the work. Works of art that were known to have been forged were found to have more brushstrokes when compared to genuine works.

6 The difference in value between a forgery and a genuine piece can run into millions of dollars, so there's a lot at stake. Not only that, but anyone who appreciates art wants to see the handiwork of the original artist and not be fooled by the copycat efforts of a forger. However, experts now have a growing arsenal of forensic techniques, which may well make it harder to pass off forged works of art in the future.

Reading tip

Writers often use the first paragraph of a text to set out a problem to which the rest of the text will offer solutions.

Lesson D *Artistic fakes*

1 Reading

- **Set the scene** Books closed. Ask, "How often do you visit art museums or galleries? Have you seen any really valuable paintings? Why do you think some art sells for large amounts of money? Whose paintings are the most valuable?" Have a short class discussion.

A Prepare

- **Preview the task** Write *Artistic fakes* on the board. Ask, "What's a fake?" [something that isn't real] Say, "Look at the title of the article. What does *to authenticate* mean?" [to prove something is real, not fake] Read the instructions aloud. Say, "Here are two examples." Write *painting* and *forgery* on the board.

- **Do the task** Have Ss complete the task and then call out their words. Write them on the board (e.g., *forge, masterpiece, authenticate, expert, age, verify, paint, canvas, genuine,* and so on). Check that Ss understand the meaning of each word. If there are any questions, have the S who provided the word give a definition or an example to explain it.

B ⬇ www.cambridge.org/viewpoint/audio
Read for main ideas

- **Preview the task** Books open. Read the instructions aloud. If desired, play the downloadable recording. Ss listen and read along.

- **Do the task** Ss read the article and write their answers. Have Ss compare their list of techniques with a partner. Check answers with the class. [Some techniques used are to . . .
  ask the artist
  rely on expert and academic opinion
  trace ownership of a piece of art
  analyze the signature of the artist
  carbon date the pigment in paint or canvas
  use a camera to find fingerprints
  use digital imaging techniques to analyze brushstrokes]

- **Present *Reading tip*** Read the information aloud. Say, "After reading the first paragraph, what kind of solutions could you expect?" Elicit answers (e.g., *ways to establish authenticity, how to recognize forgeries*). Say, "It's useful to know that this is a common pattern in articles, because it helps you to predict what you will read about. Being able to predict helps you be a better reader."

Extra activity – pairs

Pairs read through the article and make a list of new vocabulary. They exchange the list with another pair, who have to find and explain the meanings.

C Read for detail

- **Preview and do the task** Read the instructions aloud. Tell Ss to read the questions; check that they understand them. Say, "Find the answers in the article and write brief notes. Note the paragraph where you found your answer." Have Ss do the task and compare answers.
- Check answers with the class.

Answers

1. Forged works of art change hands for large sums of money. (para. 1)
2. The dealer met the artist by chance on the same day. (para. 2)
3. Experts and academics were the main sources for authentication, rather than scientific proof. (para. 3)
4. The forged ones have more brushstrokes. (para. 5)
5. Because the difference in value between a fake and a genuine piece is very great, and people prefer to see a genuine piece of art. (para. 6)

D Read for inference

- **Preview and do the task** Read the instructions aloud. Ask Ss to read all of the questions before they begin. Check that Ss understand all the questions. Have Ss complete the tas k and compare answers with a partner.
- Check answers with the class.

Answers

1. NG; 2. NG; 3. F; 4. T; 5. F; 6. NG

② Focus on vocabulary

A
- **Preview the task** Say, "This exercise focuses on guessing words in context instead of using a dictionary all the time. You can get a general idea of a word's meaning from the sentence it's in and the surrounding sentences."
- **Present *Tip*** Say, "Developing this skill will help you read faster and more efficiently."
- **Do the task** Read the instructions aloud. Have Ss complete the task and compare their answers.

Answers

1. *lucrative*: profitable
2. *taken in*: fooled
3. *come to light*: be made known
4. *tracing*: making a connection to
5. *laborious*: difficult, challenging
6. *arsenal*: a collection of tools or techniques; *forensic*: investigation of material evidence
7. *pass off*: present as if real

About you

B Pair work
- **Preview and do the task** Read the instructions aloud. Walk around the class and help as needed.
- **Follow-up** For each word, have a few Ss say what they learned about art forgery.

③ Listening

A ◀》 CD4, Track 19
- **Preview the task** Say, "A profile is a short description of someone's life or work." Read the instructions aloud.
- **Play the recording** Audio script p. T-280 Ss listen for the answer. Say, "Tell your partner the reason you heard." Check the answer with the class. [He is not an ordinary artist because he specializes in painting copies of famous original art works, such as Monet's.]

B ◀》 CD4, Track 20
- **Preview the task** Books closed. Ask, "What do you remember about John Myatt?" Have Ss call out answers (e.g., *He's a painter. He wrote a song. His wife left him. He sold a painting. He went to prison.*).
- Books open. Read the instructions aloud. Tell Ss to read the sentences before they listen.

- **Play the recording** Audio script p. T-280 Ss listen and write their answers. Have Ss compare their answers with a partner. Replay the recording so Ss can check their answers. Check answers with the class.

Answers

1. less than two	5. fake works of art
2. stranger than fiction	6. around 40,000
3. in the 1970s	7. 12 months
4. two young children	8. take up painting again

About you

C
- **Preview and do the task** Read the instructions aloud. Have a class discussion.

C Read for detail **Answer the questions about the article.**

1. What is not uncommon in the art world?
2. How was the Chagall forgery uncovered?
3. Why has authenticating art been unreliable in the past?
4. How can experts tell if a van Gogh painting is genuine?
5. Why is it important to be certain about a work of art's authenticity?

D Read for inference **Are the sentences below true (T) or false (F) or is the information not given (NG)? Write T, F, or NG.**

1. It's easy to make money from forging art. _____
2. The New York art dealer was a longtime friend of Marc Chagall. _____
3. The New York art dealer had arranged to meet Marc Chagall after he bought the paintings. _____
4. Few experts are as lucky as the New York art dealer. _____
5. Experts all agree that the da Vinci painting is authentic. _____
6. Van Gogh's signature was analyzed on 23 of his paintings. _____

② Focus on vocabulary Words in context

Tip

If you don't understand a word, look back or ahead in the text for clues to help you.

A **What do the words in bold mean? Which parts of the article help you guess their meaning? Explain your guesses to a partner.**

1. Forgery can be a **lucrative** business. (para. 1)
2. Collectors all over the world have repeatedly been **taken in** by art forgeries. (para. 1)
3. The fact that they were fakes may never have **come to light**. (para. 2)
4. . . . **tracing** the ownership of a piece of art can help to determine if it is an original work. (para. 3)
5. . . . the process can be very **laborious**. (para. 3)
6. However, experts now have a growing **arsenal** of **forensic** techniques . . . (para. 6)
7. . . . (it) may well make it harder to **pass off** forged works of art. (para. 6)

About you **B** Pair work **Take turns using the words and expressions in Exercise A to say something you have learned about the topic of art forgery.**

③ Listening *Fakes of art!*

A ◀))CD 4.19 **Listen to a radio profile of artist John Myatt. Why is he no ordinary artist?**

B ◀))CD 4.20 **Listen again. Complete the sentences in no more than four words.**

1. A collection of John Myatt's watercolors sold out in _____ months.
2. The story of John Myatt's life is a case of truth being _____.
3. Myatt co-wrote a song _____ called "Silly Games," which was a hit.
4. When his wife left, he had _____ to support.
5. Soon after, he put an ad in a magazine offering to paint _____.
6. An auction house sold one of his paintings for _____ dollars.
7. He went to prison for _____.
8. A police investigator persuaded Myatt to _____ again.

About you **C** **What do you think of Myatt's story? Should he have been given a longer sentence?**

Writing *So what if it's fake?*

In this lesson, you . . .
- report other people's views and give your own.
- use academic conjunctions and adverbs.
- avoid errors with *provided that*.

Task Write an opinion essay.

Producing or selling fake designer goods is illegal. Yet many people buy them. Is it possible to stop these illegal enterprises?

A **Look at a model** Read the extracts from six essays. Which say that selling fake goods can be stopped (Y)? Which say it can't (N)? Write Y or N. Do you agree with the arguments they make?

1. I would argue that sellers of counterfeit products are unlikely to be stopped irrespective of any efforts to do so given the demand for cheap goods. _____

2. Clearly, people are attracted to fake goods regardless of the economic consequences. Yet if the law were enforced, this industry could be shut down. _____

3. It is inevitable that this activity will continue given that there is a market for fake goods. _____

4. The law can be changed, assuming that there is enough political will to do so. _____

5. I consider buying fake goods to be a form of stealing in view of the fact that it deprives the designers of income. However, it would be naïve to think that it can be stopped. _____

6. This activity can be stopped provided that the authorities take decisive action. _____

B **Focus on language** Read the chart. Then circle the expressions used in the extracts above.

Conjunctions and adverbs in academic writing

"If": *as long as, assuming (that), provided / providing (that)* ; "But + despite this": *Yet*
*This activity can be stopped **as long as** the authorities take decisive action.*
*Counterfeiting is a serious problem. **Yet** people are attracted to cheap, fake goods.*

"Because": *considering (that), in view / light of [the fact (that)], given (that)*
*It will continue **in view of the fact / given that** there is a market for fake goods. / **given** the demand.*

"Despite": *regardless of, irrespective of, no matter (who / what / how / etc.)*
*People buy fake goods **regardless of / irrespective of / no matter** how much it hurts the economy.*
                    ***regardless of / irrespective of / no matter what** the consequences.*

C **Complete the sentences with appropriate expressions. There may be more than one answer.**

1. People buy fake goods to save money _____ how much harm they are doing to the industry.
2. _____ the time that designers put into creating their work, we should pay the full price.
3. It is illegal to buy counterfeit goods. _____ some people continue to do this.
4. People think it is acceptable to buy fake goods _____ they are for their own personal use.
5. _____ legitimate businesses lose massive profits from the sale of counterfeit products, it is imperative that the law be enforced.

D **Write and check** Write the essay in the Task above. Then check for errors.

Common errors

Don't use *provided that* to give reasons.
*Counterfeit items should not be sold **given that** this is illegal.* (NOT ~~provided that~~. . .)

Writing *So what if it's fake?*

In this lesson

- Ask a S to read the lesson aims (*In this lesson, you . . .*) aloud. Say, "When you write an essay that reports other people's views in addition to your own, you are writing an opinion essay.
- **Preview the writing** Say, "In this lesson, you will write an opinion essay." Point out the writing topic in Task and read it aloud. Explain that Ss will end the lesson by writing an essay that will practice the three aims presented in this lesson.

A Look at a model

- **Preview the task** Write on the board:

  counterfeit   *irrespective of*

  deprive   *naïve*

  Say, "Read extracts 1 and 5 and find these words. Guess the meaning of each word from its context. Check your guesses with a partner or in the dictionary." [*counterfeit*: illegal copies of a real product; *irrespective of*: despite; *deprive*: stop someone having something; *naïve*: too trusting or foolish]

- **Do the task** Say, "Now read all of the extracts. Which say that selling fake goods can be stopped? Which say it can't? Write Y or N." Have Ss complete the task and compare answers with a partner. Check answers with the class.

Answers

1. N; 2. Y; 3. N; 4. Y; 5. N; 6. Y

- Ask, "Do you agree with the arguments they make?" Have individual Ss read each extract aloud. Ask Ss to raise their hands to vote yes or no for each extract.

B ⬇ www.cambridge.org/viewpoint/audio

Focus on language

- **Present the grammar for writing chart** Read the information in the chart aloud. If desired, play the downloadable recording. Ss listen and read along.
- **Understand the grammar for writing** Say, "You saw some more formal prepositions in Unit 4. This chart shows more formal conjunctions and adverbs used in formal writing."
- Have Ss look at the first section on expressing *if*. Have Ss say the example, replacing *as long as* with the other conjunctions. Ask, "What is another word for *yet* here?" [however] Say, "You saw these more formal ways to express *because* in Unit 9 with the Conversation strategies for supporting opinions." Ask, "When do you use *that* or *the fact that*?" [when they are followed by a clause, not a noun]

- Point out the formal expressions for *despite*. Ask, "What pronouns can be used after these?" [*who, what, how, when*, etc.] Say, "Notice that *regardless* and *irrespective* are followed by *of. No matter* is not."
- Say, "Circle the expressions used in the extracts above." Have Ss complete the task. Check answers with the class.

Answers

1. irrespective of
2. Yet
3. given that
4. assuming that
5. in view of the fact that
6. provided that

- Say, "Look at the sentences in the model (Exercise A) again. Rewrite the section of the extract that follows the conjunction or adverb that you circled in Exercise B." Have Ss complete the task. For each extract, have a few Ss read their sentence aloud to the class. Alternatively, have Ss read their sentences aloud to a partner.

C
- **Preview and do the task** Read the instructions aloud. Have Ss complete the task. Check answers with the class.

Answers

1. regardless of / irrespective of / no matter
2. Considering / In view of / In light of / Given
3. Yet
4. as long as / assuming (that) / provided (that) / providing (that)
5. Considering (that) / In view of the fact (that) / In light of the fact (that) / Given (that)

D Write and check

- **Preview and do the task** Read the instructions aloud. Have Ss complete the task.
- **Present *Common errors*** Books closed. Read the information aloud.

Extra activity – class

Ss leave their essays on their desk for classmates to read. Ss go around the class reading each other's work. How many people believe it can be stopped, and how many believe it cannot?

Vocabulary notebook *Use it or lose it.*

If done for homework

Briefly present the Learning tip and the task directions. Make sure Ss understand what they need to do.

If done in class

- **Present *Learning tip*** Read the information aloud. Ask a S to read the example in the box. Ask the class for more examples of sentences containing the expression *turn into*.

A • **Preview and do the task** Read the instructions and the expressions in the box aloud. Ask Ss which expression completes sentence 1. [turned out] Have Ss complete the task. Check answers with the class. Ask individual Ss each to read sentences aloud.

Answers

1. turned out
2. turned over a new leaf
3. turn back the clock
4. turn to
5. turned down

- **Present *How do we turn?*** Say, "This box contains the top collocations with *turn*. You have 15 seconds to read and try to remember them." Say, "Go!" and give Ss 15 seconds. Ss close their books and write as many of the collocations as they can remember. Tell Ss to open their book and see how well they did.

B • **Preview and do the task** Read the instructions aloud. Ask a S to read the expressions aloud. Say, "A two-line conversation for each word is enough." Have Ss complete the task. Ss read their conversations aloud to a partner. Have a few Ss read their sentences aloud to the class.

Possible answers

1. **A** Did you enjoy college?
   B Oh, yeah. It was a turning point in my life. I met my husband there.
2. **A** So, you were offered a job in advertising?
   B Yeah, but I turned it down. I decided I wanted to do an MBA.
3. **A** So, are you going back to work after you have your baby?
   B I think so. I don't want to turn my back on my career.
4. **A** Is it difficult raising teenagers?
   B In some ways. I mean, you have to turn a blind eye to some things they do. I mean, we don't always approve of every choice they make.
5. **A** How's business?
   B Well, we were heading for bankruptcy, but I think we've turned the company around now.

Extra activity – groups

Group members write 15 *turn* expressions found in the exercises on this page on separate slips of paper. The slips are placed facedown on a table. Group members take turns picking up a slip and making a sentence with the word on their slip.

C **Word builder**

- **Preview the task** Read the instructions aloud. Have a S read the expressions aloud.
- **Do the task** Have Ss complete the task. Check answers with the class.

Possible answers

1. **A** I love my new jacket. You can turn it inside out and wear it that way, too.
   B That's awesome.
2. **A** How was your hiking trip?
   B Actually, it turned into a nightmare. I went off the trail and got lost for several hours.
3. **A** You know I lost my wallet, right? Well, I turned my apartment upside down looking for it. But I couldn't find it anywhere.
   B So, it's gone?
4. **A** Do you remember my ex-boyfriend? He turned up at my party last Friday.
   B No way.

D Focus on vocabulary, page 123

- **Preview and do the task** Read the instructions and the words in the box aloud. Have Ss complete the paragraph and compare answers with a partner. Check answers with the class.

Answers

Passing off fake goods as original designer products is a lucrative business. While some consumers may be taken in by these products, many buy the goods knowing they are fake. Tracing the criminals who make the goods is not always easy. The work is laborious and requires forensic investigations. However, as more of these products come to light, law enforcement is adding to its arsenal of tactics to deal with the problem.

Vocabulary notebook *Use it or lose it.*

Friend: Have you read The Hunger Games?
Me: No, but they turned it into a movie, and I saw that.

A Complete the conversations with the expressions from the box. You may need to change the form of the verbs.

turn back the clock	turn down	turn out	turn over a new leaf	turn to

1. *A* How was your summer?
   B Actually, it _____ great. It was a little busy, but it was fun.

2. *A* How are things going?
   B Really well. Actually, I've _____ and started going to the gym every day.

3. *A* Did you grow up around your cousins?
   B Yeah. I remember being devastated when we moved away. I wish I could _____ . They were good times.

4. *A* So, are you close to your parents?
   B Oh, yeah. They're the first people I _____ when I need help.

5. *A* You know, I didn't get into college. They _____ my application.
   B Oh, that's too bad. Well, something else is bound to come along.

How do we turn?

The top collocations with *turn* include *turn out / into / to / around / down / upside down / over / off / up, twists and turns.*

B Use the expressions below to write your own conversations.

a turning point	turn down	turn your back on
turn a blind eye to	turn something around	

C Word builder Find the meanings of these expressions. Then write a conversation using each one.

turn inside out	turn into	turn upside down	turn up somewhere

D (Focus on vocabulary) Complete the paragraph with the words in the box. Refer to Exercise 2A on page 123 to help you.

arsenal	forensic	lucrative	taken in
come to light	laborious	passing off	tracing

_____ fake goods as original designer products is a _____ business. While some consumers may be _____ by these products, many buy the goods knowing they are fake. _____ the criminals who make the goods is not always easy. The work is _____ and requires _____ investigations. However, as more of these products _____ , law enforcement is adding to its _____ of tactics to deal with the problem.

Unit 12 Psychology

Lesson A *Being independent*

Grammar *Describing complex situations and events*

(See Student's Book p. 127.)

In this lesson, Ss learn to use objects + *-ing* forms after prepositions and verbs. The forms are presented here in the context of an article on becoming independent.

Form

You can put a noun or pronoun between a preposition and an *-ing* form or between some verbs and an *-ing* form. The noun or pronoun is the object of the preposition or verb and the subject of the *-ing* form.

- Verb + preposition + noun / pronoun + *-ing* form

  They always **insisted on us** making our own decisions.

- Adjective + preposition + noun / pronoun + *-ing* form

  There's nothing **wrong with children** relying on their parents.

- Noun + preposition + noun / pronoun + *-ing* form

  They were big **believers in children** being responsible for themselves.

- Verb + noun / pronoun + *-ing* form

  Examples of verbs are *love, hate, not mind, recall, remember, like, dread, imagine, envisage,* and *resent.*

  I **remember us** setting off on a trip.
  My mom and dad **dreaded me** leaving.

> ### Corpus information
> #### Writing vs. Conversation
> In formal writing and speaking, possessive determiners are often used before the *-ing* form. These are considered more correct, especially in formal writing.
>
> They always insisted on **our** making our own decisions.

Grammar extra *Common verbs, adjectives, and nouns + object + -ing*

(See Student's Book p. 166.)

Grammar extra provides more practice with object + *-ing* patterns.

Lesson B *Love is blind.*

Vocabulary in context *Phrasal verbs*

(See Student's Book p. 128.)

The lesson presents phrasal verbs in the context of a podcast about relationships on the Internet.

Vocabulary notebook *Pick and choose*

(See Student's Book p. 135.)

The Learning tip tells Ss to create their own thesaurus. In writing, Ss often need to refer to the same idea more than once, so it's a good idea to learn synonyms. Ss get more practice with the vocabulary from Lesson B.

The Dictionary tip reminds Ss that some expressions, including some phrasal verbs, are too informal for writing. If a dictionary says an expression is "spoken" or "informal," it is not suitable for use in academic writing.

- **Focus on vocabulary** reviews and practices vocabulary introduced in Lesson D (p. 132).

Grammar *Referring to people and things*

(See Student's Book p. 129.)

This lesson teaches uses of reflexive pronouns and *each other / one another.*

Form

- Singular reflexive pronouns

  Singular reflexive pronouns are: *myself, yourself, himself, herself, itself,* and *oneself.*

  She hadn't written much about **herself** on her profile.

- Plural reflexive pronouns

  Plural reflexive pronouns are: *ourselves, yourselves,* and *themselves.*

  Even the smartest people can fool **themselves** into thinking they're communicating with a real person.

- *Each other / one another*

  They had been writing to **one another** for two months.

Use

Reflexive pronouns are used when the subject and object of a verb refer to the same person or thing. They are also used for emphasis: *As he **himself** put it, he'd been "had."*

You don't need reflexive pronouns with *meet* and *marry.*

Use *each other* or *one another* when the subject does something to an object and the object does the same thing to the subject.

They wrote to **each other / one another**. (= He wrote to her, and she wrote to him.)

Corpus information

Common errors with *each other* and reflexive pronouns

Ss may confuse *each other* with *themselves, ourselves,* or *yourselves.*

Helen and I looked at each other. = She looked at me, and I looked at her.

We looked at ourselves in the mirror. = I looked at my reflection. She looked at hers.

 Corpus information

In conversation

In conversation, *each other* is eight times more frequent than *one another. One another* is almost four times more frequent in academic writing than in conversation.

 Corpus information

Writing vs. Conversation

Oneself is mostly used in formal writing. It is not common in conversation.

*One might think of **oneself** as immune to such tricks.*

Grammar extra *More on reflexive pronouns; Referring to unknown people*

(See Student's Book p. 167.)

Grammar extra presents more ways to use reflexive pronouns.

Speaking naturally *Stress with reflexive pronouns*

(See Student's Book p. 143.)

In this section, Ss practice saying reflexive pronouns. Reflexive pronouns are stressed when they are used for emphasis. They are generally unstressed in other cases.

Lesson C *I can see it from both sides.*

Conversation strategy *Exploring arguments*

(See Student's Book p. 130.)

Speakers often signal that they are considering different aspects of an argument with expressions like *I can see it from both sides. By the same token* shows that the speaker is going to give different information with the same significance.

Strategy plus *To put it mildly*

(See Student's Book p. 131.)

Speakers use *to put it mildly* to show that they could say something in a stronger or more extreme way.

This helps speakers avoid sounding too harsh or judgmental. In addition to *to put it mildly,* speakers can also use the sentence *And that's putting it mildly* after something they've said. Note that *to put it mildly* is 10 times more frequent than *And that's putting it mildly.* If speakers want to be very direct, they say *to put it bluntly.*

 Corpus information

In conversation

In conversation, other expressions are *to put it simply / politely / crudely.*

Lesson D *Brain matters*

Writing *Teen drivers*

(See Student's Book p. 134.)

This lesson teaches Ss to plan and write a report on a road safety recommendation. The grammar for writing presents ways to make more complex statistical comparisons in writing.

• Expressions

With adjectives and adverbs

*Girls are **twice as likely as** boys to use a cell phone.*

*Teens are **four times more likely** to have a crash **than** adults.*

*Teens are **four times as likely** to have a crash **as** adults.*

*Boys communicate with people outside of the car **twice as often / much**.*

With nouns and pronouns

*Teen drivers have **four times more** crashes **than** adults.*

*Teen drivers have **four times as many** crashes **as** adults.*

*The cost of insurance for teens can be **five times as much as** for adults.*

 Corpus information

Common errors with *twice*

Ss often use *twice* + a comparative adjective.

*They **are twice as safe** with an adult in the car.*

(**NOT:** *They are ~~twice safer~~ . . .*)

Two times or twice?

In writing, *twice* is more than 40 times more frequent, especially in comparisons such as *twice as likely.*

 Corpus information

Writing vs. Conversation

You can use *more* or *as* in phrases like *six times more / as likely. More* is more frequent than *as.*

As is more frequent in writing than in conversation.

Psychology

In Unit 12, you . . .
- talk about independence, attraction, and the brain.
- use objects + *-ing* forms after prepositions and verbs.
- use reflexive pronouns and *each other / one another*.
- explore arguments with expressions like *at the same time*.
- use expressions like *to put it mildly* and *to put it bluntly*.

Lesson A *Being independent*

1 Grammar in context

A In what ways should young adults be independent? Tell the class.

B 🔊 CD 4.21 **Listen. What experience did each person have of becoming independent?**

BECOMING INDEPENDENT

In psychology, young people between the ages of 17 and 22 are often characterized as experiencing "early adult transition." At this age, they might leave home to attend college, get their first job, or think about starting their own family. It's a time when young people start to separate from their family attachments and become truly independent. We asked readers to tell us about their experiences of becoming independent.

"Actually, I've always been independent. My parents raised me and my brother that way. They always insisted on us making our own decisions. I guess they were big believers in children being responsible for themselves and their own choices. Like I remember us setting off on a trip one time, and it was snowing, and I wouldn't wear a coat. And I was *frozen* and sobbing. And I remember my mom saying, 'It's your own fault.' She's always hated people complaining about things that are their own fault." CHRIS, 24

"Interestingly enough, I didn't find it hard leaving home. I think actually my parents had a much harder time dealing with me becoming independent. But at the time, they encouraged me to leave without me realizing how difficult it was for them. My mom said later that she and my dad dreaded me leaving and hated the thought of them becoming 'empty nesters.' But for me, it was all just a big adventure." LARRY, 22

"I left home with little experience of being independent. I'd always depended on my parents being there and doing everything for me. Leaving home was a big shock to me. I couldn't cook, didn't know how to do laundry. I mean, there's nothing wrong with children relying on their parents. But it's a balance. I wish mine had been more supportive of me doing things by myself." PAULA, 46

About you **C** Pair work **Discuss the questions.**

1. What do you think about Chris's mother's philosophy?
2. Do you know any parents that have suffered from becoming "empty nesters"?
3. Why do you think some parents find it hard when their children leave home?
4. Do you think Paula's experience is common?
5. Whose experience is most similar to your own or is most likely to be?

Psychology

Introduce the theme of the unit Say, "There are various branches of psychology. The two main areas of study are cognitive and behavioral. Cognitive psychology studies how people perceive and remember things and solve problems, for example. Behavioral psychology is concerned with people's behavior and how behavior can be learned or changed."

Lesson A *Being independent*

① Grammar in context

- **Set the scene** Books closed. Say, "The title of this lesson is *Being independent*. What do you think 'being independent' means?" Have a short class discussion.

A • **Preview and do the task** Ask, "In what way should young adults be independent?" Elicit ideas from the class. Write the ideas on the board. (If doing the Extra Activity after Exercise 1C, do not erase the board.]

B 🔊 CD4, Track 21

- **Preview the task** Write on the board:

  transition (introduction)

  to sob (Speaker 1: Chris)

  to dread (Speaker 2: Larry)

  empty nester (Speaker 2: Larry)

  Say, "If you know the meaning of any of these, tell the class." Write the correct Ss' definitions on the board. [*transition*: a gradual change from one thing to another; *to sob*: to cry in a noisy way; *to dread*: to worry about something that hasn't happened yet; *empty nester*: a person whose children have grown up and moved out of the house] If Ss cannot define a word, tell the class to listen for it and use the context to guess.

- Read the instructions aloud. Add, "There are three speakers."

- **Play the recording** Say, "Just listen the first time you hear the recording." Replay the recording. Tell Ss to listen to the article and write brief answers. Have Ss compare their notes with a partner.

- Books open. Tell Ss to read the article and complete their answers. If desired, play the recording again while Ss read along. If any of the words on the board were not defined, tell Ss to scan the article for the word and to guess its meaning.

- Check answers with the class. [*Chris*: He's always been independent. His parents believed he and his brother should be responsible for themselves. *Larry*: He didn't find it hard leaving home. His parents had a much harder time with him becoming independent. *Paula*: Leaving home was a big shock for her. Her parents had always been there and done everything for her.]

About you

C Pair work

- **Preview and do the task** Read the instructions aloud. Ask a S to read the questions aloud. Check that Ss understand them.

- Have Ss discuss the questions. Walk around the class and help as needed. Have several pairs report to the class.

Extra activity – groups

Groups decide the appropriate age to introduce various duties and responsibilities to their children to help them become independent.

Ss use the ideas on the board from Exercise 1A and add their own ideas.

Groups report their ideas to the class.

---

② Grammar

A ⬇ www.cambridge.org/viewpoint/audio

- **Preview the task** Say, "Circle the correct options to complete the sentences. Use the interviews to help you."

- **Do the task** Have Ss complete the task and compare answers with a partner. Check answers with the class.

Answers

1. us making   2. them becoming   3. saying

- **Focus on the form** Ask, "What form do the three verbs you chose have?" [*-ing* form] Say, "Look at sentence 1. What kind of word comes before *us making*?" [preposition] Ask, "In sentence 2, what kind of word comes before *them becoming*?" [preposition] "Look at sentence 3. What kind of word comes before *my mom saying*?" [verb]

- **Focus on the use** Say, "You can use an object and an *-ing* form after prepositions and verbs."

- **Present the grammar chart** Read the information aloud. If desired, play the downloadable recording.

- Have Ss look at the example in the *verb + preposition* section of the chart. Ask, "What's the object of *insisted on*?" [us] Ask, "What's the subject of *making*?" [us]

- Have Ss look at the section for *adjective + preposition*. Ask, "What's the object of *wrong with*?" [children] Ask, "What's the subject of *relying*?" [children]

- Ask Ss to look at the example with *noun + preposition*. Ask, "In the phrase *believers in*, what's the object of *in*?" [children] Ask, "What's the subject of *being*?" [children]

- Tell Ss to look at the bottom section. Ask, "What's the object of *remember* and the subject of *setting off*?" [us] Ask, "What's the object of *dreaded* and the subject of *leaving*?" [me]

③ Listening

A 🔊 CD4, Track 22

- **Preview the task** Have Ss look at the cartoon. Write *helicopter parents* on the board. Ask if Ss can explain the term. Have Ss call out their ideas. Say, "Helicopter parents hover over their children, watching them carefully."

- Read the instructions aloud. Say, "Just listen the first time. Then we'll listen again. Write brief notes to answer the questions."

- **Play the recording** Audio script p. T-281 Ss listen. Replay the recording. Ss listen and write. Have Ss compare their notes to make more complete answers.

- **Play the recording again** Ss listen and check their answers. [Mark and his mom agree that "helicopter" parents are ridiculous and keep their children from learning how to be independent.]

B 🔊 CD4, Track 23

- **Preview the task** Read the instructions aloud. Have Ss read the three sentence stems before they listen.

- **Present *Writing vs. Conversation*** Read the information aloud. Write on the board:

  My mom and dad dreaded me leaving.

  There's nothing wrong with them relying on parents.

- Say, "Rewrite these sentences using the more formal form." Have Ss complete the task. Check answers with the class. [Change *me* to *my* and *them* to *their*.]

  (For more information, see Language notes at the beginning of the unit. For more work on object + *-ing* forms, go to Grammar extra, p. 166.)

About you

B • **Preview and do the task** Say, "Rewrite the underlined parts of the sentences in the conversations. Use an object and an *-ing* form." Do the first underlined section with the class.

- Have Ss complete the task and compare their answers with a partner. Check answers with the class.

- Say, "Now ask a partner the same questions. Give your

Answers

1. **B** . . . I remember my brother taking me . . . My parents weren't really concerned about us (or our) getting lost or falling or anything . . .
   C . . . They couldn't even deal with us (or our) going . . . I hated them (or their) fretting so much.

2. **B** Well, I'm a supporter of kids learning to . . . I didn't mind my dad telling me to . . . There's nothing wrong with kids having to . . .
   C . . . I'm a big believer in kids needing . . . I don't like the thought of them (or their) growing up too early. I don't recall my parents giving us . . . It resulted in them (or their) raising two happy, carefree kids.

own answers." Remind Ss to use object + *-ing* forms. Walk around the class and help as needed.

- **Play the recording** Audio script p. T-281 Ss listen and complete the task. Have Ss compare their answers with a partner. Replay the recording. Ss listen and check their answers. Check answers with the class.

Answers

1. . . . parents storming into class and complaining about a failed test or a bad grade.
2. . . . kids forgot their lunch money or if they'd forgotten to take in their homework.
3. . . . insists on him calling five times a day and she's always calling his professors.

About you

C Pair work

- **Preview and do the task** Read the instructions aloud. Have Ss complete the task.

- **Follow-up** Have several pairs report their opinions to the class.

2 Grammar Describing complex situations and events

Figure it out

A **Circle the correct options to complete the sentences. Then read the grammar chart.**

1. My parents always insisted on **we make / us to make / us making** our own decisions.
2. She hated the thought of **become / them becoming / them to become** empty nesters.
3. I remember my mom **say / saying / to say**, "It's your choice."

Objects + -ing forms after prepositions and verbs ⬇

Grammar extra
See page 166.

You can put a noun or pronoun between a preposition and an -ing form, or between some verbs and an -ing form. The noun or pronoun is the object of the preposition or verb and the subject of the -ing form.

verb + preposition	They always **insisted on us** making our own decisions.
adjective + preposition	There's nothing **wrong with children** relying on their parents.
noun + preposition	They were big **believers in children** being responsible for themselves.
verb (e.g., *love, hate, not mind, recall, remember*)	I **remember us** setting off on a trip. My mom and dad **dreaded me** leaving.

Writing vs. Conversation

In formal writing and speaking, possessive determiners are often used before the -ing form.
*They dreaded **my** leaving.*

About you

B **Rewrite the underlined parts of the sentences. Use an object and an –ing form. Then ask and answer the questions with a partner.**

1. *A* How independent were you when you were a kid?
   B Very. I <u>remember that my brother took</u> me off to explore the neighborhood. My parents weren't really <u>concerned about the fact that we might get lost</u> or <u>fall</u> or anything.
   C Not at all. My parents were really protective. They couldn't even <u>deal with the fact that we went away</u> for summer camp. I <u>hated the fact that they fretted</u> so much.

2. *A* Do you think it's good for young children to be independent?
   B Well, I'm a <u>supporter of the idea that kids should learn</u> to be independent at a young age. I <u>didn't mind that my dad told</u> me to get a job when I wanted a new bike. I was only 12, but I did. There's nothing <u>wrong with the idea that kids should have</u> to do things for themselves.
   C Well, I'm not so sure. I'm a <u>big believer in the idea that kids need</u> to be kids. I don't like the <u>thought that they grow up</u> too early. I don't <u>recall that my parents gave</u> us much responsibility. It resulted in <u>the fact that they raised</u> two happy, carefree kids.

3 Listening "Helicopter" parents

A ◀))CD 4.22 **Listen to the conversation between a mother and her college-age son, Mark. What do they both think of "helicopter" (i.e., overprotective) parents? Do they agree?**

I DON'T MIND MY MOM BEING CONCERNED, BUT WHY DOES SHE HAVE TO BE SO LITERAL?

B ◀))CD 4.23 **Listen again and complete the sentences.**

1. Mark remembers parents storming into class and . . .
2. Mark's mom recalls moms rushing in if kids . . .
3. Mark says his roommate's mom insists on . . .

About you

C **Pair work** **What are your views on helicopter parents? Do you know any?**

Lesson B *Love is blind.*

1 Vocabulary in context

A 🔊 CD 4.24 **Listen to the podcast. What happened to Dr. Epstein? Why is it ironic?**

Who are YOU talking to?

Robert Epstein could rightly describe himself as an expert in human relationships. One might even say a leading expert, if being a former editor of *Psychology Today* is anything to **go by**. However, he proved himself to be as vulnerable as the rest of us when it comes to matters of the heart. A cousin **talked him into** trying online dating, and he **picked out** a photo of an attractive young woman on a dating website. She hadn't written much about herself on her profile, but he liked the photo and wrote to introduce himself. She replied, revealed herself to be Russian, and though her English wasn't good, they started getting to know each other through regular email correspondence. Her letters were warm and affectionate, and he felt that they were attracted to each other. Epstein found it odd that she didn't respond to specific questions, in particular to his suggestion that they might meet. Then, after they had been writing to one another for two months, the realization dawned on him. So he wrote a nonsense message of random characters, to which she replied as usual. The reason for her evasive replies suddenly presented itself. It turned out that he had been conversing with a so-called "chatterbot" – software that interacts with humans on the Internet. As he himself put it, he'd been "had." The clues that should have **given "her" away** were all there, but he had failed to **pick up on** them.

One might think oneself immune to such tricks – that one's judgment would be better – but Epstein's story shows that even the smartest people can fool themselves into thinking they are communicating with a real person. Any one of us might **go about** finding our life partner in this way, and Epstein estimates there are thousands of chatterbots on the Web. So in case you think you could never **be taken in** by a chatterbot yourself, think again. History does repeat itself. At least it did in Dr. Epstein's case. Some time later, he was again fooled by a dating site chatterbot. Interestingly enough, instead of keeping it quiet and **putting it behind him**, Epstein used his experiences in his work, **playing down** in interviews and articles the fact that he corresponded with a chatterbot twice. (He is, after all, also an expert in human-computer interaction.)

In the end, it **comes down to** this: No matter how smart we are, we all want to be loved – and love, as they say, is blind.

About you

B **Rewrite the underlined phrases with phrasal verbs from the article. You may need to change the verb forms or word order. Which sentences do you agree with? Compare with a partner.**

1. If his profession is anything to <u>be considered</u>, this shouldn't have happened to him.
2. He shouldn't have let his cousin <u>persuade him to try</u> online dating.
3. He couldn't have known when he <u>chose</u> the photo that it was a fake.
4. The poor English in the emails should have <u>revealed</u> "her" <u>secret</u> immediately.
5. It's odd that he didn't <u>notice</u> the fact that it wasn't a real person sooner.
6. <u>It's a matter of someone</u> looking for love, and anyone can <u>be fooled</u> by a chatterbot.
7. It could happen to anyone if they know how to <u>do</u> online dating.
8. If it had happened to me, I'd try to <u>stop being upset by</u> it. Or I'd try to <u>make</u> it <u>seem less serious</u>.

Word sort

C **Make charts of phrasal verbs like this. Add other verbs you know. Compare with a partner.**

Verb = GO	Meaning	Example sentence
go by	consider, judge, take into account	If you go by his experience, . . . If his experience is anything to go by, . . .
go on	happen	He didn't understand at first what was going on.

Vocabulary notebook

See page 135.

Lesson B *Love is blind.*

1 Vocabulary in context

- **Set the scene** Books closed. Write *Love is blind* on the board. Ask if anyone in the class knows this saying. [Some people can't see the faults that the person they love might have.] Ask Ss if they agree or disagree with the statement.

A 🔊 CD4, Track 24

- **Preview the task** Ensure that Ss know what an ironic situation is. [a situation that is the opposite of what you expected] Read the instructions aloud.
- **Play the recording** Say, "Just listen the first time you hear the recording." Replay the recording. Tell Ss to listen to the article and write brief answers. Have Ss compare their notes with a partner.
- Books open. Ss listen, read along, and complete their answers. Check answers with the class. [Dr. Epstein was fooled by a chatterbot, a computer robot that mimics real human communication. It's ironic because he is an expert in human communications.]
- Check for any remaining vocabulary questions.

About you

B • **Preview and do the task** Say, "Rewrite the underlined phrases with phrasal verbs from the article. You may need to change the verb forms or word order." Do sentence 1 with the class. Ask, "What phrasal verb replaces *be considered*?" [go by] Ask, "Do you need to change the verb form or word order?" [no] "Why not?" [The verb follows *to*, so the simple form is correct.] Have Ss complete the task and compare answers with a partner. Check answers with the class.

Answers

1. If his profession is anything to <u>go by</u>, this shouldn't have happened to him.
2. He shouldn't have let his cousin <u>talk him into</u> online dating.
3. He couldn't have known when he <u>picked out</u> the photo that it was a fake.
4. The poor English in the emails should have <u>given</u> "her" <u>away</u> immediately.
5. It's odd that he didn't <u>pick up on</u> the fact that it wasn't a real person sooner.
6. It <u>comes down to</u> looking for love, and anyone can <u>be taken in</u> by a chatterbot.
7. It could happen to anyone if they know how to <u>go about</u> online dating.
8. If it had happened to me, I'd try to <u>put</u> it <u>behind me</u>. Or I'd try to <u>play</u> it <u>down</u>.

- Say, "Which sentences do you agree with? Compare with a partner. Use the phrasal verbs when you compare opinions."

Word sort

C • **Preview and do the task** Read the instructions aloud. Say, "Look at the examples of the phrasal verbs made with *go*." Ask a S to read the meanings for *go by* aloud. Ask individual Ss to complete and read aloud the example sentences. Have Ss complete the task.
- Check answers with the class. Have Ss call out their phrasal verbs and give their meanings. Write the verbs on the board. Ss add any new phrasal verbs to their own charts (e.g., *end up, take in, talk into, talk out of, see through*).

Extra activity – class / pairs

Randomly circle five of the phrasal verbs on the board. Ss write a sentence for each verb.

Ss read their sentences aloud to a partner. Ss decide if their partner's phrasal verb has been used correctly.

Tell Ss to turn to Vocabulary Notebook on p. 135 of their Student's Books. Have Ss do the tasks in class or assign them for homework. (See the teaching notes on p. T-135.)

Vocabulary notebook

2 Grammar

Figure it out

A 🔊 www.cambridge.org/viewpoint/audio

- **Preview the task** Say, "Which of the two options is the one given in the article? What would the other option mean? Circle the correct option, and write a few words to answer the second question."

- **Do the task** Have Ss complete the task and compare their answers with a partner. Check answers with the class.

Answers

1. *himself* "Introduce him" would mean that he is introducing another person to the woman.
2. *yourself* "Taken in yourselves" would mean that the writer is addressing a group of people, not just one person.
3. *themselves* "Fool one another" would mean that one set of people are trying to deceive a second set of people, and the second set are also fooling the first set of people at the same time.

- **Focus on the form** Say, "Look at sentence 1. What's the subject of the verb *wrote*?" [Epstein] "What's the object of the verb *wrote*?" [himself] "Who does *himself* refer to?" [Epstein]

- Say, "In sentence 2, what's the subject of the phrasal verb *taken in*?" [you] Ask, "In this sentence, is *you* singular or plural?" [singular] "What's the object of the phrasal verb *taken in*?" [yourself] Ask, "Is *yourself* singular or plural?" [singular]

- Say, "In sentence 3, what's the subject of the verb *fool*?" [people] Ask, "What's the object of the verb *fool*?" [themselves] "Who does *themselves* refer to?" [people]

- **Focus on the use** Say, "Pronouns that end in -*self* or -*selves* are called reflexive pronouns. Reflexive pronouns are used when the subject and object of a verb refer to the same person or thing."

- **Present the grammar chart** Read the information aloud. If desired, play the downloadable recording.

- **Understand the grammar chart** Have Ss look at the first section of the chart. Ask, "What are the singular reflexive pronouns?" [myself, yourself, himself, herself, itself, oneself] Ask, "What are the plural reflexive pronouns?" [ourselves, yourselves, themselves]

- Say, "Look at the first sentence. Who does *himself* refer to?" [the subject *he*] "In the second sentence, who does *herself* refer to?" [the subject *she*] "In the third sentence, what does *itself* refer to?" [the subject *history*] Ask Ss to look at the bottom section. "Who do *each other* and *one another* refer to?" [the subject *they*]

- Add, "You don't need reflexive pronouns for the verbs *meet* and *marry*."

- Ask Ss to look at the middle section of the chart. Say, "You can also use a reflexive pronoun to add emphasis. The reflexive pronoun must refer to the noun or pronoun it emphasizes."

- Have Ss look at the bottom section of the chart. Point out that *each other* and *one another* mean the same thing.

- **Present *Common errors*** Read the information aloud.

  (For more information, see Language notes at the beginning of the unit. For more work on reflexive pronouns, go to Grammar extra, p. 167.)

B • **Preview and do the task** Say, "Complete the conversation with appropriate pronouns." Have Ss complete the task and then compare answers with a partner.

- **Play the recording** Ss listen, read along, and check their answers.

Answers

B each other / one another, herself, himself
A themselves, each other / one another
B myself, herself, each other / one another, each other / one another, himself, yourself, itself

- Ask, "What do you think of the *Catfish* story?" Elicit opinions from the class.

Extra activity – pairs

Write these sentence stems on the board.

1. You can _____ yourself.
2. My best friend and I _____ each other every week.

Have Ss write as many verbs or verbs + prepositions as they can to complete the sentences. Elicit or give examples before you start (e.g., 1. *burn* 2. *speak to*).

---

3 Viewpoint

Group work

- **Preview the task** Read the instructions and questions aloud. Check that Ss understand the questions.

- **Present *In conversation*** Read the information aloud. Ask a S to read the example aloud.

- **Do the task** Have Ss complete the task. Walk around the class and give help as needed.

- **Follow-up** For each question, ask Ss to share their ideas with the class.

Speaking naturally

- Tell Ss to turn to Speaking naturally on p. 143. (For more information, see Language Notes at the beginning of this unit. See the teaching notes on p. T-143.)

2 Grammar Referring to people and things

Figure it out

A Which of the two options is the meaning given in the article? What would the other option mean? Then read the grammar chart.

1. Epstein wrote to the woman in the photo to introduce **himself** / **him**.
2. If you think you could never be taken in **yourself** / **yourselves**, think again.
3. People fool **one another** / **themselves** that they're communicating with a real person.

Pronouns

Grammar extra
See page 167.

Use reflexive pronouns when the subject and object of a sentence refer to the same person or thing.
*He could rightly describe **himself** as an expert in human relationships.*
*She hadn't written much about **herself** on her profile.*
*One might think **oneself** immune to such tricks, but history often repeats **itself**.*

Reflexive pronouns can also be used for emphasis.
*As he **himself** put it, he'd been "had."*

Use *each other* or *one another* when the subject does something to an object and the object does the same thing to the subject.
*They wrote to **each other** / **one another** for months.*

Common errors

Don't confuse *each other* with *themselves, ourselves, yourselves.*
*Helen and I looked at **each other**.*
= She looked at me and I looked at her.
*We looked at **ourselves** in the mirror.*
= I looked at my reflection. She looked at hers.

B Complete the conversation with appropriate pronouns.

A Have you ever been taken in by someone?

B Not that I can think of. But did you ever see that movie *Catfish*? It's about this guy and someone he met online. They wrote to _____ for months. And she'd described _____ as this young woman and sent him these songs that she said she'd written. And he kind of convinced _____ that he was really attracted to her.

A Oh, I've heard those stories, where people fall in love online and then when they meet, they find _____ in this awkward situation where they don't really like _____ at all.

B I know. See, I don't think I'd ever let _____ get into a situation like that. But anyway, he started picking up on these weird things, like that she hadn't written the songs _____. And even though they'd seen photos of _____ and spoken to _____, he realized something wasn't right. So he talked _____ into driving across the country to meet her. Anyway, I don't want to spoil the ending! You'll have to see the movie _____. I guess the story _____ isn't that unusual, but it was interesting that they were able to document it.

3 Viewpoint *It's easy to be taken in . . .*

Group work **Discuss the questions.**

- What are some ways that people get taken in by others online?
- Can you get to know someone online? Is it the same as meeting face-to-face?
- How can people protect themselves from situations like the ones in the lesson?
- Do you consider yourself an expert on relationships?
- Do you know anyone who falls in love easily?

"People get taken in by those lottery emails. I got one myself last week, as a matter of fact."

In conversation . . .

You can use *As a matter of fact* to give new or surprising information.

Speaking naturally
See page 143.

Lesson C *I can see it from both sides.*

1 Conversation strategy Exploring arguments

A Do you ever judge people by their appearance? How do you form an impression of someone?

B ◀))CD 4.25 Listen. What does Sydney think about judging people by their appearance? How about Nate?

Sydney	We were talking in class today about how much appearance matters in society.
Nate	Yeah?
Sydney	Yeah. Apparently, they say that more attractive people do better in job interviews, and they earn more. I mean, it seems unfair – to put it mildly – that the good-looking ones are more likely to get hired and promoted.
Nate	Well, I suppose if you look at it from an employer's perspective, the people who make an effort to look good are probably the ones who make more of an effort at work.
Sydney	Possibly. But at the same time, surely your skills and education are more important than how you look.
Nate	True. They always say, "Never judge a book by its cover." But equally, shouldn't we try to make ourselves look as good as we can?
Sydney	I suppose. But to put it bluntly, there's something not right about employers only hiring people that are attractive.

C **Notice** how Sydney and Nate use expressions like these to consider different aspects of an argument. Find examples in the conversation.

> **Considering different points of view:**
> *I can see it from both sides.*
> *If you look at it from someone's point of view / perspective, . . .*
>
> **Giving different information with the same significance:**
> *at the same time, by the same token, equally*

D ◀))CD 4.26 **Read Speaker A's views below. Then listen and complete the various responses. Which views, if any, do you agree with? Discuss the ideas with a partner.**

1. *A* They say you're more likely to stop and help attractive people on the street. That's awful, really.
   B Yeah, but _____ people probably don't do it deliberately. It's probably just instinct.
   C Actually, _____ , you might not feel *safe* stopping and helping a stranger.
   D I guess _____ . I think we're all probably influenced by looks in some way.

2. *A* You should always trust your first instinct about someone, don't you think?
   B Well, it depends. I mean, instincts can be right. But _____ , sometimes you need time to get to know someone new. Like, I don't like it when people think I'm unfriendly because I'm shy. _____ , I guess I prefer people who are more friendly than I am.
   C Well, _____ . Trust your instincts *and* give people the benefit of the doubt.
   D Yeah. I mean, what if you just met them on a bad day? You should either trust your instincts and hope you're right, or _____ , you can be cautious and let them prove you wrong.

Lesson C *I can see it from both sides.*

① Conversation strategy

Expressions to use for exploring arguments

Speakers use various expressions to show they are considering different aspects of an argument. By using these expressions, speakers show that they are receptive and open-minded. An expression such as *I can see it from both sides* shows that the speaker is considering different points of view. *By the same token* shows that the speaker is going to give different information with the same significance.

(For more information, see Language notes at the beginning of this unit.)

- **Set the scene** Books closed. Write *appearance* on the board. Ask, "When you want to describe someone's appearance, what do you talk about?" Elicit ideas from the class (e.g., *physical traits such as height and hair color / style, clothing preferences, how tidy / untidy a person is*).

A • **Preview and do the task** Read the instructions aloud. Say, "For example, would you assume that a tidy person does tidy work? Is a tidy person more likely to be honest?" Have Ss call out their opinions.

B 🔊 CD4, Track 25

- **Preview the task** Write *perspective* on the board. Ask Ss to call out a definition. [the way you think about something]
- Read the instructions aloud. Tell Ss to make brief notes to answer the questions. Say, "Sydney is the first speaker."
- **Play the recording** Ss listen only. Replay the recording. Ss listen and take notes. Have Ss compare their notes in pairs.
- **Play the recording again** Books open. Ss listen, read along, and check their answers. Check the answers with the class. [Sydney thinks it's bad to judge people by their appearance. She thinks it's unfair that good-looking people are more likely to get the best jobs. She thinks skills and personality are more important than looks. Nate sees it both ways. He thinks people who take care of their appearance probably pay more attention to their work. He thinks people should take care of their appearance.]

C • **Present *Notice*** Read the information and the examples aloud.

- Say, "Read the conversation again. Find the examples." Have a S read them aloud. [*Nate*: Well, I suppose if you look at it from an employer's perspective, . . . *Sydney*: But at the same time, surely your skills and education . . . *Nate*: But, equally, shouldn't we try to make ourselves . . . ?]
- **Practice** Tell Ss to practice the conversation in pairs, taking turns playing each role.

D 🔊 CD4, Track 26

- **Preview the task** Say, "Read Speaker A's views below. Then listen and complete the various responses."
- **Play the recording** Ss listen and write. Replay the recording as needed. Have Ss compare their answers with a partner. Play the recording again and have Ss check their answers. Check answers with the class.

Answers

1. **A** They say you're more likely to stop and help attractive people on the street. That's awful, really.
   B at the same time
   C if you look at it from a passerby's point of view,
   D I can see it from both sides

2. **A** You should always trust your first instinct about someone, don't you think?
   B equally; By the same token
   C I can see it from both sides
   D equally

- Say, "Which views, if any, do you agree with? Discuss the ideas with a partner." Have Ss discuss the views. Walk around the class and help as needed.
- **Follow-up** Have several Ss share their opinions with the class.

Extra activity – pairs

Write on the board:

Personality is more important than job skills when you hire someone.

Ss write a conversation similar to Sydney and Nate's discussing the topic on the board. Pairs present their conversation to another pair. Remind Ss to use expressions to consider different sides of an argument.

② Strategy plus

Why use *to put it mildly?*

Speakers use *to put it mildly* to show that they could say something in a stronger or more extreme way. This helps speakers avoid sounding too harsh or judgmental. On the other hand, if speakers want to be very direct, they can use the expression *to put it bluntly*.

(For more information, see Language notes at the beginning of this unit.)

◀)) CD4, Track 27

- **Present *Strategy plus*** Read aloud or play the recording of the information and examples. Ss listen and read along. Add, "You can also use the sentence *And that's putting it mildly* after something you've said. When you use *to put it bluntly*, you are speaking in a very direct way. It tells the listener that you feel very strongly about the issue."

- Tell Ss to read Sydney and Nate's conversation on page 130 again and find these expressions. [*Sydney*: I mean, it seems unfair – to put it mildly – that the good-looking ones . . . But to put it bluntly, there's something not right . . .]

③ Strategies

A ◀)) CD4, Track 28

- **Preview the task** Say, "Read the information and circle the best expressions in the people's reactions." Check that Ss understand what it means to stereotype a person. [to have a fixed idea about what someone is like based on age, appearance, or ethnicity instead of actually knowing the person] Tell Ss to read through the conversation before they begin.

- Have Ss complete the task.

- **Play the recording** Ss listen and check their answers. Check answers with the class.

Answers

1. *Mindy*   That seems ridiculous, <u>to put it mildly</u>. . . .
   Leo   Actually, people probably react to names all the time. I mean, <u>to put it bluntly</u>, they might draw conclusions, . . .
   Harriet Well, <u>I can see it from both sides</u>. . . .

2. *Yvette*   That's not fair. I mean, older people have a wealth of experience to contribute. <u>At the same time</u>, it's true they might not . . .
   Grant   Well, <u>if you look at it from an employer's perspective</u>, I think it's justified . . . <u>To put it simply</u>, they're more likely to get sick.
   Susan   Well, <u>I can see it from both sides</u>: . . .

- **Present *In conversation*** Write on the board:

  a. *nicely*

  b. *in an unsophisticated way, or somewhat offensively*

  c. *without a lot of details*

  Say, "Read the information in the box. Match the expression with the meaning on the board." Have Ss call out their answer. [a. politely; b. crudely; c. simply]

About you

- **Preview and do the task** Say, "Read what people say about looks. Read sentences 1 to 5 and then read *a* to *e*." Check for vocabulary questions. Say, "Match the two sentences that go together." Have Ss complete the task and compare their answers with a partner. Check answers with the class.

Answers

1. a; 2. e; 3. b; 4. d; 5. c

- Say, "Now discuss the views with a partner. Do you agree?"

- **Follow-up** Have a short class discussion about the views.

About you

B Pair work

- **Preview and do the task** Read the instructions and the example aloud. Have Ss discuss the questions.

- **Follow-up** Have pairs share interesting points with the class.

Extra activity – pairs

Pairs write a conversation similar to Sydney and Nate's on the topic of stereotyping. Pairs read their conversation to another pair.

2 Strategy plus *To put it mildly*

◀)) CD 4.27 You can use **to put it mildly** to show that you could say something in a stronger or more extreme way.

When you want to be very direct about what you say, you can use **to put it bluntly**.

I mean, it seems unfair – **to put it mildly** – that . . .

But **to put it bluntly**, there's something not right about it.

In conversation . . .
Other expressions are *to put it simply / politely / crudely.*

About you | **Match the two parts of each comment. Write the letters a–e. Then discuss the views with a partner. Do you agree?**

1. They often say people choose a life partner who looks like them. _____
2. People are often suspicious of people who look and dress differently. _____
3. TV is responsible for our obsession with looks. _____
4. People should make an effort to look good. _____
5. Some people care too much about their appearance. _____

a. Though that seems like the last reason to marry someone, to put it mildly.
b. To put it simply, the media just creates unrealistic expectations.
c. To put it bluntly, they should be more concerned with their personality.
d. I mean, to put it bluntly, there's nothing worse than people looking like a mess.
e. Which is pretty shallow, to put it politely. I personally think it makes people interesting.

3 Strategies Stereotypes

A ◀)) CD 4.28 **Read the information. Circle the best expressions in the people's reactions. Then listen and check.**

1. *Researchers say certain names on résumés receive more callbacks than other names.*
   Mindy   That seems ridiculous, **to put it mildly / equally**. Why should a name matter?
   Leo   Actually, people probably react to names all the time. I mean, **at the same time / to put it bluntly**, they might draw conclusions, for example, about a guy with a feminine name like Lee.
   Harriet Well, **I can see it from both sides / by the same token**. Either those interviewers are stereotyping people, or maybe it's that they really don't think the person is suitable for the job.

2. *Employers often consider elderly people as less productive and are therefore less likely to employ them.*
   Yvette That's not fair. I mean, older people have a wealth of experience to contribute. **At the same time / To put it mildly**, it's true they might not be able to do physically demanding work.
   Grant   Well, **I can see it from both sides / if you look at it from an employer's perspective**, I think it's justified because, um, older people are more likely to have health issues. **To put it simply / Equally**, they're more likely to get sick.
   Susan   Well, **I can see it from both sides / to put it bluntly**: Older people may cost a company more, but they're probably reliable.

About you | **B** Pair work **Discuss the information and views in Exercise A. Do you agree? What other stereotypes do people have? Are stereotypes ever justified?**

"I have to say it seems unfair, to put it mildly, to judge someone by a name.
After all, you don't choose your name."

Lesson D *Brain matters*

1 Reading

A Prepare Which statements do you think are true? What do we know about the brain?

1. Scientists have a clear understanding of the brain.
2. The brains of men and women are different.
3. Brains don't fully develop until the age of 12.
4. Girls are better at language than boys.

B Read for main ideas Read the article. Were your guesses in Exercise A correct? How is the brain different across gender and age?

THE DEVELOPING BRAIN

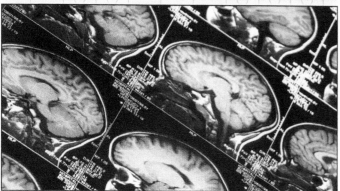

1 At the heart of psychology is understanding behavior, and understanding behavior has much to do with understanding the brain, an endeavor that has proved somewhat elusive. However, as neuroscientists become more efficient at mapping the brain, and as they gain more insight into how the brain develops and functions, scientists believe they may be closer than ever to an understanding of why we behave in the way we do. Differences in behavior as we age and between genders may well be accounted for by the physical state of and changes in our brains.

2 At the age of six, the brain is about 95 percent of its adult size. Over the coming years, it continues to thicken and develop extra connections. Around the age of 12, it is believed that the areas of the brain that are used most will strengthen in terms of neural connectivity. Cells in the brain that are not used tend to wither and die. The implications are enormous. What you do with your brain in your teen years may well determine how your brain functions for the remainder of your life. If a teen spends endless hours watching TV, the neural connections that help the brain process TV are what will strengthen. It is clear, therefore, that how young people spend their time really is of great importance.

3 Surprisingly, and contrary to earlier beliefs, the brain is still developing even in the early twenties. Areas of the brain that are related to emotion, decision making, reasoning, and problem solving are still not fully matured. This may go some way toward explaining impulsive behavior in teens and why vehicular accident rates in young people are significantly higher than those among older people. Young people just don't have the capacity, that is, the set of skills necessary, to make complex judgments while driving.

4 There are also differences in the way brains develop across gender. It appears that girls are ready to process more challenging information earlier than boys, with the area of the brain responsible for this activity peaking at the age of 14 to 16 in boys, a full two years later than girls. In addition, studies have demonstrated that girls and boys process language input in different parts of their brains. Girls typically tend to display stronger language skills than boys. Girls have more brain matter dedicated to language skills. "If there's more area dedicated to a set of skills, it follows that the skills will be more refined," says David Geary, PhD, professor of psychological sciences at the University of Missouri.

5 This kind of research raises important questions about how boys and girls should be taught in schools to maximize their learning. For example, the idea of single-sex education should perhaps be taken into consideration. Experts say that we would do well to revisit the timing of the subjects taught in school, given that some parts of the brain develop before others. Additionally, what we understand about the adolescent brain should perhaps inform public policy and the laws we make with regard to the minimum driving age.

C Read for detail Complete the sentences. Then compare with a partner.

1. Mapping the brain is important because _____.
2. How your adult brain works may largely be a result of _____.
3. In their early twenties, young people probably still don't have the skills to _____.
4. The brains of young girls and boys differ in that _____.
5. Understanding the brain may have a social impact – for example, in areas of _____.

Lesson D *Brain matters*

1 Reading

- **Set the scene** Books closed. Write *gray matter* on the board. Ask, "What is referred to as 'gray matter'?" [the brain] Say, "In the expression 'gray matter,' *matter* refers to the substance or thing. *Matter* can also refer to a subject that you need to think about or discuss."

- Write *Brain matters* on the board. Say, "This is the title of this lesson. What do you think we'll read and talk about?" Elicit ideas (e.g., *What our brains are made of, the structure of our brains, how our brains work / function, the study of the brain*).

A Prepare

- **Preview and do the task** Books open. Ask, "Which statements do you think are true?" Say, "Check (✓) the statements you think are true." Have Ss complete the task.

- Ask a S to read each statement aloud. The S finds out, using a show of hands, if the class thinks the statement is true. A second S counts and records the total numbers on the board. (Note: If using the Extra Activity after Exercise 1B, do not erase the numbers.)

- Ask, "What do we know about the brain?" Have a short class discussion. Write brief notes of the Ss' ideas on the board.

Extra activity – class

Write on the board:

endeavor (1)

elusive (1)

neuroscientist (1)

connectivity (2)

wither (2)

reasoning (3)

impulsive (3)

vehicular (3)

Call out one of the new words on the board. Ss look for the word and raise their hand when they find it. When all Ss have raised their hands, have one S read the definition aloud. Have other Ss use the word in a sentence to show its meaning.

B ⬇ www.cambridge.org/viewpoint/audio

Read for main ideas

- **Preview the task** Read the instructions aloud. If desired, play the downloadable recording. Ss listen and read along.

- **Do the task** Ss read the article. Ask, "How many of your guesses were correct?" [statements 2 and 4 are true] Ask, "How is the brain different across gender and age?" Check answers with the class. [Across gender, brains develop differently. Girls are able to process more challenging information earlier than boys, and they typically display stronger language skills than boys. Across age, young people do not have fully matured decision-making, reasoning, and problem-solving skills compared to older people. Younger people are also more impulsive.]

C Read for detail

- **Preview the task** Tell Ss to read the five sentence stems. Read the instructions aloud.

- **Do the task** Have Ss complete the task and compare their answers with a partner. Check the answers with the class.

Answers

1. Mapping the brain is important because <u>it gives insight into how the brain develops and functions</u>. (para. 1)
2. How your adult brain works may largely be a result of <u>what you did with your brain in your teen years</u>. (para. 2)
3. In their early twenties, young people probably still don't have the skills to <u>make decisions, reason, and solve problems</u>. (para. 3)
4. The brains of young girls and boys differ in that <u>girls are ready to process more challenging information earlier than boys, and girls tend to display stronger language skills than boys</u>. (para. 4)
5. Understanding the brain may have a social impact – for example, in areas of <u>education and public policy</u>. (para. 5)

D Paraphrase

- **Preview the and do the task** Read the instructions aloud. Ask a S to read the five sentences aloud. Have Ss complete the task and compare their answers with a partner.
- Check answers with the class.

Answers

1. Over the coming years, it continues to thicken and develop extra connections. (para. 2)
2. What you do with your brain in your teen years may well determine how your brain functions for the remainder of your life. (para. 2)
3. Surprisingly, and contrary to earlier beliefs, the brain is still developing even in the early twenties. (para. 3)
4. There are also differences in the way brains develop across gender. (para. 4)
5. For example, the idea of single-sex education should perhaps be taken into consideration. (para. 5)

2 Focus on vocabulary

A • **Preview the task** Say, "This exercise focuses on expressions with *be, do, go, have,* and *take*. Scan the article on p. 132 to find the expressions in the box below. Use the context to decide what they mean. Then rewrite the questions using the expressions. Change the forms of the verbs if necessary."

- **Do the task** Have Ss complete the task and compare their answers with a partner. Check answers with the class.

Answers

1. has to do with	4. take into consideration
2. is at the heart of; are close to	5. is of great importance
3. would do well to	6. goes some way toward

About you

B Pair work

- **Preview and do the task** Read the instructions aloud. Walk around the class and give help as needed.
- **Follow-up** For each question, have a few Ss share their answers with the class.

3 Listening

A ◀))) CD4, Track 29

- **Preview the task** Read the instructions aloud. Have Ss read through the answer choices. Check that they understand what each choice means. Say, "You will hear the following in the lecture." Write on the board:

  circuitry (of the brain)

  obesity

  optimal

  Ask the class if anyone can provide definitions. If yes, write the definitions on the board. Provide any definitions the class doesn't know. [*circuitry*: the connections in the brain that are considered as a single system; *obesity*: being extremely overweight; *optimal*: best or most likely to bring success]

- **Play the recording** Audio script p. T-281 Ss listen and circle a, b, or c. Have Ss compare their answers with a partner.
- **Play the recording again** Ss listen and check their answers. Check answers with the class.

Answers

1. b; 2. c; 3. a; 4. a

B ◀))) CD4, Track 30

- **Preview the task** Read the instructions aloud.
- **Play the recording** Audio script p. T-281 Ss listen and make notes. Pause the recording after each lecture to give Ss time to write. Have Ss compare their notes for each lecture. Replay the recording if necessary.
- **Play the recording again** Ss listen and check their answers. Check answers with the class.

Answers

1. It is certain to affect how companies train employees and promote them into senior roles.
2. We are coming closer to an understanding of how certain foods affect the brain.
3. We may be able to design programs for learning that teach subjects at the time in development when the brain is most receptive to learning.
4. It will be easier to treat the millions who suffer from addictions.

About you

C Pair work

- **Preview and do the task** Read the instructions aloud. Have Ss discuss the questions. Walk around the class and help as needed.
- **Follow-up** For each question, have several Ss give their opinions.

Extra activity – groups

Groups decide which of the areas of research from the lecture should be given the highest priority and why. Groups present their opinions to the class.

D Paraphrase Read the sentences below. Underline the sentences in the article that they paraphrase.

1. After the age of six, the brain continues to mature.
2. How you use your brain as a youngster may well impact the efficiency of your brain as an adult.
3. The brain is still not fully grown in early adulthood, which is the opposite of what was previously believed.
4. Male and female brains mature differently.
5. It is worth thinking about educating male and female students in different schools.

2 Focus on vocabulary *be, do, go, have, take*

A Find the expressions in the box below in the article on page 132. What do they mean? Rewrite the questions using the expressions. Change the forms of the verbs if necessary.

be at the heart of	be of great importance	have to do with	would do well to
be close to	go some way toward	take into consideration	

1. Do you think how we behave **relates to** how our brains are hardwired at birth?
2. What do you think **is the key to** understanding how people behave? Do you think we **are near** an understanding?
3. Do you think lawmakers **should** reconsider the legal age for driving as a result of this research?
4. What aspects of the teenage brain and behavior should schools **think about**?
5. Do you believe that understanding the teenage brain **is essential**? Why?
6. Do you feel the article **gives part of** an explanation of why teens behave differently from adults?

About you **B** Pair work Ask and answer the questions in Exercise A.

3 Listening *Understanding the brain—outcomes*

A ◀))CD 4.29 Listen to four experts lecture about brain research and how it impacts their areas of expertise. Choose the most likely profession of each speaker. Circle a, b, or c.

1. a. education consultant   b. management consultant   c. IT consultant
2. a. marketing consultant   b. chef   c. psychologist
3. a. education consultant   b. mathematician   c. management consultant
4. a. psychiatrist   b. education consultant   c. specialist in aging

B ◀))CD 4.30 Listen again. How will research impact these areas in the future according to the experts? Complete the notes using as many words as you need.

Lecture 1: What is the research certain to affect?

Lecture 2: What are we coming closer to understanding?

Lecture 3: What may we be able to design in the future?

Lecture 4: What will be easier to treat in the future?

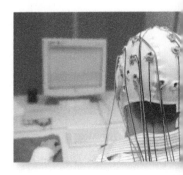

About you **C** Pair work Discuss the impact of the research in the different fields mentioned. Which field do you think would benefit most from research? In what ways?

Writing *Twice as likely*

In this lesson, you . . .
- discuss statistics.
- make statistical comparisons.
- avoid errors with *twice*.

Task | Write a report with a recommendation.

Write a report on safety issues for a social studies class, and make some recommendations for state policy. Use at least one statistic to support your argument.

A **Look at a model** **Which of the sentences do you think are true? Then read the report and check.**

a. Girls use phones more than boys while driving.

b. Girls are less likely to eat while driving than boys.

c. Boys talk to people outside the vehicle more.

d. Boys are less likely to turn around while driving.

Per mile driven, teen drivers have four times as many crashes as adult drivers.* According to research by the AAA Foundation for Traffic Safety, teen girls are . . .

- twice as likely as teen boys to use a cell phone while driving.
- nearly 50 percent more likely than males to reach for an object in the vehicle.
- nearly 25 percent more likely to eat or drink while driving.

The same report shows that teen boys . . .

- are roughly twice as likely as girls to turn around in their seats while driving.
- communicate with people outside of the vehicle twice as often.

*Centers for Disease Control

B **Focus on language** **Read the chart. Then underline the statistical comparisons in Exercise A.**

Statistical comparisons in writing

You can make comparisons with adjectives, adverbs, nouns, or pronouns.
*Girls are **twice as likely as** boys to use a cell phone.*
*Teens are **four times more likely** to have a crash **than** adults.*
    OR   **as likely** to have a crash **as** adults.
*Boys communicate with people outside of the car **twice as often / much**.*
*Teen drivers have **four times as many** crashes **as** adults.* OR ***four times more** crashes **than** adults.*
    OR   **four times the number of crashes** that adults do.
*The cost of insurance for teens can be **five times as much as** for adults.*

Writing vs. Conversation

You can use *more* or *as* in phrases like *six times more / as likely*. *More* is more frequent than *as*. *As* is more frequent in writing than in conversation.

C **Complete the sentences with the information given. Then write the report in the task above.**

1. Sixteen-year-old drivers are _____ to be in a fatal crash when there are three or more young passengers in the car _____ when they are driving alone. (four times / likely)

2. A 16-year-old is only _____ to be involved in a fatal crash with one young passenger in the car. (3% / likely) However, a 17-year-old driver is _____ be involved in a fatal crash. (66% / likely)

3. With an adult passenger over 35, teen drivers are _____ when they are alone. (twice / safe)

4. Boys turn around in their seats while driving _____ girls. (twice / times)

5. Girls use a cell phone while driving _____ boys. (twice / often)

6. If there is loud talk, teen drivers are _____ to have a serious incident. (six times / likely)

7. Insurance costs for a 16-year-old driver can be _____ for an 18-year-old. (twice / much)

D **Write and check** **Write the report in the Task above. Then check for errors.**

Common errors

Don't use *twice* + a comparative adjective.
*They are **twice as safe** with an adult.* (NOT *They are ~~twice safer~~ . . .*)

Writing *Twice as likely*

In this lesson

- Ask a S to read the lesson aims (*In this lesson, you . . .*) aloud. Say, "The report you'll write will be based on statistics on teens' bad driving habits." Ask, "What common error do you learn about in this lesson? Scan the page." [Don't use *twice* + a comparative adjective.]
- **Preview the writing** Say, "In this lesson, you will write a report with a recommendation." Point out the writing topic in Task and read it aloud. Explain that Ss will end the lesson by writing a magazine article that will reinforce the three aims presented in this lesson.

A Look at a model

- **Preview and do the task** Say, "Cover the statistics and look at the sentences in Exercise A. Which of the sentences do you think are true? Put a check (✓) beside them."
- Ask individual Ss each to each read a sentence aloud. After each sentence, Ss raise their hand if they think it is true.

Culture note:

The Centers for Disease Control and Prevention (CDC) is headquartered near Atlanta, Georgia. In addition to monitoring diseases, the CDC also conducts studies on health and safety.

- Say, "Read the report and check your answers." Check answers with the class.

Answers

a. T   b. F   c. T   d. F

B 🔽 www.cambridge.org/viewpoint/audio

Focus on language

- **Present the grammar for writing chart** Read the information in the chart aloud. If desired, play the downloadable recording. Ss listen and read along.
- **Understand the grammar for writing** Say, "The chart shows you how to make statistical comparisons in writing." Say, "You can make comparisons with adjectives. What adjective is used in the first example sentence?" [likely] Ask, "What does *twice* mean?" [two times] Say, "After *twice*, use *as* + adjective + *as* to compare two things." Say, "Read the next two examples. These are two ways to say the same thing. How are they different?" [One uses *four times more likely*; the other uses *four times as likely*.] Ask, "What word do you use after *more* + adjective to introduce the second item in the comparison?" [*than*] "How about after *as* + adjective?" [*as*] Say, "Read the first three examples again. Which one has a different word order from the other two?" [the first *as boys* comes immediately after the adjective] Say "You can put the second item after the adjective – here, it's *likely* – or after the whole adjective phrase as in *likely to have a crash*. Put it after the adjective if you have a very long phrase."
- Say, "You can also make comparisons with adverbs. What adverbs are used in the fourth example sentence?" [often, much]

- Say, "Look at the example sentence about teen drivers. A noun is used in the comparison. What noun is used?" [crashes] Ask, "What type of noun is it?" [plural, countable] Write the first sentence on the board and erase *crashes*. Ask, "If you replace the word *crashes* with the word *confidence*, what other word would you need to change, and how?" [*Many* changes to *much* because *confidence* is an uncountable noun.] "Ask, "What's another way of saying 'four times as many crashes as adults'?" [*four times more crashes than adults* or *four times the number of crashes that adults have*] Write the last sentence in the noun section on the board, and erase *crashes*. Ask, "What change would you make if you changed *crashes* to *confidence*?" [Change *the number of* to *the amount of*.]
- Say, "Look at the last sentence. Here *much* is a pronoun. What does it mean here?" [the cost]
- **Present *Writing vs. Conversation*** Read the information aloud.
- **Do the task** Read the instructions aloud. Have Ss complete the task. Check answers with the class.

Answers

Per mile driven, teen drivers have <u>four times as many crashes as</u> adult drivers. . . . teen girls are . . .
- <u>twice as likely as</u> teen boys to use a cell . . .
- nearly <u>50 percent more likely than</u> males to . . .
- nearly <u>25 percent more likely</u> to eat or drink while driving.

The same report shows that teen boys . . .
- are roughly <u>twice as likely as</u> girls to turn . . .
- communicate . . . <u>twice as often</u>.

C

- **Preview and do the task** Read the instructions aloud. Have Ss complete the task. Check answers with the class.

Answers

1. . . . are <u>four times more / as likely</u> to be . . . in the car <u>than / as</u> when they are driving alone.
2. A 16-year-old is only <u>3% more likely</u> to be . . . However, a 17-year-old driver is <u>66% more likely</u> to . . .
3. . . . , teen drivers <u>are twice as safe as</u> when . . .
4. . . . while driving <u>twice as many times as</u> girls.
5. Girls use . . . driving <u>twice as often as</u> boys.
6. . . . <u>six times more / as likely</u> to have . . .
7. . . . be <u>twice as much as</u> for an 18-year-old.

- **Present *Common errors*** Books closed. Write on the board:

  Teens are twice safer with an adult in the car.

  Ask a Ss to come to the board and correct the sentence. The correct sentence will read:

  Teens are twice as safe with an adult in the car.

D Write and check

- **Preview and do the task** Read the instructions aloud. Have Ss complete the task. Have Ss read each other's work and decide on three recommendations they think will work.

Vocabulary notebook *Pick and choose*

If done for homework

Briefly present the Learning tip and the task directions. Make sure Ss understand what they need to do.

If done in class

- **Present *Learning tip*** Read the information aloud. Say, "This will help you not to sound repetitive and will give your writing variety." Ask a S to read the example in the box.

- **Present *Dictionary tip*** Have a S read the tip aloud. Add, "Make sure that you identify informal expressions in your thesaurus."

A • **Preview and do the task** Read the instructions and the expressions in the box aloud. Tell Ss to read the sentences before they begin. Make sure they understand them. Have Ss complete the task. Check answers with the class: Ask individual Ss each to read a sentence aloud.

Answers

1. Charismatic individuals can often <u>persuade</u> other people <u>to do</u> things they don't want to do. . . .
2. . . . Their expressions do not <u>show their true feelings</u>.
3. Many people would like to find the right partner but do not know how to <u>proceed</u>. . . .
4. Also when <u>it's a matter of</u> deciding whether or not to get married, you need to be sure. . . .
5. It is important to play down your shortcomings and <u>minimize</u> your failures in job interviews.

B • **Preview and do the task** Read the instructions aloud. Have Ss complete the task and compare their answers with a partner. Check answers with the class.

Answers

1. *d.* It is not always easy to <u>notice</u> other people's moods.
2. *c.* If you only <u>take into consideration</u> looks, you may choose the wrong partner.
3. *b.* It is easy to <u>be fooled</u> by people who seem sincere.
4. *a.* You have to <u>stop being upset by</u> difficult or unpleasant experiences.

C Word builder

- **Preview and do the task** Read the instructions aloud. Ask a S to read the four sentences aloud.

- Have Ss complete the task and share meanings they found with the class. Check answers with the class: Ss call out the meaning and say whether they think it's too informal for writing.

Possible answers

1. *brush off*: ignore, disregard
2. *get to someone*: bother, irritate, annoy; *get to* is probably too informal for writing.
3. *hit it off*: get along; *hit it off* is probably too informal for writing.
4. *give in*: concede (defeat), accept you cannot win or achieve something

Extra activity – class

Ss write new sentences using the expressions in bold in Exercise B. For each expression, several Ss read their sentence aloud.

D Focus on vocabulary, page 133

- **Preview and do the task** Read the instructions aloud. Have Ss match the expressions. Check answers with the class.

Answers

1. e; 2. d; 3. a; 4. b; 5. f; 6. c

Vocabulary notebook *Pick and choose*

A   **Replace the bold expression in each essay extract to avoid the repetition. Use a word or an expression in the box, and make any other necessary changes.**

be a matter of	minimize	persuade	proceed	show their true feelings

1. Charismatic individuals can often **talk** other people **into doing** things they don't want to do. It can be difficult to resist someone who is good at talking people into things.
2. Some people are good at hiding how they feel and not giving anything away. Their expressions do not **give them away**.
3. Many people would like to find the right partner but do not know how to **go about it**. For example, they don't know how to go about finding places to meet people.
4. When it comes down to finding a partner, it is not always easy to make the best choice. Also when it **comes down to** deciding whether or not to get married, you need to be sure.
5. It is important to play down your shortcomings and **play down** your failures in job interviews.

> **Dictionary tip**
>
> Some expressions are too informal for writing. Check in a dictionary. If it says "spoken" or "informal," don't use the expression in formal writing.
>
> **hit it off**
> INFORMAL
> to like someone and become friendly immediately

B   **Match the expressions in bold with the words and expressions on the right. Write the letters a–d. Then rewrite the sentences using the alternatives.**

1. It's not always easy to **pick up on** other people's moods. _____
2. If you only **go by** looks, you may choose the wrong partner. _____
3. It's easy to **be taken in** by people who seem sincere. _____
4. You have to **put** difficult or unpleasant experiences **behind you**. _____

    a. stop being upset by
    b. be fooled
    c. take into consideration
    d. notice

C   **Word builder Find the meaning of the expressions in bold, and write a word or expression with a similar meaning. Which are too informal for writing?**

1. It may be necessary to **brush off** criticism. _____
2. Life can **get to** people sometimes. _____
3. Some people never **hit it off**. _____
4. Often it is better to **give in**. _____

D   **(Focus on vocabulary)**   **Match the expressions on the left with the ones on the right. Write the letters a–f. (See Exercise 2A on page 133 to help you.)**

1. be at the heart of _____
2. have to do with _____
3. be close to _____
4. be of (great) importance _____
5. go some way toward _____
6. would do well to _____

    a. be near
    b. be essential
    c. should, be advised to
    d. relate to
    e. be the key to
    f. help, make progress with

Checkpoint 4 *Units 10–12*

1 Change in the workplace

A Change the underlined verbs to continuous forms. Then complete the sentences with reflexive pronouns. One blank needs *each other* or *one another*.

be undergoing

Economists say that society will <u>undergo</u> some critical changes in the near future, especially in the workplace. Women seem <u>to graduate</u> in larger numbers than men, although they appear <u>not to take</u> as many graduate courses in science, business, and engineering. Women also appear <u>to have gained</u> momentum in the workplace _____ . They are said <u>to gain</u> in confidence, according to a study by N. Scott Taylor of the University of New Mexico, and now rate _____ as equal to men in terms of leadership qualities. Ask any young professional woman today if she can see _____ in a top job in 15 years from now, and she'll likely say yes. Given that employers will <u>need</u> a more highly educated workforce, it's likely that we are going <u>to see</u> more women in top jobs. What's more, an increasing number of women might well <u>earn</u> more than their spouses. A man who sees _____ as a "traditional" male partner and thinks he ought <u>to earn</u> more than his partner is more likely to feel the relationship _____ is not satisfactory. However, men with "progressive" attitudes are more likely to have high-quality relationships, where respect for _____ is more important than income.

B Pair work Discuss the information in Exercise A. Highlight the topics you talk about.

"It's interesting, more women are graduating from college. I wonder why that is?"

2 Pick out the real problem.

A Add a word to each bold expression. Then complete the sentences using the verbs given. Some need passive verbs.

1. **Q:** Would you <u>turn</u> **your back** on an old friend if she <u>were to do</u> (be to / do) something really bad? A friend of mine was recently arrested for stealing from her employer. She _____ (be to / go) to court next month. She's trying to _____ **it down**, but when it **comes** _____ to it, I don't want to **be** _____ **in** by someone who's dishonest.
   A: *If your friendship _____ , (be to /continue), then your friend should face up to what she's done. You can't **turn back the** _____ , but anyone can **turn over a new** _____ and **turn their** _____ **around**. Tell your friend how you feel. She may appreciate having someone to **turn** _____ . Then try to **put it** _____ **you**.*

2. **Q:** A friend is trying to **talk me** _____ setting up a business with her. I don't want to **turn** the offer _____ , but I'm not sure. She spends a lot of money and I don't. I know I won't be able **to turn a** _____ **eye to** that. I don't know how to _____ **about** telling her. She's beginning to **pick** _____ **on** my reluctance, though.
   A: *This is a common problem, if my inbox is **anything to** _____ **by**. It could **turn** _____ to be a success, or it could **turn** _____ a nightmare. If we _____ (be to / believe) the statistics, many new businesses fail in their first year. Therefore, you are right to be cautious. Maybe you've reached a **turning** _____ **in your lives** and friendship. Your email **gives** _____ one thing – you have different attitudes toward money. You need to talk. Otherwise, it _____ (be bound to / end) in failure.*

B Pair work Discuss the problems and solutions above. Use expressions like *to me, I can see it from both sides,* and *at the same time* to express different points of view.

Checkpoint 4 *Units 10–12*

Before you begin the Checkpoint, tell Ss to think of three language points from Units 10–12 (grammar, vocabulary, or conversation strategies) that they are unsure of. Have Ss make note of them, find them in the units, and review them.

1 Change in the workplace

↻ Exercise A recycles the continuous infinitive forms of verbs and reflexive pronouns. During the pair work discussion in Exercise B, Ss review highlighting topics by putting them at the start or end of what they say. (e.g., *My girlfriend, she watches news channels all the time.*)

A (10A Grammar; 12B Grammar)

- **Preview and do the task** Say, "Before you begin the exercise, read the paragraph." Check that the class has no questions with vocabulary or content. Say, "Change the underlined verbs to continuous forms." Point out that the first underlined verb has been done as an example. Have Ss complete the task and compare their answers with a partner.

- Say, "Then go back and complete the sentences with reflexive pronouns. Look at the first blank. What reflexive pronoun completes the sentence correctly?" [itself] Ask why. [It refers to *workplace*, which is singular and a "thing."] Have Ss complete the task and then compare answers in pairs. Check answers with the class.

Answers

Economists say that society will **be undergoing** some critical . . . Women seem **to be graduating** in larger numbers than men, although they appear **not to be taking** as many . . . Women also appear **to have been gaining** momentum in the workplace <u>itself</u>. They are said **to be gaining / to have been gaining** in confidence, . . . and now rate <u>themselves</u> as equal . . . if she can see <u>herself</u> in . . . Given that employers **will be needing** a more . . . we are going **to be seeing** more . . . women might well **be earning** more . . . A man who sees <u>himself</u> as . . . thinks he ought **to be earning** more . . . the relationship <u>itself</u> is not satisfactory. . . . where respect for <u>each other /</u> <u>one another</u> is more important than . . .

B (10C Conversation strategy)

Pair work

- **Preview and do the task** Read the instructions aloud. Ask a S to read the example aloud. Ask, "How does this example show highlighting the topic?" [The pronoun *it* is used and then it's followed by the information it refers to.] Ss work in pairs to discuss the information.

- **Follow-up** Have several pairs share one of their discussions with the class.

2 Pick out the real problem

↻ Exercise A recycles expressions with *be to*. It also recycles expressions with *turn* (e.g., *turn your back on*) and phrasal verbs. The pair work discussion gives Ss an opportunity to practice two conversation strategies: considering different sides of an argument (*I can see it from both sides / at the same time*) and using *to me*.

A (11B Vocabulary; 12B Vocabulary; 11A Grammar)

- **Preview the task** Read the instructions aloud. Tell Ss to read the conversations before they begin. Say, "Follow the instructions in the order they are written."

- **Do the task** Have Ss complete the task and compare their answers with a partner. Check answers with the class.

Answers

1.
Q: Would you <u>turn</u> **your back on** an old friend, if she <u>were</u> <u>to do</u> something really bad? . . . She <u>is to go</u> to court next month. She's trying to <u>play</u> **it down**, but when it **comes** <u>down</u> **to** it, I don't want to **be** <u>taken</u> **in** by someone who's dishonest.
A: *If your friendship* <u>is to continue</u>, *then . . . You can't* **turn** **back the** <u>clock</u>, *but anyone can* **turn over a new** <u>leaf</u> *and* **turn their** <u>life</u> **around** . . . *someone to* **turn** <u>to</u>. *Then try to* **put it** <u>behind</u> *you*.

2.
Q: A friend is trying to **talk me** <u>into</u> setting up . . . I don't want to **turn** the offer <u>down</u>, but . . . I know I won't be able **to turn a** <u>blind</u> **eye to** that. I don't know how to <u>go</u> **about** telling her. She's beginning to **pick** <u>up</u> **on** my reluctance, though.
A: . . . *my inbox* **is anything to** <u>go</u> **by**. *It could* **turn out to** *be a success, or it could* **turn into** *a nightmare. If we are to believe the statistics, . . . Maybe you've reached a* **turning** <u>point</u> **in your lives** *and friendship. Your email* **gives** <u>away</u> *one thing . . . Otherwise, it's* <u>bound to end</u> *in failure.*

B (12C Conversation Strategy; 11C Strategy plus)

Pair work

- **Preview and do the task** Read the instructions aloud. Have Ss complete the task.

- **Follow-up** Have Ss report one of the problems and solutions they discussed with the class.

3 A true story

This exercise recycles passive verb complements; the conversation strategy of highlighting topics with *this*, *these*, *that*, and *those*; and the conversation strategy of using *to put it mildly* to say something in a stronger way.

A (11B Grammar)

- **Preview the task** Read the instructions aloud. Ask Ss to read the entire article before they begin. Point out that the first answer has been done for them.
- **Do the task** Have Ss complete the task. Tell Ss to compare their answers. Check answers with the class.

Answers

Maybe every young person <u>wants to be known</u> as a hero, . . . Chesley Sullenberger probably <u>didn't expect to be called</u> a national hero . . . Passengers on Flight 1549 <u>recall being terrified</u> as . . . A flock of geese <u>appears / appeared to have been sucked</u> into the plane's engine. . . . perhaps, he <u>deserves / deserved to be admired</u>. It was an incident that many passengers no doubt <u>would rather forget</u>. . . . the industry <u>needs to remember</u>.

B (10C Strategy plus; 12C Strategy plus)

Pair work

- **Preview and do the task** Read the instructions aloud. Ask, "What other expressions do you remember?" Have Ss call out the expressions. Ask a pair of Ss to read the example aloud. Have Ss complete the task.
- Say, "After you've added the words and expressions, read your version to a partner. Listen to your partner and make a note of where your versions differ. Compare the paragraphs and decide on a final version." Have Ss complete the task. Check answers with the class.

Answers

"I'm sure <u>those</u> passengers were pleased [to put it mildly] when <u>that</u> plane landed safely. <u>Those</u> geese caused a few problems [to put it mildly]. Just think what could have happened if <u>that</u> pilot hadn't been so skilled. <u>That</u> guy must have nerves of steel [to put it mildly]. He must have analyzed the problem instantly to bring <u>that</u> aircraft down safely. Then he made sure all <u>those</u> people were safe. I read <u>this</u> story recently about <u>this</u> pilot who fell asleep, which is scary [to put it mildly], and <u>these</u> passengers woke him up."

4 In the news?

This exercise recycles objects + -*ing* forms after prepositions and verbs; collocations in news reports; the subjunctive, and comments that can be used to express concern.

A (10A Vocabulary; 12A Grammar)

- **Preview and do the task** Say, "Replace the underlined words in the reports with expressions from Unit 10, Lesson A. Have Ss complete that part of the task.
- Say, "Now complete the verb phrases to express the ideas given in brackets." Tell Ss to read the entire paragraph before they begin. Have Ss complete the task and compare answers with a partner. Check answers.

Answers

1. The failure . . . to <u>greet a delegation</u> of foreign . . . has <u>fueled speculation</u> about . . . She <u>underwent</u> surgery . . . However, . . . doctors are insisting <u>on her having</u> more surgery before they can <u>agree to her carrying out</u> her normal duties. This comes . . . political rival <u>announced his campaign</u>. Analysts . . . there is <u>a danger of the stock market being affected</u>. They say they cannot <u>rule out the possibility of the economy collapsing</u>. Stocks <u>plunged</u>.

2. A bomb <u>went off</u> near . . . A protest group has said it <u>caused the explosion</u>. If . . . it could result <u>in the government taking action</u>. Riot squads may be <u>mobilized</u>. . . . victims will be <u>compensated</u> and . . . need to be <u>contained</u>. It is . . . is already <u>filing a lawsuit / considering legal action</u> against one group.

B (10B Grammar)

- **Preview and do the task** Read the instructions aloud. Have Ss complete the task. Check answers with the class.

Answers

1. [should] <u>pass / take</u>
2. [should] <u>speak / write</u>
3. [should] <u>be</u>
4. [should] <u>stay / study</u>
5. [should] <u>be</u>

C (11C Conversation Strategy)

Pair work

- **Preview and do the task** Read the instructions aloud. Ask, "What other expressions do you remember?" (e.g., *That doesn't seem right. / That would be my concern.*) Have Ss discuss the editorial.
- **Follow-up** Have pairs share ideas with the class.

❸ A true story

A Complete the story using the verbs given. Many have passive verb complements.

Maybe every young person _wants to be known_ (want / know) as a hero, but very few people get the opportunity. As he left for work one morning, pilot Chesley Sullenberger probably _____ (not expect / call) a national hero later that day. Passengers on Flight 1549 _____ (recall / terrify) as their plane headed into the Hudson River. A flock of geese _____ (appear / suck) into the plane's engine. Sullenberger landed the plane safely on the water. He also made sure that every passenger and crew member was safely out of the plane before leaving the aircraft himself. For this above all, perhaps, he _____ (deserve / admire). It was an incident that many passengers no doubt _____ (would rather / forget). However, it is a feat that the industry _____ (need / remember) for many years to come.

B Pair work Retell this comment on the story. Use *that* and *those* to refer to ideas your partner knows and *this* and *these* to introduce or highlight ideas. Add *to put it mildly* in two more places.

those   to put it mildly

"I'm sure ~~the~~ passengers were pleased ^when the plane landed safely. The geese caused a few problems. Just think what could have happened if the pilot hadn't been so skilled. The guy must have nerves of steel. He must have analyzed the problem instantly to bring the aircraft down safely. Then he made sure all the people were safe. I read a story recently about a pilot who fell asleep, which is scary, and some passengers woke him up."

❹ In the news?

A Replace the underlined words in the reports with expressions from Unit 10, Lesson A. Then complete the verb phrases to express the ideas given in brackets [ ].

greet a delegation

1. The failure of the president to <u>meet a group</u> of foreign heads of state this week has <u>encouraged rumors</u> about the state of her health. She <u>had surgery</u> earlier this year. However, it is thought that doctors are insisting **on** _her having_ [= *insisting that she should have*] more surgery before they can **agree to** _____ [= *agree that she can carry out*] her normal duties. This comes in a week when her main political rival <u>stated he was running for office</u>. Analysts say with the political uncertainty, there is **a danger of** _____ [= *that the stock market be affected*]. They say they cannot <u>exclude the idea</u> **of** _____ [= *idea that the economy may collapse*]. Stocks <u>fell sharply</u>.

2. A bomb <u>exploded</u> near a central market in the capital early this morning. There were no injuries. A protest group has said it <u>was responsible</u>. If these protests continue, it could result **in** _____ [= *have the result that the government will take action*]. Riot squads may be <u>put on the streets</u>. A government spokesperson said that victims will be <u>paid damages</u> and that the protest movements need to be <u>controlled</u>. It is thought the government is already <u>preparing a legal case</u> against one group.

B Complete the sentences from an editorial column with an appropriate verb in the subjunctive.

1. The requirement that every student _____ an advanced English exam to graduate is a good one.
2. It is essential that everyone _____ English well.
3. Our recommendation is that English exams _____ harder.
4. Colleges should demand that any student who fails _____ in college for another year.
5. It is crucial that our country _____ better at English than neighboring countries.

C Pair work Do you agree with the editorial in Exercise B? What subjects do you think should be mandatory? Signal your concerns with expressions like *That doesn't sit right with me.*

Speaking naturally

Unit 1, Lesson C Stressing auxiliaries for emphasis

The audio for the Speaking naturally activities can be found at www.cambridge.org/viewpoint/audio 📥

A 📥 www.cambridge.org/viewpoint/audio

Preview the task Read the instructions aloud. Say, "Here is more practice of adding stressed auxiliary verbs and stressing other types of auxiliary verbs and the main verb *be*."

Play the recording Ss listen, read along, and repeat the example sentences. Ask Ss to read and repeat the example sentences again, this time without listening to the audio.

B 📥 www.cambridge.org/viewpoint/audio

Preview the task Read the instructions aloud.

Play the recording Ss listen, check their answers, and repeat.

Answers

A I <u>do</u> **know** . . . but I <u>do</u> **think** they . . .
B Well, . . . I <u>did</u> **worry** that using . . .
A . . . it <u>has</u> **been shown** that math students . . .
B And it <u>is</u> true . . .
A But I <u>have</u> **noticed** that students . . .
B Yeah, I <u>had</u> **hoped** that wouldn't happen, . . .

About you

C Pair work

Preview and do the task Read the instructions aloud. Have Ss complete the task.

Unit 2, Lesson A Stress in noun phrases

A 📥 www.cambridge.org/viewpoint/audio

Preview the task Read the instructions aloud.

Play the recording Ss listen, read along, and repeat the example noun phrases. Ask Ss to read and repeat the example phrases again, this time without listening to the audio.

B 📥 www.cambridge.org/viewpoint/audio

Preview the task Read the instructions aloud. Say, "Read all the comments before we start."

Play the recording Pause the recording after the first comment. Check Ss understand the task. Play the rest of the recording. Ss listen, underline, and circle.

Play the recording again Ss listen, check their answers, and repeat. Check the answers.

Answers

1. <u>atti</u>tudes toward (pri)vacy . . . <u>infor</u>mation once considered (pri)vate
2. <u>pro</u>ducts on the (Inter)net. . . . <u>ads</u> for similar (pro)ducts.
3. <u>pass</u>word based on my (birth)date. <u>any</u>thing (ob)vious.
4. <u>pho</u>tos posted by my (friends) . . . <u>some</u>thing to (think) about.

About you

C Pair work

Preview and do the task Read the instructions aloud. Have Ss complete the task.

While Ss do the activity, walk around the class and listen for the correct word stress. If necessary, have Ss listen to and repeat the phrases in Exercise A again.

Speaking naturally

Unit 1, Lesson C Stressing auxiliaries for emphasis

People often add the stressed auxiliary verbs *do, does, did,* or stress the full form of the auxiliary verbs with *be* or *have* (e.g., *am, was, have,* and *had*) to emphasize an idea.

*I'm not surprised John didn't come to the party, but I **am** surprised he didn't call! I mean, I **had** asked him to let me know if he couldn't come, so I really **did** think he would call me.*

A 📥 Read and listen to the information above. Repeat the example sentences.

B 📥 Read the conversation. Rewrite the phrases in bold to emphasize the speakers' ideas. Then listen, check, and repeat.

    I do know
A I **know** computers help people learn, but I **think** they often make it difficult to concentrate.
B Well, at one point I **worried** that using computers in class was a mistake, but now I don't.
A Yeah, no. I mean, **it's been shown** that math students learn algebra faster on a computer.
B And **it's true** that students often pay more attention to a good computer program. . . .
A But I**'ve noticed** that students spend a lot of time doing other things instead of studying.
B Yeah, I**'d hoped** that wouldn't happen, but there are lots of distractions on the Internet.

About you **C** Pair work **Practice the conversation. Then discuss the ideas. Which do you agree with?**

Unit 2, Lesson A Stress in noun phrases

Notice the stress in these noun phrases. The primary stress is on a word after the noun or pronoun. The main noun or pronoun gets the secondary stress.

information online   *attitudes toward privacy*   *information considered private*

people on social networks *ads requesting private information* *something to worry about*

A 📥 Read and listen to the information above. Repeat the phrases.

B 📥 Listen. In the bold phrases, underline the syllable with the secondary stress and circle the syllable with the primary stress. Then listen, check, and repeat.

1. I often feel that **attitudes toward privacy** are changing for the worse. It seems like **information once considered private** is now shared freely on social networks.
2. I ran into a problem after checking out some **products on the Internet**. On every website I went to, I got all these **ads for similar products**.
3. Someone hacked into my email, probably because I used a **password based on my birthdate**. Now when I choose passwords, I never choose **anything obvious**.
4. I have maximum privacy settings on my social networks so my boss won't see the **photos posted by my friends**. That really is **something to think about**.

About you **C** Pair work **Have you or has anyone you know had these problems? Tell your partner.**

Speaking naturally

Unit 3, Lesson C Stress in expressions of contrast

A ⬇ www.cambridge.org/viewpoint/audio

Preview the task Read the instructions aloud.

Play the recording Ss listen, read, and repeat. Ask Ss to read and repeat the example sentences again, this time without listening to the audio.

B ⬇ www.cambridge.org/viewpoint/audio

Preview the task Read the instructions aloud.

Play the recording Ss listen and circle the stressed word.

Play the recording again Ss listen, read along, check their answers, and repeat. Check each answer with the class.

Answers

1. Having (said) that, though . . .
2. But then (again). . .
3. . . . but even (then) . . .
4. But even (so), . . .
5. Having (said) that, . . .

About you

C Pair work

Preview and do the task Read the instructions aloud. Have Ss complete the task.

Speaking naturally

Unit 3, Lesson C **Stress in expressions of contrast**

Notice which words are stressed in these expressions introducing a contrasting view.

It's important to get a college degree, **but even** *then, you won't necessarily find a job.* **Having** *said* **that, though,** *your chances are better if you finish college.*

There's a lot of competition for jobs these days. **But then** *again, there always has been.* **Even** *so, the competition is probably more intense now than ever.*

A 🔊 Read and listen to the information above. Repeat the example sentences.

B 🔊 Listen. Circle the stressed word in each bold expression. Then listen, check, and repeat.

1. I think you should attend the best college that accepts you. **Having said that, though**, you need to make sure you can afford the housing and tuition costs.
2. I think it's great that people have a shorter workweek than they used to. **But then again**, many people now work two jobs in order to earn enough money to live on.
3. More people are working overtime, **but even then**, many have a hard time paying their bills.
4. I think it's good that people are getting married later, when they're more mature. **But even so**, the divorce rate doesn't seem to be going down.
5. There *is* competition for jobs. **Having said that**, there aren't enough candidates for some jobs.

About you **C** Pair work **Discuss the comments. Which views do you agree with?**

Unit 4, Lesson C **Stress in adding expressions**

Notice which words are stressed in these expressions that add information.

Overfishing decreases the fish population, **not to** *mention that many fish are killed by pollution.* **On top of** *that, fish consumption continues to increase every year.*

What's *more, no one seems interested in finding a solution to the problem.* **In** *any* **case,** *someday people will have to consume less fish, or there won't be any left to eat.*

A 🔊 Read and listen to the information above. Repeat the example sentences.

B 🔊 Listen to these conversations. Circle the stressed word in each bold expression. Then listen, check, and repeat.

1. *A* No one seems to agree on the causes of global warming. **What's more**, they don't agree on any solutions, either.
   B I suppose it's hard to identify the causes, but **in any event**, we need to do something.
   A I agree. I mean, we need to prepare for higher temperatures, **not to mention** extreme weather events like hurricanes. And **on top of that**, there's rising sea levels.
2. *A* The world uses way too much oil, and **what's more**, demand is increasing every year.
   B Yeah. **Not to mention** the fact that the supply of oil is decreasing pretty quickly.
   A And **on top of that**, people aren't trying very hard to develop different energy sources.
   B You're right. **In any case**, we'll need to do something soon. We're running out of oil.

About you **C** Pair work **Practice the conversations. Then discuss the issues. What's your view?**

Speaking naturally **139**

Unit 4, Lesson C Stress in adding expressions

A ⬇ www.cambridge.org/viewpoint/audio

Preview the task Read the instructions aloud.

Play the recording Ss listen, read along, and repeat the example words.

Ask Ss to read and repeat the example words again, this time without listening to the audio.

B ⬇ www.cambridge.org/viewpoint/audio

Preview the task Say, "Read the conversations first."

Play the recording Ss listen and circle the stressed words.

Play the recording again Ss listen, read along, check their answers, and repeat. Check each answer with the class.

Answers

1. *A* What's (more) . . .
   B . . . in (any) event, . . .
   A . . . not to (mention). . . on top of (that) . . .
2. *A* . . . what's (more), . . .
   B Not to (mention). . .
   A . . . on top of (that) . . .
   B In (any) case, . . .

About you

C Pair work

Preview and do the task Read the instructions aloud. Have Ss complete the task.

Extra activity – pairs

Pairs choose a climate-related issue and have a short discussion. Ss need to use expressions to add ideas. Partners monitor each other's stress.

Speaking naturally

Unit 5, Lesson C Stress in expressions

A 🔊 www.cambridge.org/viewpoint/audio

Preview the task Say, "This unit looks at stress in another type of conversational expression – expressions that introduce a point that contains an alternate view."

Read the instructions aloud. Remind Ss that the larger red box is above the syllable with primary stress and the smaller red box is above the syllable with secondary stress.

Play the recording Ss listen, read along, and repeat the example sentences.

B 🔊 www.cambridge.org/viewpoint/audio

Preview the task Read the instructions aloud.

Play the recording Ss listen and complete the task.

Play the recording again Ss listen, read along, check their answers, and repeat. Check each answer with the class.

Answers

1. *B* look at it (this) way:
2. *B* (one) way to look at it is; To put it an(oth)er way,
3. *B* Let me put it (this) way; Or to look at it an(oth)er way,

About you

C Pair work

Preview and do the task Read the instructions aloud. Have Ss complete the task.

Unit 6, Lesson A Prepositions in relative clauses

A 🔊 www.cambridge.org/viewpoint/audio

Preview the task Say, "Look at the examples of relative clauses with pronoun + *of*. Which word in each example receives the primary stress?" [the pronoun] "Why?" [It contains the important information.] Read the instructions aloud. Say, "When you read the sentences, be sure to give extra stress to the words in red."

Play the recording Ss listen, read along, and repeat the example sentences.

Have Ss read and repeat the sentences again, this time without listening to the audio.

B 🔊 www.cambridge.org/viewpoint/audio

Preview the task Read the instructions aloud. Tell Ss to read the sentences first.

Play the recording Ss listen and repeat.

About you

C Pair work

Preview and do the task Read the instructions aloud. For each sentence ask, "Do you agree? If so, raise your hand." Have Ss complete the task.

Speaking naturally

Unit 5, Lesson C   Stress in expressions

Notice that in these expressions, which introduce different perspectives on an issue, the primary stress is on the determiners, and the secondary stress is on the verbs.

■   ■
One **way** to **look** at it is that space exploration is a good investment.

I don't really agree. Let **me put it** this **way**: If money's limited, you need to set priorities.

■   ■
To **put it** another **way**: As long as people are hungry, we can't waste money on space.

A 🔊 Read and listen to the information above. Repeat the example sentences.

B 🔊 Listen to these conversations. In the bold expressions, circle the primary stress and underline the secondary stress. Then listen, check, and repeat.

1. *A* I think we need to cut back on government spending, including education.
   B Well, yes, but **look at it this way**: Education is the key to our children's future.
2. *A* I think we spend too much on infrastructure – you know, highways, bridges, and things.
   B Well, **one way to look at it is** investing in infrastructure creates jobs, which we need. **To put it another way**, it makes the economy grow.
3. *A* They should eliminate taxes on gasoline. Gas costs too much these days.
   B Well, I'm not too sure. **Let me put it this way**: Taxes help lower consumption. Or **to look at it another way**, if we don't tax gas, consumption rises and it'll cost more.

About you   **C** Pair work Practice the conversations. Then discuss the ideas. Who do you agree with, Speaker A or Speaker B?

Unit 6, Lesson A   Prepositions in relative clauses

Notice how the prepositions before the relative pronouns are reduced. Notice also which word has the primary stress in each phrase.

■
Online coupons bring in new customers, **some of whom** become regular customers later on.

■   ■
These coupons generate income for gyms, **many of which** have equipment that isn't used for long periods during the day.

A 🔊 Read and listen to the information above. Repeat the example sentences.

B 🔊 Listen and repeat these sentences. Pay particular attention to the weak forms of the prepositions and the stressed words in the bold expressions.

1. Online coupons don't always work for small restaurants, **most of which** have low profits.
2. The steep discounts, **some of which** attract lots of customers, often don't continue long term.
3. Restaurants get paid a low fee for their meals, **half of which** goes to the coupon website.
4. Coupons attract particular types of people, **many of whom** never return for a full-price meal.
5. Often a restaurant's regular customers, **all of whom** pay full price, get annoyed that others are getting better deals.

About you   **C** Pair work Discuss the ideas in the sentences. Which do you agree with?

140 Speaking naturally

Speaking naturally

Unit 7, Lesson B Binomial pairs

A ⬇ www.cambridge.org/viewpoint/audio

Preview the task Read the instructions aloud.

Play the recording Ss listen, read, and repeat.

Ask Ss to read and repeat the sentences again, this time without listening to the audio.

B ⬇ www.cambridge.org/viewpoint/audio

Preview the task Read the instructions aloud. Have Ss complete the task and compare their answers with a partner.

Play the recording Ss listen, check their answers, and repeat. Check each answer with the class.

Answers

B wait and see if
A slowly but surely
B ups and downs
A above and beyond, I just got sick and tired of it.
B stop and think
A time and energy!

About you

C Pair work

Preview and do the task Read the instructions aloud. Have Ss complete the task.

Speaking naturally

Unit 7, Lesson B   Binomial pairs

Notice how *and* and *but* are reduced in these binomial expressions. Notice also that the primary stress is on the second word of the pair and the secondary stress on the first.

■ ■
I'm sick and tired of getting work calls at night. When I'm home, I need peace and quiet.

■ ■
I suspect that, slowly but surely, phone calls will become an issue between me and my wife.

A ⬇ Read and listen to the information above. Repeat the example sentences.

B ⬇ Read the conversation. Circle the bold words that have the primary stress. Underline the bold words with secondary stress. Then listen, check, and repeat.

A Guess what! I just quit my job. I gave notice on Friday.
B Really? I thought you were going to **wait and see** if things got better.
A Yeah, but you know, **slowly but surely**, things were getting worse, so . . .
B Well, you and your boss certainly had your **ups and downs**.
A That's for sure. I mean, I went **above and beyond** most of the other staff, and he'd still criticize me. I just got **sick and tired** of it.
B Yeah. But did you **stop and think** what you might do? I mean, now you have no job to go to.
A Well, actually, I might do a PhD now that I have the **time and energy**!

About you **C** Pair work Practice the conversation. Then discuss the situation. Did Speaker A do the right thing? Why, or why not?

Unit 8, Lesson A   Saying perfect infinitives

Notice that in perfect infinitives, *to* is not reduced, but *have* is reduced.
My grandfather seems to have had an extremely interesting career as a journalist.
I'd like to have known him, but he died before I was born.
I'd like to have spoken to him about his experiences in war zones.

A ⬇ Read and listen to the information above. Repeat the example sentences.

B ⬇ Listen and repeat these sentences. Pay attention to the pronunciation of the perfect infinitives.

1. I'd like **to have studied** math with Einstein. He's said **to have been** a great teacher.
2. I would love **to have gone** to the moon with Neil Armstrong.
3. People seem **to have lived** much simpler lives 100 years ago – certainly less stressful.
4. My grandparents' generation seems **to have had** more time to spend with family.
5. We're supposed **to have made** great progress in how we handle conflict, but I'm not so sure.
6. People are said **to have lived** healthier lives until about 20 years ago.

About you **C** Pair work Discuss the sentences. Do you agree?

Unit 8, Lesson A Saying perfect infinitives

A ⬇ www.cambridge.org/viewpoint/audio

Preview the task Read the instructions aloud. Say, "In conversation, the reduced form of *have* sounds like the preposition *of.*"

Play the recording Ss listen, read along, and repeat the example sentences.

Have Ss read and repeat the sentences again, this time without listening to the audio.

B ⬇ www.cambridge.org/viewpoint/audio

Preview the task Read the instructions aloud. Tell Ss to read through the sentences before listening.

Play the recording Ss listen and repeat.

About you

C Pair work

Preview and do the task Read the instructions aloud. Ask, "Do you agree with the sentences. Why or why not?" Have Ss complete the task.

While Ss do the activity, walk around the class and listen for the correct pronunciation. If necessary, have Ss listen to and repeat the sentences in Exercise B again.

Extra activity – pairs

Partners each write five sentences that refer to a past time in their lives. Partners read their sentences aloud to each other.

Speaking naturally

Unit 9, Lesson C Intonation of background information

A 📥 www.cambridge.org/viewpoint/audio

Preview the task Read the instructions aloud.

Play the recording Ss listen, read, and repeat.

B 📥 www.cambridge.org/viewpoint/audio

Preview the task Read the instructions aloud. Tell Ss to read the conversation before you play the recording.

Play the recording Ss listen and circle the answers.

Play the recording again Check answers with the class.

Answers

A . . . given all the damage.
B . . . in light of rising sea levels, . . .
A . . . given the huge populations.
B . . . given how serious this is.
A . . . considering the incredible cost.
B in view of the fact that 15 of the world's 20 largest cities are in flood zones

About you

C Pair work

Preview and do the task Read the instructions aloud. Have Ss complete the task.

Unit 10, Lesson C Stress and intonation

A 📥 www.cambridge.org/viewpoint/audio

Preview the task Read the instructions aloud.

Play the recording Ss listen and read along.

Play the recording again Ss listen and repeat the example sentence.

B 📥 www.cambridge.org/viewpoint/audio

Preview the task Read the instructions aloud.

Play the recording Ss listen and circle.

Play the recording again Ss listen, check their answers, and repeat. Check answers.

Answers

1. Those shopping channels, / I never watch them. / They can be addictive.
2. This friend of mine, / he's always on his smartphone, / checking the financial news.
3. The weather channels, / now they're useful. / The weather reports / are constantly updated.
4. The cooking channels, / they're a lot of fun. / You can learn to cook / simply by watching them.
5. My mother and father, / they leave the TV on / pretty much all day / I guess they like it / when there's background noise.

About you

C Pair work

Preview and do the task Read the instructions. Have Ss complete the task.

Speaking naturally

Unit 9, Lesson C Intonation of background information

Expressions that give background information, or information you expect your listener to know, have a fall–rise intonation: *considering . . . , given (that / the fact that) . . . , in view of (the fact that) . . . , in light of (the fact that). . . .*

Space exploration is expensive. **Considering the cost**, it makes no sense at all to go to Mars.

It makes no sense at all to go to Mars, *considering the cost*.

A 📥 Read and listen to the information above. Repeat the example sentences.

B 📥 Listen to this conversation. Circle the stressed words where the fall-rise intonation starts in the underlined parts of the sentences.

A I'm getting worried about the storms we've had recently, given all the damage.
B Well, in light of rising sea levels, I think this is just the beginning. Frankly, I think it's time for people to start moving away from the coasts.
A Maybe. But what are we going to do about places like New York, Bangkok, and Rio? We can't just move entire cities, given the huge populations.
B No, but we could build sea walls for protection, given how serious this is.
A I don't think that's going to happen anytime soon, considering the incredible cost.
B But in view of the fact that 15 of the world's 20 largest cities are in flood zones, we can't ignore the problem. We have to find ways to protect the people in these cities.

About you **C** Pair work Practice the conversation. Which ideas do you agree with?

Unit 10, Lesson C Stress and intonation

Notice how longer sentences can be broken up into parts. Each part has a primary stress, where the intonation changes, and often a secondary stress as well. Notice also the fall–rise intonation for background information and falling intonation for new information.

My girlfriend, / she's always watching / those cooking shows.
[Background] [New] [New]

A 📥 Read and listen to the information above. Repeat the example sentences.

B 📥 Each phrase has two stressed syllables shown in bold. Listen and circle the syllable with the primary stress.

1. Those **shopping** channels, / I never **watch** them. / They can be ad**dic**tive.
2. This **friend** of mine, / he's always on his **smart**phone, / **check**ing the financial news.
3. The **weather** channels, / now they're **use**ful. / The **weather** reports / are constantly up**dat**ed.
4. The **cooking** channels, / they're a **lot** of fun. / You can **learn** to cook / simply by **watch**ing them.
5. My **mother** and father, / they leave the TV on / pretty **much** all day. / I **guess** they like it / when there's **back**ground noise.

About you **C** Pair work Rewrite each comment with your own information. Discuss with your partner.

142 Speaking naturally

Unit 11, Lesson B Stress in longer idioms

A www.cambridge.org/viewpoint/audio

Preview the task Read the instructions aloud. Remind Ss that the larger red box indicates the primary stress and that the smaller red box indicates the secondary stress.

Play the recording Ss listen, read along, and repeat the example sentences.

Ask Ss to read and repeat the examples again, this time without listening to the audio.

B www.cambridge.org/viewpoint/audio

Preview the task Say, "Listen. Circle the word that has the primary stress in the bold expressions."

Play the recording Ss listen and circle the answers.

Play the recording again Ss listen, check their answers, and repeat. Check the answers with the class.

Answers

1. **life**	2. **back**	3. **eye; in**
4. **leaf**	5. **clock**	6. **opportunity**

About you

C Pair work

Preview and do the task Read the instructions aloud. Have Ss complete the task.

Speaking naturally

Unit 11, Lesson B Stress in longer idioms

Phrasal verbs are usually stressed on the particle. However, in idioms that are phrasal verbs with a noun object, the object has the primary stress.

I *turned around* and looked in the mirror.

I realized that I needed to *turn my life around*.   BUT   I *turned it around*.

A Read and listen to the information above. Repeat the example sentences.

B Listen. Circle the word that has the primary stress in the bold expressions. Then listen, check, and repeat.

1. Have you ever known anyone who was in a bad situation but was able to **turn his life around**?
2. Have you ever needed to **turn your back on** friends who were doing things you didn't approve of?
3. If you knew some friends were cheating on exams, would you **turn a blind eye to** what they were doing? Or would you **turn them in** to the teacher?
4. Have you ever wanted to **turn over a new leaf** for any reason?
5. Do you ever feel you want to **turn back the clock** to a time when life was more fun?
6. Have you ever regretted **turning down an opportunity** of some kind?

About you **C** Pair work **Take turns asking and answering the questions.**

Unit 12, Lesson B Stress with reflexive pronouns

Notice how reflexive pronouns are stressed when they are used for emphasis. They are generally unstressed in other cases.

Once my parents found **themselves** in trouble because some harassing emails had been sent from their computer. They **themselves** hadn't sent the messages, of course.

I **myself** have never had a problem with my email. But once I let **myself** be tricked into giving money to a con artist on the street.

A Read and listen to the information above. Repeat the example sentences.

B Listen. Circle the stressed reflexive pronouns. Then listen, check, and repeat.

1. People allow **themselves** to taken in by the same scams again and again. If you think you'll never get taken in **yourself** think again. History repeats **itself**.
2. I wouldn't describe **myself** as terribly cautious, but I never open emails if I don't recognize the sender. I've never had a virus **myself**, but I just want to protect **myself**.
3. You have to be careful not to let **yourself** be fooled when you meet people online. They often say things about **themselves** that are simply untrue.
4. My brother got so upset with **himself** because he was spending too much time on social media, so he deleted all his accounts. It was a decision he made **himself**.

About you **C** Pair work **Read the comments aloud. What do you think of the ideas they express?**

Unit 12, Lesson B Stress with reflexive pronouns

A www.cambridge.org/viewpoint/audio

Preview the task Read the instructions aloud.

Play the recording Ss listen, read, and repeat.

Ask Ss to repeat the example sentences again without listening.

B www.cambridge.org/viewpoint/audio

Preview the task Say, "Listen. Circle the stressed reflexive pronouns. Read through the sentences before you begin." Point out that first answer has been circled as an example.

Play the recording Pause the recording after sentence 1. Check that Ss heard the heavier stress. Play the rest of the recording. Ss listen and circle.

Play the recording again Ss listen, check their answers, and repeat. Check answers.

Answers

1. yourself
2. myself
3. —
4. himself

About you

C Pair work

Preview and do the task Read the instructions aloud. Have Ss complete the task.

While Ss do the activity, walk around the class and listen for the correct word stress. If necessary, have Ss listen to and repeat the sentences in Exercise B again.

Grammar extra Unit 1, Lesson A

These activities look at using auxiliary verbs with more verb forms and *too, either, so, neither,* and *(to) do so* to avoid repetition.

1 More on auxiliary verbs to avoid repetition

If done for homework Briefly present the grammar chart. Go over the task instructions to make sure Ss understand what to do.

If done in class

Present the grammar chart Read the explanation at the top of the chart and the verb tenses and forms aloud.

Understand the grammar Tell Ss to review the example sentences in the chart. For each example, elicit the reason the auxiliary in bold was used (i.e., for the first example: *my friend does* means *my friends takes risks*). Elicit alternate

sentences. (e.g., *I didn't often take risks in college, but my friend did.*)

Preview and do the task Read the instructions aloud. Ss complete the task and then compare answers in pairs. Check answers with the class.

Answers

1. were; are
2. hasn't; are
3. had; can
4. 'm not; does
5. has; do
6. hadn't; does

2 too, either, so, neither, and (to) do so

Present the grammar chart Have Ss read the examples aloud.

Understand the grammar Ask, "What do you have to do after *so* and *neither*?" [change the order of the auxiliary and the subject] Say, "What type of verb do you use before *either*?" [negative] "How about with *neither*?" [affirmative] "Why?" [*Neither* is a negative form, so the auxiliary is affirmative.]

Ask Ss to look at the bottom section of the chart. Ask, "What does *to do so* replace?" [to give me confidence; to buy their home; to publish novels; to take a career break]

Preview and do the task Read the instructions aloud. Have Ss complete the task and compare their answers with a partner. Check answers.

Answers

1. my wife **doesn't** either / neither does my wife; **do so**
2. **to do so**; my friend **can**, too / so can my friend
3. **do so**
4. I **am**, too / so am I; **to do so**
5. **to do so**; my sisters **are**, too / so are my sisters

⊙ Corpus information

Do so is mostly used in the infinitive form, *to do so,* especially after the verbs *continue, fail, choose, want, require, refuse,* and *plan;* the nouns *opportunity, time, money, reason,* and *(be in a) position;* and adjectives *(un)able, appropriate, prepared, possible, happy,* and *free.*

Unit 1, Lesson A   Grammar extra

1 More on auxiliary verbs to avoid repetition

- You can use auxiliary verbs to avoid repetition of these verb tenses and forms.

Simple present or past	I don't often take risks, but my best friend **does** all the time.
Present or past continuous	I was hoping to graduate last year. One of my friends **was**, too.
Present perfect (or continuous)	I've been thinking about settling down, but my friends **haven't**.
Past perfect (or continuous)	I'd never had straight A's till this year, though my friends all **had**.
Modal verbs	My dad can't understand why I want to travel, but my mom **can**.

Use auxiliary and modal verbs to complete what these people say about the different topics. Use the same tense and form as the first verb.

1. *Work:* Well, I was trying to get a job in TV. Actually, I know a couple of other people who _____ , too. But I'm finding it difficult to get *any* job, as many people _____ these days.
2. *Family:* I've never really thought about starting a family, and I know my husband _____ either. I'm getting so involved in my career at the moment, as we all _____ , I guess.
3. *Relationships:* I hadn't really met anyone serious until now, though a couple of my friends _____ . I mean, I can really imagine getting married now – I just hope my girlfriend _____ !
4. *Social life:* It's funny. Some of my friends are going to parties still, but I _____ . I'm not interested. I want to do other things with my life now. I think my closest friend _____ , too.
5. *Hobbies:* I haven't had much time to do anything, but my wife _____ . She's been learning how to edit videos. I don't often use my computer now; well, I _____ a bit but not a lot.
6. *Travel:* My sister and I went to Italy last fall. I hadn't gone overseas before that, and she _____ , either. We had a fabulous time. Now I want to go away again – and my sister _____ , too.

2 too, either, so, neither, and (to) do so

- You can use auxiliaries with *too, either, so,* and *neither* to show similarity. After *so* and *neither,* change the order of the auxiliary and subject.
  I am saving for a trip, and **my best friend is, too.** OR . . . and **so is my best friend.**
  She doesn't enjoy her work, and **I don't, either.** OR . . . and **neither do I.**
  She can't afford to go away next year, and **I can't, either.** OR . . . and **neither can I.**

- Use *(to) do so* to avoid repeating a verb + object or complement.
  Learning to play sports has given me confidence and will **continue to do so** for many years.
  Many people want to buy their own home but are not in a **position to do so.**
  A lot of people want to publish novels but are **unable to do so.**
  Anyone who wishes to take a career break **can do so** if they plan it carefully.

Complete the bold phrases with an auxiliary and the sentences with *(to) do so*. Then write another way to state the bold phrases using *so* or *neither*.

1. To get ahead in your career, you often have to move to another city. I don't really want to uproot my family, and **my wife** _____ , **either,** but if necessary, we'll _____ .
2. A friend asked me to go to a debate club last year with him, and you know, I was happy _____ . And actually, I'm glad I did. I can speak much more confidently now, and **my friend** _____ , too.
3. It's easier than ever now to take a year off before college if you can _____ .
4. My friend's thinking of studying in Paris. I _____ , too, if I can get the money _____ .
5. I've always wanted to go on a cycling tour, but I've never had the time _____ . But finally my sisters and I are planning to go next spring. I'm looking forward to it, and **my sisters** _____ , too.

Grammar extra *Unit 1, Lesson B*

These activities look at more issues involved in using *to* to avoid repeating verbs phrases and *one / ones* to avoid repeating countable nouns.

① More on using *to* to avoid repeating verb phrases

Present the grammar chart Ask a S to read the information aloud.

Understand the grammar Ask Ss to look at the top section of the chart. Say, "In the example sentences, what words would complete the infinitive phrase?" [write a journal] Have Ss look at the middle section. Say, "Notice that *to* is optional after *agree, ask, promise, forget,* and *try*." Say, "Look at the bottom section. When is *be* required after *to*?" [when *be* is used in the first clause]

Preview and do the task Read the instructions aloud. Say, "The first answer has been done. Why is it correct?" [*To* follows *promise*, so it is optional.]

Ss complete the task and then compare answers in pairs. Check answers with the class.

Answers

1. promised (<u>to</u>); tried (<u>to</u>); forgot (<u>to</u>)
2. expects <u>to</u>
3. wanted <u>to</u>; intend <u>to</u>
4. deserve <u>to be</u>
5. want (<u>to</u>); mean <u>to</u>
6. hope <u>to be</u>
7. hopes <u>to</u>
8. prefer not <u>to</u>

Unit 1, Lesson B   *Grammar extra*

① More on using *to* to avoid repeating verb phrases

- You can use *to* to avoid repeating an infinitive verb phrase when it is clear what you mean. Use *to* after *choose, deserve, expect, hate, hope, like, mean, intend, need, prefer, want, 'd like.*
  I've never written a journal. I keep meaning **to**. / *But I hope* **to**. / *I'd prefer* **not to**.
- You don't need *to* after *agree, ask, promise, forget, try,* or after *want, like, wish* in *if* clauses.
  "*I want to get my novel published. I've tried* **(to)** *but can't.*" "*I'll look at it if you* **want / like / wish**."
- When you use *be* in the first clause, including in the passive, use *to be* in the second clause.
  My parents **aren't** *interested in poetry, and they've never pretended* **to be**.
  In college, I **was** *asked to enter a short-story contest, though I didn't expect* **to be**.

Complete the comments with *to* or *to be*. Write parentheses where *to* is not needed.

1. A classmate asked me to comment on her poems. Well, I promised ___(to)___ , and I really tried _____ . But they were really bad. After a month, she asked, "Did you read them?" I said, "Sorry, I forgot _____ ."
2. My friend has entered a few writing contests. She's never won, though she always expects _____ .
3. I'd love to see a Shakespeare play in English. I've always wanted _____ , and I intend _____ one day.
4. I was voted the best fiction writer in high school, though I didn't deserve _____ .
5. You can borrow my e-reader if you want _____ . I lost some books off it. I didn't mean _____ , but . . .
6. I'm just not very good at writing, and I'll never hope _____ , really. I'll stick to math!
7. My sister wants to work in publishing. Well, she hopes _____ .
8. I think I'm going to have to play the lead role in the school play, but I'd prefer not _____ .

② More on *one / ones* to avoid repeating countable nouns

- You need to use *one / ones* after *the, the only, the main, every,* and after adjectives.
  I read six plays last week – a **long one** *and five* **short ones**. *The one I liked best was the* **long one**.
- You don't need *one / ones* after *which, superlatives, this, that, either, neither, another, the other.*
  "*Can I borrow a book?*" "*Sure.* **Which (one)** *do you want? You can take* **this (one)** *or* **that (one)**."
- Don't use *one / ones* after *these, those, my, your, Dan's,* etc., *some, any, both,* or numbers.
  "***Both (books)*** *are good. They're both* **mine**." (NOT . . . *my ones.*)
- In formal English, especially writing, use *that / those* or a possessive instead of the *one / ones*.
  Keats's poems are better than **those of Byron / Byron's**.

> **Common errors**
> Notice the spelling of *ones*.
> *I love books. The* **ones** *I like best are . . .*
> (NOT . . . *once / one's I like*)

Replace the underlined words with *one / ones* if possible or make other changes to avoid repeating.

1. *A* Can I take a look at one of your magazines? I mean, these <u>magazines</u> on your desk.
   B Sure. Which <u>magazine</u> do you want to read?
   A Either <u>magazine</u>. Oh, actually, I'll take a look at that <u>magazine</u>. It's an expensive <u>magazine</u>.
   B Actually, that's the only <u>magazine</u> worth reading. It's the <u>magazine</u> I prefer, anyway. The other <u>magazine</u> doesn't have very many interesting articles.
2. *A* My literature classes are fun. Are your <u>literature classes</u>? I have three <u>literature classes</u> a week.
   B Well, Mrs. Brown's classes are the hardest <u>classes</u>. She said in her lecture last week, "My class is more demanding than Mr. Smith's <u>class</u>." And honestly, the homework is hard. I mean, listen to this: "The works of J.K. Rowling are as important as <u>the works</u> of Shakespeare. Discuss."

Grammar extra **145**

---

② More on *one / ones* to avoid repeating countable nouns

Present the grammar chart Read the information aloud.

Understand the grammar Have Ss look at the chart. For each section of the chart, elicit more examples from the class.

Present *Common errors* Ss may misspell *ones. I love books. The* **ones** *I like best are . . .* (NOT . . . *once / one's I like . . .*) Another common error is to use *one / ones* to refer to people without it being clear who is meant. [e.g., We started a book club for all the **people** interested. (not *ones*) People who read a lot are often the ones with the widest vocabulary. ✓]

Preview and do the task Read the instructions aloud. Tell Ss to read the conversation before they begin. Say, "*Work* is normally an uncountable noun, which means it can't be used with *a*, can't be plural, and you can't use *one / ones* to replace it. However, one use of *work* is countable and plural, as in 'a *work* of literature' or 'a *work* of art.' So in conversation 2, *works* is a plural countable noun." Have Ss complete the task. Check answers with the class.

Answers

1. *A* . . . I mean, these **–** on your desk.
   B Sure. Which (<u>one</u>) do . . .
   A Either <u>one</u>. . . . at that <u>one</u>. It's an expensive <u>one</u>.
   B . . . only <u>one</u> worth . . . the <u>one</u> I prefer, anyway. The other <u>one</u> . . .
2. *A* . . . Are yours **–** ? I have three **–** a week.
   B . . . hardest <u>ones</u>. . . . than Mr. Smith's **–** ." / than that of Mr. Smith **–** ." . . . important as <u>those</u> of Shakespeare. / as **–** Shakespeare's. . . .

Grammar extra *Unit 2, Lesson A*

These activities look at more ways to add information to nouns, including adjectives after nouns and negatives.

1 Adjectives after nouns

Present the grammar chart Read the information aloud.

Understand the grammar Ask, "Which adjectives often come after nouns?" [available, possible, concerned, responsible, involved, necessary, extra]

Ask, "What measurement is followed by an adjective?" [decade] "What indefinite pronouns are used in the examples?" [nothing, anyone] Say, "A complement of an adjective completes its meaning of the adjective." Ask, "What are the adjectives in the examples?" [worth, full] "What are the complements?" [taking, of personal data] Ask, "If you remove the complements, do these sentences make sense?" [no]

Preview and do the task Read the instructions aloud. Ss complete the task and compare answers. Check answers with the class.

Answers

1. . . . personal information available online . . .
2. . . . there's anything wrong . . .
3. . . . any means possible . . .
4. . . . the people responsible for hacking . . .
5. People unaware of . . .
6. The victims concerned . . .
7. . . . the steps necessary . . .

2 Negative phrases after nouns

Present the grammar chart Read the information aloud.

Understand the grammar Ask, "When you want to add information that is negative after a noun, where do you put *not*?" [after the noun]

A

Preview and do the task Read the instructions aloud. Have Ss complete the task and compare their answers with a partner. Check answers with the class.

Answers

1. not wishing
2. not protected
3. not to ignore / not to be ignored
4. not familiar
5. not to post / not to be posted
6. not in your contacts list
7 not to do / not to be done
8. not to discuss / not to be discussed
9. not to click / not to be clicked

About you

B

Preview and do the task Read the instructions aloud. Ask a S to read the example aloud. Have Ss complete the task.

Follow-up Have several Ss read their opinion to the class. Alternatively, put Ss in small groups to read and discuss each group member's opinion.

Unit 2, Lesson A **Grammar extra**

1 Adjectives after nouns

- Adjectives usually come before nouns, but these adjectives often come after nouns: *available, possible, concerned, responsible, involved, necessary, extra.*
  Cybercrime is a problem, and the people **responsible / involved** should be punished.
  There are various antivirus programs **available**.
  Look for the easiest solution **possible**.

- Adjectives come after nouns in measurements and after indefinite pronouns.
  Social media sites are only about a **decade old**.
  There's **nothing unusual** about getting spam mail.
  Anyone interested in protecting themselves from cybercrime should talk to an expert.

- Adjectives with complements come after nouns.
  One action **worth taking** is changing your password regularly.
  Websites **full of personal data** can be targets for identity thieves.

Unscramble the sentences. Put the adjectives after the nouns.

1. a great deal of / personal information / Some people / have / available online
   Some people have a great deal of personal information available online.
2. with doing this / wrong / don't think / They / there's anything
3. your personal data / any means / eager to get / However, hackers / will try / possible
4. responsible for hacking / It can be / the people / to find / difficult
5. may "lose" / People / confidential information / what hackers / are doing / unaware of
6. The victims / problems with / concerned / their credit / may end up having
7. the steps / You need to / take / necessary / to protect yourself

2 Negative phrases after nouns

- Phrases that come after nouns can be negative. You can add *not* after the noun.
  Some information can be hidden from people **not in your group of "friends."**
  Individuals **not willing to give personal information** shouldn't have to do so.
  Emails **not to trust** often have the subject "Hi."
  Credit card numbers are one example of the kind of data **not to be shared**.
  Social networking sites can be a mystery to anyone **not belonging to one**.
  Any computer **not protected by antivirus software** is vulnerable.

A **Complete the sentences using the words given. Sometimes there is more than one answer.**

1. These days anyone_____ (not / wish) to have their information online may find it impossible.
2. Computers _____ (not / protect) by antivirus software are unsafe.
3. If you think you've been hacked, there are some warning signs _____ (not / ignore).
4. There are some basic rules for first-time users _____ (not / familiar) with social networks.
5. Your phone number is one example of information _____ (not / post).
6. Don't allow people _____ (not / in your contacts list) to read your profile.
7. Another thing _____ (not / do) is to post photos of yourself doing silly things.
8. Remember that your problems at work are a subject _____ (not / discuss) on social media sites.
9. Online ads _____ (not / click) on are the ones that say you won a prize.

About you **B** **Choose a sentence from Exercise A that you agree with. Explain why.**

I agree. It's almost impossible for people not wishing to have their information online to stop it from happening. Every time you sign up to a website you have to give personal information.

Grammar extra *Unit 2, Lesson B*

These activities look at more ways to use correlative or two-part conjunctions.

1 More on two-part conjunctions

Present the grammar chart Read the information aloud. Have Ss read the examples.

Understand the grammar Ask, "Where do two-part conjunctions go in a sentence?" [The first conjunction goes before the first choice or alternative, and the second conjunction goes before the second choice or alternative.] Ask, "Can two-part conjunctions connect different parts of speech?" [no]

Present *Common Errors* Read the information aloud.

Preview and do the task Read the instructions aloud. Ss complete the task and then compare answers in pairs. Check answers with the class.

Answers

1. . . . both convenient and innovative.
2. . . . both temperature and lighting.
3. Either remote computers or smartphones . . .
4. . . . not only simpler but also more efficient.
5. . . . not only list their contents but also suggest . . .
6. Neither cookbooks nor recipe cards will be needed . . .
7. . . . both displays the recipes . . . and reads the recipes . . .

Unit 2, Lesson B   *Grammar extra*

① More on two-part conjunctions

- You can use two-part conjunctions to combine nouns, adjectives, and verbs.

Nouns	My TV can play **either** *DVDs* **or** *Internet movies.* **Both** *the mouse* **and** *the keyboard* are wireless. My friend has **neither** *a TV* **nor** *a computer* in her home. The kitchen has **not only** *a self-cleaning oven* **but also** *a robot* that cleans the floors.
Adjectives	Some high-tech products are **either** *very expensive* **or** *very complicated.* Housework is **both** *boring* **and** *tiring.* Housecleaning with modern appliances is **neither** *difficult* **nor** *time-consuming.* Using a microwave to cook is **not only** *simple* **but also** *fast.*
Verbs	You can **either** *raise* **or** *lower* all the blinds with a remote control. My alarm clock **both** *flashes lights* **and** *sounds an alarm* to wake me up. Older cell phones **neither** *play music* **nor** *take pictures.* I'd like a robot that **not only** *cleans the house* **but also** *cooks the meals.*

> **Common errors**
>
> Don't use *neither . . . nor* when you have already used a negative verb. Use *either . . . or.*
> We do not have **either** *a dishwasher* **or** *a washing machine.* (NOT ~~We do not have neither a . . .~~)
> If you use a modal verb, put it before the first conjunction.
> My TV **can either** *stream movies* **or** *play DVDs.* (NOT ~~My TV either can stream . . .~~)

Rewrite the sentences using the two-part conjunctions in parentheses.

1. Many features in high-tech homes are convenient. They are innovative. (both . . . and)
   Many features in high-tech homes are both convenient and innovative.
2. In high-tech homes, one control manages temperature. It manages lighting. (both . . . and)
3. Remote computers can control the central systems. Smartphones can control them. (either . . . or)
4. In new, high-tech homes, cooking is simpler. It is more efficient. (not only . . . but also)
5. Refrigerators list their contents. They suggest recipes for the foods available. (not only . . . but also)
6. Cookbooks won't be needed anymore. Recipe cards won't be needed anymore. (neither . . . nor)
7. A computer displays the recipes on your kitchen counter. It reads the recipes aloud. (both . . . and)

② Two-part conjunctions with phrases and clauses

You can turn on the oven **either** *from work* **or** *in the car on the way home.* (phrases)
                              either *before you leave work* **or** *as you drive home.* (clauses)
High-tech homes are good **not only** *in summer* **but also** *in winter.* (phrases)
                              not only *because they are innovative* **but** they **also** *make life easier.* (clauses)

A Rewrite the sentences using two-part conjunctions to combine phrases and clauses.

1. You can control the systems when you're at home. You can control them when you're somewhere else. (either . . . or)
2. With a sophisticated security system, you can monitor your house at work. You can monitor your house on vacation. (both . . . and)
3. A high-tech home can adjust the temperature when it gets cold outside. It can adjust the temperature after it warms up. (not only . . . but also)

 About you

B Write three sentences about a home you'd like to live in. Use two-part conjunctions.

I would like to live in a home that has both a modern kitchen and a nice entertainment system. . . .

Grammar extra **147**

---

2 Two-part conjunctions with phrases and clauses

Present the grammar chart Read the information aloud.

Understand the grammar Say, "Look at the first example. What are the two phrases here?" [from work, in the car on the way home] Ask, "Where do the two parts of the conjunction go?" [before each phrase]

Say, "A clause has a subject and a verb. What type of clauses are in the second sentence, and what are they?" [time clauses: *before you leave work, as you drive home*] Have Ss change the example using *not only . . . but also.*

Have Ss comment on the second set of examples, identifying the phrases [in summer, in winter] and clauses [because they are innovative, because they make life easier].

A

Preview and do the task Read the instructions aloud. Have Ss complete the task. Check answers with the class.

Answers

1. . . . either when you're at home or when you're somewhere else.
2. . . . both at work and on vacation.
3. . . . not only when it gets cold outside but also after it warms up

About you

B

Preview and do the task Read the instructions and the example aloud. Have Ss complete the task. Have a few Ss share a sentence with the class.

Grammar extra *Unit 3, Lesson A*

These activities look at more ways to link events and add information about time or reason using clauses with prepositions and conjunctions + *-ing*. Also presented and practiced are passive forms of participle and time clauses.

❶ Clauses with prepositions and conjunctions + *-ing*

Present the grammar chart Read the information aloud.

Understand the grammar Say, "A preposition is always followed by a noun or an *-ing* form of a verb. A conjunction can be followed by other types of words. *While* and *when* are only conjunctions. Some words, like *before* and *after*, are both prepositions and conjunctions."

Say, "Look at the first two examples. These are clauses with prepositions and *-ing*." Ask, "What's the subject of *after completing*?" [I] "Look at the third example. What's the subject of *while studying*?" [many students] Say, "Notice the last example. What follows *after*?" [*having* + past participle] Add, "*After working* is also possible here."

Preview and do the task Read the instructions aloud. Complete the first blank with the class. Have Ss complete the task and compare answers. Check answers with the class.

Answers

After having spent / After spending; after graduating; In looking back; upon boarding; while staying; before leaving; when going; by making; after starting; Since coming; by making; through writing

❷ Passive forms of participle and time clauses

Present the grammar chart Read the information aloud. Have Ss read the examples.

Understand the grammar Ask, "In what two ways can you start a passive participle clause?" [a past participle; *having been* + past participle] "Are clauses with *being* + past participle often used?" [no]

Ask, "Can you use any conjunction before a past participle?" [no] "Which conjunctions can you use?" [*when, while, as, if,* and *though*] Say, "The first two examples in the bottom half of the chart have a similar meaning. Which structure is more commonly used?" [after being laid off] Say, "Look at the last sentence. What is another say to say *When told* here?" [When they / people were told] Ask, "Can you use *Before* in this sentence?" [No, because it's not one of the conjunctions you can use before a past participle.]

Preview and do the task Read the instructions aloud. Ask a S to call out the first answer. [Before being elected] Have Ss complete the task and compare their answers with a partner. Check answers with the class.

Answers

Before being elected; while employed; Faced (delete *and*); given / having been given (delete *and*); Having been raised; when informed; compared; When asked

---

Unit 3, Lesson A   *Grammar extra*

❶ Clauses with prepositions and conjunctions + *-ing*

- Clauses with prepositions (e.g., *after, by*) + *-ing* or conjunctions (e.g., *while, when*) + *-ing* are common in writing. The subject of the *-ing* clause and the main clause should be the same.
  After completing *my masters, I felt pressured to study for a PhD.* (Formal: ***On / Upon completing*** . .)
  By taking *extra classes, and **without telling** anyone, my sister was able to graduate early.*
  *Many students take on part-time work **while studying** for their masters.*
  *I changed careers and became a writer **after having worked** in accounting all my life.*

Complete the blog. Use *-ing* clauses with the words given.

(After / spend) _____ my college years at home, I was ready to set off into the world. So, (after / graduate) _____ , I flew to New York on a one-way ticket. (In / look back) _____ , I feel I became truly independent (upon / board) _____ the plane. However, (while / stay) _____ with a friend for a week, I felt the initial excitement begin to wear off. Luckily, I had gotten in touch with her (before / leave) _____ home. But I didn't want to overstay my welcome. I also realized, (when / go) _____ for my first job interview, how much pressure I felt. I had to find a job *and* a place to live quickly. I soon found a paid internship at a design company (by / make) _____ dozens of phone calls, and shortly (after / start) _____ work, I was invited to rent a room in a colleague's apartment. (Since / come) _____ to New York, I have felt the pressure of city living, but I enjoy it. Of course, I've often felt homesick, but (by / make) _____ use of social media, I keep in touch with people. I also make sense of my experience of post-college life (through / write) _____ this blog.

❷ Passive forms of participle and time clauses

- Passive participle clauses can start with a past participle or *having been* + past participle. Clauses that start with *being* + past participle are not common.
  Presented *with a chance to change careers, my father bought a café.* (= when he was presented)
  *My boss doesn't have many friends, **compared to** his co-workers.* (= if he is compared)
  Having been born *in the country, she found it hard to live in the city.* (= because she had been born)

- You can use prepositions or conjunctions before *being* + past participle or *having been* + past participle. Use only the conjunctions *when, while, as, if,* and *though* before a past participle.
  After being laid off, *most workers moved to other cities to find employment.* (more common)
  After having been laid off, . . . (less common)
  When told *that the company was closing, most people felt relieved.* (NOT *After told.* .)

Rewrite the underlined clauses with a participle or time clause, as in the chart above. In two cases, you need to delete *and* from the sentence.

Before he was elected, a politician said that if more women managed corporations and more men stayed at home with their families, the world would be a better place. I heard the speech while I was employed at a bank, and I took it to heart. At the time, my wife, who held a higher position than me, and I were expecting our first child. She was faced with the prospect of interrupting her career, and she suggested that I should be the primary caregiver. So, I was given the chance to take care of our child, and I immediately agreed to do so. As I had been raised in a traditional family, I knew my parents would pressure me to pursue my career. Indeed, when they were informed of our decision, they were clearly disappointed. Twelve years later, I still believe I made the right choice. In fact, I feel fortunate, if I am compared to many of my friends. When I'm asked if I made the right choice, I say it's the best decision I ever made. My wife agrees. She is now the president of a large company.

Grammar extra *Unit 3, Lesson B*

These activities look at more ways to use *so* and *such* and *even* and *only*.

❶ More on *so* and *such*

Present the grammar chart Read the information aloud. Have Ss read the examples.

Understand the grammar Ask Ss to look at the first section. Say, "While *such* means 'big' when placed before nouns, it is also commonly used along with the adjective *big*, for example, *such a big difference*, *such a big idiot*, *such a big mess*. In these cases, *such* is used for added emphasis." Ask, "In the second section, what idea does *such a way* refer to?" [you have time for a social life] For each use of *so* and *such* in the chart, have Ss give more examples.

Preview and do the task Say, "Use *so* or *such* to complete the posts on a website about the challenges of marriage."

Have Ss complete the task and then compare answers in pairs. Check answers with the class.

Answers

1. no such **thing** . . . so much **harder** . . . such **a lot** . . . so **little**
2. such **an impact** . . . so **many**
3. so **much** . . . such **a disaster** . . . so **many**
4. so **much** . . . such **a great experience** . . . in such **a way**

Say, "Now write a post of your own on a topic of your choice using *so* or *such*." Have Ss complete the task.

Follow-up Put Ss into small groups where they take turns reading their post aloud.

Unit 3, Lesson B *Grammar extra*

❶ More on *so* and *such*

- You can use *such* before some nouns to add emphasis. It means "big."
  *It makes **such a difference** to keep your desk neat. Mine was **such a mess**. I was **such an idiot**.*

- With some nouns, *such* can refer forward to what will be mentioned.
  *Organize your time in **such a way** that you have time for a social life.*

- You can use *so* and *such* with determiners and pronouns: *so much / many / few / little; such a lot.*
  *In my first semester, there were **so many** parties that served pizza and soda. I ate **so much** (pizza) and drank **such a lot** (of soda) that I gained weight.*

- You can use *so much* as an adverb and before comparative adjectives and adverbs.
  *I enjoyed college **so much**. It was **so much better / more fun** than I expected. The time went by **so much more quickly** than I thought it would.*

Use *so* or *such* to complete the posts on a website about the challenges of marriage. Then write a post of your own on the topic of marriage using *so* or *such*.

1. There's no _____ **thing** as an easy marriage. It was _____ **much harder** at first than I imagined. I worked _____ **a lot**, and my husband and I spent _____ **little** time together that we almost broke up.
2. Getting married had _____ **an impact** on some of my friends. They had a lot of arguments at first, but my husband and I didn't have _____ **many**. You just have to take responsibility for making things work.
3. I've always loved my single life _____ **much** that I can't imagine getting married. Married life has been _____ **a disaster** for some of my friends, and I've seen _____ **many** of them get divorced.
4. I've enjoyed being married _____ **much** more than I thought. It's been _____ **a great experience**. My advice is to live your life in _____ **a way** that nothing takes precedence over your marriage.

❷ More on *even* and *only*

- *Even* and *only* usually go after *be*, after an auxiliary verb, or before a main verb.
  *Semesters **are only** 14 weeks. I've **even** made friends. I **only called** home a few times.*

- *Even* and *only* can also go before other words or phrases to add emphasis.

Nouns / pronouns	*The test was easy – **even weak students** passed. **Even I** got an A.*
Numbers	***Only one student** got a B.*
Adverbs	*I worked **even harder** in my last year. I missed class **only once**.*
Prepositions	*It was hard, **even in** the first week. It got easier **only after** spring break.*
Conjunctions	*I was tired **even before** classes started. I was tired **only because** I was sick.*

Note: *She **only missed** two classes because she was sick* can have two meanings. You can make the meaning clear by moving the position of *only*.
*She missed **only** two classes because . . .   She missed two classes **only** because . . .*

About you

Cross out the incorrect uses of *even* and *only*. Then answer the two questions about yourself.

A Do you remember your first job? I remember mine. I was nervous, **even** after the first month. But that's **only** because my boss **only** was so scary. She used to yell at everyone.

B Oh, that makes you feel **even** worse, if you have a boss like that.

A Yeah. I think **only** there was **only** one person that my boss liked. And **even** he **even** didn't like her. I **only** stayed in that job three weeks. Then I moved to another city. Have you ever had to move?

B Um, just once. We moved when I **only** was eight, and that was **only** because Dad got a new job. My parents **even** hadn't considered it before – they hadn't **even** been on a vacation.

Grammar extra **149**

---

❷ More on *even* and *only*

Present the grammar chart Read the information in the first two sections aloud.

Understand the grammar Ask Ss to look at the middle section of the chart. For each part of speech listed, elicit new example sentences from the class. Then have Ss close their books. Write on the board:

> *She only missed two classes because she was sick.*

Ask, "In this sentence, what does *only* emphasize? There are two possibilities." Have Ss call out their ideas. Have Ss open their books. Ask a S to read the two solutions aloud.

About you

Preview and do the task Say, "Cross out the incorrect uses of *even* and *only*." Have Ss complete the task. Check answers with the class: Ask a pair of Ss to read the conversation with the corrections.

Answers

A even; only; ~~only~~
B even
A ~~only~~; only; even; ~~even~~; only
B ~~only~~; only; ~~even~~; even

Say, "Now answer the two questions about yourself." Have Ss complete the task.

Follow-up Call on several Ss to read their responses aloud. Alternatively, have Ss read their responses to a partner. Then have a few pairs read a question and their response the class.

These activities look at more ways to use the future perfect, including more time expressions, the passive form, and the use of the future perfect to make predictions and state assumptions.

1 More on the future perfect

Present the grammar chart Read the information aloud.

Understand the grammar Ask, "What are the patterns for future perfect verbs? [active: *will (not) have* + past participle; *won't have* + past participle; passive: *will have been* + past participle; *will not have / won't have been* + past participle.]

Call on a few Ss to say a true sentence using each time expression.

Preview and do the task Read the instructions aloud. Say, "Be sure to read through both paragraphs before you begin."

Have Ss complete the task and compare their answers with a partner. Check answers with the class.

Answers

By; will have disappeared; <u>by</u>; will have died out; <u>within</u>
By; have been lost; <u>By</u>; will have risen; <u>within</u>; will have been affected

2 The future perfect for predictions and assumptions

Present the grammar chart Read the information aloud.

Understand the grammar Ask Ss to read the first example. Ask, "Is this sentence about the future?" [no] "Does it mean the same as *you will read*?" [no] "What's another way of saying it?" [I'm sure you have read.] Ask, "What's another way to say the second sentence?" [I'm sure many people haven't seen the documentary.] Ask various Ss to each make an affirmative prediction or assumption and a negative one.

Preview and do the task Read the instructions aloud. Tell Ss to read through the entire blog before they begin. Point out that the first answer has been done for them. Have Ss complete the task and compare their answers with a partner. Check answers with the class.

Answers

Note: *will* may also be contracted here (*you'll*) as this is a blog and not academic writing.

will not have heard / won't have heard; will have reacted; will have noticed; will have heard; will not have realized / won't have realized; will have saved; will have motivated

---

Unit 4, Lesson A *Grammar extra*

1 More on the future perfect

- The future perfect describes events that at a future point will be in the past, or in a time leading up to that future point in time. It can emphasize the completion of the events.
  *In two months, it will be winter and many birds **will have migrated** south.* (The migration is complete.)
- Time expressions, especially with *by*, are often used with the future perfect to show the time by which an event will be complete, e.g., *by then, by that time, by the time (that) . . ., by 2030, by the end of the century, by the age of six, within 30 days, within a decade, within the next 20 years.*
  ***Within the next 10 years**, many species **will have become** extinct.*
- The future perfect has a passive form – *will have been* + past participle – but it is not very common.
  *In the time it takes you to do this lesson, hundreds of sharks **will have been killed**.*

Complete the time expressions with *by* or *within*. Then rewrite the verbs in bold using either the active or passive form of the future perfect.

_____ the time our children reach adulthood, hundreds of species **disappear** off the face of the planet. One study estimated that _____ 2050, 37 percent of terrestrial species **die out** or will be in danger of extinction. That is well over a third _____ the next 30 years.

Sea life is also in danger._____ the time that sea levels rise 50 centimeters (about 20 inches), one-third of nesting beaches in the Caribbean **lose**, leading to the decline in turtle populations. _____ the end of this century, it is believed that seawater temperatures **rise** enough to affect the food supply of some ocean species. This impacts various species in different ways. For example, it is believed that _____ only a few decades, the reproductive cycle of the sperm whale **affect**, which threatens the very survival of the whale itself.

2 The future perfect for predictions and assumptions

- You can use the future perfect to state predictions or assumptions about the present or to say what you think has happened in the past. It suggests you are certain.
  *No doubt you **will have read** about the melting ice caps.*
  *Many people **will not have seen** the recent documentary about this.*
- The negative with *won't* with this meaning is mostly used in speaking and informal writing.
  *"A lot of people **won't** even **have heard** about it."*

Rewrite the underlined parts of the blog using the future perfect.

will not / won't have heard

It is unlikely that there is anyone who <u>has not heard</u> about the threat to certain species on the planet. No doubt you <u>have reacted</u> to the news that species such as polar bears are under threat. But what can we as individuals do? In recent years, perhaps you <u>have noticed</u> the appeals for help that come in the mail or that are on TV. They are certainly having an impact on my children. I'm sure that in addition to sending donations to various charities, you <u>have heard</u> about the "adopt an endangered animal" programs. I suspect what you <u>haven't realized</u> is how expensive these "adoptions" are. Not that I mind donating $50 for my child to adopt an orangutan or a Sumatran rhino. It's all for a good cause. And no doubt donations <u>have saved</u> some obscure species from the brink of extinction, and certainly the programs <u>have motivated</u> many children to become involved. What I hadn't expected was for a cuddly stuffed toy version to arrive in the mail. Now my daughter wants the entire collection, which is all very well – except there are more than 100 endangered species that she can sign up to help!

150 Grammar extra

Grammar extra *Unit 4, Lesson B*

These activities look at more ways combine ideas with formal prepositions, *the fact that*, and prepositions + perfect forms.

1 Formal prepositional expressions

Present the grammar chart Read the information aloud. Have Ss read the examples.

Understand the grammar Explain to Ss that the prepositions on the left are common basic prepositions, but that in writing there are other expressions that they can use to make their writing sound more formal or academic. For each example, ask various Ss to call out an additional example using a formal prepositional phrase. Point out that in the *about* section, these phrases are used to link or raise topics and can't always replace the preposition *about*. Write examples on the board, for example:

More could be done <u>in relation to</u> protecting the environment.

Preview and do the task Read the instructions aloud. Have Ss complete the tasks and then compare answers in pairs. Check answers with the class.

Answers

(Note: Correct expressions are in bold; alternate expressions are in italic)

with regard to / *with respect to / in relation to / regarding;*
with respect to / *with regard to / regarding / in relation to;*
Given / *Owing to / On view of / On account of;* **in conjunction with** / *alongside / along with / together with;* **on account of** / *in view of / owing to / given;* **following** / *subsequent to;*
together with / *alongside / along with / in conjunction with;*
In view of / *Given / Owing to / On account of*

Unit 4, Lesson B *Grammar extra*

1 Formal prepositional expressions

- Some prepositional expressions are very frequent in academic writing. You can use them instead of more common prepositions to make your writing sound more formal.

after	One desert spread **subsequent to / following** the introduction of new farming practices.
before	Delegates will meet **ahead of / in advance of / prior to** the conference.
with	Talks will take place **in conjunction with / alongside** an exhibition on deserts. Small mammals, **together with / along with** larger ones, survive in harsh climates.
about	There is concern **with respect to / with regard to / regarding / in relation to** agriculture.
because of	It is classified as a desert **owing to / in view of / on account of / given** its lack of rainfall.

Circle the correct expressions to complete the paragraph. Then rewrite each sentence using an alternative expression from the chart above. More than one expression is possible.

Environmental concerns, especially **with regard to / in advance of** desertification, are growing. Desertification is a huge problem **prior to / with respect to** loss of habitats and agricultural land. **Given / Alongside** the problems that desertification causes, the United Nations adopted a convention in 1994. This convention proposed returning land to its original state (land rehabilitation) **in conjunction with / owing to** programs of sustainable land management. Many countries signed up to the convention **on account of / together with** the economic problems that desertification was causing. Projects that have emerged **prior to / following** the adoption of the convention include the mapping of desertification using satellite imagery **together with / on account of** a variety of educational programs. **In view of / Subsequent to** the severity of the issue, it appears that much more still needs to be done.

2 More on *the fact that;* prepositions + perfect forms

- The prepositional expressions *apart from, because of, besides, by virtue of, despite, due to, except for, including, in spite of, in view of, owing to, thanks to,* and *given* are often followed by *the fact that.*
  *The Antarctic is classified as a desert **in view of the fact that** it has low rainfall.*
  Despite the fact that it is extremely cold, Antarctica is a desert.

- Prepositions can be followed by *having* + past participle to refer to events in a period of time up to the present or up to a point in the past.
  *The government takes credit **for having initiated** a tree-planting program to halt desertification. Agricultural practices were criticized **as having been** partly responsible for the growth of deserts.*

Complete the sentences. In some, you need to add *the fact that;* in others, add *having*.

1. The Atacama desert is considered *the* driest region by virtue of _____ some parts have no rain.
2. Apart from _____ it is so dry, much of the land is also at high elevation.
3. It is surprising that over a million people are recorded as _____ settled there given _____ it is so arid.
4. Population centers developed in several areas despite _____ it is so inhospitable.
5. Teams of astronomers operate observatories in the desert due to _____ its skies are so clear.
6. Crops can now be grown owing to _____ farmers have developed irrigation systems.
7. Communities in northern Chile no longer import water into the region thanks to _____ they can now collect water from fog. Lives have improved.
8. A Canadian development team can be credited for _____ helped to develop this system.

Grammar extra **151**

2 More on *the fact that;* prepositions + perfect forms

Present the grammar chart Read the information aloud.

Understand the grammar Write on the board:

The Antarctic is a desert _____ it has low rainfall.

in view of

Ask, "Can I just put *in view of* into this sentence?" [no, because *it has low rainfall* is a clause and *in view of* is a preposition] Ask, "How can I use *in view of* in the sentence?" [add *the fact that*] Add *in view of the fact that* to the sentence on the board.

Have a S read out the prepositional expressions that are often followed by *the fact that.* Ask, "What follows *the fact that?*" [a clause] Have Ss look at the bottom section of the chart. Ask a S to read the first sentence aloud. Ask, "When did the government do this?" [sometime in the past / in a time period up to now] Ask a S to read the second sentence aloud. Ask, "When were the agricultural practices responsible for the growth of deserts – before or after they were criticized?" [before]

Preview and do the task Read the instructions aloud. Have Ss complete the task. Check answers with the class.

Answers

1. the fact that
2. the fact that
3. having; the fact that
4. the fact that
5. the fact that
6. the fact that
7. the fact that
8. having

These activities present and practice positions of adverbs in present and past verb phrases.

1 Adverbs in present and past passive verb phrases

Present the grammar chart Read the information aloud.

Understand the grammar Ask, "In present and past passive verb phrases, what is the usual position for an adverb?" [after *be*, or after *not* in negative phrases] Ask, "When an adverb describes a participle, where does it often go?" [before the participle] Explain to Ss that these are the *most common* positions for adverbs, but they may see adverbs in other positions, too.

Preview and do the task Read the instructions aloud. Tell Ss to read the paragraphs before they begin. Have Ss complete the task and then compare answers in pairs. Check answers with the class.

Answers

are often required; was originally invented; was reportedly heard; was already infected; was fortunately discovered

is still being used; was not initially recognized; were increasingly used; was eventually eradicated; was finally recorded

are not currently being developed; have already been approved; are being effectively protected

2 Adverbs in perfect verb phrases

Present the grammar chart Read the information aloud.

Understand the grammar Say, "Adverbs in a sentence with perfect verb phrases follow similar rules." Ask, "In a sentence with a perfect verb phrase, where can an adverb go?" [before or after *has / have / had*] "Where does it usually go, before or after?" [after] "When is it used before?" [for emphasis] Ask, "Where can you use *yet* in a negative statement?" [after *not* or at the end of a clause] Explain that *yet* after *not* is more formal than *yet* at the end of the clause.

Preview and do the task Say, "Read the clues. Write the underlined words in the correct order." Have Ss complete the task and check answers with a partner. Check answers with the class.

Answers

1. has been widely used
2. had originally been invented
3. had apparently been created; had obviously been used
4. had been carefully wrapped
5. has not yet been discovered / has not been discovered yet
6. has still not completely materialized

Say, "Close your books. Can you guess the product?" Ss call out their guesses. Have Ss open their books and find the answer [paper] upside down at the bottom of the page.

Unit 5, Lesson A *Grammar extra*

1 Adverbs in present and past passive verb phrases

- In present and past passive verb phrases, adverbs usually go after the verb *be*. In negative statements, adverbs usually go after *not*. This is the most frequent position for most adverbs.

Simple present passive
New discoveries are **apparently** made every day.

Present continuous passive
GPS software is **continually** being upgraded.

Simple past passive
Asbestos was **widely** used until the 1960s.

Past continuous passive
Alternatives were not **yet** being developed.

- Some adverbs usually go before *not*, e.g.: *also, still, just, probably, certainly, reportedly,* attitude adverbs.
Alternatives were **simply** not developed until later.   Alternatives were **still** not being developed.

- Adverbs that describe the participle (e.g., to say "how" or "how much") often go before it.
Some inventions are not being **widely** reported or are being **completely** ignored by the media.

Write the adverbs given into the underlined verb phrases.

              <u>often</u>
Vaccinations are required for entry to kindergarten. (often) For many parents, it's a nuisance. Yet where would we be without them? One of the first vaccines was invented in 1776 by Edward Jenner, a British country doctor. (originally) A milkmaid was heard to say that she would never develop smallpox because she was infected with the cowpox virus. (reportedly / already) Jenner understood the significance, and thanks to him, a vaccine for smallpox was discovered. (fortunately)

    Jenner's smallpox vaccine is being used today, but his work was not recognized. (still / initially) However, smallpox vaccines were used around the world and were even made compulsory by law, until 200 years later, when the disease was eradicated. (increasingly / eventually) The last case of smallpox was recorded in 1977. (finally)

    While vaccines are not being developed for every disease, they have been approved for many life-threatening ailments. (currently / already) As a result, children are being protected from disease, which has to be anything *but* a nuisance. (effectively)

2 Adverbs in perfect verb phrases

- Adverbs usually go after *has / have / had*. Some can also go before for emphasis.
In negative statements, adverbs usually go after *not*.
Some progress has **clearly** been made. OR . . . **clearly** has been made. (more emphatic)
The difficulties of research had not **always** been understood.

- Adverbs that describe the participle to say "how" or "how much" often go before it.
Scientists have not always been **widely** praised. Some have even been **sharply** criticized.

- *Still* goes after *has / have / had*. In negative statements, *yet* goes after *not* or at the end of a clause.
Liquid water has **still** not been found on Mars. Liquid water has not **yet** been found on Mars.
OR Liquid water has not been found on Mars **yet**. (less formal)

Read the clues. Write the underlined words in the correct order. Can you guess the product?

1. A variation of this product <u>widely been used has</u> for millennia – since 4000 B.C.E., in fact.
2. A number of my friends said they thought that it <u>had invented originally been</u> by the Egyptians.
3. However, the first "recipe" for the product as we know it today <u>been had created apparently</u> by the Chinese. Historians say it <u>used had been obviously</u> to protect bronze mirrors in the second century.
4. In addition, records show that medicines <u>had wrapped been carefully</u> in it for safekeeping.
5. A replacement product <u>yet been discovered not has</u>, unless you consider computer technology.
6. The idea we can live without it <u>not has materialized completely still</u>, but will it ever be obsolete?

Exercise 2 Answer: Paper

152 Grammar extra

Grammar extra *Unit 5, Lesson B*

These activities present and practice adverbs with past modals and questions with passive past modals.

1 Adverbs and past modal verb phrases

Present the grammar chart Read the information aloud.

Understand the grammar Point to the art in the exercise and explain that the examples relate to a jump someone made off an electrical tower. Say, "Negative past modal statements are not very common, especially in the passive."

Preview and do the task Read the instructions aloud. Have Ss complete the task. Check answers.

Answers

(Note: These are the most frequent possible answers.)
1. could easily have died
2. might also have been
3. probably should not have allowed
4. definitely should have checked
5. could have actually been crippled
6. probably should have followed
7. should never have watched

Unit 5, Lesson B   *Grammar extra*

1 Adverbs and past modal verb phrases

- In past modal verb phrases, adverbs like *probably, certainly,* and *definitely* often go before the modal.

Active
He **never** should have tried to jump.
He **probably** should not have jumped.

Passive
The jump **certainly** could have been stopped.
It **probably** should not have been allowed.

- Within the verb phrase, adverbs can go after the modal or after *have*. After the modal is more frequent.
He should **never** have gone there.
Something bad could **easily** have happened.

It should **never** have been allowed.
Someone could **easily** have been killed.

Read the post from a video website and the various comments. Put the words in a correct order. There is more than one correct answer.

In 2012, a young Russian base-jumper jumped off a tall electrical tower not knowing that his parachute wouldn't open. He crashed into the ground below and miraculously survived. He was able to walk again three months later after fracturing his legs and hip.

Comments
1. Not a good idea. He easily / have / could / died by jumping off that tower.
2. He also / have / been / might electrocuted!
3. His friends probably / should / have / allowed / not him to jump.
4. He checked / should / have / definitely his parachute before jumping!
5. He been / have / crippled / actually / could for life.
6. He looked nervous. He have / should / probably / followed his gut instinct and not jumped.
7. I never / watched / have / should this video. It was scary!

2 Questions with passive past modals

- Questions with passive past modals are not very common. In writing, they are often rhetorical.
Would these problems **have been avoided** if there had been more support?
Should this trip **have been prevented**?
Could more money **have been raised** in another way?

Read the excerpt from an editorial news column. Then read the comments. Complete the questions in the passive form, using the verbs given.

The youngest British woman ever to climb Mount Everest was welcomed home by her family and friends this week. Such is the danger of climbing Everest that the return of any climber must be met with relief. However, the young Briton reported treacherous conditions. She had to climb past several badly-injured people and even some who had died. She had also experienced a dangerous 100-person "snarl up," as people rushed to the summit during a period of calm weather. It raises important questions about such dangerous expeditions. For example:

1. Should people *have been allowed* (allow) to climb in such treacherous conditions?
2. Could the injured climbers _____ (help)?
3. Could more _____ (do) to make the climb safer?
4. Would deaths _____ (prevent) if people had shown better judgment?
5. In the past, should people rescued off the mountain _____ (make) to pay for their rescue?
6. Should climbers _____ (charge) for failing to help other injured climbers?

Grammar extra **153**

2 Questions with passive past modals

Present the grammar chart Read the information aloud.

Check that Ss understand the meaning of *rhetorical question*. [A question that is asked without the expectation of an answer; the answer is implied or clear from the context. Rhetorical questions can be used especially in writing to make an argument or to raise issues.] Say, "In fact, questions with passive past modals are four times more frequent in writing than in speaking."

Understand the grammar Ask, "What's the pattern for a question with passive past modals?" [modal + subject + *have been* + past participle]

Preview and do the task Read the instructions aloud. Have Ss complete the task. Check answers with the class.

Answers

1. Should people <u>have been allowed</u> to climb in such treacherous conditions?
2. Could the injured climbers <u>have been helped</u>?
3. Could more <u>have been done</u> to make the climb safer?
4. Would deaths <u>have been prevented</u> if people had shown better judgment?
5. In the past, should people rescued off the mountain <u>have been made</u> to pay for their rescue?
6. Should climbers <u>have been charged</u> for failing to help other injured climbers?

These activities introduce more types of relative clauses starting with pronouns, numbers, and nouns.

① Pronouns and numbers in relative clauses

Present the grammar chart Read the information aloud.

Understand the grammar Tell Ss to read the first example sentence. Ask, "What do *neither* and *both* refer to?" [two new products] Ask, "Why was *which* used?" [Products are things.] Ask similar types of questions for the other examples.

Present *Common Errors* Read the information aloud.

Preview and do the task Read the instructions aloud. Have Ss complete the task. Check answers with the class.

Answers

1. . . . most of whom are on tight budgets . . .
2. . . . the majority of which offer more or less the same thing.
3. . . . much of which is misleading . . .
4. . . . two of whom are avid coupon users . . .
5. . . . both of which are major players in the coupon business . . .
6. . . . none of which was / were easy to navigate.
7. . . . neither of which is / are particularly well-known . . .
8. . . . each of which specializes in grocery coupons . . .
9. . . . 80 percent of which offered email alerts . . .

② Nouns in relative clauses

Present the grammar chart Read the information aloud.

Understand the grammar Ask Ss to circle the noun that the words in bold refer to. Elicit the answers. [in which = a world; for whom = a staff; a copy of which = the end-of-year report; a person for whom = the CEO]

Present *Common Errors* Read the information aloud.

Preview and do the task Read the instructions aloud. Have Ss complete the task and compare their answers with a partner. Check answers with the class.

Answers

Imagine a perfect economic environment **in which no business fails**. Unfortunately, the truth is that the rate **at which start-up companies fail is high**. The high failure rate, **the main reasons for which are given below**, is concerning. Many owners, **for whom start-up costs are high**, are deterred by the risk of failure.

1. The frequency **at which new businesses fail** is high when they're started for the *wrong* reasons.
2. Many new business owners lack basic skills, **the importance of which** cannot be underestimated. Above all, they need to be able to manage finances, **an understanding of which** is critical.
3. The employees **to whom the owner entrusts the business** often have the wrong skills.
4. A new business must have a website, **the functions of which can vary** and **without which the business will fail**.
5. Many new business owners underestimate the prices **at which their products must sell** to make a profit.

Unit 6, Lesson A *Grammar extra*

① Pronouns and numbers in relative clauses

- Relative clauses can start with a pronoun (*both, each, much, neither, none, several,* etc.) + *of* or with numbers and quantity words (*half, 30 percent, the majority,* etc.) + *of.*
  In 2013, we launched two new products, **neither of which** was successful. / **both of which** failed.
  The company had four directors, **each of whom** made a fortune. / **none of whom** stayed after the sale.
  There are over 2 million businesses in Canada, **the majority of which** have fewer than 100 employees.
  One company has 500 employees, **half of whom** are part-time.

  > **Common errors**
  > Don't start these types of relative clauses with *which* or *whom.*
  > There are 100 companies, **most of which** have one employee. (NOT . . . ~~which most of them have~~ . . .)

Rewrite each pair of sentences from a report using a relative clause. You may delete words.

Consumers, most of whom are on tight budgets, are looking to save money when they shop.
1. Consumers are looking to save money when they shop. Most consumers are on tight budgets.
2. There are thousands of online coupon sites. The majority of these offer more or less the same thing.
3. So how do you know which sites to use or which information to trust? Much of it is misleading.
4. Our staff researched 10 options. Two of them are avid coupon users.
5. Two sites we researched had out-of-date coupons. Both are major players in the coupon business.
6. Our staff identified four more sites. None was easy to navigate.
7. On two sites, staff found much better deals than on other sites. Neither site is particularly well-known.
8. These two sites had coupons with discounts up to 30 percent. Each one specializes in grocery coupons.
9. Of the 10 sites we surveyed, three had too many distracting banner ads. Eighty percent offered email alerts.

② Nouns in relative clauses

- Relative clauses can begin with a preposition, or a noun + preposition, + *which* or *whom.*
  Imagine a world **in which** there is no profit motive and a staff **for whom** nothing is a problem.
  The end-of-year report, **a copy of which** was sent to the press, painted a gloomy picture.
  The CEO of this company, **a person for whom** I have great respect, just retired.

  > **Common errors**
  > Don't start these types of relative clauses with *which* + noun.
  > We read the research, **the results of which** were unclear. (NOT ~~which results were unclear.~~)

Rewrite the underlined parts of the report as relative clauses that begin with the bold words.

in which no business fails.
Imagine a perfect economic environment that no business fails in. Unfortunately, the truth is that the rate that start-up companies fail at is high. The high failure rate, and the main reasons for this are given below, is concerning. Many owners, and start-up costs are high for them, are deterred by the risk of failure.

Reasons for failures of start-up companies

1. The frequency that new businesses fail at is high when they're started for the *wrong* reasons.
2. Many new business owners lack basic skills, and the importance of this cannot be underestimated. Above all, they need to be able to manage finances, and an understanding of this is critical.
3. The employees that the owner entrusts the business to often have the wrong skills.
4. A new business must have a website, and the functions can vary and without it the business will fail.
5. Many new business owners underestimate the prices that their products must sell at to make a profit.

154 Grammar extra

Grammar extra Unit 6, Lesson B

These activities present more ways to refer to people and things using *other*, *every other*, *other than*, and *another*.

1 Other, every other, other than

Present the grammar chart Read the information aloud. Have Ss read the examples.

Understand the grammar Ask, "If you do something every other week, how many times will you do it in a year?" [26]

Present *Common Errors* Read the information aloud.

Preview and do the task Read the instructions aloud. Ask, "What is the first answer?" [other] "Why is it correct?" [It follows *all*, so it can't be *every other* or *other than*. You can't use *others* before a noun.]

Ss complete the task and then compare answers in pairs. Check answers with the class.

Answers

1. other; other; other; other
2. other; others
3. other; others
4. other; other; every other

Unit 6, Lesson B   Grammar extra

1 other, every other, other than

- Before *other*, you can use *the*, *any*, *some*, *all*, *many*, *much*, *most*, *no*, *(a) few*, *every*, *this / that*, etc.
  One retailer outsells **all other** stores. **No other** store can compete. **Few other** stores do as well.
  There is **no other** business news. If **any other** information comes to light, it will be reported.

- You can also use these words: *several*, *various*, *numerous*, *whole*, *certain*, *countless*.
  Online shopping is **a whole other** problem for small retailers. There are **several other** threats too.

- Every other can mean "alternate" and is often used with time words (*day*, *week*, *year*, etc.).
  We go to the grocery store **every other weekend**.

- Other than means "except" or "apart from."
  Salesclerks need to speak a language **other than** English.

Common errors

Don't use *others* before a plural noun.
Retailers face **other** threats.
(NOT ~~others threats~~)

Use *other*, *others*, or *every other* to complete the sentences in this business report.

1. While many retailers are struggling, one electronics retailer outperforms all _____ stores. No _____ company attracts such a loyal consumer base. In fact, many consumers will *not* be seen with products _____ than these smartphones or tablets, which must be the envy of most _____ retailers.
2. Selling print magazines has been difficult in recent years. One magazine recently announced that it will now publish only online, and numerous _____ magazines are considering doing the same. Many _____ have simply gone out of business.
3. Maintaining sales is a problem for any small business, but supporting online sales is a whole _____ issue. Some simply don't create user-friendly sites, while some _____ often don't know how to make their sites visible on the Web.
4. While some stores are concerned about the loss of sales to online retailers, certain _____ stores are tackling the issue head-on. One retailer lets customers pick up goods that they ordered online at the store the same day. It's a huge advantage over all _____ competing stores, which deliver their goods only _____ week.

2 More on *another*

- *Another* can mean "an additional" or "an alternative." You can use it before a singular countable noun, the pronoun *one*, numbers, and *few*, or as a pronoun instead of a singular count noun.
  I bought **another** sweater. I liked it so much I bought **another** (*one*) in **another** color.
  I actually bought **another three** sweaters. In **another few** weeks, I'll buy some more.

Read the blog. Find seven more places where you can replace words with *another*.

                                                                                another
I recently bought a sweater online, but when it arrived, it didn't fit. I decided to order a different one in a different size, and return the first sweater. It was a long process. I called customer service, and they promised to send me a return label. Only they didn't. I emailed them, made a second call, and then sent an additional email. Finally, I got the return label and went to the post office. I had to make a further trip, however, as I had forgotten to wrap the sweater in the original packaging. Now I have to wait an additional five days before it ships. I'll have to wait an extra couple of weeks before the refund appears on my credit card statement. Meanwhile, I ordered a new sweater, which was out of stock. Next time I'll just go to the store.

---

2 More on *another*

Present the grammar chart Read the information aloud.

Understand the grammar Say, "Notice that *another* immediately precedes a singular countable noun. To use *another* with a plural countable noun, you need a number or an expression, such as *couple of*, between *another* and the noun." Have student find each use of *another* in the examples.

Preview and do the task Read the instructions aloud. Point out that the first answer has been done. Ask why it is correct. [*a different one* is an "alternative one"] Have Ss complete the task. Check answers with the class.

Answers

I recently bought a sweater online, but when it arrived, it didn't fit. I decided to order **another** one in **another** size, and return the first sweater. It was a long process. I called customer service, and they promised to send me a return label. Only they didn't. I emailed them, made **another** call, and then sent **another** email. Finally, I got the return label and went to the post office. I had to make **another** trip, however, as I had forgotten to wrap the sweater in the original packaging. Now I have to wait **another** five days before it ships. I'll have to wait **another** couple of weeks before the refund appears on my credit card statement. Meanwhile, I ordered **another** sweater, which was out of stock. Next time I'll just go to the store.

This activity reviews and extends Ss' knowledge of inversions for hypothesizing about the present and past.

More on inversions

Present the grammar chart Read the information aloud.

Understand the grammar Have Ss read the first two examples, which review the patterns taught in Lesson A. Ask, "Which sentence refers to the past?" [second one] Ask, "How can you express these clauses using *if*?" [If he had a child . . . If he had known . . .] Ask, "How do you make these negative?" [put *not* after the subject]

Have Ss look at the second section. Say, "These are patterns with 'dummy *it*.'" Have a S read the examples with *were*. Say, "These sentences can be expressed in two ways. They mean 'If my parents didn't exist.' It's a hypothetical – or imaginary – statement about now." Ask, "Is the speaker continuing his or her education?" [yes] Have Ss contribute other ideas to continue the sentence. Write them on the board. You may also want to tell Ss that it is also possible to follow both clauses here with a clause that has a past modal form. For example, *If it weren't for my parents, I couldn't have made it through college.* This pattern is not shown, however, in order to keep the chart simple.

Have a S read the next examples with *had*. Ask, "Is this a hypothetical statement about now?" [no, the past] Say, "Which do you think is more formal: the clause with *If* or the clause with the inversion?" [The clause with the inversion is more formal.]

A

Preview and do the task Read the instructions aloud. Ask, "How would you rewrite the first underlined section?" [if it weren't for the advice in parenting magazines] Have Ss complete the task and then compare answers in pairs. Check answers with the class.

Answers

If it weren't for the advice in parenting magazines; Had these magazines existed; had my wife and I not had; If it hadn't been for our neighbor in particular; Had we been able to see; Had she not done so
1. Were I suddenly to find myself
2. Had I thought you would listen
3. Were it not for

Had it not been for; Were she

B

Preview and do the task Read the instructions aloud. Ask, "How could you complete the first blank?" [were it not / if it weren't / if it hadn't been / had it not been] Have Ss complete the task and then compare answers in pairs. Check answers with the class.

Answers

were it not / if it weren't / if it hadn't been / had it not been . . . Were it not / If it weren't . . . were . . . to close . . . had they had . . . had we not kept . . . if it hadn't been / had it not been

---

Unit 7, Lesson A *Grammar extra*
More on inversions

- Inversions are generally used in formal English. Use *were* + subject (+ infinitive) to describe an imaginary situation in the present or future. Use *had* + subject + past participle for the past.
  Were he to have a child, my son would take classes.   Negative: *Were he **not** to have . . .*
  Had they known about the classes, my friends would have taken them.   Negative: *Had they **not** known . . .*

- You can also use *If it weren't for . . .*, *If it hadn't been for . . .*, *Were it not for . . .*, and *Had it not been for* + noun phrase. They mean "If someone or something didn't exist or something hadn't happened."
  If it weren't for my parents, I wouldn't be able to continue with my education.
  OR **Were it not for** my parents, I . . . (hypothetical statement about the present)
  If it hadn't been for my parents, I wouldn't have been able to continue with my education.
  OR **Had it not been for** my parents, I . . . (hypothetical statement about the past)

A Rewrite the underlined parts of the blog about parenting teenagers, using a structure in the chart. Start with the word in bold.

There are many challenges associated with parenting, especially parenting teens. Some parents claim that **if** the advice in parenting magazines didn't exist, they would not know how to deal with their teenage children. If these magazines **had** existed when we were younger, we could certainly have learned from them. We relied instead on our friends for advice. Indeed, if my wife and I **had** not had the support of other parents with the same challenges, we may not have survived the journey. **If** our neighbor in particular hadn't existed, life would have been much harder. We had it tough, or so we thought. However, as you get older, you realize your "mistakes." If we **had** been able to see things from our teenager's perspective, we may have realized that it was our daughter who needed the advice – on how to handle us, her parents. Now a parent herself, she discussed this with us recently. If she **had** not done so, we may not have formed the close bond that we have today. She said:

1. If I **were** suddenly to find myself a parent of teenagers, I'd trust them to make good decisions.
2. If I **had** thought you would listen without judging me, I would have talked to you more openly.
3. If it **weren't for** the fact that you were always so busy, I would have spent more time with you.

If it **hadn't been for** that conversation, we would probably have interfered too much as grandparents, too. Now we trust her decisions as a new parent. If she **were** a teenager today, our daughter would be proud of us!

B Complete the company article extracts about its family-friendly policies. Use the words given and a structure from the chart.

All parents complained of high childcare costs before our childcare center opened 10 years ago. Many say that _____ (it / not be) for their own parents' help, they could not have continued to work when their children were small. The center is highly valued by employees. "_____ (it / not be) for the care center, I simply couldn't do this job," is a typical comment. The costs of running this facility are high, but _____ (be) the center _____ (close), the company would lose experienced employees. Flexible working is also important. Most parents said that _____ (they / have) the opportunity to work part-time when their children were small, they would have done so. Others said they needed two incomes. One told us, "_____ (we / not keep) working, we couldn't have managed financially." Trying to juggle family life and career is still an issue. Many non-parents report that _____ (it / not be) for their careers, they might start families earlier.

Grammar extra *Unit 7, Lesson B*

These activities present and practice more patterns with and functions of *what* clauses as the subject or object of a sentence.

1 More on *what* clauses

Present the grammar chart Read the information aloud.

Understand the grammar Have Ss look at the top section of the chart. Ask a few Ss to each choose a *what* clause and complete it with information that could describe or analyze a current topical problem or situation. Repeat this with the next two sections of the chart.

Preview and do the task Read the instructions aloud. Say, "Look at number 2. This is something these people have *done* – they're not talking about a place they have *gone to*. So you need the verb *do*. What is the verb form in this item?" [present perfect] Say, "When you change the underlined phrase to a *what* clause, you need the present perfect of *do*."

Ask, "What verb form will you need after *is*?" [base form; go] Have Ss complete the task and then compare answers in pairs. Check answers with the class.

Answers

What we're seeing today is; What we do know is;
1. What we're doing is
2. What my husband and I have done is go
3. What we want to do is stay; What we've found is
4. What it boils down to is
5. What it comes down to is

2 *what* clauses with passive verbs and modals in writing

Present the grammar chart Read the information aloud.

Understand the grammar Ask, "What's the pattern for the first section of the chart?" [*what* + *be* + past participle] Ask Ss to look at the middle section of the chart. Say, "In writing, you might need to define expressions or terms. These phrases are useful to help you do that." Ask Ss to look at the bottom section of the chart. Say, "Look at the words in bold. What kinds of words are joined?" [the affirmative and negative forms of the same modal verbs]

Preview and do the task Read the instructions aloud. Have Ss complete the task. Check answers with the class.

Answers

1. what is known as
2. What is considered; what is called
3. what is called; could and could not wear; must and must not do
4. what is required; what is . . . termed

Unit 7, Lesson B *Grammar extra*

1 More on *what* clauses

- Speakers often use a *what* clause as the subject of a verb to do the things below.

Describe and analyze situations	What we're seeing is . . . What we do know is . . . What we've seen is . . . What we've found is . . . What's happening now is . . . What it comes / boils down to is . . .
Say what is being done	What we're doing is . . . What we've done is . . . What we're (really) trying to do is . . . What we don't want to do is . . .
Say what is needed or wanted	What we need to / have to do is . . . What we want to do is . . . What we're looking for is . . . What we would like to do is . . .

Rewrite the underlined sentences in the article. Use *what* clauses and add the verb *is*.

An organization recently released a report on the state of families today. The report said, "We're seeing today the unprecedented breakdown of relationships." While the cause of the breakdowns is complex, the report emphasized, "We do know that divorce is tearing families apart." Their survey asked people, "How do you keep your relationship strong?" Here are some excerpts from the responses.
1. "We're creating more family time."
2. "My husband and I have gone to counseling."
3. "We want to stay together. We've found that it gets easier with time."
4. "It boils down to being more tolerant of other people."
5. "It comes down to small things, like doing something special for each other every day."

2 *what* clauses with passive verbs and modals in writing

- In some *what* clauses, *what* is the subject of a passive verb.
  What was intended to be a small, quiet wedding became a huge affair.
  There may be a problem if your income falls short of **what is needed** to run your home.

- You can use these phrases in writing to define words and expressions: what is / are called, what is / are known as, what is / are termed.
  When planning a wedding, many couples choose **what is known as** a "full wedding package."
  My grandparents had **what is called** an "arranged introduction."

- This is a common pattern with modal verbs in object *what* clauses:
  We are always being told what we **can and cannot** do, what we **should and should not** think.

Complete the article extracts about the "worst marriage trends." Use the words given.

1. In Japan, some couples get _____ (what / know) the "Narita divorce." It's named after the airport near Tokyo and refers to the fact that the couple starts divorce proceedings on returning from their honeymoon.
2. _____ (what / consider) by most people to be a private experience after the wedding – the honeymoon – is becoming a family and friends affair. A group honeymoon, or _____ (what / call) by some a "buddymoon," is the latest "worst trend."
3. An email to four bridesmaids from a bossy bride – or _____ (what / call) a "bridezilla" – has gone viral. The bride told them what they _____ (could / wear) and what they _____ (must / do).
4. In case you're not sure _____ (what / require) to create a cost-effective wedding, it is _____ now _____ (what / term) a "drive through" ceremony. Couples are getting married at fast-food restaurants!

Grammar extra *Unit 8, Lesson A*

These activities look at using perfect infinitives after verbs in the present and past and after adjectives and nouns.

1 More on perfect infinitives

Present the grammar chart Read the information aloud.

Understand the grammar Say, "You can also use an infinitive instead of a perfect infinitive of some stative verbs, such as *have, be,* and *love,* in sentences about the past, but with action or dynamic verbs you need to use a perfect infinitive." Write on the board:

> *He was said to have had special powers.*
>
> OR *He was said to have special powers.*

Have Ss read the negative statements. Elicit the three patterns.

Preview and do the task Read the instructions aloud. Have Ss complete the task. Check answers with the class.

Answers

Harry Houdini was known to have suffered; he was said to have refused; was believed to have caused; is still thought to have been; seems to have caused; Harry Houdini himself claimed to have been; doesn't appear to have been / appears not to have been; appears not to have deterred / appears to have not deterred / doesn't appear to have deterred; is known to have tried; seem not to have been / seem to have not been / don't seem to have been; appears to have gotten

2 The perfect infinitive after adjectives and nouns

Present the grammar chart Read the information aloud.

Understand the grammar For each example sentence, have Ss identify the adjective or noun that the perfect infinitive follows. Ask Ss to suggest who might say each sentence and why. Have Ss write new sentences, replacing the perfect infinitive with another perfect infinitive and explain the situation. Elicit several of the new sentences.

Preview and do the task Read the instructions aloud. Have Ss complete the task and compare their answers with a partner. Check answers with the class.

Answers

1. to have seen
2. to have strived
3. to have received
4. to have come out
5. to have become
6. to have heard
7. to have become
8. to have met
9. to have contributed

Follow up Have Ss write six sentences about an important person in their country to share with the class.

Unit 8, Lesson A — *Grammar extra*

1 More on perfect infinitives

- You can use perfect infinitives after verbs in the present or past.
  He **seems to have fooled** everyone. (= It seems now that he fooled everyone.)
  He was **said to have had** special powers. (= It was said in the past that he had special powers.)
- There are three negative forms. The first is the most frequent and the third the least frequent.
  His wealth **does not appear to have changed** him.
  His wealth **appears not to have changed** him.
  His wealth **appears to have not changed** him.

Rewrite the underlined parts in this biography. Change the *it* clauses, using perfect infinitives, and change the punctuation. Sometimes there is more than one correct answer.

Harry Houdini was known to have suffered
Near the end of his life, the great magician Harry Houdini, it was known, suffered from appendicitis, for which, it was said, he refused treatment. However, as part of a challenge, a Canadian student unexpectedly punched him in the stomach, which, it was believed, caused Houdini a fatal injury. It was a sad ending for a man who people still think is the greatest magician of all time. As in death, his life was shrouded in mystery and, it seems, caused great speculation. It was Harry Houdini himself who claimed to be a native of Appleton, Wisconsin. However, he was actually born in Budapest, Hungary, and moved to the U.S. when his family emigrated in 1878. His family, it appears, wasn't wealthy. But the poverty in which he lived, it appeared, did not deter him from seeking success. Houdini, it is known, tried all kinds of magic tricks early in his career. However, his early tricks, it seems, weren't successful. He, it appears, got his biggest break with an act where he freed himself from a pair of handcuffs. It was the start of an extraordinary career as an escape artist.

2 The perfect infinitive after adjectives and nouns

- You can use perfect infinitives after some adjectives and nouns.
  He was **fortunate to have escaped**.   It was an **honor to have been** there.
  I'm very **lucky to have met** her.   It was a terrible **thing to have done**.
  I was **too young to have understood**.   She was the only **person to have achieved** that.

Read the information about Nelson Mandela. Rewrite the underlined parts of the sentences by using the perfect infinitive.

1. Many students today are too young and didn't see Nelson Mandela released from jail in 1990.
2. He is one of many activists who strived for racial equality in South Africa in the 1960s.
3. While he was dismayed when he received a life sentence in prison for his activist work, he remained true to his beliefs for a free and equal society. He spent 27 years in prison.
4. It was a remarkable accomplishment when he came out of jail without any anger or resentment.
5. It was also an achievement that he became president of South Africa in 1994.
6. It must have been an honor hearing his first speech after his release.
7. He is one of only two people that became an honorary citizen of Canada.
8. Many of the celebrities who have visited South Africa say they feel privileged because they met him.
9. I'm sure he was proud that he contributed so much to his country's history.

Grammar extra *Unit 8, Lesson B*

These activities look at more ways to give ideas extra focus using cleft sentences with *it + be* and *it + be* + noun phrase in writing.

❶ More on cleft sentences with *it + be*

Present the grammar chart Read the information aloud.

Understand the grammar Ask, "Why are cleft sentences useful?" [They give extra focus to an idea.] Ask, "In the first example, what is the subject of the verb *changed*?" [the Internet] Say, "The *Internet* is the important item in the cleft, and it is the subject of the main verb in the next clause."

Ask, "In the second example, what is the object of *invented*?" [the cell phone] Say, "*The cell phone* is the important item in the cleft, and it is the object of the main verb in the next clause. When can you leave out *who, that,* and *which* in a cleft sentence with *it + be*?" [when the idea being focused on is the object]

Preview and do the task Read the instructions aloud. Have Ss complete the task. Check answers with the class.

Answers

(Note: The answers given here are for the full form, *it is*, because of the formality of the text. However, the contraction *it's* is also correct.)

but it was my grandpa who / that influenced; It was an adventure (that / which) I will never forget; it was the exhibit that explained . . . scientists that / which had; it was NASA scientists (who / whom / that) we have to thank; it was NASA technology that / which put; It is / was that / the day that / which changed; I recall it is / was those NASA scientists (who / that) were; it was my grandpa (who / whom / that) I told; It was his response that / which convinced

---

Unit 8, Lesson B   *Grammar extra*

❶ More on cleft sentences with *it + be*

In cleft sentences with *it + be*, the item that you focus on can be the subject or object of the next clause. When it is the object, you can leave out *who, that,* or *which*.

Subject   *The Internet changed everything in the twentieth century.*
→ **It was the Internet that** *changed everything in the twentieth century.*

Object   *Martin Cooper invented* **the cell phone**.
→ **It was the cell phone (that / which)** *Martin Cooper invented.*
I remember studying **Edison** *for a history project.*
→ **It's Edison (who / that)** *I remember studying.*

Read the story. Rewrite the sentences, using *it + be* clefts to focus on the words in bold.

There were many influential figures in my past, but **my grandpa** influenced me most. When I was still an impressionable child, he took me to the Kennedy Space Center in Florida. I will never forget it as an **adventure**. I remember staring in awe at the space shuttle and riding in the simulators. However, the **exhibit** that explained how NASA needed children like me to become scientists had the biggest impact on me. I realized we have **NASA scientists** to thank for many of the things we see in daily life: baby formula, freeze-dried food, and ear thermometers. Not only that, but **NASA technology** put people into space. That **day** changed everything for me all those years ago. Looking back on my childhood, I recall **those NASA scientists** as being my heroes. Today **I'm** a scientist, and I told **my grandpa** first about my ambition to become one. **His response** convinced me. "Of course you can be a scientist. You can be anything you want to be," he said.

❷ *It + be* + noun phrase in writing

- In writing, some cleft sentences with *it + be* + noun are used to introduce issues, e.g.:
  It is no coincidence that . . . , It is a fact that . . . , It is no accident that . . . , It is no wonder that . . . , It is no surprise that . . . , It is a shame / pity that . . .
  It is no coincidence that *countries with strong economies became politically dominant.*

- Other expressions refer back to something that has just been mentioned, e.g.:
  It is an issue that . . . , It was a decision that . . . , It is a story that . . . , It is a system/process that . . . , It was a reminder that . . . , It was a moment that . . .
  In 1919, the atom was first split. **It was a moment that** *changed history forever.*

Complete the sentences in the article. Use *it + be* + the noun phrase given + *that*.

On July 20, 1969, the Apollo 11 spacecraft landed on the moon. <u>It was an event that</u> (an event) will forever be remembered in history, and _____ (no surprise) more than half a billion people watched it on television. During the previous decade, _____ (no coincidence) other countries had been developing rockets of their own. _____ (a period) became known as the "Space Race," as countries competed to develop superior space technologies.

In 1961, a Russian cosmonaut named Yuri Gagarin became the first human to go into space. _____ (a move) spurred President John F. Kennedy to announce a program to land people on the moon by the end of the decade. _____ (a decision) energized the entire nation. However, in 1967, during a launch test, three U.S. astronauts were killed. _____ (a tragedy) almost derailed the whole program. After an overhaul of the entire operation, the Apollo 11 mission was ready. As Neil Armstrong stepped onto the surface of the moon in 1969, he declared, "That's one small step for man, one giant leap for mankind." For those watching, _____ (a day) they will never forget, and for everyone else, _____ (a moment) defined an era.

Grammar extra   **159**

❷ *It + be* + noun phrase in writing

Present the grammar chart Read the information aloud.

Understand the grammar Check that Ss know the meaning of the nouns in the examples. Explain that *It is no* + noun means *It is not a / an . . .* Ask, "What issue is 'no coincidence' in the first example?" [that countries with strong economies became politically dominant] Ask, "What relative pronoun is used with *it + be* + noun to introduce issues?" [that] Have Ss suggest different examples using other introductory phrases.

Say, "Look at the example at the bottom of the chart. What does the expression in bold refer to?" [when the first atom was split in 1919]

Preview and do the task Read the instructions aloud. Point out that the first blank has been completed. Have Ss complete the task. Check answers with the class.

Answers

It is / was an event that; it is / was no surprise that; it is / was no coincidence that; It is / was a period that

It was a move that; It was a decision that; It was a tragedy that; it is / was a day (that); it is / was a moment that

Grammar extra *Unit 9, Lesson A*

These activities look at how to use *whatever*, *whichever*, and *whoever* as the subject or object of a verb and patterns with *however* and *whatever the* + noun.

 whatever, whichever, and whoever as subjects and objects

Present the grammar chart Read the information aloud.

Understand the grammar Say, "The *-ever* words can be the subject or object of a verb. A clause that begins with an *-ever* word can also be the subject or object of a verb."

Present *Common Errors* Books closed. Write on the board:

whatever   *whether*

Ask, "Which word introduces alternatives?" [whether] "What does *whatever* mean?" [*any at all* or *it doesn't matter what*]

Books open. Ask a S to read the information aloud.

Say, "Another error is to use *whatever* to mean *but*. What *-ever* word also means *but*?" [However] "Also, be careful of the spelling of *whatever* – it is one word."

Preview and do the task Read the instructions aloud. Ss complete the task and then compare answers in pairs. Check answers with the class.

Answers

1. whatever / whichever
2. whatever
3. Whichever / Whatever
4. whoever
5. whatever / whichever
6. Whatever
7. whoever
8. whether

② Patterns with *however* and *whatever*

Present the grammar chart Read the information aloud.

Understand the grammar Ask, "Which *-ever* word comes before *much*, *many*, adjectives, and adverbs?" [however] Ask Ss how to express the examples in a different way [e.g., *. . . it doesn't matter how many years or how much it costs.*] "Which *-ever* word comes before *the* + noun?" [whatever] Say, "Notice that you don't need to use the verb *be* in this pattern. So you can say in the first example sentence, *whatever the cost is* or just *whatever the cost*."

Present *In Writing* Read the information aloud.

Preview and do the task Read the instructions aloud. Have Ss complete the task and compare their answers with a partner. Check answers with the class.

Answers

1. **However much** you aim to earn in life – and **however** hard you try – you won't find a better career than engineering, in my view.
2. Engineering is a good choice, **whatever the cost** and **however demanding** the course.
3. **Whatever the cause**, there are simply not enough engineers.
4. **However many** engineers we train, there will never be enough.
5. **Whatever the financial merits** of a career in engineering, nothing beats the feeling of creating solutions to problems, **however challenging they are**.

Unit 9, Lesson A — *Grammar extra*

① whatever, whichever, and whoever as subjects and objects

- *Whatever*, *whichever*, and *whoever* can be the subject or object of a verb.
  - **Subject** — *Whatever* happened to the idea of building things to last?
  - **Object** — *Whichever* (*program*) you choose, make sure it's one that you're interested in.
- Sometimes a clause with *whatever*, *whichever*, or *whoever* is the subject or object of a verb.
  - **Subject** — *Whatever happens in your career* is your responsibility.
  - **Object** — We don't just take *whoever applies to this program*.

Common errors
Don't confuse *whatever* and *whether*. *Whether* introduces alternatives.
Whether you are an employer or an employee, come to our job fair. (NOT *Whatever you . . .*)

Read the report about women in STEM professions. Complete the sentences with *whatever*, *whichever*, *whoever*, or *whether*. Sometimes there is more than one correct answer.

1. Researchers found gender bias against women in _____ jobs they chose in the fields of science, technology, engineering, and math – also known as STEM fields.
2. Women are often considered as less capable than men _____ their qualifications are.
3. _____ STEM field they pursued, women were often also seen as less likable than men.
4. High school test scores now show that _____ wants to excel in STEM subjects can do so.
5. If the school environment is right, girls can excel in _____ STEM subject they choose.
6. _____ else high school teachers may do, however, they must focus on teaching spatial skills to girls.
7. Colleges should not just accept _____ applies for STEM majors. They should actively recruit girls into these courses.
8. All students, _____ male or female, should be mentored in college.

② Patterns with *however* and *whatever*

- *However* can be used before *much / many* and before adjectives and adverbs.
  *Engineering is well worth studying, **however many** years it takes, **however much** it costs. We will solve the problem, **however complex** (it may be), and **however long** it takes.*

- The pattern *whatever the* + noun means "it doesn't matter what the (noun) is."
  *We should make efforts to train a new generation of engineers, **whatever the cost**. **Whatever the reason**, engineering isn't attracting as many students as we need.*

In writing . . .
The most common collocations in *whatever the* + noun are *reason(s)*, *case*, *outcome*, *cause*, *merits*, *explanation*, *price*, *cost*.

Rewrite the underlined parts of the comments using *however* or *whatever* + an adjective or adverb, or *whatever the* + noun.

1. It doesn't matter how much you aim to earn in life – and it doesn't matter how hard you try – you won't find a better career than engineering, in my view.
2. Engineering is a good choice, no matter what the cost is and no matter how demanding the course.
3. It doesn't matter what the cause is, there are simply not enough engineers.
4. It doesn't matter how many engineers we train, there will never be enough.
5. It doesn't matter what the financial merits are of a career in engineering, nothing beats the feeling of creating solutions to problems, no matter how challenging they are.

160 Grammar extra

Grammar extra *Unit 9, Lesson B*

These activities review, extend, and practice using negative adverbs to begin a sentence followed by inversion of subject and verb.

1 More on inversion

Present the grammar chart Read the information aloud.

Understand the grammar Ask, "When you start a simple present statement with a negative adverb, what do you add before the subject?" [do / does] "And when the verb is simple past?" [did] "When the verb is present perfect or past perfect?" [has / have; had] Ask, "Which expressions need a particular word to begin a second clause, and what are they?" [*No sooner + than; Hardly / Scarcely + when; Not only + optional but*] Say, "*Hardly* and *scarcely* are tested in some international exams."

Present *In Writing* Read the information aloud. Have Ss write their own sentences with *Nowhere* and a comparison. Have Ss say their sentences to the class and ask if other Ss agree.

Preview and do the task Read the instructions aloud. Ask, "What's the negative equivalent of *anywhere*?" [nowhere] Elicit the answer. [**Nowhere in the world is there** a more famous sight . . .] Have Ss complete the task. Check answers.

Answers

Nowhere in the world is there . . . ; However, by no means did its designers intend . . . ; No sooner had . . . than . . . ; Hardly had work begun . . . when . . . ; not only did it lean . . . ; Only after it . . . did . . . close . . . ; And only then was there . . . ; No sooner had it closed than . . . ; Hardly a day went . . . ; not only has the tower reopened . . .

Unit 9, Lesson B   *Grammar extra*

1 More on inversion

- Use inversion when these adverbs begin a sentence. Notice the words that begin a second clause.

  Negative adverbs: *Not only . . . (but), Never, Nowhere, No sooner . . . than, No longer*
  Adverbs with negative meaning: *Hardly / Scarcely . . . when, Little, Rarely, Seldom*
  Only + adverb, prepositional phrase, or clause: Only then, Only after, Only when . . .
  Expressions with *no: At no time, At no point, By no means, Under no circumstances*

  *Not only **does** it **wobble** as people walk across it, **(but)** it also causes nausea.*
  *No sooner **had** the paint **dried** at one end **than** it needed repainting.*
  ***Hardly had** construction **begun when** there were problems.*
  *It opened. **Only then / Only after** the ceremony / **Only when** it opened **did** they **see** the problem.*
  ***At no time did** anyone **raise** any objections to the construction of this bridge.*

- Do not use inversion after *only, hardly,* and *scarcely* when they modify a noun, or after *In no time*.
  ***Hardly** a week went by* that there wasn't a problem. ***In no time, they built** the main structure.*

  In writing . . .
  After *Nowhere*, there is often a comparison.
  *Nowhere was the need for redevelopment **more evident than** here.*

Rewrite the information, starting with the bold negative adverb or a negative equivalent (e.g., *As soon as → No sooner*). Use inversions where necessary.

There isn't a more famous sight **anywhere in the world** than the Leaning Tower of Pisa. However, its designers did not intend the tower to lean **by any means. As soon as** construction started, problems began. Work had **hardly** begun on the tower in 1173 **when** engineers noticed it was leaning. In the following centuries, it **not only** leaned farther, but it also seemed like it would collapse. It was **only after** it became unsafe in the early 1990s that authorities finally closed the tower. And it was **only then** that there was an effort to stabilize it. **As soon as** it closed, work started. A day **hardly** went by that there wasn't a danger of collapse. Nevertheless, the tower was restored. Today, the tower has **not only** reopened to the public, it has been declared safe for 200 years.

2 Inversion with modals and in passive sentences

- After negative adverbs, the inversion with modal verbs is modal + subject + verb.
  *Never again **would** anyone **achieve** anything of this size.*

- In simple present and past passive sentences, the inversion is *be* + subject + past participle.
  *Under no circumstances **is / was** this project **allowed** to be delayed.*

- In present or past perfect passive sentences, the inversion is *have* + subject + *been* + past participle.
  *Never **has / had** such a large project **been completed** on time.*

Unscramble the sentences, starting with the negative adverb.

Hong Kong International Airport at Chek Lap Kok is a remarkable feat of engineering.
1. attempted / nowhere before / been / a more complex airport project / had
2. nowhere in the world / an island / had / constructed / on which to build an airport / been
3. completed / been / had / a project this size / under budget / rarely
4. could / bringing in thousands of workers / only by / the project / be accomplished
5. however, under no circumstances / permitted / the project / to fail / was
6. no sooner / were / finished / than work began / the designs
7. was / not only / completed on time, / but it was finished under budget / the project

---

2 Inversions with modals and in passive sentences

Present the grammar chart Read the information aloud.

Understand the grammar Ask, "What's the pattern for a clause that begins with a negative adverb and includes a modal?" [negative adverb + modal + subject + verb] Ask, "In simple present or past passive sentences that begin with a negative adverb, what is inverted?" [*be* + subject] "In perfect passive sentences that begin with a negative adverb, what is inverted?" [*have* + subject]

Preview and do the task Read the instructions aloud. Have Ss complete the task. Check answers with the class.

Answers

1. Nowhere before had a more complex airport project been attempted.
2. Nowhere in the world had an island been constructed on which to build an airport.
3. Rarely had a project this size been completed under budget.
4. Only by bringing in thousands of workers could the project be accomplished.
5. However, under no circumstances was the project permitted to fail.
6. No sooner were the designs finished than work began.
7. Not only was the project completed on time, but it was finished under budget.

Grammar extra *Unit 10, Lesson A*

These activities look at more ways to report events using single and continuous infinitives and perfect continuous infinitives.

❶ Simple vs. continuous infinitives

Present the grammar chart Read the information aloud.

Understand the grammar Ask, "What kinds of events do continuous infinitives describe?" [ongoing or temporary; possibly not complete] "What kinds of events do simple infinitives describe?" [single or repeated events, which are possibly complete] Say, "Simple forms generally describe events in a factual way. Continuous verbs describe events as ongoing activities. Both are often correct."

Preview and do the task Read the instructions aloud. Tell Ss they can identify perfect infinitives because *have* is the word before the blank. Have Ss complete the task. Check answers with the class.

Answers

Note: Perfect infinitives are also included here where they are possible but not prompted by the exercise.

improved; become; be increasing / have increased / have been increasing; do / be doing / have done / have been doing; been listening / listened; been hoping / hoped; to move; had; survived; stopped; been preparing; be working; get; had; ignored / been ignoring

❷ More on perfect continuous infinitives

Present the grammar chart Read the information aloud.

Understand the grammar Say, "Look at the bold verbs in the first two example sentences. Are they the same form?" [no] "What forms are they?" [simple present and simple past] "What follows both bolded verbs?" [perfect continuous infinitives]

Say, "Look at the bold verbs in the last two example sentences. Are they the same form?" [no] "What forms are they?" [simple present (active) and present passive] "What follows both bolded verbs?" [perfect continuous infinitives]

Preview and do the task Read the instructions aloud. Point out that the first *it* clause has been changed as an example. Have Ss complete the task and compare their answers with a partner. Check answers with the class.

Answers

1. Unemployment rates appear to have been declining; the economy is not believed to have been making
2. were alleged to have been traveling
3. Workers' unions are said to have been talking
4. The man is thought to have been suffering
5. the coal mining industry appears to have been declining; clean coal technology is reported to have been revitalizing
6. who was believed to have been diving

Unit 10, Lesson A   *Grammar extra*

❶ Simple vs. continuous infinitives

- Infinitives can be simple or continuous. The simple form describes single or repeated events in a factual way. It can also suggest that an event is complete.
  *A scientist claims **to have found** a cure for malaria. She hopes **to publish** her research soon.*

- The continuous form describes events as activities that are ongoing or temporary. It can suggest that the event is not complete.
  *The team appears **to have been working** on their research for several decades.*
  *They seem **to be making** great progress.*

Complete the infinitives in the editorial with the verbs given. Sometimes both simple and continuous forms are correct.

Weather-forecasting techniques appear to have _____ (improve). Certainly, the predictions of the scale and timing of major weather events, such as hurricanes, seem to have _____ (become) more accurate – fortunately so, because the frequency of strong storms appears to _____ (increase). However, what we, as a society, appear not to _____ (do) is to recognize how serious forecasters' warnings are and take appropriate action. As another huge storm hits the coast, some residents of low-lying areas appear not to _____ (listen) to the reports on TV and radio that urged them to evacuate. They seem to have _____ (hope) that the forecasts were exaggerated. Others were too poor _____ (move) and seem to have _____ (have) no help from officials. Now, looking at the devastation, many are lucky to have _____ (survive). The whole city appears to have _____ (stop) working even though officials are likely to have _____ (prepare) for a state of emergency for several days and despite the efforts of utility companies, which we believe to _____ (work) around the clock to restore power. They hope to _____ (get) the city back to normal in the next few days. We are fortunate to have _____ (have) the warnings, but many of us are unwise to have _____ (ignore) them.

❷ More on perfect continuous infinitives

- Verbs that are followed by perfect continuous infinitives can be present or past, active or passive.
  *The hacker **seems** to have been working alone.*
  *The economy **appeared** to have been growing steadily until 2008.*
  *The government **appears** to have been negotiating secretly with unions on a new pay deal.*
  *A terrorist group **is believed / is alleged** to have been planning attacks for several months.*

Rewrite these news excerpts without using *it* clauses.

Unemployment rates appear to have been declining
1. It appears that unemployment rates have been declining in recent months. However, it is not believed that the economy has been making a sufficient recovery.
2. Twenty soccer fans, who, it was alleged, had been traveling to an international match with the intention of causing a riot, have been arrested and banned from all future European matches.
3. It is said that workers' unions have been talking with employers in the auto industry this week.
4. A man was arrested after disrupting a flight en route to Miami. It is thought the man had been suffering from an anxiety attack.
5. While it appeared that the coal mining industry had been declining in the last part of the twentieth century, it is reported that clean coal technology has been revitalizing the industry.
6. A man who, it was believed, was diving for sunken treasure has been reported missing.

These activities look at using the subjunctive to refer to the past, with passive verbs, and in conditional sentences.

 More on the subjunctive

Present the grammar chart Read the information aloud. Have Ss read the examples.

Understand the grammar Ask, "What is the form of the subjunctive?" [the base form of the verb] "Does the subjunctive form change for the past tense?" [no] "How do you make the subjunctive negative?" [Use *not* before the verb] Ask, "Can the subjunctive be used in the passive?" [yes] "What's the pattern?" [*be* + past participle]

Preview and do the task Read the instructions aloud. Say, "Look at the chart on p. 109 for help, if needed." Have Ss complete the task and then compare answers in pairs. Check answers with the class.

Answers

. . . a reporter **leave** a war zone . . . they **be allowed** to stay . . . locations **not be revealed** to ensure . . . journalists **provide** detailed . . . **be recognized** . . . media **respect** their privacy . . . work **not be abandoned** . . . **be publicized** . . . reporter **not be forgotten** . . . she **be remembered** for her courage . . .

Unit 10, Lesson B   *Grammar extra*

❶ More on the subjunctive

- The subjunctive form is used for both the present and the past. It does not change.
  *An editor may require that a journalist **reveal** his or her sources.*
  *The military instisted that all reporters **leave** the war zone.*

- The negative subjunctive is *not* + verb. Do not use *do / does / did*.
  *It is often advisable that a local journalist **not report** the truth about corrupt officials.*

- Passive forms of the subjunctive are *be* + past participle and *not be* + past participle.
  *It is essential that interviewees **be treated** with respect.*
  *We requested that the exact location of the journalists **not be broadcast**.*

Read the editorial. Find 10 verbs you can change to the subjunctive form, either by deleting a verb or changing the form of a verb.

Journalists who cover combat zones often pay the ultimate price for their determination to report the news. While media outlets may not require a reporter to leave a war zone, they often encourage him or her to do so. Even so, journalists often insist that they should be allowed to stay. Typically, they request that their exact locations are not revealed to ensure their safety. While viewers demand that journalists should provide detailed reporting on conflicts worldwide, it is essential that the dangers they face in doing their work are recognized. One such courageous reporter died this week. Her family asked the media to respect their privacy. However, she herself requested that her work should not be abandoned. Indeed, in a video made shortly before her death, she said that it was critical that the plight of civilians in the cross fire is publicized. This editor asks that this reporter should not be forgotten. It is important that she is remembered for her courage in reporting the truth.

❷ The subjunctive and conditional sentences

- The subjunctive can also be used in conditional sentences after *on condition that*.
  *A witness agreed to testify on condition that he **remain** anonymous / he **not be named**.*

- You can use *whether it / they be . . . or . . .* OR *be it / they . . . or . . .* to introduce alternative ideas. They mean "whether we are talking about one thing or another, the issue is the same."
  *One way to read the news, **whether it be** print or broadcast media, is to question what you read.*
  *The problem with news reporting, **be it** live or recorded, is that it is always selective.*

Rewrite the underlined parts of this editorial with *on condition that, whether it be,* or *be it* (both may be possible) with the same meaning. Make any other changes necessary.

Writing vs. Conversation
The subjunctive is rarely used in conversation. However, *whether it / they be . . . or . . .* is more frequent in conversation than in writing.

It makes no difference if it's a television report or a printed news article, bias exists. Research shows 1 in 6 adults perceive bias in the news, both liberal and conservative. Reporting should be balanced, either in terms of reporting a range of perspectives or reflecting the diversity of public opinion. There are other problems with the way in which stories are reported, both in the use of biased language and in the fact that certain stories are given more coverage. One reporter stated, and he insisted that he did not want to be identified, that the media represent the views of the sources of their funding. Media outlets, and the issue is the same if they are transparent or not, show bias, so read as many sources as possible.

---

❷ The subjunctive and conditional sentences

Present the grammar chart Read the information aloud.

Understand the grammar Ask, "What expression introduces a conditional clause in the subjunctive?" [on condition that] Point out that in the example sentence, *remain* is a subjunctive form. Also point out the alternative negative sentence ending. Ask, "What verb form is this verb?" [passive negative subjunctive] Elicit the pattern. [subject + *not* + *be* + past participle] Add, "In addition to after *on condition that*, the subjunctive can be used after *providing / provided that*, but this is very rare."

Have Ss look at the information about *whether it be* and *be it*. Ask, "What are the alternative ideas in each sentence?" [print media and broadcast media; live news and recorded news] Say, "In the example in the chart, the pronoun *it* is used between *whether* and *be*. There can be other subjects, mostly pronouns, between *whether* and *be*, but mostly the subject is *it* or *they*."

Preview and do the task Read the instructions aloud. Have Ss complete the task. Check answers with the class.

Answers

Whether it be / be it; whether it be / be it . . . or . . . ; whether it be / be it; whether it be / be it . . . or . . . ; on condition that he not be identified; whether they be / be they

Grammar extra *Unit 11, Lesson A*

These activities look at more ways to use *be to* and related expressions, including for instructions.

 More on *be to; be due to, meant to*

Present the grammar chart Read the information aloud.

Understand the grammar Have Ss read each section and suggest true examples for each one about events Ss know of. Elicit the form of a passive verb after *be to*. [*be* + past participle] Ask, "Which examples in the last section include a passive verb after a *be to* expression?" [be published, be announced] Ask, "In negative statements, where do you put *not*?" [after *be*] Say, "*Be to, be due to,* and *be meant to* are much more common in writing than in conversation."

Preview and do the task Read the instructions aloud. Ask Ss to call out the answer for the first blank. [are due to attend] Check that Ss understand why this is correct.

Have Ss complete the task and then compare answers in pairs. Check answers with the class.

Answers

are due to; is to consider; 's meant to teach; is about to end; was due to end; is to be believed; are about to be launched; are about to be killed; is about to be destroyed; is to be ignored; are to be believed; were to be interrupted; were to be forced out; is to hold

---

 be to for orders and instructions

Present the grammar chart Read the information aloud.

Understand the grammar Ask the class to provide more example sentences that describe orders or instructions set down by the school.

Preview and do the task Read the instructions aloud. Have Ss complete the task. Check answers with the class.

Answers

1. All fire doors are to be kept shut at all times.
2. Fire alarms and sprinkler systems are not to be tampered with.
3. If the fire alarms sound, staff members are to leave all personal belongings and exit the building.
4. Staff members are not to stay in the building under any circumstances.
5. No one is to use the elevators in the event of a fire.
6. All staff members are to meet in the parking lot.
7. Each department head is to take a roll call once staff is assembled in the parking lot.
8. No one is to leave the lot until notified that it is permissible to do so.
9. Under no circumstances is anyone to return to the building without notification from the fire department.

Unit 11, Lesson A   *Grammar extra*

① More on *be to; be due to, be meant to*

- You can use *be to* to describe fixed events in the future, especially official or scheduled events.
  The president **is to** host a summit of world leaders in May. World leaders **are to** meet in May.

- You can use passive verbs after *be to* expressions.
  Meetings **are to be held** in July, and a report **is to be published** in the fall.
  The government is looking at new technology, which **is about to be tested** in national trials.

- *Be to* can be used in conditional sentences to state what is expected or assumed.
  If we **are to** believe scientists, weather patterns are changing. (= If we are expected to believe)

- *Be due to* suggests that the time is or was known. *Be meant to* means "what is or was intended."
  The report **is not due to** be published until next week. Results **were due to** be announced last week.
  The law **is meant to** protect citizens from cyberattacks. It **was not meant to** restrict freedoms.

Read the article and complete it with the prompts given. Use the passive where necessary.

State officials _____ (due / attend) a national disaster conference next month as part of a series of events. The upcoming conference _____ (be / consider) how to cope with major disasters. "It _____ (mean / teach) us how to survive," the governor stated, "in the event of a major catastrophe." With so many in the media declaring, "The world _____ (about / end)," it would serve us well to know how to survive. But how likely is such an event? The world _____ (due / end) in 2012, but it didn't. In fact, if the media hype _____ (be / believe), disasters would have struck the world several times over in the last decade. Disaster theories have suggested that nuclear weapons _____ (about / launch) accidentally, that millions of people _____ (about / kill) by a deadly virus, or that the northern United States _____ (about / destroy) by a super volcano. While much of the hype _____ (be / ignore), there are other real dangers if experts' warnings _____ (be / believe). Perhaps, then, we really *should* prepare for disaster. If water supplies _____ (be / interrupt), what would you do? If your family _____ (be / force out) of the area, where would you go? If your community _____ (be / hold) a disaster awareness event next month, attend – it could save your life.

② be to for orders and instructions

- *Be to* is used to give or describe orders and instructions, mostly in official notices or written instructions.
  No one **is to use** the fire exits except in an emergency. Staff members **are not to open** windows.
  These doors **are to be kept** closed at all times. They **are not to be left** open.

Read this emergency fire plan from a company website. Rewrite the plan, using *be to*.

1. Keep all fire doors shut at all times. *All fire doors are to be kept shut at all times.*
2. Do not tamper with fire alarms and sprinkler systems.
3. If the fire alarms sound, staff members should leave all personal belongings and exit the building.
4. Staff members should not stay in the building under any circumstances.
5. No one should use the elevators in the event of a fire.
6. All staff members should meet in the parking lot.
7. Each department head should take a roll call once staff is assembled in the parking lot.
8. No one should leave the lot until notified that it is permissible to do so.
9. Under no circumstances should anyone return to the building without notification from the fire department.

164 Grammar extra

Grammar extra Unit 11, Lesson B

These activities focus on passive perfect infinitive verb complements and *would rather* + passive.

1 More on passive perfect infinitives

Present the grammar chart Read the information aloud.

Understand the grammar Ask, "How many passive verbs are in the first example?" [one, the perfect infinitive] Ask, "And the second?" [two, *is believed* and the perfect infinitive] Ask, "Can passive perfect verb complements follow both active and passive verbs?" [yes]

Preview and do the task Read the instructions aloud. Have Ss look at the first blank. Elicit the two possible answers. Have Ss complete the task and compare their answers with a partner. Check answers with the class.

Answers

seems not to have been resolved / does not seem to have been resolved; appear to have been kept; seem to have been divided

1. are / were believed to have been composed
2. are / were reported to have been hidden
3. are / were rumored to have been written; were found to have been used
4. are / were alleged to have been written; is / was reported to have been kidnapped; seems not to have been found / does not seem to have been found; are said to have been included
5. appear to have been given

Unit 11, Lesson B   Grammar extra

1 More on passive perfect infinitives

- Passive perfect infinitives can follow active or passive verbs. The most frequent active verbs are *seem, appear, claim*. The most frequent passive verbs are *be believed, be known, be reported, be found, be rumored, be alleged, be said*, and the expression *be supposed to*.
  Shakespeare's plays **appear to have been enjoyed** by Queen Elizabeth I.
  Shakespeare **is believed to have been born** in 1564.

Complete the sentences in the article using the verbs given. Sometimes the first verb in each pair can be present or past. Each verb phrase has a passive perfect infinitive.

The movie *Anonymous* reignited interest in the English poet and playwright Shakespeare. The plot of the movie focuses on the debate, which _____ (seem / not /resolve), about whether Shakespeare wrote his own plays. Few records of his personal life _____ (appear / keep), which makes verifying his work difficult. Here are some of the issues on which scholars _____ (seem / divide) for many years.

1. Shakespeare's plays _____ (believe / compose) in collaboration with other authors.
2. Secret codes about the political climate of the time _____ (report / hide) in his plays.
3. The plays _____ (rumor / write) by his rival, Christopher Marlowe. In one study, identical word patterns _____ (find / use) by both writers.
4. In the movie *Anonymous*, the plays _____ (allege / write) by Edward de Vere, Earl of Oxford. A well-traveled lawyer, de Vere _____ (report / kidnap) by pirates and left on the shores of Denmark, which was supposedly the inspiration for *Hamlet*. However, this event _____ (seem / not / find) in written sources used for the play, which raises the question: How did Shakespeare know some of the details? Many of the other places that de Vere visited _____ (say / include) in Shakespeare's plays.
5. Supporters of Shakespeare as the author of the plays dismiss these theories, saying that they _____ (appear / give) too much credibility.

2 would rather

- After *would rather*, you can use a passive base form.
  He would rather **be remembered** for his philanthropy. He'd rather **not be remembered** for his crimes.

- Notice the patterns in comparisons.
  Passive + active: He would rather **be killed** than **give up** his beliefs.
  Passive + passive: He'd rather **be loved** than **(be) respected**.

Read the article and complete it with passive base forms of the verbs given.

In law enforcement, many crimes go unsolved and sometimes remain a mystery. Not so in the case of a Florida grandmother. While she would probably rather _____ (know) for her good deeds than _____ (remember) for her crimes, this "pillar of the community" shocked neighbors when she was arrested 34 years *after* her crimes were committed. She was sent to jail, and while it's understandable that anyone would rather _____ (give) probation than _____ (sentence) to five years in prison, the woman shocked the community again. Two months later, she escaped from prison, obviously feeling that she would really much rather _____ (leave) alone to live her life out of jail than _____ (serve) a prison sentence.

Grammar extra **165**

2 would rather

Present the grammar chart Read the information aloud.

Understand the grammar Say, "Look at the first example sentence. What does it mean?" [He wants people to remember him for his philanthropy.] "Look at the next example. What does it mean?" [He doesn't want people to remember him for his crimes.]

Say, "Look at the bold verbs in the example sentences in the second half of the chart. What word is used between the verbs?" [than] "If you have a second passive verb after *than* what word can you leave out?" [be]

Preview and do the task Read the instructions aloud. Tell Ss to write *be* in parentheses when it can be omitted. Have Ss complete the task and compare their answers with a partner. Check answers with the class.

Answers

In law enforcement, many crimes go unsolved and sometimes remain a mystery. Not so in the case of a Florida grandmother. While she would probably rather be known for her good deeds than (be) remembered for her crimes, this "pillar of the community" shocked neighbors when she was arrested 34 years *after* her crimes were committed. She was sent to jail, and while it's understandable that anyone would rather be given probation than (be) sentenced to five years in prison, the woman shocked the community again. Two months later, she escaped from prison, obviously feeling that she would really much rather be left alone to live her life out of jail than serve a prison sentence.

Grammar extra *Unit 12, Lesson A*

These activities provide more practice with object + *-ing* patterns.

1 Common verbs, adjectives, and nouns + object + *-ing*

Present the grammar chart Read the information aloud.

Understand the grammar Say, "These are the verbs, adjectives, and nouns that are some of the most common words used in this pattern. The object in these patterns can be a noun or a pronoun. Look at the examples below. In the first example sentence, what noun is the object in the object + *ing* pattern?" [my father] "What pronoun is the object in the second sentence?" [you] Say, "Pronouns can be people, for example *him, her, us, them*, and so on." Write on the board:

I remember him saying . . .

You'll hate me saying this, but . . .

Say, "Pronouns can also be indefinite, such as *someone, everybody*, and *anything*." Write on the board:

I don't remember anyone doing that . . .

I remember that happening . . .

For each pattern in the chart, elicit an example sentence for three of the verbs, adjectives, and nouns.

A

Preview and do the task Read the instructions aloud. Say, "The first sentence has been done as an example." Have Ss complete the task and then compare answers in pairs. Check answers with the class.

Answers

happy about their adult children moving back; the thought of their offspring returning; worries about their privacy being invaded; supportive of their children finding

1. uncomfortable with your adult children living; don't mind them living; insist on them moving out
2. count on their parents doing; see their children taking; to leave you feeling; wrong with them wanting
3. chances of your adult children being; serious about your kids figuring out
4. probability of unemployed children remaining; you insist on them paying; Don't worry about your children going without; possibility of them being
5. adamant about you supporting; responsible for them needing to find; appreciate them doing chores and working

B

Preview and do the task Read the instructions and the example aloud. Ask, "Which are the more formal words in the example?" [their, children's] Have Ss complete the task and then compare answers in pairs.

Check answers with the class: have several Ss read one the sentences aloud.

(Note: *Any of the pronouns above can be made into possessive determiners in formal English. In theory, the nouns can also be made possessive, but this is extremely formal and is now seen as archaic.*)

Unit 12, Lesson A　　　*Grammar extra*

Common verbs, adjectives, and nouns + object + *-ing*

- Here are some common verbs, adjectives, and nouns that introduce object + *-ing* patterns.

Verbs + prepositions	*keep, appreciate, remember, leave, mind, get, hear, see, feel, watch hear about, listen to, worry about, result in, count on, depend on, think of, insist on*
Adjectives + prepositions	*interested in, tired of, sick of, supportive of, worried about, wrong with, responsible for, excited about, (un)comfortable with, aware of, serious about, good about, happy with / about, fine with, grateful for, crucial / critical to, crazy about*
Nouns + prepositions	*picture / photo / video of, thought of, report of, questions of / about, probability of, possibility of, chance(s) of, danger of, worries about, way of*

*I remember **my father giving** me a lot of advice.*
*But he also said, "I'm not **responsible for you repeating** my mistakes!"*
*I said, "There's no **chance of me doing** that!"*

A Read the advice to parents of young adults. Rewrite the underlined parts of the sentences, using a pattern in the chart. You may need to delete or add words and change the verb forms.

After college – what then?
happy about their adult children moving back
Many parents are happy if their adult children move back into their home after college, and in many families, it's expected that they will do so. For others, though, the thought that their offspring will return home raises worries that their privacy will be invaded. What's more, while parents mostly want to be supportive so their children will find their way in life, there is a limit to the financial support they can offer.

1. If you're uncomfortable that your adult children might live at home, then say so. Say you don't mind if they live with you for a fixed period of time. Then insist that they move out.

2. Set ground rules from the outset. If children count on the fact that their parents will do everything for them, they may never do anything for themselves. Parents often see that their children are taking advantage of them. You don't want this to leave you in a situation where you feel resentful toward your children, so speak up. There's nothing wrong if they want to do things their own way, but they are in your home.

3. If the chances that your adult children will be financially dependent on you for a long time are high, then you should probably do something about it. You need to be serious so your kids will figure out how to manage their own money. Don't pay for everything.

4. The probability that unemployed children will remain unemployed is higher if you don't insist that they pay their own way. Don't worry if your children go without luxuries or even basics. There's a good possibility that they will be more motivated to find work if they can't buy the things they want.

5. If your adult children are adamant that you should support them, be firm. Say you are not responsible for the fact that they need to find work. On the other hand, say you would appreciate the fact that they do chores and work around the home in return for rent.

B Look at the sentences you rewrote. Choose six and make them more formal by using a possessive determiner (*their, your, 's*) before the *-ing* form.

Many parents are happy about their adult children's moving back home after college.

Grammar extra Unit 12, Lesson B

These activities look at more ways to use reflexive pronouns.

1 More on reflexive pronouns

Present the grammar chart Read the information aloud.

Understand the grammar Have different Ss suggest examples for each verb in the first section.

Ask Ss to look at the second section and say what *itself* refers to in each example. Ask, "What does *itself* refer to in each example?"

Present Common Errors Read the information aloud. Write on board (Ss close books):

   1. *I found _____ in a difficult situation.*

   2. *I felt _____ terrible.*

   3. *I couldn't relax _____ .*

   4. *I usually pride _____ on knowing what to do.*

   5. *Then I remembered _____ .*

Have Ss put reflexive pronouns where they fit. [1, 4] Then ask individual Ss to call out an answer for each item.

Preview and do the task Read the instructions aloud. Have Ss complete the task. Check answers with the class.

Answers

yourself; yourself; itself; ourselves; ourselves; themselves; itself; yourself; herself; himself; himself; X; X; itself; itself; herself; X; X

Unit 12, Lesson B   *Grammar extra*

1 More on reflexive pronouns

- Reflexive pronouns are often used after *find, protect, defend, consider / see, call, ask, kill, describe, identify, pride . . . on* (= be proud), *distance, express, reinvent, introduce, see for.*
  *He **prides himself on** being an expert, but even he **found himself** "dating" a piece of software.*

- *Itself* is often used after *in, lend,* and *speak for.*
  *Identifying who you are writing to is a problem **in itself.*** (= without considering other issues)
  *This tale of Internet deception **lends itself** to a movie adaptation.* (= is suitable for)
  *His willingness to talk openly about the event **speaks for itself.*** (= is clear)

> **Common errors**
> You don't need a reflexive pronoun after *apologize, complain, develop, feel, relax, remember.*
> *I **felt** unhappy at first, but then I began to **relax.*** (NOT . . . felt myself . . . relax myself)

Read the article and complete it with reflexive pronouns. If one is not needed, write an X.

Even if you pride _____ on being a good judge of character, when it comes to online relationships, ask _____ if you are sure about who you are in touch with. Meeting people online is a challenge in _____ . Many of us who have found _____ in a problematic online relationship say we didn't see it coming – even those of us who call _____ experts. People often reinvent _____ online, and email doesn't lend _____ to getting to know someone well. You may have to protect _____ from dangerous people. Take my friend Ana, who considers _____ a cautious person. This guy introduced _____ via a dating site and described _____ as caring *and* single. The relationship developed _____ , but on their first real date, he apologized _____ for being evasive, which in _____ was a warning sign. How the story ends speaks for _____ . He turned out to be married. She distanced _____ from him, but he started turning up at her home. She couldn't relax _____ and complained _____ to the police.

2 Referring to unknown people

- If you refer back to an unknown person, you can use *he or she, him or her,* and *himself or herself.* People often say *they, their,* and *themselves,* especially after *everyone,* etc., but do not write this.
  *It is up to the person **himself or herself** whether to see a doctor when **he or she** needs to.*
  *Everybody needs sympathy when **their** problems affect their health.*

> **Common errors**
> Don't use *itself* for people or to refer back to plural nouns.
> *The patient was in fact a doctor **herself.*** (NOT The patient was a doctor itself.)
> *My friends do online dating **themselves.*** (NOT My friends do online dating itself.)

Complete the sentences. Then rewrite sentences 1–4 as you might tell a friend in a conversation.

1. Everyone should make sure that <u>his or her</u> personal details are not online.
   <u>Everyone should make sure their personal details are not online.</u>
2. An online dater can always ask for a background check if _____ wishes to.
3. Nobody should let _____ guard down when they meet _____ date.
   Meet several times, ask to meet _____ friends, and find out where _____ works.
4. Everybody should ask _____ if _____ is a good judge of character.
   If not, ask a friend to come along and meet your new date.
5. People can protect _____ by meeting in a public place.

---

2 Referring to unknown people

Present the grammar chart Read the information aloud.

Understand the grammar Write on the board

   1. *Everyone wants to keep _____ identity safe online.*

   2. *Someone once asked me to give _____ my address.*

   3. *I didn't know the person, so I deleted _____ email.*

   4. *Everybody has to take care of _____ online.*

Ask, "How can you complete these sentences when you don't know if the person is male or female?" [1. his or her; 2. him or her; 3. his or her; 4. himself or herself]

Ask, "When people are in conversation, how do they complete the sentences?" [1. their; 2. them; 3. their; 4. themselves] Ask, "Which should you use in writing?" [*his or her, him or her*, etc.]

Present Common Errors Write the two example sentences on the board with the pronouns missing. Ask Ss to complete them and then check their answers. Have a Ss read the information aloud.

Preview and do the task Read the instructions aloud. Have Ss complete the task. Check answers.

Answers

1. his or her
2. he or she
3. his or her; his or her; his or her; he or she
4. himself or herself; he or she
5. themselves

Language summaries

Unit 1

Nouns
avid reader
battle
blogosphere
chef
fate
implication
means
memoirs
microblog
nonfiction
oral history
poem
plagiarism
prophecy
trashy novel
values
verse

Adjectives
abstract
agrarian
compassionate
compelling
continuing
enduring
exhausted
lasting
lucrative
ongoing
pre-literate
rhythmic

Verbs
compose
consist of
contemplate
determine
dye
evolve
hold dear
implicate
impress
predict
record
register
reinvent (oneself)
retain
value

Expressions

Understanding
come to grips with
get something out of
get (your) head around
I can't make heads or tails
   of . . .
It's beyond me.
see the point of

Remembering
come to mind
lose (your) train of thought
It's on the tip of my tongue.
learn by heart
off the top of (my) head
stick in (your) mind

Avoiding repetition

Auxiliary verbs

He's obviously enjoying it — as I am.
I think it's a great idea, but my family doesn't.
She took a risk, which is what I did too.
I haven't been abroad. My friends haven't either.
She changed careers — a lot of people do.
I hope it works out. It did for me.

Infinitive verb phrases; *one, ones*

I would love to write like her, but I'll never be able to. I mean,
   I'd like to, but . . .
We had to read Shakespeare's plays in college. Well, we were
   supposed to.
I shouldn't read trashy novels, and I try not to, but . . .
I used to read a lot, but these days I prefer not to.
I've read all her books. Her best one is . . .
Of the books I read, the ones I like best are nonfiction.

Emphasizing ideas
I do like the fact that anyone can write a blog
I do think that anyone can be a writer.
It does seem that everyone's writing something these days.

If so, if not
And if not, then does that mean anything goes?
Are there implications of this for literature? And if so, what?
That's just as important, if not more important.

Linking adjectives in writing
George is a compassionate and caring friend.
George is a compassionate, caring friend.
Lennie is a physically large but gentle man. . . .
A short yet powerful novel, . . .
Its dramatic, though not unexpected, ending . . .
It is compelling, if at times depressing.
Their dream will be difficult, if not / (or) even impossible, to
   fulfill.

Viewpoint 2 © Cambridge University Press 2014 photocopiable

Unit 2

Nouns	Adjectives	Verbs	Adverbs
adopter	cautious	adopt	**Predict**
adoption	domestic	appear	predictably
application	harmful	assume	inevitably
assumption	harmless	bombard	invariably
caution	intimate	categorize	
concept	millennial	classify	**Expect**
consumers	obsolete	get into	presumably
conventional	phenomenal	innovate	supposedly
fingerprint	poor	monitor	
innovation	radical	multitask	**Don't expect**
innovators	recreational	penetrate	ironically
laggards	so-called	presume	
life cycle	skeptical	regard	**Assume to be true**
marital status		represent	evidently
millennium	**Compound adjectives**	revise	apparently
multitasker	air-conditioned	target	supposedly
multitasking	carbon-neutral		
online store	climate-controlled		**Think is possible**
penetration	computer-controlled		potentially
phenomenon	custom-built		theoretically
pop-up ads	energy-efficient		
privacy	high-speed		**Think is ideal**
recreation	high-tech		ideally
revision	home-cooked		
section	human-like		**Expressions**
social networks	labor-saving		can't possibly
technology	last-minute		couldn't possibly
theory	net-savvy		invasions of privacy
updates	not-too-distant		that is
voicemail	self-cleaning		
	solar-powered		
	state-of-the-art		
	wind-powered		

Combining ideas

It plays either easy-listening music or birdsong.
It either reads your messages or gives you a traffic report.
Both solar-powered and wind-powered energy supplement
    the regular electricity supply.
Dishwashers and vacuum cleaners are regarded neither as
    remarkable objects nor as luxuries.
Many homes boast not only high-speed Internet connections
    but also high-tech entertainment systems.

Referring to charts, diagrams, and graphs in writing

The graph shows / illustrates . . .
As can be seen in the graph . . .
. . . as shown in the table.
In 2012, Internet users accounted for / represented
    32.7 percent of the world population.
North America had a high percentage of users in comparison
    to / compared to Africa.
In comparison / contrast, Africa had the lowest percentage of
    Internet users.

Signaling expectations

Multitasking is supposedly an essential skill.
Theoretically, you can pack 12 hours into an 8-hour day.
You can't possibly concentrate on more than one thing.
Evidently, you're either doing things badly or not at all.
Apparently, "high multitaskers" had poor memories and
    couldn't switch tasks easily.
It's almost invariably more efficient.

Adding information to nouns

the guy upstairs
someone next door
people on the other side of the world
people happy to give away this information
an easy concept to define
the subject to be discussed
ads offering personal recommendations
applications programmed to monitor your messages

Unit 3

Nouns

consensus
convention
dialect
issue
(peer) pressure
rat race
rebel
social life
social status

Adjectives

anxious
assertive
contemporary
controversial
dominant
elderly
extra-curricular
geographical
neutral
offensive
overwhelming
regional
ripe
sexist
tremendous
valid

Synonyms

accent – way of speaking
consensus – agreement
conventions – rules
distinct – different
evaluate – assess
frequently – often
inferior – less good
inherently – essentially
regarded / considered – seen
reveal – show
seldom – rarely
superior to – better than

Verbs

conform
regret
rethink
struggle

Expressions with *take*

take advantage of
take charge
take credit for
take heart
take into account
take note of
take part in
take personally
take precedence over
take refuge
take responsibility for
take steps
take stock of
take the initiative

Expressions

bearing in mind
generally speaking
get laid off
golden opportunity
speaking of
talking of
thinking about it

Linking events

Growing up, I was always branded a rebel.
I never met anyone, working as hard as I do.
Having built up a successful career, I'm happy with my life choices.
I've never conformed to social norms, not having had any children.

Adding emphasis

You'll be so excited that you can only think of the fun ahead.
Time goes so fast you won't notice.
It's such an overwhelming experience that many students drop out.
You don't even realize.
It may even take a year to adjust to college.
That will make things even worse.
Even the best students don't always get A's.
You only want to take refuge in your room.
It will only make things worse.
It's only natural to feel anxious.
Only you can take charge of your situation.

Changing views

Having said that, there were other pressures.
But then, I suppose there always was.
But then again, they say women still do more of the household chores.
Even so, their options were limited.
But even then, you're not guaranteed a good job.

Expressing results in writing

There was too much reading, leaving little time for evening activities.
She spoke so quickly that students could not understand her.
She spoke quickly, so students . . .
Group work was part of the course. As a result, / Consequently, the classes were lively.
It was an excellent course, and I would therefore recommend it.

Viewpoint 2 © Cambridge University Press 2014 photocopiable

Unit 4

Nouns

adhesive
apathy
biomimicry
breeding grounds
climate
colony
desertification
grasslands
landscape
lifespan
overfishing
predator
(fat) reserves
species
subsidy
wasteland

Adjectives

apathetic
arable
arid
barren
diverse
feasible
hard to imagine
money-making
noteworthy
rich (in)

Adjectives with the suffix -able

affordable
considerable
demonstrable
dependable
measurable
notable
profitable
reliable
remarkable
unimaginable
viable
workable

Verbs

Nature

adapt
adhere
encroach
expand
exploit
preserve
replicate

Animal behavior

attack
build nests
build up
dig a burrow
hatch (eggs)
feed and raise their young
go into hibernation
hibernate
keep warm
lay (an egg)
mate
store food
survive the winter months

Prepositions and prepositional expressions

amongst
apart from
as a result of
beneath
by means of
by virtue of
due to
far from
in addition to
in line with
in spite of
in terms of
on account of
per (year)
prior to
throughout
to a large extent
within

Expressions

Animal idioms

be a fish out of water
be a guinea pig
be in the doghouse
beat a dead horse
clam up
get off your high horse
have ants in your pants
have butterflies in your stomach

Expressions from nature

a dying breed
a nest egg
a running mate
grounds for divorce
hatch a plan
the goose that lays the golden egg
the young

Talking about the past in the future

How far will the tern have flown?
It will have flown 70,000 kilometers.
How long will it have been hibernating?
It will have been hibernating for six months.

Combining ideas

In line with USGS definitions, a desert has less than 250 millimeters of rain per year.
A camel can go up to eight days without drinking.
As a result of experiencing severe dust storms, China started planting trees.
Antarctica is a desert, apart from the fact that it is one of the coldest places on earth.
The Gobi desert has spread due to the fact that agricultural practices have changed.

Adding ideas

Not to mention all the other industries that depend on it.
Additionally, governments give subsidies.
Big commercial fleets are more efficient at finding fish as well.
On top of that, consumers got used to having a wide variety of fish available.
Also, fish became much more affordable.
What's more, the public has been pretty apathetic.
In any case, apathy has contributed to the problem.
In any event, it's impacting the ocean.

Prepositions in academic writing

Each organism depends upon another.
It is a subject of debate within the academic community and amongst scientists. . . .
In terms of our survival, this has not proved critical.

One for general statements

One might think this is a major problem and that one's worst fears will materialize.

Nouns

Risk-taking

expedition
feat
harm's way
risk
stunt
terrain
willingness

Ideas

amusement
brilliance
comfort
convenience
ease (of use)
effectiveness
efficiency
innovation
instrument
invention
inventor
originality
popularity
radiation
simplicity
willingness

Gadgets

abacus
compass
GPS (Global Positioning System)
lodestone
microwave
satellite
smartphone
smoke detector

Adjectives

Devices

archaic
compact
countless
elementary
everyday
functional
groundbreaking
humble
innovative
integral
major
obsolete
practical
portable
rudimentary
significant
standard

Verbs

Invention

apply
consider
engineer
incorporate
innovate
invent
label

Risk-taking

be / put (yourself) in harm's way
ensure
pursue an ambition

Expressions

Making a point

Absolutely (not).
Definitely (not).
Maybe (not).
Not necessarily.
Probably (not).

Sharing information

Adverbs within continuous verbs

Compasses are still being made.
They were continually being improved in the last century.
Alternatives to the compass were being intensively developed.

Adverbs within perfect passive verbs

GPS has already been incorporated into aircraft.
It had originally been developed for military use.
It has been widely used.

Past modals and the passive

He could easily have been killed.
The trip might well have been cut short.
He shouldn't have been permitted to do it.
It ought (not) to have been allowed.

The verb *make* in the passive

He was made to sleep in police cells.

Making a point

One way to look at it is that all kinds of things have been discovered through space exploration.
I look at it this way: there are other things we could spend the money on.
Let me put it another way: maybe we *should* explore space, but not till we've made our own world a better place.
Just think what could have been done to research alternative fuels.
Let's put it this way: there are better things to spend money on.
Think about it: that in itself does more for the planet.

Passive *it* clauses

It is often said that technological progress is important.
It is generally accepted / widely recognized / well known . . .
It has also been reported / shown / suggested that . . .

Unit 6

Nouns

Business

(the) bottom line
community
coupon
customer
deal
discount
economy
enterprise
entrepreneur
life saver
markets
merchant
multimillionaire
promotion
retailer
start-up company
subscriber
word of mouth

Organizational threats

data leakage
electronic data
espionage
hacking
intellectual property
logon information
password
protocol
strategic plans

Adjectives

confidential
corporate
ethical
granted
insecure
legitimate
malicious
mundane
savvy
secure
sensitive
retail
vulnerable
widespread

Verbs

Attract

appeal
attract
coax
convince
draw (someone) in
entice
induce
lure
persuade
pressure into
prompt
tempt
urge
woo

Deter

alienate
deter
discourage
dissuade
intimidate
put (someone) off
scare (someone) off
unnerve

Organizational threats

boycott
collaborate
communicate
encourage
estimate

Adding and modifying information

The company had more than 85 million customers, all of whom "opt in" to the site.

The Internet provided a new opportunity to coupon businesses, many of which have been successful.

Over 90 percent of companies, most of which are small businesses, said the promotion attracted customers.

Mason had an idea: Attract subscribers to whom you email special deals.

Shoppers clip coupons from newspapers, with which they can save money.

Referring to people and things

Lower prices will tempt some people, and some will be attracted by special offers.

Any store that makes people feel at ease will probably generate more business.

Stores need to find other ways to attract customers.

Other evidence suggests music can actually irritate people.

It needs to be like your home, not some other unfamiliar place.

Another store might offer self-service ordering. Yet another might create a "third place."

Persuading

Don't you think companies should listen to their customers?

It makes sense for any corporation, doesn't it?

Consumers don't have that much influence, do they?

It's more complex than that, isn't it?

Conceding a point

Well, granted, the notion is very popular.

Use modal verbs in writing

These factors can cause data leakage.

Some devices might / may / could be shared with others

It would be advisable not to allow employees to take work home.

We could also enforce the rules on using private computers.

Unit 7

Nouns

compromise
generation
in-laws
instant messaging
interactions
resentment
substitute
workshop

Adjectives

absorbed
computerized
dysfunctional
encouraging
face-to-face
isolated
immersed
mandatory
parallel
sociable
sophisticated
substitute
virtual
worrisome

Verbs

benefit (from)
compete
contend
drive apart
enable
enhance
establish
improve
inhabit
interpret
perceive
pursue
replace

Expressions

Binomials

above and beyond
back and forth
far and away
give-and-take
husband and wife
(in this) day and age
last but not least
live and work
now and then
now or never
out and about
over and above
pain and suffering
pick and choose
sick and tired
slowly but surely
sooner or later
stop and think
success or failure
time and energy
to and from
ups and downs
wait and see

Number and amount

a few
a great deal of
a huge amount of
a little
a number of
a range of
a small amount of
a variety of
an enormous amount of
few
little
several
various

Summarizing points

at the end of the day
in a word
in that case
in the end
then
when all's said and done

Hypothesizing

Ask any new parent the question, and you'll get the answer, "Absolutely!"
Were I in charge of education, I would make this class mandatory.
Had I known it would be this hard, I would have waited.
Should you think your experience will be any different, think again.
Let's make them mandatory. Otherwise, parents will be unprepared.

Finishing a point

When all's said and done, surely it's better to get to know them first.
At the end of the day, you probably don't have time for a boyfriend.
In a nutshell, we're all too busy.
In the final analysis, there is no difference between them.
In the end, it's a lot cheaper.
In a word, it's safer, too.

Expressing information

Is how you spend money a problem right now?
What many couples fail to do is (to) discuss the important issues.
How you resolve differences can be critical.
Can you agree how often your partner's family can visit without arguing?
Tell each other now whether / if you intend to work long hours.
Agree now on what your financial goals are.

Drawing a conclusion

So you think it's OK, then?
In that case, do you have time to date?

Expressing number and amount in writing

There are a number of / several factors that lead to improved relationships.
They don't take a great deal of time / effort.
It takes little time / a little thought.

Unit 8

Nouns

alliance
contribution
dispute
empress
figure
pharaoh
philosophy
weapon

Unearthing the past

ancestor
anthropologist
archaeologist
database
fragment
manuscript
paleographer
papyrus

Adjectives

ancient
archaeological
charismatic
considerable
courageous
detailed
distorted
groundbreaking
influential
insignificant
meaningless
minute
painstaking
philosophical
significant
superficial
tantalizing
thorough
undisturbed
unimportant

Changes

apparent
brief
conspicuous
fleeting
gradual
immediate
imperceptible
insignificant
lasting
local
long-term
major
massive
minor
minute
permanent
profound
rapid
slight
striking
sudden
superficial
temporary
universal
unseen
visible
world-changing

Verbs

decipher
engage
foresee
negotiate
nominate
observe

Expressions

Ordering events

after
after a while
as soon as
eventually
finally
in the end
once
previously
subsequently

Metaphors

bring (something) to life
brush over
feed a hunger for
kill an idea
look into a crystal ball
look into a window on
paint a detailed picture of
piece together
roll out (a project)
sit alongside
sift
starve (of something)
wind down

Referring to past time

He seems to have had a lot of respect for older people.
She is considered to have formed some extremely effective
    political alliances.
I'd love to have met Leonardo da Vinci.
Li-yun would like to have spoken with Confucius.

Giving ideas extra focus

It was scientists who / that started alerting us to the fact that
    the climate was changing.
Generally, it is not the small things that we worry about.
It is only when we are personally affected that we describe
    events as "world-changing."

Avoiding a topic

Don't get me started on that.
But that's another / a whole other story.
Let's not go there.
Let's not get into / talk about that.
I'd rather not talk about it / that.

Focus your viewpoint

That's what I'm saying.
That's what I mean / meant.

Ordering events in writing

After / Once / As soon as the war ended, they married.
On arriving at the station, she met my father.
Arriving at the station, she met my father.
Saddened by this tragedy, she decided to leave the city.
She had previously lived in the city.
They subsequently / eventually had four children.
In the end, / After a while, they married.

Unit 9

Nouns

agriculture
application
boundaries
caregiver
ceramics
construction
cosmetics
creativity
delays
dilemma
feat
forestry
impact
landmark
micro-robots
mining
reluctance
robotics
skyscraper
solution
steel
surgeon
therapies
urban planning
warfare

Adjectives

artificial
complete
concrete
ethical
fade-resistant
groundbreaking
hazardous
humanoid
lifesaving
scratchproof
urban

Fields of engineering

biomedical
chemical
civil
materials science

Verbs

accomplish
assemble
attempt
conduct
construct
deploy
design
determine
develop
elevate
engineer
erect
identify
install
interact
maneuver
monitor
perform
position
relate to
transform

Expressions

ahead of schedule
check on
complete (something) on
   time
fall behind schedule
get along with
in a short time frame

Talking about unknown people and things

however
whatever
whenever
wherever
whichever
whoever

Emphasizing ideas

Not only does it ease traffic congestion, but it has become
   a landmark.
Not once did the engineers fail to find a solution.
Never before had engineers attempted to build a bridge
   like this.
Only by elevating the highway were the architects able
   to achieve the stunning visual impact.

Using facts to support opinions

In view of the fact that it takes seven months to get there,
   that's a long way off.
There's one that's kind of surprising, given the weather.
That's pretty basic considering we're in the twenty-first
   century.
It make sense in light of the fact that some places got no rain
   at all last year. I mean none whatsoever.

Stating alternatives and preferences in writing

Robots are used in industry in place of / instead of / rather
   than humans.
Human caregivers as opposed to robots are best at caring for
   patients.
Robots are a good alternative to / substitute for humans in
   space.
Most people would rather have a human caregiver than a
   robot.
Robots are no substitute for humans in some areas.

Viewpoint 2 © Cambridge University Press 2014   photocopiable

Unit 10

Nouns

News topics

campaign
deficit
demonstrations
explosion
income
legal action
livelihood
oil spill
recovery

People involved in the news

candidate
correspondent
delegation
fact-checkers
investigators
investors
journalist
officials
politician
press secretary
protestors
senator
speechmakers
spokesperson
terrorist
victims

Reporting the news

accuracy
airtime
appearance
misinformation
myth
networks
news organization
news ticker
possibility
ratings
reputation
speculation
standards
statistics

Adjectives

balanced
biased
breaking
committed
conscientious
controversial
conventional
distorted
enterprising
exaggerated
extensive
fabricated
in-depth
measured
misleading
reliable
rumored
satirical
suspicious
trustworthy

Verbs

arise
broadcast
demonstrate
escalate
loot
mobilize
plummet
plunge
sue

Reporting the news

confirm
deceive
distort
establish
exaggerate
fabricate
materialize
mislead
misrepresent
overstate
prove
publish
report
trust
verify

Expressions

Breaking news

announce a campaign
bomb went off
cause the explosion
compensate the victims
consider legal action
contain the oil spill
fuel speculation
jump on the bandwagon
mobilize riot squads
rule out the possibility
run for office
stock market plunged
stocks. . . . making . . .
   recovery . . . markets
tensions escalate
undergoing routine surgery

Reporting events in progress

Efforts to contain the oil spill appear to be working.
The senator seems not to be announcing her campaign
   just yet.
Police were said to be searching for a red pickup truck.
Markets are said to have been gaining confidence.
The president will be undergoing routine surgery.
Investors might have been worrying unnecessarily.

Describing what should happen

The judge demands that the jury reach its verdict.
They insist that everything be edited.
The requirement that a journalist check the facts can mean
   time is lost.
It is important that the story be instantly available.
It is essential that its reputation not be damaged.

Highlighting topics

My girlfriend, she watches news channels all the time.
It drives me crazy, hearing the same thing all the time.
This guy at work, he has all these news apps on his phone.
Those news tickers, they're another thing I hate.

Subject-verb agreement in writing

News is easily misreported.
Information needs to be checked.
The public is concerned.
The number of websites has grown.
A number of websites have appeared.
Political reporting and campaigning are in danger of
   misleading the public.
The reasons for inaccurate news coverage are varied. People
   pass on inaccuracies.

Nouns

Imagined threats

arsenal
asteroid
dinosaur
debris
documentary
doomsayer
national grid
NASA

Hard to believe

con artist
forgery
deception
fraud

Artistic fakes

academic
analyst
arsenal
authenticity
brushstroke
carbon dating
digital-imaging
dishonesty
forger
handiwork
ownership
pigment
techniques

Adjectives

forensic
genuine
imagined
imminent
lighthearted
lucrative
notorious
perceived
recognized
unethical
unreliable

Artistic fakes

copycat
fortunate
genuine
high-resolution
laborious
multi-spectral
straightforward
uncommon

Verbs

appreciate
apprehend
authenticate
collapse
con
establish
exaggerate
forge
illustrate
panic
prepare
stockpile
threaten
trace
uncover

Expressions

be drawn into
be taken in
call someone on
come to light
pass off

Be to expressions for the future

be to
be bound to
be set to
be sure to

Idioms and phrasal verbs with *turn*

turn a blind eye (to)
turn back the clock
turn down
turn over a new leaf
turn into
turn out
turn (something) around
turn to
turn your back on
turning point

Talking about the future

A TV documentary is to air later this week.
If we are to survive a catastrophe, we'd better shape up.
If society were to collapse, these people are well prepared.
Civilization is not about to collapse. There's bound to be debris falling on us.
They said the world was to end in 2012. It was bound to happen, they said.

Information focus

He'd rather be remembered for his work with the FBI.
He'd rather remember his work with the FBI.
Abagnale deserves to be admired.
A 12-year prison term appears to have been considered harsh even then.
He avoided being apprehended for several years.

Expressing concerns

I'm not comfortable with (that).
I'm not too happy about (that).
That doesn't seem right.
That doesn't sit right with me.
That's my concern.
That's not good.
To me, it was a lie.

Conjunctions and adverbs in academic writing

This activity can be stopped as long as the authorities take decisive action.
Counterfeiting is a serious problem. Yet people are attracted to cheap, fake goods.
It will continue in view of the fact / given that there is a market for fake goods. / given the demand.
People buy fake goods regardless of / irrespective of / no matter how much it hurts the economy.

Unit 12

Nouns

attachment
chatterbot
correspondence
empty nesters
perspective
profile
realization
transition

Brain matters

capacity
consideration
endeavor
input
insight
neuroscientist
psychology

Adjectives

evasive
independent
responsible
shallow
supportive

Love is blind

affectionate
attractive
immune
particular
vulnerable

Brain matters

adolescent
efficient
elusive
impulsive
neural
vehicular

Verbs

account
characterize
dread
encourage
interact
maximize
mature
minimize
persuade
promote
rely
reveal (oneself)
sob

Expressions

Idioms and phrasal verbs

be accounted for
be (anything) to go by
be at the heart of
be close to
be immune to
be of great importance
be taken in
be the key to
brush off
come down to
dawn on (someone)
get to
give (someone) away
give in
give part of
give them away
go about (doing something)
go by
go some way toward
have to do with
hit it off
pick out
pick up on
play down
put (something) behind (you)
relate to
show (your) true feelings
take into consideration
talk (someone) into
think about
would do well to

Describing complex situations and events

They always insisted on us making our own decisions.
There's nothing wrong with children relying on their parents.
They were big believers in children being responsible for themselves.
I remember us setting off on a trip.
My mom and dad dreaded me leaving.

Referring to people and things

each other
herself
himself
itself
one another
oneself
ourselves
themselves
yourself
yourselves

Exploring arguments

I can see it from both sides.
If you look at it from a passerby's point of view, people probably don't do it deliberately.

At the same time, surely your skills and education are more important.
By the same token, I guess I prefer people who are more friendly than I am.
Equally, you can be cautious and let them prove you wrong.

Commenting on your choice of words

It seems unfair, to put it mildly.
It's pretty shallow, to put it politely.
To put it bluntly, there's something not right about it.
To put it simply, the media just creates unrealistic expectations.

Statistical comparisons

twice as likely . . . as
twice as often / much
three times as many . . . as
three times as much as
four times more . . . than
four times more likely . . . than
five times more / as likely

VIEWPOINT

TESTING PROGRAM

Contents

Note: *Speaking quizzes: sample answers* are available on the CD-ROM.

Introduction to the *Viewpoint* testing program

The *Viewpoint* testing program contains a wide range of tests and quizzes for you to assess the progress of your students. You can use all these tests right away, or you can use the Word versions provided on the CD-ROM to customize the tests and quizzes to suit your needs.

Three kinds of assessment

The *Viewpoint* testing program offers a comprehensive range of tests and quizzes, giving you lots of options for how you want to test your students. All quizzes and tests contain three parts:

- **General**

  Students complete a range of tasks (including listening and reading tasks) that cover the grammar, vocabulary, and conversation strategies they have been learning. Teachers score the tests using the answer keys provided.

- **Speaking**

  Students ask each other discussion questions on the topics from the units and then do a role play activity, with a particular focus on the conversation strategies they have been learning. Teachers assess their performance following suggested criteria and using the sample answers provided.

- **Writing**

  Students write short texts with a similar format to the ones they studied in class. Teachers score their answers following suggested criteria and using the sample answers provided.

The difference between quizzes and tests

- **Quizzes** can be used after each unit. You can either photocopy the quizzes from the *Viewpoint* Level 2 Teacher's Edition book, or you can print out PDFs from the CD-ROM. Word versions of all quizzes, answer keys, and scripts are also available on the CD-ROM.

- **Tests** can be used for mid-terms and end-of-book assessment. There are tests for Units 1–6, Units 7–12, and Units 1–12. The tests, answer keys, and scripts are available on the CD-ROM as both PDFs and Word documents.

Using the quizzes and tests

The *Viewpoint* testing program provides lots of options – and you can choose the best way to use the quizzes and tests to suit your needs and your situation. For example, you may want to give all three parts of every quiz and test, or you may decide you only want to do the general quiz after each unit and then give the writing quizzes for homework. It's up to you to decide the best fit for you and your students.

Available on the CD-ROM

General tests

    Administration and scoring guide
    Units 1–6 General test
    Units 7–12 General test
    Units 1–12 General test

Speaking tests

    Administration and scoring guide
    Speaking test: assessment sheet
    Units 1–6 Speaking test
    Units 7–12 Speaking test
    Units 1–12 Speaking test

Writing tests

    Administration and scoring guide
    Writing test: assessment sheet
    Units 1–6 Writing test + sample answers
    Units 7–12 Writing test + sample answers
    Units 1–12 Writing test + sample answers

Answer key and audio scripts

    Units 1-6 Tests: answer key and audio scripts
    Units 7-12 Tests: answer key and audio scripts
    Units 1-12 Tests: answer key and audio scripts

(*Plus* Word files for all tests, quizzes, audio scripts, and answer keys.)

Score record sheet

This scoring sheet can be used to record general (G), speaking (S), and writing (W) quiz and test scores.

Students' Names	Quiz	Unit 1	Unit 2	Unit 3	Unit 4	Unit 5	Unit 6	Unit 7	Unit 8	Unit 9	Unit 10	Unit 11	Unit 12	Units 1–6 test	Units 7–12 test	Units 1–12 test
1.	G															
	S															
	W															
	Total															
2.	G															
	S															
	W															
	Total															
3.	G															
	S															
	W															
	Total															
4.	G															
	S															
	W															
	Total															
5.	G															
	S															
	W															
	Total															
6.	G															
	S															
	W															
	Total															
7.	G															
	S															
	W															
	Total															
8.	G															
	S															
	W															
	Total															
9.	G															
	S															
	W															
	Total															
10.	G															
	S															
	W															
	Total															

Students' Names	Quiz	Unit 1	Unit 2	Unit 3	Unit 4	Unit 5	Unit 6	Unit 7	Unit 8	Unit 9	Unit 10	Unit 11	Unit 12	Units 1–6 test	Units 7–12 test	Units 1–12 test
11.	G															
	S															
	W															
	Total															
12.	G															
	S															
	W															
	Total															
13.	G															
	S															
	W															
	Total															
14.	G															
	S															
	W															
	Total															
15.	G															
	S															
	W															
	Total															
16.	G															
	S															
	W															
	Total															
17.	G															
	S															
	W															
	Total															
18.	G															
	S															
	W															
	Total															
19.	G															
	S															
	W															
	Total															
20.	G															
	S															
	W															
	Total															

General quizzes

Administration and scoring guide

Contents and purpose

The general quizzes help teachers assess students' mastery of the material in *Viewpoint* Level 2. Each of the twelve quizzes covers one unit in the Student's Book. All quizzes assess listening, grammar, vocabulary, conversation strategies, and reading.

Students' performance on the general quizzes helps teachers determine what target language has been successfully acquired and what may need more attention. Quizzes can be used as part of student grading and assessment. They also give students a sense of accomplishment.

The separate speaking and writing quizzes (see pages T-236 and T-252) can be given in conjunction with the general quizzes.

Getting ready for a general quiz

- Plan to give a quiz shortly after Ss have completed a unit. Tell Ss that there is going to be a quiz and when it is to be given. Tell Ss to review the entire unit to be tested. If Ss have difficulty with any particular language point, suggest that they spend extra time reviewing it. Encourage Ss to work together and help one another or to ask you for additional help as needed.

- Explain the purpose of the quiz: Tell Ss that the quiz helps them see how well they have learned the target language and what language they may need to review further. Explain how their score will be used, especially if it will be used as part of a final grade.

- Copy the quiz – one copy for each S in the class.

- Schedule about 30 minutes of class time for the quiz.

- Locate the audio for the listening task on the Assessment CD-ROM, which can be played from a computer or on a CD player. (The audio scripts are included in this Teacher's Edition, beginning on page T-224.)

Giving a general quiz in class

- On the day of the quiz, have Ss take out a pencil and an eraser. Tell Ss they are not allowed to use their Student's Books or dictionaries during the quiz.

- Hand out one copy of the quiz to each S.

- Encourage Ss to take a few minutes to look through the quiz without answering any of the items. Go through the instructions to make sure Ss understand them.

- Tell Ss they will have 30 minutes to complete the quiz. Write this time on the board: *30 minutes.*

- Tell Ss that about five minutes of the quiz time will be used for the listening task in Exercise A. Although this is the first exercise in the quiz, it can be done at the beginning or end of the quiz time.

- During the listening section of the quiz, you may choose to pause the audio if you feel that Ss require more time to complete their answers. You may also choose to play the listening section a second time.

- After the quiz begins, change the time shown on the board every five minutes so that Ss know how much time is left.

Giving a general quiz as homework

- It is possible to give a quiz as homework. Hand out one copy of the quiz to each S. Tell Ss to complete all parts of the quiz at home except the Exercise A listening task.

- Tell Ss to spend 25 minutes on the quiz.

- Remind Ss that they may not use books, dictionaries, or notes when doing the quiz.

- Tell Ss not to talk to other Ss about the quiz.

- In class – the class session either preceding or following the homework quiz – complete the listening task, Exercise A, according to the instructions above.

Scoring a quiz

- You may collect quizzes and grade them yourself. Alternatively, have Ss correct their own quizzes by going over the answers in class, or have Ss exchange quizzes with a partner and correct each other's answers as you go over them.

- Each quiz has a total score of 50 points. (Point values for exercises and individual questions vary.)

- Scores may be interpreted roughly as follows:

  45–50 points = Excellent

  40–44 points = Good

  35–39 points = Average

  34 points or below = Needs improvement

- To record quiz results, use the Score Record Sheet on page T-184.

Scoring particular task types

When the answer key designates that two check boxes must be checked, then *both* need to be checked in order to receive credit for that item.

For the reading tasks, students should mark T (true) if the statement appears in the text or can be inferred from the text, F (false) if the statement is refuted by the text, or NG (not given) if the statement is not mentioned in the text.

Unit 1 General quiz

Total Score

_____ / 50 points

A 🔊 **Listen to a man and a woman talking about their reading habits. Check (✓) True or False for each sentence.**

	True	False
1. The woman doesn't see the point of reading short stories.	☐	☐
2. The woman thinks online games are fun.	☐	☐
3. The man mainly reads books that have been assigned in class.	☐	☐
4. The woman is struggling with her course work.	☐	☐
5. The woman will probably read the short stories the man recommends.	☐	☐

A _____ **/ 10 points** (2 points each)

B **Complete the conversation. Use the correct forms of the auxiliary verbs be, have, and do. Some are negative.**

A Do you ever read poetry?

B No, I guess I _____ (1), really. But not many people _____ (2). But I _____ (3) when I was younger, sometimes. We had to write poems at school, and I was quite good at them. I remember many of my friends often asked me to write their poems for them – and I _____ (4)! I wrote lots of them.

A Well, maybe you should try again sometime. Do you ever write songs? I hear your brother _____ (5). Do you?

B No. My brother's written a few songs for our band, but I _____ (6) – I don't have the time, actually. Anyway, why do you want to know?

A Well, you're always reading – as I _____ (7). And I thought it might be cool to set up some kind of reading group, but for poetry, you know? My cousin _____ (8) that last year, at another college, and it worked really well.

B Yeah, good idea!

B _____ **/ 8 points** (1 point each)

C **Match the situations on the left with the expressions on the right. Write the letters on the lines.**

1. Your friend asked you where you got your shoes. You can picture the store, but can't remember its name. _____
2. You're telling your friends why they should see a new movie, and suddenly you can't remember what you wanted to say. _____
3. You found it hard to understand a difficult concept. _____
4. You were asked to give a presentation without any time to prepare. _____
5. You had to prepare to recite a poem from memory in front of your class. _____

a. Sorry, I just lost my train of thought.
b. I had to learn it by heart.
c. I just did it off the top of my head.
d. It's on the tip of my tongue.
e. I couldn't get my head around it.

C _____ **/ 10 points** (2 points each)

D Circle the correct words to complete each sentence.

1. I like reading fashion blogs, and many of the **one** / **ones** I read are really good.
2. I used to buy fashion magazines, but now there are so many good blogs that I don't really **need** / **need to**.
3. There are a lot of blogs out there. Every time I look there seems to be **a new one** / **a new**.
4. You can usually comment on a blog, though I generally prefer **to** / **not to**.
5. The longest blogs are not always **the best one** / **the best**, of course.
6. Anyone can start a blog, and in fact, I think I'd **like to** / **like**.
7. I hope to have links to other sites on my blog – at least to some of **the better** / **the better ones**.
8. I'd like to get started as soon as I can, but I know I won't be **able** / **able to** for a while.

D _____ / **8 points** (1 point each)

E Complete the introduction to a class with the phrases from the box. There is one phrase you do not need to use.

I do	I do believe	I do like	if not	if so

Well, I'm very glad to see so many of you here today, and _____ I recognize some
                                                                                    (1)
of you from last year's class. _____ hope I'll get to meet you all individually in the
                                              (2)
next few weeks to discuss dissertations. You may be having trouble choosing a topic for your

dissertation – _____, do come and discuss it with me as soon as you can. In the
                              (3)
meantime, you should have received the reading list for the class, but _____, please
                                                                                            (4)
come and see me afterward.

E _____ / **4 points** (1 point each)

(continued)

F Read the article. Then read the statements and write **T** for true, **F** for false, or **NG** if the information is not given.

Although autobiographies have been around for almost as long as books have existed, they were not considered a genre in their own right until the late eighteenth century. An autobiography is most simply defined as the story of a person's past, written by the person him- or herself. Some critics, however, believe this definition to be too broad. They consider that unless the writer reflects on personal development as well as objective facts and events, the book is not a true autobiography.

It is certainly the case that many early works of autobiography were designed to be explanations of the writer's actions, rather than simply a record of their achievements. In the fourth century the philosopher Augustine of Hippo called his autobiographical work *Confessions*, as did the French philosopher Jean-Jacques Rousseau nearly 1400 years later. The earliest known autobiography in English is that of a woman named Marjory Kempe, describing her life and travels. Although she wrote it in the late fifteenth century, the manuscript was not actually published until 1936.

In the sixteenth century, the Italian sculptor Benvenuto Cellini famously said that no one under the age of 40 should embark on their autobiography. This advice was generally followed until the nineteenth century, when it became the norm for celebrities — including writers, politicians, and actors — to write them. Since then, celebrity culture has become an even more important force in society. Interest in anyone famous is now so intense that people are producing autobiographies at a younger and younger age.

1. Autobiographies became recognized as a literary genre in the late 1800s. _____
2. Some of the earliest known autobiographies included personal information and thoughts. _____
3. Jean-Jacques Rousseau's biography is very similar to that of Augustine of Hippo. _____
4. The first autobiography in English was written by a woman in 1936. _____
5. Most autobiographies in the past 100 years have been written by celebrities. _____

F _____ **/ 10 points** (2 points each)

Unit 2 General quiz

Name: _____

Date: _____

Total Score

_____ / 50 points

A 🔊 **Listen to Tom and his friend Maria talking about their attitudes toward technology. Check (✓) the correct answer for each question.**

1. What has the man just bought?
   A. ☐ a cell phone
   B. ☐ a laptop
   C. ☐ a TV
2. What does the woman say about her cell phone?
   A. ☐ She doesn't know how to use all the functions.
   B. ☐ She just bought it.
   C. ☐ It's a nice color.
3. Why does the man keep getting new gadgets?
   A. ☐ He likes to have the latest ones.
   B. ☐ He needs them for work.
   C. ☐ He gets them for free.
4. How does the woman find out about new technology?
   A. ☐ from reviews on the Internet
   B. ☐ from her friend
   C. ☐ in magazines

A _____ **/ 8 points** (2 points each)

B **Complete the conversation with the words from the box. Some words are used more than once.**

also	and	both	either	neither	nor	not only	or

A It's interesting, isn't it, how cell phones have changed so much in just a few years. I mean, not so long ago they were _____ really expensive, but _____ really big and bulky.
(1)   (2)

B I know what you mean. My dad had this huge thing. He was always complaining about it. He said they were _____ affordable _____ convenient.
(3)   (4)

A Yeah. I mean, half the time you couldn't even make a call because you were out of range.

B I know. You _____ had to find a payphone _____ just wait until you got home and then
(5)   (6)
make a call.

A Wow. Can you imagine having to do that today?

B No way. People have _____ the time _____ the patience to do that.
(7)   (8)

A Right. Everyone needs to be in constant contact. I mean, everyone I know has _____ a
(9)
smartphone _____ a tablet. You know, so they're never out of touch.
(10)

B _____ **/ 10 points** (1 point each)

C Choose one word from each column to form a compound adjective. Write the letters (a–e) on the lines. Then complete the sentences with the compound adjectives.

1. custom-_____	a. called
2. last-_____	b. saving
3. solar-_____	c. minute
4. labor-_____	d. powered
5. so-_____	e. built

6. I don't know how people had time to do anything other than housework before we had all the _____ - _____ appliances that are now available!

7. If I make a lot of money when I'm older, I'll buy a _____ - _____ car so I can have everything exactly as I want it, and mine will be different from everyone else's!

8. If you want a cheap vacation, you can find some really good _____ - _____ deals on the Internet.

9. I'm tired of _____ - _____ experts giving me the wrong information about how to fix my computer!

10. Because my radio is _____ - _____, it can take some time to recharge the battery when it's cloudy!

C _____ / 10 points (1 point each)

D Replace the words in italics with the type of phrase given in parentheses.

1. People *who commute to work* _____ on public transportation spend a lot of time on their computers. (present participle)

2. If you want to buy a new laptop online, I know a good website *that you should try* _____. (active infinitive)

3. There are lots of elderly people *who are eager to adopt new technology* _____. (adjective phrase)

4. The kids *who live in the apartment* _____ next door all have cell phones, even the little ones. (prepositional phrase)

D _____ / 8 points (2 points each)

E Replace the words in parentheses by writing the adverb forms of the words in bold.

1. (In **theory**,) _____, all this high-tech stuff we have these days should be making our lives easier, but sometimes I wonder if that's actually true.

2. (It **appears** that) _____, a lot of people receive so many emails that they don't have time to read them.

3. Being able to communicate with other people anytime, anywhere, is (**supposed** to be) _____ a good thing.

4. In fact, having all these devices can become a problem, (which is **ironic**) _____.

5. (You have to **presume** that) _____, when they were first developed, nobody considered the downsides.

6. We now know that (there is the **potential** that) _____ our addiction to gadgets may be harmful.

E _____ / 6 points (1 point each)

F Read the article. Then read the statements and write T for true, F for false, or NG if the information is not given.

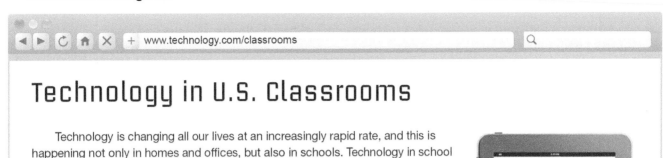

Technology in U.S. Classrooms

Technology is changing all our lives at an increasingly rapid rate, and this is happening not only in homes and offices, but also in schools. Technology in school will potentially revolutionize both the way students learn and the methods used by teachers. A study on how widely technology is used in U.S. schools has produced some interesting findings.

Sixty-three percent of all teachers reported that students in their schools had access to high-speed Internet in the classroom. When this data was broken down according to the grades the teachers taught, 49 percent in high school grades had high-speed Internet access in their classrooms, compared with 55 percent in middle school grades and 72 percent in elementary grades. It is worth noting that there were no significant differences in classroom Internet access associated with the places where schools were located: Typically, rural, suburban, and urban schools offer similar levels of Internet access. Nor, apparently, were there any major differences across the range of subjects taught.

Another issue highlighted by the study is how wide the variation is in teacher technology competency between states. Only 27 states (52 percent) have minimum technology competency standards, and only 11 (21 percent) provide data on how well teachers meet these standards. The methods used to evaluate teacher competency in this area also vary greatly. The states that reported the percentage of teachers meeting minimum standards of technology competency gave figures that varied from 8 to 100 percent. There is clearly more work to be done.

1. The older the students, the more likely they are to have Internet access in the classroom. _____

2. In general, students in rural schools have less access to the Internet than students in urban schools. _____

3. It is more appropriate to teach some subjects than others by using the Internet. _____

4. Most states do not keep data on how well teachers meet technology competency standards. _____

F _____ / **8 points** (2 points each)

Unit 3 General quiz

Name: _____

Date: _____

Total Score

_____ / 50 points

A 🔊 **Listen to a man and a woman talking about living at home. Check (✓) True or False for each sentence.**

	True	False
1. The woman wants to leave home because of an argument with her parents.	☐	☐
2. The woman's parents would like her to pay them rent.	☐	☐
3. The woman is not discussing her plans with her parents at the moment.	☐	☐
4. The man left home after finishing college.	☐	☐
5. They both agree their views may change in the future.	☐	☐

A _____ **/ 10 points** (2 points each)

B **Complete the conversation. Write participle clauses, using the verbs in parentheses.**

A When I was at school, I remember everybody talking about this new TV series. I couldn't join

in the conversations, though, _____ (not see) it. I felt really left out of things.
    (1)

B So it bothered you?

A Yeah, it did. My parents, you know, _____ (be) serious academics, never let
    (2)

us watch much TV. And certainly not any of the popular shows.

B That must have been hard. My family loved TV shows, but _____ (have) four
    (3)

older brothers and sisters, I invariably had to watch their favorite shows.

A I wish I'd had a large family. I mean, _____ (live) with just my mom and dad,
    (4)

I was often lonely.

B But you had friends, right?

A Yeah, but _____ (not know) about all the latest fashions and stuff, I was
    (5)

never one of the cool kids at school.

B Well, you presumably had other advantages. _____ (be) one of the so-called
    (6)

cool kids when I was at school, I now wish I'd focused on my schoolwork a bit more!

B _____ **/ 6 points** (1 point each)

C **Replace the paraphrases in bold with expressions from the box. There is one expression that you do not need to use.**

> take advantage of   take credit for   take heart   take stock of   take part in   take precedence over
> take refuge in   take responsibility for   take steps   take note of   take the initiative

My friend Jon took a break from his career last year, feeling he needed time to **think about**

and assess _____ some aspects of his life and **do some positive things**
                (1)

_____ to change what he didn't like about it. Having worked as a
        (2)

sales consultant since leaving college, he found his work tended to **take priority over**

_____ everything else, leaving him little free time.
        (3)

Jon's employer had asked his staff to take unpaid leave. So Jon decided to **make use of** _____ (4) the situation and do something different for a year. He loves sailing, but rarely had time to **participate in** _____ (5) competitions. So he volunteered at a sailing center, and now he's been offered a job as an instructor.

Jon's story allows me to **have courage** _____ (6) when my work gets me down. I know I can **take control of** _____ (7) my own life rather than **hide in** _____ (8) the safety of my regular job. He's taught me that I need to **do something before others suggest it** _____ (9) and change my life if I need to. I really think he should **accept praise for** _____ (10) inspiring me!

C _____ / **10 points** (1 point each)

D Complete the sentences with *even, only, so,* and *such.*

1. Our lives have changed _____ much that our great-grandparents wouldn't recognise many of the things we take for granted.
2. I didn't tell my grandparents I was planning to go traveling by myself. They'd _____ worry about me.
3. Some people love routine and _____ making the smallest changes in their lifestyle can be a huge challenge for them.
4. I often feel overwhelmed with work, but I can't do everything. There are _____ so many hours in a day.
5. There's _____ a wide range of subjects you can study at college that it's sometimes hard to choose.
6. Not everyone is academic. Some people don't _____ want to go to college, but feel they have to because everyone else is going.
7. It's _____ hard for some people to resist peer pressure that they just do what their friends are doing.
8. Starting college is hard, but starting a new job can be _____ more stressful.
9. The first few days of college can be _____ exhausting that you'll need to get some extra sleep.
10. A lot of people say that it's _____ natural to feel anxious the first few days of work or school.
11. My friends are _____ kind people that I couldn't imagine life without them!

D _____ / **11 points** (1 point each)

E Match the comments on the left with the contrasting views on the right. Write the letters on the lines. There is one contrasting view that you do not need to use.

1. Nobody seems to have time to talk these days. _____

2. Most people don't get enough exercise. _____

3. It's great that people can communicate so easily online. _____

4. Living in a big city gets me down sometimes. _____

5. People should not be allowed to drive in the city. _____

a. Then again, the countryside can be so boring!
b. Having said that, a lot of my friends are going to fitness classes.
c. But then, that's apparently the best way to do it.
d. But then, the public transportation system is really pretty bad.
e. Then again, people are always chatting with their friends online.
f. Even so, you have to take steps to protect your privacy.

E _____ / **5 points** (1 point each)

F Read the course descriptions. Then read the questions. Which course covers each question? Write the course letter (A, B, or C).

Spring Semester Courses in Sociology

Course A

Sociology of Work

The purpose of this course is to examine how work has evolved over the past 30 years and how it has been affected by radical recent changes in the U.S. economy. These changes have been so enormous that understanding the full extent of their impact on our daily lives is a challenge. They affect family life, individual life chances, and personal identity within the wider community. There have also been consequences for American culture as a whole, and the course will consider these, too.

Course B

Sociology of Language

There is such a close connection between language and society that discussing diversity in language can be almost meaningless if we do not also consider how it relates to culture. Variations in language frequently reflect social and cultural diversity. When someone does not use language in the same way as we do, do we feel prejudiced toward them? This course will introduce the linguistic diversity in the U.S., as well as look at how we respond to people who speak in different ways.

Course C

Sociology of Culture

In the field of sociology, "culture" includes areas such as how people spend their free time, what they buy, how they dress, and how they interact with the arts. In this course, we look at how our social status affects the choices we make concerning things like leisure activities, friends, and personal style. We will look at the way society influences our cultural behavior, and how we distinguish between ourselves and those we consider "different."

1. What factors influence a person's choice of clothes? _____
2. Do people's accents affect the way they are treated by others? _____
3. Does the economy play a role in people's sense of identity? _____
4. Does social status influence people's choice of friends? _____

F _____ / 8 points (2 points each)

Viewpoint 2 • Unit 3 General quiz © Cambridge University Press 2014 photocopiable

Unit 4 General quiz

Name: _____

Date: _____

Total Score

_____ / 50 points

A 🔊 **Listen to part of an interview with a wildlife photographer. Check (✓) A, B, or C to answer the questions.**

1. Why did Daniel become a wildlife photographer?
   A. ☐ He thought it would be a well-paid career.
   B. ☐ He couldn't get into college to study veterinary science.
   C. ☐ He wanted to be out in nature.

2. What is Daniel's favorite photograph a picture of?
   A. ☐ an animal that is being attacked by a predator
   B. ☐ birds migrating in the early evening
   C. ☐ a colorful parrot

3. What will have happened by the end of this year?
   A. ☐ Daniel and his wife will have published their first book.
   B. ☐ Daniel will have changed his job.
   C. ☐ He will have collected his third award for his work.

4. What does Daniel's wife do?
   A. ☐ She's a publisher.
   B. ☐ She's also a photographer.
   C. ☐ She studies wildlife in the Antarctic.

5. What was the most exciting moment in Daniel's career?
   A. ☐ seeing giant pandas in a reserve
   B. ☐ seeing turtle eggs hatch
   C. ☐ observing penguin colonies

A _____ **/ 10 points** (2 points each)

B **Circle the correct words to complete the conversation.**

A I'm concerned that by the time (1) **I'm / 'll have been** 50 years old, most of the Arctic sea ice
(2) **will have been disappearing / will have disappeared**!

B Well, it's certainly possible, as it (3) **will probably have been melting / has probably melted** steadily for years by then.

A And if that (4) **will have happened / happens**, our planet (5) **will have lost / will have been losing** some important animal and plant habitats – with all the ice melting away.

B Yeah, and if so, there's a danger that many species (6) **will have been becoming / will have become** extinct.

A I know. We really ought to do something about it, so our children (7) **won't say / won't have said** that we didn't try to stop it!

B _____ **/ 7 points** (1 point each)

C Complete the sentences with words from the box. There is one word you do not need to use.

burrow	colony	ground	hatch	lay	mate	migration	nest	predator	raise

1. A place where animals breed and _____ their young is called their breeding _____.
2. Some animals dig a hole, called a _____, for shelter.
3. Many species of birds build a _____ in which they can _____ their eggs.
4. A large group of penguins is called a _____.
5. Birds have to sit on their eggs to keep them warm until they _____.
6. Some animals, such as beavers, stay together and _____ for life.
7. An animal that attacks and eats other animals is called a _____.

C _____ / **9 points** (1 point each)

D Circle the correct words to complete the article.

The Amazing African Elephant

AFRICAN ELEPHANTS ARE THE LARGEST LAND ANIMALS ON EARTH. They can be distinguished from Asian elephants (1) **apart from / by virtue of** their larger size and the fact that their ears are larger.

(2) **Far from / In line with** simply being a long nose used for smelling and breathing, an elephant's trunk contains about 100,000 different muscles and is used for a wide variety of activities. (3) **As a result of / Apart from** drinking through them, elephants also use their trunks to grasp things – especially a potential meal. (4) **Thanks to / Apart from** two fingerlike features on the end of their trunk, African elephants can even pick up small objects.

(5) **Despite / Due to** the fact that elephants can release body heat through their ears, sometimes the African heat is too much for them. These large animals love water and like to take a cold shower (6) **in line with / by means of** their trunks, sucking water into them and spraying it all over their bodies.

(7) **In addition to / As a result of** taking these water showers, they often take "dust baths," spraying themselves with a fine layer of dust, which protects their skin from the sun and repels insects.

Both male and female African elephants can dig for food and water and strip bark from trees (8) **by means of / far from** their long, sharp, ivory tusks. Many elephants have been killed (9) **apart from / on account of** the fact that ivory is so valuable. (10) **In spite of / As a result of** the fact that the trade in ivory is illegal today, it has not been completely eliminated, and some African elephant populations remain endangered.

D _____ / **10 points** (1 point each)

(continued)

E Match the opinions on the left with the comments on the right. Write the letters on the lines. There is one response that you do not need to use.

1. Plastic bags do so much damage to fish and birds if they end up in the oceans. Stores really shouldn't use them. _____

2. I try to buy organic meat because I think it's much healthier. _____

3. I think deforestation is one of the biggest threats to our planet. _____

4. People are eager to protect cute animals like polar bears, but it's important to remember that less attractive species are endangered, too. _____

5. I think it's great that some schools have a garden so the kids can learn to grow vegetables. _____

6. I think it's better to watch wildlife documentaries than go to the zoo. _____

a. Also, forests are important habitats for wildlife. We need to protect those trees.

b. Additionally, it's worth improving it.

c. What's more, they're often not biodegradable.

d. Not to mention the fact that they can then use them for healthy lunches.

e. And on top of that, the animals are generally treated better – so it's best for everyone.

f. Right. And what's more, things like insects are often threatened, and they're an important part of the food chain.

g. Yeah, and then you can see the animals in their natural habitat.

E _____ / **6 points** (1 point each)

F Read the article. Then read the statements and write T for true, F for false, or NG if the information is not given.

Inventions based on nature

Plastics that can repair themselves and aircraft wings that can change their shape during flight? Far from being ideas dreamed up by science-fiction writers, these are two examples of biomimicry – inventions inspired by nature. This technology is apparently viable, and before too long it will have been incorporated into aircraft design.

The first example mimics the ability of the human body to repair itself. If you accidentally cut your finger, your body heals itself and in the process creates a protective scab over the injury. It may seem unimaginable, but scientists are working on new plastics, called "self-healing plastics," which will be able to do the same thing. If a crack develops in the material, a substance will be released that forms the equivalent of a scab over it. Thanks to this remarkable technology, safer and more fuel-efficient cars and even spacecraft could soon be built out of self-healing plastics.

In the case of the aircraft wings, scientists at Penn State University were inspired by birds. On account of the fact that they fly in different ways, different species of birds have evolved wings of different shapes. As a result, some are able to fly long distances quickly and efficiently. The scientists have designed adaptable wings called "Morphing Airplane Wings," which can change shape depending on how fast the aircraft is flying and how long the flight is. This should allow aircraft to fly farther and faster, using less fuel.

1. The inventions above have been inspired by science fiction as well as by nature. _____
2. The article discusses how self-healing plastics will be used to repair human bodies. _____
3. Self-healing plastics should allow spacecraft to spend more time in outer space. _____
4. Morphing Airplane Wings will allow aircraft to be more efficient. _____

F _____ / **8 points** (2 points each)

Unit 5 General quiz

Name: _____

Date: _____

Total Score

_____ / 50 points

A 🔊 **Listen to two friends talk about an unusual activity. Check (✓) True or False for each sentence.**

		True	False
1.	The man has heard of geocaching.	☐	☐
2.	The man has been given a new cell phone.	☐	☐
3.	The man prefers the rural areas to the city.	☐	☐
4.	The man agrees to go geocaching next week.	☐	☐

A _____ **/ 8 points** (2 points each)

B **Complete the second sentence in each pair so that it has a similar meaning to the first. Add the adverbs in parentheses to the verb phrase. Use *by* if necessary.**

1. Downloadable music files have replaced CDs as far as most people are concerned.

    CDs _____ as far as most people are concerned. (largely)

2. By the late 1990s, manufacturers had abandoned the production of audio cassettes.

    By the late 1990s, the production of audio cassettes _____. (generally)

3. Retailers are selling vinyl records in surprisingly large numbers.

    Vinyl records _____ in surprisingly large numbers. (still)

4. More and more people are appreciating the richer sound from a vinyl record.

    The richer sound from a vinyl record _____. (apparently)

5. Engineers are developing new high-resolution formats for recording music.

    New high-resolution formats for recording music _____. (reportedly)

B _____ **/ 10 points** (2 points each)

C **Match the adjectives on the left with the more formal adjectives on the right. Write the letters on the lines. There is one letter that you do not need to use.**

1. out of date, not used _____	a. compact
2. modest, ordinary _____	b. countless
3. necessary _____	c. functional
4. small _____	d. humble
5. simple, basic _____	e. innovative
6. new, creative _____	f. integral
7. useful _____	g. obsolete
8. important, big _____	h. portable
9. usual, not special _____	i. rudimentary
10. easy to carry _____	j. significant
	k. standard

C _____ **/ 10 points** (1 point each)

D Rewrite the sentences (1–4) in the passive. Use the adverbs in parentheses and *by* if necessary.

In 2007, three athletes ran 4,000 miles across the Sahara Desert in 111 days. They battled extreme heat and sandstorms, relying on their GPS devices for direction much of the time.

1. Sandstorms could have delayed the athletes during their marathon run.
   The athletes _____ during their marathon run. (easily)

2. Sheer exhaustion could have prevented the runners from finishing the race.
   The runners _____. (also)

3. GPS devices must have made the run much easier.
   The run _____. (surely)

4. People might have made the organizers cancel the event if athletes had become seriously ill.
   The organizers _____ if athletes had become seriously ill. (well)

D _____ / 8 points (2 points each)

E Circle the correct expressions to complete the conversation.

A I don't think people should be allowed to do extreme sports.

B Why not? I mean, you can't stop them!

A (1) **Let me put it this way / Maybe not / Just think**, but I still think they should be prevented from doing really dumb things.

B So what would you do – have an age limit for some sports?

A (2) **Not necessarily / Just think / One way to look at it**. But I do think people should only do things if they're fit enough and avoid having to be rescued from dangerous places.

B Yeah, that always puts other people's lives in danger. And you're right, nowadays people can do things thanks to technology that could never have been done before. (3) **Definitely / Just think / Absolutely not**, I could go sky-diving tomorrow, if I could afford it! So people don't always really understand that they need to prepare properly. But like I said, how can they be stopped?

A Well, maybe not stopped, exactly, but (4) **not necessarily / one way to look at it / to put it another way**, I think people should be made to take out special insurance, at least.

E _____ / 4 points (1 point each)

F Read the article. Then read the sentences and write T for true, F for false, or NG if the information is not given.

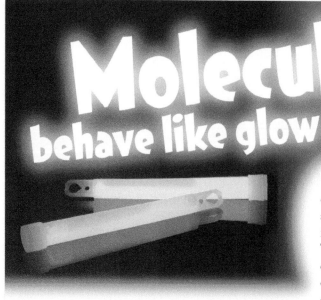

Molecules
behave like glow sticks°!

A new family of molecules has been developed thanks to the hard work and persistence of researchers at the University of Notre Dame, in Indiana, U.S.A. What is so special about them? They behave just like tiny glow sticks, and amazingly, the researchers can control the color emitted by each molecule!

When one of these new molecules has been warmed to body temperature, it glows, behaving like a tiny flashlight. This phenomenon, known as "chemiluminescence," provides amusement for children around the world as they wave glow sticks around in the dark. After being stored in a kitchen freezer, the molecules are warmed up and start to glow. The new molecules can have their chemical structure changed by the researchers, causing them to emit light of different wavelengths. So they can produce visible colors like red and green, or invisible light that can only be detected by special night vision cameras.

These molecules are promising to be incredibly useful in the field of diagnostic medicine. They may possibly be turned into little lights that can be sent into the body to search out cancer cells. This would allow doctors to see where exactly a tumor is located. The international medical community eagerly awaits further developments in this field.

°*glow stick* a plastic tube that contains two chemicals that combine when the tube is bent, producing a luminescent glow

1. The researchers discovered the new molecules by chance. _____
2. The molecules are going to be used in flashlights. _____
3. The researchers store the molecules in kitchen freezers. _____
4. The researchers know what type of light will be produced by each molecule. _____
5. These molecules have successfully detected cancer cells. _____

F _____ / **10 points** (2 points each)

Unit 6 General quiz

Name: _____

Date: _____

Total Score

_____ / 50 points

A 🔊 **Listen to a man and a woman talking about supporting local businesses. Check (✓) True or False for each sentence.**

	True	False
1. The man rarely shops at small stores like Walter's.	☐	☐
2. The man thinks Main Street needs more chain stores.	☐	☐
3. The man says chain stores don't pay good salaries.	☐	☐
4. The woman intends to support stores like Walter's more.	☐	☐

A _____ / 8 points (2 points each)

B Complete the sentences with *which, of which, whom,* and *of whom.*

1. Our business is looking for office space downtown from _____ to operate.
2. We have interviewed our largest customers, many of _____ say they are pleased with our products.
3. We started off with a few loans, most _____ we have already paid off.
4. Our friends and family, most _____ supported us from the beginning, are impressed by how much we have achieved.
5. It was their help, without _____ we would have struggled, that gave us the confidence to continue.
6. We have tried advertising our business in various ways, not all _____ have been successful.
7. A number of friends, some _____ also run businesses, have given us good advice.
8. Our employees, most _____ are women, say they enjoy working in such a friendly environment.

B _____ / 8 points (1 point each)

C Circle the correct words to complete the paragraph.

Many people are (1) **tempted / lured** to set up their own businesses. Other people's success stories (2) **coax / persuade** them that they can do as well themselves. The idea of not having an employer also (3) **attracts / intimidates** them, and of course, the hope that they will make a lot of money (4) **alienates / entices** them, too. The work required (5) **woos / discourages** some people, especially at the beginning, but the challenge (6) **convinces / appeals to** others. The risk of failure naturally (7) **scares off / draws in** some entrepreneurs, although many are (8) **convinced / coaxed** from the beginning that they will succeed. New enterprises are being set up all the time, so people are obviously not (9) **attracted / put off** by the difficulties involved.

C _____ / 9 points (1 point each)

D Circle the correct words to complete the sentences.

1. **Some / Any** online retailers send their customers too many emails about new products and special offers.

2. **Other / Any** website that is well designed will allow customers to browse the products quickly and easily.

3. If you can't find what you want on one website, it takes only a few seconds to find **another / other** one.

4. If you don't want to give your bank details to an online retailer, **another / other** payment options are usually available.

5. Although many people like buying clothes online, **another / others** prefer to try things on before buying them.

6. I like the atmosphere in malls, but **another / other** people think they're too crowded and noisy.

7. Malls often have those big, noisy food courts, too. There has to be **some other / other** way to design those so that they're more inviting.

D _____ / **7 points** (1 point each)

E Complete the conversation using tag questions.

A I was just looking at an article about Internet security. It's scary when you think how easy it is for people to get your personal data, _____?
(1)

B Yeah, I know. But there are all kinds of software these days to protect companies from hackers, _____?
(2)

A Sure, but these days employees often take work home, _____? And that's when
(3)
problems can occur.

B Granted, but companies are taking the threat more and more seriously, _____?
(4)

A That's true, though they can't always prevent staff from checking their personal emails at work, _____? And a lot of confidential records have been lost or stolen,
(5)
_____?
(6)

B Yeah, granted, it isn't always easy to make sure everyone observes security protocol.

A And employees often leave computers on without logging off, _____?
(7)

B You're right, I suppose. A fail-safe solution hasn't been found yet, _____?
(8)

E _____ / **8 points** (1 point each)

Viewpoint 2 • Unit 6 General quiz © Cambridge University Press 2014 photocopiable

F Read the article. Then read the statements and write T for true, F for false, or NG if the information is not given.

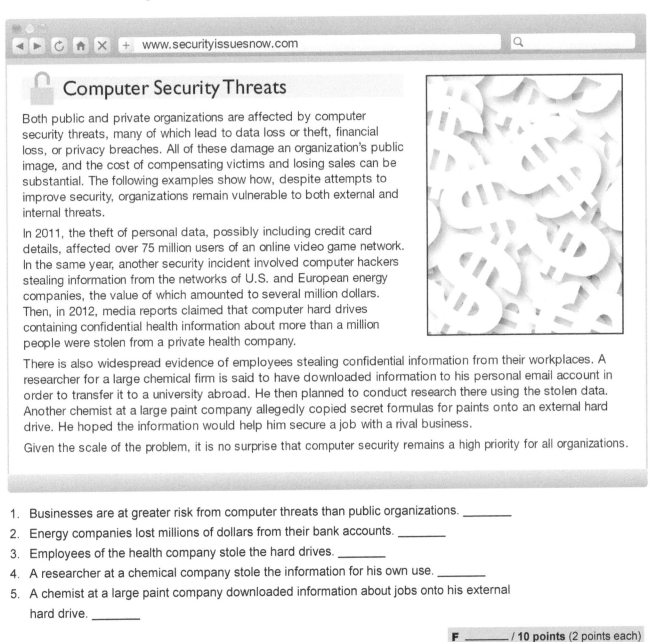

www.securityissuesnow.com

Computer Security Threats

Both public and private organizations are affected by computer security threats, many of which lead to data loss or theft, financial loss, or privacy breaches. All of these damage an organization's public image, and the cost of compensating victims and losing sales can be substantial. The following examples show how, despite attempts to improve security, organizations remain vulnerable to both external and internal threats.

In 2011, the theft of personal data, possibly including credit card details, affected over 75 million users of an online video game network. In the same year, another security incident involved computer hackers stealing information from the networks of U.S. and European energy companies, the value of which amounted to several million dollars. Then, in 2012, media reports claimed that computer hard drives containing confidential health information about more than a million people were stolen from a private health company.

There is also widespread evidence of employees stealing confidential information from their workplaces. A researcher for a large chemical firm is said to have downloaded information to his personal email account in order to transfer it to a university abroad. He then planned to conduct research there using the stolen data. Another chemist at a large paint company allegedly copied secret formulas for paints onto an external hard drive. He hoped the information would help him secure a job with a rival business.

Given the scale of the problem, it is no surprise that computer security remains a high priority for all organizations.

1. Businesses are at greater risk from computer threats than public organizations. _____
2. Energy companies lost millions of dollars from their bank accounts. _____
3. Employees of the health company stole the hard drives. _____
4. A researcher at a chemical company stole the information for his own use. _____
5. A chemist at a large paint company downloaded information about jobs onto his external hard drive. _____

F _____ / **10 points** (2 points each)

Unit 7 General quiz

Name: _____

Date: _____

Total Score

_____ / 50 points

A 🔊 **Listen to a man and his sister talking about speed dating. Check (✓) the correct answers.**

1. The man says he heard about speed dating
   A. ☐ from a friend.
   B. ☐ online.
   C. ☐ at work.

2. Where did the speed dating event take place?
   A. ☐ in a café
   B. ☐ in a hotel
   C. ☐ in a stadium

3. What surprised the man when he first arrived?
   A. ☐ He recognized a friend of his.
   B. ☐ There were a lot of people there.
   C. ☐ Some people had brought friends along.

4. The first woman the man spoke to was
   A. ☐ a teacher.
   B. ☐ a doctor.
   C. ☐ an actress.

5. What is the man planning to do?
   A. ☐ try speed dating again
   B. ☐ look at the speed dating website
   C. ☐ meet someone from the speed dating event

A _____ / **10 points** (2 points each)

B **Rewrite the sentences without *if*. Start with the words in parentheses or use an imperative and *and*.**

1. If I moved to a different city, I'd miss all my friends. (*Were*)

   _____

2. If I'd realized how friendly people at the gym are, I'd have joined earlier. (*Had*)

   _____

3. If you let children choose their own friends, they'll probably be happier. (imperative)

   _____

4. Go to the student cafeteria at lunchtime. If you don't, you won't meet many new people. (*Otherwise*)

   _____

5. If I'd listened to my sister's advice, I wouldn't have gotten married. (*Had*)

   _____

6. If you have problems with your roommate, you can always talk to an adviser. (*Should*)

   _____

7. If you get a dog, you'll meet people in your neighborhood when you're out walking it. (imperative)

   _____

8. If you tried talking to your new classmates, you'd probably find they are really nice. (*were*)

   _____

9. I'm so glad my mom called yesterday. If she hadn't, I'd have forgotten it was my brother's birthday. (*otherwise*) _____

10. If you need any more information about student clubs, check online. (*should*)

_____

B _____ / 10 points (1 point each)

C Complete the sentences with words from the box. There is one word that you do not need to use.

| age | beyond | choose | energy | forth | see | suffering | take | think | tired | work |

1. I'm sick and _____ of hearing people complain about kids' behavior. You'd think they'd never been young themselves!
2. Family life is all about give and _____.
3. Some people spend a lot of time and _____ trying to make their relationships work.
4. It's sad to hear that in this day and _____ there are still families who can't afford to feed their children.
5. Some parents spend a lot of time traveling back and _____, taking their children to and from sports activities.
6. When parents split up, it causes everyone in the family a lot of pain and _____.
7. When people get married, they have to think about a lot of issues above and _____ immediate concerns like finances and accommodation.
8. I think couples should stop and _____ before having children; it's a huge responsibility.
9. Families often have to raise children in small apartments. Not everyone can afford to pick and _____ where they live.
10. I don't know whether my baby's a boy or a girl. We'll just have to wait and _____ when it's born!

C _____ / 10 points (1 point each)

D Rewrite the two sentences as one sentence. Keep the clauses in the same order.

1. New parents have to decide this. Will one of them stay at home instead of going to work?

_____

2. How do you raise a child? It's a joint responsibility.

_____

3. Is it important to think about this? How many children do you both want to have?

_____

4. What do some couples have to do? They live with older relatives for financial reasons.

_____

5. People have to consider this. Do they want to go to parenting classes before having children?

_____

6. Parents need to agree on this. What time should teenagers go to bed?

_____

7. How much should children help with the chores? This is something families often argue about.

   _____

8. Does anyone know this? Is family life easier in the city or the country?

   _____

D _____ / 8 points (1 point each)

E **Match the two parts of each comment. Write the letters on the lines. There is one extra sentence that you do not need to use.**

1. Teenagers should be taught about the realities of parenthood. _____

2. Parenting classes are essential for everyone, I think. _____

3. Nobody can teach anyone else how to raise a family. _____

4. It isn't better to have children in your twenties rather than later on. _____

a. At the end of the day, we all have to figure it out for ourselves.

b. In a nutshell, we know they understand.

c. In a word, they should be compulsory.

d. In the end, there are advantages and disadvantages to both.

e. When all's said and done, most of them will have children themselves one day.

E _____ / 4 points (1 point each)

F **Read the article. Then read the statements and write T for true, F for false, or NG if the information is not given.**

Cell Phones & the Family

Leading psychologists have produced a report on the impact of personal devices on our relationships with other people. One of the areas they have looked into is how parents and their children are affected by the ways in which they use their cell phones.

The research shows how from an early age children have to compete with these devices for their parents' attention. At sporting events, for example, rather than watching their kids, parents are often texting on their phones. And whether they are in a car or taking public transportation, parents and kids are often on the phone, missing out on conversations they could be having with each other instead.

According to some psychologists, children's insistence on texting at mealtimes is something that many parents complain about. However, it is hard for parents to insist on their children giving them their full attention at the dinner table when they themselves are constantly distracted by their own cell phones during the rest of the day. One suggestion psychologists make is for families to agree to not bring their phones with them to breakfast or dinner, so that there is at least one meal a day when all the family are together, and talk.

The way in which texting has largely come to replace face-to-face conversations is another concern that the report addresses. Should a teenager need to cancel an arrangement with another family member, for example, many prefer to send a brief text rather than have a potentially awkward conversation. The experts worry that our cell phones come between us, rather than connect us, as families.

1. The report looked at how families are affected by their use of cell phones. _____

2. The research shows that young children are eager to use their parents' devices _____

3. Some psychologists believe parents set a bad example for their children in their texting habits. _____

4. The psychologists say that texts can create misunderstandings between family members. _____

F _____ / 8 points (2 points each)

Unit 8 General quiz

Name: _____

Date: _____

Total Score

_____ / 50 points

A 🔊 Listen to a woman telling her friend about her experience of volunteering on an archaeological dig in England. Check (✓) the correct answers.

1. The woman says she decided to volunteer on a dig because
   - A. ☐ she had seen a TV show about archaeology.
   - B. ☐ she wanted to go to Egypt.
   - C. ☐ she had wanted to since she was a child.
2. How did the woman feel when she arrived at the dig?
   - A. ☐ worried that she had chosen the wrong dig
   - B. ☐ shy about meeting so many new people
   - C. ☐ confused about where to go
3. What does the woman say she'd like to have done?
   - A. ☐ spoken to a Roman emperor
   - B. ☐ lived in the village they were excavating
   - C. ☐ seen some of the objects when they were new
4. How will the experience help her in the future?
   - A. ☐ It will help her with a class she's taking next year.
   - B. ☐ She'll have to do fewer archaeology projects next year.
   - C. ☐ Some of the people she met will help her with her project next year.

A _____ / 8 points (2 points each)

B Complete the sentences with the verbs in parentheses and a perfect infinitive. Some verbs are passive.

1. I _____ ('d love / interview) Martin Luther King.
2. He _____ (acknowledge / be) an important figure in U.S. history.
3. He _____ (consider / play) a major role in gaining equal rights for all citizens.
4. He _____ (know / believe) in non-violent protest.
5. I _____ ('d like / ask) him about his childhood.

B _____ / 10 points (2 points each)

C Circle the correct words to complete the sentences.

1. Atatürk was an important leader who had a **profound** / **slight** impact on twentieth century Turkey.
2. Cleopatra was a very influential leader and a **minor** / **significant** figure in ancient Egypt.
3. Marie Curie may not have known that her work on radioactivity in the early twentieth century would have such a **long-term** / **rapid** effect on medicine over the next 100 years.
4. Even **imperceptible** / **universal** changes in global temperature can turn out to be important for our planet.
5. Simón Bolivar had a **sudden** / **lasting** effect on Latin America that can still be felt.
6. Events that seem unimportant or **insignificant** / **visible** at the time can have a great influence on the course of history.
7. People don't always notice change because it is so **massive** / **gradual**.
8. The first moon landing had a **minute** / **universal** impact.

9. Catherine the Great was the longest ruling female leader of Russia. She was a **major** / **superficial** political figure.

10. Some events only have a **major** / **temporary** effect and are soon forgotten.

D **Rewrite the numbered sentences as cleft sentences with *it* + *be* to give extra focus to the underlined words.**

The English mathematician and physicist Isaac Newton was born in 1643. (1) He became interested in physics <u>at Cambridge University</u>. He built a functional reflecting telescope in 1668. (2) <u>This achievement</u> drew the attention of other scientists. (3) <u>Newton's work on the nature of light</u> established the modern study of optics. (4) Newton published his most famous work <u>in 1687</u>. Called *Philosophiae Naturalis Principia Matematica*, it described universal gravitation and the three laws of motion. (5) <u>These ideas</u> dominated scientific views of the physical universe for the next 300 years.

1. _____
2. _____
3. _____
4. _____
5. _____

E **Complete the conversation with the expressions in the box. There is one expression that you do not need to use.**

But don't get me	But that's another	I'd rather not talk about	Let's not get into
Let's not go			

Ann   Have you finished your history assignment, Jay?

Jay   Yeah, though I wish we'd been given more time to write it.

Ann   I know. _____ started on that. You already know what I think about it!
(1)

Jay   Yeah. Three days is nowhere near enough time to research and write an essay.

Ann   Oh, definitely not. But the other thing that got to me, you know, was the topic. _____
(2)
story. I'm just not that interested in science, I guess. So I don't really want to learn about its history!

Jay   Well, I suppose you have to see how all kinds of different things are connected, don't you?

Ann   But I mean, we're expected to learn about such a wide variety of topics that we don't always get to study any one thing in much depth. But anyway, we've already talked about that!

Jay   Yeah. _____ that again.
(3)

Ann   Actually, I'm glad I chose this course – at least most of the time. I just hope I get a good grade.

Jay   Yeah. Me too. But _____ my grades so far this semester!
(4)

F Read the article. Then read the statements and write T for true, F for false, or NG if the information is not given.

Grass Roots History

People all over the country are getting involved in local history projects to explore their community's past, sometimes literally digging it up. More than 500 new projects have now been set up nationwide. And it's not just groups of local people getting involved, but also college archaeologists and historians.

The aim of the scheme is to allow thousands of people, wherever they live, to explore their own local heritage. They will have the opportunity to find out about the history, customs, and traditions that matter to them, at a truly grass roots level.

The idea for each project comes from the local group, and experts will advise them as they carry out their research. People of all ages and backgrounds will be given the chance to participate in the discoveries and excavations. It's not only community histories that will be rewritten, but it is hoped that each project will also provide new data for academic research.

A wide range of projects are receiving funding under the scheme, from research into the lives of working women to the setting up of local history trails. A number of groups are hoping to uncover the remains of early settlements around their villages, about which there appears to have been little documentary evidence. Archaeologists will help the volunteers to understand how their local landscape has developed through the ages.

Many advisers say they have built strong relationships with the local groups they are working with, and are very pleased that the ideas for the new projects can now be put into action.

1. The scheme is based on partnerships between amateurs and professionals. _____
2. Experts from colleges have chosen the research topics for the projects. _____
3. It will be possible for children to be involved in the project. _____
4. Some groups have already dug up ancient objects. _____

F _____ / **8 points** (2 points each)

Unit 9 General quiz

Name: _____

Date: _____

Total Score

_____ / 50 points

A 🔊 **Listen to two friends talking about ways to save energy. Check (✓) True or False for each sentence.**

	True	False
1. The woman is surprised that so much energy is wasted at the man's college.	☐	☐
2. The man has been trying to encourage energy saving at his college.	☐	☐
3. The woman is hoping to have a career in engineering.	☐	☐
4. The man and the woman agree that a solution will be found to global energy problems.	☐	☐

A _____ / **8 points** (2 points each)

B **Complete the conversation with** *whatever, whichever, whoever, whenever, wherever,* **or** *however.*

A _____ designed these radios was clever, don't you think? It's so neat that you
     (1)
can wind it up if you don't have batteries.

B Yeah, I suppose you can use it _____ you are – as long as there's a signal, of
                                    (2)
course.

A Exactly. On the website I got it from, there are three different sizes. But I guess

_____ one you get, the functions are basically the same.
     (3)

B So do you use it a lot?

A Oh, yeah – _____ I go camping. And sometimes at home, though I tend to listen
                   (4)
to the radio on my computer at home.

B Well, _____ often you use it, I guess you're saving a little money every time. I
            (5)
mean, I listen to the radio _____ I'm home, _____ I'm doing, really.
                              (6)   (7)
I mean, that probably uses a lot of power every year.

A Sure, and they're great in remote places, too, you know, where people can't get batteries.

B Yeah, that's true. So, I guess _____ you're located, it's a pretty useful thing to
                                    (8)
have. Especially for emergencies, too. Actually, I might ask my girlfriend to get me one for my

birthday. Usually I like _____ she chooses. But I think I'd really like one of these!
                          (9)

A Yeah, I think you'll like it.

B _____ / **9 points** (1 point each)

C Complete the speech with the words or phrases from the box. There is one extra option.

to assemble	complete the project on time	constructing	delays	elevate	engineer
fall behind schedule	in a short time frame	maneuvering	position	steel	

As a civil _____ (1), I'm part of a team responsible for designing and _____ (2) roads and bridges throughout the country. Our projects often need to be delivered _____ (3), so we're usually under pressure. Inevitably, _____ (4) occur, so then we _____ (5) and have to make a huge team effort to _____ (6). So my job doesn't only involve knowing about how materials like _____ (7) and concrete behave but also requires me to work long hours and be flexible.

A bridge that looks straightforward to build on paper can sometimes be a challenge _____ (8) and erect. As you can imagine, the practical problems involved in _____ (9) large blocks of concrete into _____ (10) are sometimes immense.

C _____ / **10 points** (1 point each)

D Rewrite the sentences starting with the words given.

1. People are not only using cars more often, but they are also using more energy in their homes.
   Not only _____

2. Oil companies will only be able to supply this demand by drilling for oil that is hard to reach.
   Only by _____

3. Engineers have never had to deal with such a high demand in the past.
   Never _____

4. We didn't realize the effects of our energy use on the environment.
   Little _____

5. We didn't think that alternative sources of energy would take so long to be developed, either.
   Nor _____

D _____ / **10 points** (2 points each)

E Match the comments on the left with the supporting ideas on the right. Write the letters on the lines. There is one supporting idea that you do not need to use.

1. Developing low-carbon electricity is a priority for many engineers these days, _____

2. Engineers are helping to develop efficient and sustainable ways of growing and harvesting crops, _____

3. It would be good if engineers could find an effective way to use wave power, _____

4. Engineers have to try to come up with low-cost solutions to environmental problems, _____

5. It isn't clear that energy-saving heating systems will save the planet, _____

a. especially considering so much of the world's population lives in coastal areas.

b. in light of the need to feed a rapidly increasing global population.

c. given the growing demand for energy that does not harm our environment.

d. and, in fact, they may have no impact on global warming whatsoever.

e. considering the fact that people need clean water to survive.

f. in view of the fact that many people do not want to pay more to protect the planet.

E _____ / **5 points** (1 point each)

F Read the article. Then read the statements and write T for true, F for false, or NG if the information is not given.

Biomedical Engineering

Biomedical engineering is the application of engineering principles to the fields of medicine and biology. The problem-solving and design skills of engineering are used to benefit medical science. Every stage of the process in creating new devices and instruments involves biomedical engineers: from inventing a device, through the years it may take to develop it, to making sure that it is used properly.

Biomedical engineering is not a new concept. Not only have 3,000-year-old mummies been discovered with artificial toes attached to their feet, but people are known to have used wooden teeth as well as specially designed shoes and crutches for hundreds of years. The invention of the optical microscope in 1590 gave an enormous boost to medical science. Several centuries later, in the late nineteenth century, the German physicist Wilhelm Röntgen was experimenting with the way electric current flowed through a glass tube when he accidentally discovered a type of electromagnetic radiation that could pass through solid objects. Little did he know then that X-rays would come to be routinely used in medicine.

Today, biomedical engineering is a wide and varied field that is continually expanding. Medical device engineers, for example, create new machines such as pacemakers for heart patients, hearing aids, and artificial lenses for the eyes. Medical imaging engineers work to improve scanning techniques, refining X-ray, MRI, CT scanning, and ultrasound equipment. Tissue engineers are currently developing artificial tissues and organs, which they hope will be suitable for use in human patients. As a result, organs are now being grown in the laboratory which may one day be used as transplants.

1. Engineers are better at solving problems and designing things than medical doctors are. _____
2. The optical microscope was designed to help medical doctors carry out research. _____
3. Röntgen was researching medical scanning techniques when he discovered X-rays. _____
4. Tissue engineers are working on ways to replace human tissues and organs with ones that do not originate from other human beings. _____

F _____ / **8 points** (2 points each)

Viewpoint 2 • Unit 9 General quiz © Cambridge University Press 2014 photocopiable

Unit 10 General quiz

Name: _____

Date: _____

Total Score

_____ / 50 points

A 🔊 **Listen to two friends talking about the news. Check (✓) the correct answers.**

1. How does the woman feel about the news at the moment?
   A. ☐ bored
   B. ☐ anxious
   C. ☐ confused

2. What does the man want to find out more about?
   A. ☐ the economy
   B. ☐ an oil spill
   C. ☐ a political campaign

3. How does the man prefer to keep up with current events?
   A. ☐ He watches TV.
   B. ☐ He uses a phone app.
   C. ☐ He reads an online newspaper.

4. What does the woman say about news reports on TV?
   A. ☐ They give too little information.
   B. ☐ They are prepared too quickly.
   C. ☐ They are often well written.

A _____ **/ 8 points** (2 points each)

B **Complete the news report using the verbs in parentheses in a continuous infinitive form.**

Insurers are going to _____ (hold) talks next week with the legal representatives of
(1)
flood victims. This comes after claims that, for the last six months, some insurance companies
appear _____ (ignore) all attempts to reach an agreement on compensation.
(2)
Over 1,000 people whose homes were damaged in last summer's floods are still believed
_____ (live) in temporary accommodation or with friends and families. Many of
(3)
them appear _____ (not receive) the help they were promised shortly after being
(4)
forced to leave their homes. It is also feared that many may now _____ (suffer)
(5)
from a range of health problems as a result of their difficult living conditions.

B _____ **/ 10 points** (2 points each)

C **Complete the collocations with the words from the box. There is one word that you do not need to use.**

| announce | consider | contain | compensate | escalate | fuel | go off |
| make | plunge | rule out | undergo | | | |

1. The security services had not expected the bomb to _____.
2. A special fund has been set up to _____ the victims.
3. The police cannot _____ the possibility of another attack because those responsible have not yet been found.
4. Tensions will no doubt _____ if a solution to the crisis is not found soon.

5. The prime minister will _____ routine surgery next month, and his deputy will step in until he has made a full recovery.

6. People often _____ taking legal action if they suffer an injury at work.

7. The news of these losses is likely to _____ speculation about the health of the economy.

8. Every effort is being made to _____ the oil spill.

9. All the candidates are expected to _____ their campaigns by the end of the month.

10. Economists predict that stocks will _____ a recovery within the next six months.

C _____ / 10 points (1 point each)

D Read the comments, then complete the news report below with subjunctive verbs.

Protestors: "You must listen to our concerns." "You must not give permission for the plan." "Please meet with us." "You have to understand our concerns."
The company: "We must be operational 24 hours a day." "We have to build this year."

Protests continue against a proposal to build a factory close to a residential area of the city.

Protesters demand that the planning authority _____ to their concerns and
_____ permission for the plan to go ahead. They have requested that the CEO
(2)
of the company _____ with their representatives and say it is crucial that she
(3)
_____ the reasons for their concerns. The company's insistence that the factory
(4)
_____ operational 24 hours a day has added to residents' concerns. The
(5)
company says it is essential that the factory _____ this year or jobs will go overseas.
(6)

D _____ / 6 points (1 point each)

E Rewrite the sentences to highlight the underlined words, as in the example.

Example: In our family, my mom is the news addict.
My mom, she's the news addict in our family.

1. My dad's always listening to the news when he's in the car. I wish we could play music instead!
_____ when he's in the car. I wish we could play music instead!

2. One thing I don't like about news websites is all that celebrity news.
_____.

3. Another thing I hate is the way they never report on anything in depth.
_____.

4. The ones I like to listen to are the reporters who really check out their stories.
_____.

E _____ / 8 points (2 points each)

(continued)

F Read the article. Then read the statements and write T for true, F for false, or NG if the information is not given.

Lying to Discover the Truth

A few years ago, an American journalist invented a completely fictitious company and pretended it was behaving unethically. He then approached public relations professionals and asked them to help him present the company's actions in a favorable light. He discovered that they were prepared to do the work, even though they knew that their actions were morally wrong. When the journalist wrote an article revealing what he had learned, the reaction was surprising. Instead of the PR people being criticized, it was the journalist who was considered to have behaved particularly badly. The general opinion was that journalists should not lie, and that in doing so, they discredited their entire profession.

For decades, journalists have gone "undercover," using false

identities to discover and expose the truth about individuals and organizations. On some occasions they have done so to gain access to, and then write about, establishments such as psychiatric hospitals or prisons. At other times, they have, for example, taken jobs in factories and then reported on the working conditions they experienced there. The justification they give for lying, or at least withholding the truth about their real reason for being there, is that they would not find out as much as quickly if they simply went to the organizations concerned and asked questions openly, as journalists.

Critics of such methods insist that journalists be open and keep to the truth at all times during their investigations. If journalists lie to get a story, they say, how can we believe what they report?

1. The American journalist told the PR professionals the truth before writing the story. _____
2. Most people praised the journalist for exposing the bad behavior of others. _____
3. Journalists claim to have valid reasons for sometimes telling lies. _____
4. Critics of undercover journalism say that undercover journalists cannot be trusted. _____

F _____ / 8 points (2 points each)

Unit 11 General quiz

Name: _____

Date: _____

Total Score

_____ / 50 points

A 🔊 Listen to two friends talking about buying fake goods. Check (✓) True or False for each sentence.

		True	False
1.	The woman regrets that she paid so much for the bag.	☐	☐
2.	The man agrees with the woman's point about buying fake goods.	☐	☐
3.	The woman says there is little people can do about the problem.	☐	☐
4.	The man says that the trade in fake goods is expensive for taxpayers.	☐	☐
5.	The man has some sympathy for people who want to look fashionable.	☐	☐

A _____ / 10 points (2 points each)

B Complete the sentences using a correct form of the expressions in parentheses. Some are negative.

Apparently, the earth's magnetic poles _____ (be bound to) reverse at some point in
(1)
the future, but nobody knows exactly when this _____ (be set to) take place. If it
(2)
_____ (be to) happen within our lifetime, then it would affect all our technological devices,
(3)
which _____ (be to bound to) to cause problems. Some also fear it might cause natural
(4)
disasters. Fortunately, this switch _____ (be about to) happen soon, but in the next few
(5)
thousand years.

Many people believe that in the future, healthcare _____ (be bound to) be far more
(6)
focused on preventing people from becoming sick than it is today. If people _____ (be to)
(7)
have regular check-ups, for example, this would help medical staff pick up on problems at an
early stage. Experts say that within the next 10 years, most organizations _____ (be to)
(8)
introduce schemes that reward employees who participate in health education programs.

B _____ / 8 points (1 point each)

C Match the idioms on the left with the meanings on the right. Write the letters on the lines. There is one option that you do not need to use.

1. She wished she could **turn back the clock** to avoid having that argument. _____
2. He was worried about losing his job, but it **turned out** that he didn't need to worry at all, because he got promoted. _____
3. She decided to become an honest citizen and **turn her back on** her previous life of crime. _____
4. He could always **turn to** his parents for help. _____
5. She hoped that the therapist could help her **turn** her life **around**. _____
6. That experience was an important **turning point** in his life. _____
7. She knew that if she didn't **turn over a new leaf** and cut down on junk food soon, her health wouldn't improve. _____

a. a moment of change
b. become
c. become apparent
d. do something helpful
e. go back in time
f. go to, approach
g. ignore
h. make a change for the better
i. refuse
j. stop a bad habit
k. stop being involved in

8. He was determined to **turn a blind eye to** the fact that he was very unlikely to succeed. _____

9. Her friends were surprised to see her **turn into** a hard-working student. _____

10. It was an invitation he just couldn't **turn down**. _____

C _____ / 10 points (1 point each)

D Circle the correct words to complete the sentences.

I know what I'd like to (1) **be remembered / remember** for. It's for always (2) **refusing / being refused** to tell lies, even when it would have been much easier to do so. I recall (3) **be tempted / having been tempted** to say I liked a birthday gift, even when I really didn't. Though I did avoid (4) **offending / being offended** my friend by talking about how much I always enjoy (5) **being given / be given** presents for my birthday.

My mother says I deserve (6) **having been congratulated / to be congratulated** for working so hard in college, but everyone else is doing the same, so I guess it's normal. But of course I love (7) **being told / telling** I'm doing the right thing! If they made a movie about my life, it would be pretty boring though. Having said that, I don't regret (8) **to be seen / being seen** as a serious student, because it's what I actually am! Those guys who manage (9) **to be awarded / having been awarded** good grades without seeming to do much work are often studying harder than they'll admit. They're not always telling the whole story.

D _____ / 9 points (1 point each)

E Complete the conversation with the words from the box. There is one option that you do not need to use.

That doesn't seem right   That would be my concern   To her   To him   To me   To them

A You know what I think? It's easy to say to kids that they should never lie, but they have to learn to be kind, too. _____, that's the most important thing.
(1)

B I know what you mean, but when you're raising children, you should be consistent. And if you told them not to lie, and then they saw you lying yourself, they might get pretty confused. _____.
(2)

A Yeah, but you can't let them just ignore other people's feelings, can you? _____.
(3)

B No, I agree. But my brother has young kids, and he sometimes worries about the way they tell lies to get out of trouble. _____, it's a big deal, you know?
(4)

A Yeah, but most people grow out of that, don't they? Your brother's kids are just doing what most kids do. _____, it's probably just a case of getting an awkward conversation over
(5)
with as fast as they can!

E _____ / 5 points (1 point each)

F Read the article. Then read the statements and write T for true, F for false, or NG if the information is not given.

---

www.healthandmedicine.com/fake_drugs

Fake Medicines – a Global Threat

Fake drugs are causing great suffering and even deaths all over the world. These medicines contain either little or no active ingredient, or worse still, they may actually contain toxic substances. It is not known exactly how much fake medicine is being sold, but over 100,000 people are thought to be killed every year by substandard or fake drugs for cancer, heart disease, and other illnesses. In one country, a well-known medical aid charity was fooled into buying fake drugs used in the treatment of a major autoimmune disease. Thousands of patients are known to have been given them before the fraud was discovered.

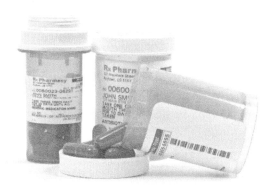

This is a global problem, and unless countries agree to cooperate and take strong action, the number of victims is expected to increase. International police and government agencies have already managed to track down and close a number of fraudulent online pharmacies run by organized criminal groups. In many countries, however, the main issue is how to prevent these products from being allowed into the supply chain for pharmacies and health clinics.

More research needs to be done to find out precisely where these drugs are being made and how they are being distributed. If international laws were to be put in place making their trafficking a crime, this would also be hugely beneficial. Additionally, if a global agreement were to be negotiated, backed by pharmaceutical companies, governments, and nongovernmental organizations, this would be a major step forward on the road to a safe drug supply for all.

---

1. Some fake drugs are ineffective rather than poisonous. _____
2. Most fake drugs are sold to medical charities. _____
3. Government agencies have identified where the majority of the fake drugs are being produced. _____
4. There are now international laws that ban the sale of fake drugs. _____

F _____ / **8 points** (2 points each)

Unit 12 General quiz

Name: _____

Date: _____

Total Score

_____ / 50 points

A 🔊 **Listen to two friends talking about dating. Check (✓) the correct answers.**

1. How does the woman feel about being single?
   A. ☐ She prefers it to being in her previous relationship.
   B. ☐ She hopes she won't remain single for too long.
   C. ☐ She wishes she were happier about it.
2. What does the man think about meeting people online?
   A. ☐ It's a convenient way of making friends.
   B. ☐ There's a risk that he might be fooled.
   C. ☐ He believes it's an unusual thing to do.
3. What does the woman say about online dating?
   A. ☐ She has tried it herself.
   B. ☐ She thinks it's a reasonable thing to do.
   C. ☐ She doesn't understand the man's attitude toward it.
4. The man agrees that dating agencies
   A. ☐ only suit certain types of people.
   B. ☐ can't help him find a girlfriend.
   C. ☐ put people into categories.

A _____ **/ 8 points** (2 points each)

B **Rewrite the underlined parts of the sentences. Use an object and an –ing form, and add a preposition if necessary, as in the example.**

Example
Some parents are uncomfortable <u>if their adult child lives with them</u>.
Some parents are uncomfortable with their adult child living with them.

1. There's nothing <u>wrong with the idea that parents should know</u> exactly where their kids are.

   _____

2. I remember <u>that my mother let</u> me play outside on my own.

   _____

3. She's a great <u>believer in the idea that children should be</u> allowed to grow up at their own pace.

   _____

4. Some parents <u>insist that their teenage children should call</u> them every day when they're away from home.

   _____

5. My dad never <u>minded when my older brother came</u> home late.

   _____

B _____ **/ 10 points** (2 points each)

C Complete the sentences with the phrases from the box. There is one option that you do not need to use.

came down to	gave away	looked up to	picked out	picked up on	played down
put behind	taken in	talked into	went about	went by	

1. One of my friends was _____ agreeing to meet someone he'd chatted to online.
2. If you _____ people's looks rather than their résumés, you'd be breaking the law.
3. I couldn't invite all my friends to my birthday dinner, so I _____ a few and sent them invitations.
4. My brother felt better when all his bad experiences had been _____ him.
5. My sister was _____ by her neighbor's charm and didn't realize he was lying to her.
6. When it _____ making the final decision about who they should rent their apartment to, my parents decided to meet prospective tenants in person rather than trust what they said about themselves online.
7. My brother _____ his plans for my surprise party by accidentally mentioning it to me.
8. My colleague _____ his work as if he'd been doing it for a long time, even though he had only just started at the company.
9. My friend soon _____ the fact that a person she was emailing was concealing his true identity.
10. My cousin had been really upset by his car accident, but _____ that fact when he told his parents what had happened.

C _____ / **10 points** (1 point each)

D Complete the sentences with the words from the box. There is one option that you do not need to use.

another	herself	himself	itself	myself	oneself	other
ourselves	themselves	yourself	yourselves			

1. My parents never helped me clean my room because they believed I should do it _____.
2. Our parents always expected us to look after one _____.
3. The Internet _____ is not to blame for the problems people complain about – it's the people who misuse it.
4. If you find _____ wondering if someone you're chatting to online is a fake, you should probably trust your instincts.
5. My grandparents don't think of _____ as being good with computers, but they email me regularly.
6. We are always being reminded not to give too much information about _____ to strangers online.
7. My parents were introduced to each _____ by a personal friend.
8. On his dating site profile, a friend of mine described _____ as a great athelete.
9. Whenever we asked my dad for help he'd say: "Do it _____, kids!"
10. My sister's always annoyed with _____ whenever she gets into embarrassing situations.

D _____ / **10 points** (1 point each)

E Circle the correct expressions to complete the conversation.

A Did you hear that report on how political candidates with deeper voices are more likely to be trusted?

B That's ridiculous, (1) **by the same token** / **to put it mildly**. I mean, whether or not you have a deep voice has nothing to do with your character.

A Well, I don't know... (2) **equally** / **I can see it from both sides**. Of course, a person's voice shouldn't really make any difference, but maybe people unconsciously associate deep voices with confidence and authority. (3) **By the same token** / **To put it mildly**, people are said to trust older candidates more because they believe they are wiser than younger ones.

B So (4) **if you look at it from the candidate's perspective** / **I can see it from both sides**, it may be worth learning to speak in a deeper voice if you want people to vote for you.

E _____ / **4 points** (1 point each)

F Read the article. Then read the statements and write T for true, F for false, or NG if the information is not given.

Training for Young Brains

School is generally accepted to be a place children attend in order to acquire new skills and knowledge. Young children start school more or less ready to learn, and their teachers do their best to ensure they do so, whatever the child's personality or background. According to some psychologists and educators, however, schools should also be places where children's brains are trained to help them pay attention, persevere, and exercise self-control.

Researchers point to many children being unable to learn effectively because they find it difficult to focus or give up too easily when they experience difficulties. If children are to succeed both at school and in later life, experts say, then they need to be given training to develop the psychological traits that will help them to achieve. With this in mind, programs have been designed for social and emotional learning and are becoming more and more popular in schools.

The skills the programs aim to cultivate, such as focus, drive, and self-control, are known as executive functions. The psychologists who designed the programs say executive functions are essential for anyone planning and carrying out a goal-directed activity. The training involves a variety of activities. In one, repeated two or three times a day, children are encouraged to focus on their breathing, which helps them to direct their attention to the present moment. The children are told that if they find themselves not paying attention in class, they should bring their awareness to their breathing for a few seconds. According to the researchers, this can reduce anxiety and promote better emotional control.

1. Some people believe that teachers could do more to help children learn. _____
2. Children who do not succeed in school are unlikely to succeed in later life. _____
3. The psychologists say their programs should be compulsory. _____
4. Children are taught to constantly focus on their breathing. _____

F _____ / **8 points** (2 points each)

General quizzes: audio scripts

Unit 1

Woman Hey. What's up? What are you doing? Playing a game?

Man Oh, just reading a short story.

Woman Yeah? You know, I never really got into short stories. I mean, I know some people like them, but I don't. The thing is, you just start getting into a story and getting to know the characters, and then it's all over! I mean, I think you're more likely to get something out of a full-length novel.

Man Yeah, I know what you mean, but actually I do like them. They're good to read on the train, you know, and during lunch break or something, because they *are* so short. And I've found some really good ones online, so I read them a lot now.

Woman Really? Huh. Well, that's good. I guess it's better than playing games and stuff – especially if you have a short commute. I can't believe how many people waste their time on those things.

Man Though online games are fun, especially, uh, you know – the ones you can play against other people. Though I have to say, I do spend most of my free time reading – though it's not always the books I should be reading for my course. I mean, I have a big pile of philosophy books I need to get through by the end of the semester. Well, I'm supposed to, at least.

Woman Oh, yeah, I bet you have to read some heavy stuff for Philosophy! We had to read some . . . oh . . . who is that? Um . . . um, some well-known philosopher. It's on the tip of my tongue . . . um . . . Well, anyway, it was heavy going . . . it was beyond me, really. Actually, I'm trying to get to grips with my work at the moment, but it's hard. I'm finding it tough.

Man Yeah. It *is* tough, isn't it? I do find it hard to get my head around some of my work sometimes. But you seem to be studying hard, well, as everyone is, I guess.

Woman Yeah . . . I'm trying to take breaks, though – or it all gets too much. I mean, I do feel a bit stressed at times.

Man Exactly. That's why I read these short stories. It's a change of scene, like a bit of an escape.

Woman Yeah, you're right. So where do you find all these good stories then?

Man Oh, this website. I can't remember it off the top of my head, but hold on – let me find it for you. I think you might like them.

Woman OK, thanks. Though honestly, I'll never have the time to look at them, I mean, I'd like to . . . but I have so much work. . . . Anyway, do you want a coffee? I'm just going to get one.

Unit 2

Tom Hey, Maria, take a look at this. I've been shopping again!

Maria Uh oh. . . . What did you get now? You can't possibly need another gadget! You have all the high-tech stuff anyone could need.

Tom Well . . . yeah, but wait . . . I've got a picture of it on my cell phone.

Maria Is it a new laptop?

Tom No. I got a new TV. It's really cool. Look! It's way better than my old one.

Maria Well, you can't really see it. I mean, it looks just like a regular TV to me.

Tom It's neat. It not only has one of those smart screens, but it also has 3D.

Maria Really? That's kind of neat. So do you get 3D glasses with it?

Tom Yeah. It's really fun.

Maria By the way, this is a cool cell phone. It's a nice color.

Tom This? Yeah . . . I didn't buy it myself, I got it from work. But it's OK. I'd prefer one of the latest ones though, with more functions.

Maria Yeah? Well, I just have a plain old black phone that I've had for ages. And I still can't use all the functions! It's fine though. I guess I'm not into all the latest gadgets and stuff. I mean, I'm glad we have things like air-conditioning, but sometimes I think all these so-called labor-saving devices and gadgets actually create more work. It takes ages to figure out how to use them.

Tom Well, maybe. . . . I mean, I know I spend too much on high-tech stuff, but I just enjoy it – when I hear about something new, I mean, I read all the reviews online and everything and then I want to try it out for myself.

Maria Yeah? To be honest, I'm neither interested in nor particularly good at using new technology. In fact, the only way I hear about new stuff is when you tell me about it!

Unit 3

Jim Hi, Anita, what's up? You don't look too happy.

Anita Oh, I'm OK, just thinking about things. I'm trying to figure out what to do. I kind of want to move out of my parents' house and rent a studio downtown, but my mom and dad are so upset about it I'm not sure I can.

Jim	But you're 25 years old! I mean, most people have left home by now. Though having said that, I heard some people are moving back in with their parents – you know, to save money.
Anita	I know. I don't even want to leave right away. But I just want to start planning my future, you know?
Jim	Knowing you, I'm sure you don't want to upset your parents. But then, you're only trying to live your own life, so. . . . So what do they say about it?
Anita	Well, they don't see it that way. They think I already have a comfortable home, so why go and live in a small studio and start paying rent?
Jim	Well, they do have a point there. But then again, you have to leave home some day, don't you?
Anita	Well, they think I should wait. But you know, having got a good job now and everything, I just think it's time to move on. I guess they only left home when they got married. You know, my mom can't understand why I even want to live alone. She thinks I'll get lonely.
Jim	Really? So what are you going to do? I mean, don't they realize you need your independence, too?
Anita	I don't know. It's such a difficult decision that I can't even make a decision!
Jim	Well, something will work out for sure.
Anita	Yeah. But then I don't want to upset them either. I know they want what's best for me. I mean, when they were my age, their lives were so different.
Jim	Yeah, but even so, they still left home at some point.
Anita	Yeah, I just don't think they realize how I feel.
Jim	Well, uh, not having lived with my parents since leaving college, it's hard for me to understand your parents' point of view. But then, I don't have any kids yet!
Anita	Yeah . . . um . . . you know, maybe I'll feel just like my parents one day!
Jim	Yeah, right. Being a parent changes everything, supposedly, but even so, I hope I'd be able to let my kids go.
Anita	Yeah. . . .

Unit 4

Interviewer	And in our studio this morning, we have Daniel Treece. Daniel, good morning.
Daniel	Good morning.
Interviewer	Um, Daniel you have a fascinating job as a wildlife photographer. How did you get into wildlife photography as a career? Have you always been interested in wildlife?

Daniel	Um, actually, yes I have. But it took me a while to get started. I actually went to school to study veterinary science – um, I've always loved animals, growing up on a farm as I did. But half way through my studies I realized – by the time I finish my degree I will have been here for *eight* years, without really spending much time outdoors – and I just wanted to get back out into nature. I missed it. So I quit school and set off with my camera. Apart from anything else, I didn't think you could actually earn a good living in wildlife photography – so it was a risk, but . . . in any case, one that paid off, I guess!
Interviewer	Uh-huh. So you eventually got work for a well-known nature magazine, and now you travel all over the world, taking photographs. Do you have a favorite photograph?
Daniel	Well, one photograph I took won an award. It was a zebra being attacked by lions. It's a great picture but it's not my favorite. My favorite was taken in Alaska. It's a huge flock of birds, migrating at sunset. They're flying over the water and the colors are spectacular.
Interviewer	And I believe by the end of this year, you will have published a new book that shows a collection of your best, award-winning pictures? And I believe that is as a result of collaboration with your wife? Your first joint project?
Daniel	Yes. It's a project that we will have been working on for five years by the time the book comes out. My wife is a specialist, doing research on penguin colonies in Antarctica. And we have some extraordinary photos from those research trips, too.
Interviewer	Well, we'll look forward to seeing it. Now, what would you say has been the most exciting moment in your career so far?
Daniel	Well, there are always exciting moments. Um, especially when you see wildlife in its natural habitat. You know, like seeing a giant turtle lay its eggs or watching the eggs hatch – that kind of thing. But um, the *most* exciting thing? I think that was last year. I saw giant pandas on a trip to China, and I went to a wildlife reserve where they live. That was very special, just watching and observing them for days. You really get a sense of how important it is to protect these endangered animals.
Interviewer	Daniel, thank you for your time, and we look forward to seeing your new book, *Into the Wild – with a Camera.*
Daniel	Thank you.

Unit 5

Jim	Hi, Li-Hua! How're you doing?
Li-Hua	Good, thanks. I just had a great day out in the forest.
Jim	Yeah? Did you go camping?
Li-Hua	No, I went geocaching!
Jim	Really? Is that when you have to find a hidden box with a GPS – kind of like a treasure hunt, but using satellite technology?
Li-Hua	Exactly. You go out looking for a waterproof container that has been hidden by another geocacher. They put the details of where it is on a website, and people use GPSs to find the exact location.
Jim	Then what do you do?
Li-Hua	Well, you write in a logbook in the box, and small objects have often been left in it, too, like plastic toys or key chains. You can take one as a souvenir, and you can leave something in exchange, if you want.
Jim	Sounds like fun, and it gets you outdoors, too. So do you have to buy expensive equipment?
Li-Hua	Not necessarily. You do need some kind of portable GPS system, though, or at least one person in the group does. Though you know, they're an integral part of most cell phones these days. So you probably have one already.
Jim	Yeah – my new cell has GPS. My brother just gave me one because my old one finally died.
Li-Hua	So do you think you'd enjoy geocaching yourself?
Jim	Yeah, I love city life, but it sure is good to get some fresh air now and then!
Li-Hua	Well, you certainly do that. I don't know why you like the city so much, though. I wish I lived in a cabin, up in the mountains!
Jim	Well, I look at it this way: There's always something fun to do in the city, and when I need to get away, I can take a break and enjoy nature. I would hate to live in a rural area all the time, though.
Li-Hua	So do you want to come with us next week? And try it out?
Jim	Oh I don't know. . . . Well, yeah, I guess. Why not? I'd like to try.
Li-Hua	OK, I'll be in touch!

Unit 6

Danielle	Hey, Ned, I like your scarf! Where did you get it from?
Ned	Oh, a small shop on Main. It's called Walter's.
Danielle	Really? I've never been there. But I heard it sells nice things.
Ned	Yeah, it's a little expensive, but I like to buy as much as I can from locally owned businesses.
Danielle	Yeah? I'd probably shop in local places, too, if they weren't so expensive.
Ned	I know, but don't you think it's worth paying a little bit more to keep all the small stores open? Main Street would lose all its character if they were replaced by chain stores, wouldn't it? Most of which sell the same stuff anyway.
Danielle	Well, granted it wouldn't be the same. And in theory, I guess people should support local businesses. But some people just can't afford the prices.
Ned	Well, it's like when I buy a gift for someone, I'd prefer to go to Walter's and get something smaller, you know, rather than go to a mall. I mean, you end up spending the same, so. . . . Yeah, it makes sense, doesn't it?
Danielle	Well, I hadn't thought of it that way. But some people just want the cheapest deal. I guess that's why people shop online, too. It's just cheaper.
Ned	Yeah. I still prefer to actually go in a store and look at something before I buy it. It's just better, isn't it?
Danielle	Yeah, I'm the same way.
Ned	But you know, another good thing about supporting local businesses is that smaller stores put more money back into the local economy than chain stores, some of which pay very low wages, too.
Danielle	Well, to some extent, maybe. But small businesses don't always hire that many people. I mean, those big stores employ a lot of people. And that's important, isn't it?
Ned	Maybe. But I still think we need local stores. I mean, they're an important part of the community, and not everyone can drive to the big malls so easily, can they?
Danielle	No, you're right. . . . But I'm still not sure I'll be shopping at Walter's anytime soon!

Unit 7

Man	Hey! You'll never guess what I did yesterday!
Woman	What?
Man	I went speed dating!
Woman	You did what? That doesn't sound like you!
Man	No, I know. In fact, I'd never heard of it before last week.
Woman	Really? I thought everybody knew about it in this day and age!
Man	Well, I didn't! But anyway, I overheard these two guys talking about it at work. Otherwise, I'd never have known about it. It isn't something any of my friends do. At least, I don't think so! So yeah, I decided to look online to find out more about it, and I researched a few events, and in the end, I decided to go to one.

Woman	So where was it? In a hotel? Was it fun?
Man	Actually, It was in that café near the stadium – I guess the company hired the place for the evening.
Woman	And was it good? I mean, did you meet anyone?
Man	Well, it was OK, but what I hadn't realized was that you could take someone with you if you wanted. I guess that's what a few people did. I mean, had I known, I would have gone with someone, too, I think, because I was a little nervous. But anyway, I didn't recognize anyone, which actually, at the end of the day, I was glad about.
Woman	So did you meet anyone nice?
Man	Well, the first woman I talked to looked like a famous actress – oh, what's her name? Oh, it's on the tip of my tongue. Anyway, she was very pretty. She was actually a doctor. Anyway, she was nice. But, in a nutshell, she was a bit serious for me.
Woman	So you didn't like her, then. So how about the other people you met?
Man	Well, there were two women I'd like to meet again, and when I checked the website afterwards, one of them had said she'd like to see me again, too! So I have a date with her later this afternoon! I'm just glad someone was interested, like, it'd be a bit embarrassing if not. And then I'd have to sign up and go all over again, which I'm not sure I want to do, when all's said and done. It takes a lot of time and energy!
Woman	Well, good luck on your date then.
Man	Yeah, I'll have to wait and see how it turns out. . . .

Unit 8

Man	So did you do anything interesting this summer?
Woman	Actually, yeah! I spent two weeks in England volunteering on an archaeological dig.
Man	Cool! What made you do that? Was it part of your history course?
Woman	No, not exactly. It's something I've always wanted to do, though I never really thought I'd get the chance. Like, when I was a kid I used to look at the pictures in *National Geographic*, you know, and think I'd like to do the same thing too one day. I mean, you can watch the TV shows, and everything, about digs in Egypt, but it isn't the same as actually going yourself, is it? So anyway, I asked my professor for advice, and he suggested this dig in England.
Man	Really? So how was it? I mean, what was it like?
Woman	Well, it was amazing. I actually didn't know much about the Romans before I went, but it was so interesting. And I was made to feel like part of the team right away, which was great – because I didn't feel too confident when I got there. I guess I was kind of nervous about not knowing anyone

and meeting all those new people. But it helped that we were camping right by the site, so we spent a lot of time together in the evenings. And actually, I met some great people. Like from all over. One guy was an engineer and – I really liked him – but that's a whole other story!

Man	Wow. You seem to have met some interesting people.
Woman	Oh, totally. And just being there brought everything to life. I'd love to have been able to talk to a real Roman – not an emperor or ruler or anything, but you know, just someone ordinary. Actually, I'd really like to have lived there in Roman times – you know, like in the little village. Just to see what it was like.
Man	Yeah? I'm not sure I'd want to do that. Though I guess if it was for a short time. . .
Woman	Yeah, that's what I'm saying. I mean, it'd be just fascinating. Anyway, I want to go back next year. It was the people that made it really special: They taught me so much. It'll all be incredibly useful for my archaeology class next year, and I already have a few ideas for a project I'd like to do.

Unit 9

Man	Hi, Ferda, I haven't seen you in ages! What are you doing here?
Woman	Oh, hi! I'm doing a class on energy efficiency in buildings as part of my course. And your college buildings are so new and modern, you know. So a group of us are being shown around by an engineer. We're looking at energy-saving features that they've built into the design.
Man	That's interesting. Well, it's good to hear that you're doing that, given the need to save energy these days.
Woman	Sure, and building design can make a big difference. I had no idea so much had been done here to reduce waste.
Man	Well, I'm glad. I think more could be done, though. Some friends and I have asked the college to put up signs in every room, encouraging people to turn the lights out whenever they leave it empty.
Woman	That's a good idea. But considering the way so many people ignore notices like that, they should maybe install sensors that can detect if a room is empty, and then turn the lights off automatically.
Man	Great idea! Though it might be a little expensive to install.
Woman	They'd probably get the money back in a couple of years, though, given the price of electricity!
Man	Yeah, and not only would they be more environmentally friendly, but they'd also save money. . . . Anyway, it sounds like you're going to be a good engineer!

Woman	I'm actually studying architecture, but I'll be working closely with engineers when I'm finally qualified.
Man	Cool. I sometimes wonder, though, if we really can do much as individuals. I mean, whatever we do, the problems facing the world are so enormous. . . . Does switching the lights off when we leave a room really make any difference whatsoever?
Woman	I think it does. . . . I mean, every little bit counts, don't you think?
Man	Um . . . I'm not too sure about that. . . .

Unit 10

Lucas	Hey, Diana!
Diana	Lucas! What are you doing here?
Lucas	Just hanging out till my next class. Did you hear about the explosion outside that store?
Diana	Oh, yeah, that was terrible! All the news is bad at the moment, isn't it? I just feel worried all the time when I think about it, you know what I mean?
Lucas	Yeah, no, definitely!
Diana	I suppose good news is boring, so we don't hear too much of that, you know?
Lucas	No, I know. But that explosion, you know, I think it was an accident, not a bomb or anything, and at least nobody was hurt.
Diana	Yeah, it could have been worse, I suppose. Anyway, you seem to be following the news pretty closely.
Lucas	Yeah, well, it's one of my interests, I guess. . . .
Diana	So, uh, that oil spill, I guess you know all about that, too.
Lucas	Yeah, well, the state's said to be considering legal action against the company.
Diana	Yeah, I read that. Someone needs to do something.
Lucas	Well, I know that a new green candidate may be about to run for office. In fact, I must check that story out and see who it is. But the economy is what most people are concerned about, really.
Diana	Yeah, no, you're right. At least the stock market, you know, that's making a bit of a recovery, apparently. Let's just hope it lasts! So, anyway, do you have one of those apps on your phone so you can keep up with all the news as it happens? Or do you watch TV, like I do?
Lucas	Actually, I have all the news apps on my phone but rarely look at them. I subscribe to a couple of online newspapers, and I prefer to read the news, really – you know, read well-written articles that actually analyze the issues.

Diana	Yeah, I tend to turn on the TV when I'm getting ready for work in the morning. I'm always in a rush then, and usually only see a couple of minutes of each news story. But even when I have time to sit and watch, I don't really feel I'm fully informed. They're very superficial and don't go into much detail.
Lucas	Yeah, I know. . . .

Unit 11

Julie	Do you like my new designer purse?
Marco	Yeah, it's a great color. Was it expensive?
Julie	Yeah, it was pricey. Like $100.
Marco	Really? You could have bought one just like it for $10 from a street vendor.
Julie	Yeah, but those are usually fake. And to me, that wouldn't be right.
Marco	Well, that's true. You're right. They must be fake at that price, I guess.
Julie	Oh, yeah. And they shouldn't even be selling them – in view of the fact that all that stuff is imported illegally. I mean, I don't think I could carry around a purse that's been made illegally. That wouldn't sit right with me.
Marco	Yeah, no, you're right. I guess anyone buying those purses and fake watches and things is turning a blind eye to the fact that a lot of those guys who make these things are criminals. I mean, they're bound to get caught at some point.
Julie	Yeah. And actually the people who make them are probably not getting a fair wage. That would be my concern. They're being exploited, you know.
Marco	Right.
Julie	I mean, to some people, a cheap bag or some fake perfume may be just a good bargain, but it's actually a lot more complicated than that. I saw a program on TV about it once, in fact. And, like, the people who design the real products are losing business. So that's not right either. Apparently, it's a growing problem, and they're about to spend millions of dollars to try and tackle it. And that's all to be funded by the taxpayer, you know.
Marco	Wow. I never thought about the business all those real companies lose. I guess the problem is getting people to stop buying fake goods. People like a cheap deal. And all just to look good. But don't get me started on that. To me, it's crazy that people are so desperate to have all these designer clothes and accessories.
Julie	Well, I think that's OK. But the designer companies deserve to be protected. And people shouldn't be buying fake stuff. . . .

Unit 12

Man	Hey, Gina, how are you doing? I was just thinking about you – I saw your boyfriend studying in the library this morning, so. . .
Woman	Oh, hi there. I'm doing good. How about you? By the way, he isn't actually my boyfriend anymore. We split up a few weeks ago.
Man	Oh, I'm sorry to hear that.
Woman	Yeah, it's not been easy, but we're both fine now. Actually, I'd say I've managed to put the whole thing behind me now. I'm getting pretty used to being single again, and honestly, to put it bluntly, I'm actually a lot happier now than when we were together.
Man	Well, that's good. I haven't dated anyone myself in a while, but I must say I'd rather be in a relationship. It's more fun, you know.
Woman	Well, I expect you'll meet someone soon enough. Though it's not always easy meeting people. I guess we can always try online dating, can't we?
Man	Yeah, I suppose. . . . Though really, I don't feel comfortable about meeting a girlfriend in cyberspace. And some of the people using those sites, well, you just don't know who they are, really. And by the same token, I'd be afraid of someone taking me in. You know, pretending to be something they're not.
Woman	Well, they're mostly just people like you and me, aren't they? I mean, it's not that different than meeting someone at a club – you're just chatting online and then arranging to meet one another if you think you might get on well together.
Man	Yeah, but when it comes to dating, I guess I'm just a little old-fashioned.
Woman	Well, I can see it from both sides, and I do know what you mean. A friend's trying to talk me into joining a dating website myself, but I don't think I'll do it either. Those sites tend to stereotype people. You know, they label you as this or that and put you into a box so you fit a certain profile.
Man	Yeah, I don't really agree with that. It certainly seems to be true of many dating agencies, whether or not they're online.

General quizzes: answer key

Unit 1

A

1. True
2. False
3. False
4. True
5. False

B

1. don't
2. do
3. did
4. did
5. does
6. haven't
7. am
8. did

C

1. d   2. a   3. e   4. c   5. b

D

1. ones
2. need to
3. a new one
4. not to
5. the best
6. like to
7. the better ones
8. able to

E

1. I do believe
2. I do
3. if not
4. if so

F

1. F   2. T   3. NG   4. F   5. NG

Unit 2

A

1. C   2. A   3. A   4. B

B

1. not only
2. also
3. neither
4. nor
5. either
6. or
7. neither
8. nor
9. both
10. and

C

1. e
2. c
3. d
4. b
5. a
6. labor-saving
7. custom-built
8. last-minute
9. so-called
10. solar-powered

D

1. commuting to work
2. to try
3. eager to adopt new technology
4. in the apartment

E

1. Theoretically
2. Apparently
3. supposedly
4. ironically
5. Presumably
6. potentially

F

1. F   2. F   3. NG   4. T

Unit 3

A

1. False   2. False   3. True
4. True   5. False

B

1. not having seen / having not seen
2. being
3. having
4. living
5. not knowing
6. Being / Having been

C

1. take stock of
2. take steps
3. take precedence over
4. take advantage of
5. take part in
6. take heart
7. take responsibility for
8. take refuge in
9. take the initiative
10. take credit for

D

1. so
2. only
3. even
4. only
5. such
6. even
7. so
8. even
9. so
10. only
11. such

E

1. e   2. b   3. f
4. a   5. d

F

1. C   2. B   3. A   4. C

Unit 4

A

1. C   2. B   3. A
4. C   5. A

B

1. I'm
2. will have disappeared
3. will probably have been melting
4. happens

5. will have lost
6. will have become
7. won't say

C

1. raise, ground
2. burrow
3. nest, lay
4. colony
5. hatch
6. mate
7. predator

D

1. by virtue of
2. Far from
3. Apart from
4. Thanks to
5. Despite
6. by means of
7. In addition to
8. by means of
9. on account of
10. In spite of

E

1. c   2. e   3. a
4. f   5. d   6. g

F

1. F   2. F   3. NG   4. T

Unit 5

A

1. True
2. False
3. False
4. True

B

1. have been largely replaced by downloadable music files / have largely been replaced by downloadable music files
2. had generally been abandoned by manufacturers / had been generally abandoned by manufacturers
3. are still being sold by retailers
4. is apparently being appreciated by more and more people
5. are reportedly being developed by engineers

C

1. g   2. d   3. f   4. a
5. i   6. e   7. c   8. j
9. k   10. h

D

1. could easily have been delayed by sandstorms / could have easily been delayed by sandstorms
2. could also have been prevented from finishing the race by sheer exhaustion / could have also been prevented from finishing the race by sheer exhaustion
3. must surely have been made much easier by GPS devices / surely must have been made much easier by GPS devices
4. might well have been made to cancel the event

E

1. Maybe not
2. Not necessarily
3. Just think
4. to put it another way

F

1. F
2. NG
3. T
4. NG
5. F

Unit 6

A

1. False   2. False
3. True   4. False

B

1. which
2. whom
3. of which
4. of whom
5. which
6. of which
7. of whom
8. of whom

C

1. tempted
2. persuade
3. attracts
4. entices
5. discourages
6. appeals to
7. scares off
8. convinced
9. put off

D

1. Some
2. Any
3. another
4. other
5. others
6. other
7. some other

E

1. isn't it
2. isn't there
3. don't they
4. aren't they
5. can they
6. haven't they
7. don't they
8. has it

F

1. F   2. F   3. NG   4. T   5. F

Unit 7

A

1. C   2. A   3. C   4. B   5. C

B

1. Were I to move to a different city, I'd miss all my friends.
2. Had I realized how friendly people at the gym are, I'd have joined earlier.
3. Let your children choose their own friends, and they'll probably be happier.
4. Go to the student cafeteria at lunchtime. Otherwise, you won't meet many new people.
5. Had I listened to my sister's advice, I wouldn't have gotten married.
6. Should you have problems with your roommate, you can always talk to an adviser.
7. Get a dog, and you'll meet people in your neighborhood when you're out walking it.
8. Were you to try talking to your new classmates, you'd probably find they are really nice.

9. I'm so glad my mom called yesterday. Otherwise, I'd have forgotten it was my brother's birthday.

10. Should you need any more information about student clubs, check online.

C

1. tired
2. take
3. energy
4. age
5. forth
6. suffering
7. beyond
8. think
9. choose
10. see

D

1. New parents have to decide if / whether one of them will stay at home instead of going to work.
2. How much it costs to raise a child is hard to figure out, isn't it?
3. Is it important to think about how many children you both want to have?
4. What some couples have to do is live with older relatives for financial reasons.
5. People have to consider if / whether they want to go to parenting classes before having children.
6. Parents need to agree on what time teenagers should go to bed.
7. How much children should help with the chores is something families often argue about.
8. Does anyone know if / whether family life is easier in the city or the country?

E

1. e   2. c   3. a   4. d

F

1. T   2. F   3. T   4. NG

Unit 8

A

1. C   2. B   3. B   4. A

B

1. 'd love to have interviewed
2. is / 's acknowledged to have been
3. is / 's considered to have played
4. is / 's known to have believed
5. 'd like to have asked / 'd have liked to ask

C

1. profound
2. significant
3. long-term
4. imperceptible
5. lasting
6. insignificant
7. gradual
8. universal
9. major
10. temporary

D

1. It was at Cambridge University that he became interested in physics.
2. It was this achievement that drew the attention of other scientists.
3. It was Newton's work on the nature of light that established the modern study of optics.
4. It was in 1687 that Newton published his most famous work.
5. It was these ideas that dominated scientific views of the physical universe for the next three hundred years.

E

1. But don't get me
2. But that's another
3. Let's not get into
4. I'd rather not talk about

F

1. T   2. F   3. T   4. NG

Unit 9

A

1. False
2. True
3. False
4. False

B

1. Whoever
2. wherever
3. whichever
4. whenever
5. however
6. whenever
7. whatever
8. wherever
9. whatever

C

1. engineer
2. constructing
3. in a short time frame
4. delays
5. fall behind schedule
6. complete the project on time
7. steel
8. to assemble
9. maneuvering
10. position

D

1. Not only are people using cars more often, but they are also using more energy in their homes.
2. Only by drilling for oil that is hard to reach will oil companies be able to supply this demand.
3. Never have engineers had to deal with such a high demand in the past.
4. Little did we realize the effects of our energy use on the environment.
5. Nor did we think that alternative sources of energy would take so long to be developed.

E

1. c   2. b   3. a   4. f   5. d

F

1. NG   2. NG   3. F   4. T

Unit 10

A

1. B   2. C   3. C   4. A

B

1. be holding
2. to have been ignoring
3. to be living

4. not to have been receiving / to not have been receiving
5. be suffering

C

1. go off
2. compensate
3. rule out
4. escalate
5. undergo
6. consider
7. fuel
8. contain
9. announce
10. make

D

1. listen   4. understand
2. not give   5. be
3. meet   6. be built

E

1. My dad, he's always listening to the news
2. All that celebrity news, that's / it's one thing I don't like about news websites
3. The way they never report on anything in depth, that's another thing I hate
4. The reporters who really check out their stories, those are / they're the ones I like to listen to

F

1. NG   2. F   3. T   4. T

Unit 11

A

1. False
2. True
3. False
4. True
5. False

B

1. are bound to
2. is set to
3. were to / is to
4. is bound to
5. is not about to
6. is bound to
7. were to / are to
8. are to

C

1. e
2. c
3. k
4. f
5. h
6. a
7. j
8. g
9. b
10. i

D

1. be remembered
2. refusing
3. having been tempted
4. offending
5. being given
6. to be congratulated
7. being told
8. being seen
9. to be awarded

E

1. To me
2. That would be my concern
3. That doesn't seem right
4. To him
5. To them

F

1. T
2. NG
3. F
4. F

Unit 12

A

1. A
2. B
3. B
4. C

B

1. wrong with parents knowing
2. my mother letting
3. believer in children being
4. insist on their teenage children calling
5. minded my older brother coming

C

1. talked into
2. went by
3. picked out
4. put behind
5. taken in
6. came down to
7. gave away
8. went about
9. picked up on
10. played down

D

1. myself
2. another
3. itself
4. yourself
5. themselves
6. ourselves
7. other
8. himself
9. yourselves
10. herself

E

1. to put it mildly
2. I can see it from both sides
3. By the same token
4. if you look at it from the candidate's perspective

F

1. T   2. NG   3. NG   4. F

Speaking quizzes

Administration and scoring guide

Contents and purpose

The speaking quizzes examine students' ability to communicate orally using the language presented in *Viewpoint* Level 2. Each of the 12 speaking quizzes covers one unit. Speaking quizzes may cover any of the language in a unit; they also require students to use the conversation strategies presented in the unit.

The speaking quizzes can be used in conjunction with the general quizzes and/or writing quizzes. Students' performance on the speaking quizzes helps the teacher determine what target spoken language has been successfully acquired. The speaking quizzes can be used as part of student grading and assessment.

Getting ready for a speaking quiz

- Plan to give a quiz shortly after the class has completed a unit. The speaking quizzes should be given either on the same day as the general quizzes, or in the class period before or after.

- Suggest that students prepare for each quiz by reviewing the unit and by practicing speaking to a classmate or friend in English.

- Copy the quiz for the unit. Cut the page to separate the individual sets: *Student A, Student B, Student C,* and *Student D.*

- Make one copy of the Speaking quiz assessment sheet per S and use these for scoring students' performance on the speaking quiz.

- Schedule class time by deciding if Ss will be tested individually, in pairs, or in groups. Calculate the total testing time based on the times indicated for individual, pair, or group speaking tests (see details under "Giving a speaking test").

- Arrange an appropriate space for testing speaking.

Giving a speaking quiz

- Each speaking quiz is divided into four sets: *Student A, Student B, Student C,* and *Student D.* Each student is tested on similar language points.

- Speaking quizzes can be administered in several ways:

Individuals: Lead a one-on-one conversation with a single S. Take the role of *Student A,* and assign the S the role of *Student B.* Give the S a copy of only his or her part. Take turns asking and answering the questions. You may choose to include other questions and prompts of your own. Individual testing may take approximately 3 to 4 minutes per student.

Pairs: Quizzes can be taken by pairs of Ss. Assign the students in each pair the roles of *Students A* and *B* or of *Students C* and *D.* Give each S a copy of only his or her part. Ss take turns asking and answering questions. The teacher should only assess one S at a time. Pair testing may take approximately 4 to 6 minutes per pair.

Groups (3 or 4 students): Group testing is similar to pair testing. Assign each S one set of questions – *Student A, B, C,* or *D.* Give each S a copy of only his or her part. Ss take turns asking and answering their questions. This may be structured in any of several ways: (1) Each S consistently asks questions to the same partner; (2) Ss ask their questions either to the Ss sitting on their right or on their left. Group testing may take approximately 7 to 9 minutes per group.

Note: You should only assess one S at a time. For the Questions and topics to discuss, it is the S who is answering the questions in each set. For the Conversation, it is the S who is asked to use the conversation strategies.

Scoring a speaking quiz

- Each speaking quiz is worth 25 points. Ss are graded in five categories: Communication, Grammar, Vocabulary, Fluency, and Pronunciation. (See the category guidelines on the Speaking quiz assessment sheet on page T-238.) Each category is worth five points: 1 is low, 5 is high.

- To score the speaking quizzes, use a Speaking quiz assessment sheet. Use a separate sheet for each student.

- Scores may be interpreted as follows:

  22–25 points = Excellent

  18–21 points = Good

  14–17 points = Average

  13 or below = Needs improvement

- It is important to provide students with written comments and positive feedback. There is space on the Speaking quiz assessment sheet for these comments.

- To record test results, use the Score Record Sheet on page T-184 or print one out from the CD-ROM.

Scoring particular task types

For the Conversation section of the speaking quizzes, only one of the speakers is being tested at a time, depending on which partner in the conversation the conversation strategy is aimed at.

In the sample answers section, only pairs are shown, and these are all referred to as *A* and *B*.

Speaking quiz: assessment sheet

Name: _____

Unit: _____ Date: _____

	Poor	Fair	Good	Very good	Excellent
Communication	1	2	3	4	5
Grammar	1	2	3	4	5
Vocabulary	1	2	3	4	5
Fluency	1	2	3	4	5
Pronunciation	1	2	3	4	5

Comments and suggestions: Total: _____/25 points

_____

_____

_____

_____

Communication: ability to comprehend, interact, make oneself understood, and get one's message across (effective, natural use of conversation strategies)

Grammar: accurate use of grammar structures

Vocabulary: correct and effective use of vocabulary

Fluency: ability to speak naturally, without many long pauses

Pronunciation: correct use of stress, rhythm, and intonation patterns

- -

Speaking quiz: assessment sheet

Name: _____

Unit: _____ Date: _____

	Poor	Fair	Good	Very good	Excellent
Communication	1	2	3	4	5
Grammar	1	2	3	4	5
Vocabulary	1	2	3	4	5
Fluency	1	2	3	4	5
Pronunciation	1	2	3	4	5

Comments and suggestions: Total: _____/25 points

_____

_____

_____

_____

Communication: ability to comprehend, interact, make oneself understood, and get one's message across (effective, natural use of conversation strategies)

Grammar: accurate use of grammar structures

Vocabulary: correct and effective use of vocabulary

Fluency: ability to speak naturally, without many long pauses

Pronunciation: correct use of stress, rhythm, and intonation patterns

Speaking quiz: assessment sheet

Name: _____

Unit: _____ Date: _____

	Poor	Fair	Good	Very good	Excellent
Communication	1	2	3	4	5
Grammar	1	2	3	4	5
Vocabulary	1	2	3	4	5
Fluency	1	2	3	4	5
Pronunciation	1	2	3	4	5

Comments and suggestions: Total: _____/25

_____

_____

_____

_____

> **Communication:** ability to comprehend, interact, make oneself understood, and get one's message across (effective, natural use of conversation strategies)
>
> **Grammar:** accurate use of grammar structures
>
> **Vocabulary:** correct and effective use of vocabulary
>
> **Fluency:** ability to speak naturally, without many long pauses
>
> **Pronunciation:** correct use of stress, rhythm, and intonation patterns

---

Speaking quiz: assessment sheet

Name: _____

Unit: _____ Date: _____

	Poor	Fair	Good	Very good	Excellent
Communication	1	2	3	4	5
Grammar	1	2	3	4	5
Vocabulary	1	2	3	4	5
Fluency	1	2	3	4	5
Pronunciation	1	2	3	4	5

Comments and suggestions: Total: _____/25 points

_____

_____

_____

_____

> **Communication:** ability to comprehend, interact, make oneself understood, and get one's message across (effective, natural use of conversation strategies)
>
> **Grammar:** accurate use of grammar structures
>
> **Vocabulary:** correct and effective use of vocabulary
>
> **Fluency:** ability to speak naturally, without many long pauses
>
> **Pronunciation:** correct use of stress, rhythm, and intonation patterns

Unit 1 Speaking quiz

Student A

Part 1: Questions and topics to discuss

Ask these questions. Answer your partner's questions.

1. Would you like to write a memoir about your life? If so, why? If not, why not?
2. What kinds of books do you like to read? Why?
3. Do you think that people share too much information through social media and blogs?
4. Do you think poetry is important to society? Why or why not?

Part 2: Conversation

1. **What kinds of books should people read more of?**

Use conversation strategies to make your conversation flow. The strategies you learned in this unit are:
- Use stressed auxiliary verbs (*do*, *does*) before main verbs to add emphasis.
- Use *if so* to mean "if this is true" and *if not* to mean "if this is not true."

2. **Listen and react to your partner's opinion.**

Student B

Part 1: Questions and topics to discuss

Ask these questions. Answer your partner's questions.

1. Do you enjoy reading memoirs? If so, what kind do you read? If not, why not?
2. Is there a book that really sticks in your mind? If so, why? If not, why not?
3. Do you prefer to read books and newspapers, or blogs and articles online? Why?
4. Have you ever written poetry? What was it about? If not, what do you prefer to write? Why?

Part 2: Conversation

1. **Would you enjoy writing books for a living?**

Use conversation strategies to make your conversation flow. The strategies you learned in this unit are:
- Use stressed auxiliary verbs (*do*, *does*) before main verbs to add emphasis.
- Use *if so* to mean "if this is true" and *if not* to mean "if this is not true."

2. **Listen and react to your partner's opinion.**

Student C

Part 1: Questions and topics to discuss

Ask these questions. Answer your partner's questions.

1. What would you say in a memoir about your life? Is there anything you would leave out?
2. What kinds of books do you dislike reading? Why?
3. Do you share much information through social media or blogs? If so, why? If not, why not?
4. Why do you think some people enjoy reading poetry so much?

Part 2: Conversation

1. **Do you think people read enough, or should they read more?**

Use conversation strategies to make your conversation flow. The strategies you learned in this unit are:
- Use stressed auxiliary verbs (*do*, *does*) before main verbs to add emphasis.
- Use *if so* to mean "if this is true" and *if not* to mean "if this is not true."

2. **Listen and react to your partner's opinion.**

Student D

Part 1: Questions and topics to discuss

Ask these questions. Answer your partner's questions.

1. Name a person whose memoir you would like to read. Why?
2. Is there a book you've been wanting to read? What is it?
3. Do you read many blogs? If so, why? Would you write your own blog?
4. Do you think kids should read more poetry?

Part 2: Conversation

1. **If you could only read nonfiction or fiction books, which would you choose?**

Use conversation strategies to make your conversation flow. The strategies you learned in this unit are:
- Use stressed auxiliary verbs (*do*, *does*) before main verbs to add emphasis.
- Use *if so* to mean "if this is true" and *if not* to mean "if this is not true."

2. **Listen and react to your partner's opinion.**

Unit 2 Speaking quiz

Student A

Part 1: Questions and topics to discuss

Ask these questions. Answer your partner's questions.

1. Is there anything that you wish people would not share online?
2. What labor-saving device would you most like to have in your home? Why?
3. Do you enjoy multitasking? Why or why not?
4. Would you rather buy new technology as soon as it's released or wait a while? Why?

Part 2: Conversation

1. **Do you think kids are too involved with technology?**

Use conversation strategies to make your conversation flow. The strategies you learned in this unit are:
- Use adverbs like *predictably* and *apparently* to express what you predict, expect, etc.
- Emphasize that something is impossible with *can't / couldn't possibly.*

2. **Listen and respond to your partner.**

Student C

Part 1: Questions and topics to discuss

Ask these questions. Answer your partner's questions.

1. What kinds of information do you prefer to keep private rather than share online?
2. Do you think it's important for people to use energy-efficient appliances? Why or why not?
3. Do you think you're good at multitasking? Why?
4. Is it important to you to buy the latest gadgets? Why or why not?

Part 2: Conversation

1. **What kind of new technology do you expect to see in the future?**

Use conversation strategies to make your conversation flow. The strategies you learned in this unit are:
- Use adverbs like *predictably* and *apparently* to express what you predict, expect, etc.
- Emphasize that something is impossible with *can't / couldn't possibly.*

2. **Listen and respond to your partner.**

Student B

Part 1: Questions and topics to discuss

Ask these questions. Answer your partner's questions.

1. Are you very concerned with privacy issues online? Why or why not?
2. Would you like to have a computer-controlled home? Why or why not?
3. Do you ever multitask while you're driving? If so, what do you do? If not, why not?
4. Why do you think some people don't care to keep up with the latest technology?

Part 2: Conversation

1. **Do you think there is too much emphasis on technology today?**

Use conversation strategies to make your conversation flow. The strategies you learned in this unit are:
- Use adverbs like *predictably* and *apparently* to express what you predict, expect, etc.
- Emphasize that something is impossible with *can't / couldn't possibly.*

2. **Listen and respond to your partner.**

Student D

Part 1: Questions and topics to discuss

Ask these questions. Answer your partner's questions.

1. How would you feel if someone posted private information about you online? Has this happened before? What did you do?
2. If you had a human-like robot in your home, what tasks would you want it to perform?
3. What are two tasks that you sometimes do at the same time? Do you do them both well, or poorly?
4. New technology makes our lives both better and more complicated. Do you agree?

Part 2: Conversation

1. **How has technology changed since you were a child? Is life better because of these changes?**

Use conversation strategies to make your conversation flow. The strategies you learned in this unit are:
- Use adverbs like *predictably* and *apparently* to express what you predict, expect, etc.
- Emphasize that something is impossible with *can't / couldn't possibly.*

2. **Listen and respond to your partner.**

Unit 3 Speaking quiz

Student A

Part 1: Questions and topics to discuss

Ask these questions. Answer your partner's questions.

1. What is one social pressure that you face? How do you take action to deal with it?
2. What was one pressure that was difficult for you to deal with growing up?
3. Do you think the pressure to "be cool" affects many young people today? How?
4. What word from your language is it important for learners of English to speak without an accent? Why?

Part 2: Conversation

1. **Generally speaking, what challenge do you think is hardest for college students to face?**

   Use conversation strategies to make your conversation flow. The strategies you learned in this unit are:
   - Express a contrasting view with expressions like *having said that* and *then again*.
   - Use *even so* and *even then* to introduce a contrasting idea.

2. **Listen and react to your partner's opinion.**

Student C

Part 1: Questions and topics to discuss

Ask these questions. Answer your partner's questions.

1. How can students take steps to cope with the pressures of college?
2. Which do you think is tougher for young people today, social pressure or academic pressure?
3. What is one way that you take care of yourself?
4. Is it important for learners of English to speak without an accent? Why? Why not?

Part 2: Conversation

1. **Do you think people in our society feel pressured to dress or look a certain way? Why?**

   Use conversation strategies to make your conversation flow. The strategies you learned in this unit are:
   - Express a contrasting view with expressions like *having said that* and *then again*.
   - Use *even so* and *even then* to introduce a contrasting idea.

2. **Listen and react to your partner's opinion.**

Student B

Part 1: Questions and topics to discuss

Ask these questions. Answer your partner's questions.

1. Why do you think that so many students drop out of college during their first year?
2. What is one social pressure that you think young people face today? How do they handle it?
3. What is something you take very seriously? Why is it so important to you?
4. What is the most difficult part of learning another language for you? How do you deal with it?

Part 2: Conversation

1. **What social pressure do you think is the most difficult for people to deal with in our society?**

   Use conversation strategies to make your conversation flow. The strategies you learned in this unit are:
   - Express a contrasting view with expressions like *having said that* and *then again*.
   - Use *even so* and *even then* to introduce a contrasting idea.

2. **Listen and react to your partner's opinion.**

Student D

Part 1: Questions and topics to discuss

Ask these questions. Answer your partner's questions.

1. What kinds of pressures do you think people in our society face at work?
2. What advice would you give to a college student struggling with classes?
3. What is something that you think people take for granted in our society?
4. Do you think learners of English should use slang when they speak English? Why? Why not?

Part 2: Conversation

1. **Do you think young people today face different social pressures than they did 20 or 30 years ago?**

   Use conversation strategies to make your conversation flow. The strategies you learned in this unit are:
   - Express a contrasting view with expressions like *having said that* and *then again*.
   - Use *even so* and *even then* to introduce a contrasting idea.

2. **Listen and react to your partner's opinion.**

Unit 4 Speaking quiz

Student A

Part 1: Questions and topics to discuss

Ask these questions. Answer your partner's questions.

1. What animal do you find particularly interesting? Why?
2. Describe an animal that hatches from an egg. What do you know about this animal?
3. What interesting facts do you know about deserts?
4. What two animals do you think will have become extinct by the year 2050? Why?

Part 2: Conversation

1. **What are some lessons that people could learn from animals?**

Use conversation strategies to make your conversation flow. The strategies you learned in this unit are:
- Use expressions like *What's more, In addition,* and *not to mention* to add and focus on new ideas.
- Use *in any case* and *in any event* to strengthen arguments and reach conclusions.

2. **Listen and react to your partner's opinion.**

Student C

Part 1: Questions and topics to discuss

Ask these questions. Answer your partner's questions.

1. What kind of animal behavior do you think is interesting? Why?
2. Describe an animal that migrates. What do you know about this animal?
3. What problems are caused by the spread of deserts?
4. Do you think that the polar ice caps will have melted by 2040? Why? Why not?

Part 2: Conversation

1. **Are wild animals important to humankind? Why?**

Use conversation strategies to make your conversation flow. The strategies you learned in this unit are:
- Use expressions like *What's more, In addition,* and *not to mention* to add and focus on new ideas.
- Use *in any case* and *in any event* to strengthen arguments and reach conclusions.

2. **Listen and react to your partner's opinion.**

Student B

Part 1: Questions and topics to discuss

Ask these questions. Answer your partner's questions.

1. How does throwing trash in the oceans affect wildlife there?
2. Describe an animal that is a predator. What do you know about this animal?
3. All deserts are not the same. How do they differ?
4. Do you think that much of the world's drinking water will have been polluted by 2030? Why or why not?

Part 2: Conversation

1. **Are you concerned about the future of our natural world?**

Use conversation strategies to make your conversation flow. The strategies you learned in this unit are:
- Use expressions like *What's more, In addition,* and *not to mention* to add and focus on new ideas.
- Use *in any case* and *in any event* to strengthen arguments and reach conclusions.

2. **Listen and react to your partner's opinion.**

Student D

Part 1: Questions and topics to discuss

Ask these questions. Answer your partner's questions.

1. Do you enjoy watching nature documentaries? Why or why not?
2. Describe an animal that builds a nest. What do you know about this animal?
3. Describe a plant or animal that lives in the desert. How does it survive there?
4. In your opinion, how will global warming have affected agriculture in your country by the year 2050?

Part 2: Conversation

1. **What are ways that people can protect the natural world?**

Use conversation strategies to make your conversation flow. The strategies you learned in this unit are:
- Use expressions like *What's more, In addition,* and *not to mention* to add and focus on new ideas.
- Use *in any case* and *in any event* to strengthen arguments and reach conclusions.

2. **Listen and react to your partner's opinion.**

Unit 5 Speaking quiz

Student A

Part 1: Questions and topics to discuss

Ask these questions. Answer your partner's questions.

1. Do you use a GPS? Do you think it's a useful gadget? Why or why not?
2. What would be the hardest part about cycling around the world?
3. In what ways has everyday life been affected or not affected by space exploration?
4. If the Internet had not been invented, how would your life have been different?

Part 2: Conversation

1. **Do you think people will ever be able to live in space?**

Use conversation strategies to make your conversation flow. The strategies you learned in this unit are:

- Make important points by using *(let's) put it this way, just think about it,* and similar phrases.
- Use expressions like *absolutely (not)* and *not necessarily* for agreement and disagreement.

2. **Listen and react to your partner's opinion.**

Student C

Part 1: Questions and topics to discuss

Ask these questions. Answer your partner's questions.

1. Have you been in a situation where it would have been useful to have a compass? If not, can you imagine a situation where you might need one?
2. Would you like to run a marathon? Why or why not?
3. Should governments spend money on space programs? Why or why not?
4. How might your life have been different if computers had not been invented?

Part 2: Conversation

1. **Do you think people own or use too many gadgets?**

Use conversation strategies to make your conversation flow. The strategies you learned in this unit are:

- Make important points by using *(let's) put it this way, just think about it,* and similar phrases.
- Use expressions like *absolutely (not)* and *not necessarily* for agreement and disagreement.

2. **Listen and react to your partner's opinion.**

Student B

Part 1: Questions and topics to discuss

Ask these questions. Answer your partner's questions.

1. What is a gadget that has been greatly improved over time? How has it been modified?
2. In recent years, many people have died climbing Mt. Everest. Should they have been allowed to attempt this dangerous feat?
3. Do you think it will ever be possible for humans to live on another planet? Why?
4. What is an invention that you think is silly or not very useful? Why?

Part 2: Conversation

1. **Have apps changed the way people live?**

Use conversation strategies to make your conversation flow. The strategies you learned in this unit are:

- Make important points by using *(let's) put it this way, just think about it,* and similar phrases.
- Use expressions like *absolutely (not)* and *not necessarily* for agreement and disagreement.

2. **Listen and react to your partner's opinion.**

Student D

Part 1: Questions and topics to discuss

Ask these questions. Answer your partner's questions.

1. What is a gadget you use often? How could it have been made better, in your opinion?
2. Have you ever been in an unsafe situation where you could have been injured? What happened?
3. What is one area of research that you think is important? Why?
4. Has your life been made better by a specific invention? What? How is your life better now?

Part 2: Conversation

1. **What object or technology do you think may soon be obsolete?**

Use conversation strategies to make your conversation flow. The strategies you learned in this unit are:

- Make important points by using *(let's) put it this way, just think about it,* and similar phrases.
- Use expressions like *absolutely (not)* and *not necessarily* for agreement and disagreement.

2. **Listen and react to your partner's opinion.**

Unit 6 Speaking quiz

Student A

Part 1: Questions and topics to discuss

Ask these questions. Answer your partner's questions.

1. Do you ever use online coupons? For what? If not, would you try online coupons?
2. Why do you think online shopping has grown so much in recent years?
3. What are some of the ways in which small retail businesses have been affected by large chain stores?
4. Is it reasonable for companies to ask employees to take work home? Why or why not?

Part 2: Conversation

1. **What kinds of store promotions do you think are the most effective?**

   Use conversation strategies to make your conversation flow. The strategies you learned in this unit are:
   - Use negative questions and tag questions to persuade others of your point of view.
   - Use *granted* to concede points.

2. **Listen and react to your partner's opinion.**

Student B

Part 1: Questions and topics to discuss

Ask these questions. Answer your partner's questions.

1. Do you wait until stores offer promotions before you buy things? Why?
2. What are some aspects of customer service that are most important to you?
3. What are some reasons to support small, local businesses? Do you think this is important?
4. Should employees be allowed to access their personal email at work? Why or why not?

Part 2: Conversation

1. **Do you think businesses do enough to keep your personal information secure? Why or why not?**

   Use conversation strategies to make your conversation flow. The strategies you learned in this unit are:
   - Use negative questions and tag questions to persuade others of your point of view.
   - Use *granted* to concede points.

2. **Listen and react to your partner's opinion.**

Student C

Part 1: Questions and topics to discuss

Ask these questions. Answer your partner's questions.

1. Do you ever use store coupons? Why? Why not? If yes, where do you get them?
2. What are some advantages that stores have over online shopping?
3. Would you rather shop at a local, neighborhood store or at a big-box store? Why?
4. Why might an employee steal confidential data from the company they work for?

Part 2: Conversation

1. **What is a new business from the last 10 years that has had great success? Why do you think it has done so well?**

   Use conversation strategies to make your conversation flow. The strategies you learned in this unit are:
   - Use negative questions and tag questions to persuade others of your point of view.
   - Use *granted* to concede points.

2. **Listen and react to your partner's opinion.**

Student D

Part 1: Questions and topics to discuss

Ask these questions. Answer your partner's questions.

1. If you could start your own business, what kind of business would it be?
2. Do you prefer to shop online or in stores? Why?
3. Some companies give a lot back to the community, while others do less. Do you believe it is important for companies to give back? Why or why not?
4. What are some ways to keep your personal data secure when using computers?

Part 2: Conversation

1. **Are there any businesses you prefer to buy from? Are there any you prefer not to buy from? Why?**

   Use conversation strategies to make your conversation flow. The strategies you learned in this unit are:
   - Use negative questions and tag questions to persuade others of your point of view.
   - Use *granted* to concede points.

2. **Listen and react to your partner's opinion.**

Unit 7 Speaking quiz

Student A

Part 1: Questions and topics to discuss

Ask these questions. Answer your partner's questions.

1. What life skills do you think should be taught to high school students? How should they be taught?
2. In what ways can work contribute to ups and downs in a marriage?
3. What are the pros and cons of online dating?
4. In what ways can technology enhance relationships with family and friends?

Part 2: Conversation

1. **Discuss how give and take is important in any relationship. Give examples from different types of relationships.**

   Use conversation strategies to make your conversation flow. The strategies you learned in this unit are:
   - Summarize and finish points with expressions like *at the end of the day* and *in the end*.
   - Use *then* and *in that case* to draw a conclusion from what someone just said.

2. **Listen and react to your partner's opinion.**

Student C

Part 1: Questions and topics to discuss

Ask these questions. Answer your partner's questions.

1. What class do you wish you had been able to take in high school?
2. What are different ways to resolve conflicts in a marriage or relationship?
3. What are the best ways to meet new people in this day and age?
4. Do you think technology can be a substitute for face-to-face interaction in relationships? Why or why not?

Part 2: Conversation

1. **In the end, how similar or different is online dating to traditional dating?**

   Use conversation strategies to make your conversation flow. The strategies you learned in this unit are:
   - Summarize and finish points with expressions like *at the end of the day* and *in the end*.
   - Use *then* and *in that case* to draw a conclusion from what someone just said.

2. **Listen and react to your partner's opinion.**

Student B

Part 1: Questions and topics to discuss

Ask these questions. Answer your partner's questions.

1. Do you think parenting classes for high school students are a good idea? Why or why not?
2. At the end of the day, what factors do you believe are most important to the success or failure of a marriage?
3. Describe how you met someone important in your life (for example, your best friend or husband or wife).
4. Do you think that technology makes relationships with family and friends more dysfunctional? Why or why not?

Part 2: Conversation

1. **Do you think it's possible to teach relationship skills to young people? Why or why not?**

   Use conversation strategies to make your conversation flow. The strategies you learned in this unit are:
   - Summarize and finish points with expressions like *at the end of the day* and *in the end*.
   - Use *then* and *in that case* to draw a conclusion from what someone just said.

2. **Listen and react to your partner's opinion.**

Student D

Part 1: Questions and topics to discuss

Ask these questions. Answer your partner's questions.

1. If you were a high school principal, what two classes would you make mandatory for students?
2. What are the most important questions for a couple to discuss before they become husband and wife?
3. Does technology enhance our opportunities to meet people? Why or why not?
4. How do younger people and older people use technology differently?

Part 2: Conversation

1. **The divorce rate in many Western countries is worrisome because it is so high. What are some reasons for this?**

   Use conversation strategies to make your conversation flow. The strategies you learned in this unit are:
   - Summarize and finish points with expressions like *at the end of the day* and *in the end*.
   - Use *then* and *in that case* to draw a conclusion from what someone just said.

2. **Listen and react to your partner's opinion.**

Unit 8 Speaking quiz

Student A
Part 1: Questions and topics to discuss

Ask these questions. Answer your partner's questions.

1. What questions would you like to have been able to ask a famous person from history?
2. What is something that has had a significant effect on your local economy?
3. Do you feel it is important for people to know a lot about their country's history? Why or why not?
4. What documents and materials would paint a detailed picture of your life if archaeologists found them in the future?

Part 2: Conversation

1. **What is a major event in history that you feel the world has either learned or not learned from?**

   Use conversation strategies to make your conversation flow. The strategies you learned in this unit are:
   - Use expressions like *Don't get me started* or *Let's not go there* to avoid talking about certain topics.
   - Use expressions like *That's what I'm saying* to focus on your viewpoint.

2. **Listen and react to your partner's opinion.**

Student C
Part 1: Questions and topics to discuss

Ask these questions. Answer your partner's questions.

1. Who are two people from history you would love to have had dinner with? Why?
2. What invention of the twentieth century do you believe has had the most profound impact on the world? Why?
3. To what extent do you believe that historical facts become distorted over time?
4. Describe how volunteers can help archaeologists piece together the jigsaw puzzle of the past.

Part 2: Conversation

1. **How important is it for students to study controversial events from history? What can be learned?**

   Use conversation strategies to make your conversation flow. The strategies you learned in this unit are:
   - Use expressions like *Don't get me started* or *Let's not go there* to avoid talking about certain topics.
   - Use expressions like *That's what I'm saying* to focus on your viewpoint.

2. **Listen and react to your partner's opinion.**

Student B
Part 1: Questions and topics to discuss

Ask these questions. Answer your partner's questions.

1. Who is someone widely believed to have made significant contributions to your country's history? What did he / she do?
2. What medical discovery do you think has had the most profound and lasting effect on the world?
3. Do you think it is important for adopted children to be able to learn about their biological family's history? Why or why not?
4. What kind of citizen participation project would you most like to volunteer in? Why?

Part 2: Conversation

1. **If you could have lived in a different time in history, what time period would you like to have lived in? Why?**

   Use conversation strategies to make your conversation flow. The strategies you learned in this unit are:
   - Use expressions like *Don't get me started* or *Let's not go there* to avoid talking about certain topics.
   - Use expressions like *That's what I'm saying* to focus on your viewpoint.

2. **Listen and react to your partner's opinion.**

Student D
Part 1: Questions and topics to discuss

Ask these questions. Answer your partner's questions.

1. Who is considered to have had a major influence on culture and the arts in your country?
2. What discovery or invention seemed to have been insignificant at first, but has actually had lasting effects?
3. How much do you know about your family's history? Do you think this is important?
4. Do you think areas of study such as anthropology or archaeology are useful? Why or why not?

Part 2: Conversation

1. **Describe a gradual change that is happening in the world that you believe may eventually have long-term or major effects.**

   Use conversation strategies to make your conversation flow. The strategies you learned in this unit are:
   - Use expressions like *Don't get me started* or *Let's not go there* to avoid talking about certain topics.
   - Use expressions like *That's what I'm saying* to focus on your viewpoint.

2. **Listen and react to your partner's opinion**

Unit 9 Speaking quiz

Student A

Part 1: Questions and topics to discuss

Ask these questions. Answer your partner's questions.

1. What skills are needed to become an engineer? Why?
2. What are some of the engineering challenges in building major structures like bridges and tunnels?
3. Given the challenges society faces today, are engineers more likely to resolve energy problems or the issue of access to clean water first? Why?
4. Describe different ways robots are already being deployed in society.

Part 2: Conversation

1. **In light of world population growth, what will be the biggest engineering challenges in the next 50 years?**

Use conversation strategies to make your conversation flow. The strategies you learned in this unit are:
- Give facts to support your opinions, using expressions like *considering* or *given (that / the fact that)*.
- Use *at all* or *whatsoever* to emphasize a negative phrase.

2. **Listen and react to your partner's opinion.**

Student C

Part 1: Questions and topics to discuss

Ask these questions. Answer your partner's questions.

1. What kind of engineering seems most interesting to you? Why?
2. What is the most impressive engineering feat in your country? Describe how it was constructed.
3. Considering that the infrastructure (subways, roads, etc.) in many cities is old, is it a high priority to deal with this problem?
4. What activities would you like a robot to perform in your everyday life?

Part 2: Conversation

1. **What are some potential ethical issues with humanoid robots?**

Use conversation strategies to make your conversation flow. The strategies you learned in this unit are:
- Give facts to support your opinions, using expressions like *considering* or *given (that / the fact that)*.
- Use *at all* or *whatsoever* to emphasize a negative phrase.

2. **Listen and react to your partner's opinion.**

Student B

Part 1: Questions and topics to discuss

Ask these questions. Answer your partner's questions.

1. What would be the most and least interesting aspects of being an engineer?
2. Think of a structure in your town or city. Explain how it was constructed.
3. What is an engineering solution that has had an impact on your everyday life?
4. How likely is it that robots will become more powerful than humans?

Part 2: Conversation

1. **What do you think is the most impressive engineering feat in the world? Why?**

Use conversation strategies to make your conversation flow. The strategies you learned in this unit are:
- Give facts to support your opinions, using expressions like *considering* or *given (that / the fact that)*.
- Use *at all* or *whatsoever* to emphasize a negative phrase.

2. **Listen and react to your partner's opinion.**

Student D

Part 1: Questions and topics to discuss

Ask these questions. Answer your partner's questions.

1. What skills do you think a good engineer needs to have? Why?
2. What has been the most challenging structure to engineer in the world? Why?
3. What gets in the way of solving engineering challenges: money, politics, lack of technology, or something else?
4. How do you think robots might transform everyday life in the future?

Part 2: Conversation

1. **What is an engineering challenge that needs to be solved now? Why?**

Use conversation strategies to make your conversation flow. The strategies you learned in this unit are:
- Give facts to support your opinions, using expressions like *considering* or *given (that / the fact that)*.
- Use *at all* or *whatsoever* to emphasize a negative phrase.

2. **Listen and react to your partner's opinion.**

Unit 10 Speaking quiz

Student A

Part 1: Questions and topics to discuss

Ask these questions. Answer your partner's questions.

1. What news stories do people seem to be worrying about these days?
2. What are the pros and cons of obtaining news from conventional sources?
3. What is an aspect of news broadcasting that drives you crazy? Why?
4. How do you know if you can trust the accuracy of different news sources?

Part 2: Conversation

1. **Describe how our access to news seems to be changing. Do you think this is good or bad?**

   Use conversation strategies to make your conversation flow. The strategies you learned in this unit are:
   - Highlight topics by putting them at the start or end of what you say.
   - Use *this* and *these* to highlight information and *that* and *those* to refer to known information.

2. **Listen and react to your partner's opinion.**

Student C

Part 1: Questions and topics to discuss

Ask these questions. Answer your partner's questions.

1. What is a news story where someone is said to be considering legal action?
2. Do you think it is necessary that newspapers continue to be a source of news? Why or why not?
3. What types of news (e.g. sports, politics, etc.) are you most interested in? Why?
4. Do you think news stories are often misleading?

Part 2: Conversation

1. **What are some of the major issues in reporting news these days?**

   Use conversation strategies to make your conversation flow. The strategies you learned in this unit are:
   - Highlight topics by putting them at the start or end of what you say.
   - Use *this* and *these* to highlight information and *that* and *those* to refer to known information.

2. **Listen and react to your partner's opinion.**

Student B

Part 1: Questions and topics to discuss

Ask these questions. Answer your partner's questions.

1. Are there any news stories that may be running for some time to come?
2. What are the pros and cons of reporting the news via social networking media?
3. Do you think it is advisable that journalists try to influence or change situations? Why or why not?
4. Do you think news stories are often fabricated? Can you think of any that have been fabricated?

Part 2: Conversation

1. **Do you think some news sources are more trustworthy than others? Why?**

   Use conversation strategies to make your conversation flow. The strategies you learned in this unit are:
   - Highlight topics by putting them at the start or end of what you say.
   - Use *this* and *these* to highlight information and *that* and *those* to refer to known information.

2. **Listen and react to your partner's opinion.**

Student D

Part 1: Questions and topics to discuss

Ask these questions. Answer your partner's questions.

1. Do you think people's opinions about the news generally appear to be changing?
2. Do you feel it is essential that news be instantly available? Why or why not?
3. Do you think that people can be addicted to news? Why or why not?
4. What are some reasons that facts might be misrepresented or distorted in news stories?

Part 2: Conversation

1. **Describe a current news story you believe that people will be discussing for a long time.**

   Use conversation strategies to make your conversation flow. The strategies you learned in this unit are:
   - Highlight topics by putting them at the start or end of what you say.
   - Use *this* and *these* to highlight information and *that* and *those* to refer to known information.

2. **Listen and react to your partner's opinion.**

Unit 11 Speaking quiz

Student A

Part 1: Questions and topics to discuss

Ask these questions. Answer your partner's questions.

1. People have said the world was to end many times, yet it hasn't happened. What do you think about these kinds of predictions?
2. What challenges do you think people face when they try to turn their lives around?
3. How much do you think people lie on social network sites?
4. If your friend bought a designer product that he or she loved and you knew it was fake, would you tell him or her? Why or why not?

Part 2: Conversation

1. **Do you think that "white lies" are ever acceptable? Why or why not?**

> Use conversation strategies to make your conversation flow. The strategies you learned in this unit are:
> - Use expressions like *That's my concern* or *That doesn't sit right with me* to express your concern.
> - Use *To me* or *To* + other pronouns or nouns to mean "that's how it seems to me or someone else."

2. **Listen and react to your partner's opinion.**

Student C

Part 1: Questions and topics to discuss

Ask these questions. Answer your partner's questions.

1. Have you prepared for problems or situations that may arise in the future? Why or why not?
2. Think of someone important in your country's history. What is he or she remembered for?
3. Have you or anyone you know been taken in by something that wasn't true?
4. What time in your life would you want to turn back the clock to, if you could? Why?

Part 2: Conversation

1. **If you really believed a serious catastrophe was about to happen near you, what would you do?**

> Use conversation strategies to make your conversation flow. The strategies you learned in this unit are:
> - Use expressions like *That's my concern* or *That doesn't sit right with me* to express your concern.
> - Use *To me* or *To* + other pronouns or nouns to mean "that's how it seems to me or someone else."

2. **Listen and react to your partner's opinion.**

Student B

Part 1: Questions and topics to discuss

Ask these questions. Answer your partner's questions.

1. Some scientists say that a global disease pandemic is bound to happen at some point. Do you agree? Why or why not?
2. What piece of advice do you think every child deserves to be given?
3. Are there any behaviors that many people consider acceptable that don't sit right with you?
4. Do you think there will be more or less forgery in the art world in the future? Why?

Part 2: Conversation

1. **Describe a major turning point in your life. How did it change you?**

> Use conversation strategies to make your conversation flow. The strategies you learned in this unit are:
> - Use expressions like *That's my concern* or *That doesn't sit right with me* to express your concern.
> - Use *To me* or *To* + other pronouns or nouns to mean "that's how it seems to me or someone else."

2. **Listen and react to your partner's opinion.**

Student D

Part 1: Questions and topics to discuss

Ask these questions. Answer your partner's questions.

1. What do you think about people who are convinced that civilization is about to end and are preparing for survival?
2. What quality or qualities would you most like to be known for?
3. Do you think it's possible for someone who tells a lot of lies to turn over a new leaf?
4. Would you buy a piece of art or designer product you liked, even if you knew it was fake?

Part 2: Conversation

1. **How important is it for us to know whether a work of art that is centuries old is forged or not?**

> Use conversation strategies to make your conversation flow. The strategies you learned in this unit are:
> - Use expressions like *That's my concern* or *That doesn't sit right with me* to express your concern.
> - Use *To me* or *To* + other pronouns or nouns to mean "that's how it seems to me or someone else."

2. **Listen and react to your partner's opinion.**

Unit 12 Speaking quiz

Student A

Part 1: Questions and topics to discuss

Ask these questions. Answer your partner's questions.

1. What is something that your parents insisted on you doing when you were growing up?
2. Do you know any stories about people being taken in by someone or something online?
3. What does the expression "Never judge a book by its cover" mean to you?
4. What aspects of brain research do you think society would do well to take into consideration?

Part 2: Conversation

1. **How do you think it affects children when parents are very overprotective?**

Use conversation strategies to make your conversation flow. The strategies you learned in this unit are:
- Use expressions like *I can see it from both sides* or *at the same time* to consider different aspects of an argument.
- Use *to put it mildly* to show that you could say something in a stronger or more extreme way.

2. **Listen and react to your partner's opinion.**

Student C

Part 1: Questions and topics to discuss

Ask these questions. Answer your partner's questions.

1. How independent were you when you were a child?
2. How easy do you think it would be to be taken in by "chatterbot" software that interacts with humans online?
3. Are there any situations where you think it is acceptable to judge a person based on his or her appearance?
4. How much do you think schools should take differences in brain development between girls and boys into consideration?

Part 2: Conversation

1. **What do you think motivates people who present themselves in an untrue way online?**

Use conversation strategies to make your conversation flow. The strategies you learned in this unit are:
- Use expressions like *I can see it from both sides* or *at the same time* to consider different aspects of an argument.
- Use *to put it mildly* to show that you could say something in a stronger or more extreme way.

2. **Listen and react to your partner's opinion.**

Student B

Part 1: Questions and topics to discuss

Ask these questions. Answer your partner's questions.

1. What were your parents big believers in when raising you?
2. What are different ways that people might be taken in by others online?
3. How much do you trust your first instincts about people? Why?
4. What aspects of brain research do you think are most interesting or helpful for us to learn about?

Part 2: Conversation

1. **How much do you think behavior has to do with how we are hardwired at birth, and how much has to do with our environment as we grow up?**

Use conversation strategies to make your conversation flow. The strategies you learned in this unit are:
- Use expressions like *I can see it from both sides* or *at the same time* to consider different aspects of an argument.
- Use *to put it mildly* to show that you could say something in a stronger or more extreme way.

2. **Listen and react to your partner's opinion.**

Student D

Part 1: Questions and topics to discuss

Ask these questions. Answer your partner's questions.

1. Why do you think some parents are overprotective, or helicopter, parents?
2. What are the differences between meeting someone online and meeting face-to-face?
3. Describe someone that you hit it off with immediately. Why do you think it happened?
4. What is something you remember saying or doing as a teenager that fits in with research about brain development?

Part 2: Conversation

1. **What do you think is at the heart of stereotypes? How or why are they created?**

Use conversation strategies to make your conversation flow. The strategies you learned in this unit are:
- Use expressions like *I can see it from both sides* or *at the same time* to consider different aspects of an argument.
- Use *to put it mildly* to show that you could say something in a stronger or more extreme way.

2. **Listen and react to your partner's opinion.**

Writing quizzes

Administration and scoring guide

Contents and purpose

The writing quizzes examine students' ability to communicate in writing using the language presented in *Viewpoint* Level 2. Each of the twelve writing quizzes covers one unit. Writing quizzes may cover any of the language in a unit, but specifically focus on the language and strategies taught in the Writing section of the unit.

The writing quizzes can be used in conjunction with the general quizzes and speaking quizzes. Students' performance on the writing quizzes helps determine what target written language has been successfully acquired. The writing quizzes can be used as part of student grading and assessment.

Getting ready for a writing quiz

Plan to give a quiz shortly after the class has completed a unit. The writing quizzes should be given either on the same day as the general quizzes, or in the class period before or after.

- Suggest that Ss prepare for each quiz by doing the writing assignment for the unit.
- Explain to students how their score will be used, especially if it will be used as part of a final grade.
- Schedule about 30 minutes of class time for the quiz.

Giving a writing quiz

On the day of the quiz, have Ss take out a pencil and an eraser. Tell Ss they are not allowed to use their Student's Books or dictionaries during the quiz.

- Hand out one copy of the quiz to each S.
- Go through the instructions to make sure Ss understand them.
- Tell Ss they will have 30 minutes to complete the quiz. Write this time on the board: *30 minutes*
- After the quiz begins, change the time shown on the board every five minutes so that Ss know how much time is left.
- Make one copy of the Writing quiz assessment sheet for each S.

Scoring a writing quiz

Each Writing quiz is worth 25 points. The score received is multiplied by 2.5 to reach the final point total.

Follow these guidelines for scoring the content and language of the writing quizzes:

5 points = All content and language points of the assignment have been addressed and are clearly communicated. There are only a few errors, and these do not impede meaning.

4 points = An attempt has been made at addressing all content and language points of the assignment, but they are not all fully or clearly communicated. There are only a few errors, and these generally do not impede meaning.

3 points = Not all content and language points of the assignment have been attempted, but those that are attempted have generally been clearly communicated. There are some errors, but the majority of them do not impede meaning.

2 points = Not all content and language points of the assignment have been attempted, and some of those that are attempted have not been clearly communicated. There are quite a few errors, a number of which impede meaning.

1 point = Not all content and language points of the assignment have been attempted, and many of those that are attempted have not been clearly communicated. There are many errors, a substantial number of which impede meaning.

It is important to provide Ss with written comments and positive feedback. On the next pages are an example of a Writing quiz question and some sample answers plus the scores that a teacher might give. Three sample answers are given – showing an excellent, average, and poor answer.

Unit 2 Writing quiz

A Look at the table about how ownership of high-tech devices in the U.S. has changed in recent years.

Percentage of American adults (age 18+)
who own high-tech devices (2006–2011)

Date	Desktop computer	Laptop computer	Cell phone
Apr 2006	68%	30%	73%
Dec 2007	65%	37%	75%
Apr 2008	65%	39%	78%
Apr 2009	64%	47%	85%
Sep 2009	62%	47%	84%
May 2010	62%	55%	82%
Sep 2010	59%	52%	85%
May 2011	57%	56%	83%
Aug 2011	55%	57%	84%

B Write one or two paragraphs about how the ownership of high-tech devices in the U.S. has changed over time. Use information from the table in Part A.

Make sure that you:

- describe the table.
- describe and compare statistics.
- use expressions like *as can be seen, as shown,* etc.

Sample answers, scores, and teacher's comments

Score: 10 (excellent)

While many people feel that video games have a negative effect on children, we need to look closely at this argument. In fact, playing video games can have many advantages for children. **First**, children can learn a lot from playing video games. They learn to solve problems and make choices. They also learn how to deal with winning and losing. **Second**, playing video games can help children pay attention. They have to concentrate to play the games. Video games can help children focus on one task. **Lastly**, children can be social with video games. Some people say children who play video games are not social, but children play games together, and many children enjoy talking about video games with each other. In conclusion, playing video games can have a positive effect on children.

Teacher's comment:

All three content points and the language point (give reasons using *first, second, third,* and *finally / lastly*) are clearly and fully communicated. There is a clear <u>topic sentence</u> that shows that the writer disagrees with the statement. There are **three reasons** that are clearly developed. There are no errors in grammar or usage.

Score: 6 (good)

While many people feel that video games have a negative effect on children, we need to look closely at this argument. In fact, playing video games can have many advantages for children. **First**, children can learn a lot from *play* video games. They learn to solve problems and make choices. They also learn how *deal* with winning and losing. **At last**, children *is social* with video games. Some people say children who play video games are not social, but children do play games together, and *any children* enjoy talking about video games with each other. In conclusion, playing video games can have a positive effect on children.

Teacher's comment:

Only two of the three content points are clearly and fully communicated. There is a clear <u>topic sentence</u> that shows that the writer disagrees with the statement. However, there are only **two (rather than the required three) supporting reasons** that are clearly developed. There are some minor grammatical errors but these do not impede communication (*play* should be *playing; be social* should be *can be social; deal* should be *to deal; any children* should be *many children*). The language point is attempted but is not fully accomplished (*first* and *second* are used correctly, but *at last* is used instead of *finally / lastly*).

Score: 2 (poor)

Play video games has many advantages for children can learn from video games. They learning solve problems and make choices and win and lose is also important. Play video games make children be aggressive. They often with family and friends after playing video games for long periods of time. At last play video games have positive and negative for children.

Teacher's comment:

The three content points are not clearly and fully communicated. There is no clear topic sentence. Only one of the three reasons (*children can learn from video games*) is communicated successfully. Another one (*video games make children aggressive*) is attempted, but this is not an advantage, so it is not clear whether the writer agrees or disagrees with the statement. There are grammar errors that impede communication. (*They often with* is not comprehensible without a verb. The meaning of *positive and negative for children* is not clear.) The language point (give reasons using *first, second, third,* and *finally / lastly*) is not attempted.

Writing quiz: assessment sheet

Name: _____

Unit: _____ Date: _____

	Poor	Fair	Good	Very good	Excellent
Content: All points successfully addressed	1	2	3	4	5
Language: Accurate and meaning is clear	1	2	3	4	5

Comments and suggestions:

Total: _____/10 points

Score × 2.5 = _____/25 points

_____
_____
_____
_____
_____
_____
_____
_____
_____

✂ -

Writing quiz: assessment sheet

Name: _____

Unit: _____ Date: _____

	Poor	Fair	Good	Very good	Excellent
Content: All points successfully addressed	1	2	3	4	5
Language: Accurate and meaning is clear	1	2	3	4	5

Comments and suggestions:

Total: _____/10 points

Score × 2.5 = _____/25 points

_____
_____
_____
_____
_____
_____
_____
_____

Unit 1 Writing quiz

A Read the book review from the blog below.

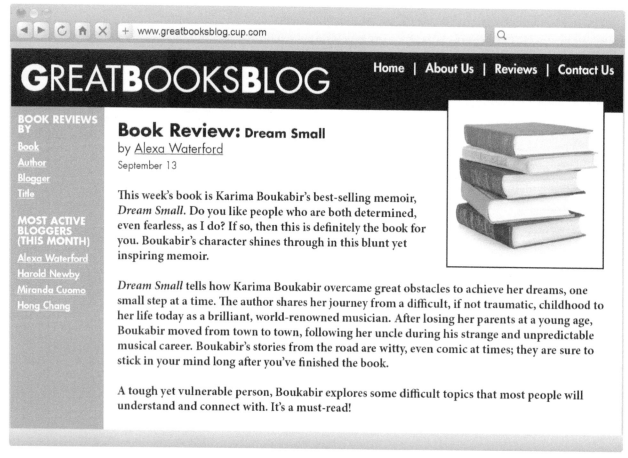

B Write a book review recommending a book you enjoyed. Use the blog from Part A as a model.

Make sure that you:

- explain what the book is about, including information about the setting, plot, characters, and themes.
- give three or more reasons why you liked the book.
- use coordinating adjectives as you describe the book, linking them with words like *and, but, yet, though, if, if not,* and *(or) even.*

Sample Answer

One More Lap Around the Track is a simple but enjoyable memoir by James Jenson, a race car driver from Vermont. In his book, Jenson tells the amusing and unlikely story of how he made it to the top in the competitive world of stock car auto racing. He also writes about the supportive people in the small town where he grew up. I found it fascinating, if not inspiring!

Jenson knew from an early age that he wanted to race cars. When he was just 10 years old, he started building his own race car with the help of his father. His father was a mechanic – talented, though untrained – and he started Jenson off on his exciting, if sometimes dangerous, career. Indeed, it was Jenson's mechanical skills that first earned him a spot on the pit crew of a rich and famous NASCAR driver. From there, his own driving career took off. Jenson's behind-the-wheel stories are bizarre yet hilarious, and truly entertaining to read.

The writing is always sincere, if not brutally honest, and his style is simple yet effective. It is an entertaining read from the first page to the last.

Unit 2 Writing quiz

A Look at the table about how ownership of high-tech devices in the U.S. has changed in recent years.

Percentage of American adults (age 18+) who own high-tech devices (2006–2011)

Date	Desktop computer	Laptop computer	Cell phone
Apr 2006	68%	30%	73%
Dec 2007	65%	37%	75%
Apr 2008	65%	39%	78%
Apr 2009	64%	47%	85%
Sep 2009	62%	47%	84%
May 2010	62%	55%	82%
Sep 2010	59%	52%	85%
May 2011	57%	56%	83%
Aug 2011	55%	57%	84%

B Write one or two paragraphs about how the ownership of high-tech devices in the U.S. has changed over time. Use information from the table in Part A.

Make sure that you:

- describe the table.
- describe and compare statistics.
- use expressions like *as can be seen, as shown,* etc.

- -

Sample Answer

The table shows the percentage of American adults who owned different high-tech devices from 2006 to 2011. During this period, the percentage of people who owned cell phones and laptops increased. Ownership of laptop computers accounted for the greatest change, with a jump from 30 percent in 2006 to 57 percent in 2011. Cell phone ownership also increased by 14 percent.

In contrast, ownership of desktop computers actually decreased by 13 percent. As illustrated in the table, the percentage of people who owned a desktop computer dropped from 68 percent in 2006 to 55 percent in 2011. This shows a clear trend toward an increase in ownership of laptop computers as compared to desktop computers.

Unit 3 Writing quiz

A You were on the planning committee for a recent conference. The aim of the conference was to help students prepare for life after college. Read the notice and the notes evaluating the conference.

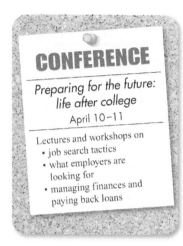

CONFERENCE

Preparing for the future:
life after college
April 10–11

Lectures and workshops on
• job search tactics
• what employers are looking for
• managing finances and paying back loans

Conference feedback and ideas

• Good topics. Feedback positive from attendees.

• Central location of conference good. Easy to get to.

• Conference was held too late in year. Too late to use information? Schedule earlier.

• Expert speakers gave useful information.

• Not enough opportunity for attendees to ask questions!

• Great to have social time in evening – good for networking.

• Need a place to buy drinks and snacks.

B You have been asked to evaluate the conference in order to help the planners for next year. Use ideas from Part A and / or your own ideas and write a report.

Make sure that you:

• express results using present participle clauses, *so / such . . . that . . .* or *so*.

• express results using words and phrases like *as a result, consequently,* and *therefore*.

• avoid errors with *therefore*.

- -

Sample Answer

The purpose of this report is to evaluate our first conference, which was intended to help students prepare for life after they finish their studies. As requested, I will present both positive and negative feedback on the conference.

There were many positive aspects to the first conference. The location was central and therefore easy for attendees to get to. Feedback on the topics was positive, and all the expert speakers gave useful information. As a result, conference attendees left with ideas and resources to help them. The social time on Saturday evening was very good, giving people a chance to network. In fact, people enjoyed it so much that they didn't want to leave.

On the negative side, the conference was held too late in the school year. Consequently, it may be too late for students to take advantage of the ideas and resources presented. Also, there was no scheduled time for questions after lectures, leaving many attendees feeling frustrated. Finally, drinks and snacks were not available nearby, so people had to run between sessions if they needed a snack!

In conclusion, this conference was a success, considering it was our first effort. Having said that, there are definitely some improvements we can make. However, if we take these points into consideration and work to improve them, the conference next year will be even better.

Unit 4 Writing quiz

A Read the list of arguments for and against logging* in rainforests. Add any other examples you can think of.

The pros and cons of logging

FOR LOGGING	AGAINST LOGGING
☐ Logging provides much needed jobs in some countries.	☐ Tourism may provide more sustainable jobs.
☐ Cleared land can be used for other purposes, such as agriculture.	☐ Rainforests keep the environment in balance.
☐ People need wood for fuel and to build homes.	☐ Species of plants and animals may disappear.
☐ _____	☐ _____
☐ _____	☐ _____

logging cutting down trees for wood

B Write a short persuasive essay either for or against logging in rainforests. Use ideas from Part A and / or your own ideas

Make sure that you:

- state your opinion clearly in the introduction and conclusion.
- give details that support your opinion.
- use academic prepositions (e.g. *upon, in terms of*) and *one* to mean "people in general."
- avoid errors with *upon*.

- -

Sample Answer

Logging in rainforests is a topic that has gained much attention within the last few years. It is an issue that people will probably never agree upon. Although logging can have some harmful effects, one can argue that it is beneficial, even necessary.

In terms of the benefits of logging, people's need for wood is without question. Wood is used to build homes, make furniture, and as a source of fuel, among other things. In addition, many people throughout the world rely upon jobs in the logging industry in order to make a living. Moreover, people benefit from the land that is cleared. They can grow crops to feed their families or use the land to raise livestock, which they can then sell. One could also point out that rainforests are frequently destroyed by natural forces, such as fires or flooding. Therefore, people should use the trees rather than let them go to waste.

As outside observers, it is easy for us to say that people should not cut down the rainforest. However, when one's livelihood depends upon such logging, the issue is not so simple. In my view, we must count the needs of people above any other consideration. Therefore, we need to continue logging in rainforests until we develop alternate means of providing the resources they offer us.

Unit 5 Writing quiz

A Some people believe that young people today are too dependent on technology such as computers, tablets, and cell phones. Others disagree and believe that technology is beneficial for young people's development. Read the opinions below. Which are for technology (✔)? Which are against technology (✗)? Write ✔ or ✗.

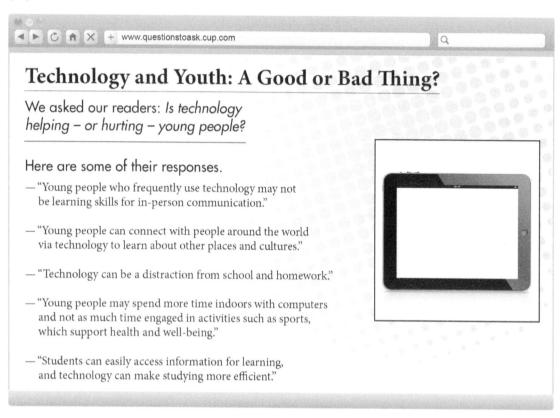

Technology and Youth: A Good or Bad Thing?

We asked our readers: *Is technology helping – or hurting – young people?*

Here are some of their responses.

— "Young people who frequently use technology may not be learning skills for in-person communication."

— "Young people can connect with people around the world via technology to learn about other places and cultures."

— "Technology can be a distraction from school and homework."

— "Young people may spend more time indoors with computers and not as much time engaged in activities such as sports, which support health and well-being."

— "Students can easily access information for learning, and technology can make studying more efficient."

B Write an opinion essay about the question in the readers' survey in Part A. State your view and summarize the arguments for both sides in your introduction and conclusion. Use ideas from Part A and / or your own ideas. Give reasons and examples for your views.

Make sure that you:

- compare and contrast arguments.
- use *it* clauses + passive to say what people think.
- avoid errors with *affect* and *effect*.

Sample Answer

It has been said that young people are becoming too dependent on technology such as computers, tablets, and cell phones. While this may be true to some extent, it is also generally accepted that there are clear benefits that support young people's education and development.

It is widely recognized that laptops or tablets in the classroom and Internet access in schools provide more and more learning opportunities. This technology also allows young people to communicate with people around the world, which may teach them new ways to socialize and to learn about places and cultures.

On the other hand, parents and teachers should be aware of possible concerns with technology. It can be a distraction from important activities such as homework. It has also been suggested that young people may not develop appropriate social skills because they communicate only via cell phones and social networking sites.

These potential negative effects of technology are real concerns. Nevertheless, overall, I believe that the positive effects of these technologies on young people's development outweigh the negative effects.

Unit 6 Writing quiz

A Read the case study about a small business. What do you think are the causes of the problems with the store?

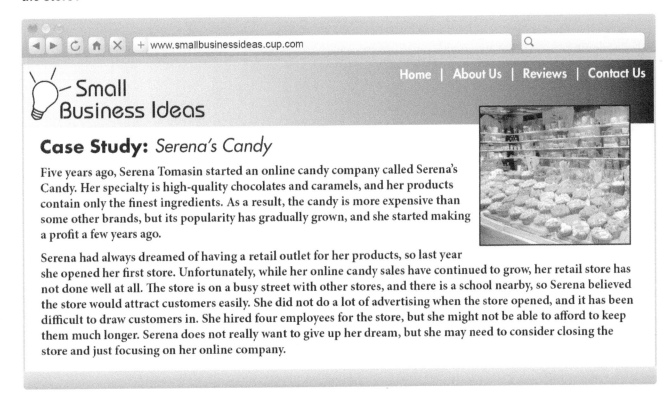

Small Business Ideas

Home | About Us | Reviews | Contact Us

Case Study: *Serena's Candy*

Five years ago, Serena Tomasin started an online candy company called Serena's Candy. Her specialty is high-quality chocolates and caramels, and her products contain only the finest ingredients. As a result, the candy is more expensive than some other brands, but its popularity has gradually grown, and she started making a profit a few years ago.

Serena had always dreamed of having a retail outlet for her products, so last year she opened her first store. Unfortunately, while her online candy sales have continued to grow, her retail store has not done well at all. The store is on a busy street with other stores, and there is a school nearby, so Serena believed the store would attract customers easily. She did not do a lot of advertising when the store opened, and it has been difficult to draw customers in. She hired four employees for the store, but she might not be able to afford to keep them much longer. Serena does not really want to give up her dream, but she may need to consider closing the store and just focusing on her online company.

B Write a report describing the possible causes of the problems with Serena's small business and proposing some potential solutions.

Make sure that you:

- write about the causes of and solutions to the problem.
- use modals to avoid being too assertive and to make recommendations.
- avoid errors with *can* and *could*.

- -

Sample Answer

Serena has several problems with her store, some of which are quite serious. However, it may be possible for her to resolve the issues and save the store, if she is willing to make some changes.

One reason for her problems is that she did not advertise when she opened the store. She assumed too much, but it is not too late for her to deal with this. Serena should use her online candy store, as well as other online sites, to advertise the store. She could consider working with online organizations to offer deals to customers and increase awareness of her business. Also, if her neighborhood has a local newspaper, she could publish coupons in it for customers to use at the store.

Another possible cause of problems is the type of customer in the neighborhood. Serena thought that a school nearby would easily attract customers to her candy store, but that did not happen. This might be the result of the price of her products. Students may like to buy candy, but not if it is too expensive. It would be a good idea for her to make a less expensive line of candy for the store with which she could attract some students.

It would be advisable for Serena to establish a timeline to make changes. She should allow enough time to see if business at her store improves. If it does not, she might want to close her retail store and concentrate on the online sales only.

Unit 7 Writing quiz

A Look at these topics. Check (✔) the ones that might be included in an article about how to get along with colleagues at work. Add ideas of your own.

☐ being considerate
☐ spending a lot of time together on weekends
☐ being professional
☐ listening and being respectful
☐ doing hobbies together
☐ _____
☐ _____
☐ _____

B A workplace magazine has asked you to write an article called *Getting along: How to have successful relationships at work*. Use ideas from Part A and / or your own ideas and write an article.

Make sure that you:

- use expressions like *a number of* and *a little*.
- avoid errors with *a number of*, etc.

- -

Sample Answer

Most of us spend a great deal of time at work each week. As a result, while our relationships with our co-workers may not be as deep or important as those we have with family and friends, they can certainly have an impact on our job satisfaction.

There are a number of factors that contribute to good relationships at work. These include being considerate of colleagues, as well as listening and being respectful in interactions. Above all, it is important to be professional. Gossiping with co-workers can quickly create problems and have a negative effect on the workplace atmosphere.

It is a good idea not to assume that your co-workers will become close friends, but spending at least a little time socializing can enhance your connections with colleagues.

There are sometimes ups and downs in relationships at work, but with a little thought and consideration, it is usually possible to improve them.

Unit 8 Writing quiz

A Read a student's notes about Abraham Lincoln. Then write notes about an important person in your country's cultural or political history.

Abraham Lincoln . . .
- Born in Kentucky in 1809
- Became the 16th president of the United States in 1861
- Worked hard to eliminate slavery through the Thirteenth Amendment, which was passed in 1865
- Was assassinated in 1865

NOTES

_____

_____

_____

_____

_____

_____

B Write a historical narrative of the person you chose in A.

Make sure that you:
- order events in the past.
- avoid errors with *in the end* and *at the end.*

- -

Sample Answer

Abraham Lincoln, who eventually became president of the United States, was born in a log cabin in Kentucky in 1809. His family was not rich, and Lincoln had to work hard as a child. After his mother died, when he was nine years old, his father remarried. Encouraged by his stepmother, Lincoln started reading a lot. It is believed that he only had about a year of formal education during his life.

Once he turned 22, Lincoln moved out on his own. Working various jobs, Lincoln started developing the social skills that would serve him in his political career. After some time working, he decided to become a lawyer. He taught himself by reading books about the law in England.

In 1842 he married Mary Todd, who came from a wealthy family in Kentucky. The couple subsequently had four boys, but only one son survived into adulthood. One child died from tuberculosis. Then, after battling typhoid fever for two months, their 11-year-old son died. Saddened by this tragedy, Mary apparently never fully recovered from it.

After winning the presidential race in 1860, Lincoln was inaugurated as the 16th president of the U.S. in 1861. Within months, the South seceded from the Union and the Civil War had begun. Lincoln managed to win a second term as president. He worked hard to eliminate slavery in the U.S. Finally, in 1865, Congress passed the Thirteenth Amendment, abolishing slavery. On April 14, 1865, just weeks after being inaugurated for his second term, Lincoln was assassinated.

Unit 9 Writing quiz

A Read the comments from engineers. Write the correct type of engineering from the box next to each name.

What kind of ENGINEERING do you like – and why?

computer software engineer	aerospace engineer	electrical engineer
civil engineer	biomedical engineer	mechanical engineer

1. I grew up interested in airplanes, jets, and space exploration. This field fits my talents and interests perfectly. Also, many people don't realize how many inventions that we use every day came from this type of work.
Maggie Chen _____

2. I've always been good at anything to do with electronics. I started taking apart radios and TVs when I was a teenager so that I could figure out how they worked. Work in this field has a huge impact on people's daily lives.
Ricardo Klein _____

3. It's satisfying for me to help build large structures like bridges and dams that help people live better lives.
Frederick Jones _____

4. I really want to help people who are living with disease or illness. I'm just starting out, but I hope I can do something that will help patients have a better quality of life.
Alma Santos _____

B Write a classification essay about how different types of engineers benefit society.

Make sure that you:

- express alternatives.
- avoid errors with *would rather* and *rather than*.

- -

Sample Answer

The field of engineering can be divided into a number of different specialty areas, or types, of engineering. For example, one type of engineering is mechanical engineering. Engineers in this field design and build machinery to produce products more cheaply and efficiently. Another type of engineering is civil engineering. Rather than focus on machines, civil engineers plan, design, and maintain structures such as buildings, bridges, dams, and roads. This work benefits society by improving public infrastructures. Yet another type is biomedical engineering. Biomedical engineers apply engineering principles to the medical field. They develop procedures and devices for the human body, as opposed to the external environment, and improve the lives of people who are ill or disabled. These are some of the ways in which engineering benefits society.

Unit 10 Writing quiz

A Look back at the article, *Why it is essential that "old" news survive,* on page 108. Check the three sentences that are suitable to use in a summary of the article.

_____	Events these days are instantly broadcast around the world via text messages, social media, etc.
_____	A devastating earthquake is an important news event.
_____	Major news organizations may take more time to check facts.
_____	All journalists should check facts for a news story.
_____	Major news organizations may be perceived as a source of old news.

B Write a summary of the article on page 108. Use no more than 150 words.

Make sure that you:

- appropriately summarize the article.
- correctly choose singular or plural verbs.
- avoid errors with verbs in relative clauses.

- -

Sample Answer

The number of ways in which people can access news has grown enormously. News is always available via smartphones and other devices, and major events these days are instantly broadcast around the world through text messages, blogs, social media, and so on. Mainstream news organizations may take more time to check facts, and they may insist that stories be investigated carefully. As a result, their stories may take longer to appear, and there is a danger that people view these organizations as a source of old news. However, this type of news is essential. It is crucial that consumers have access to this type of news, which is more in-depth and trustworthy.

Unit 11 Writing quiz

A Read the topic for an opinion essay. Then read the extracts from essays on the topic. Which essay writers believe this is a serious problem?

> Write an opinion essay on the topic of counterfeit medications for pets. Is this a serious problem or not? If you believe it is, what can be done about it?

1. I do not believe this is a serious concern. The problem of counterfeit medications for humans is much more worrying.

2. For many people, pets are almost like family and, therefore, I consider this to be a major concern. However, in light of the fact that most of the sales are transacted on the Internet, I believe it would be very difficult to stop.

   DISCOUNT PET DRUGS! NO PRESCRIPTION REQUIRED!

3. I would argue that law enforcement authorities have more urgent matters to pursue. This may be a problem, but there are illegal activities that can endanger human life. I regard that as a higher priority for law enforcement.

4. Since most of these sales happen online, I consider this to be only a small part of the larger issue of online fraud. I believe this is a significant issue that needs to be dealt with by authorities. Yet, not enough is being done.

B Write an opinion essay on the topic in Exercise A.

Make sure that you:

- report other people's views and give your own.
- use academic conjunctions and adverbs (e.g., *as long as, yet*).
- avoid errors with *provided that*.

- -

Sample Answer

Some people may not consider the issue of counterfeit medications for pets to be a serious problem, but I disagree. Many veterinarians regard it as a widespread problem that harms or even kills many animals. Clearly, this makes it a serious issue, at least for pet owners. However, I would argue that it also highlights a broader problem that needs to be considered. Most counterfeit pet medications are sold online, as are countless other goods and products, many of which could also be counterfeit. In view of this, I believe that the authorities should take decisive action against all online fraud. Consumers should also do their part. As long as consumers do not report and follow up on any fraud encountered, criminals will be able to continue their activities. Irrespective of whether you believe fake pet medications are an issue or not, online fraud is an issue that everyone should be aware of and concerned about.

Unit 12 Writing quiz

A Read the statistics about cycling and the safety recommendations for cyclists. Can you add more recommendations to the list?

Bicycling statistics	Safety recommendations

• Cyclists aged 5–15 make four times as many trips as cyclists aged 40–46.
 • Twice as many men as women make bike trips.
 • Cyclists under 16 have 21% of all injuries.
 • Males are three times more likely to have cycling injuries than women.
 • More than 70% of car–bicycle crashes happen at intersections.
 • Helmets are 85–88% effective in making head injuries less serious.
 • Only about 20–25% of cyclists wear helmets.
 • Every dollar spent on bike helmets saves society $30 in indirect medical costs and other costs.
	• Obey all traffic laws.
	 • Wear a helmet.
	 • Wear brightly colored clothing.
	 • Use lights and reflectors when riding at night.
	 • _____
	   _____
	   _____
	 • _____
	   _____
	   _____

B Write a report about bicycle safety with recommendations. Use some of the statistics in Exercise A to support your argument.

Make sure that you:
- include statistics.
- make statistical comparisons.
- avoid errors with *twice as*.

- -

Sample Answer

Cycling is an activity enjoyed by many people, especially children. Children aged 5–15 make four times as many bicycle trips as adults over 40 years old. It is also more popular among men than women. Among adults, twice as many men as women make bike trips. However, despite its popularity, cycling has its dangers. Not surprisingly, perhaps, given the number of male cyclists, males are three times more likely than females to have injuries from cycling. More than 70 percent of crashes between cars and bikes happen at intersections.

There are a number of measures that can be taken to prevent serious injuries, including the wearing of helmets. Helmets are 85–88 percent effective in making head injuries from accidents less serious, but only about 20–25 percent of cyclists wear them. Therefore, wearing a helmet should be made mandatory. Other recommendations to prevent cycling injuries include wearing brightly colored clothing and using lights and reflectors for nighttime riding. Finally, cyclists should obey all traffic laws.

Unit 1 *A great read*

Lesson C, Ex. 2A (p. 15), CD 1, Track 7

1.

Student 1 You know, everyone uses the Internet to research information for papers and everything, as I do, but I do think it's a problem sometimes because often you just don't know the source of the information, or the source is unclear.

2.

Student 2 I do know that some students take information they find online and just copy and paste it straight into their own essays. I know they do. But isn't that cheating?

3.

Student 3 It's sometimes confusing when you read about research studies on the Internet. Sometimes different researchers get different, if not contradictory, results.

4.

Student 4 The thing is, there's so much information out there. And I do think a lot of people find it difficult, if not overwhelming. Sometimes I even panic when I have to research and write something because there's so much to read.

5.

Woman One problem with all this information on the Web is that people think they can become an expert at something. Like people look up a medical problem and decide what's wrong with them. I know I have!

Lesson C, Ex. 3A (p. 15), CD 1, Track 8

Presenter Are there any questions? If not, let's move on and look at blogging. As you all know, there are literally millions of blogs on the Internet and they are being read by millions and millions of people on a daily basis. So bloggers have a huge reach and are able to access huge numbers of readers – something writers of any literary material would dream of! So let's look at who the bloggers are and why blogging has become so popular.

Well, first, let's look at some of the facts about blogging. Two-thirds of blogs appear to be written by men. So, it does seem to be mostly a male activity, which in itself is interesting. Additionally, blogs are largely written by younger people – indeed, 60 percent of blogs are written by people between the ages of 18 and 44. And um, this data is something that I will refer back to later in the presentation, and I will examine the possible reasons behind these trends. So, male, largely written by younger people. Furthermore, bloggers also tend to be more educated. In fact, the majority of blogs are created by college graduates – so it does seem that the blogosphere is dominated by young, educated males.

A small but sizable percentage of bloggers – around 15 percent, in fact – spend a huge amount of time blogging: 10 hours each day, if not more. So some people are indeed extremely dedicated to this activity.

As far as their motivation for blogging is concerned, the, the reasons for blogging do appear to be quite diverse. It does seem that only a relatively small proportion of bloggers report writing blogs as a source of revenue or income. As many as 72 percent report that they do not generate any income as a result of their blogging activities. So, in this sense, these bloggers can be considered as hobbyists – people who write as a hobby, if not for fun.

Lesson C, Ex. 3B (p. 15), CD 1, Track 9

Presenter So, bloggers' main motivation for writing blogs does appear to be more about sharing their views and opinions. Many also say they write to share their expertise in a particular area or field. Others say their blog enables them to have more visibility professionally, in their company or workplace. If so, um, the motivation to blog in a professional environment does seem to be more practical. Bloggers are more focused on career promotion, building professional contacts, etc., etc. And then, interestingly, some bloggers do say that blogging makes them more committed to, if not passionate about, the things they believe in. If so, then there is a sense that bloggers are blogging because they really do want to have influence. And this seems to be supported in some of the data, which shows that those people who do derive supplementary income from their blog sites tend to add advertisements for products that they really believe in. . . .

So, yes, let's see. Let's move on to what kinds of blogs are successful. What are the most popular kinds of blogs? It does seem like that . . .

Lesson D, Ex. 3B (p. 17), CD 1, Track 11

Woman I guess I must have read thousands of poems, and the ones I like best are short ones where the poet uses just a few words and it suggests a whole situation or a feeling and a mood – just like this one does. You can see the whole picture before you. Yeah, it's a lovely poem. I have to say I really like Amy Lowell's poetry, and this one is one of my favorites. I do think it's so beautiful and, well, . . . moving. I really do.

She's obviously talking about a person she loves very much. And what I love is just, just the way she describes that person's voice – like bells ringing in the early morning – you can picture it: one of those beautiful early mornings when the sky is silvery gray, with maybe a hint of red and orange . . . the sun just rising. And the rooftops and bells ringing. And she talks about the sky changing to a lighter color – the darkness going away and a bird flying across the sky. I'm sure the poet is feeling, like that feeling of waking up and starting a wonderful new day. That's how she feels when she hears the person's voice. It's like when you're in love with someone, and you just want that person to call to hear their voice. I know I do, anyway.

So yeah, she's telling the person she loves – her beloved – to speak, say a few words so that she can hear them, as she puts it: her ears can . . . can catch the words and send them to her heart.

I mean, how great to be able to write like that! I'd never be able to . . . but yeah, the poem makes me feel so calm and so encouraged.

Unit 2 *Technology*

Lesson A, Ex. 3B (p. 21), CD 1, Track 14

Mary   You know what drives me crazy?

Mark   What?

Mary   When you go to a store and they ask for all your personal information, and you know, you're just buying a T-shirt or something.

Mark   I hate that, too. I mean, I don't mind giving them my zip code but nothing else.

Mary   Me too. I just say "No, thank you" when they ask for my phone number. It's too much.

Mark   I know. We took the kids to a theme park last summer, and I couldn't believe it. I mean, the kids were all excited and everything, and we spent an hour in line waiting to get into the place, and then when we got to the front of the line, we found out you had to give your fingerprint or you couldn't get in.

Mary   You're kidding!

Mark   I'm not kidding. I wanted to walk right out of there – and I told them I didn't think it was right, you know, to ask someone for their fingerprint to get into a theme park. And the guy behind us in line, was like, "Dude, just do it and stop holding up the line."

Mary   Wow. I guess there are people happy to just do it. So what did you do?

Mark   Well, my wife was like, "We can't disappoint the kids – they've made a list of rides they want to go on, and they're so excited.'

Mary   Well, of course. And they know that – at that theme park. I mean, basically you have no choice. How can you turn away when you have kids in tow? I mean, who's going to do that?

Mark   Exactly. I mean, I really didn't want to give them permission to take my fingerprint, but yeah, I had to give my fingerprint.

Mary   It's ridiculous. I mean, did they say *why* they need your fingerprint?

Mark   Oh, yeah. They say it's so you can use the lockers – you get a locker that only opens with your fingerprint. Like, so you don't need a locker key.

Mary   Well, I guess that's kind of useful. At least you can't lose the key. But what if there's an employee who's prepared to steal your identity? I mean, what do they do with all the fingerprints at the end of the day?

Mark   Well, they said they delete them from the system. But who knows?

Mary   Yeah, I think I'd rather give up the convenience and know that my personal information is secure.

Mark   Well, actually, it wasn't that convenient in the end, anyway. My wife had to go back to the locker because we'd forgotten the camera. It took her like half an hour to get back to it – right across the park in all the crowds. And then when she got there, she realized she couldn't open it, anyway, because it had my fingerprint on there.

Mary   Oh, no! What a pain! There's a lot to be said for sticking with the old-fashioned way!

Lesson C, Ex. 2A, 2B, and 2C (p. 25), CD 1, Tracks 18–20

1.

Man   Well, if you get distracted – not only by your cell phone but also by someone sitting next to you, talking. I mean, potentially, you might end up killing someone. You should concentrate on the road. A car is like the one place where you definitely shouldn't be multitasking. It's just stupid.

2.

Woman   One thing that interests me is that when you interrupt a task like, say, to check email or answer the phone, it takes about 25 minutes to get back into the task, supposedly. I mean, that's a lot of time. It's no wonder a lot of people say they work better at home and do more.

3.

Man   What interests me about the research is that it's the high multitaskers who can't concentrate on the one thing they were asked to do. So it sounds like it's not good for your ability to think or concentrate for any length of time.

4.

Woman   I don't know – I'm a bit skeptical about all this research. You know, supposedly, psychologists claim you can't do more than one thing at a time. But I mean, what's so hard about cooking and talking on the phone? Or watching TV and answering an email? It's just not that difficult.

5.

Man   I have to say you can't really expect young people *not* to multitask all the time. I mean, it's what they were brought up with. They watch TV at the same time as surfing online, or they're checking messages when they're doing homework, or whatever. I mean, you'd like them to do one thing at a time, ideally – but it's not going to happen. It's what they do.

Lesson C, Ex. 3A and 3B (p. 25), CD 1, Tracks 21 & 22

CONVERSATION 1

Man   Work is always crazy for me – especially at lunchtime, when we get the office crowd in.

Woman   Yeah? I can imagine – cooking all those different orders. I've always thought being a cook must be stressful.

Man   Well, it's not just that. I mean, invariably, I have to *remember* all the different orders I'm working on. You know, you're remembering it's hamburgers for one order and fried chicken for another, and then if we're short-staffed and there's only two of us there, then not only am I cooking, but I'm also serving the customers. It's not an easy job to do. Most people leave eventually. It's just impossible to work under pressure constantly.

Woman   I'm not surprised. You can't possibly expect people to do three or four things at the same time and do each thing properly. I know I'd get all the orders mixed up.

Man   Well, that's not usually the problem. The problem is I sometimes burn the food, and then I have to start all over again – you know, when it gets really pressured.

CONVERSATION 2

Man   It's pretty frustrating at work. There's this one guy in our office – he's one of the managers – and he's, he's just so demanding. Like he asks me to do all these different things, and he wants everything done at the same time.

Woman   So what kind of things do you have to do for him as a personal assistant?

Man   Oh, things like printing out reports, and I'll be doing that, and then he asks me to set up some appointments for him. And then I'll be going through and checking his mail at the same time. But it's hard to concentrate. . . .

Woman   I bet. Inevitably, I end up making mistakes when I try to do more than one thing at once. It's usually better to take your time.

Man   Oh, I know. Ideally, that would be nice, but in a fast-paced office like ours, that never happens. But yeah,

I sometimes make mistakes – like I'll write down the appointment for the wrong time – he'll get mad.

Woman   But presumably, he realizes that you can't possibly do all that and do it properly.

Man   No. Ironically, he has no idea. He's too busy texting and checking his email.

Woman   That's what drives me crazy – trying to have a conversation with someone and they're checking messages on their phone. Invariably, I just make an excuse and leave.

CONVERSATION 3

Woman   I don't know about you, but I couldn't possibly just sit and watch a TV show. I have to do other stuff at the same time. Otherwise, I feel like I'm not making good use of my time. So like, yeah, I update my social network page and do my homework.

Man   Really? You can do all that and still do your homework? Is that what everyone does in high school?

Woman   Oh, yeah. I do it all the time. Supposedly, it's a good skill to have, you know, to be able to juggle several things at once like that.

Man   Well, theoretically. But can you really do your homework properly while you watch TV? I couldn't possibly concentrate.

Woman   Oh, it's fine. I mean, sometimes I get some of my math problems wrong, but . . .

Man   Huh. I mean, I can see you can listen to music and study – it helps you concentrate, presumably. I mean, that kind of multitasking seems fine. But you can't possibly watch TV and study at the same time.

Unit 3 *Society*

Lesson C, Ex. 2A and 2B (p. 35), CD 1, Tracks 27 & 28
(Highlighted text appears only on Track 28.)

1.

Woman 1   Thinking about the school I work in, one of the things I see, as the school counselor, especially among girls, is that a group will start to pick on other girls, you know . . . just to be mean to other girls to be part of the cool crowd. Then again, a lot of it goes on outside of school, too, kids going on social networking sites. Fortunately, our school is really strict on bullying. Having a zero-tolerance policy, we can pretty much stop this sort of thing. But even so, we still see some cases of this kind of behavior.

2.

Student   There's this huge pressure to compete and to do well in sports, you know, so you can use it to get scholarships for college and stuff. And I'm just not a sporty type of person. Having said that, I enjoy watching some sports, but anyway it just seems unfair to me. Why not let the guys who are good at sports do it? Then they can compete for the scholarships. And even then, they're not guaranteed to get a place in college.

3.

Man   Growing up, we had things a lot easier. I think it's much harder to be a teenager these days. I think they're expected to grow up too quickly. Like my daughter's friends wear makeup, and they all look a lot older than their age – and some are only 12. I think she'd be a lot happier, not having pressure like this on her. So we always try to encourage her, you know, to make her own choices and to ignore peer pressure. But even so, they all still want to fit in with their friends.

4.

Woman 2   Watching my younger brother grow up – he's 10 years younger than me, so he's 21 now – I think it was harder for him in high school. There was a tremendous pressure from other boys *not* to do homework, you know, like it wasn't cool to be studying and doing well academically. I tried hard to contradict that, keeping him on track with his exams and stuff. Even then, I'm sure he got lower grades than he could have – deliberately.

Viewpoint 2 © Cambridge University Press 2014   photocopiable

Lesson C, Ex. 3A and 3B (p. 35), CD 1, Tracks 29 & 30

Troy Did you know, traffic accidents are the biggest cause of death in teens? It's not surprising really, though. They're allowed to drive at such a young age. We really shouldn't let kids drive till they're 21. Even then, you can't be sure they'll be safe.

Lucy True. But it's easier said than done, too. A lot of kids pressure their parents. Some of the kids I know just pestered their parents, you know, to let them start driving as soon as they turned 16. Having said that, some parents encourage their kids to drive, too. You know, I guess parents get so tired of driving their kids around, they feel like they've done enough of being a taxi service and they think that the kids are legally old enough to drive, so . . .

Troy Yeah. They're legally old enough, but even so, I think it's too young. Young drivers take too many risks.

Lucy I know. They get so easily distracted by their friends and music and stuff. Really, it's terrifying. And you read all these stories. You even hear of kids texting at the wheel. Then again, adult drivers do that, too. So you can't say it's just young people.

Troy I know. It's such a dangerous thing to do, you can't believe they do it. Just irresponsible. But you know, it must be hard for parents, when their kids want to do things that they feel they're not ready for.

Lucy Oh, without a doubt. Like my friend's daughter is nine and she wants a cell phone, which is ridiculous at that age. She's wearing makeup and stuff, you know, trying to be grown up. Her friends all do, too, but it's causing a lot of problems.

Troy Yeah, a lot of my friends have stories about their kids growing up too fast. But then, thinking about it, I guess we caused problems for our parents, too.

Lucy You mean like hanging around in malls and staying out too late? Yeah, I guess it's just part of growing up – doing stuff your parents don't like.

Troy Yeah. We pushed the boundaries, too. Even so, I wasn't so bad. In fact, I think I was good most of the time. I only got into trouble a couple of times. I think I was an easy kid to raise. Having said that, though, my mom probably wouldn't agree!

Lucy Yeah. With my two coming up to 11 and 13, I'm beginning to sympathize with my mom and see what she used to go through. But then, thinking about it, my mom didn't worry so much about us – not like we do about our kids.

Troy That's true. They didn't care if we rode bikes without helmets and things like that. Maybe we all just worry too much!

Lesson D, Ex. 3A and 3B (p. 37), CD 1, Tracks 31 & 32

Woman Good morning and welcome to the first lecture on language and gender. So . . . you should have seen the course outline and assignment schedule on the website, but I'd just like to add a brief overview before we begin.

The study of language and gender has always been such a controversial and sensitive issue that there are huge debates – even arguments – about it, not just in universities, but also in the media. There are a great many general books on the subject – not all of these are reliable, being based on the authors' beliefs and opinions and not on research. So please keep to the reading list, also on the website.

Now, the purpose of this course is to enable you to analyze the relationship between language and gender on the one hand and society on the other, and to do so on the basis of evidence or facts and not simply popular belief. Having said that, evidence can be very difficult to acquire and we'll look at why later on.

In Lecture 1, we start by looking at some common stereotypes about the language of men and women and we will explore questions such as:

Do women talk more than men?

Are women better listeners?

Are women less confident and therefore less assertive?

These are the kinds of issues that the media love to debate. However, we will look at the various studies that have been done on this and find different answers. One researcher – Janet Hyde is the reference – took all the combined studies and found there was little or no difference between the sexes on most of these issues.

Having said that, in Lecture 2 we return to the first of these questions: Do women talk more than men? While there have been very different results in various studies, the general consensus is that men often talk more than women. However, we need to be careful here. Because it is also true that people who have a high social status tend to talk more than lower-status people. So could the finding that men talk more be because traditionally in our society men have been dominant? We look also at studies where status is not an issue and we find in most informal situations, the two sexes contribute about equally to conversations.

In Lecture 3, we look at gender-marked language, which is regarded by many as sexist language. Some terms are now falling out of use: *fireman* is outdated; we say *firefighter*. Others are still in use: The word *actor* can mean both male and female actors, but some people still describe female actors as *actresses*. What about the term *male nurse*? Is this sexist? Some writers still use the word *man* to mean all humans, for example, in discussions about man and nature. In many pairs of male / female family members, we usually put the male first. However, with parents we say *mother and father*, but in many other cases, we say, for example, *brother and sister, husband and wife*. Is this to be regarded as sexist? If so, what should we do if this is the way people speak?

In Lecture 4, we look at the suggestion by Deborah Tannen that communication between men and women should be considered as "cross-cultural" communication – like communicating with people of different cultures. Tannen says that having been raised differently, men and women come from different cultures.

Finally, having looked at all the issues above, in week 5, we ask the question: Is it fair to compare men and women's language as distinct and separate? In doing so, are we suggesting that one type of talk is inherently superior to another? Or should we look only at differences between speakers in different situations, without considering their gender? Maybe we should ask not what are the differences between men and women, but what are the differences between different people in the same situation?

So, let's start on . . .

Unit 4 *Amazing world*

Lesson B, Ex. 3A (p. 45), CD 2, Track 4

PART 1.

Interviewer Is it a desert, and if so, why?

Cynan It's very much a desert. A desert is defined as having a very low precipitation, rainfall. The standard rule is around 10 inches of rainfall per year. Anything less than that would be regarded as a desert. We basically would be lucky in some parts of Antarctica to get an inch of rain; in some you get absolutely none at all. It's very much the driest part of the planet, and so it's a desert. But it's all ice and snow, so it's also a very cold desert.

Interviewer: What kind of temperatures do you get there and what kind of weather?

Cynan Well, this is really cold on Antarctica. It is the coldest, the coldest temperatures that have ever been recorded on Earth – minus 89.6 degrees centigrade has been recorded at a location in the middle of Antarctica. If you look at summer temperatures in the main part of the Antarctic plateau, so just talking about the center of Antarctica, again you're looking at summer temperatures of minus 20 degrees centigrade; in winter that'll go to minus 60 degrees centigrade. It's very cold. It's also incredibly windy in very large parts of the continent, and so it's not the most pleasant place to live, it has to be said. It's a very challenging place for life.

Lesson B, Ex. 3B (p. 45), CD 2, Track 5

PART 2.

Interviewer Why is Antarctica an important area for scientists?

Cynan Well, there are a number of reasons. One is the fact that there's nothing quite like it anywhere on the planet. Yes, there's the Arctic, but the Arctic is an ocean surrounded by warm continents, one of them being North America. But in the Antarctic we have this cold, cold continent. It's been cold like that for 30 to 40 million years, and it's surrounded by this cold ocean which circulates very quickly, and so it's a very, very isolated place. The environment is harsh for life, so it's really interesting to find out how life can tolerate these sort of extreme conditions. This is the sort of information we need if we're going to establish where the possibilities are for life on other planets. But it also tells us a lot about how we ourselves cope with extremes and indeed lots of people do spend the winter in the Antarctic – on bases and, you know, in research stations, places like

that. People live in the Arctic in a similar way, but they have to have all sorts of technologies, they have to have all sorts of adaptations of the clothing that they wear and the way that they deal with like day-to-day existence. And they also have to, in some cases, actually adapt themselves. So sometimes their physiology has changed. That's particularly noticeable more among some of the animals that you find in the Antarctic waters, for instance, where temperatures don't rise above plus two degrees centigrade in the ocean around Antarctica. If you're going to survive there as a fish, for instance, you need to have antifreezes in your bloodstream, and we have found this there. Animals on the land have antifreezes as well, which help them to survive.

Interviewer What did you miss when you lived there?

Cynan Curiously, there weren't a lot of things that I missed because for me it was the greatest adventure that I'd been on. I was the only microbiologist working in my field. I had effectively been given an entire environment to myself. It's funny the things you do miss: I missed fruit and vegetables. We actually had on this station where I was based for my winters, a greenhouse where we grew tomatoes – very unsuccessfully, it has to be said. We grew one tomato and we divided that tomato 18 ways and that way, you know, I can still remember tasting that fresh tomato. We were waiting for six months for fresh fruit and vegetables, so it was a fantastic thing there. But I think there's very little not to like about it.

Lesson D, Ex. 3A and 3B (p. 49), CD 2, Tracks 10 & 11

Man There are insects in the natural world that live in large communities. There may be millions of them in one square mile, and yet these insects, when they fly around, never collide. They never hit each other. They don't hit each other and fall from the sky. Remarkable, isn't it? And scientists know that the reason for this is because of one neuron in the insect's brain – one tiny part of the insect's brain. Now imagine if we could take that cell in the insect's brain, see how it works, and apply it to a problem in the real world. Which problem could we solve?

Yes. Just imagine in 20, 30, 40 years, perhaps we will have found a way to prevent car accidents. To prevent cars from colliding with each other. And all because of an insect. And on top of that, millions of lives will have been saved.

One problem we had in the past was in the field of medicine – well, in transporting medicine and vaccines, really. And it's a great example of how nature inspired a solution. There's an organism that scientists discovered. It can dry itself out completely for months on end – but still stay alive. Then it brings itself back to life, so to speak, and rehydrates itself. Scientists used that technique – of that organism – and applied it to a real-world problem. And that problem was having to keep medicine and vaccines refrigerated. It made transporting them to remote places very difficult – besides being expensive. There was no dependable way to do this. But now scientists can dry out the vaccines and transport them without needing to keep them cool.

The lotus flower – a beautiful flower – has little bumps on it that makes rainwater roll off its petals. As the water rolls off, it collects dust and leaves the flower clean. Now if only you could create a material that keeps itself clean like that. Unimaginable? Not at all. A German company did just that – and they created something that would,

apart from anything else, save homeowners a lot of money. And that would be extremely profitable for the company.

A self-cleaning paint! And this we don't have to imagine. It's here. You can actually buy a paint that is self-cleaning. It will stay clean. A fabulous example of a problem, and scientists finding a workable solution from nature.

One thing that was a challenge for scientists was how to keep things warm efficiently. Scientists were looking for a building material that would help insulate buildings and keep them warm. And what's more, they needed something affordable. They looked to nature and studied polar bears, which as we know, have the ability to keep warm in spite of the fact that they live in frigid temperatures.

So, scientists studied the fur of polar bears and found a way to replicate, to copy, the hollow shafts of hair. And the result? An insulation material that keeps buildings warm and stops them from losing heat.

Unit 5 *Progress*

Lesson B, Ex. 3A and 3B (p. 55), CD 2, Tracks 14 & 15

Host   Hi, everyone. This is *Changing Lives – the podcast.* This week we feature extreme skier Kristen Ulmer, who Jodie interviewed earlier this week.

Jodie   Yes. I did.

Host   So how did it work out?

Jodie   It was so interesting talking with her. You know, when we asked her to do an interview, she could easily have said no – but she got right back to us and said "Sure," which was nice.

Host   Yeah. So what did you learn?

Jodie   Well, Kristen is such a fascinating person. She's been *so* successful, and you want to know like *why* did she do that stuff, . . . how she became not only a world-class skier but *the* best . . . extreme . . . female skier in the world.

Host   Right. So how did she?

Jodie   I guess it all really started when she was in college, you know, she fell in with the wrong crowd, you know, the wrong kind of friends. . . .

Host   Uh-oh.

Jodie   . . . And that's when she started jumping off cliffs and mountains, . . . and doing crazy stuff. But, she became a *really great* skier. What's interesting is that she wasn't actually an expert skier or anything when she was a kid. So it's not like she had planned all this. She *liked* to ski as a kid, but she didn't take ski lessons or anything.

Host   So she just "fell into it"? *(jokingly)*

Jodie   Very funny. Yeah. Kind of.

Host   So what kind of person is she?

Jodie   Well, one thing you notice about Kristen is that she has great self-awareness. Looking back, she said she realized that her entire self-esteem was tied up with

being pretty and with being a great skier. So she decided one summer to take a trip to Asia – and she had two rules: One, she had to not focus at all on her appearance, and two, she wouldn't talk about skiing at all. All her friends spent the summer skiing and training, and she could easily have stayed and done that, too.

Host   So did she have some good stories?

Jodie   Oh, yeah. She has all these fascinating stories. Like she got robbed at one point – held up at gunpoint – when she could easily have been killed. And another time, she got sick – her leg got infected, and she might well have lost her leg – but fortunately someone helped her and actually saved her life.

Host   Wow!

Jodie   She said the trip changed her whole attitude toward life, and that changed her way of thinking. And it had a real impact on her performance. And when she got back, she was a better skier than all the friends who had spent the summer training.

Host   So Kristen made it onto the U.S. ski team.

Jodie   She did. Though she eventually quit. She couldn't afford to stay on it and pay for her training. And that's when she started doing film work, when her professional career as an extreme skier started.

Host   Like doing movies, right? By the way, what *is* extreme skiing?

Jodie   Kristen's definition of *extreme* is "If you risk your life doing it, then it's extreme."

Host   Boy. She risked her life?

Jodie   Yeah. You know, she could easily have died – she had more than 30 near-death experiences. It's *so* dangerous. But she got paid *big* money . . . doing flips off cliffs, jumping out of helicopters, and skiing down, like, vertical mountains. I mean, it's crazy, but yeah, she was constantly being invited to shoot these movies . . . and contacted by sponsors and paid to fly all over the world. I mean, she was *famous*. And it became an addiction for her. But then, she decided to turn her back on it all.

Host That must have been hard.

Jodie Actually, she says it was an easy decision. And now she's been training in Zen, doing life coaching – helping people be the best they can be. And she says she really understands how powerful the mind is. And she wants to help athletes change the way they train – focusing on mental training, not just on physical training, and so transform their performance.

Host Amazing. So let's listen to the interview.

Lesson C, Ex. 3A and 3B (p. 57), CD 2, Tracks 19 & 20

Woman Don't you think a lot of money has been completely wasted in recent years? I mean, on unnecessary research? Like one thing I read about was how research is being done on how far crickets walk in a day. It just seems a waste to me. I mean, there's no point.

Man Maybe. Maybe not. See, I look at it this way. It all depends on *why* they're doing the research. It might give them some really useful information. Like maybe they wanted to find out how much crop damage a cricket can do in a day or something. Scientists need to know that kind of thing so they can protect crops, and ensure food security, which is really important.

Woman Oh, definitely. But there's some research that seems to have no purpose at all. Let's put it this way: Unless research saves lives or improves life, then it's not worth doing.

Man Well, again, maybe. Maybe not. You can't always be sure.

Woman What do you mean?

Man Well, I mean, one way to look at it is that you don't really know if you're going to make progress and improve lives until you do the actual research. That's just the way it is.

Woman Well, . . .

Man To put it another way, you can't always know exactly what you're going to discover. Or why something is important. It's like there are studies of snails that are now being done to see how they learn and remember things. And they've found they learn and remember things best when their brains have a certain protein or something. And they think it might ultimately help scientists see how people remember. Just think – the potential applications of that in teaching and learning. I mean, it could improve people's ability to learn, for example.

Woman Well, yeah, I guess.

Man And think of the medical applications, too. This research might help find a treatment for people recovering after a brain injury, or people who have a disease that affects their brains, and so on. But if you'd just been asked, "Should we study snails?" you could easily have said no.

Woman Well, not necessarily. And these guys must have known the type of thing they were looking for, no? I mean, put it this way: They knew they were looking at snails' brains and not where they live or something.

Man Probably. But not necessarily. That's what I'm saying. You don't always know before you start. So you can't say to people they should or shouldn't do research on something because you don't know what they're going to find.

Unit 6 *Business studies*

Lesson A, Ex. 3A and 3B (p. 63), CD 2, Tracks 22 & 23

Woman 1 Stores have all kinds of promotions, most of which aren't really such a good deal at all. For example, the one that I find annoying is when you buy something in a store, like a printer or a camera or something – it's usually electronics – and they give you lots of receipts to send in for a rebate of, say, $50. But in fact, most people don't send them in – or they send them in too late. So what seems like a good deal at first, really isn't if you forget or just can't be bothered to send the receipts in.

Woman 2 Eating out can be expensive, and consumers are always trying to find good deals. So if you look online and see what coupons there are, you'll probably find that there are a number of two-for-one specials and so on. So you'd get two entrées for the price of one, which sounds good. But . . . the problem is when people *know* they're getting a free meal, they tend to think, "Oh, OK. Let's get an appetizer each, too, and then maybe dessert and coffee," all of which adds up. So if

you're not careful, you end up spending a lot more than if you had just bought an entrée each!

Man 1 When many consumers go shopping for clothes, they see lots of different promotions – some of which are good – but you need to be cautious because a lot of them really aren't. One that I would advise against are the "buy one, get one half price" promotions. Because actually, what often happens is that you buy something because it's cheap, but it might not be something you really want. So I always advise shoppers to buy only what you really like. Ask yourself if you'd buy it at full price. If the answer's no, then don't get it.

Man 2 These days at any mall, you'll probably see promotions like "get a 10-minute massage free." And if you've been shopping all morning, it looks exactly like something you'd want to do. So you sit in one of their chairs and they massage your neck and back for 10 minutes, after which you get up. So what do you do then? Just say thank you and leave? Most of us just can't do that, and you end up tipping them so you don't feel bad. And then the free massage wasn't really free at all.

Lesson D, Ex. 3A and 3B (p. 69), CD 2, Tracks 28 & 29

Interviewer So, John, presumably in any organization, you have to be prepared for things to go wrong, don't you?

John Correct. When you're running a large organization – or even a small business – you do indeed have to be prepared for anything at all.

Interviewer And that's your field of expertise – helping companies to assess risks and plan for how to deal with threats to their organizations.

John That's right. All companies have to assess risks and have a plan to deal with them. Um, that's critical for any organization because there are so many threats – all of which can have a devastating impact on a business.

Interviewer Can you give us some examples? I mean, are we talking here about things like losing your key employees?

John Well, when key talent walks out the door and goes to a competitor, that is serious. But it's not one of the top threats to an organization. Um, org– organizations can prepare for things like that. Many employees these days have contracts, saying that that they cannot give confidential information to other companies.

Interviewer So is that the biggest threat a corporation faces?

John Actually, no. Interestingly enough, losing staff is not the main threat that companies fear. Um, recent research shows that the greatest threat companies worry about is unplanned IT outages. If your telecommunications and computer systems fail, um, go down, um, that can have a huge financial impact: It can be extremely costly. Businesses rely so much these days on being connected to the Internet, on their computer systems. If they're not connected, they can't do business.

Interviewer And what about actually losing data?

John That's the next threat CEOs worry about. Losing data can happen when your computer systems go down, especially if it's not backed up. Another way companies lose data is, is when hackers get into the systems and steal sensitive data. The problem there is extremely serious. Um, companies really can be badly affected there – their plans for a new product can be stolen, for example.

Interviewer Which can be devastating for a company, can't it?

John Yes, absolutely. And then the next biggest threat that companies reported was cyber attacks, like malware – malicious software – infecting computers, was the next biggest threat they are concerned about. The problem there is that a business can lose hundreds of working hours, getting that fixed.

Interviewer Right. So it's important to have software that protects your data and –

John Absolutely. Definitely.

Interviewer So a lot of concern about information and data systems.

John Right, but then, there are more down-to-earth things: like companies are worried about weather. A weather event such as a tornado or flooding can cause immense problems. Granted they don't happen very often – but if they do, their effects may be huge. A flood might destroy all the goods or stock in your warehouse, for example. Or maybe –

Interviewer Which again means a huge loss of revenue, doesn't it?

John Yes. And equally, problems with electricity, gas, or water supplies, for example, can have a similar effect. The problem there is that it can simply close you down. No power, no business. I mean, there are many more threats, but these are the ones that seem to concern businesses the most.

Unit 7 *Relationships*

Lesson A, Ex. 3A and 3B (p. 75), CD 3, Tracks 3 & 4

Woman Oh, really. I didn't know you'd done that. How interesting. So tell me about it. Like when did you do this?

Brandon I did it my freshman year – when I was 14.

Woman And was it like for a class or something?

Brandon Yeah. It was part of a required health class, but I can't remember the actual class name, but yeah, something I guess we had to do.

Woman So was it mandatory?

Brandon It wasn't a mandatory class until a couple years before I had to take it, when one of the new phys ed teachers thought it would be necessary for teenagers to take this class at a younger age, to be more aware.

Woman So what *did* you have to do?

Brandon What I had to do was like take care of a baby simulator by changing its diapers, feeding it, rocking it, and burping it. They were all sound sensitive, so it could start crying if there was a sudden loud noise, and there were sensors on different parts of the body to detect abuse or neglect or whatever and that would cause it to start crying, too.

Woman Oh, wow. So did it cry a lot?

Brandon Oh, yeah. It seemed like it would cry all the time, and it was really time-consuming to take care of it. The worst part about it was having to wake up during the middle of the night at least like three or four times to take care of it.

Woman I bet. Had you known how hard it would be, would you still have done it?

Brandon I guess I had no choice, really. But yeah, I think it was worth having the experience of knowing what it's like and it could certainly make people think twice before having kids, especially at a young age. At first, before getting the baby simulator, I was thinking, "How hard could it really be?" To me it was just an easy A. It wasn't until the first few hours of having it that I realized it was going to take a lot more work.

Woman Do you think you learned a lot from it, then?

Brandon I guess I learned that it's pretty much a full-time job just taking care of a kid – especially at such a young age – and it should definitely require some thought before having one.

Woman So it did change your views about parenting.

Brandon Yes, it did – mostly because of how much work and time is necessary to raise a child.

Woman Did your friends all do it, too? Did they have the same experience as you?

Brandon Every freshman took the class because it was mandatory, so yes, I knew a lot of people who did and they all were talking about how hard and annoying it was to take care of the baby simulators.

Woman So do you think all high school freshmen should have to do it, or do you think that's too young to have to learn about parenting?

Brandon I don't think it would be needed for people even younger than I was to go through the experience, but it was a great program for people at my age at that time. Otherwise, how would you know how hard it is to take care of a baby? You know?

Woman That's really interesting. So, were you a parent of teenagers, you'd want them to do it, too, then.

Brandon Yeah, definitely.

Lesson D, Ex. 3A and 3B (p. 81), CD 3, Tracks 9 & 10

Host Today we're talking about technology and the family in particular, keeping tabs on our loved ones. And with us is Gloria Marshall, a counselor specializing in family relationships, to discuss why you might want to monitor different members of the family and whether you should do it at all.

Gloria, I see you have a cell phone there. . . .

Gloria Yes. What I wanted to talk about first is an application for a smartphone that's been designed for parents of teenage children to track their children's driving. It can tell you where your teen is, so at any point when your teen is out, you can find out where he or she is. But perhaps more importantly, it can tell you whether your teen is driving safely. So, for example, you get a text if your teen is speeding.

Host So this sounds like a good thing, then?

Gloria Well, the manufacturers say that the evidence is that these GPS tracking devices can prevent a lot of pain and suffering because teens are less likely to speed or be reckless, and so the number of accidents is greatly reduced. Nevertheless, I have to say that, were I the parent of a teenager, this is definitely something I would *not* do.

Host You wouldn't?

Gloria Because your teen might interpret this as a lack of trust. At the end of the day, it's better to have an open and trusting relationship with your teen. So if you can't trust your teen to be responsible and he or she asks to use the car, then in a word, just say no.

Host Of course tracking devices are not all for teens.

Gloria No, that's right. A lot of us have an elderly parent who lives independently in their own home. But as we know, as they get older, sooner or later, they might fall and – and falls are especially dangerous for seniors. It's a real cause for concern for families. Now these gadgets are worn on the body and they can alert you, either by phone or text, if a person is not moving. So you can get help to any person who's maybe fallen or is unconscious much quicker.

Host Which can be a matter of life or death.

Gloria Exactly. Had I had this when my mother was alive, I would have used it. So, should you have an elderly parent, I would highly recommend this to you.

Host And it's less intrusive than, say, cameras around the house?

Gloria Right. And another technology that I wanted to talk about, going back to children again, is a device that allows you to limit the amount of time your children spend on any kind of electronic equipment, like a computer or TV.

Host Basically anything with a screen, right?

Gloria That's right. And this is something I would recommend for parents of younger children. It allows you to set the amount of time that you want your kids to use something – say, a computer game – or you can use it to limit their TV viewing.

Host So this isn't like parental controls where you control *what* they see or do?

Gloria No. This is a timing device. The kids decide when they use whatever device it is, but at the end of the time you set, it turns the computer or TV off. So your kids have control over *when* they do something, but you have control over *how much* they do it.

Host Sounds like a perfect compromise. Gloria, thank you so much. And now we move on to . . .

Unit 8 *History*

Lesson C, Ex. 3A and 3B (p. 89), CD 3, Tracks 17 & 18

Patrick Mmm, you make the best lasagna, Jennifer.

Jennifer Thanks. It's one of my great-grandmother's recipes. She was from a little village in central Italy – you know how they are with their food. They take great pride in their cooking.

Patrick I didn't know you were of Italian descent.

Jennifer Yeah. My great-grandparents emigrated to New York. It was my great-grandfather who wanted to come here, I think – to start a new life. My grandmother would have been happy to stay in her village. I mean, it was a major event for her and they seemed to have had a happy family life there, but still, they moved . . . I mean, it's more than 80 years ago now that they arrived here.

Patrick That must have been hard, to leave family behind and all. It's a massive change.

Jennifer Oh, yeah. But apparently my great-grandfather was said to have been a real character. I'd love to have met him. Everyone loved him. He had his own bakery business when he was younger. He baked amazing pastries and breads.

Patrick So how do you know all this stuff about them? I hardly know anything about my family background.

Jennifer Well, I asked my grandma and she told me a lot. And then I searched all the documents I could find online – like old census data, birth certificates, et cetera. I traced our family back several generations.

Patrick Really? That's amazing.

Jennifer Yeah, and you find out all this amazing stuff. You really get a sense of who you are and where you came from. And of course you discover some really interesting stories. Have you never tried to trace your family history?

Patrick Well, it's not easy. See, I was adopted. . . . But that's another story.

Jennifer Oh, I didn't know that. Hmm, yeah. I can see that would be tricky.

Patrick I mean, I'd like to, but my mom, well, she would never tell me anything about my birth family – well, except my birth mother's name. But don't get me started on that. I tried to find them once, but it's only when you start trying to find your original family that you find out how hard it is. But I would like to have known the identity of my birth mother when I was growing up.

Jennifer Oh, I'm sure. It's important to know where you came from – who your family is and stuff.

Patrick That's what I mean. You need to know who your family is. I mean, I love my adoptive parents and they're great and everything.

Jennifer But isn't there a law, saying that you can access information about your biological parents?

Patrick Not in my state. It's crazy. I mean, being adopted has had a profound impact on me. But let's not get into that. But it's not right, you know, that there's no law or anything. . . .

Jennifer Huh. I guess if you have your family name, you could . . . well, maybe you could try going to a family history center. . . .

Lesson D, Ex. 3A and 3B (p. 91), CD 3, Tracks 19 & 20

Speaker So, the, um, Ancient Lives Project is a, an important and significant piece of work with thousands of volunteers, deciphering all those ancient texts. And, of course, it's the painstaking work of the public, these so-called "citizen volunteers" that makes all this possible – something that a small team of paleographers could never have done alone. So the public really has made a major contribution to this project. Ancient Lives is just one of many projects that call on the public to actively volunteer their time to help decipher or uncover information that will help scientists and others working on massive research projects: People are sitting at their computers, and these are people from all walks of life – ordinary everyday people, from students to homemakers.

There are . . . there is a wide variety of other projects, um . . . that have been rolled out, using citizen volunteers. For example, some are exploring the surface of the moon, looking at images of the moon and counting the number of visible craters. In another project, people are helping scientists to understand more about the language of whales. They listen to the sounds from whales and then categorize them . . . in order to help researchers understand what the whales are saying to each other.

What these volunteers can achieve is quite amazing. For example, it's estimated that one project would have taken more than 28 years to complete if the team of scientists alone had worked on it, but with public help, they believe it can be done in less than six months, which is incredible. So these projects really seem to have captured the imagination of the public, and there are more than 500,000 volunteers working on different projects right now.

Um, another project, and this is a good example of how we can look at historical data and use it today, is the Old Weather Project. In this project, people study old weather records that were made from navy ships during World War I. And this work will be important in two ways. First, these historical measurements will help climatologists. They'll be able to see any gradual changes in weather patterns, or even any sudden extreme weather, in the past, and, and the data will mostly be used to predict future weather patterns. And this data is not insignificant . . . these ships are known to have traveled around the world, so the measurements they took were very valuable.

Second, historians will use the information to track the movements of these ships during the war and to uncover some of the stories of the crews and other people on board. So it's very important historically, too.

Unit 9 *Engineering wonders*

Lesson B, Ex. 3A and 3B (p. 97), CD 3, Tracks 25 & 26

1.

Presenter Engineers faced a huge challenge when it came to this project – building the gigantic viewing-window of the tank. Never before had engineers tried to build a tank of this size. It was an engineering feat like no other. Not only did it have to hold seven and a half million liters of water, but it had to be earthquake-proof, too. *And* it had to hold three of the largest species of whale sharks. Clearly, ambitious aims.

Engineers wanted to create a window that visitors wouldn't even notice. Only by using a special process did it become possible. The window was made from seven panels, each made up of layers of acrylic glued together, rather than glass, which wouldn't be as strong. At 60 centimeters thick, it was, at the time, the largest of its kind in the world. Little did anyone realize how *spectacular* it would look once installed. An amazing experience that two to three million visitors enjoy every year. . . .

2.

Presenter Seldom has a project taken so long to get off the ground as this one. Proposals for a way to link the two nations were first made in the 1800s. But it wasn't until the late *1980*s that work actually began. The key challenge was how to *dig* through rock 50 meters below the seabed. That in itself presented engineers with unique problems. But the aim was clear: Build two railway lines for high-speed trains, and a third emergency tunnel. Thirteen thousand engineers, technicians, and laborers worked on the project, which was completed in just six years. On completion, it was the longest undersea tunnel in the world. Little did they know that construction would come in more than 80 percent over budget. But there's no doubt that the project was a success. Approximately 15 million people travel through the tunnel each year. . . .

3.

Presenter This is one of the most amazing feats of engineering this century. The biggest problem was making her profitable. Only by competing with planes would that be possible. She had to be luxurious – like a first-class resort. The aim was to make her bigger than any other liner so there was more space for paying passengers. But not only did they have to make sure she could fit under a New York bridge, they had to ensure she was not too wide for the Panama Canal. To do this, engineers had to rewrite the rules of shipbuilding – and do it all in less than two years. Every day the project ran over would cost almost $500,000. When finished, this would be the largest and most luxurious liner in the world. A magnificent cruise ship with first-class spas and world-class restaurants. Ninety-one thousand seven hundred passengers sail every year across the Atlantic. . . .

Lesson D, Ex. 3B and 3C (p. 101), CD 3, Tracks 30 & 31

Minnie Today we're talking about humanoid robots – and specifically about a robot that has been developed by a professor from Osaka University in Japan. It – or should I say "she"? – even has a name. Not a girl's name, granted, but *Geminoid F.* Our guest – Mark Spock – first set eyes on Geminoid F at a Valentine's Day exhibition at a department store . . . in, um, Tokyo, Japan. Mark, Geminoid looks very realistic. I mean, she looks like a young Japanese woman.

Mark Yes, Minnie, she really does. It's amazing. Actually, the faces of several young Japanese women were scanned and an average Japanese woman's face was created. She certainly looks very realistic, even though her skin is made from synthetic material.

Minnie So what was she doing in the department store?

Mark Well, actually, she was there in a glass display case, sitting, waiting for someone to meet her. She interacted with people around her, so she could respond to smiles, for example. Her maker actually said part of the reason for her being there was to see how people would actually interact with her.

Minnie And what were people's reactions to her?

Mark I'd say people were curious. Interested to see her. I mean, on a previous engagement in Hong Kong, she sang and smiled at a huge crowd of people who were taking photos and they were completely fascinated by her. I mean, considering that she is a robot, it's amazing to think that she got as much attention as a real pop star. She was a hit.

Minnie So she sings?

Mark She sings, she talks, you know, she responds to people. She has 65 facial expressions – so she can smile, she can frown, and she can blink and even look as though she's breathing. And you know, she has modeled clothes, and actually, she has been in a play starring alongside a real actress. I mean, she has limitations, obviously, but whatever you think of her, it . . . she represents an amazing technological advance.

Minnie And what applications for robots of this kind does her inventor anticipate in the future?

Mark Well, he has been quoted as saying that there's no reason whatsoever that in the future, with the right technology, he wouldn't be able to build robots that think and act like real people. He really believes he can get humanoids to copy human behavior. And then he says the applications are basically endless. I mean, if you think about it, she could be a substitute teacher, a caregiver – anything, really.

Minnie A caregiver?

Mark Yes, he believes that humanoids can become our friends.

Minnie And will people *want* robots as friends?

Mark Well, considering the reactions people have around here – that robots are a little creepy – maybe not. But that may be cultural. In Japan, for example, there's no doubt whatsoever that people are more accepting of robots. Maybe it's only a matter of time here. . . .

Unit 10 *Current events*

Lesson C, Ex. 3B and 3C (p. 111), CD 4, Tracks 8 & 9

Host Recent events in the news have highlighted the work of journalists around the world. It's work that can be dangerous – foreign correspondents often find themselves in difficult and hostile places – reporting on wars or on other crises like famines, floods, etc. This is no nine-to-five job, and it can be tough. On today's show, we're talking about the work of journalists, trends in journalism, and how technology has changed journalists' work. With us is Stanley Stuffenberg, who has written a book called *Journalism Today*. Stanley, welcome to the show. What are some of the issues you talk about in your book?

Stanley Well, thank you. Um, clearly one of the main issues we are seeing in journalism – and how news is disseminated – has to do with how quickly events are reported. Gone are the days when journalists wrote their reports, filed them with the news agency, and a day later they would appear in a newspaper. But these days, many of our news reports, they're being filed, filmed or, or published live, as events are still happening and unfolding. It's immediate.

Host Right. We see news helicopters filming car chases live. Or cameras are there when people are being arrested.

Stanley Right. And there are more sources of news and information these days, too. We don't just rely on *reporters* at the scene of an event. Ordinary people and citizens, they're sending in photos and reports. It gives a much wider range of voices and opinions.

Host Right. Now let's take a question from a caller. This is Louis calling in from San Diego. Louis, go ahead.

Louis Um, yes, thank you for taking my call. Um, one of the things I find worrisome with this instant news reporting is that we see many more really shocking or upsetting images. I mean, of people who have been killed or badly injured, and I wonder, should we be seeing these pictures? Do we even need to? Is it ethical?

Stanley Well, the caller raises an important question. Do we really need to see those kinds of graphic pictures? The problem is that many news organizations are very concerned with ratings – they're very competitive. So using pictures like this is one way to boost the ratings, get more viewers. Is it ethical? In my opinion, it isn't.

Host Which brings me to another question. Is the role of a journalist to simply report news as an observer, or is the role of the reporter to be someone who can help change a situation?

Stanley I think many people believe that journalists can influence or change situations and that by exposing what is going on in a region, it can have an enormous political impact. But in reality, I think what they can do is limited. They have influence but only to a certain extent. As journalists, they can report what's happening, show the pictures, and maybe offer their own comments, their own perspective. But at the end of the day, it's then up to leaders or, indeed the public, to make change happen.

Unit 11 *Is it real?*

Lesson C, Ex. 2A and 2B (p. 121), CD 4, Tracks 15 & 16

1.
Woman It's interesting. I mean, the kinds of white lies people tell. I mean, some of the time it's not that people are telling a lie. It's like they're exaggerating or something. Like my dad is always talking about the fish he catches – he likes fishing – and he's like, "Yeah, this fish I caught was *this* long." Not really!

2.
Man I guess one reason people tell white lies is to avoid hurting someone. I mean, for example, you might say to someone, "Oh, I've been meaning to call you all week," even if you haven't even *thought* of calling – because if you told the truth, "Um, sorry, I haven't even thought about calling you," I mean, that would just damage your relationship.

3.
Woman So when you think about it – there's a big difference between, you know, saying, "I love your shirt" when you really don't mean it – and telling an outright lie – like to your parents or something.

4.
Man Apparently, people who lie about themselves – like saying they're better at something than they are – tend to be more confident. And actually, they really *do* become better at whatever it is. So it's kind of a self-fulfilling thing – say you're better at something and you become better at it. So I suppose in that case white lies actually serve a useful purpose.

5.
Woman To me, it's kind of obvious when someone's telling a white lie, but it can be kind of sad, you know? Like when people tell them to make up for the fact that they feel inadequate in some way. Like they feel as if they're not interesting enough or clever enough, so they invent all these stories to make themselves sound really fascinating.

Lesson C, Ex. 3A and 3B (p. 121), CD 4, Tracks 17 & 18
(Highlighted text appears only in Track 18.)

Chad Do you think most people post things on social network sites that are untrue?

Debra	Not sure. I know I have. I've listed a fake birthday, and I actually use a nickname. And to me, that's OK. I'm just protecting my identity. But some people change things like their marital status. But that doesn't sit right with me – saying you're single when you're actually married.
Chad	So have you ever changed other information, like, you know, your qualifications or . . . ?
Debra	No. I've never done that. But I know people who have. But to me, that's just plain wrong. I mean, giving a different birthday is harmless. Except I got a birthday card one time on my fake birthday, from like this old friend who saw it on my page.
Chad	Oh, that's funny. But you know, I read that people lie online all the time. Like six times a day on average or something – to work colleagues and family and friends. I mean, to everyone!
Debra	Wow. That's not good. But it's really not that surprising to me. I mean, it's easier to lie online, I suppose.
Chad	Well, that's what they say. Like face-to-face, people can tell if you're lying. Well, sometimes.
Debra	But you can't tell that when you get a text or email or whatever.
Chad	Right. Though my sister says she's always really careful with email. She keeps reminding me that what you write on email is there forever, and to her, that's important to remember.
Debra	Yeah, I suppose so.
Chad	Hmm. But anyway, what are all these people lying about?
Debra	Well, I suppose the number one lie is people saying "I'm fine" when you ask how they are. And they're not fine at all. Though I would think that's a lie people tell face-to-face all the time, too.
Chad	Right. Or their age. People don't like to tell their age oftentimes.
Debra	I'm pretty sure people who are using online dating sites tell a lot of white lies, too. Like exaggerate and make things up about themselves.
Chad	Oh, yeah.
Debra	I heard, like, they lie about their height and what they earn and . . . how attractive they are! Supposedly, men tell more lies than women. Or so they say. Though I'm not sure how they know that stuff.
Chad	See, to me, that's a bit pointless. Like what happens when you finally meet the person for a date and they find out you're not a tall, dark-haired, attractive guy in your thirties.
Debra	Yeah, and you're actually 45 and short and ugly! That's hilarious. But yeah, that doesn't seem right to me.
Chad	Yeah, at least if you're with someone, you can usually tell if they are lying. They kind of don't look at you.
Debra	Yeah. I heard people who lie touch their nose a lot.
Chad	Yeah, no. They always seem kind of suspicious, that's for sure.
Debra	Gosh. It makes you wonder if you can trust anything anyone says.
Chad	I know.

Lesson D, Ex. 3A and 3B (p. 123), CD 4, Tracks 19 & 20

Host	Our special segment today is called "Fakes of Art." It's an in-depth look at the world of fake art and how some people make a lucrative living from it. Michael Simmons brings us this report.
Michael Simmons	John Myatt is a successful painter. But he's no ordinary artist. He paints in the style of other world-famous artists. One of his early collections – a series of watercolors painted in the style of the famous French artist Monet – sold out in less than two months.
	But the story of his life is a fascinating one, and the road to his success as an artist is quite unconventional. It's a case of truth being stranger than fiction.
	Myatt's first taste of success came with a hit song he co-wrote in the 1970s. It was called "Silly Games," and it went to number one on the UK charts.
	But that success was short-lived, and he soon found himself in desperate circumstances when his wife walked out, divorcing him and leaving him with two young children to support.
	As an art teacher on a fairly low income, he needed to find a way to earn a better living but also be able to work from home and take care of his small children. Myatt placed an advertisement for his work in a magazine, offering to paint fake works of art for a fee. It soon became a business – and a legitimate one at that. Myatt made it clear that his works were entirely fake.
	It wasn't until some years later that things went terribly wrong. Myatt had become involved with a business partner who found buyers for his works. One day this partner told Myatt that an auction house had been taken in by one of his pieces of art and had sold it for more than 25,000 pounds – around 40,000 dollars. Myatt received payment for the work, which to him was a huge amount of money.
	With a young family to support, Myatt needed that money. And even though he was uncomfortable with being involved in this business, he continued to paint and his business partner continued to sell. Over 200 paintings are believed to have been sold in this way. Eventually, he stopped, but two years later, the police became involved and an investigation began. After four years, Myatt was sentenced to 12 months in prison – a lenient sentence because he had helped with the investigation. He said he would never paint again, but a police investigator, who had become a close friend, persuaded him to take up painting again.
	Myatt has gone on to become a fine artist in his own right – running a very lucrative and *legitimate* business.
Host	John Myatt's work is documented in a book and a movie. Read more about his story online at . . .

Lesson A, Ex. 3A and 3B (p. 127), CD 4, Tracks 22 & 23

Mark Hmm, this article's interesting. I'm glad you weren't one of those "helicopter" parents. I would have hated that.

Mom Oh, I know. We always believed in you making your own decisions – even in elementary school. Otherwise, how do you learn how to be independent?

Mark I know. But I remember in middle school, some of my friends' moms storming into class and complaining about a failed test or a bad grade. The kids were always like embarrassed.

Mom I bet. And even in high school, I remember the moms of some kids – they would rush in if their kids forgot lunch money or if they'd forgotten to take in their homework. It was ridiculous.

Mark Yeah. One time I didn't have lunch money, and I remember the other kids giving me some of their lunch.

Mom Oh, yeah. That happened a few times. But the point is you never expected us to rescue you every time something went wrong. Which is good, really. We always insisted on you taking responsibility for yourself.

Mark Yeah. It's not good when parents hover over their kids and micro-manage everything. And interfere and everything.

Mom Well, apart from anything else, you need to be self-reliant and you have to be able to sort out problems and conflict . . . so there's no point in parents doing that for their kids.

Mark You'd be surprised, though. It still happens in college. Like my roommate – his mom insists on him calling like five times a day to make sure he's OK and she's always calling his professors. I'm glad you don't do that. I'd resent you doing that, actually.

Mom Oh, I know. Mind you, I don't have time to do that for you. So it's just as well, really!

Lesson D, Ex. 3A and 3B (p. 133), CD 4, Tracks 29 & 30

1.

Woman One of the biggest challenges for organizations in this day and age is adapting to changing situations. Those organizations that can change are the ones that are more likely to be successful. So what does this have to do with brain research? Well, people tend not to like change, um, they tend not to be good at it. And research into how the brain works goes some way toward understanding why that is, so we can work with people to create more effective change.

It also tells us how the brain manages information, how people make decisions or solve problems, how they work together in a team, and so on. And if we can understand these kinds of things, then we can begin to understand how to manage people and choose the best people to run organizations.

In the future, this research is certain to affect how companies train employees and promote them into senior roles so that they'll have the best people to lead their organizations and make the best decisions in times of change.

2.

Man One of the exciting areas in brain research is understanding how, how changes in the circuitry of the brain affect hunger and eating. It's in the early stages, but there is promising research in this area. And the impact it could have in the future is extremely exciting – because we are beginning to understand more fully what factors prompt obesity and eating disorders, which of course is of great importance if we are to treat these problems more effectively than we currently do.

We are also coming closer to an understanding of how certain foods affect the brain. Of course, a lot has been done in this area already – um, we already see on the market drinks that – if manufacturers are to be believed – promote brain health, for example. But maybe one day we will discover more about which foods affect different parts of the brain so that we could create diets that help people to deal with their eating problems. And know which foods help with learning skills – for example, what foods a musician or a gymnast needs. The potential is huge.

3.

Woman One of the interesting things is that as we understand more about how the brain develops, we can get a deeper understanding of how we acquire new knowledge and skills throughout life. So we can start to understand perhaps if there are optimal ages at which it's best to learn a specific skill. So it has often been claimed that the younger you are, the easier it is to learn a new language. The same may also be true of other subjects such as mathematics, say. But is it really true? Does the evidence back this up? Researchers are starting to look at these exciting questions. And . . . and the implications for educational policy are sure to be significant; in the future, we may be able to design programs for learning that teach subjects at the time in development when the brain is most receptive to learning.

4.

Man We already know so much about the brain – and the work that neuroscientists have already done needs to be recognized – but recent developments have been especially exciting. We are beginning to understand how addiction has a great deal to do with how the brain is wired, and that it is in fact a brain disorder.

And as we understand more about addictions – what it is that makes the brain become addictive in its behavior – then we can begin to treat the millions of addicts there are. And of course it's not just drugs that people are addicted to, but shopping, gambling, eating – so many different things. And I mean, *really* effectively treat them to overcome their addictions. However, going back to the subject of drugs, the impact on society in the future would be enormous – especially when you consider the amount of drug-related crime we have, for example.

Workbook answer key

Unit 1 *A great read*

Lesson A Grammar (p. 2)

Exercise A

1. am 2. am 3. doesn't 4. haven't 5. do; do 6. did

Exercise B

1. do 2. did 3. has 4. am 5. didn't; does 6. haven't; don't

Exercise C

Answers will vary.

Lesson B Vocabulary (p. 3)

Exercise A

sticks in my mind / learn it by heart / It was on the tip of my tongue / off the top of my head / see the point / can't make heads or tails of / got something out of / lose my train of thought

Exercise B

Answers will vary.

Lesson B Grammar (p. 4)

Exercise A

1. *B* Yes, sometimes. The old Greek tragedies are the **ones** I like most.
2. we were supposed to
3. No changes.
4. *B* Well, I prefer not to read them, but sometimes if I'm waiting at the doctor's office I might look at **one**.
5. *B* Yes, I know her novels (not *one / ones* after *her*). I think her more recent **one** is much better than her first **one**.
   A Yeah, I agree. Actually, she's working on a new **one** now.

Exercise B

A I need something to read. Have you read anything good lately?

B Well, I've been reading a lot of crime novels lately. You can borrow **one** if you like. Do you **want to / want to borrow one?**

A Thanks, but I don't like to read books about murders. I generally prefer **not to** or I get nightmares.

B OK. How about a classic like *Great Expectations*?

A Yeah, that sounds good. I've never read that **one** and I've always **wanted to.**

B We read it in our literature class a few years ago. Well, actually we were **supposed to**, but I watched the movie instead.

A You did? That's funny. There are so many movies of the classics nowadays. But usually I don't watch the movie until after I've read the book, or at least I **try not to.** Usually the books are better.

B Yeah. I have to say I usually prefer the movie. Anyway, take *Great Expectations*. Or I have some Shakespeare plays, too. I think I have most of his plays (not *ones* after *his*). Here, take that **one**, *Romeo and Juliet,* or *Hamlet.* You can borrow **both** (plays) (not *ones* after *both*) if you like. I hope Hamlet doesn't give you nightmares, though!

A OK. Thanks.

Exercise C

Answers will vary.

Lesson C Conversation strategies (p. 5)

Exercise A

1. do appreciate 2. does feel 3. does make
4. do need 5. do think

Exercise B

1. If not 2. if so 3. if not 4. If so 5. If not

Exercise C

1. if so; do; do 2. if not; does

Lesson D Reading (p. 6)

Exercise A

Item 3 is true.

Lesson D Reading (p. 7)

Exercise B

1. c 2. b 3. b 4. c 5. a 6. c 7. b

Exercise C

1. T
2. F—Slams are open to everyone who wishes to sign up and can get into the venue.
3. NG
4. F—Each poem must be of the poet's own construction.
5. T
6. F—The poet may not use props, costumes, or musical instruments.
7. NG
8. F—Poets are free to do work in any style on any subject.

Exercise D

Answers will vary.

Writing (p. 8)

Exercise A

dark yet thrilling; thoughtful though arrogant; terrible, even brutal; tense, dramatic; unpredictable though perhaps realistic; disturbing, if not depressing

Exercise B

1. yet 2. , 3. and 4. yet 5. even 6. and

Exercise C

1. Dostoevsky's novels are complex, **if not / even** difficult.
2. His work has often been described as thought-provoking, **if not / even** philosophical.
3. The vocabulary in the book is rich, **if / though / but / yet** at times obscure.
4. Correct
5. Readers may find the initial plot development slow, **if not / even** boring.
6. For me, reading a Dostoevsky novel is an intriguing, **if not / even** fascinating experience.
7. However, his novels can leave the reader feeling saddened, **if not / even / if not, even** depressed.

Exercise E

Answers will vary.

Listening extra (p. 9)

Exercise A

Answers will vary.

Exercise B

Try to publish a story in a school or student newspaper. / Attend a writer's workshop. / Self-publish an e-book. / Try to get accepted to a writer's conference. / Take a creative writing class.

Unit 2 *Technology*

Lesson A Grammar (p. 10)

Exercise A

1. to be taken   2. based on data   3. collected
4. designed to search   5. in my class
6. no doubt hoping to reassure me
7. directly targeted   8. on their account   9. around the world OR living around the world   10. to worry about
11. to be shared OR to share   12. existing

Exercise B

1. displaying; based   2. providing; to welcome / to be welcomed; to welcome   3. programmed

Lesson B Vocabulary (p. 11)

Exercise A

1. air-conditioned   2. high-speed   3. last-minute
4. climate-controlled   5. solar-powered
6. energy-efficient   7. home-cooked

Exercise B

1. human-like   2. labor-saving   3. custom-built
4. carbon-neutral

Exercise C

Answers will vary.

Lesson B Grammar (p. 12)

Exercise A

1. not only   2. but also   3. neither   4. nor   5. either
6. or   7. both / not only   8. and / but also

Exercise B

1. Masdar City not only relies on technological innovation, but also it also draws on traditional Arabic architecture.
2. In Masdar City, both solar power and wind farms will be used to generate energy.
3. Neither biological nor industrial waste will be thrown away.
4. The completion of Masdar City will either be in 2020 or in 2025.
5. The walls surrounding the city were not only designed to keep out gas-powered cars, but also for protection from the hot, desert winds. OR The walls surrounding the city were designed not only to keep out gas-powered cars, but also for protection from the hot, desert winds.
6. Both clean-tech companies and major research institutes are expected to occupy some of the city's buildings.

Exercise C

1. T   2. F   3. F   4. T   5. F   6. F

Exercise D

1. 22   2. freshman   3. student newspaper   4. corporate
5. Jenny Davis   6. powerful

Exercise E

Answers will vary.

7. According to the plans, wastewater will be used either for crop irrigation or to maintain the city's parks.

Exercise C

Answers will vary.

Lesson C Conversation strategies (p. 13)

Exercise A

Predictably / evidently / potentially / apparently / inevitably / Ideally

Exercise B

1. can't possibly   2. potentially   3. couldn't possibly
4. Evidently   5. ironically   6. can't possibly   7. ideally

Exercise C

Answers will vary.

Lesson D Reading (p. 14)

Exercise A

Answers will vary.

Lesson D Reading (p. 15)

Exercise B

✓ People who read e-books read more often than those who read printed books.
✓ The development of e-books has created economic problems for traditional bookstores.
✓ People who read to children prefer printed books to e-books.

Exercise C

1. 7   2. 15   3. 16   4. 3, 4   5. 5   6. 13   7. 9   8. 6

Exercise D

1. a   2. a   3. a   4. c

Exercise E

Answers will vary.

Writing (p. 16)

Exercise A

shows / can be seen / as compared to / In contrast to / in comparison to

Exercise B

1. illustrates   2. In comparison with   3. accounted
4. represented   5. As can be seen   6. In contrast

Exercise C

1. As can be seen in the graph, the number of people using smartphones has increased.
2. In 2010, the number of Americans owning cell phones represented / accounted for 85 percent of the total population.
3. China has the highest number of Internet users, in comparison to other countries.
4. According to the Pew Internet and American Life Project, e-book users read 24 books per year, compared to / with print book readers, who only read 15 books per year.
5. In the past, a small group of "innovators," who accounted for 2 percent of consumers, were the first to buy hi-tech products.
6. As is shown / As shown in the graph, the number of people who use the Internet on their phones has doubled.

Listening extra (p. 17)

Exercise A

Answers will vary.

Exercise B

cell phones and computers; consumers who buy electronics; possible health problems; environmental problems; recycling

Exercise C

1. F   2. F   3. T   4. F
5. T   6. F   7. T   8. T

Exercise D

1. 50 million   2. 30 million   3. 15–20%   4. 80–85%

Exercise E

Answers will vary.

Unit 3   *Society*

Lesson A **Grammar (p. 18)**

Exercise A

1. growing up   2. speaking   3. not being   4. bearing
5. having worried

Exercise B

Natalie:
Coming from a family that didn't have a lot of money, I couldn't have all the things I wanted. / As a teenager, I often felt embarrassed, having never had the same phone as my friends.

Armando:
Growing up in a low-tech home, I never felt the need to have all the latest technology. / These days, living in a university environment, I feel much more pressure to keep up. / Not wanting to look like I'm totally behind the times, yesterday I went out and spent a fortune on a new phone.

Chung-hee:
Being a communications major, I need to buy the latest phones, gadgets, apps, etc. / Having thought about it, I've stopped worrying about all the money I'm spending.

Exercise C

Answers will vary.

Lesson B **Vocabulary (p. 19)**

Exercise A

precedence over / refuge / into account / stock of / advantage of / charge of / part in / credit for

Exercise B

steps / take / take responsibility / take for granted / take time / take note / take into account / take the initiative / take refuge / take advantage

Exercise C

Answers will vary.

Lesson B **Grammar (p. 20)**

Exercise A

so / Even / only / such / even / so / such / only / so / so

Exercise B

1. Starting a new job is such a stressful experience that even the most self-confident person can get nervous.
2. Learning new skills can be such a demanding task that new employees often feel overwhelmed.
3. Employees are often so embarrassed about not knowing something that they're afraid to ask for help.
4. Understanding a company's culture is such an important part of fitting in that new employees need to make it a major priority.
5. Most employees eventually become so comfortable in their jobs that they completely forget how hard things were in the beginning.

Lesson C **Conversation strategies (p. 21)**

Exercise A

1. again   2. so   3. Having   4. though   5. but   6. then

Exercise B

1. a   2. c   3. e   4. d   5. f   6. b

Exercise C

Answers will vary.

Lesson D **Reading (p. 22)**

Exercise A

Answers will vary.

Lesson D **Reading (p. 23)**

Exercise C

1. b   2. b   3. a   4. b   5. a   6. a

Exercise D

1. rapidity   2. a sharp reproach   3. the jury is still out
4. exotic signifiers   5. is / has become synonymous with
6. neologisms   7. at the mercy of / trending

Exercise E

Answers will vary.

Writing (p. 24)

Exercise A

Consequently, / Because of / giving / As a result of / so /
such / Having said that, / helping / Therefore,

Exercise B

1. Our summer course was incredibly useful. Therefore,
   I strongly recommend that you sign up for it. / Our
   summer course was extremely useful, and therefore,
   I strongly recommend that you sign up for it.
2. The teachers always prepared their lessons carefully. As a
   result, we never wasted any class time.
3. Sometimes the guides were in such a hurry to finish their
   talks that it was hard to follow them.
4. The wildlife cruise was led by a brilliant naturalist.
   Consequently, it was very informative.
5. Some of the lectures were so technical that they
   demotivated some students.

Exercise C

1. The summer course was excellent. **Therefore,** I'm
   planning to major in wildlife management. / The summer
   course was excellent, **and therefore,** I'm planning to
   major in wildlife management.

2. The ocean mammals course was **so** difficult **that** some
   students lost interest.
3. The classes finished late, **giving** us no time to relax
   before the field trips.
4. I had never seen a whale before. **Therefore,** I was excited
   to go on the wildlife cruise. / I had never seen a whale
   before, **and therefore,** I was excited to go on the wildlife
   cruise.
5. Correct.
6. Our group project was **such a** success **that** we got the
   highest grade in the class. / Our group project was so
   successful that we got the highest grade in the class.

Exercise D

Answers will vary.

Listening extra (p. 25)

Exercise A

1. d   2. e   3. a   4. b   5. c

Exercise B

1. T   2. F   3. F   4. T
5. T   6. F   7. F   8. F

Exercise C

1. is not   2. several organizations   3. single   4. did
5. documentaries   6. difficult

Exercise D

Answers will vary.

Unit 4   Amazing world

Lesson A Vocabulary (p. 26)

Exercise A

1. c   2. b   3. d, f   4. a   5. e, g

Exercise B

1. hibernate   2. mate   3. lay   4. hatch   5. feed
6. predators

Exercise C

Answers will vary.

Lesson A Grammar (p. 27)

Exercise A

will have gained / will have been gaining
will have dropped
will have decreased
will have hibernated / will have been hibernating
will have lost

Exercise B

1. will have been resting / will have rested
2. will have been hibernating / will have hibernated
3. will have lost
4. will have eaten
5. will have consumed
6. will have gained

Exercise C

Answers will vary.

Lesson B Grammar (p. 28)

Exercise A

1. b / f   2. d   3. a / c   4. a / c   5. b / f   6. e

Exercise B

By virtue of / Thanks to / On account of / In spite of / in
addition to / Apart from / as a result of / due to

Lesson C Conversation strategies (p. 29)

Exercise A

1. also   2. top   3. mention   4. In   5. event

Exercise B

1. c   2. e   3. d   4. a   5. b

Exercise C

in any case / Not to mention / And then / In any case

Lesson D Reading (p. 30)

Exercise A

Answers will vary.

Exercise B

They detect the earth moving. / They notice changes in
chemistry. / They leave their mating sites.

Lesson D Reading (p. 31)

Exercise C

1. paragraph 6 2. paragraph 7 3. paragraph 1
4. paragraph 3 5. paragraph 9 6. paragraph 2

Exercise D

1. b 2. c 3. c 4. a

Exercise E

1. F—3 days 2. NG 3. T 4. T 5. NG
6. F—did not follow

Exercise F

Answers will vary.

Writing (p. 32)

Exercise A

Possible answer: The author's argument is that animals have the ability to detect environmental changes before certain kinds of natural disasters. The evidence the author presents as support is that toads change their breeding and migration patterns before an earthquake, fish are sensitive to electromagnetic pulses like those of an earthquake, and dogs tend to bark more before an throughout upon within prior to earthquake.

Exercise B

1. Throughout 2. upon 3. beneath 4. within
5. Amongst 6. in terms of

Exercise C

1. Many scientists disagree <u>with</u> / [**delete disagree**] **dispute** the idea that animals can predict earthquakes.
2. Scientists are now looking ~~upon~~ <u>at</u> changes in animal behavior before natural disasters in greater detail.
3. Scientists cannot rely <u>on / upon</u> anecdotal evidence to prove their point.
4. If you look ~~upon~~ <u>at</u> the facts, it seems certain that the climate is changing.
5. In the future, humans might depend <u>on / upon</u> our pets to predict natural disasters.
6. Correct.

Exercise D

Answers will vary.

Listening extra (p. 33)

Exercise A

Answers will vary.

Exercise B

a. adaptable / d. curious / f. skillful / g. smart

Exercise C

1. b 2. c 3. a 4. b 5. b

Exercise D

Answers will vary.

Unit 5 *Progress*

Lesson A Vocabulary (p. 34)

Exercise A

1. integral 2. innovative 3. functional 4. portable
5. compact 6. obsolete

Exercise B

1. standard 2. countless / significant
3. rudimentary 4. humble 5. significant / countless

Exercise C

Answers will vary.

Lesson A Grammar (p. 35)

Exercise A

1. been eagerly anticipated
2. continually being invented / being continually invented
3. reportedly been injected / been reportedly injected
4. being heavily invested
5. apparently been done
6. still being worked on

Exercise B

1. Hybrid cars were being intensively developed
2. hybrid cars have apparently been made
3. A hybrid car had already been built
4. That hybrid car had originally been presented (more common) / That hybrid car had been originally presented
5. hybrid cars were finally being mass produced (were being finally mass produced is possible, but not common)
6. only 300 hybrid cars had reportedly been sold (had been reportedly sold is possible, but not common)

7. the designs are continually being improved / are being continually improved; hybrid cars are increasingly being driven / are being increasingly driven

Exercise C

Answers will vary.

Lesson B Grammar (p. 36)

Exercise A

1. she could easily have been killed.
2. She could have been attacked by pirates
3. Her sailboat could have been hit by larger vessels
4. her boat might well have been damaged or destroyed by heavy seas
5. she might have been attacked by sharks
6. such a young person should not have been allowed by her parents
7. People say it ought not to have been permitted

Exercise B

1. Her parents should have been made to stop her.
2. She might have been made to call the authorities every day.
3. Her parents shouldn't have been made to feel guilty.
4. She could have been made to go with an older person.
5. She should have been made to gain more experience before her first solo trip.
6. She could have been made to wait until she was older to take the trip.

Exercise C

Answers will vary.

Lesson C Conversation strategies (p. 37)

Exercise A

just think about it / not necessarily / look at it this way: / To put it another way, / Maybe not / one way to look at it is

Exercise B

1. c   2. e   3. a   4. d

Exercise C

1. Not necessarily   2. Let me put it another way / Look at it this way   3. Absolutely   4. Maybe   5. Let me put it another way / Look at it this way

Lesson D Reading (p. 38)

Exercise A

Answers will vary.

Exercise B

b

Lesson D Reading (p. 39)

Exercise C

a. 4   b. 5   c. 2   d. 6   e. 3   f. 1

Exercise D

1. NG   2. F—4000 BCE   3. T   4. T   5. F—6 steps
6. NG   7. F—Chinese man   8. F—tree bark, plant fibers, cloth, and water   9. NG   10. F—after Ts'ai Lun   11. T
12. F—the printing press only   13. T   14. NG

Exercise E

Answers will vary.

Writing (p. 40)

Exercise A

c

Exercise B

1. It is generally accepted that there will be less need for paper in the future.

2. It is widely recognized that fewer people are printing documents because they can store them electronically.
3. It is often suggested that there are many aspects of our current lives that will not be preserved for the future because of the absence of paper documents, such as personal letters.
4. It has also been suggested that the reading process on a screen may differ from the process of reading a printed book.
5. It is generally recognized that digital storage is an environmentally friendly option.

Exercise C

1. Do you believe that writing on a screen, rather than paper, ~~effects~~ **affects** creativity in any way?
2. ~~Nevertheless~~ **Even though** writing on a computer might be faster than writing by hand, many wonder whether writing skills are being lost in the process.
3. Researchers are not yet sure whether the ~~affects~~ **effects** of new technology are positive or negative for students.
4. ~~In~~ **On** the one hand, writing on a computer or tablet is faster. On the ~~one~~ **other** hand, it doesn't work if there is a power outage and your battery runs out.

Exercise D

Answers will vary.

Listening extra (p. 41)

Exercise A

Answers will vary.

Exercise B

1. b   2. a   3. b   4. c

Exercise C

1. F   2. F   3. T   4. F   5. F   6. T   7. T   8. F

Exercise D

Answers will vary.

Unit 6 *Business studies*

Lesson A Grammar (p. 42)

Exercise A

1. of whom   2. of which   3. which   4. whom
5. of which   6. of whom

Exercise B

1. Pop-up ads are an interesting topic, with which I'm only too familiar, unfortunately.
2. Every day I struggle with pop-up ads, some of which can't be closed with a simple click.
3. I don't pay much attention to pop-up ads, most of which advertise products I'm not interested in anyway.
4. Absolutely — I can tell you that none of my friends, most of whom spend long hours on the Internet, can stand pop-up ads.
5. Well, this is an interesting phenomenon about which a lot has been written.
6. Well, I subscribe to an Internet service for which I pay a lot of money every month.
7. This is a difficult problem to which there seems to be no obvious solution.
8. Yes, websites are offering us a valuable service for which they have to pay with advertising.

Exercise C

Answers will vary.

Lesson B Vocabulary (p. 43)

Exercise A

1. woo   2. put them off   3. scare them off; appeal
4. discourage   5. pressure clients into   6. attract

Exercise B

1. convinced   2. pressure . . . into   3. attract   4. lured / attracted   5. draw . . . in   6. puts . . . off   7. discourage

Exercise C

Answers will vary.

Lesson B Grammar (p. 44)

Exercise A

Some / others / Some / Some / Any / Any / other / Any / any / another / some / some / other

Exercise B

1. Some   2. others / some   3. some
4. another / some / some other   5. other   6. any   7. Some
8. others   9. some other / another   10. Any   11. other

Exercise C

Answers will vary.

Lesson C Conversation strategies (p. 45)

Exercise A

1. So, that's a good thing, isn't it?
2. That's still a big gap, don't you think?
3. Couldn't that be the reason for the gap?
4. So, it really isn't fair, is it?
5. But aren't things changing?
6. So shouldn't they earn just as much as men?

Exercise B

1. Isn't that a good thing?
2. Don't you think that's still a big gap?
3. That could be the reason for the gap, couldn't it?
4. Isn't it unfair? / So, really, isn't it unfair?
5. Things are changing, aren't they?
6. They should earn just as much as men, shouldn't they?

Exercise C

1. *A* Doesn't the government need more money for infrastructure projects? / The government needs more money for infrastructure projects, doesn't it?
   B Granted the government needs more tax revenue, but corporation also benefit from government project, so they should pay higher taxes, too.
2. *A* Don't companies have a responsibility to ensure that they don't cause any environmental damage? / Companies have a responsibility to ensure that they don't cause any environmental damage, don't they?
   B Well, the government really needs to pass more legislation to protect the environment, but companies should take more responsibility, granted.
3. *A* Isn't it really unfair when a company doesn't have equal numbers of male and female managers? / It's really unfair when a company doesn't have equal numbers of male and female managers, isn't it?
   B Well, granted it is unfair. But it can be difficult to fix that.

Lesson D Reading (p. 46)

Exercise A

Answers will vary.

Exercise B

records and files (both hardcopy and electronic); raw materials and product inventory; computers

Lesson D Reading (p. 47)

Exercise C

1. b   2. c   3. c

Exercise D

1. e   2. c   3. h   4. b   5. g   6. d   7. f   8. a

Exercise E

Answers will vary.

Writing (p. 48)

Exercise A

1. One reason for this / might / may   2. Another possible reason that / could / could   3. This is possibly because
4. It may also be a result of / can / can / could / would / could

Exercise B

1. Our website often scares people off. This may be a result of the very complicated design.
2. Our customers often don't complete their orders. One reason for this might be because / that it's very confusing to go through the ordering process.
3. People get very frustrated on our website. A possible cause could be all the dead links and out-of-date information.

Exercise C

1. If our website had a better design, people ~~can~~ **could** navigate through it more easily.
2. People tell us that they are using our new website and they ~~could~~ **can** find things more easily.
3. I just discovered a great website where you ~~could~~ **can** order foods from all over the world.
4. Some news sites have so many pop-up ads that you ~~could~~ **can** hardly read the articles.
5. correct
6. There used to be a site where I ~~can~~ **could** get discounts on designer clothing, but it's gone now.

Exercise D

Answers will vary.

Listening extra (p. 49)

Exercise A

Answers will vary.

Exercise B

b

Exercise C

1. a   2. b   3. a   4. c   5. a   6. c   7. b

Exercise D

Answers will vary.

Unit 7 *Relationships*

Lesson A **Grammar (p. 50)**

Exercise A

1. Ask any parent about the challenges of a new baby, and
2. Had we known   3. Were we to do it again
4. Had I been   5. Otherwise

Exercise B

1. Were   2. Had   3. Should   4. Talk   5. Should
6. Otherwise

Exercise C

Answers will vary.

Lesson B **Vocabulary (p. 51)**

Exercise A

1. stop and think   2. wait and see   3. sooner or later
4. ups and downs   5. sick and tired   6. above and beyond
7. give-and-take   8. time and energy   9. success or failure

Exercise B

1. and age   2. and suffering   3. and work   4. or later
5. but surely   6. and think   7. and energy   8. and forth

Exercise C

Answers will vary.

Lesson B **Grammar (p. 52)**

Exercise A

1. Why some couples have problems is usually obvious.
2. What many couples don't understand is that daily communication is necessary.
3. It's important to agree on where and when you can talk every day.
4. How you resolve differences can be a big problem.
5. You should discuss how you express opinions kindly in an argument.
6. It's a good idea to decide how much free time you want to spend together.
7. Should you tell your husband or wife which of his or her hobbies you don't enjoy doing?
8. You should discuss how often you want to go out separately with your own friends.
9. It's important to consider how much you can compromise in order to accommodate your partner's needs.

Exercise B

1. What successful couples do is talk about their problems.
2. How you communicate helps determine the success or failure of your relationship.
3. How many hours you work in a week can easily become a problem.
4. Discuss whether or not you want to have children before you get married.
5. Agree now on where you want to live and work.
6. What many parents fail to understand is that their child might need independence.
7. How children and parents approach problems in their relationship makes a difference.

Lesson C **Conversation strategies (p. 53)**

Exercise A

1. e   2. c   3. a   4. d

Exercise B

1. You don't have to try to work it out, then, do you?
2. So, in that case, it must be a good way to meet people.
3. Really? In that case, it's not ideal if you want to settle down.
4. In that case, maybe you should try online dating.
5. You should talk to him, then.

Exercise C

1. In a word   2. then / in that case   3. in that case
4. At the end of the day   5. then / in that case

Lesson D **Reading (p. 54)**

Exercise A

Answers will vary. The true statements are 1 and 3.

Lesson D **Reading (p. 55)**

Exercise B

1. F — do not frequently   2. T   3. T
4. F — in vocabulary and reading   5. F — do not depend
6. T   7. F — may decrease the amount; do affect   8. T

Exercise C

1. c   2. c   3. a   4. c   5. b

Exercise D

1. rarely   2. promoting   3. high school   4. active
5. intake   6. High-risk

Exercise E

Answers will vary.

Writing (p. 56)

Exercise A

a number of / little / a wide variety of / lead to / in / many / little / several / a range of

Exercise B

1. several   2. few   3. leads   4. number   5. result in
6. creates

Exercise C

1. There ~~is~~ **are** a number of situations that can lead to tension in relationships.
2. It takes a great deal **of** time to fully trust someone.
3. A wide range of factors ~~effect~~ **affect** how well roommates get along.
4. Most people agree that face-to-face communication leads **to** greater satisfaction.
5. A large number of people ~~is~~ **are** trying online dating these days.
6. It only takes a ~~few~~ **little** effort to be a respectful roommate.
7. There ~~is~~ **are** various ways that you can improve any relationship.
8. There are a number of factors that **make** family dinners more enjoyable for everyone.

Exercise D

Answers will vary.

Listening extra (p. 57)

Exercise A

Answers will vary.

Exercise B

2. ✓ 5. ✓ 6. ✓

Exercise C

1. F 2. T 3. T 4. T
5. F 6. F 7. T 8. F
9. T 10. F

Unit 8 *History*

Lesson A Grammar (p. 58)

Exercise A

1. would like to have met   2. is widely acknowledged to
have advanced   3. is said to have established
4. is considered to have been   5. is also known to have
influenced   6. seems to have had

Exercise B

1. Many human rights activists would like to have discussed
   passive resistance with Mahatma Gandhi.
2. According to Nostradamus, the 16th century prophet,
   the world was supposed to have come to an end on
   December 21, 2012.
3. Sir Isaac Newton's 1687 work *Mathematical Principles of
   Natural Philosophy* is said to have laid the foundations for
   most of classical mechanics.
4. Jack Nicklaus is more than a great golfer – he happens to
   have won 18 major championships.
5. As an art student, I would love to have watched Leonardo
   da Vinci create one of his masterpieces.
6. Singapore statesman Lee Kuan Yew is acknowledged to
   have helped trigger the Asian economic miracle.

Exercise C

Answers will vary.

Lesson B Vocabulary (p. 59)

Exercise A

1. significant   2. gradual   3. visible / apparent   4. profound
5. lasting   6. visible / apparent   7. universal

Exercise B

rapid / Universal / a major / massive

Exercise C

1. insignificant   2. superficial   3. immediate   4. sudden
5. local   6. long-term   7. temporary

Exercise D

Answers will vary.

Lesson B Grammar (p. 60)

Exercise A

Copernicus
1. It was   2. who / that   3. It wasn't   4. that
5. it is   6. that   7. it is   8. that
Newton
1. It is   2. who / that   3. It was   4. that   5. it is
6. that   7. it was   8. who / that

Exercise B

1. It's thanks to of Michael Faraday that electricity makes
   our lives easier.

2. It was his discovery of using electricity and a magnet to
   rotate a wire that led to the development of the electric
   motor.
3. It was Faraday who became the first person to produce
   an electric current by moving a wire through a magnetic
   field.
4. It was largely due to his efforts that electricity became
   practical for use in technology.

Exercise C

Answers will vary.

Lesson C Conversation strategies (p. 61)

Exercise A

1. I'm dreading my history class.   2. Don't get me started!
3. I can't believe how they just accept one view.
4. That's always a big debate in our class.
5. let's not get into that.   6. I feel like that, too.
7. That's a whole other story.
8. I'd rather not talk about that now.

Exercise B

1. c   2. a

Exercise C

Don't get me started.
That's what I'm saying.
But that's another story. / That's what I mean.
I'd rather not talk about it.

Lesson D Reading (p. 62)

Exercise A

Answers will vary.

Exercise B

2. ✓   3. ✓

Lesson D Reading (p. 63)

Exercise C

1. c   2. d   3. e   4. a   5. b

Exercise D

1. F — James Marshall found gold while working on John
   Sutter's ranch.   2. NG   3. T
4. F — because it became a popular port for all the
   immigrants arriving from overseas
5. F — Gold was free to whoever found it.   6. NG
7. F — The individuals who became the richest were the
   entrepreneurs who created businesses to support the
   prospectors.   8. F — Lawlessness was rampant.
9. NG   10. T

Exercise E

1. a   2. b   3. a   4. b   5. c

Exercise F

Answers will vary.

Writing (p. 64)

Exercise A

As soon as / subsequently / arriving / saddened / Once / previously / Resigned / Excited / hoping / In the end

Exercise B

1. On arriving at Ellis Island, he was given a new last name.
2. Once he settled in / had settled in, he looked or a job and eventually found one washing dishes in a restaurant.
3. He bought a book to teach himself English as soon as he had saved enough money. / As soon as he had saved enough money, he bought a book to teach himself English.
4. After a while, he became the restaurant manager, marking the beginning of a successful era for the restaurant.
5. In the end, he started his own restaurant, which my family still owns today.

Exercise C

1. ~~In~~ **At** the end of the war, my great-grandmother tried to find her daughter.

2. My great-aunt wanted to find her birth family, and thanks to the TV show, she ~~at the end~~ **finally** found her siblings.
3. ~~At~~ **In** the end, the family members were reunited.
4. ~~In~~ **At** the end of the TV show, the brothers and sisters exchanged contact details and promised never to lose touch.

Exercise D

Answers will vary.

Listening extra (p. 65)

Exercise A

Answers will vary.

Exercise B

1. ✓   2. ✓   5. ✓

Exercise C

1. T   2. F   3. T   4. F   5. F
6. T   7. T   8. F   9. T   10. T

Exercise D

1. 2 and a half   2. 950   3. 14th   4. 2   5. 1800

Exercise E

Answers will vary.

Unit 9 *Engineering*

Lesson A **Grammar** (p. 66)

Exercise A

whenever / wherever / wherever / whenever / however / whatever / whenever / whoever

Exercise B

whichever / wherever / whatever / wherever / Whenever / Whoever / however

Exercise C

Answers will vary.

Lesson B **Vocabulary** (p. 67)

Exercise A

1. in a short time frame; maneuvered   2. constructed
3. delayed; ahead of schedule
4. assembled; erected; positioned; installed

Exercise B

1. constructed / erected   2. constructed / erected
3. fell behind schedule   4. installed   5. completed on time
6. steel   7. concrete   8. in a short time frame
9. ahead of schedule

Lesson B **Grammar** (p. 68)

Exercise A

they had / had they / engineers had / the site posed / was the soil / the foundation was / a Y-shaped floor plan was devised to / did the engineers feel / did it solve / the team began / did they know / financial obstacles were

Exercise B

1. Never before had such a large urban highway project been undertaken in the United States.

2. When excavation began in 1991, little did the planners know that the projected wouldn't be done until 2007.
3. Nor did they imagine that it would cost $18 billion more than projected.
4. Not only was the project over budget, (but) there were also many construction problems.
5. Rarely do highway projects have so many problems with the quality of materials and construction.
6. Not only was some of the concrete defective, (but) the tunnel light fixtures started to fall down.
7. Only by replacing all 2,500 light fixtures was the lighting problem solved.
8. The project is now complete, and no longer is the "Big Dig" the main topic of conversation in Boston.

Lesson C **Conversation strategies** (p. 69)

Exercise A

both / considering / both / In light of / given that / in view of

Exercise B

no need whatsoever / no need at all
no sense whatsoever
no interest whatsoever
nothing whatsoever / nothing at all
no doubt whatsoever / no doubt at all
no effect whatsoever / no effect at all

Exercise B

1. at all / whatsoever; considering / in light of
2. considering / given that / in view of the fact; considering, in light of; at all / whatsoever
3. considering / given that / in view of the fact that; at all / whatsoever

Lesson D Reading (p. 70)

Exercise A

Ss' views will vary. The article says call center and clerical jobs will be replaced by computers and robots

Lesson D Reading (p. 71)

Exercise B

1. c   2. d   3. b   4. a

Exercise C

1. b   2. a   3. b   4. b   5. c   6. c

Exercise D

Answers will vary.

Writing (p. 72)

Exercise A

there are a number of / can be classified by / The first type / The second type / Another type / Yet another type

Exercise B

1. When creating the islands, the engineers used natural materials like rocks and sand as a substitute for more traditional construction materials like concrete and steel.
2. To build the foundation of the islands, the marine engineers decided to use calcified rock from under the seabed instead of desert sand.
3. Engineers created 16 narrow channels to allow water to circulate every 13 days because they wanted clean, flowing water around the islands as opposed to stagnant water.
4. Because there was so little time in the schedule, the engineers made all their decisions on the job rather than researching / research the project ahead of time.

Exercise C

1. Robots are better at some rescue efforts ~~rather~~ than humans.
2. Correct.
3. The military **would rather / would prefer** to use robots in many types of combat situations.
4. ~~Both~~ The police and the military use robots, as opposed ~~for~~ to humans, to dismantle bombs.
5. "Virtual" robots ~~are~~ **can be** used as an alternative ~~of~~ to humans to search the Web.
6. For certain tasks, people would rather have a human ~~rather~~ than a robot.
7. Most people would want a human server in a restaurant rather than ~~to have~~ / **having** a robot.
8. In many cases, robots simply cannot substitute ~~to~~ **for** humans.

Exercise D

Answers will vary.

Listening extra (p. 73)

Exercise A

1. c   2. a   3. d   4. b

Exercise B

1. c   2. a   3. b   4. a   5. a

Exercise C

1. 20 percent   2. 5.6   3. 10,000   4. 700   5. 1.3   6. 15; 20

Exercise D

Answers will vary.

Unit 10 *Current affairs*

Lesson A Vocabulary (p. 74)

Exercise A

1. plunged   2. made   3. compensate   4. mobilize
5. escalated

Exercise B

1. went off   2. caused the explosion   3. ruled out the possibility   4. contain the spill   5. considering legal action   6. fueled speculation   7. undergoing routine surgery   8. announced his campaign

Lesson A Grammar (p. 75)

Exercise A

be turning / have been regaining / be reaching / have been negotiating / may have been holding out / be considering

Exercise B

1. to be preparing   2. will have been discussing
3. to be fading   4. be taking
5. not to be listening / not to have been listening
6. to have been increasing   7. to be monitoring

Exercise C

1. The president's health problems are said to be hindering / have been hindering his re-election campaign.
2. Hopes of a lasting peace appear to have been growing since the ceasefire agreement.
3. The public prosecutor is thought to be considering legal action against corrupt banking CEOs later this year.
4. Sporting officials say that the games seem to have been going / be going smoothly so far.

Exercise D

Answers will vary.

Lesson B Grammar (p. 76)

Exercise A

1. maintain   2. be applied   3. consult   4. check
5. be; correct   6. be published; be

Exercise B

1. b   2. c   3. a   4. a   5. c   6. b

Exercise C

Answers will vary.

Lesson C Conversation strategies (p. 77)

Exercise A

1. c   2. d   3. f   4. e   5. g   6. b

Exercise B

1. this   2. those   3. that   4. That   5. these   6. those
7. that

Exercise C

Answers will vary.

Lesson D Reading (p. 78)

Exercise A

Answers will vary.

Exercise B

N / Y / N / Y

Lesson D Reading (p. 79)

Exercise C

✓ 2, 3, 7, 9

Exercise D

1. seventeenth   2. slowly   3. detailed news coverage
4. charge only for print   5. want   6. a thing of the past

Exercise E

1. T   2. T   3. NG   4. T   5. F – Free online content
continues to be the predominant model.   6. F – They
think the online model won't support newspapers.   7. T
8. F – It remains anybody's guess

Exercise F

Answers will vary.

Writing (p. 80)

Exercise A

is / was / has / has / are / struggle / has / concludes

Exercise B

1. was   2. was   3. has grown / is growing   4. expect /
have expected   5. charge / are charging; need   6. are

Unit 11   *Is it real?*

Lesson A Grammar (p. 82)

Exercise A

1. is to strike   2. are about to hit   3. is set to continue
4. is set to occur   5. is / was bound to happen   6. is set to
change   7. are actually set to intensify
8. is about to hit

Exercise B

1. were to; are bound to   2. was to; was to
3. are bound to; is to; are to

Exercise C

Answers will vary.

Lesson B Vocabulary (p. 83)

Exercise A

1. d   2. b   3. a   4. e   5. f

Exercise B

1. turned into   2. turn back the clock   3. turned over a
new leaf   4. turning point   5. turn (his) back on

Exercise C

1. The number of blogs that **analyze** the news ~~have~~ **has**
   grown during the past five years.
2. The amount of spam that arrives in my inbox **seems** to be
   increasing.
3. The most exciting opportunities for someone who has
   been trained as a reporter ~~is~~ **are** in online news.
4. The quality of news reporting that ~~are~~ **is** available online
   ~~are~~ **is** not always consistent.
5. The use of microblogs that ~~is~~ **are** read by most young
   people ~~have~~ **has** dramatically changed news reporting.
6. Satirical news and stories which **appear** on some websites
   are often believed to be true.

Exercise D

Answers will vary.

Listening extra (p. 81)

Exercise A

1. c   2. f   3. d   4. e   5. b   6. a

Exercise B

Answers will vary. The topic is whether journalists should
be regulated.

Exercise C

1. a   2. b   3. c   4. b   5. a   6. a

Exercise D

1. not hack into people's   2. entire profession of journalism
3. look for the truth   4. final outcome   5. might save lives
6. make difficult decisions

Exercise E

Answers will vary.

6. turned out / have turned out turn   7. have turned (their
lives) around

Exercise C

Answers will vary.

Lesson B Grammar (p. 84)

Exercise A

1. to be recognized   2. to be placed   3. to have been taken
over   4. being caught up   5. to have achieved
6. persuade / have persuaded   7. be left
8. being made   9. to be respected   10. being forced

Exercise B

1. I'd like to be remembered for the charity work I do in the
   community.
2. I remember being taught to appreciate the funny side of
   life by my grandmother. / I remember being taught by my
   grandmother to appreciate the funny side of life.
3. I don't think I deserve to have been labeled / to be labeled
   the class clown by my English teacher.

4. Sensitive viewers shouldn't be allowed to watch a movie about me!
5. I didn't enjoy being given all my sister's old clothes by my mother.
6. I wouldn't want my life to be portrayed dishonestly by scriptwriters.
7. I didn't expect to be / to have been offered a graduate school scholarship by my college.

Exercise C

1. What qualities do you want to be appreciated for?
2. What kind of advice should be given to children today?
3. How would you want to be portrayed in a movie of your life?

(Other answers will vary.)

Lesson C Conversation strategies (p. 85)

Exercise A

1. doesn't seem right; I'm not comfortable with; be to happy about   2. that's not good; that would be my concern; doesn't sit right with me

Exercise B

1. B To me, that's rude, but to some people, that's perfectly fine.   2. B To me, that's not right. To them, it's probably normal.   3. B To me, that's also an issue.

Exercise C

1. To me; That's my concern   2. that doesn't seem right; that doesn't sit right with me; To me

(Other answers will vary.)

Lesson D Reading (p. 86)

Exercises A, B

Answers will vary.

Lesson D Reading (p. 87)

Exercise C

1. T   2. NG   3. T   4. F — four countries: England, America, Italy, and Switzerland   5. F — discovered using an elementary mathematical test   6. T
7. F — The Isleworth version is larger.   8. T   9. NG
10. F — more evidence is needed (not more experts)

Exercise D

1. a   2. b   3. a   4. b   5. b   6. a   7. a

Exercise E

Answers will vary.

Writing (p. 88)

Exercise A

no matter / considering that / Yet / regardless / as long as / in view of the fact

Exercise B

1. provided   2. regardless of / irrespective of   3. in light of
4. irrespective of / regardless of   5. Yet   6. given that

Exercise C

1. Some people think that the rhino horn ban can work **considering that / in view of the fact that / in light of the fact that / given (the fact) that** the ivory ban worked.
2. The illegal trade of animal body parts continues **regardless of / irrespective of** the fact that many animal species are close to extinction.
3. **Yet** some people think a legal trade in rhino horn would endanger wild rhinos.
4. Endangered species can be saved **as long as / provided / providing (that)** the authorities start exploring alternative ideas to protect them.

Exercise D

Answers will vary.

Listening extra (p. 89)

Exercise A

Answers will vary. Sample answers: grades, their job titles, companies they worked at, levels of responsibility, interests

Exercise B

[✓] last salary

Exercise C

1. a   2. b   3. b   4. b   5. a   6. b   7. a

Exercise D

Answers will vary.

Unit 12   *Psychology*

Lesson A Grammar (p. 90)

Exercise A

1. she wouldn't take kindly to me relaxing   2. she insisted on us going   3. I didn't enjoy her driving   4. my concerns about her causing   5. I remember her looking   6. we were dealing with her getting

Exercise B

1. didn't like me living   2. comfortable with them handling   3. believer in people being   4. recall her always saying   5. insist on her giving up the car

Exercise C

Answers will vary.

Lesson B Vocabulary (p. 91)

Exercise A

picked out / go by / picked up on / was taken in by / gave the game away / comes down to

Exercise B

1. gave; away   2. talk; into   3. go about   4. put; behind
5. play down

Exercise C

Answers will vary.

Lesson B Grammar (p. 92)

Exercise A

1. each other / one another   2. ourselves   3. himself
4. herself   5. yourself   6. each other / one another
7. yourself   8. itself   9. oneself   10. themselves

Exercise B

1. each other / one another   2. myself   3. himself
4. one another / each other   5. herself   6. ourselves
7. himself   8. yourself (or yourselves)   9. itself

Exercise C

Answers will vary.

Lesson C Conversation strategies (p. 93)

Exercise A

1. a   2. b   3. a   4. b

Exercise B

1. d   2. c   3. b

Exercise C

1. A to put it mildly
   B if you look at it from; at the same time, equally; to put
   it bluntly
2. A I can see it from both sides
   B by the same token, at the same time; To put it bluntly

Lesson D Reading (p. 94)

Exercise A

Answers will vary.
[✓] Girls write better than boys. / [✓] Boys are better at
reading maps than girls.

Lesson D Reading (p. 95)

Exercise B

1. paragraph 1   2. paragraph 4
3. paragraph 8   4. paragraph 11

Exercise C

1. a   2. b   3. b   4. c   5. b   6. c   7. c

Exercise D

[✓] 1. The idea that all gender differences are natural is
   old-fashioned.
[✓] 4. Dr. Eliot's book has been written in a way that
   ordinary people will be able to understand.
[✓] 6. We force gender stereotypes onto young people.
[✓] 8. The book gives a balanced view of how nature and
   nurture influence our development.

Exercise E

Answers will vary.

Writing (p. 96)

Exercise A

as many / as / as / than / as many / as / than / as high as / as

Exercise B

1. 1.5 times more likely; than   2. twice as likely; as
3. five times as many; as   4. twice as many times as

Exercise C

1. The incidence of respiratory allergies is twice ~~more~~ **as**
common in children with poor health.
2. Children in single-mother families are more likely to
have learning disabilities and ADD **than** children in
two-parent families.
3. Uninsured children are more than four times **as** likely to
have unmet dental need as children with private health
insurance.
4. In families with an income of less than $35,000, the
percentage of children with a learning disability is twice
~~higher~~ **as high** as children in families with an income of
$100,000 or more.

Exercise D

Answers will vary.

Listening extra (p. 97)

Exercise A

Answers will vary.

Exercise B

[✓] online dating / [✓] Marty's appearance / [✓] Marty's
job / [✓] household chores / [✓] leaving home / [✓] Marty's
motorcycle

Exercise C

1. T   2. F   3. F   4. T   5. F   6. F   7. T   8. T

Exercise D

1. on the Internet   2. isn't   3. less   4. sometimes
5. moving out of   6. completely

Exercise E

Answers will vary.

Workbook audio scripts

Unit 1 *A great read*

Listening Extra, Ex. B, C, and D (p. 9)

Host Welcome! Today we're speaking with 22 year-old Rebecca Jackson, who just published her first novel, *2050*. Her self-published e-book has become an overnight sensation. Rebecca we are delighted to have you with us.

Rebecca Thanks so much.

Host Well, I'd like to begin by asking you about your experience as a writer before you wrote *2050*.

Rebecca Well, during my freshman year in college, I took a creative writing class. I remember the professor outlined some steps you should take to get published. The one that really stuck in my mind was the idea of starting small – like publishing a short story in the student newspaper, or trying to get accepted to a writer's conference. The point he was making is that you have to build a name and reputation for yourself before a major publisher would take you seriously. So, I diligently tried to follow his advice, but it took me some time to come to grips with how difficult it can be. My short story got rejected from the student newspaper. I applied to writer's conferences, but didn't get into the ones I wanted, and I only got a 'B' in my writing class.

Host Did you get discouraged? And if not, how did you stay motivated?

Rebecca I tried not to. While I did experience a lot of rejection along the way, I still felt this great urge to communicate with people. So I decided to take a year off from school to work on my novel. I thought this was a great plan, but my parents didn't. They didn't see the point of pursuing something I hadn't been successful with. But I followed my instincts and began writing.

Host It was something you had to do for yourself.

Rebecca That's right. I was going to a local, free writer's workshop and one of the participants told us how we could publish an e-book. I really got a lot out of that workshop. I loved this idea that I wouldn't have to contend with the large, corporate publishers and I'd actually have something to show for my hard work.

Host It does sound like you had to be extremely driven to get to where you are now. Now let's discuss *2050*. The main character is Jenny Davis. . . .

Rebecca Yes, she's a shy but intelligent young woman, who spends most of her time alone reading and studying in the library.

Host Yes. I saw Jenny as soft-spoken yet rather powerful.

Rebecca Exactly. It was a challenge to find the right balance between shyness and strength for her character.

Host Well, she's certainly a fascinating character. When we come back we'll talk more about *2050*, Rebecca Jackson's new book.

Unit 2 *Technology*

Listening Extra, Ex. B and C (p. 17)

Documentary Filmmaker Can you imagine living in a world without technology? Thanks to computers, we're able to work more efficiently and with greater freedom. And smartphones have enabled us to stay in touch with family and friends in ways we couldn't have dreamed of 50 years ago. Yet, despite all the benefits of technology, there is a darker issue, which is largely hidden from most consumers. This twenty-first century problem is electronic waste, otherwise known as e-waste.

We interviewed several savvy customers who purchased new cell phones or laptops. And we discovered that not many of them really know what happens to their old phones and laptops once they've been discarded. So let's take a journey to learn more about this issue. Dr. Priya Adani is an expert on the health issues resulting from heavy metal leakage into the environment.

Dr. Adani As you know, electronics include many different elements – some precious metals such as silver and gold and heavy metals like cadmium, lead, silicon etc. Now, the elements by themselves may not all be dangerous . . . but we don't really know about all the possible dangers when the materials are separated from the other elements used in electronics.

Documentary Filmmaker So you mean when the computers or phones are taken apart?

Dr. Adani Yes, exactly. Old electronics are often shipped to recycling facilities in developing countries where they are disassembled . . . and there may not be a lot of regulation to protect workers there. Workers might not be given protective equipment . . . so they might touch dangerous materials without masks or gloves and they may breathe in toxic fumes during the work.

Documentary Filmmaker Do we know about possible health effects?

Dr. Adani Good question . . . Very little research has been done, so it's hard to say. But we do know about health problems from many of these substances individually. For example, lead, as scientists have known for years, can cause substantial damage to the central and peripheral nervous systems, which can result in many serious health problems. And, mercury can affect your memory . . . it can also cause a loss in sight or hearing.

And so on. . . . This is a serious problem, which unfortunately is not receiving the attention it should.

Documentary Filmmaker E-waste also creates environmental problems. Dr. Steven Jien is an environmental researcher who specializes in e-waste. . . .

Dr. Jien The amount of waste produced is astounding. According to recent reports, approximately 50 million tons of e-waste is produced on a yearly basis. The U.S. alone gets rid of at least 30 million computers per year. Naturally, these figures are expected to rise dramatically as the population increases and the price of electronics decreases. And not enough of this e-waste is being recycled. Figures vary, but it's approximately 15 to 20 percent. The rest of the materials – up to 85 percent – go to landfills.

Documentary Filmmaker The resulting impact on the earth is startling. Dr. Jien again . . .

Dr. Jien Improper disposal of electronics harms the environment. For example, toxic elements can seep through the soil into the ground water, which is a major source of fresh water for many communities. Or they can be released into the air. There have been attempts at regulation to deal with this, but they have not been effective enough.

Listening Extra, Ex. D (p. 17)

Dr. Jien The amount of waste produced is astounding. According to recent reports, approximately 50 million tons of e-waste is produced on a yearly basis. The U.S. alone gets rid of at least 30 million computers per year. Naturally, these figures are expected to rise dramatically as the population increases and the price of electronics decreases. And not enough of this e-waste is being recycled. Figures vary, but it's approximately 15 to 20 percent. The rest of the materials – up to 85 percent – go to landfills.

Unit 3 *Society*

Listening Extra, Ex. B and C (p. 25)

Host Good afternoon! Today we're talking about something I'm sure we've all experienced at some time in our lives, – "social pressure." We've invited three guests who have personal experience about the effects of social pressure. First, I'd like to introduce Susan Ward, who is the author of two fascinating books on peer pressure, Jason Thompson, a sculptor, who has some interesting stories to tell about his own personal experience. And finally, Dr. Cassie Jones, a surgeon whose career takes her all over the world. Thank you for joining me today. Now, I'd like to start with Jason and Dr. Jones, to hear about the kinds of pressure people face when they choose a career that is not what people expect. So, Dr. Jones, let's start with you.

Dr. Jones Well, as you mentioned, I'm a surgeon. However, unlike most doctors, I, I work for different international organizations, which means I'm traveling almost all the time, working in hospitals all over the world.

Host So why has this resulted in social pressure for you? I mean, what is it that you've experienced?

Dr. Jones Well as you can imagine, I don't really have much of a home base. I mean, I don't have a house, a husband, children, which is not something that has worried me at all. But my friends keep telling me I ought to settle into a more traditional life. For some reason they find my lifestyle difficult to accept.

Host Let's come back to your experience in a moment, but Jason, tell us about your own experience.

Jason Well, Uh, I guess I should begin at the beginning. Over a hundred years ago, my great-grandfather started a clothing company. Since then every member of my family – cousins, aunts, uncles – they've all worked for this company. Obviously, from the time I was born, the plan was that I would join the family business. But unfortunately, I wasn't interested in the fashion industry; I was only interested in art, painting, sculpture. . . .

Host So did your family put a lot of pressure on you?

Jason Well, yes. But I defied all the family traditions and became a sculptor. And I'm the first and only person in my family to do so.

Host So let's turn to Susan Ward. . . . Susan, here are two people who have resisted pressure in order to pursue their goals. What kind of personality does it take to do this?

Susan Well, it's difficult to say because, naturally, everyone is unique. Having said that, there are generalizations we can make. First, people who resist pressure like this have a strong sense of personal identity and a need for independence. And they often have such a clear sense of their ambitions from an early age that they follow their own path despite all the obstacles.

Host So, Jason, did you have a clear sense of your identity from an early age?

Jason Oh, definitely. As far back as I can remember I knew that I wanted to be an artist. Growing up, all I wanted to do was draw and paint. Eventually I got interested in sculpture. Naturally, my parents were trying to steer me toward the clothing business, having me work in the factory on Saturdays alongside my brother and sister. They never really understood. But I knew I wasn't cut out for a career in business.

Host And what about you, Dr. Jones?

Dr. Jones Well, I never wanted to do the same things as the other kids in my neighborhood. They all wanted to watch cartoons and action movies on TV and

I wanted to watch the shows on science and nature and hospital dramas! I always knew I wanted to be a doctor.

Host Susan, can you comment on the challenges people face when they try to resist social pressure?

Susan Sure . . . well, it's not easy to resist social pressure. Humans are social creatures by nature. We naturally want to fit in and be part of a community. That means conforming to certain rules and conventions. Resisting these conventions can be extremely challenging – most people aren't able to do it.

Host Let's take a break.

Unit 4 *Amazing world*

Listening Extra, Ex. B and C (p. 33)

Interviewer Welcome to the *Amazing Nature Show*. By the end of this segment, you will have learned far more about raccoons than you ever expected from biologist Dr. William Bailey, who's our guest today.

Dr. Bailey Thanks for having me on the show.

Interviewer Now, when most people think of raccoons, they imagine an adorable, furry creature that is a bit troublesome because it gets into their trash and sometimes destroys the roof. But in your research, you have made some interesting discoveries.

Dr. Bailey That's right. I've been researching raccoon behavior for over 10 years now, and I have really come to appreciate their intelligence and problem-solving skills.

Interviewer Yes, I read one of your recent reports where you said that raccoons are actually becoming more intelligent as a result of living in urban environments. Could you explain that?

Dr. Bailey Well, yes. Raccoons originally lived in tropical areas. But they migrated north. During this migration they expanded their diet and adapted their behavior to survive in different environments. You see, raccoons are very adaptable; in other words, they can adjust to new situations quickly. Thanks to this ability to change their behavior, they've been very successful, even in urban areas. For example, in the cities they've learned how to open trashcans, or how to climb inside buildings for shelter.

Interviewer Yes, I remember last summer when a very annoying raccoon kept getting into our trashcan; it seemed to eat everything – from pizza crust to apple cores.

Dr. Bailey Yeah. That's true. As I said, raccoons' feeding habits have changed drastically. As you witnessed, in cities, raccoons eat just about anything that humans eat. In the wild, they eat nuts, berries, fruits, eggs, insects, and fish. So they're what we call "opportunistic eaters" – that is they eat whatever they find.

Interviewer So these animals are pretty smart in terms of their ability to survive?

Dr. Bailey Absolutely. Raccoons are incredibly skillful. They seem to be able to learn, remember things, and then change their behavior. Let me give you an example. Kassel, Germany, they have the largest raccoon population in the country. And houses were being damaged as a result of all these raccoons who were climbing on the roof using the drainpipes. So, after consulting biologists, homeowners created protection devices to keep the raccoons off their drainpipes. But in time, the raccoons learned how to climb over these protection devices.

Interviewer Remarkable. And presumably, this knowledge is passed down to young raccoons, too?

Dr. Bailey Yes, in terms of raising their young, mother raccoons are very good about teaching them survival skills. Mothers stay with their young for up to a year. By the end of that year, she will have taught them how to find food and shelter and avoid danger. She takes them out with her and helps them learn by example, by watching how she does things.

Interviewer Do they reproduce frequently, have lots of young?

Dr. Bailey No actually, in terms of their breeding habits, raccoons mate between January and June. And um, the mother raccoon gives birth after about 65 days and will have between two to five babies.

Interviewer So not a huge number. Now do raccoons have many predators?

Dr. Bailey Actually, raccoons have very few predators. In the wild they might sometimes be attacked by a coyote. However, in the cities their main problem is cars and of course, human beings. In general, not having any major threats has allowed the species to thrive.

Interviewer I'm sure our listeners want to know if raccoons are dangerous. In other words, will they attack humans?

Dr. Bailey No. They generally won't attack humans. However, people should keep in mind that they are wild animals, which means that they will bite or scratch if provoked or threatened. In general, they seem to be more curious about humans than anything else. If a raccoon sees a non-threatening human, it will probably stop and stare for a minute and then walk away.

Interviewer Well, that's good to know. Let's take a break.

Unit 5 *Progress*

Listening Extra, Ex. B and C (p. 41)

Pieter   I just downloaded this great app . . . when I hear a song I like, I just hold up my phone and it gives me information about it . . . the name of the song, who sings it and all that.

Aisha   Oh, yeah, I have that one. I think it's been around for a while. It's really useful. . . . I like to know who's singing a song, especially if I want to buy it. I love it. But then I have dozens of apps on my phone that I love.

Pieter   Yeah. Just think about it . . . it's not *that* long since apps have even been developed. It's hard to believe really. I don't even know how many I have now.

Aisha   I know . . . it's kind of crazy how many there are. And new ones are constantly being developed and released. There seems to be an app for pretty much everything.

Pieter   Maybe. . . . Maybe not. . . . I think there are still some apps that we could use that haven't been developed yet. Or to put it another way, I keep thinking of apps I'd like to have that don't seem to have been developed yet. It'd be fun to invent a really popular one, don't you think?

Aisha   Yeah. So what would yours be if you were going to create one?

Pieter   Well, I was thinking the other day that there should be one for services that you use a lot . . . like ATMs or subway stops. You'd choose the things you use the most and then they'd be flagged on a map. So wherever you are, you open the app and a map shows the nearest bank, subway station, or whatever. I'd call it "Where's the nearest?"

Aisha   Well, look, I have one like that already. I use it a lot.

Pieter   Oh, I guess that wasn't such an original idea then! What about you . . . have you ever thought of any apps you'd like to develop?

Aisha   Well . . . I have a couple of ideas, like one's more practical and functional and the other's kind of silly . . . but it'd be fun. So the serious one is an app that would calculate my taxes for me every year. You know, you could choose your country or state, enter all your income and other information each week. You'd also have to put in things like expenses and if you have any dependents and so on. . . . I think it could be helpful. People worry about their taxes so much.

Pieter   Absolutely. I tried one kind of like that, but it wasn't very easy to use. I think I read somewhere that simplicity and ease of use are the key things when they develop apps – or they won't sell. So what's your other idea?

Aisha   OK, so you choose an animated cartoon face . . . like from a movie or TV cartoon character, then when you make a video call to a friend they just see the face you chose. But that's not all . . . the character actually looks as if it's speaking your words! I guess if they're famous cartoon characters you might have to pay more, say 10 or 20 dollars, but just think how cool it would be for your friends. And for an upgrade the app could alter your voice to sound like the character too!

Pieter   Hey, that sounds like fun. So what cartoon character would you be?

Aisha   Oh, I don't know, maybe . . . . [fade out]

Unit 6 *Business studies*

Listening Extra, Ex. B and C (p. 49)

Narrator   Workplace Communication Part 1

Lecturer   Are you good observer of human behavior? What about at your workplace? Are you good at observing people there? If you are, you've probably seen many instances of miscommunication. It happens in every type of workplace and sometimes it feels like the problem is just getting worse. So why is miscommunication such a common occurrence? Well, first of all, it's probably inevitable whenever you have people working together, most of whom do not know each other very well. Second, it often happens with a group of people between whom there are hierarchical relationships – everyone has a boss, even most bosses do – and there are always cases of miscommunication in boss–employee relationships. And miscommunication unfortunately can lead to hostility and bad feelings, and eventually to wasted time and decreased productivity, all of which will severely affect the bottom line of a business.

You may not think that communication problems exist at your particular place of work, but if you are a good observer, you will probably notice that they do. What you need to know is why they exist and how to combat them. So let's start with the question "why"? In this part of the program, I'm going to talk about one of the most common causes of miscommunication, and that is the overuse of written electronic communication. Email, instant messaging, and texting have become so easy that they now have become preferable to face-to-face communication. And they have certain advantages. When you send an email message to staff, yes, you can communicate with a lot of people at once, and as the communicator, you can have total control over the message and flow of communication. But there is nevertheless a big disadvantage. It doesn't allow you, the communicator, to gauge how well the messages, some of which may be of critical importance, are being understood. In face-to-face communication, you get much more feedback on whether a message has been understood and how it has been received. Also, it is a common misconception that written communication saves time. Frequently it doesn't save any time at all. It often leads to a confused series of email that are sent back and forth asking for clarification and sometimes causing hard feelings. And of course you only hear from a few people – there are probably others who haven't actually tried to understand the message.

There is another problem with written communication, and that is related to problem of giving employees bad news. Research has shown that when bad news, negative feedback, or any type of criticism has to be communicated, it is more effective to do it face-to-face. This may be a result of the fact that negative information is often likely to be misunderstood. A person might feel that they are being blamed unfairly. Feelings will definitely be affected. In these tense situations, egos can get in the way of accurate comprehension. And how would you, the communicator, be aware of that if the communication is not a face-to-face, two-way process? Unfortunately, you probably wouldn't. OK, we've spent a little time today talking about miscommunication caused by the overuse of written communication, particularly email. In Parts 2, 3, and 4 of this program I will be talking about some of the other common causes of miscommunication, and in Part 5, I will give you some easy solutions, but for the moment, I want to return to my original question. Are you a good observer? If not, the first thing you should do is work on improving your observation skills. This is also your first homework assignment. Take some time this week to observe how your staff members communicate. Keep an eye and ear out for problems. Do some detective work and try to locate the source of the problem. Have some informal conversations with staff members to confirm your conclusions. Make notes and bring them to your discussion group for this topic.

Narrator That ends Part 1 of Workplace Communication.

Unit 7 *Relationships*

Listening Extra, Ex. B, C, and D (p. 57)

Host Hello, this week we're talking about relationships on the program . . . and, Dr. Antonio Borgo is with us again. Dr. Borgo has been a psychologist for more than 20 years, and has published a number of bestselling books. Welcome Dr. Borgo.

Dr. Borgo Thank you.

Host Our first caller, Sally, is on the line. Hi Sally!

Sally Hi. I'm having a problem with my boss. I never know what mood he'll be in. One day he might be super nice – complimenting me on my work and making small talk – and the next day he'll be really mean, tell me my work is terrible and that I have to re-do everything. In a word he's just totally unpredictable. I mean I understand that maybe he has personal problems, and we all have our ups and downs, but at the end of the day shouldn't he leave those at home? I just don't know how I should act around him.

Dr. Borgo Unfortunately this is complicated. After all, he *is* your boss and he has the ability to fire or promote you. So it's important to approach the situation with care. First, don't take his negative criticisms too personally. As you noted, he probably has personal problems or he could actually have psychological issues. Second, always act professionally and stay positive regardless of his mood swings. Don't avoid him; instead try to get him to clearly articulate his expectations on all the work he assigns. In the end, this is a tough situation. I wish you the best of luck.

Host Great advice. Now we have Tarek . . . Hi Tarek. What's troubling you these days?

Tarek I'm a freshman in college and my roommate and I just don't get along. I mean, we're total opposites. I know I need to be tolerant, but I'm getting sick and tired of the way he acts.

Dr. Borgo What exactly does he do?

Tarek Well I guess the main thing is that he uses my stuff without asking *all* the time! Like, he'll eat all my food or he'll take my headphones to the gym and then I won't be able to find them. One time, I couldn't find my laptop. I freaked out and called campus security. Turns out, my roommate had taken it to the library to do his homework. I mean, I don't mind sharing but you should ask first!

Dr Borgo Hmm . . . In that case, I think the best solution is to have a face-to-face conversation with him. You don't need to bring up past issues. Just explain to him in a polite manner that you expect him to ask before using your things. This might seem like a difficult issue, but I think it can be resolved by setting up some boundaries.

Host An easier problem to solve, then? Now, our next caller, Camilla, has a problem with her mother. Hi Camilla.

Camilla Hi, thank you. Well, my mother always goes above and beyond to help. I mean, I really do appreciate her help but sometimes she just doesn't know when to stop. She calls me at least five times a day to check on me. And, one time she actually called my professor about a bad grade on an exam. I'm 20 and I want to be more independent. I just don't know how to tell her.

Dr. Borgo She sounds like a typical helicopter parent. In theory you should feel grateful for all this love and attention. However, too much interference can result in resentment. So, I suggest that you sit down with her, thank her for all she's done for you. Then, gently explain that you are an adult and that you really need your independence.

Be sure to reassure her that you still want her in your life – but, you also need some space. It's a hard transition for a lot of parents, but, when all's said and done, I'm sure it'll work out.

Unit 8 *History*

Listening Extra, Ex. B, C, and D (p. 65)

Host   Good day and welcome to the history show. Today we're looking at the history of the English language, spoken by millions of people around the world. We're going to examine where it comes from and how it is thought to have developed into the English we speak today.

Now it's interesting to know that English wasn't originally from England. In fact, the earliest form of English happens to have come from Denmark and northern Germany. People from these countries invaded England about two-and-a-half thousand years ago, and they brought their language with them. That developed into what linguists call Old English, and about half of our modern English words are known to have originated from this early form of the language – words like *be*, *water*, and *strong*, for example. Yet despite these connections, Old English was very, very different from the English we speak today.

Then about 950 years ago England was invaded again, this time by people from France. They brought a version of French with them, and it was French that then became the language of the ruling class and the business class in England. Eventually the language of the French invaders was absorbed into English, but for a period there were two languages spoken in England: The upper classes spoke French, and the lower classes spoke the local English.

By the 14th century English had become dominant again, but it had undergone a major change. Thousands of French words had been added to it, easily identified by prefixes like c-o-n, *con-*, and d-e, *de-*, and suffixes like m-e-n-t, *-ment*, and a-n-c-e, *-ance*. Some examples of these words are *concierge*, *decor*, *parliament* and *resistance*. This language was called Middle English, and just like Old English, it would be difficult for native English speakers to understand it today. English again then developed from about the 16th century onwards into what linguists call Modern English.

Modern English is further divided into two time periods: Early Modern English, and Late Modern English. Now, it was the invention of the printing press that is acknowledged to have had a massive impact on the development of Early Modern English. A lasting and visible effect of printing was the standardization of English spelling and grammar. This was done so that everyone could read and understand the same form of the language. Also, most of the printing houses were in London, so it was London English that became the standard version of the language.

The start of the Late Modern English period can be traced to about the year 1800. The many inventions of the Industrial Revolution had created a need for new technology words, and those words were added to English. Secondly, the British Empire was at its peak, and English is known to have adopted many words from foreign languages at that time. The British Empire was also responsible for the different varieties of English that developed in the former British colonies. These include American English, Australian English, New Zealand English, Canadian English, South African English, Indian English, and Caribbean English. American English is particularly influential today, mainly because of the universal impact of American cinema, TV, music, trade, and technology, but that's a whole other story which we'll save for a future edition of the show.

Of course, as we have seen, English itself is influenced by other cultures and technology, and these are the main reasons why it's still changing. Recent additions to English from other cultures are *latte* from Italian, and *karaoke* from Japanese. New technology words include *internet*, *sms*, and *cyberbully*.

So, in conclusion, let me leave you with the fact that English, like all languages, is bound to experience gradual change as it responds to changing circumstances. Indeed, it's very unlikely that today's English will be adequate for – or even comprehensible to – future generations of English speakers.

Unit 9 *Engineering wonders*

Listening Extra, Ex. B and C (p. 73)

Professor
Robinson   OK, so today we begin our student presentations. And our first presenter is Marco Riera, um . . . So I'll turn it over to Marco.

Marco   Good morning, everyone. Today, I want to introduce you to an engineering project that's

not only unique, but also extremely relevant to some global problems we face today. After I've talked about it, I'll give you the chance to ask questions.

The project is the Netherlands North Sea Protection Works, and I'll describe a specific part of that project which is called the Delta Works.

Something you probably know is that the Netherlands, for over 1,000 years, has been building dikes and other structures to protect its land and citizens from the North Sea. And it has been doing this for a very good reason: Not only is 20 percent of the land below sea level, but about two-thirds of their total land is in danger of flooding.

What I want to focus on is a recent phase of this project, the Delta Works, which was in reaction to the flood of 1953. In 1953 a storm surge caused massive flooding in the Netherlands, particularly in the Southwest and there were a total of 1,836 deaths in the Netherlands, a real tragedy. In light of the fact that the storm surge caused the water to rise to 5.6 meters above sea level – that translates to 18.4 feet above sea level – they realized that they needed to do something quickly to protect the land and the citizens.

It's important to understand that in this part of the Netherlands there is not just a sea coast, there is also a river delta, where three different river estuaries flow into the North Sea. So there can be flooding both on the coast and all along the rivers. The Dutch have built an elaborate system of dikes to protect the land and the people along the rivers. The purpose of the Delta Works is to provide additional protection to the people living around the network of estuaries that forms this river delta in Southwest Netherlands. An incredible fact is that this system has been carefully designed to withstand the type of storm that only occurs once in every 10,000 years!

The Delta Works consists partly of storm surge barriers, or sea walls, that actually close the mouths of the river estuaries. If you look at the map I have here, you can see that these sea barriers in effect make the sea coast shorter to better protect the 700 kilometers of dikes on the estuaries. Most of the barriers keep the salt water out of the rivers, but two of the barriers are normally open so that the sea water flows in and out with the tides. They only close when the sea water rises above 3 meters.

The project was largely finished by 1997, but considering that the climate continues to change, the work will never really end. The planning commission for the North Sea Protection Works says that the Netherlands needs to be ready for a rise in the North Sea of 1.3 meters by the year 2100 and 4 meters by the year 2200.

We all know that extreme weather events are becoming more and more frequent, but maybe not everyone realizes that 15 of the world's 20 largest cities are on flood plains. Given that so many major cities are vulnerable to flooding, countries all over the world are studying what the Netherlands has done to protect its citizens. Little did the people of the Netherlands realize in 1953 how influential and relevant their ideas would become in the 21st Century.

Now does anyone have questions?

Unit 10 *Current events*

Listening Extra, Ex. B, C, and D (p. 81)

Host Welcome to our show. Today we are discussing the question: Should we regulate how journalists get information for their stories? Let me introduce our guests. First, we have Dr. James Gilmore, professor and former journalist who recently published a book on ethics in journalism. Welcome.

Dr. Gilmore Thanks for inviting me.

Host Next, we have Marion McCall a journalist with over 20 years' experience. Thanks for joining us.

Ms. McCall It's my pleasure to be here.

Host Let's begin with Dr. Gilmore, who thinks it important that there be strict regulations on information gathering.

Dr. Gilmore Thank you. The question I'd like to start with is this: Should we require that journalists follow a code of ethics? The answer, of course, in my view, is yes. Therefore, it follows that we should be demanding that journalists **not** hack into people's e-mail accounts. Nor should they use secret recordings, or generally trick people into giving information. Simply put, it's essential that journalists maintain the highest professional standards at all times. Because if we don't insist on that, there may well be serious consequences. Take the recent case of those journalists who went to jail for hacking into celebrity voice mails. Like everyone else, I was shocked by what they had done. We all know there is interest in celebrities – that's only natural – but that doesn't mean journalists should employ these kinds of tactics to get a story. Cases like that have had negative consequences for the entire profession of journalism. Basically, we have lost public trust. Journalists have to win back that trust, and for that reason we need to insist that strict regulations on information gathering be implemented.

Host Thank you Dr. Gilmore. Now, let's turn to Ms. McCall. Ms. McCall what is your view on this issue?

Ms. McCall Well, clearly journalists should not be encouraged to do anything illegal. However, having said that, I believe it is every journalist's responsibility to look for the truth. Like any other citizen, I depend on journalists to be whistle blowers and report any wrongdoings or illegal activities. If there are too many rules and regulations, those kinds of stories would never be written. And those are the stories that result in significant, positive changes for the average citizen. In other words, it's important that one consider the final outcome of a story, the social changes that it might bring about. Yes, there are unprofessional journalists, but that doesn't mean the entire profession behaves in the same way. You see Dr. Gilmore, my question is: Do you think that creating a new set of regulations for journalists is necessary because a small number of unprofessional reporters seem to have been engaging in unethical activities? Is it not an overreaction that could have serious implications for the role of journalism in society?

Host Good point. Dr. Gilmore?

Dr. Gilmore Well, I don't think it's an overreaction. As I said earlier, the public has a right to demand that some areas of our lives be private. Off limits!

I mean, don't you think that most readers prefer professional journalism to criminal activity?

Ms. McCall Well, first of all, let me say that I am in no way supporting criminal activity. But sometimes the public needs to know the truth. A journalist could be going onto a social networking site or into an email account to find information that might save lives, for example. And it's essential that any new rules should not prevent journalists from finding a way to do that. In other words, there are always going to be exceptional cases where journalists have to make difficult decisions. Now ethical journalists, they've been doing that for years, and the world is a better place for it.

Host Thank you. When we return from our break, we'll continue our discussion.

Unit 11 *Is it real?*

Listening Extra, Ex. B and C (p. 89)

Bill Good morning everyone, and welcome to *Employment Today*, the program that gives you news and information about the job market. Today we're talking to Sarah Lim, who is the Director of Human Resources for a multinational company. Welcome to the program, Sarah.

Sarah Good morning, and thanks for inviting me.

Bill Now Sarah, as Director of Human Resources, you have a lot of experience when it comes to analyzing résumés from job applicants. I'm sure you know a lot about fake résumés, and how recruiters can identify fake information before making a bad hire. So to begin, perhaps you could tell us how much of an issue fake résumés are for businesses these days?

Sarah Yes, well everyone wants to look good on their résumé, so there's bound to be a bit of exaggeration on most people's résumés. But there are some people who try to fake important information, like their qualifications, for example. And that's not right. I mean, apart from being morally wrong, lying on a résumé can lead to wasted time and money for the company that is trying to hire someone.

Bill Yes, that's not good at all. So how can managers avoid wasting time and money on someone with fake credentials?

Sarah Well, what we recommend is that managers do an initial phone interview to check the accuracy of a candidate's résumé information. That can save you the time of interviewing unsuitable candidates face-to-face.

Bill And what should managers look for if they suspect they're dealing with a fake résumé?

Sarah Well, candidates often avoid putting in information that might turn off or deter potential employers. You know, things like being fired from a job, or only holding a job for a short time. I get suspicious when I see unexplained periods of unemployment on a résumé. I'm also not comfortable with people who claim to be self-employed for very long periods. So gaps in experience ring alarm bells.

Bill Now you mentioned earlier that people provide false education information. I guess you look at that section of a résumé pretty closely.

Sarah Yes, we do check that closely. We always instruct our recruiters to call the schools listed on the résumé in order to check that the information is accurate. If it isn't, the applicant is turned down immediately. Unfortunately you find candidates who list degrees they didn't complete – sometimes even from schools that don't exist.

Bill And what about job experience? What's the best way to check that information?

Sarah One thing to watch for is the company names that the candidate lists as part of his or her work experience. If there are too many company names with for example, info, tech, tele, or net . . . etc., and if that doesn't seem right to you, don't turn a blind eye to it, check it out. They're probably fake. And when you do the telephone interview, ask for the name and phone number of previous managers.

Bill That's a good point. Now, I guess salaries are something else to check for.

Sarah Yes, to me that's very important. We find that it's often salespeople who claim to be worth more than they deserve. For example, they tend to add their salaries to their sales commission and present that as their current salary. It's always best to ask candidates to send you their last pay check so you can check that the salary listed on their résumé is accurate.

Bill Right. Now do you have any final tips for employers who are checking résumés?

Sarah Hmm . . . Yes, be careful of the references that candidates provide. We've had cases where candidates list friends or relatives as references, who of course will try to make the candidate sound really good when you call them. So always check the website of previous employers, and use the contact information provided there to check on a candidates work experience.

Bill OK, those sound like very useful tips indeed. Thank you for sharing your knowledge and experience with us on Employment Today. And if any of our listeners are about to send a résumé, remember that honesty is the best policy! You don't want a fake résumé to turn into a bad record.

Unit 12 *Psychology*

Listening Extra, Ex. B and C (p. 97)

Jules So, anyway, how's Marty doing? We haven't seen each other for ages.

Caitlin Marty? He's doing OK. But I think you'll notice some changes when you see him again.

Jules Yeah? The last time I saw him he said he'd met this really cool girl online. Are they still together?

Caitlin Yes, and it seems to be working out. Even though they're a little different in some respects.

Jules Really? He thought they had a lot in common when they were chatting online.

Caitlin Yeah, I think Marty got excited about some stuff in her profile. Like you know how he's into hiking and kayaking and camping and stuff?

Jules Yeah?

Caitlin Well she'd written that she was into nature in a big way, but it turns out she's really a city girl. The only time she goes outdoors is when she walks in the park on her lunch break.

Jules That's not so serious. I'm sure he can forgive her for that! So how else are they different?

Caitlin Hmm, she's more focused and organized. And she's taken it upon herself to organize him too, like insisting on him changing his appearance. No more ponytail and jeans for Marty.

Jules You're kidding. Marty's had a ponytail since high school.

Caitlin She told him he was too old to look like a student. And if he wanted to stop waiting on tables for a living, he needed to change his appearance.

Jules I guess I can see it from both sides. She probably thinks it's time for Marty to be more responsible about stuff.

Caitlin Yep, so now he works as a supervisor at a grocery store. And he only wears the pants and shirts she's picked out for him.

Jules Marty has a responsible job?

Caitlin Uh-huh. And get this she's got him cooking meals for the two of them. He's even doing his own laundry these days.

Jules No way! You mean he doesn't get his mom to do that anymore?

Caitlin Oh, you haven't heard? He finally moved out of his parent's house!

Jules Wow! Now that can't have been easy! I mean, he's always depended on his parents being there and doing everything for him.

Caitlin Actually, I think it was quite difficult for his parents. They've always dreaded him leaving home one day, and now it's finally happened.

Jules Yeah, but at the same time they must be relieved that he's becoming more independent. So what else has changed in Marty's life? Don't tell me there's more. . . .

Caitlin Hmm . . . Actually there is. You remember his old motorcycle? His girlfriend talked him into selling it. Now he drives an ordinary everyday safe car!

Jules OK, well that figures. I mean, look at it from her point of view it can't be comfortable riding around on the back of an old motorcycle. It must have been embarrassing, to put it mildly.

Caitlin Exactly. She wasn't going to put up with that!

Jules Well, I'd sure like to meet his girlfriend. It sounds like she's good for him. And Marty sounds like a new man!

Illustration credits

Photography credits

Text credits

Corpus

Development of this publication has made use of the Cambridge English Corpus (CEC). The CEC is a computer database of contemporary spoken and written English, which currently stands at over one billion words. It includes British English, American English and other varieties of English. It also includes the Cambridge Learner Corpus, developed in collaboration with the University of Cambridge ESOL Examinations. Cambridge University Press has built up the CEC to provide evidence about language use that helps to produce better language teaching materials.